CULTURAL GEOGRAPHY

THIRD EDITION

MICHAEL D. MATTHEWS

BJU PRESS
Greenville, South Carolina

NOTE: The fact that materials produced by other publishers may be referred to in this volume does not constitute an endorsement of the content or theological position of materials produced by such publishers. Any references and ancillary materials are listed as an aid to the student or the teacher and in an attempt to maintain the accepted academic standards of the publishing industry.

CULTURAL GEOGRAPHY
THIRD EDITION

Michael D. Matthews

CONTRIBUTING AUTHORS
Ramona Dunckel, PhD
Linda Hayner, PhD
Lauren Kowalk
Nathan Lentfer
Dennis Peterson
Bryan Smith, PhD

EDITOR
Manda Kalagayan

BIBLE INTEGRATION
Adam Mayo
Bryan Smith, PhD

COVER & BOOK DESIGN
Drew Fields
Elly Kalagayan

PAGE LAYOUT
Drew Fields
Carol Jenkins
Megan Eshleman
Dan Van Leeuwen

PROJECT MANAGERS
Elena Emelyanova
Kevin Neat
Malachy Pierre

PHOTO ACQUISITION
Joyce Landis
Rita Mitchell
Sarah Strawhorn

ILLUSTRATION
Preston Gravely, Jr.
Dave Schuppert

Photograph credits are listed on pages 621–24.

Battleship is a registered trademark of Milton Bradley Company.

Produced in cooperation with the Bob Jones University Departments of History and Social Studies of the College of Arts and Science, the School of Education, and Bob Jones Academy.

© 2008 BJU Press
Greenville, South Carolina 29614

First Edition © 1987
Second Edition © 1998

Printed in the United States of America

ISBN 978-1-59166-496-3

15   14   13   12   11   10   9   8   7   6   5   4   3   2   1

GOD'S GRANDEUR

The world is charged with the grandeur of God.

It will flame out, like shining from shook foil;

It gathers to a greatness, like the ooze of oil

Crushed. Why do men then now not reck his rod?

Generations have trod, have trod, have trod;

And all is seared with trade; bleared, smeared with toil;

And wears man's smudge and shares man's smell: the soil

Is bare now, nor can foot feel, being shod.

And for all this, nature is never spent;

There lives the dearest freshness deep down things;

And though the last lights off the black West went

Oh, morning, at the brown brink eastward, springs—

Because the Holy Ghost over the bent

World broods with warm breast and with ah!

bright wings.

—Gerard Manley Hopkins (1844–89)

CONTENTS

Pronunciation Guide

Vowels			
symbol	example	symbol	example
a	cat = KAT	aw	all = AWL
a-e	cape = KAPE	o	potion = PO shun
ay	paint = PAYNT	oa	don't = DOANT
e	jet = JET	o-e	groan = GRONE
eh	spend = SPEHND	oh	own = OHN
ee	fiend = FEEND	u	some = SUM
i	swim = SWIM	uh	abet = uh BET
ih	pity = PIH tee	oo	crew = CROO
eye	icy = EYE see	oo	push = POOSH
i-e	might = MITE	ou	loud = LOUD
ah	cot = KAHT	oy	toil = TOYL
ar	car = KAR		

Consonants			
symbol	example	symbol	example
k	cat = KAT	th	thin = THIN
g	get = GET	th	then = THEN
j	gentle = JEN tul	zh	fusion = FYOO zhun

The pronunciation key used in this text is designed to give the reader a self-evident, acceptable pronunciation for a word as he reads it from the page. For more accurate pronunciations, the reader should consult a good dictionary.

Stress: Syllables with primary stress appear in LARGE CAPITAL letters. Syllables with secondary stress and one-syllable words appear in SMALL CAPITAL letters. Unstressed syllables appear in lowercase letters. Where two or more words appear together, hyphens separate the syllables within each word. For example, the pronunciation of Omar Khayyam appears as (OH-mar kie-YAHM).

READY REFERENCE TO MAPS

FEATURES OF THE BOOK

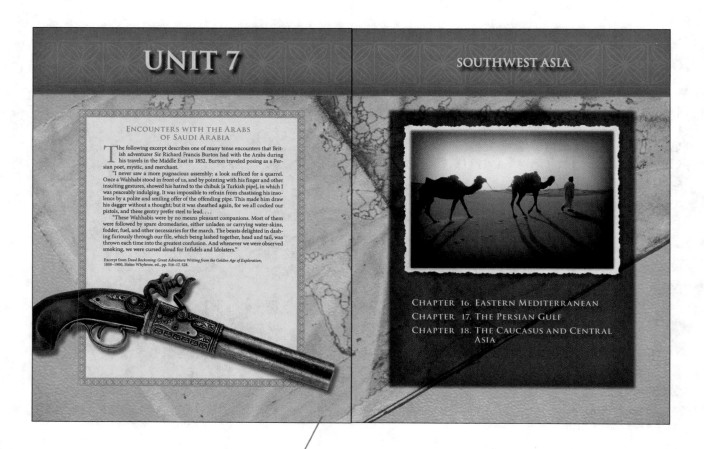

UNIT 7

SOUTHWEST ASIA

ENCOUNTERS WITH THE ARABS OF SAUDI ARABIA

The following excerpt describes one of many tense encounters that British adventurer Sir Richard Francis Burton had with the Arabs during his travels in the Middle East in 1852. Burton traveled posing as a Persian poet, mystic, and merchant.

"I never saw a more pugnacious assembly: a look sufficed for a quarrel. Once a Wahhabi stood in front of us, and then, by pointing with his finger and other insulting gestures, showed his hatred to the chibuk [a Turkish pipe], in which I was peaceably indulging. It was impossible to refrain from chastising his insolence by a polite and smiling offer of the offending pipe. This made him draw his dagger without a thought; but it was sheathed again, for we all cocked our pistols, and these gentry prefer steel to lead. . . .

"These Wahhabis were by no means pleasant companions. Most of them were followed by spare dromedaries, either unladen or carrying water-skins, fodder, fuel, and other necessaries for the march. The beasts delighted in dashing furiously through our file, which being lashed together, head and tail, was thrown each time into the greatest confusion. And whenever we were observed smoking, we were cursed aloud for Infidels and Idolaters."

Excerpt from Dead Reckoning: Great Adventure Writing from the Golden Age of Exploration, 1800–1900, Helen Whybrow, ed., pp. 516–17, 528.

CHAPTER 16. EASTERN MEDITERRANEAN

CHAPTER 17. THE PERSIAN GULF

CHAPTER 18. THE CAUCASUS AND CENTRAL ASIA

Unit openers offer brief first-person accounts relating to the unit and unifying the book along the theme of a "Grand Tour."

Cultural openers offer short essays that emphasize key geographic principles and highlight important information about the region covered in the unit.

400

PROMISE AND PERIL

CULTURAL SNAPSHOT

The broad, rich culture of the region comprising the Eastern Mediterranean, the Persian Gulf, and the Caucasus/Central Asia is built on dozens of ancient civilizations, including Sumer, Akkad, Israel, Babylon, Persia, Assyria, and many others. Although vestiges of those various cultures still exist today, the region is dominated by three major religions and the cultures that flow from each of them: Judaism, Islam, and Christianity.

The first two of these three religions have their origins in the biblical Abraham. God promised Abraham an heir in his old age, but Abraham tired of waiting for God's promise and tried to achieve it himself by having a child by his wife's handmaid, Hagar. The child who was born was named Ishmael. He became the father of the modern-day people known as Arabs, who made important contributions in such fields as mathematics, astronomy, and medicine. From those people also came the religion of Islam. Over the centuries, Islam has spread beyond the Middle East to become the predominant religion of not only that area but also the Persian Gulf, the Caucasus and Central Asia, and much of Africa and southern and eastern Asia.

When Abraham's child of the promise arrived in God's perfect time, a second nation was born. Isaac became the father of the Israelites, from whom came the religion of Judaism. Judaism contributed, through the Old Testament, influential literature and a moral code (the Ten Commandments) among other things.

The culture of modern Israel is based on two key factors: Judaism and Zionism. Judaism itself is divided between Orthodox Jews, who want to adhere strictly to the religious rules, and secular Jews, who are more liberal and tend to follow Judaism only as an ethnic and racial tradition. (Secular Jews have always outnumbered Orthodox Jews.) The Zionist movement began as a reaction against the growing anti-

Semitism around the world. It promoted the creation of a Jewish homeland and resulted in the founding of the state of Israel in 1948. Today, Zionists are hard-line supporters of the development and advancement of Israel. They violently oppose any accommodation of the Arabs. Zionism is central to the national self-image of Israel, and it is a lightning rod for anti-Semites around the world.

Israel also was the birthplace of Jesus Christ, Whose life, death, resurrection, and ascension produced the religion of Christianity. Christianity built upon the moral code of Judaism but raised the standards and expectations for moral and spiritual life. Simultaneously, it offered hope where Judaism offered only the hopelessness of human tradition.

Judaism, Islam, and Christianity have had an uneasy coexistence in this region, punctuated by frequent periods of tension and warfare. At the center of the controversy is Israel. Generally, the Muslims have sought the destruction of Israel. As recently as 2006, the Palestinian terrorist organization Hamas (winner of the 2006 parliamentary elections in Palestine) refused to renounce its pledge to destroy Israel. The same year, the president of Iran declared that Israel should be wiped off the map.

Throughout the conflict between Jews and Muslims, Christianity has sought not only to defend Israel's right to exist but also to broker peace between the two groups. Despite such efforts, the Christian countries of the West have been the target of Islamic terrorists (e.g., the September 11, 2001, attacks on the World Trade Center and the Pentagon; the train bombings in Spain; the bombings in the London subway system; Muslim riots in France).

Some people, considering this apparent "no-win" situation, ask, "Why bother working for peace in these regions?" As counterproductive as it might seem, this search for peace is actually commanded of believers. Psalm 122:6 commands, "Pray for the peace of Jerusalem." In doing so, we are actually praying for the return of the Prince of Peace, Who is the only One Who can bring true peace to our troubled world.

CHAPTER 7

The Spasskaya (Savior's) Tower is the main gate to the Kremlin in Moscow.

RUSSIA

I. HISTORY AND GOVERNMENT
  A. FROM THE CZARS TO THE PRESENT
  B. FEDERATION GOVERNMENT
II. NORTHERN EUROPEAN RUSSIA
  A. MOSCOW
  B. NORTHWEST RUSSIA
III. SOUTHERN EUROPEAN RUSSIA
  A. THE VOLGA RIVER
  B. THE DON RIVER BASIN
  C. CAUCASUS MOUNTAINS
IV. ASIAN RUSSIA
  A. URAL MOUNTAINS
  B. SIBERIA

Amazing color photographs throughout help the students "see" the sites and people along the Grand Tour of Cultural Geography.

The **chapter outline** lists the major topics that will be covered.

The **Chapter Review** asks students about terms, people, places, and concepts to help them prepare for the test.

---

562   *Australia and New Zealand*

Can You:
Define These Terms?

wattle	station
jumpbuck	aquifer
lignite	outbackr
artesian well	Aborigine

Locate These Places?

Oceania	Tasmania
Great Divid- ing Range	Great Barrier Reef
	Western Plateau
Central Lowlands	Hamersley Range
Botany Bay	Ayers Rock
Mount Kosciusko	Simpson Desert
Lake Eyre	North Island
Great Austra- lian Bight	South Island
	Cook Strait
Murray River	Mount Cook

Explain the Significance?

Captain James Cook	Adelaide
	Perth
Canberra	Sydney
Melbourne	Maori
Brisbane	Auckland

CHAPTER REVIEW
22

HOW MUCH DO YOU REMEMBER?

1. Name four outstanding features of Australia that appear on its coat of arms.
2. What is Australia's tallest mountain? In what range is it located?
3. What are the three major geographic features of Australia?
4. What was the First Fleet?
5. What is Australia's largest city?
6. List ten memorable features of the outback.
7. Give the state of Australia that best fits each description.
    a. largest area
    b. largest population
    c. largest city
    d. first settled
    e. last settled
    f. island
    g. lignite
    h. opals
    i. cattle stations
8. Give the island of New Zealand that best fits each description.
    a. most populous
    b. highest peak
    c. geothermal activity
    d. Canterbury Plain
9. Describe the differences between the Aborigines and the Maori.

WHAT DO YOU THINK?

1. The land west of the Appalachians is wet, but west of the Great Dividing Range it is dry. Why the difference? (Hint: Compare currents and wind patterns.)
2. How has Australia's location as "the Land Down Under" affected its history and economy?
3. List five important similarities and five differences between Australia and New Zealand.
4. Why do you think Australia used to be called "the lucky land"?
5. Compare the histories of the Aborigines of Australia, the Maoris of New Zealand, and the American Indians of the United States.

Fast Facts present a wealth of information about each country/region discussed in the chapter.

Margin info boxes offer intriguing bits of extra information.

Section quizzes help the students remember what they have learned so far.

"Through Christian Eyes" boxes present important issues from a Christian perspective and encourage development of higher-order thinking skills.

"Let's Go Exploring" provides opportunities to practice and develop various map skills.

402   *Chapter 16*

While the jagged peninsulas of southern Europe have plentiful harbors and a mild mediterranean climate, the coasts along the eastern Mediterranean Sea have few good ports, scarce water, and almost no natural resources. Yet the strategic location of this region has placed it at the center of the world stage.

The countries at the eastern edge of the Mediterranean touch three continents. Turkey is anchored in Europe, Israel borders Africa,

			Eastern Mediterranean Fast Facts				
Flag	Country	Capital	Area (sq. mi.)	Pop. (M)	Pop. Density (per sq. mi.)	Per Capita GDP ($US)	Life Span
	Cyprus	Nicosia	3,571	0.78	218	$20,300	77.65
	Israel	Jerusalem	8,019	6.28	783	$20,800	79.32
	Jordan	Amman	35,637	5.76	162	$4,500	78.24
	Lebanon	Beirut	4,015	3.83	953	$5,000	72.63
	Syria	Damascus	71,498	18.45	258	$3,400	70.03
	Turkey	Ankara	301,384	69.66	231	$7,400	72.36

Australia and New Zealand   549

became a major railroad junction and Australia's most populous inland city.

Victoria is home to Australia's largest oil field and a major natural gas field off the coast. Coal is also mined in the state. The Latrobe Valley holds the world's largest deposit of **lignite** (brown coal). Lignite is the lowest grade of coal, however, because its high moisture produces little heat but a lot of smoke. Three vast power plants in Latrobe Valley produce nearly 90 percent of Victoria's electricity.

SECTION QUIZ

1. List six ways that Australia is an unusual continent.
2. What mountain system runs along Australia's eastern coast?
3. What is the highest peak in Australia?
4. Where did the first European settlers land in Australia? What year did they arrive?
5. What are jumpbucks?
6. What is the capital of Australia, and where is it located?
♦ Why do most Australians live on the east coast?

THE CENTRAL LOWLANDS

On the other side of the Great Dividing Range is the continent's dry interior, where rain is scarce. Runoff water from the Great Dividing Range is vitally important. This low area just west of the mountains is known as the **Central Lowlands.**

Australians and Sports
Australians are avid sports fans. Their most popular spectator sport is cricket. They also enjoy playing golf, tennis, and lawn bowling and engaging in water activities on the beaches. Sailing is popular in Sydney's beautiful harbor.

Through Christian Eyes
Is it possible for recreation and sports to glorify God? Why or why not?

LET'S GO EXPLORING

LAND USE OF AUSTRALIA AND NEW ZEALAND

1. What type of farming occurs in the tropics?
2. What is the most widespread type of land use in Australia and New Zealand?
3. What is the main commercial grain grown in Australia?
4. What two types of farming appear to be common in the Murray River basin?
♦ Find the geographic names of the four main primitive hunting grounds (of the Aborigines).

CENTRAL PLAINS

Larger than either Italy or the United Kingdom, Poland has played a central role in the history of Europe. The best farmland and most of the nation's major cities lie on the Central Plains. Warsaw lies on the **Vistula** (VIS chuh luh) **River**, the major artery of shipping through the Central Plains. Poland's farms rank second worldwide in rye, sixth in potatoes, seventh in oats, and eighth in hogs. Poland's sausages are world renowned.

Few people live on the plains near the coast, where glaciers have left many lakes and rocky moraines. The Masurian Lakeland lies east of the Vistula on the coastal plains, and the Pomeranian Lakeland lies in the west. These lakes, nestled among low hills, are popular among campers. The Great Poland Lakeland is located west of Warsaw.

Near the mouth of the Vistula is Gdańsk (formerly Danzig), Poland's largest port and once its most populous city. The hard-working shipbuilders of Gdańsk formed Solidarity, the first trade union in the Iron Curtain. **Lech Walesa**, the head of the union, demanded changes in the 1980s that helped to bring about the end of communism in Eastern Europe. He later became the first president of free Poland, introducing many reforms to the economy.

SOUTHERN UPLANDS

The Polish plains rise into a series of hills and scattered mountains in southern Poland. Mines produce zinc, lead, and sulfur; Poland ranks ninth worldwide in copper and fifth in silver production. A coal field that crosses the border with the Czech Republic is the largest source of coal in Europe outside the German Ruhr.

Gdańsk, formerly called Danzig, has been an important trade center on the Baltic Sea for one thousand years. For centuries Gdańsk was a German city, a fact reflected in the town's early architecture.

Terms in bold type draw attention to important facts, ideas, people, or definitions.

GEOGRAPHER'S CORNER

CITY PLANNING MODELS

Few cities in the world were planned. Instead, their layout reflects the events of their history. As businesses grew and as people moved into the city, the city spread out and developed. Today, city planners in every country are attempting to foresee future growth and decline so that they can avoid problems of congested roads, pollution, or abandoned neighborhoods.

Like scientists, city planners use models to help them summarize and analyze complex information. Most city models break down the city into at least five components. The central business district (CBD) refers to the original skyscrapers and office buildings, where property value is at a premium.

Cities have changed rapidly with the rise of suburbs and high-tech industries, such as e-commerce, that allow people to work on computers at home. Examine these three models of cities typical in the early twentieth century and then answer the questions.

1 = Business
2 = Industrial
3 = Low-income residential
4 = Middle-income residential
5 = High-income residential

Concentric Zone Model
Sector Model
Multiple-Nuclei Model

1. What type of building is near the CBD in every model?
2. What type of housing is near industry in every model?
3. Which model appears the least planned?
4. Which model appears to show development along roads?
5. Which model is most similar to a city... different from any of these models...

"Geographer's Corner" provides opportunities to apply geographic knowledge.

Maps, charts, and diagrams help the students visualize geographic locations and information.

Agricultural Regions of the United States

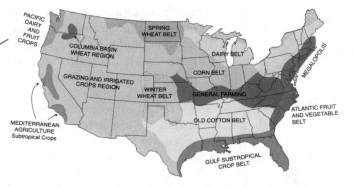

PACIFIC DAIRY AND FRUIT CROPS
COLUMBIA BASIN WHEAT REGION
SPRING WHEAT BELT
DAIRY BELT
GRAZING AND IRRIGATED CROPS REGION
CORN BELT
MEGALOPOLIS
WINTER WHEAT BELT
GENERAL FARMING
MEDITERRANEAN AGRICULTURE Subtropical Crops
OLD COTTON BELT
ATLANTIC FRUIT AND VEGETABLE BELT
GULF SUBTROPICAL CROP BELT

AMERICA'S PASTIME: BASEBALL

Baseball has long been called "America's pastime." Alexander Cartwright invented the game in 1845 and founded the New York Knickerbocker Base Ball Club. The first recorded game was in 1846 between Cartwright's club and the New York Base Ball Club. Cartwright's team lost. Baseball was also played by soldiers during the War Between the States.

The first salaried team was the Cincinnati Red Stockings in 1869. The first professional baseball league was formed two years later as the National Association of Professional Base Ball Players, and the first formal major league, the National League, began in 1876. A rival American League was formed in 1893. These same two leagues have competed ever since.

At first, the teams played other teams in their own league and then the winners of each league played each other in the World Series. Today, some interleague play is scheduled during each season.

Initially, only white Americans played professional baseball. Blacks had their own league, the Negro League, but they did not get to play in the World Series. In the 1940s, however, Branch Rickey, owner of the Brooklyn Dodgers, hired the black player Jackie Robinson. This breaking of the color barrier opened the door for extensive black participation. Soon, players of still other races and nationalities were allowed into baseball. Today, teams include whites, blacks, Hispanics, and Asians. Baseball is no longer merely a sport; it is big business, with players demanding—and getting—multimillion dollar contracts.

Although baseball must now compete with other professional sports for both participants and spectators, the names of baseball's legends—such men as Babe Ruth, Lou Gehrig, Ty Cobb, Willy Mayes, Hank Aaron, and others—still carry great meaning among Americans today.

General feature boxes provide a deeper look at a person, event, or concept mentioned in the text.

UNIT 1

OFF ON A GRAND TOUR

In the late eighteenth century and throughout the nineteenth century, many parents sent their young adult children on what was to be the culmination of their education: the "Grand Tour." The goal was for the students to immerse themselves in foreign cultures, learn the languages, broaden their minds, increase their self-reliance, establish relationships, and develop into well-rounded, culturally refined individuals who were prepared to assume the responsibilities of adulthood as dependable stewards of their inheritance.

At first, such trips were restricted to the British aristocracy, but peace, prosperity, improved transportation, and reduced costs opened the opportunity to the upper middle class. Americans soon joined their British cousins on their own Grand Tours. They often recorded their experiences and observations in journals and letters home. Most people who started such writing projects never finished, but some did. A few of these journals still exist.

Most Grand Tours lasted from a few months to two years and some as long as eight years. Young single females usually traveled with an older female, often a spinster aunt, as chaperon. Some people traveled with a servant or a tutor.

The length of the Grand Tour and the variety of climates encountered required a lot of luggage, including one's own set of silverware. A passport and a health certificate (proving that the traveler was healthy and not carrying any infectious diseases) were mandatory, as were both casual and formal clothing. Gentlemen were advised to take weapons, usually pistols and knives.

The modes of transportation—ships, canal boats, stagecoaches, and trains—were often as important as the scenery. One traveler lamented that the canal boats moved too fast for him to enjoy points of interest. His solution was to land whenever he wanted to proceed at a more leisurely pace and there engage a stagecoach—or even a farmer's wagon.

You—through the text, photographs, and maps of your geography book—are embarking on your own *virtual* Grand Tour. This tour, however, is not limited to continental Europe. Beginning in Great Britain, it takes you around the world to every continent and even under the sea. Each unit opens with an excerpt from someone's writings about a place discussed in that unit. As you read, imagine yourself as part of that person's entourage, experiencing the same adventure. You will thereby become a knowledgeable, more refined person, better prepared to fulfill your role as a faithful steward of God's creation.

THE WORLD AS GOD MADE IT

Cunard Line promotional brochure for the 'Franconia' c.1926–30 (colour litho) by American School (20th century) ©Private Collection/ Ken Welsh/ The Bridgeman Art Library

MEET MR. LIP!

Why should I have to study geography? What is geography anyway? And what does it have to do with me?

Geography is an important subject for many reasons, and it has a lot to do with not only you but also everyone around you. We often take for granted, however, the many ways geography affects and influences us. Studying the many aspects of geography will make you more aware of your connection to geography and how it influences you, your actions, and your interactions with others.

The word *geography* literally means "a description of the earth," but it involves much more than that. In fact, geography is of many different kinds, including physical geography, political geography, economic geography, cultural geography, and others. Essentially, though, one can divide geography into two broad categories: physical and human. *Physical* geography (covered in Unit 1) involves the world as God created it (e.g., land forms, resources, and climate). *Human* geography (covered in Unit 2) involves what humankind has done or is doing on and to the earth and how humans interact with each other and their environments.

Throughout all of the kinds of geography, however, run several consistent themes or central topics. These themes can best be remembered using the acronym MR. LIP. The individual letters of that acronym stand for the basic geographic themes: movement, region, location, interaction, and place.

Movement—This theme involves how people, goods, ideas, diseases, and other things move from one location to another. Examples of this theme in action include travel, trade, and mass communication (radio, television, telephone, etc.). In some places, movement is quite easy. In other places, it is more difficult because of geographic features (e.g., high mountain ranges or raging rivers), cultural differences, or disagreements between governments. Modern technology and modes of transportation have made the earth smaller, so it is important that you understand this theme.

Region—This theme is defined by formal boundaries, functions, or languages. In many instances, formal boundaries are not open to dispute (e.g., those formed by mountain ranges or rivers). Other boundaries that have been determined by political decisions have stood undisputed for centuries, and they usually continue undisputed because they are so widely acknowledged. Some boundaries, however, are disputed and have changed many times over the course of history. Most geography books are organized using the basic theme of region, and this book is no exception. You will "travel" in your studies—(Did you catch the theme of movement there?)—from region to region, studying in each region the other three themes: location, interaction, and place.

Location—"Where are we?" The answer to that question may be either absolute or relative. An absolute location is specific, a precise "address" (either a street address or a scientific location called latitude and longitude). For example, if you are calling for help with a flat tire and the repairman asks where you are, you might reply, "We're at the corner of Main Street and Third Avenue." A relative location describes a place in relation to the things around it. For example, you might tell someone that the resort town of Gatlinburg is in East Tennessee at the boundary of the Great Smoky Mountains National Park, west of North Carolina, and northeast of Georgia. The location of a place often affects the people there—the foods they eat, the clothing they wear, the industries in which they engage, and many other activities.

Interaction—This theme gets to the heart of human geography: people interacting with and responding to each other and their environment. An example of this theme in action is the aftermath of the flooding of New Orleans, Louisiana, when Hurricane Katrina struck that city. How did the people of New Orleans respond to the crisis? (Some displayed great courage and community spirit; others reacted with extreme antisocial conduct, such as looting.) How did people in other regions respond? (Some donated money or went there in person to assist rescue and clean-up efforts; others criticized the various governments' responses.) What effects did the disaster have on the economy, government, health care providers, and family units of the region? How did the flooding affect the environment? All of these issues—and more—are involved in the theme of interaction.

Place—This theme includes both physical and human characteristics. Physical characteristics include such features as the mountains, rivers, soils, and plant and animal life (called the flora and fauna) of a particular spot on earth. Human characteristics are the actions of people. They include roads, buildings, agriculture, industry, and the broad factor called *culture*.

Someone has defined *culture* as "everything people make, think, and do." Many aspects of culture change as one moves from region to region. People think and act differently in different regions. They wear different kinds of clothing. They speak different languages. They celebrate at different times and in different ways. They eat different foods. They grow different crops. They have different industries, religions, and governments. They have different motivations, fears, and goals. Yet they often share similarities as well. All of these factors are encompassed by the word *culture*.

When you understand Mr. Lip and all of the "kinfolk" in his culture family, you gain a greater appreciation of geography. And that appreciation will make geography come alive for you as you study it.

Mount St. Helens, a volcano in the American Northwest, is just one of the wonders of God's creation.

GEOGRAPHY: FINDING OUR PLACE IN THE WORLD

The Lord by wisdom hath founded the earth; by understanding hath he established the heavens.
(Prov. 3:19)

God created man and the world for a specific purpose. Every mountain and valley is exactly where He wanted it to be. This planet did not "just happen." As we behold the earth's amazing design and provisions for life, our hearts should praise the Creator.

Isaiah tells us that God made the earth to be a home for man, and He supplied it with abundant resources for humans to use and to enjoy. Genesis 1:26 gives God's reason for making each of us: "Let us make man in our image, after our likeness: and let them have dominion over . . . all the earth." God made man to show His glory by being like Him. He is the infinite Lord of the universe; humans are the finite lords of His earth. Our challenge is to use the earth's resources wisely and in a way that honors the Creator.

This unique calling to exercise dominion over the earth is called the **Creation Mandate**. It reveals that we all have a high and glorious calling. But we also bear a heavy burden of responsibility. Our task is complicated by the fact that humans are by nature sinful as a result of the Fall of Adam and Eve (see Genesis 3). In addition to the sin problem, which makes our task harder, the earth is a big and complicated place. If we are to do a good job of using the earth, we will have to study many things—and geography is near the top of the list. We cannot exercise good and wise dominion without knowing about the earth's physical features, its climates, and the ways in which humans interact on it. Thankfully, God has provided a solution to the sin problem: redemption through the sacrificial death of His Son, Jesus Christ, who paid the price of our sin by dying on the Cross in our place. Redemption also gives us hope and encouragement for our task of exercising dominion over His earth.

I. WHAT IS GEOGRAPHY?

History and geography are both necessary to help us understand the world around us. History is the study of events in *time* (*what* happened and *when*); geography is the study of *space* and *place* (*where* things happen). The basic tool of history is a timeline; the basic tool of geography is a map. One could compare history and geography to a play. History would be the actors and the plot; geography would be the stage on which those actions are played out.

It is not enough, however, just to memorize a list of dates and names of people and places. Beyond *when* and *where*, we want to know *how* and *why*. Geography helps us learn not only where places are but also how they differ and why.

BRANCHES OF GEOGRAPHY

The word *geography* comes from two roots meaning "earth" (*geo-*) and "written description" (*-graphy*). In other words, geography is a description of humanity's God-given abode—and everything and everyone on it—and how people interact with it and on it in fulfilling their God-given role as stewards of God's creation.

Geography has two main branches: *physical geography* (the study of the earth and its resources) and *human geography* (the study of man as he lives on the earth and uses its resources). This distinction is revealed by the titles of the first two units of this book: "The World as God Made It" (physical geography) and "The World as Man Subdues It" (human geography). These two branches are divided into dozens of smaller branches, such as climatology, oceanography, meteorology, and demographics.

One can study the main branches of geography in two ways. *Systematic geography* examines one branch of geography at a time, tying together examples from every region of the world. For example, a chapter titled "Urban Geography" might discuss New York City, London, and Tokyo. *Regional geography*, on the other hand, examines only one region of the world at a time, tying together all of the branches of geography simultaneously. For example, a chapter titled "The Far East" would cover not only the major cities there but also the climate, mountains, resources, and much more about the whole area.

This book combines both approaches. Chapters 1–4 are a general, systematic study of geography concepts, with two chapters on physical geography and two chapters on human geography. You get in these chapters the big picture, learning the basic terms and concepts of geography that are used in the rest of the book to examine the unique features of individual regions and the countries within each region.

THEMES OF GEOGRAPHY

The study of geography has five fundamental themes that you can remember easily using the mnemonic "MR. LIP":

1. *Movement*—of people, goods, ideas, diseases, etc.

2. *Region*—defined by formal boundaries or functions

3. *Location*—either specific (absolute) or relative to the surrounding environment

4. *Interaction*—both among people and between people and their environment

5. *Place*—physical characteristics (mountains, rivers, soils, plant and animal life, etc.) and human characteristics (roads, buildings, agriculture, industry, culture, etc.)

As you study geography, continually remind yourself of these five themes. They will recur many times throughout this book and are critical to a proper understanding of geography.

HISTORY OF GEOGRAPHY
ANCIENT VIEWS OF THE EARTH

Man probably began exploring his world in the Garden of Eden, but any written records of those explorations were lost in the Flood. After the Flood, the Lord commanded Noah to replenish the earth (Gen. 9:1); the work of geography began again. Early mapmakers supplied kings with maps to plan wars, to open new trade routes, and to build new cities. The earliest surviving map is a clay tablet from the Babylonian Empire around 2300 BC that depicts rivers and mountains.

The Greeks were the first ancient people to study the earth extensively. Early seafarers wanted to learn all about their trade routes and the people with whom they traded or might trade in the future. Alexander the Great, who rose to power in 336 BC, dreamed of conquering the world. After defeating Persia, he hired surveyors to accompany his army on a four-year journey "to the ends of the earth." His march into unexplored central Asia and India greatly expanded the Greeks' knowledge of world geography.

The first great geographer was a Greek mathematician named **Eratosthenes** (ER uh TAHS thuh NEEZ), who lived three centuries before Christ's birth. He summarized Greek understanding of the world in a book titled *Geography* and was the first man to use the word *geography*. He believed that the world was a sphere and even calculated its circumference as about 25,000 miles, which is very close to its actual 24,860-mile circumference. A century later, another Greek philosopher, **Hipparchus** (hih PAHR kus), made it easier to locate places on maps by drawing a **grid** (a regular pattern of intersecting vertical and horizontal lines).

The Romans borrowed their mapmaking techniques from the Greeks. They used maps of their vast empire to help them build roads and rule efficiently. The most famous Roman geographer was **Ptolemy** (TAHL uh mee), who lived in the second century after Christ. He promoted a **geocentric** (earth-centered) **theory**, which states that the sun, stars, and planets revolve around the earth. Ptolemy's amazing map of the world represented land from Britain to China. Both his map and his theory remained unchallenged for almost fourteen centuries.

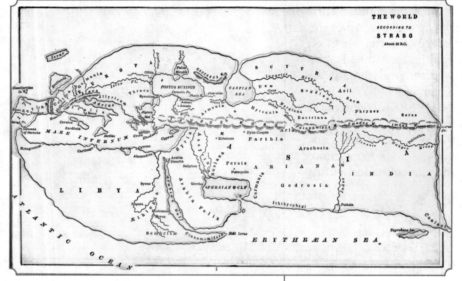

This is how Eratosthenes thought the world must look based on his calculations.

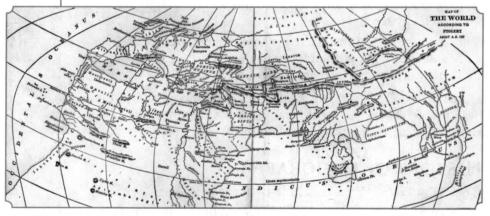

Ptolemy's map of the world (second century AD)

THE AGE OF EXPLORATION

The translation of Ptolemy's works in the early fifteenth century revived Europe's interest in maps and helped to spark the Age of Exploration. Sea captains mapped the stars and charted the winds to help them plot new sea routes to reach the spices, gold, and jewels of the Orient. After studying Ptolemy's map (which greatly exaggerated the size of Asia), an ambitious young man named Christopher

Columbus decided to try a shortcut to the Orient by sailing westward. Instead, he discovered a new, uncharted world—the Americas. In 1543, **Nicolaus Copernicus** (koh PUR nuh kus) published a lengthy argument for a **heliocentric** (sun-centered) **theory** of the universe.

Along with these advances in science, the art of **cartography** (mapmaking) reached new heights. **Gerhardus Mercator** (mer KAY tuhr) of Flanders published a map in 1569 that became the standard of his day. His well-designed grid enabled seafarers to plot their courses in a straight line. The maps of that period were beautifully illustrated with sea creatures, ships, and other designs to fill in the large areas about which geographers had no information. His system is still used today.

THE MODERN AGE

As European kings began to colonize and conquer the new-found lands, they demanded maps with increasingly more detail and accuracy. They also commissioned extensive surveys of their own lands. The new maps included symbols for **topography** (detailed land features, including their elevations) to help generals move their armies more quickly. When England became the world's leading sea power in the eighteenth century, it also became the world's leading mapmaker.

As modern states began gathering more information about their climates, populations, and resources, they produced *thematic maps* (maps designed to communicate information on particular topics) to display their abstract findings. The United States was late in joining the map race, but that quickly changed. World War II especially spurred U.S. mapmaking efforts. Today, the United States produces hundreds of maps for its troops stationed around the world. The development of airplanes and satellites made it possible to create better, more detailed maps. The U.S. Geological Survey (USGS), founded in 1879, has created a wealth of detailed maps. Radar and infrared satellites have now mapped the ocean floors and the frigid poles.

The most recent innovation is the global positioning system (GPS), which is financed and operated by the U.S. Department of Defense. Although GPS was designed specifically for military use, the government also allows many civilian uses. Twenty-four GPS satellites transmit coded signals to a receiver and calculate position, velocity, and time. It is the most precise indicator available today. Although civilian use is accurate to within 100 meters, military applications are accurate to within ten centimeters!

Although cartographers have produced very detailed and accurate maps of the earth as a result of such innovations, exploration continues. The jungles teem with myriad plant species that have never been cataloged. Millions—even billions—of undiscovered animal communities dot the ocean floor. Despite many famous expeditions, many mountain peaks still have not been climbed. Immense caves remain hidden and beg to be explored.

NON PAREM PAVLO GRATIÃ REQVIRO VENIAM PETRI NEQ POSCO SED QVAM IN CRVCIS LIGNO DEDERAS LATRONI SEDVLVS ORO

Copernicus concluded that the earth revolved around the sun, not the sun around the earth.

SECTION QUIZ

1. What is the Creation Mandate? Why is the study of geography important in relation to this mandate?

2. Define *geography* and distinguish its two main branches.

3. Who were the two greatest ancient geographers, and what did each contribute to geography?

4. What contributions from the Age of Exploration are still used today?

5. What characteristics of modern maps distinguish them from maps of the ancient world and of the Age of Exploration?

☼ Why has the United States become the leading mapmaker in the world?

II. THE GEOGRAPHIC GRID

The *Apollo 11* moon mission was one of the greatest space adventures of the twentieth century and the climax of thousands of years of human exploration and learning. "Far more than three men on a voyage to the moon," observed astronaut Buzz Aldrin, "this stands as a symbol of the insatiable curiosity of all mankind to explore the unknown."

But it was an adventure that could have ended in tragedy. In the years before the space shuttle, which lands on a runway like an airplane, early spacecraft had to splash into the open ocean, where ships would rescue them. A mistake in the calculations for the splashdown could have meant death for the entire crew. But the return trip for *Apollo 11* went smoothly. When the astronauts splashed down in the Pacific Ocean, 950 miles southwest of Honolulu, they were rescued quickly. How did the rescue ship find them so easily, although they were dwarfed by the vast surrounding ocean and virtually impossible to see? The U.S. Navy used the imaginary lines of the *geographic grid* that divide the globe into small sections.

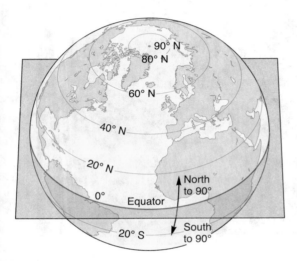

Lines of latitude

HEMISPHERES

Since the earliest times, geographers have divided the earth's sphere into two halves, calling each half a **hemisphere**. The line that divides the earth into the Northern and Southern hemispheres is the **equator**.

The *Apollo 11* astronauts landed in the Northern Hemisphere. If the earth were flat, the National Aeronautics and Space Administration (NASA) could have located them north of the equator using feet and miles. But the earth is not flat; it is round. It is easier to locate points on a circle using *degrees* (°). NASA needed only two measurements to pinpoint the astronauts' location: degrees of latitude and longitude.

LATITUDE AND LONGITUDE

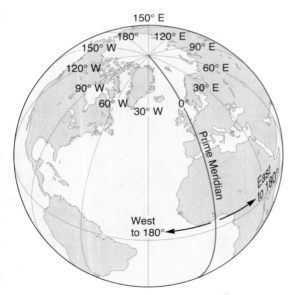

Lines of longitude

The first measurement that NASA needed was degrees of **latitude**. Imaginary lines run east and west around the earth. They form circles that are parallel to the equator and are therefore called **parallels** of latitude. They are numbered from 0° at the equator to 90° at the North and South poles. Those numbers are determined by measuring the angle of these circles from the equator. The number of the parallel is followed by an N or an S to designate whether it is north or south of the equator.

The distance from one degree of latitude to the next is about sixty-nine miles. But that still is not precise enough to find an astronaut floating in the middle of a huge ocean. Therefore, each degree of latitude is further divided into sixty *minutes* ('), with the minutes being a little more than a mile apart. Furthermore, each minute is subdivided into sixty *seconds* ("), with seconds being about one hundred feet apart. (Generally, for any activities in this book requiring you to locate places by latitude and longitude it will be sufficient to state only degrees, not minutes and seconds, but you should know how the more precise locations are designated.) A bronze marker at Meade's Ranch in eastern Kansas has been measured carefully as having a latitude of exactly 39° 13' 26.686" N (39 degrees, 13 minutes, 26.686 seconds north latitude). That location is accurate to the very inch and is used as the basis for mapping all latitudes in North America.

Even if NASA determined the latitude of the returning astronauts, it would need to know the point on that parallel where the spacecraft splashed down. To find that point, they would need to know the **longitude**. Imaginary lines called **meridians** run north and south, stretching from pole to pole. Because no equator runs north and south, one meridian is designated as the **prime meridian** from which all other meridians are numbered. That prime meridian extends through Greenwich, England, just outside of London. Scientists at the Royal Observatory there made the original calculations for modern meridians, and their meridian became the basis of all other measurements of longitude.

Like parallels of latitude, meridians are measured in degrees, minutes, and seconds but with one major difference: the highest degree for meridians is 180, not 90. Why? The farthest point from the prime meridian is halfway around the world. A full circle is 360°; half of a full circle is 180°. All other points are closer to the prime meridian and must be less than 180°.

The 180° meridian lies directly opposite the prime meridian and is actually a continuation of the same line. Together, these lines form a **great circle** and cut the earth into two equal parts (hemispheres). Every meridian except 0° and 180° is labeled as east (E) or west (W), depending on the hemisphere in which it lies. The bronze marker at Meade's Ranch has a precise longitude of 98° 32' 30.506" W (98 degrees, 32 minutes, 30.506 seconds west longitude). With the help of such exact readings, NASA easily found the astronauts' command module.

Locating places on a map using latitude and longitude uses much the same principles used to play the game Battleship. The game uses a grid with columns that are designated by letters of the alphabet and rows that are numbered. You try to locate your opponent's hidden ships by designating a spot on the game board where a lettered column and a numbered row intersect, such as E-6. To locate a place using latitude and longitude, you simply substitute degrees of latitude and longitude for the letters and numbers.

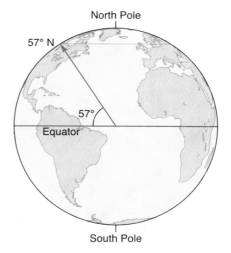

The number for a line of latitude is determined by measuring the angle of its circle from the equator.

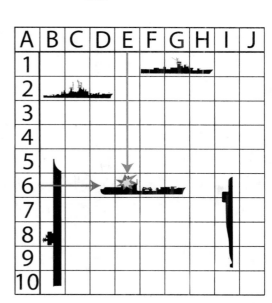

Finding a location by latitude and longitude is like playing the board game Battleship.

1. Why do humans long to explore and understand the world?
2. What are the lines of latitude called?
3. What is the 0° line of latitude called?
4. What are lines of longitude called?
5. What is the 0° line of longitude called?
6. What islands are located at the following points on the globe:

    80° N, 40° W?

    8° N, 80° E?

    0°, 90° W?

    55° N, 0°?

- ᠅ Find the approximate location of your home or school on a world map. What is the approximate latitude and longitude?

III. MAP PROJECTIONS

Globes show information about the earth's surface with almost perfect accuracy. Both globes and the earth are spheres, and both can be divided easily with lines of latitude and longitude. Although globes are useful, they are difficult to carry in a briefcase or fit into a textbook.

Flat maps are much more useful than globes, and can show much greater detail. Any method used to show the earth's round surface on a flat map is called a **map projection**.

THE PROBLEM OF DISTORTION

When a globe is transferred onto a flat map, a serious problem known as **distortion** occurs. The earth's surface is not a flat rectangle like a sheet of paper; it does not "flatten" without distorting the image. When mapmakers are making a flat map, they try to avoid or reduce distorting four features of a globe:

- area
- shape
- distance
- direction

Usually, a flat map will distort two or three of these features while minimizing or eliminating the other distortion(s). No flat map of the world can be accurate in all four ways. Manufacturers of globes must print the outer layer on a flat surface and then glue it to the globe. A typical globe is covered by twelve paper strips called **gores**.

How accurate is such a map? *Areas* of land and water are accurate, and compass *directions* are fairly accurate. *Distances* also seem to be accurate—an inch equals the same number of miles on every gore. But measuring distances *between* gores is awkward. The *shapes* have the most obvious distortions because of all the gaps. Although the gore map is fairly accurate in three respects, it is obviously not very useful as a flat map.

A globe is a model of the earth.

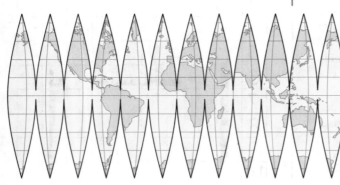

Gores

SOLUTIONS TO THE PROBLEM

In an effort to solve the problem of distortion, cartographers developed three basic types of map projections: cylindrical, planar (azimuthal), and conic. Each type of projection tries to address weaknesses inherent in other types of projections, but each also has its own problems. These projections get their names from the geometric surface onto which the globe is projected.

Although maps are drawn using mathematical equations, we can picture what takes place with the help of an imaginary globe made from wire. The wires represent lines of latitude and longitude. An imaginary light shines from the center of the globe onto the map surface.

CYLINDRICAL PROJECTIONS

Most world maps use a variation of the **cylindrical projection**. First, the mapmaker rolls a sheet of paper into the shape of a cylinder around the wire globe. Next, he traces the shadows cast by the light, and then he unrolls the paper to get a flat map.

Mercator's Projection—The first important cylindrical projection was published by Mercator in 1569. Not until the second half of the twentieth century was it replaced.

On a Mercator projection, all lines of latitude and longitude look straight. This feature means that compass *directions* are always constant. *Shapes* are also accurate. *Areas* and *distances*, however, are increasingly distorted the farther one moves north or south from the equator. Greenland, for example, looks larger than the entire continent of South America although it is really only one-eighth its size.

Goode's Interrupted Projection—The cylindrical projection has several popular variations, including a map that cuts and flattens the earth like an orange peel. It is called an **interrupted projection**. (The map made from gores before they are glued to a globe is an example.) It remains in one piece, but the image is "interrupted" with gaps or cuts. The most popular of these maps is Goode's interrupted projection. It is useful because the *areas* remain fairly accurate and the *shapes* of continents are less distorted than shapes on the gore map. Unfortunately, Goode's projection distorts *distances* and all north-south *directions*.

Robinson's Projection—Popular for textbooks is Robinson's projection, which combines the best elements from the other projections. Its greatest advantage is that it minimizes (but does not eliminate) all four types of distortions. Everything is distorted but only a little. Almost every world map in this textbook uses Robinson's projection.

AZIMUTHAL PROJECTIONS

Cylindrical projections such as Mercator's, Goode's, and Robinson's are all good for world maps.

Cylindrical projection

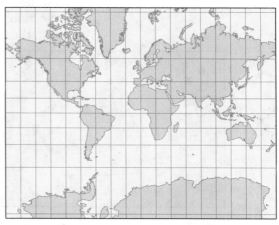

Mercator projection

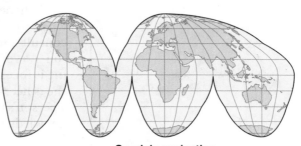

Goode's projection

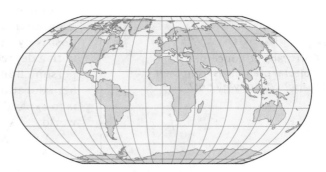

Robinson's projection

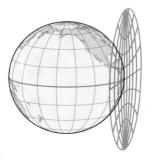

Azimuthal projection

But planar and conic projections work better on smaller-scale maps.

The planar projection, also called an **azimuthal** (AZ uh MUTH uhl) **projection**, uses a flat plane instead of a cylinder. To make the projection, one places a flat sheet of paper on an imaginary wire globe, touching only one point. The shadows traced on this paper form an azimuthal map. The map is most accurate in the center but becomes increasingly distorted near the edges. Therefore, it is useful for compact areas, such as South America and Antarctica, where land is surrounded by water.

CONIC PROJECTIONS

To make a **conic projection**, the mapmaker places a cone-shaped piece of paper on an imaginary wire globe and traces the shadow onto the cone. Then he opens and flattens the cone to make a conic projection. Unlike the planar projection, which touches a single point, the cone touches an entire line of latitude. The conic map is most accurate where the cone touches the line. Away from that line the features become gradually distorted. Thus, it is most useful for showing wide regions, such as the United States.

Choosing a projection is very important when one wants to display the whole world or a large region of the world. However, cartographers do not worry much about projections of small areas, such as cities, because distortions of such small areas are virtually undetectable.

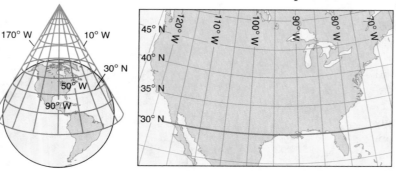

Conic projection

TYPES OF MAPS

Whenever someone asks you for directions for getting somewhere (perhaps from your school or church to your home), you consult a **mental map** to communicate the directions to the person. As you give the directions, the person to whom you are speaking is forming a mental map of his or her own based on what he or she is hearing. It might or might not be accurate. A mental map is a person's perception of the world or a part of it based on available knowledge. In addition to boundaries and major physical features (e.g., major rivers, mountains, towns), mental maps involve one's cultural perceptions, including any biases (a preference for one thing over another) or prejudices (a judgment about something or someone before you have examined all of the facts) toward the geographic region in question. One usually views his home area positively but might view "foreign" areas—rightly or wrongly—with a degree of negativity. These perceptions are influenced by a person's home life, the news and entertainment media, and his or her educational experiences. One purpose of studying geography is to expand and improve the accuracy of one's mental map of the world.

A map is a flat representation of the world or a specific portion of it. Many types of maps exist, each communicating a different type of information. The ability to read and interpret maps is essential not only in the study of geography but also in everyday living, for

Through Christian Eyes

Should Christians be concerned to remove cultural prejudices from their mental maps? Why or why not?

example, in using a road map effectively. Some of the most common map types are the following.

1. *Political maps* indicate state or national boundaries, capitals, and major cities.

2. *Physical maps* show mountains, rivers, lakes, elevation, and other natural features. Color is often used extensively to indicate bodies of water, various elevations, etc.

3. *Topographic (relief) maps* use special lines to indicate the shape and elevation of the land forms shown.

4. *Roadmaps* are used extensively by travelers, whether they are military commanders, professional truckers, or families on vacation. They show primary and secondary transportation routes.

5. *Climate maps* provide information about the type of weather in an area.

6. *Economic or resource maps* show the natural resources or economic activities of a place. Such maps might show where various industries are located, where specific types of crops are grown, or other such data.

Other specialized maps are also available, including geological, vegetation, soil, and meteorological (weather) maps. Hydrological maps give information about the water in an area, such as groundwater, runoff, and water levels in reservoirs. Ecological maps deal with the environment. Plat maps show boundaries between landowners. (If your parents own your home, they received a plat map of their property at the time of purchase, and it is on file at the county courthouse.) Nautical maps represent the waterways and bodies of water of an area and are invaluable to boaters, shippers, and engineers who design and build bridges and other structures in, over, or under the water. Military maps are essential to a nation's self-defense. There are even celestial maps for astronomers, scientists who study the stars and planets.

Regardless of the type of map, any map will usually include symbols that represent various features in an abbreviated form. Those symbols are of three basic types. *Point symbols* are used to indicate such things as cities or even such specific objects as buildings, wells, or monuments. *Line symbols* represent such things as roads, railroads, rivers, and water or power lines. *Area symbols* indicate bodies of water, swamps or marshes, glaciers, or other such physical features.

The meanings of such symbols are shown in a **legend**, which is usually located in a corner of the map that does not contain critical information. Often located near the legend are two other helpful features, a **compass rose** and a **scale**. The compass rose shows the orientation of the map, that is, whether the top of the map is north, south, east, or west. (Although north is generally the top of most maps, that is not always the case, which makes the compass rose very important.) The scale is a calibrated (marked) line that indicates

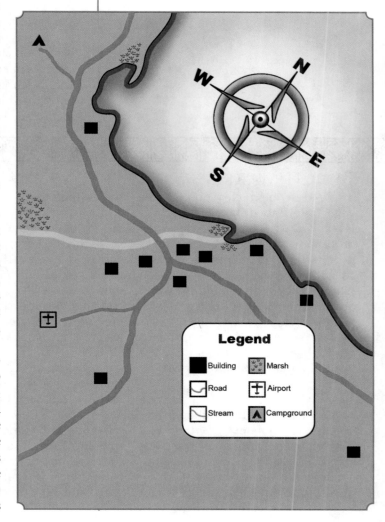

Legend

Building   Marsh
Road   Airport
Stream   Campground

distance. For maps of large areas, the scale might read, "1 in. = 200 mi." On smaller-scale maps, it might read, "1 in. = 100 ft."

SECTION QUIZ

1. What are the four types of distortion on flat maps?
2. What is an interrupted projection? Give an example of one.
3. What is the main advantage of a Mercator projection?
4. What is the main problem of a Mercator projection?
5. Which projection does this textbook use for most world maps?
6. Which two projections work better for smaller-scale maps?
7. List three of the six types of maps described in the textbook.
    - ☼ Which projection would you use to show the nation of Russia?

IV. MAP RELIEF

Map projections show the general outlines of the earth. But these two-dimensional maps are not very helpful in describing surface features, such as mountains and valleys. Soldiers, road crews, and backpackers all need detailed information about the third dimension: *altitude*, or elevation.

Any type of map that shows surface features is a physical map because it shows physical things. Physical maps that show specific changes in elevation are called relief maps. **Relief** refers to the height and depth of land features in relation to surrounding land. Many relief maps include not only water features, such as rivers, but also man-made features, such as dams.

BENCH MARKS

In describing elevation, a surveyor refers to distance above sea level. But what does he do when he cannot see the ocean? He relies on special monuments or markers called "bench marks" that have been placed in key spots around the world and give the exact altitude of the location. If you have ever hiked to the peak of a mountain, you might have seen a bench mark. It looks like the head of a giant nail and has writing on it.

How did surveyors measure the original bench marks? Although the details are complex, the theory is simple. A surveyor stands in a place where he can see the ocean with a telescope (on his theodolite). By measuring angles, he can calculate the altitude of his position and nail a marker. Then he moves farther inland and views his first marker. On and on he goes. The surveyor carries an *altimeter*, too, to check his altitude. The altimeter measures air pressure, which becomes lower as one moves up in elevation.

In the past, government surveyors hacked through dense woods to get a clear line of sight. The work was difficult and time consuming. Today, surveyors use satellites as reference points, making their work easier and more precise.

Bench marks indicate a location's elevation.

SHOWING THE THREE-DIMENSIONAL EARTH

Relief maps can show the third dimension of the earth's surface in many ways. Early maps included ink drawings of hills and mountains to show upper elevations. "Raised relief" maps, such as plaster models, are literally three-dimensional. Recent advances in technology, such as computers, satellite imagery, and aerial photography, make possible the use of color to indicate different altitudes. On most color relief maps, green represents land near sea level. Yellow or light brown represents a slight rise in land. Dark brown, gray, or white indicates mountains.

The lines that separate colors on a relief map are called **contour lines**. Each line shows all points on the map that have the same altitude. (For this reason, the line is also known as an *isoline; iso-,* "equal.") The difference in elevation between two contour lines is called the *contour interval.*

READING RELIEF MAPS

Look at the first of the three views of a landscape (diagram A). It illustrates what one region might look like to a camera, but it is not a map. It cannot show distances, directions, or the shapes and areas of the land. The second view, diagram B, shows the comparative elevations of the cross section of the same landscape. It does not, however, give any information about the other dimensions.

Three views of a landscape

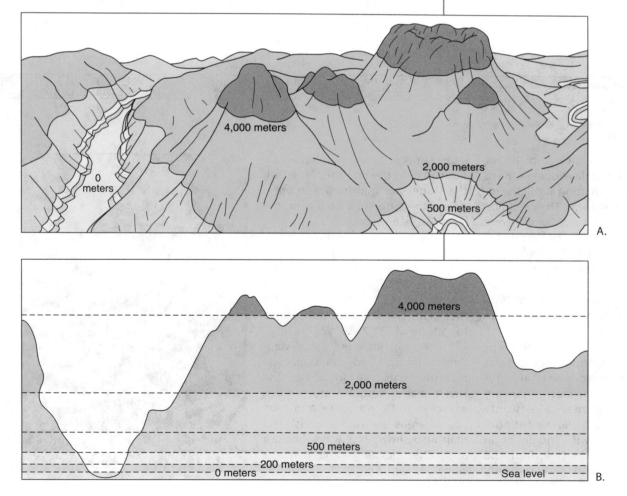

4,000 meters

0 meters

2,000 meters

500 meters

A.

4,000 meters

2,000 meters

500 meters

200 meters

0 meters

Sea level

B.

The relief map (diagram C), however, gives accurate information about all three dimensions. It helps us visualize the landforms and compare the elevations of those landforms. Relief maps also show us the general shapes, areas, distances, and directions of landforms.

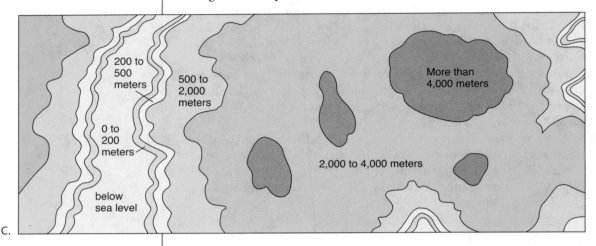

200 to 500 meters

500 to 2,000 meters

More than 4,000 meters

0 to 200 meters

2,000 to 4,000 meters

below sea level

C.

SECTION QUIZ

1. What is the term for a map that shows the altitude of land features?

2. Explain the difference between a contour line and a contour interval.

3. What color shows land between 0 and 200 meters?

   ⚲ What color shows land below sea level, and why is that color never next to the sea?

GEOGRAPHER'S CORNER

TOPOGRAPHIC MAP

Many people—including hikers, engineers, and land developers—need more specific information about the topography of small areas. Their solution is the topographic map. To someone who has never seen one before, such a map looks like a bunch of irregular lines with no apparent meaning. A trained map reader, however, can quickly visualize the entire terrain of a place. With a topographic map, a lost hiker can easily find his way again.

Unlike the colored relief maps in your textbook, topographic maps give all of the contour lines at regular intervals. On the accompanying map, the contour interval is twenty feet, and the lines are labeled at one-hundred-foot intervals. The direction of the slope is usually clear from the terrain around it. The land obviously slopes upward toward higher elevations. Where the lines are far apart, the slopes are gentle. But in areas where they are close together, the land rises steeply.

This map is a portion of the United States Geological Survey (USGS) map of a part of northern Pennsylvania. The right side of the map lies along the seventy-seventh meridian. The left side lies near a longitude of 77° 2´ 30″ W.

The map includes some standard symbols. Two exact altitude measurements are found at the bench marks. Natural features, such as creeks and ponds, appear in blue. Green areas indicate woods. The map also shows highways, houses, and other buildings and marks a cemetery with a cross.

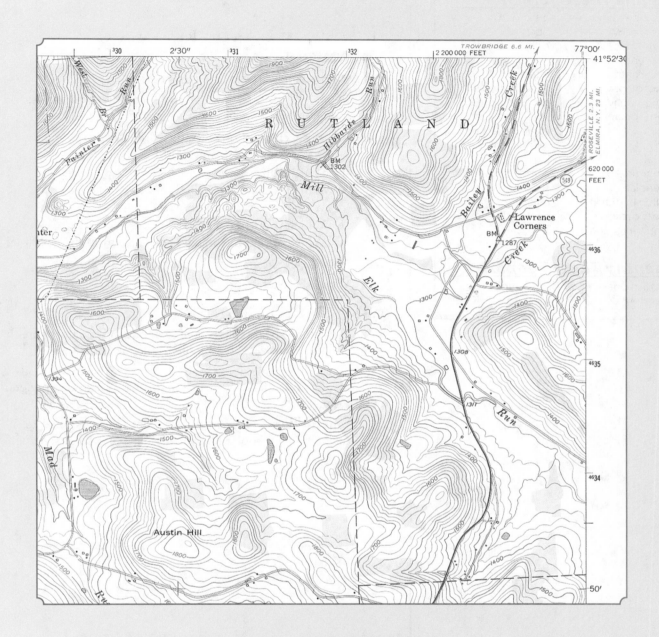

Use the information on this map to answer the questions that follow.

1. What is the altitude for the bench mark at Lawrence Corners?

2. Is Austin Hill the highest point on the map?

3. What creek flows northwest through a wide valley and empties into Mill Creek?

4. If two inches on a map equals one mile, how far is Austin Hill from Lawrence Corners?

5. What is the latitude for points along the top of the map?

☼ Can you see Austin Hill if you are standing in Lawrence Corners? Draw a picture of what you would see when looking in that direction.

Can You:
Define These Terms?

Creation mandate	distortion
geography	gore
grid	cylindrical pro-
geocentric theory	jection
heliocentric theory	interrupted
cartography	projection
topography	azimuthal pro-
hemisphere	jection
equator	conic projection
latitude	mental map
parallel	legend
longitude	compass rose
meridian	scale
prime meridian	relief
great circle	contour line
map projection	

Identify These People?

Eratosthenes	Copernicus
Ptolemy	Mercator

CHAPTER REVIEW

HOW MUCH DO YOU REMEMBER?

1. What are the two main branches of geography?

2. Who was the first great geographer?

3. Explain the difference between geography, cartography, and topography.

4. Answer each question with the word latitude or longitude:
   a. Which runs north and south?
   b. Which runs east and west?
   c. Which is called a parallel?
   d. Which is given in degrees from 0 to 90?
   e. Which is called a meridian?
   f. Which always lies an equal distance from the next line?

5. Why do all flat maps of the earth contain distortions?

6. What is a relief map?

WHAT DO YOU THINK?

1. Why were cartographers able to define the equator more than two thousand years before the prime meridian?

2. What advantages does Goode's projection have over Robinson's projection? Why do you think this textbook prefers Robinson's projection?

3. Why do most relief maps have a color scheme similar to the one in this textbook rather than some other color scheme?

THE EARTH'S SURFACE AND CLIMATE

O Lord my God, thou art very great; . . . who stretchest out the heavens like a curtain: who layeth the beams of his chambers in the waters: . . . who laid the foundations of the earth, that it should not be removed for ever.
(Ps. 104:1–5)

The psalmist reminds us that God created the earth and all that it contains. The Lord laid the foundations of not only the earth but also the sky and the ocean depths.

I. THE EARTH'S HISTORY

God's work in the earth's history can be divided into four phases: the Creation, the Flood, the current world, and the future world. We cannot understand the present world without understanding its past and its future. What we see today is the result of what happened in the past. According to the apostle Peter, however, mankind is "willingly" ignorant of God's intervention in the earth's history:

For this they willingly are ignorant of, that by the word of God the heavens were of old, and the earth standing out of the water and in the water: whereby the world that then was, being overflowed with water, perished: but the heavens and the earth, which are now, by the same word are kept in store, reserved unto fire against the day of judgment and perdition of ungodly men.
(2 Peter 3:5–7)

THE CREATION

Earth's history begins with Creation. Genesis 1 describes how God gave the earth light, atmosphere, land, and seas. A fully functioning world appeared within six days, filled with soil, tall trees, and all of the creatures—not bare rocks, seeds, and primitive life forms.

Many modern scientists ignore the biblical record, choosing to believe that the lands and seas resulted from solely natural forces working over billions of years. They assume that only the forces now active on the earth are those that shaped it. If a river is carving a canyon at a rate of one foot a century and the canyon is now one hundred feet deep, such scientists assume that it took ten thousand years to carve the canyon. People who hold this view, which is called **uniformitarianism**, are unwilling to recognize the existence of a powerful Creator, who made all things for a purpose, has at times intervened supernaturally in history, and will judge His creation at the end of time.

Flash floods, like this one in Hawaii, continue to shape the landscape.

THE FLOOD

Christians believe the earth's features were changed by a **cataclysm** (a violent upheaval or change in the earth's crust, especially a flood). Evolutionists say, however, that a universal flood, as described in Genesis 7, could not have happened because universal floods are not occurring today. But their conclusion is based on biased reasoning.

Scoffers are "willingly ignorant," Peter said. Evolutionists stubbornly reject the Flood in spite of the evidence all around us.

Only a universal flood could unleash the forces necessary to shape the world we see today. The impact of the Flood was beyond human imagination. Its waters sprang from the ground when the "fountains of the great deep" were broken up and fell from the heavens for forty days and nights. Creation scientists suggest that the superheated subterranean steam condensed in the atmosphere, making much of the rain that fell from the heavens. The water covered the earth to a height of fifteen cubits (about twenty-two feet) above the "high hills" (Gen. 7:19). Mountains as we know them today were probably formed sometime during the Flood as tectonic plates shifted and uplifted. Noah remained in the ark for a little more than a year before the Flood waters subsided. During that time, waves and water pressure reshaped the earth's surface as continents rose from the waters. Soil, rocks, dead vegetation, and animal carcasses washed from one area to another. Much of that material came to rest in layers.

A cataclysmic universal flood would explain the existence of the natural wonders along the Colorado River.

The Flood waters also softened the earth's surface greatly. Rocks that were not fully hardened were easily broken, folded, or eroded. Earthquakes, volcanoes, and local floods also had a great impact on the earth's surface. Magnificent formations, such as the Grand Canyon, formed quickly. Because the earth's surface has now hardened into rock, and because we have never again experienced a worldwide flood, we do not see such massive erosion today.

Also, the climate probably took a long time to stabilize after the Flood. Some creationary scientists believe that there was a large amount of water in the atmosphere that most likely formed thick clouds. These clouds, along with dense volcanic dust that probably existed blocked the sun's thermal energy from the earth's surface. As the earth cooled, snow and ice began to rapidly accumulate in the polar regions. In some places, many feet of snow may have accumulated each year. Huge, thick glaciers covered northern Europe, Canada, the northern United States, and similar areas in the Southern Hemisphere, killing or changing many species as a result of the drastic climatic change. The single ice age may have lasted between several hundred to over a thousand years. Evidence of glaciers can still be seen in the many landforms that they produced—landforms that could have been formed only by glaciers. Glaciers still cover the continent of Antarctica in the south and the island of Greenland in the north, as well as many mountainous and polar locations throughout the world.

Rock layers are displayed on a butte near Sedona, Arizona.

SECTION QUIZ

1. What are the four main phases in the history of the earth's surface, and what does the Bible say about each phase in 2 Peter 3:5–7?

2. What is uniformitarianism? What biblical view better explains the changes in the world's land formations?

3. Why did the earth become unstable after the Flood?

☼ How is mixing cement a useful way to explain the softness of the earth after the Flood but its hardness today?

II. The Earth's Surface

The sea is his, and he made it: and his hands formed the dry land.
        (Ps. 95:5)

God has divided the earth into three parts: the **atmosphere**, the covering of air that surrounds our planet; the **lithosphere** (LITH uh SFEER), the solid part of the earth; and the **hydrosphere** (HYE druh SFEER), the water on the earth's surface.

The Land

The earth is a *lithosphere* (literally, "rock ball"), nearly eight thousand miles in diameter. We think of the earth's surface as very rough. But when astronauts view it from space, it seems to them as smooth as the surface of an apple.

The Earth's Layers

The earth seems to be divided into several layers. The thin (4.5 to 31 miles deep) outer "skin" is called the **crust** and consists mainly of two layers. The bottom layer of basaltic rock spreads over the whole earth. Above that is the oceans and slabs of granitic rock, which are many miles thick. Where these slabs rise above the ocean, they form our continents.

Earthquakes give tantalizing hints about the secrets that lie below the earth's crust. In 1909, scientists noticed that earthquake waves decelerate abruptly and then accelerate again below the crust. They proposed that the waves were entering a layer of hot, plastic (capable of being shaped) material called the **mantle**. Earthquake waves move faster through the hot, dense mantle than through the crust.

Waves from earthquakes indicate that beneath the mantle is a **core** divided into a liquid outer core and a solid inner core. After studying the magnetism of the earth and its powerful gravity as it interacts with the moon, many scientists conclude that the core might be made of two heavy metals, iron and nickel.

The earth looks like a smooth blue gem in the blackness of outer space.

Layers of the earth

Crust (4.5-31 mi.)
Mantle
Outer core
Inner core
800 mi.
1,400 mi.
1,800 mi.

Layers of the crust

Continent
Sial
Ocean
Sima
Mantle

THE CONTINENTS

The total surface area of the earth is 197 million square miles. Of that total, 29 percent, or 57 million square miles, is land; the rest is ocean. All of the surface is divided between **continents**, the main landmasses of the earth, and **islands**, landmasses surrounded by water. The smallest continent, Australia, is more than three times larger than the largest island (Greenland).

The earth has six continental landmasses and seven continents: North America, South America, Africa, Australia, Antarctica, and Eurasia (Europe and Asia), which is divided by the Ural Mountains.

If the oceans were a little lower, the largest islands of the world would all become part of the nearby continents. We call these areas **continental islands** (for example, the British Isles). In contrast, **oceanic islands** rise from the ocean floor. If the ocean was lower, they would still be islands but slightly larger (for example, most of the islands of Micronesia in the Pacific).

Fast Facts About the Earth's Continents				
Continent	Area (sq. mi.)	*Percent of World's Land	High Point (ft.)	Low Point (ft.)
Asia	17,129,000	29.7	Mt. Everest 29,028 (Nepal)	Dead Sea -1,296 (Israel)
Africa	11,707,000	20.0	Mt. Kilimanjaro 19,340 (Tanzania)	Lake Assal -510 (Djibouti)
North America	9,363,000	16.3	Mt. McKinley 20,320 (Alaska)	Death Valley -282 (California)
South America	6,886,000	12.0	Mt. Aconcagua 22,834 (Argentina)	Salinas Grandes -131 (Argentina)
Antarctica	5,500,000	9.6	Vinson Massif 16,067	Sea Level
Europe	4,057,000	7.0	Mt. Elbrus 18,510 (Russia)	Caspian Sea -92 (Russia)
Australia	2,942,000	5.1	Mt. Kosciusko 7,316 (New South Wales)	Lake Eyre -52 (South Australia)

*(Total is not 100 percent because of rounding.)

THE MAJOR LANDFORMS

God's world is filled with a beautiful variety of land formations. Every variation in the landscape is called a **landform**. Geographers have classified three major landforms—mountains, plains, and plateaus—each of which has played a unique role in human civilization.

MOUNTAINS

Mountains stand high above the surrounding landscape. Geographers distinguish them from hills in that hills are generally smaller than mountains, but no set elevation distinguishes the two. Rather, local usage of the terms is the deciding factor.

Many mountains stand alone above the surrounding landscape. When many mountains appear together, however, such as the Rocky Mountains, the formation is called a **mountain range**. (The Rocky Mountain range is a system so large that it actually contains ranges within ranges, which are then called mountain systems.)

The highest mountain range in the world is the Himalayas (him uh LAY uhz), meaning "abode of snow." The highest peak, Mount Everest, is called Chomolungma ("Sacred Mother of the Waters"). Farmers many miles away depend on the rivers that flow from the melting snows of Mount Everest and other Himalayan peaks.

Mount Elbert, Colorado, is the highest peak in the Rocky Mountains.

In addition to influencing weather, climate, and vegetation, mountains have influenced the pattern of human settlement. Many cities arose near mines, which burrow deep into the belly of mountains. Other cities lie in the fertile valleys of mountain ranges, where they are protected from extreme weather. But in most cases, mountains are too cold, rugged, or infertile for extensive human settlement.

Mountain ranges also hinder travel and contact between people. Populations living in the mountains can easily hide from attack, and social changes are slow to reach them. As you study geography, you will see how cultures, languages, dialects, and national borders are often defined by mountain ranges.

PLAINS

In contrast to mountains, **plains** are wide areas of level land. Some plains that lie in coastal areas, such as land along the Gulf of Mexico, are called *coastal plains*. But low elevation does not define plains; plains can be found at high elevation, too. For example, nestled among the Andes Mountains of South America is the Altiplano, which averages twelve thousand feet above sea level. Plains are not totally flat, either. For instance, the Great Plains region of North America has many rolling hills.

Plains are generally thought of as being flat, such as this one, but some have rolling hills.

Plains are the most valuable landform for farmers. Rivers bring water and sediments down from the mountains, and deposits called **alluvium** settle in the flat plains. Alluvium is often rich in nutrients that enable farms to produce large quantities of food. Therefore, such *alluvial plains* are the "breadbaskets" of many nations. They are often named after the river that flows through them. For example, the Congo Basin (an area drained by a river system) is an alluvial plain named for the mighty Congo River.

PLATEAUS

Plateaus (pla TOHS), a third landform, are wide areas of relatively flat land, like plains, but they rise abruptly above surrounding lands. They are what was left after erosion of soft sedimentary material by the massive movement of the Flood waters. Steep cliffs or slopes mark at least one edge of a plateau. Indeed, plateaus are often called *tablelands* because their surface is sometimes elevated like a tabletop.

The surfaces of plateaus are much more varied than plains, often including hills, mountains, and deep canyons. For example, the Grand Canyon cuts through one of North America's largest plateaus. The most rugged plateaus of the world are often called *highlands*. Plateaus can occur at almost any elevation. The highest is the Tibetan Plateau, which lies on the northern border of the Himalayan range in Asia.

Plateaus generally have poor soils and few resources, except for grass for grazing animals. Indeed, many of the world's deserts are located on plateaus.

A plateau rises abruptly from the plain.

SECTION QUIZ

1. What are three basic landforms on the earth?

2. Which includes ranges? basins? tablelands? highlands?

3. What is the main similarity between plains and plateaus?

4. What is the main difference between plains and plateaus?

5. Choose one of the three landforms and give the main advantages and disadvantages of it for people.

III.   THE EARTH'S WATERS

Like landforms, bodies of water play a major role in human life. The three main bodies of water—oceans or seas, lakes, and rivers—are at the heart of human activity.

THE IMPORTANCE OF WATER

Without a ready supply of fresh water, we would quickly die; therefore, human settlements develop near sources of fresh water. Less than 3 percent of the earth's water is fresh, and more than two-thirds of that water is in polar ice caps and glaciers or is underground. The remaining water, in lakes and rivers, is a precious resource, essential to our growth and survival.

Large bodies of water often provide means for travel and trade. When settlers first arrived in America, they clustered along the coast and rivers rather than moving into the mountains. It was much cheaper to ship foods by water than to transport them overland. Ships could carry ten wagonloads of goods for the same price as one cart pulled over the mountains. Food on ships arrived at the marketplace much sooner; the food cost less and was fresher. Even today, water transportation is by far the least expensive way for most nations to ship products to each other, especially if they do not share a land border.

THE MAJOR BODIES OF WATER
OCEANS

The earth is unique in the solar system. Scientists have not found evidence of liquid water on any other planet or moon, yet water covers 71 percent of the earth's surface, amounting to more than three hundred million cubic miles. Although 97 percent of the water lies in oceans, traces of water can be found on almost every square inch of land.

> *He gathereth the waters of the sea together as an heap: he layeth up the depth in storehouses.*
> (Ps. 33:7)

There are four principal ocean basins in the world: the Pacific, the Atlantic, the Indian, and the Arctic oceans. (Some scientists suggest that the waters around Antarctica should be classified as a fifth ocean. More will be said about this in Chapter 24.) All of the world's seas, gulfs, and bays belong to one of these oceans. Continents generally mark the borders of each ocean. If you look at the world map, however, you will see that the divisions are not always clear. The oceans flow into each other. For this reason, the whole system is sometimes called the **world ocean**.

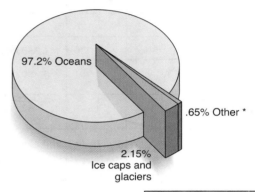

Earth's fresh water and salt water

97.2% Oceans

.65% Other *

2.15% Ice caps and glaciers

* Other	
Ground water	.62%
Freshwater lakes	.009%
Saltwater lakes	.008%
Soil water	.005%
Vapor	.001%
Streams and rivers	.0001%

The Principal Oceans of the World			
Ocean	Area (sq. mi.)	Percent of World Ocean	Lowest Point (ft.)
Pacific	70,000,000	50.0	Mariana Trench 35,840
Atlantic	36,000,000	25.5	Puerto Rico Trench 28,232
Indian	29,000,000	20.5	Java Trench 23,376
Arctic	5,400,000	4.0	Eurasian Basin 17,881

The oceans provide man with many blessings—distributing thermal energy from the sun, providing water for rain clouds, and guarding nations from foreign invasion. Ocean waters teem with tasty fish and pearl-producing clams. The most obvious but often overlooked bounty of the sea, however, is its salt. Salt has many uses: a seasoning for and preservative of food; a curer of leather; and a chemical used in refrigeration, soap manufacturing, and other industries.

If mankind could drink ocean water and pump it into his parched fields, it would solve many of his worst problems. But the high concentration of salt—about 3.5 percent of the total mass of seawater—is harmful to crops and land animals. Swallowing too much salt water leads to a quick, painful death from dehydration. Irrigating farmland with ocean water stunts the growth of plants and quickly makes the land unproductive. (We will discuss the oceans more in Chapter 24.)

RIVERS

Water is in constant motion. Unless something gets in its way, water will eventually flow to the ocean. Small streams flow into rivers, which, in turn, flow into even larger rivers. Rivers that "feed" other rivers are called **tributaries**. The main river and all of its tributaries are called a **river system**. Many of the world's great river systems flow more than two thousand miles from their *headwaters* (source) to their mouth. The "greatest" river systems are determined by comparing various features, including the following.

Length—The most obvious comparison is length. The Nile is the longest river, an impressive 4,160 miles. But depending on which tributary one designates as the headwaters, the Amazon might be longer.

The longest river in the United States, the Mississippi, does not even show up on the chart. It is only 2,340 miles long, or twelfth in the world. But this figure ignores the length of its longest tributary, the Missouri River, which is even longer than the main trunk of the Mississippi. Measuring from the headwaters of the Missouri adds another 1,600 miles to the Mississippi-Missouri River, increasing its rank to fourth place. Even this number ignores the tributaries that feed the Missouri.

Discharge—Another feature of comparison is the amount of water flowing out into the ocean—the discharge. It would take fifty rivers the size of the Nile to match the volume of water that flows from the Amazon. The volume is so large that the water from the Amazon remains fresh and drinkable two hundred miles out into the Atlantic Ocean.

Drainage Area—A third feature for comparison is the size of the **drainage basin**, the total land area drained by the main river and its tributaries. The Nile's drainage basin is small and mostly dry and has few tributaries. In contrast, the Amazon River drains a rain forest that covers 40 percent of the continent of South America. The Missouri River has the fifth largest drainage basin (1,244,000 sq. mi.).

Navigability—A fourth feature of comparison is depth, how far up a river ocean-going vessels can travel. Steamboats ply the Missouri River more than one thou-

The Longest Rivers in the World

River	Location	Length (miles*)	Discharge (cu. ft.)	Drainage Area (sq. mi.)
Nile	Africa	4,160	10,000	1,293,000
Amazon	S. America	4,000	6,350,000	2,722,000
Chang (Yangtze)	Asia	3,964	1,200,000	756,000
Huang He (Yellow)	Asia	3,395	52,900	288,000
Congo	Africa	2,718	1,458,000	1,314,000
Amur	Asia	2,744	438,000	716,000
Lena	Asia	2,734	547,000	961,000
Mackenzie	N. America	2,635	400,000	711,000
Mekong	Asia	2,600	500,000	307,000
Niger	Africa	2,590	215,000	730,000

* Estimates of length vary depending on the reference consulted and the location chosen as the river's source.

The Amazon River discharges 6.35 million cubic feet of water every second.

Jefferson
Beaverhead
Red Rock

Missouri River

Continental Divide

Mississippi River Basin

sand miles from the ocean. Barges rely on deep, **navigable rivers** for carrying goods from their distant sources to coastal cities. The Mississippi River and its tributaries include more than fifteen thousand miles of navigable water, making it the second largest inland water route in the world. The Amazon is the only river system longer than the Mississippi.

Rivers have played a central role in the history of almost every nation. Historically, explorers have used these waters as roads to the interior. Many pioneers who came after the explorers settled near these rivers, and most cities were founded beside rivers. For example, St. Louis sprang up at the point where boats floating down the Missouri entered the Mississippi River. Even where rivers are too shallow for travel, they provide drinking water, irrigation, fish, game, power generation, and recreation. The birthplace of almost every great civilization, such as ancient Egypt, was somewhere along a river.

LAKES

Bodies of water fully enclosed by land are called **lakes** and are remnants of the Flood and ice age. Many cities are located on the shores of lakes because lakes provide fish, drinking water, transportation, and recreation. Lakes make it possible for some cities to be built deep in the interior of continents.

The Great Lakes of North America are the largest system of freshwater lakes in the world. This system includes the world's largest freshwater lake (by area)—Lake Superior. The Great Lakes support many large cities, including Chicago and Detroit.

Other continents also have important freshwater lakes. Lake Titicaca, high in the Andes Mountains, is the largest lake in South America and the highest navigable lake in the world. Africa's Lake Chad has been the heart

Barges ply the Mississippi River as far inland as Minneapolis, eighteen hundred miles from the ocean.

The World's Largest Lakes

Lake	Location	Area (sq. mi.)	Depth (ft.)	Volume (cu. mi.)
Caspian Sea	Asia	143,244	3,363	19,035
Superior	N. America	31,700	1,330	2,916
Victoria	Africa	26,828	270	637
Huron	N. America	23,000	220	827
Michigan	N. America	22,300	750	1,161
Aral Sea	Asia	14,900	923	80
Tanganyika	Africa	12,700	4,823	4,659
Baykal	Asia	12,162	5,315	5,581
Great Bear	N. America	12,096	1,463	529
Nyasa	Africa	11,150	2,280	2,009

Chicago, one of the most important cities in the United States, was founded on Lake Michigan.

of great empires in central Africa. In east Africa is Lake Victoria, the largest lake on the continent and the second largest freshwater lake in the world.

Lake Baykal, located in Asia, is both the deepest lake and the largest freshwater lake (by volume). More than a mile deep, it holds almost as much fresh water as all of the Great Lakes combined, but its surface area is relatively small.

The Caspian Sea, also in Asia, is the world's largest lake. Unlike Lake Superior, however, its water is salty. While the water in freshwater lakes is kept clean by rivers or other outlets that carry dissolved minerals downstream, a few drainage basins of the world have no outlet to the ocean. Water collects at the lowest spot, called a depression. The Caspian Sea is actually *below* sea level. As the water evaporates, minerals are left behind. Though rare, such salt lakes are often large and famous. For example, the Dead Sea, which is about 30 percent salt, is the saltiest lake in the world. (Utah's Great Salt Lake is 10–25 percent salt, and ocean water is typically 3 percent salt.)

SEAS

Seas are arms of the ocean partially enclosed by land. Seas can vary greatly in size, and some even have seas within seas. For example, a map of the Mediterranean Sea reveals seven arms in the north that ancient peoples called the "seven seas." The Greek and Roman civilizations arose along their shores. Sailors prefer carrying people and goods on the smaller seas because they have smaller waves. The shores blunt the blows of most violent storms that batter ships on the "open" seas, such as the Mediterranean.

Ships need safe places to anchor while they load and unload their cargo. A sheltered body of deep water next to the shore is called a **harbor**. Good harbors are rare. The water must be deep enough that the ships do not run aground. The shore must encircle enough of the sea to shelter ships from winds and waves that might otherwise drive them into the rocks or sand. A key to the success of America's original colonies was their harbors. Boston, New York, Philadelphia, and Charleston quickly became major port cities because of their great harbors.

The World's Largest Seas		
Sea	Location	Area (sq. mi.)
Philippine Sea	Pacific Ocean	2,700,000
Coral Sea	Pacific Ocean	1,850,000
Arabian Sea	Indian Ocean	1,492,000
South China Sea	Pacific Ocean	1,148,000
Weddell Sea	Atlantic Ocean	1,080,000
Caribbean Sea	Atlantic Ocean	971,000
Mediterranean Sea	Atlantic Ocean	969,100
Tasman Sea	Pacific Ocean	900,000
Bering Sea	Pacific Ocean	873,000
Bay of Bengal	Indian Ocean	839,000

These superfreighters are being unloaded at a shipyard in a harbor.

Charleston Harbor is one of the many good harbors along the U.S. east coast.

WETLANDS

Areas of stagnant water—often referred to as bogs, swamps, moors, fens, muskegs, or marshes—are collectively known as **wetlands**. They are not actually bodies of water, but neither are they dry land. Wetlands most often form in lowland areas near coasts, rivers, and lakes, where water cannot drain away. Water saturates the ground of these areas and often collects to form murky pools a few inches deep. Wetlands are often at sea level.

Wetlands are categorized into three basic divisions according to their appearance and vegetation. **Bogs** are spongy areas that look dry but are covered with wet organic materials. These soggy lands may have formed on top of old lakes, and a layer of water may remain below the surface. Mosses commonly grow in bogs, but few other plants survive. The mosses may collect and form a thick layer of dead organic matter called peat, which in some areas of the world is cut, dried, and burned for fuel.

A **marsh** has visible standing water, and the main kinds of vegetation growing there are grasses and small water plants that survive with their roots submerged. The Florida Everglades is a very large marsh.

Like marshes, **swamps** are covered by standing water. The basic difference is that swamps are dominated by large trees whereas marshes are not. Cyprus, mangrove, and willow trees grow in swamps with their roots reaching down through the mire. Alligators, snakes, and other wild animals make swamps and marshes mysterious and somewhat scary places.

Unusual forms of plant life thrive in wetlands, as do insects and water animals. Mosquitoes, which reproduce abundantly in murky water, have been such a menace, because of the diseases they carry, that man has tried to drain many wetland areas. (Malaria and West Nile disease are but two such diseases.) In recent years, however, governments have been declaring many of the remaining wetlands protected areas because of their scenic beauty and endangered plant and animal species. They aid in flood control and water storage. They also are believed to provide the nursery for much of the world's food chain, and they effectively filter pollution from the water.

Wetlands are a source of conflict between private property owners and government regulators. Landowners have spent large sums of money to purchase prime coastal land, for example, but government regulators have rejected their plans to build on their property or to fill in mosquito-infested pools. Part of the debate concerns something as basic as the definition of a wetland. Early laws regulating wetlands defined them as places where water stands for at least seven days in the year, but property owners want to raise the number to twenty-one. Conservatives have proposed laws to compensate property owners for the value of the land that is lost as a result of government regulations.

SECTION QUIZ

1. What are the two main reasons that water is important to human activity?

2. What four factors must one consider when comparing rivers?

3. Which river system is the greatest in each category?

4. Compare and contrast the Great Lakes and Lake Baykal.

5. Why are some large lakes salty?

6. Define *sea* and *harbor* and explain why they are important to trade.

☀ Why did many major cities develop along rivers?

IV. THE EARTH'S SURFACE-CHANGING FORCES

The earth's surface is constantly changing. Since the Flood, two basic processes continue to shape the earth. Internal forces (earthquakes and volcanoes) push rocks up, and external forces (wind and water) break rocks down. Both forces help to create the mountains and other landforms we see today.

INTERNAL FORCES

Earthquakes and volcanoes are evidences of powerful forces at work deep within the earth. These internal forces are not perfectly understood, but scientists have some clues. They have known for a long time that volcanoes and earthquakes are clustered along distinct lines on the earth's surface. Using sonar (a method of using underwater sound waves, or "echoes," to detect objects or waves), scientists discovered that these lines continue under the oceans. The ocean floor is scarred by lines of deep trenches and high ridges.

PLATE TECTONICS

Basing their conclusions on this evidence, scientists proposed that the crust is broken into pieces called plates. According to the **plate tectonics** (tek TAHN iks) **theory**, the plates crash into and pull apart from one another, releasing energy from the earth's interior and causing earthquakes and volcanoes.

Some scientists suggest that the earth's crust broke suddenly into sections, or plates, during the Flood, when "all the fountains of the great deep [were] broken up" (Gen. 7:11). Those plates continue to move today, creating earth tremors and earthquakes.

One of the most noticeable evidences of tectonic activity is faulting. **Faults** are deep cracks in the earth's surface where two pieces of land have moved in different directions. Although the movement is rarely more than a few inches, it can devastate life and property. The highest land displacement ever recorded—nearly fifty feet—took place during the Alaska earthquake of 1964. Faulting is of two types: *strike-slip* and *thrust*, both of which are illustrated here.

The other notable evidence of tectonic activity is folding. Just as a piece of paper will bend when you push the edges toward the center, so unconsolidated sediment can bend upward into a **fold** when it is pushed from both sides.

Evidence of the destructive power of the earth's internal forces was seen in the 1964 Alaska earthquake.

Types of tectonic activity

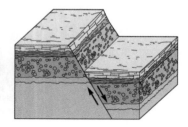

(a) Thrust fault

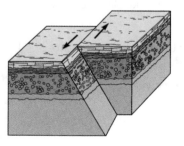

(b) Strike-slip fault

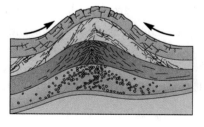

(c) Fold

The Paricutín eruptions between 1943 and 1952 caused a lot of property damage and altered the local landscape dramatically.

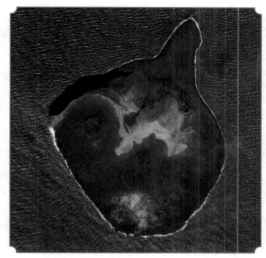

The island of Surtsey, seen in this aerial view, was born when a volcano erupted under the sea.

PANGAEA?

By putting the pieces of the earth together like a jigsaw puzzle, one might conclude that all of the continents could have been at some time in the past joined in one huge landmass. Some scientists assume that the continents must have "drifted" to their present position.

The **continental drift theory** claims to explain events that evolutionists say occurred over hundreds of millions of years. After comparing fossils and landforms on different continents, scientists concluded that all of the continents were once linked into one supercontinent, called Pangaea (pan JEE uh), 220 million years ago. Many Creationists basically agree that the earth was created with a single supercontinent. They disagree with evolutionists, however, as to the mechanism and time frame for the plate tectonics that would have broken the continent apart. To theorize what Pangaea looked like is mere conjecture.

No firm proof for such a large-scale "continental drift" exists, but if any drift did occur, we know that it would have happened relatively quickly, not over millions of years.

Whatsoever the Lord pleased, that did he in heaven, and in earth, in the seas, and all deep places.
(Ps. 135:6)

Many mountains seem to have been formed by faulting and folding. The Sierra Nevada of the western United States offer a classic example of *fault mountains*. Folding is evident in the Himalayas, the Rockies, and the Alps, but some of the best examples of *fold mountains* are in the Appalachians. Both fault mountains and fold mountains are called *deformational mountains* because tectonic forces seem to have "deformed" the rocks that were already on the surface.

VOLCANIC FORCES

A mountain-building force still active today is volcanoes. Volcanoes deposit new lava on the earth's surface, and it hardens into *depositional mountains*. In 1943, the fourteen-hundred-foot volcano Paricutín (pah REE koo TEEN) formed in a farmer's cornfield. Similarly, in 1963, a mountain rose from the sea near Iceland, creating the island of Surtsey. It now stands five hundred feet above the water and is a mile long. The world's largest active volcano is Mauna Loa, on the island of Hawaii. The island is the tip of a massive volcano that rises 33,476 feet from the sea floor—higher than Mount Everest!

EXTERNAL FORCES

Landforms do not remain the same. External forces called weathering and erosion wear away the landforms that internal forces have pushed up.

WEATHERING

Although rock might seem solid and unmoving, it is constantly weakened by the action of **weathering**, the breakdown of rocks by water, plant roots, temperature changes, and the formation of ice and mineral crystals.

Some kinds of rocks break down more easily than others. Rocks with layers are easily separated. Others shatter under extreme temperature changes. When water collects in pores and freezes, it expands, and the rock breaks. When plants take root and grow, the roots exert tremendous pressure, causing more disintegration. Natural acids (from rain, plants, and decaying matter) can dissolve some rocks. The waters of Noah's Flood, both rising and receding, would have washed away soft rocks and sediment, leaving behind harder rocks in unusual pillars.

Weathering is crucial to life on the earth because it enriches the **soil**, the thin layer of the earth's surface where plants grow.

Glaciers descend into the sea at Glacier Bay, Alaska.

Thor's Hammer at Bryce Canyon, Utah, is an example of a weathered pillar.

Tides eroded this sea stack.

Weathering produces particles of sand, silt, and clay (called **sediment**) that mix with **humus** (decayed formerly living matter) to form soil. Farmers carefully study their soils to find out which of them, combined with fertilizers, will be most productive.

EROSION

After weathering breaks down rock into small pieces, those materials are removed by the following forms of **erosion**.

Wind erosion is strongest in dry areas, particularly deserts. The abrasive action of tiny particles of sand blown by the wind can, over time, do great damage to landforms. The loss of soil through winds can also be destructive to farmers. For example, windstorms ruined American farmers throughout the Great Plains during the Dust Bowl of the 1930s. "Black blizzards" of choking dust darkened the skies as far away as New York.

Wave erosion alters the seashore, creating sea caves, sea stacks, and sea arches. Waves also deposit sand offshore, making sandbars or whole islands. That is how many of the popular barrier islands along the North American coast were formed.

> *The waters wear the stones: thou washest away the things which grow out of the dust of the earth.*
> (Job 14:19)

Glacial erosion occurs when **glaciers**, large masses of moving ice and snow, flow downhill under the pull of gravity. Like gigantic bulldozers, glaciers push and scrape the earth in their paths. When glaciers receded to their current locations, they left behind hills of debris known as *terminal moraines*. Two famous moraines extend across the entire length of Long Island, New York.

Running water, however, is the most powerful force of erosion. It quickly flows through soil and soft rocks, carrying away materials as it goes. During floods, water can carve deep gullies very quickly. But water's slow action over years can be just as devastating. Farmers are constantly battling to keep water from eroding their *topsoil* through normal runoff.

SECTION QUIZ

1. What evidence supports the plate tectonics theory?
2. What are the two most notable types of tectonic activity?
3. What is the difference between weathering and erosion?
4. List four forces that cause erosion.
5. What does weathering produce that is essential for life on earth?
- ☼ List ways by which mankind can reduce or control harmful weathering and erosion.

V. THE EARTH'S CLIMATE

Before God created the sea and dry land, He created light and the atmosphere, both of which are essential to life on earth.

Running water can erode vast amounts of fertile soil, depriving an area of valuable nutrients and leaving ugly ditches.

Volcano-rich Iceland harnesses the earth's geothermal energy to produce electricity.

This is about as dark as it gets in summer over Lake Laberge, Yukon, Canada.

Latitude Zones

90° N
North Pole

POLAR REGION   HIGH LATITUDES

66½° N

TEMPERATE
ZONE   MIDDLE LATITUDES

Tropic of Cancer   23½° N

TROPICS   LOW LATITUDES

Tropic of Capricorn

23½° S

TEMPERATE
ZONE   MIDDLE LATITUDES

66½° S

POLAR REGION   HIGH LATITUDES

90° S
South Pole

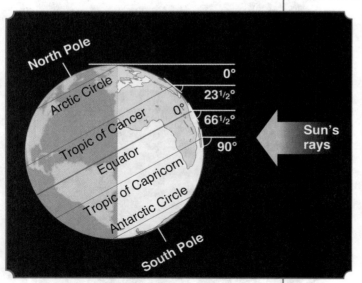

North Pole in Winter, December 21

Light is the "fuel" that drives the earth's "engine." It supplies energy for plants to grow and warms the sea and the land. The atmosphere is a blanket of air around the earth. It is part of the earth's "heating and ventilation system" that distributes thermal energy to the remote corners of the globe and draws ocean water back up to the mountaintops. Without the constant movement of thermal energy and water, the continents would become dust, the equator would be an inferno, and the polar oceans would be ice.

THERMAL ENERGY IN MOTION

Thankfully, God has designed three main systems to distribute thermal energy over the earth, thereby avoiding such extremes: seasons, winds, and ocean currents.

SEASONS

While the earth remaineth, seedtime and harvest, and cold and heat, and summer and winter, and day and night shall not cease.
(Gen. 8:22)

The sun is the source of nearly all of the thermal energy that warms the earth. The most obvious evidence of the sun's influence is in the seasons. The United States has four seasons, but some places have other kinds of seasons. Near the equator, where the air is always warm, for example, two seasons are evident: rainy and dry. Near the poles, where the air is always cold, the major seasonal change is six months of constant darkness, followed by six months of a "midnight sun." All of these changes can be considered seasons.

Seasons are caused by the slant of sunlight and the tilt of the earth's axis. These factors explain why different latitudes have different seasons. There are three distinct *latitude zones*. The **low latitudes** lie between the equator (0°) and the Tropic of Cancer (in the Northern Hemisphere) and the Tropic of Capricorn (in the Southern Hemisphere). Because the sunlight is always direct, or nearly so, this zone consistently has very warm temperatures. It is usually called the **tropics**.

In the **middle latitudes** (between the Tropic of Cancer and the Arctic Ocean in the Northern Hemisphere and between the Tropic of Capricorn and the Antarctic Circle in the Southern Hemisphere), the sunlight is nearly direct half of each year, creating seasonal changes from warm summers to cool winters. Because these regions have neither the constant warmth of the tropics nor the extreme cold of the poles, they are called the **Temperate Zone**.

During the long winter nights in the **high latitudes** (between the North Pole and the Arctic Circle in the Northern Hemisphere and between the South Pole and the Antarctic Circle in the Southern Hemisphere), sunlight is always either very slanted or nonexistent. These **polar regions** receive only a small amount of sunlight in winter.

WINDS

The sun's energy is always in motion, even after it reaches the earth's atmosphere. The air carries thermal energy between and within latitude zones. What we call *wind* is ultimately the movement of air caused by the heating and cooling of air masses.

Warm and Cold Air Masses—A large area of moving air with a similar temperature is called an **air mass**. Warm air masses are warmer than the surface of the earth over which they move; cold air masses are cooler than the surface.

Warm and cold air masses move over the earth in regular patterns. A permanent warm air mass sits over the tropics, where the rays of the sun are direct. At the same time, a cold air mass sits over the polar regions. Warm air is constantly rising at the equator and moving to the cold polar regions. As the air cools over the poles, it falls and moves back toward the equator. If the sun were the only factor affecting the circulation of air, surface winds in the United States would always blow to the south, and winds in South America would blow to the north.

In reality, however, a large portion of the tropical air mass loses its thermal energy and falls *before* it reaches the poles. The air drops in the middle latitudes near 30°. Some of the air moves back toward the poles. As the air travels along the surface, it hits frigid air from the poles at about 60° latitude and rises again. Some of this air continues its journey until it finally reaches the frigid poles, where the air drops a second time. The polar air begins moving back toward the equator. As a result of this cycle, the earth has *three* moving cells of air from the equator to the poles.

Coriolis Effect—Few winds blow strictly north or south. The rotation of the earth greatly influences wind direction in something known as the **Coriolis effect**. This phenomenon is somewhat difficult to visualize. You do not feel the earth rotating and revolving, but it is moving quite rapidly (about one thousand miles per hour at the equator and five hundred miles per hour at 30° latitude). The rotation "yanks" the land out from under the wind. The wind continues to flow straight, but the land beneath it veers away.

Wind Belts—The movement of warm and cold air masses, combined with the Coriolis effect, explains the basic movement of thermal energy around the earth. Winds flow in three belts that circle the globe. These belts influence the world's climate and have also influenced the exploration and conquest of the world.

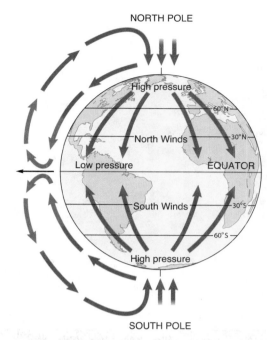

The flow of hot and cold air masses

Hurricanes are caused by rapid heating and cooling of air in the tropics.

JET STREAMS

Jet streams occur where temperate air meets air of more extreme temperature—either cold polar air or warm tropical air. Meteorologists use the jet streams in predicting weather, and scientists are trying to understand better the effect that jet streams have on weather. For example, winter jet streams looping down from Canada pull Arctic air as far south as Texas.

Jet streams were discovered during World War II when B-29 Superfortress pilots discovered that they were reaching—and overshooting—their bomb targets earlier than they had calculated. When possible, modern-day pilots flying from west to east take advantage of the jet stream to increase speeds by up to three hundred miles per hour, thereby saving both fuel and time. Because the jet stream does not flow in a straight line, however, they cannot use it for any great distance. Also, pilots flying east to west must avoid the jet stream lest it slow them down.

The hot tropics have the most powerful prevailing winds. Tropical islands are famous for the constant warm winds, called **trade winds**, that blow over the beaches. (The word *trade* once meant "a regular path.") Columbus used these steady winds to carry his ships west to the New World. European sailors called them the "northeast trades." (They named winds after the direction *from which they came*, not the direction they were going.)

The prevailing winds that blow over the middle latitudes are called the **westerlies**. They are important because they bring warm air from the tropics to lands far to the north, such as Europe. Less powerful than the trade winds, westerlies still helped Columbus and other explorers sail back east to Europe from the New World.

OCEAN CURRENTS

Like the atmosphere, the ocean absorbs thermal energy from the sun. Because water holds thermal energy much longer than air does, the oceans are even more reliable than the wind in distributing thermal energy. Temperature differences create warm and cold

LET'S GO EXPLORING

MAJOR OCEAN CURRENTS

1. What warm current begins in the tropics of North America and ends near Europe?

2. Do any warm currents flow past the west coast of South America?

3. List all of the *named* currents in the Pacific Ocean and tell if they are warm or cold.

- Guess which currents Magellan's ship followed from Europe on the first trip around the world.

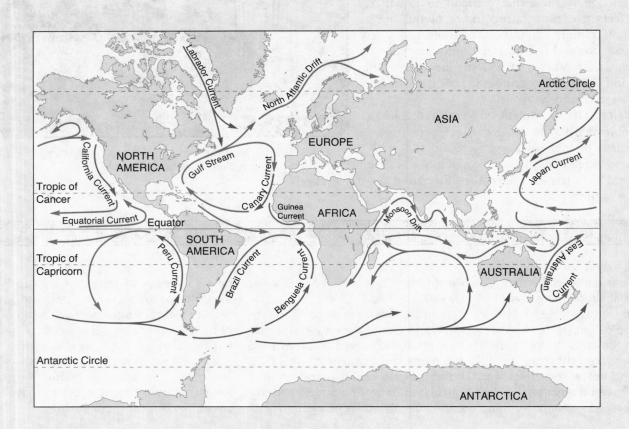

ocean currents that circle the globe, following a pattern similar to the prevailing winds. Water is heated near the equator and moves toward the poles. Cold water from the poles sinks and returns to the equator. The presence of continents causes the most obvious variations between these ocean currents.

The prevailing winds help to propel surface currents. But ocean currents move more slowly than winds. The normal speed is less than ten miles per hour. The slowest currents are called *drifts*. In some cases, however, currents may move very fast. For example, the Gulf Stream, which begins in the Gulf of Mexico, flows beyond Florida, up the U.S. Atlantic coast, and to the northeast of the British Isles near the polar region, where it finally weakens and becomes the North Atlantic Drift.

The currents flow in circular patterns. That constant circulation of thermal energy in the oceans keeps tropical water from becoming too warm for sea life, and it keeps polar water from freezing solid. Ocean currents also influence the amount of rain that enters the air and falls on the continents. Cold air contains less moisture than warm air does. Therefore, the coast of Chile is a barren desert because the cold Peru Current flows nearby, but Brazil's coast is a tropical rain forest, supplied by the warm Brazil Current.

SECTION QUIZ

1. What causes wind?
2. How does the Coriolis effect change the direction of wind?
3. Where is the jet stream?
- ☼ Compare and contrast the role of wind and ocean currents in distributing thermal energy.

WATER IN MOTION

Mount Waialeale in Hawaii receives almost *forty feet* of rain annually. In contrast, no record of rain exists for the Empty Quarter (Rub Al Khali) of the Arabian Peninsula. Few places ever see anything near these extremes because the same systems that distribute thermal energy over the land also help to distribute life-giving water.

> He causeth the vapours to ascend from the ends of the earth;
> he maketh lightnings for the rain; he bringeth the wind out
> of his treasuries.
> (Ps. 135:7)

THE HYDROLOGIC CYCLE

Water appears in three forms: solid (ice), liquid, and gas (water vapor). Ocean water must change form before it reaches plants and animals on land. This change begins as ocean water absorbs thermal energy. When the liquid water absorbs enough thermal energy, it changes into water vapor in a process called **evaporation**. When water vapor loses thermal energy, it changes back to a liquid, suspended in clouds as water droplets, in a process called **condensation**.

Warm winds carry water vapor into the interior of the continents. Warm air can hold a lot of water vapor, or **humidity**, because the molecules are very active. This humidity is not useful, however,

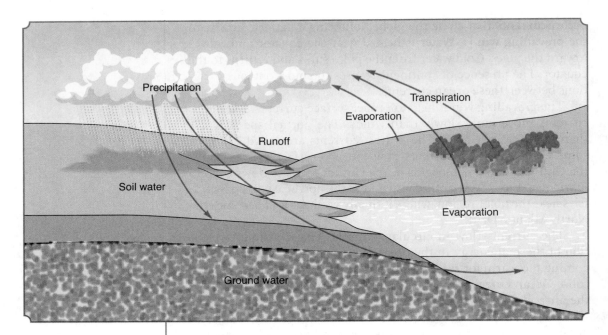

The hydrologic cycle

until it returns to the earth's surface. The point at which water begins condensation is called the **dew point**. When the temperature drops, the water vapor loses energy, condensation occurs, and water falls to the earth in a process called **precipitation**.

Most precipitation is in the form of rain, but water also can fall in solid form. A sudden drop in temperature causes water vapor to freeze, lose energy, and fall to the earth as snow, sleet, or hail.

> *For he saith to the snow, Be thou on the earth; likewise to the small rain, and to the great rain of his strength.*
> (Job 37:6)

The process of evaporation, condensation, and precipitation is called the **hydrologic cycle**. The Lord uses it to replenish the soil, lakes, and rivers with water.

About 80 percent of precipitation occurs over the oceans, but the rest falls on land. The water stays on the earth's surface, however, for only a brief time. Some runs off into rivers or lakes. Some seeps through the soil to become **ground water**. (Ground water is like a slow-moving river under the ground.) Eventually, however, all water returns to the oceans or evaporates, completing the cycle.

Three situations cause a humid air mass to cool and produce precipitation. One cause is the presence of mountains. When a warm mass of humid air passes over a mountainous area, the air moves upward and cools rapidly. Water vapor condenses into droplets, clouds form, and precipitation quickly follows. Because mountains are often bitterly cold, snow and sleet are common. This precipitation is said to be **orographic** (*oros,* "mountain," and *–graph,* "description").

Orographic precipitation is common where mountain ranges rise close to the ocean or big lakes. Large amounts of water enter the air, and prevailing winds drive the water over the mountains. The land beyond the mountains, an area called the **rainshadow**, is usually very dry because little water vapor survives the trip.

Another important cause of precipitation is the meeting of cold and warm air masses. The warmer air is lighter, so it rises above the cooler, denser air as if it were moving over a mountain range.

Rain or snow falls along the line where the two air masses meet. The line is called a **front**. For precipitation to occur, the warm air mass must have water vapor that it picked up over an ocean or large lake. Frontal precipitation is common in the eastern United States, where warm air masses move in from the Gulf of Mexico and the Great Lakes.

A third cause of precipitation is **convection**, the rise of warm air over a hot surface. In the heart of continents, the land cools at night and then heats up rapidly under the summer sun. The hot air is sometimes trapped beneath a cool air mass. When the warm, light air breaks through the cool air above, it rushes upward and cools quickly. Precipitation falls immediately and often violently. Lightning and hail may accompany such storms.

SECTION QUIZ

1. What is the difference between condensation and precipitation?
2. Explain how the dew point is related to precipitation.
3. Describe the hydrologic cycle.
4. What are the three main situations that contribute to precipitation? Which is most obvious on a climate map?

- Both sides of mountains on the East Coast of the United States are wet, but the mountains in California are wet on the west side and dry on the east side. Why?

CLIMATES

The amount of thermal energy and water that reaches each region of the world determines its basic **climate**—the typical weather in a region over a long period of time. **Weather**, on the other hand, is the atmospheric conditions of a location at a specific moment in time. Weather often changes, but climate, with only slight occasional variations, remains generally the same.

Daily changes in weather seldom determine what lives there or whether the region is good for man. Even a year of record lows or highs in temperature or rainfall does not make much of a difference. There are five broad categories of world climate. This classification system will be used on the climate maps and in the text throughout the rest of your textbook.

TROPICAL RAINY

Two climates occur in the warm tropics, where the rainfall is extremely heavy. Trees grow in the *tropical wet* areas, where rain falls all year (averaging ten inches per month). Only grasses grow in the *tropical wet and dry* areas. With only about half an inch of rain during the winter months, trees cannot survive the dry season.

DRY

In *deserts*, annual precipitation is ten inches or less. Lack of water, not high temperatures, creates deserts. Deserts are often called **arid**, which means "lacking moisture." Deserts can occur at any latitude, cold or hot. The ice-covered interior of Greenland is technically a desert!

Situations that create precipitation

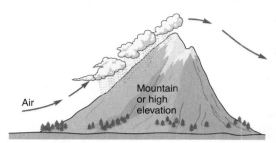

Orographic Precipitation

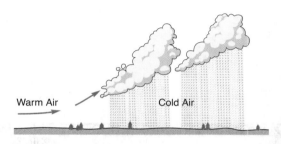

Frontal Precipitation

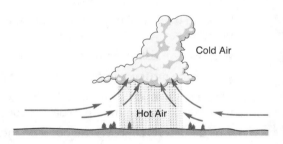

Convection Precipitation

Semiarid regions receive a few more inches of rainfall than deserts and therefore can support grasses. Pioneers once called the Great Plains of the United States the "Great American Desert," but large parts of it are actually semiarid grassland, where wheat and other grains now grow.

COLD

Some regions receive sufficient rainfall but are too cold to support many kinds of plants. For example, nothing grows on the world's two *ice caps* in Antarctica and Greenland, which have a thick layer of ice that never melts. Although *polar regions* are cold year-round, plants grow for a brief period in the middle of the summer, when some of the snow cover melts. *Subpolar regions* are not as severe in the summer, permitting hardy evergreen trees to grow. Winters are bitterly cold in all three regions, averaging less than 0°F (–18°C).

MODERATE

Most of the world's good farmland and major civilizations are located in the four climate regions with moderate rainfall and temperatures. All four climates occur in the middle latitudes, or Temperate (moderate) Zone. *Humid subtropical* refers to lands just above

LET'S GO EXPLORING

CLIMATES OF THE WORLD

1. For each type of climate, give the continent where it appears most.

2. What is the most common climate at the equator?

3. What is the most common climate at the Arctic Circle?

4. Where is a humid subtropical climate most common, on the east coast or on the west coast of continents?

💡 Why do deserts almost never occur on the equator?

Climates of the World

Tropical Rainy
- Tropical Wet (Rain Forest)
- Tropical Wet and Dry (Savanna)

Dry
- Tropical and Temperate Dry (Desert)
- Semiarid (Steppe)

Moderate
- Marine West Coast
- Mediterranean
- Humid Continental
- Humid Subtropical

Cold
- Icecap
- Polar (Tundra)
- Subpolar (Taiga)

Other
- Varied Highland

the tropics that receive about fifty inches of rain a year, mostly in the summer. The richest farmland in the world is located there.

The other three moderate climates are named after the regions where they occur in Europe: the continent, the Mediterranean Sea, and the west coast. The *humid continental* region extends far into the interior of the Eurasian continent. Rainfall is adequate but irregular because of the distance it must travel from the ocean to reach the land. Winters are colder there than in any other moderate region. In the *mediterranean* climate, little water falls during the summer, so the land supports few crops without irrigation.

In the *marine west coast*, which covers most of Western Europe, warm ocean currents bring warm, moist air that blows over the coast and provides a nice, steady rain. The rain is heavier in the winter than in the summer—about six inches per month in contrast to three inches.

VARIED HIGHLAND

Another principle is at work in mountains. There are many gas molecules near sea level, where the pull of gravity is greatest. These molecules hold much thermal energy. As the altitude increases, however,

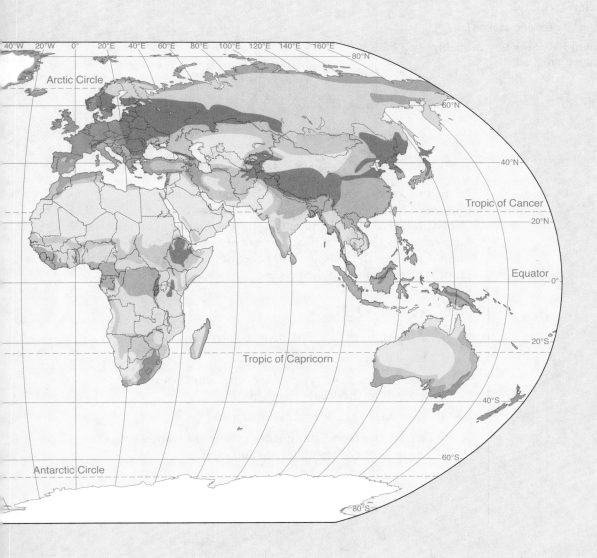

GEOGRAPHER'S CORNER

CLIMOGRAPHS

Climate charts, or **climographs**, combine two important pieces of information about the climate of a city: the average temperature and the average total precipitation during each month. Climographs help one to visualize what life is like in the city. But remember that these graphs *show averages;* daily temperatures may exceed 100°F, and monthly rainfall may be as low as 0 inches.

Use the information on the following two climographs to answer the following questions.

1. About how much rain does Miami receive during July?

2. What is the average temperature in New York City during July?

3. Which city has fairly constant temperatures throughout the year?

4. Which city has a definite rainy season?

5. During which months would freezing temperatures be common in New York City?

6. Which city has the longest growing season?

☼ In which months would New York City probably have more precipitation than Miami?

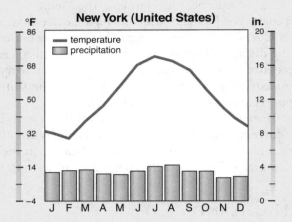

New York (United States)

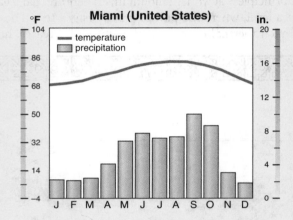

Miami (United States)

the air becomes thinner and holds less thermal energy. For every one thousand-foot increase in altitude, the temperature drops about 3½°F. This drop is called the **lapse rate**. If the temperature at sea level is 65°F, one can expect it to be 30°F at the peak of a ten-thousand-foot mountain. Climbing the mountain has the same effect as traveling three thousand miles toward the poles.

SECTION QUIZ

1. What is the difference between climate and weather?

2. What does *arid* mean?

3. List the four main types of moderate climates and tell the main differences between them.

4. How does altitude affect temperature?

☼ Why do no moderate climates exist in the tropics even though the region receives much sun and rain?

VI. The Earth's Vegetation

> *And God said, Let the earth bring forth grass, the herb yielding seed, and the fruit tree yielding fruit after his kind, whose seed is in itself, upon the earth: and it was so. . . . And the evening and the morning were the third day.*
> (Gen. 1:11,13)

The type of plants, or **vegetation**, that grows in each region depends on the climate. If you compare the vegetation and climate maps, you will see that the regions are similar. Differences between the two maps are caused by local variations in soil, mountains, and rivers.

> *He causeth the grass to grow for the cattle, and herb for the service of man: that he may bring forth food out of the earth.*
> (Ps. 104:14)

A vegetation map also indicates the types of animals that live in a region because animals in a region depend on certain types of plants for food. For example, one would expect to find koalas only in areas where there are eucalyptus trees—the koalas' only food. A **biome** is any large region where distinct populations of plants and animals are found living together. Biomes influence how people make a living, what they eat, and even what their homes look like. The unique characteristics of each biome help to explain why human cultures are so different.

Three basic biomes exist—forests, grasslands, and wastelands—and within each are many variations.

Puerto Rico is home to a tropical rain forest.

Forests

> *And out of the ground made the Lord God to grow every tree that is pleasant to the sight, and good for food.*
> (Gen. 2:9)

Wherever trees are the predominant plants, the region is called a *forest*. Because trees require a large amount of water, most forests are found in rainy climates.

Tropical Rain Forest

Tropical rain forests are found in the tropics, where many kinds of trees and animals proliferate. Teak, mahogany, and ebony are a few of the giant trees found there. The branches and leaves spread out to form a large canopy more than one hundred feet above the forest floor. The trees protect the thin soil from being washed away by the heavy rains. The forests are good for logging but not for farms. Primitive people who live in rain forests often build tree houses or temporary leaf huts.

Shrub Forest

Shrub forests occur in the mild mediterranean climate, where the dry summers do not provide enough rain for trees to reach great heights. Gnarled trees are widely scattered. Dense bushes, or shrubs, are common. This biome is sometimes called *woodlands* or *chaparral* (Spanish, "dense thicket").

Thick brush is typical of shrub forests or chaparral.

Montana includes coniferous forests.

CONIFEROUS FOREST

Conifers (KAHN uh furz) are trees that produce their seeds in a cone. Coniferous forests grow in the cold, harsh subpolar climates where most other trees cannot survive. Water does not evaporate as quickly from their needle leaves as it does from broad leaves. Nearly all needle-leaf trees stay green throughout the year and are known as evergreens. Pines and firs are among the best known evergreens.

Wood from conifers is useful for pulp in paper and for construction, but the wood produces too much soot to be burned. Limited coniferous forests are found in warm, rainy climates near the coast where the soil is poor. Examples include the giant redwoods of California and the pine forests in Florida.

DECIDUOUS FOREST

Some trees called **deciduous** (dih SIJ oo us) lose their leaves during a particular season of the year. Most deciduous trees have flat, broad leaves and require much water and a growing season of at least four months. (The **growing season** is the time between the last kill-

LET'S GO EXPLORING

VEGETATION OF THE WORLD

1. Compare the coniferous forests on this map with the climate map (pp. 38–39). In which climate are they most common?

2. Compare the deciduous forests on this map with the climate map. In which climates are they common?

💡 Compare the rain forests on this map with the rainy wet climate on the climate map. Explain the differences.

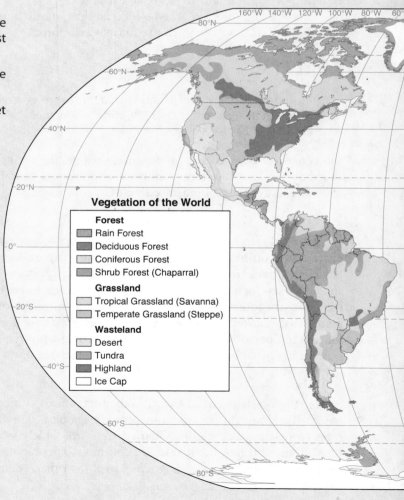

Vegetation of the World

Forest
- Rain Forest
- Deciduous Forest
- Coniferous Forest
- Shrub Forest (Chaparral)

Grassland
- Tropical Grassland (Savanna)
- Temperate Grassland (Steppe)

Wasteland
- Desert
- Tundra
- Highland
- Ice Cap

ing frost of spring and the first killing frost of fall.) Common broadleaf, deciduous trees include maple, oak, and elm. These, too, are used to make wood pulp for paper, and they are also good for heating and the making of furniture.

Many great civilizations developed near deciduous forests. The people there used the hardwoods to build homes, furniture, forts, and ships. Once settlers cleared the forest, the soil proved very fertile. Many areas that were once marked "deciduous forests" on maps are now farms or cities.

GRASSLANDS

Many tropical and temperate regions lack sufficient rainfall to support forests. They might have a substantial rainy season, but a prolonged dry season follows. Although trees can grow under such conditions, they are scattered, mostly near creeks and rivers. Grasses, on the other hand, grow quickly and produce seeds before the dry season comes. Because grasses are so

The Northeast and the Southeast in the United States have many deciduous forests.

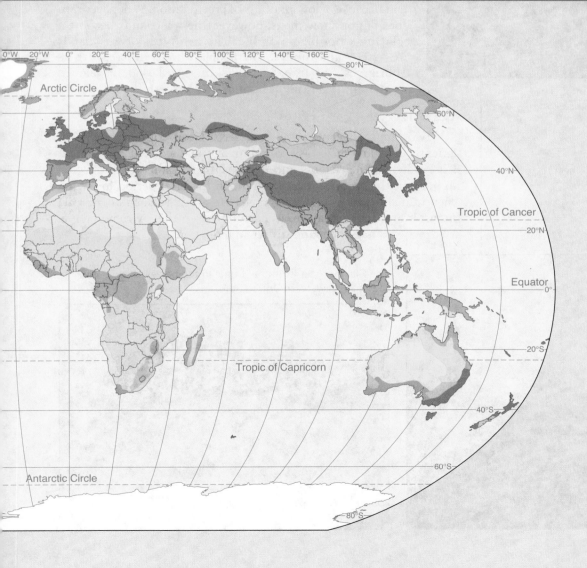

This savanna is near Mt. Kilimanjaro in Kenya, Africa.

These steppes near the Altai Mountains in Siberia are similar to the high plains of South Dakota.

common in these regions, they are called **grasslands**. With little wood available, people in the grasslands often build grass huts, sod houses, or tents from animal skins.

TROPICAL GRASSLAND

Tropical grasslands, or **savannas**, are natural "parks" with open areas and only a few scattered trees. Some grasses grow ten feet high in the rainy season, but the scorching sun soon withers the grass and makes it highly susceptible to fire. African savannas teem with wildebeests, elephants, giraffes, and lions.

TEMPERATE GRASSLAND

Temperate grasslands, often called **steppes**, are found in temperate regions where rainfall is between ten and thirty inches per year. The soil is extremely fertile, but farmers need steel plows to cut the hard ground, and their crops sometimes need to be irrigated. In North America the fertile grasslands are called prairies.

WASTELANDS

Some areas, called **wastelands**, are barren most of the year because of low amounts of precipitation. Whenever rain does fall or snow melts, however, the wastelands become a colorful sea of blooming life. The two types of wastelands are deserts and tundra. The people who live there, such as Aborigines (Australia) and Eskimos (Alaska), developed special survival skills as hunters and herders.

DESERT

Two kinds of plants grow in deserts. Cacti conserve water efficiently and are the most common of the succulent plants that store water in their stems and leaves. Other kinds of plants come to life quickly, produce seeds, and die in the brief period following each rain shower. A surprising variety of animals, such as the Gila monster and the kangaroo rat, can survive in this extreme biome. With wise management and sufficient irrigation, even deserts can be

Cacti thrive in the Arizona desert.

The Gila monster is right at home in the barren desert of the southwestern United States.

transformed into productive land, as has been the case in Israel in modern times.

TUNDRA

The cold regions near the poles are called **tundra** and support only limited vegetation. Precipitation, mainly as snow, is light, but it covers the ground most of the year. During the short summer, only the top three feet of the soil thaws, and shallow-rooted plants (mosses, lichens, and grasses) grow in the soggy soil. Melting snow does not evaporate quickly but collects in mosquito-infested bogs and lakes. When winter comes, the water freezes, and a white blanket of snow returns. The rest of the soil is **permafrost**, which remains frozen year-round. Not even coniferous trees can grow in the tundra.

Herds of caribou and reindeer migrate to the tundra during the summer. Only a few hardy animals—such as musk oxen, hares, and wolves—remain year-round.

This tundra in Canada is frozen much of the year but blossoms for a short time when the summer thaws come.

HIGHLAND VEGETATION

Many kinds of vegetation grow on mountains. In fact, it is possible to see all of the major biomes on one mountain because higher altitudes have lower temperatures (the lapse rate) and because air masses passing over the mountain drop their moisture (orographic precipitation).

MAN'S PLACE IN THE WORLD'S BIOMES

God created the world's biomes to supply man's need for food, clothing, and shelter. After the Flood, Noah's descendants encountered completely new biomes, which arose as the animals on the ark replenished the earth. Those biomes apparently went through many changes during an ice age. Some animals became extinct, but others prospered.

Mankind altered biomes, too, as he attempted to fulfill the Creation Mandate and make the earth more productive by irrigating fields, domesticating animals, draining swamps, terracing steep hillsides, and constructing dams. Unfortunately, fallen humanity has not always been a good steward of God's creation and has often had a severe impact on the environment. When merchants transport seeds to other lands, for instance, they run the risk of introducing new weeds, diseases, and harmful insects. As native plants and animals compete with foreign "invaders," only the hardiest species survive. By the end of the twentieth century, the world's vegetation had become increasingly uniform, or *homogenized.*

Modern nations have debated the effects of human activity on the world's climate and vegetation. In 1992, the United Nations hosted a historic Earth Summit at Rio de Janeiro, Brazil. The key term in the UN's discussions was *sustainable development,* the ability to meet present needs without depleting the resources to support future generations.

In 1997, many nations drafted and signed the Kyoto Treaty, which committed the industrialized nations to reduce greenhouse gasses. The leading nation, the United States, refused to sign it. The topic continues to be debated in both the United States and other countries.

As stewards of God's world, people are responsible for using the world's resources wisely, but that worthy goal must be achieved by appropriate means.

SECTION QUIZ

1. What are the three basic biomes?
2. Contrast coniferous and deciduous forests.
3. What are the two types of grasslands?
4. Why is tundra considered a wasteland?
5. What two conditions cause mountain vegetation to vary?
- ⚐ Should every country strive for sustainable development? Why or why not?

CHAPTER  REVIEW

HOW MUCH DO YOU REMEMBER?

1. What two formative events in the earth's history occurred only once and will never occur again? How do those events contradict uniformitarianism?
2. Name the two layers of the crust.
3. Name the seven continents.
4. Name the four major oceans.
5. What is tectonic activity, and what are its two most notable types?
6. What are weathering and erosion? How do they work together to shape the earth's surface?
7. What causes air masses to rise or fall?
8. What is the basic cause of all precipitation? Under what three conditions does precipitation usually occur?
9. What is permafrost, and in which climate region is it found?

WHAT DO YOU THINK?

1. What evidence contradicts the theories of uniformitarianism and plate tectonics?
2. What major landforms are in your area?
3. What future cataclysms will change the earth's surface?
4. How would the world be different if the earth did not rotate on its axis?
5. In your opinion, what is the perfect climate?
6. What kind of natural vegetation is most common near your home and why?

Can You:
Define These Terms?

uniformitarianism	wave erosion
cataclysm	glacial erosion
continent	glacier
island	air mass
continental island	Coriolis effect
oceanic island	trade winds
landform	westerlies
mountain range	ocean currents
plain	evaporation
alluvium	condensation
plateau	humidity
world ocean	dew point
tributary	precipitation
river system	hydrologic cycle
drainage basin	ground water
navigable river	orographic
lake	rainshadow
sea	front
harbor	convection
wetland	climate
bog	weather
marsh	arid
swamp	climograph
plate tecton-ics theory	lapse rate
	vegetation
fault	biome
fold	conifers
continental drift theory	deciduous
	growing season
weathering	grassland
soil	savanna
sediment	steppe
humus	wasteland
erosion	tundra
wind erosion	permafrost

Locate These Features?

atmosphere	low latitudes
lithosphere	tropics
hydrosphere	middle latitudes
crust	Temperate Zone
mantle	high latitudes
core	polar regions

UNIT 2

GRAND TOUR JOURNALS: A SAMPLE

Many people who embarked on Grand Tours kept a record of their trip in a journal. They understood, as John Elsner stated, that travel writing "is always an act of cultural appropriation. It naturalises what was seen out there; it brings home, down to earth, what was foreign; it opens a door for the people of one's own world to some understanding (however inadequate, however partial) of another world which they do not know."[1]

Consider the following excerpt from an essay in which famed journalist George Orwell describes a community of Jews he observed in Marrakech, Morocco, a predominantly Arab land.

"In the bazaar huge families of Jews, all dressed in the long black robe and little black skull-cap, are working in dark fly-infested booths that look like caves. A carpenter sits cross-legged at a prehistoric lathe, turning chair-legs at lightning speed. He works the lathe with a bow in his right hand and guides the chisel with his left foot, and thanks to a lifetime of sitting in this position his left leg is warped out of shape. At his side his grandson, aged six, is already starting on the simpler parts of the job."[2]

The unit openers in this book give you a glimpse of the people or geography of one of the places you will study in that unit. You will see it all through the eyes of one who was there. Put yourself in the travelers' shoes and enjoy the experiences they share.

[1]Elsner, John (1994). "From the Pyramids to Pausanias and Piglet: Monuments, Travel and Writing." in *Art and Text in Ancient Greek Culture*, ed. 5. Goldhill and R. Osborne, 224–254. Cambridge: Cambridge University Press.
(Quoted at https://tspace.library.utoronto-ca./citd/holtorf/5.2.9.html)

[2]Orwell, George (1939). "Marrakech," in *Collected Essays*. (Quoted from http://etext.library. adelaide.edu.au/o/orwell/george/o79e/part8.html.)

LIFE AND WORK IN COMMUNITY

CULTURAL SNAPSHOT

After God created Adam and Eve, He gave them work to do: they were to exercise "dominion" over all animal life (Gen. 1:26), to "subdue" the earth (1:28), and to "dress" and "keep" the Garden of Eden (2:15). It is important to note that this multipart assignment was not a punishment for sin; Adam and Eve had not yet eaten of the forbidden fruit. Rather, it was meant to be a natural part of human life. These facts teach us that work is a good and worthy activity, something for our benefit and God's glory, not something to be avoided or hated.

Work—whether it be dressing and keeping the Garden of Eden, mowing your lawn and weeding your mother's flower beds, studying for a test, developing a faster computer operating system, or designing high-tech equipment for exploring the ocean depths—is good. God designed people to obtain their sustenance and achieve their sense of self-worth from work. All such work is called *industry*, and industry is a major part of culture. The English Puritans strongly emphasized the concept of individual "vocation," or "calling," and the importance of viewing one's work as a way to worship and serve God.

To work more efficiently, people invent and build tools and develop systems and methods. These efforts, in turn, lead to specialization, further improvements in efficiency, increased production, and better provision for more people. Henry Grady Weaver (1889–1949), a head of customer research for General Motors, summarized this human process in his book *The Mainspring of Human Progress.*

> Through foresight, imagination, and individual initiative, man develops tools and facilities which expand his efforts and enable him to produce things which would not otherwise be possible. This is an outstanding difference between man and animal, just as it is an outstanding difference between civilization and barbarism.

Progress toward better living would never have been possible, except through the development of tools to extend the uses of human energy—tools that harness the forces of nature as a substitute for muscular effort. . . . The introduction of tools marked the beginning of man's progress in three important directions: (1) more effective use of energy; (2) specialization of effort; and (3) advances in human co-operation and improvements in living conditions, through the peaceful exchange of goods and services.*

This aspect of culture—industry—is an effort to fulfill the Creation Mandate. For industry to be effective, people within a community must get along, work together cooperatively, trade, keep the peace, ensure individual and national freedom, and control or punish all who engage in antisocial or socially harmful behavior. But Satan seeks to create chaos and impose slavery by turning humans against each other and by turning their efforts toward ungodly and harmful activities. As a result, the world includes regions that persist in economic poverty, social instability, political authoritarianism, and spiritual blindness. These problems demonstrate the importance of good government—one that ensures the maximum amount of personal freedom while ensuring both the protection of life, liberty, and property and the positive creative use of human ingenuity.

But culture involves more than work and government. It includes languages and communication; methods and organizations for transmitting regional and national values, history, and ways of life from one generation to another; and records of vital statistics about individual countries. In this unit we will focus on all of these aspects of culture under the broad headings of industry (the human use of God's resources) and society (the many interactions of people).

*Weaver, Henry Grady. *The Mainspring of Human Progress*. Irvington, N.Y.: The Foundation for Economic Education, 1953.

A ribbon of hot steel slab will soon become steel plate at the ISG Burns Harbor Plate Mill.

PASSPO

Unite

of

INDUSTRY: MANKIND'S USE OF GOD'S RESOURCES

Cursed is the ground for thy sake; in sorrow shalt thou eat of it all the days of thy life. . . . In the sweat of thy face shalt thou eat bread, till thou return unto the ground; for out of it wast thou taken: for dust thou art, and unto dust shalt thou return.

(Gen. 3:17, 19)

God made Adam in His own image, and He expected Adam to serve and honor his Creator. When Adam sinned, he brought a curse on all of the earth. Mankind must now overcome many obstacles to survive. But ironically this curse has proved to be a source of blessing. Mankind is forced to see his own limitations and to recognize his dependence on the eternal God. (See Eccles. 3:9–13.) Throughout Scripture, God has promised to bless those who work hard and depend on Him.

The word *industry* is often used to describe man's "hard work" to make a living. Although there are many types of jobs, or industries, the basic categories have been around since God made man to exercise dominion over His earth. The U.S. government has developed a system for classifying jobs. Every job can be classified under one of the categories in the chart titled "U.S. Employment by Industry." This chapter examines each category in turn and shows how industry contributes to the wealth of nations.

I. PRIMARY INDUSTRIES

All industries are either primary, secondary, or tertiary. **Primary industries** are the most basic industries. They take from the earth materials that are needed for food, clothes, and shelter. Primary industries include agriculture, fishing, forestry, and mining.

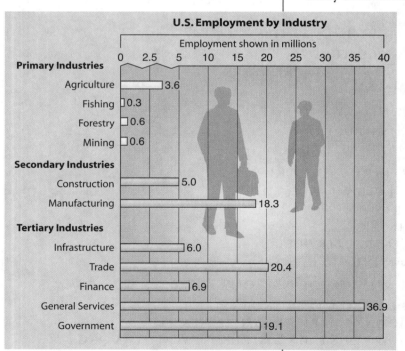

U.S. Employment by Industry

Employment shown in millions

Primary Industries
Agriculture — 3.6
Fishing — 0.3
Forestry — 0.6
Mining — 0.6

Secondary Industries
Construction — 5.0
Manufacturing — 18.3

Tertiary Industries
Infrastructure — 6.0
Trade — 20.4
Finance — 6.9
General Services — 36.9
Government — 19.1

AGRICULTURE

God said unto them, . . . have dominion over the fish of the sea, and over the fowl of the air, and over every living thing that moveth upon the earth. And God said, Behold, I have given you every herb bearing seed, which is upon the face of all the earth, and every tree, in the which is the fruit of a tree yielding seed; to you it shall be for meat.

(Gen. 1:28–29)

One part of God's Creation Mandate to Adam was control over every animal and plant in the world. God intended for Adam to be His steward, or caretaker, of the environment that He had created. The Lord Himself planted the first garden, filling it with plants and foods for man's use. In addition to using the earth to meet his needs, God intends man to make the earth both more productive and more beautiful. This requires man to be careful about how he treats the earth.

Contrary to an evolutionary view of human history, mankind did not take millions of years to figure out how to plant seeds and domesticate animals. God taught Adam to be a gardener, and his two sons specialized in the two major branches of agriculture: farming and animal husbandry. (Cain tilled the ground, and Abel kept sheep.)

Look closely at the world land-use map (pages 54-55). By comparing this map with the climate map in Chapter 2 (pages 38-39), you will see a clear pattern. First, notice that crops are raised in the moderate climates. Second, herds of animals are raised in the semiarid climates. Third, little or no agriculture takes place in the two most extreme climates—the tropics and the Arctic—where widely scattered bands of people pursue *primitive* activities, such as hunting, fishing, and gathering various foods. They must make good use of their marginal land to eke out a meager living.

FARMING

The first main branch of agriculture is farming. Throughout the ages, farming has supplied most of man's food. Planting seeds provides a much more reliable food supply than hunting wild animals and gathering wild fruits.

In the past, most farmers produced only enough food to meet the needs of their own households. They made their own clothes, furniture, and homes. Such farmers were **subsistence farmers**. Some of them raised a **cash crop**, such as rice or corn, to sell. But the money was barely enough to keep food on the table, and the household still made most of its own belongings. Billions of people in the third world still live by subsistence farming.

In the eighteenth century, an agricultural revolution took place in Europe and the United States. Farmers began applying science and machinery to increase their yields, enabling **commercial farmers** to raise large cash crops for profit and thereby freeing other people to pursue other types of work, such as manufacturing, and even cultural work, such as teaching, painting, and sculpting. Modern industrial cities depend on the steady supply of food from commercial farms.

All farms, whether subsistence or commercial, face the same challenges; they differ only in scale. Drought, disease, and insect plagues can wipe out their crops. Windstorms, hail, and floods can devastate fields. In many places, irrigation has reduced the threat of drought, insecticides have limited the threat of insects, and breeding has improved crop yields and resistance to disease. But one major problem remains: loss of soil. Wind and water can wash away soil and nutrients, and certain crops can deplete the soil's nutrients. As you study geography, notice how farmers in the various regions are dealing with these challenges.

ANIMAL HUSBANDRY

The second main form of agriculture is animal husbandry, which also can be subdivided into subsistence and commercial types. Subsistence husbandry, known as **nomadic herding**, is common in rugged mountains and dry areas where regular farming is difficult. Jabal, a descendant of Cain, became the "father of such as dwell in tents, and of such as have cattle" (Gen. 4:20). Because large herds of animals quickly consume the vegetation in an area, nomads must move constantly in search of fresh pastures.

Note the contrasts between the cornfield in Indiana (above) and the cornfield in Nigeria (below).

World's Largest Beef Producing Countries	
Country	% World's Beef
1. United States	20.9
2. European Union	15.0
3. Brazil	14.2
4. China	12.5
5. India	5.7
6. Argentina	5.6
7. Australia	3.8
8. Russia	3.7
9. Mexico	2.8
10. Canada	2.7

A farmer near Ankara, Turkey, diverts a stream into his fields.

A shepherd tends his flock in India.

Many nomads, however, became raiders and conquerors, famous for their toughness and skill with horses. Examples include the Huns of Central Asia, the Sioux Indians of North America, and the Masai of East Africa. They often built their homes of animal skins because leather was lighter than wood and more readily available in the grasslands.

LET'S GO EXPLORING

LAND USE OF THE WORLD

1. Which continent is used almost entirely for commercial farming and manufacturing?

2. Which continent has the largest proportion of subsistence farming?

3. What type of activity is most common along the equator?

4. On which continent is ranching predominant?

5. Which hemisphere, north or south, has most of the world's forestry?

6. What three continents have most of the world's manufacturing and trade?

💡 What type of activity is always found beside every manufacturing area? Why?

Land Use of the World

- Commercial Farming
- Subsistence Farming
- Manufacturing and Trade
- Ranching
- Nomadic Herding
- Forestry
- Subpolar Primitive Activity
- Tropical Primitive Activity
- Limited Activity

In the eighteenth century, Europeans developed a second method of animal husbandry called *ranching*. Wealthy landowners let their herds and flocks roam freely on vast tracts of land. In early America, ranchers let their cattle run free on the "open range" (government land to which no one had claim). Ranchers periodically rounded up their cattle to be branded or shipped to market. Sheep owners rounded up their sheep to shear the wool.

SECTION QUIZ

1. Who gave the Creation Mandate and to whom?
2. Name the two major divisions of agriculture.
3. Define *subsistence farming*.
4. Explain the difference between ranching and nomadic herding.
   ☼ Which type of agriculture did Abraham use?

Commercial fishing is an essential food industry that demands good stewardship.

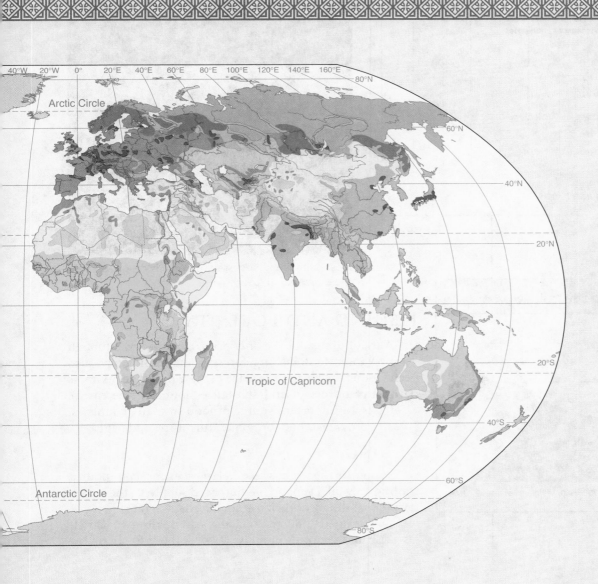

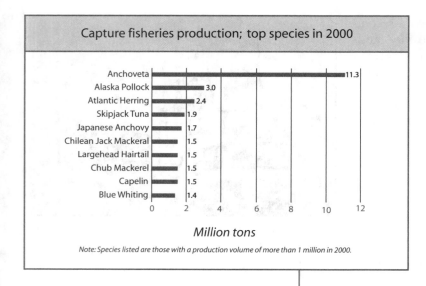

Capture fisheries production; top species in 2000

Species	Million tons
Anchoveta	11.3
Alaska Pollock	3.0
Atlantic Herring	2.4
Skipjack Tuna	1.9
Japanese Anchovy	1.7
Chilean Jack Mackeral	1.5
Largehead Hairtail	1.5
Chub Mackerel	1.5
Capelin	1.5
Blue Whiting	1.4

Million tons

Note: Species listed are those with a production volume of more than 1 million in 2000.

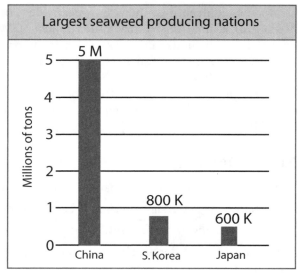

Largest seaweed producing nations

Millions of tons

- China: 5 M
- S. Korea: 800 K
- Japan: 600 K

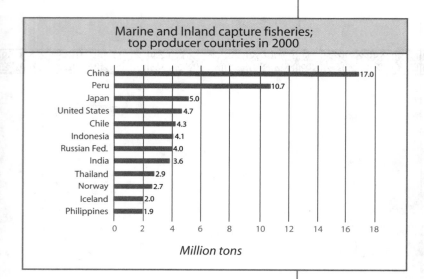

Marine and Inland capture fisheries; top producer countries in 2000

Country	Million tons
China	17.0
Peru	10.7
Japan	5.0
United States	4.7
Chile	4.3
Indonesia	4.1
Russian Fed.	4.0
India	3.6
Thailand	2.9
Norway	2.7
Iceland	2.0
Philippines	1.9

Million tons

Most of Ireland's harvested seaweed is destined for the cosmetics industry.

World capture fisheries and aquaculture production

Million tons

China

World excluding China

FISHING AND FORESTRY

Agriculture is not the only primary industry, although it is very important. Fishing, forestry, and mining have also been around for a long time. Each of these industries extracts **natural resources** (useful substances found in the earth). *Fishing* is an important source of food in many countries. *Forestry* provides wood for homes, furniture, and paper.

FISHING

Seafood is the world's second largest export commodity, trailing only oil. Demand has outpaced supply, so the industry is expanding worldwide at unprecedented rates.

The seafood industry includes essentially two varieties—fish and seaweed—and uses two methods to obtain the

World's leading exporters of wood products (2004)

Total: $65.7 Billion (up 25%)

Canada	$17.3
European Union	$10.4
U.S.	$6.2

0 5 10 15 20
Billions of dollars

World's leading importers of wood products (2004)

Total: $71.2 Billion

U.S.	$23.3
European Union	$13.2
Japan	$11.8

0 5 10 15 20 25
Billions of dollars

products: capture (products gathered in the wild, natural state) and **aquaculture** (cultivation or farming in a controlled artificial environment). The latter method is still responsible for only a fraction of total production, but it is a fast-growing part of the industry.

China *produces* the greatest amount of fish. Japan is the *consumer* of the largest amount of fish. China also produces most (68.8%) of the world's cultivated fish.

Another important aspect of the fishing industry is seaweed production, which is a $5.5 to 6 billion a year industry. About $5 billion of that is produced as food; the rest is used to obtain extracts used in making fertilizers, cosmetics, animal food additives, fuels, and wastewater treatments.

Thirty-five countries harvest seaweed, but China, Japan, and South Korea are the largest producers. They are also the largest consumers, although the emigration of those nationalities to other countries is increasing demand in those areas.

Seafood-producing countries are coming under increasing pressure both from conservationists and from within the industry to emphasize sustainability and care of the environment to ensure continuation of the industry. This pressure is leading to a united effort by scientists, conservationists, and the fishing industry. Such efforts to meet man's needs while protecting the environment and endangered species are an important part of fulfilling God's expectations of responsible stewardship.

FORESTRY

Wood is another necessity of life, and the size of the forestry products industry proves it.

How important is the wood products industry to you? Consider a few of the many products made from the following parts of a tree.

Fruit, nuts: food products

Leaves: furniture polish, car wax, crayons, lipstick, medicines, fragrances

Logging is a major industry in both the United States and Canada.

Lumber operations such as this are the starting point for numerous consumer products used throughout the world.

Gold nuggets such as this can be made into beautiful jewelry or any number of other important products.

World's Leading Silver Producers

Country	Millions of ounces
1. Mexico	93.8
2. Peru	89.2
3. Australia	60.2
4. China	46.8
5. Poland	44.3
6. Chile	41.6
7. United States	41.5

Leading Steel Producers

Country	Metric tons
1. China	272.5
2. Japan	112.7
3. United States	98.5
4. Russia	64.3
5. South Korea	47.5
6. Germany	46.4
7. Ukraine	38.7

Heavy machinery simplifies copper mining.

Branches: chemicals, plastics, various types of paper products

Bark: medicines, mulch, dyes, shoe polish

Trunk: furniture, musical instruments, plywood, baseball bats, charcoal

Sap: adhesives, ice cream, hair spray, soaps, cough syrups/drops, shampoo

Stumps: wood resin, turpentine, pine cleaners, laundry detergent, sports drinks

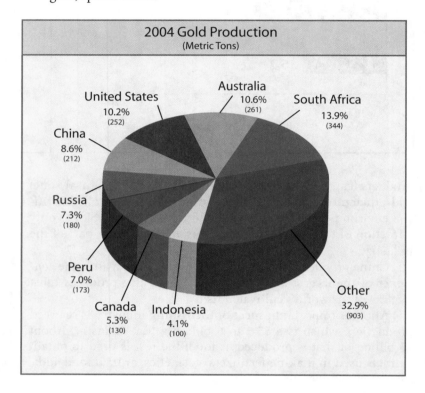

2004 Gold Production
(Metric Tons)

- United States 10.2% (252)
- Australia 10.6% (261)
- South Africa 13.9% (344)
- China 8.6% (212)
- Russia 7.3% (180)
- Peru 7.0% (173)
- Canada 5.3% (130)
- Indonesia 4.1% (100)
- Other 32.9% (903)

MINING

As important as agriculture, fishing, and forestry are, *mining* has far surpassed them in importance. Modern countries spend great sums of money mining three types of resources: metals, nonmetal minerals, and fossil fuels.

METALS

The earth's crust is composed mainly of rock that contains a variety of **minerals** (solid crystals that occur naturally and have a definite chemical composition). Scientists have identified about three thousand different minerals, but only about one hundred are common.

Metals are the most important type of mineral because of four useful properties: they are shiny, malleable (able to be hammered into sheets), ductile (able to be drawn into wire), and conductive (able to conduct electricity). Metal tools and utensils last longer and work better than tools made from stone or wood. The first metalworker was Tubal-cain, a descendant of Cain, who became "an instructor of every artificer in brass and iron" (Gen. 4:22).

Iron ore, much of it moved by trains, is essential in steel production.

Leading Iron Ore Producers	
Country	**% of world total**
1. Brazil	22.6
2. Australia	19.4
3. China	11.3
4. Russia	8.4
5. India	9.7
6. Ukraine	5.8
7. United States	4.5

Bronze workers in Benin produced this elaborate casting.

Archeologists sometimes divide ancient civilizations into three periods that reflect man's increasing skill with metals:

Stone/Copper Age (before 3000 BC)

Bronze Age (3000–1200 BC)

Iron Age (1200 BC–present)

Metals are of three types: precious metals, common metals, and alloys. The modern production of gold, silver, and platinum is small if measured in tons, but those *precious metals* are far more valuable than other metal products. They are considered precious for their beauty, durability, scarcity, and trade value.

Common metals get their name because they are mined in great quantities from the earth's surface and are therefore common. Three such metals have been used since ancient times: copper, lead, and iron.

Copper is a "native metal," like silver and gold, that can be found in pure nuggets in the earth's crust. Copper was once used to make weapons, but it is very soft. More than 60 percent of the copper mined today is used in the electrical industry because it is the least expensive conductor of electricity.

Lead does not occur alone in nature. Like most metals, it must be extracted from an *ore* (a mineral composed of several different elements). Lead is combined with sulfur in an ore called galena. A wood fire is hot enough to melt lead. Because it is such a soft metal, artists originally used lead to cast statues. Lead is now the main ingredient in car batteries.

People in the ancient world extracted *iron* too, but the process was difficult and expensive. The temperature had to be high (2,795°F), and the refined ore often contained many impurities (traces of other elements). In 1784, Britain developed a process of "puddling" (stirring) iron ore to remove the impurities. This strong, versatile metal became useful for making cannons, bridges, trains, and other modern machines. More iron is mined each year than all other metals combined.

The second most common metal on earth is *aluminum*. It was once considered a precious stone because it was so difficult to extract from its ore, **bauxite**. The bond holding the elements together in bauxite (hydrogen, oxygen, and aluminum) is so powerful that a

Sheets of galvanized steel will be fabricated into essential products.

This machine shears up to 20,000 tons of coal a day from the seam wall with the teeth of its eight-foot-diameter drum.

Oil Production by Region	
Region	**Billion barrels/year**
1. Middle East	650.7
2. Africa	75.8
3. South America	54.5
4. North America	54.5
5. Other (including Russia)	104.7

Offshore oil rigs pump crude oil from the Gulf of Mexico.

process of separating them was not discovered until 1886. This process, using electrical currents, is still used today. Aluminum's light weight and resistance to corrosion make it ideal for cars, aircraft, and other machines.

The four metals just mentioned—copper, lead, iron, and aluminum—are useful not only by themselves but also in combination with other metals. Early in history, man learned that he could combine such metals to form **alloys**. The other six common metals—chromium, manganese, zinc, nickel, tin, and tungsten—are not usually used by themselves but are combined with one or more of the first four metals.

The first useful alloys were made with copper. Copper and tin form *bronze*, from which we get the term Bronze Age. A pliable metal, bronze could be made into beautiful statues, weapons, and tools that were stronger than copper. The Romans learned to make *brass* by combining copper and zinc. It is useful in making objects with intricate designs, such as musical instruments. Bronze and brass are often confused with one another because they both have a yellow color common to all copper alloys.

Steel is the world's most important alloy. It is formed by combining iron with the carbon in coal. Early civilizations knew how to produce this metal, but the process was even more difficult and unreliable than iron-making. In 1856, Henry Bessemer devised a better process. First, he shot a jet of air into molten iron to rid it of impurities. Then, when he added coal and manganese, the iron turned into a tough steel. Nearly all of the world's iron ore is now turned into steel. In a sense, the Iron Age has become "the Steel Age."

NONMETAL MINERALS

Metals are not the only useful minerals that God has provided. Many other kinds of minerals play an important role in industry.

Limestone is formed mainly from calcite (calcium, carbon, and oxygen). When crushed and mixed with clay, it makes a powder called cement. Adding sand to cement produces mortar. Adding crushed rock to cement makes concrete, the most widely used building material in the world.

Sulfur is another versatile mineral known since ancient times. It has many modern uses. Combined with charcoal and potassium nitrate, it makes gunpowder. It is also used to process petroleum and steel, to produce fertilizer, to vulcanize (improve the strength and texture of) rubber, and even to make matches.

Other minerals that have been used since early history include clay (for bricks, plates, pitchers, cups, and bowls); sand (for making glass for windows and bottles); granite, marble, slate, and sandstone (for monuments and decorative buildings); salt (for seasoning and preserving food); and graphite (for the "lead" in pencils). From phosphates, nitrates, and potassium we get fertilizers for enriching the soil. Look at bags of fertilizer at your local home and garden shop, and you will see three numbers on the bag, perhaps 5–10–10. They indicate the percentage of those three nutrients in the bag: 5 percent nitrogen, 10 percent phosphorus, and 10 percent potassium.

A few minerals contain *uranium*, a mineral that was used in the first atomic bombs in 1945 and was later used in nuclear reactors. Its high radioactivity makes it very harmful to the human body.

FOSSIL FUELS

For centuries, man used wind, water, and wood to power his equipment for transportation and manufacture. Only in the last two hundred years has man realized the potential of another energy resource—**fossil fuels**. Coal, petroleum, and natural gas are technically not minerals but the remains of living things. Apparently, the Flood waters trapped plants and animals beneath layers of sedimentary rock. The pressure changed this *organic matter* into its present form. These fossil fuels have drastically changed our way of life.

Coal is a solid rock that occurs in various grades, or levels of quality, depending on the amount of heat produced per pound. The Chinese burned coal for heat more than a thousand years before Christ. In the late eighteenth century, Europeans used it to power steam engines. Later, it was used to make *coke,* a necessary ingredient in steel. Coal is now used to generate most of the world's electricity. Only about 18 percent of coal produced is exported; most is used by the producing countries.

Petroleum is a liquid fossil fuel. Noah used *pitch,* a thick form of petroleum, to cover the ark (see Gen. 6:14). The ancient Chinese used petroleum that had seeped into pools on the earth's surface. The first commercial oil well was not drilled until 1859. At first, Americans extracted kerosene for lamps and discarded the rest of the oil. But scientists soon realized that petroleum packs much more energy than coal. The invention of gasoline engines turned petroleum into the most important mining product in the world. All of the top five oil-producing nations are in the Middle East.

Located in many underground oil pools is a fossil fuel in gaseous form called **natural gas**. Many scientists believe it is a by-product of the process that formed petroleum. Although it was burned off as waste at the first oil wells,

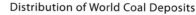
Distribution of World Coal Deposits

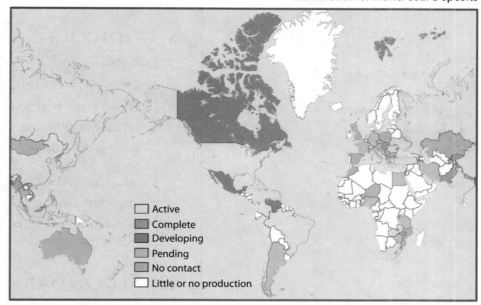

- ☐ Active
- ☐ Complete
- ☐ Developing
- ☐ Pending
- ☐ No contact
- ☐ Little or no production

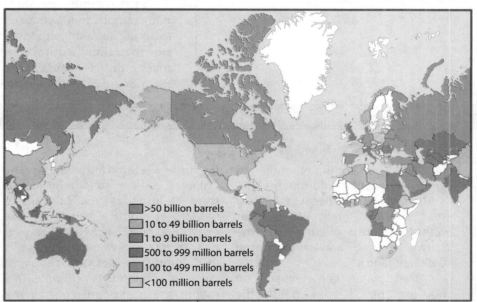

- ☐ >50 billion barrels
- ☐ 10 to 49 billion barrels
- ☐ 1 to 9 billion barrels
- ☐ 500 to 999 million barrels
- ☐ 100 to 499 million barrels
- ☐ <100 million barrels

Distribution of World Oil Deposits

Leading Coal Producers

Country	Million tons/year
1. China	1500
2. United States	900
3. India	350
4. Australia	275
5. South Africa	250
6. Russia	175
7. Poland	100

Leading Oil-Producing Countries

Country	Billion barrels/year
1. Saudi Arabia	265.3
2. Iraq	115.0
3. Kuwait	98.8
4. Iran	96.4
5. United Arab Emirates	62.8
6. Russia	54.3
7. Venezuela	47.6

Leading Natural Gas-Producing Countries

Country	Trillion cu. ft./year
1. Russia	20.5
2. United States	19.6
3. Canada	6.5
4. United Kingdom	3.8
5. Indonesia	2.3

natural gas has become an efficient fuel for furnaces, water heaters, dryers, and ovens.

SECTION QUIZ

1. Define *mineral*.
2. List four characteristics of metals.
3. Which metal is mined more than any other?
4. What is an alloy, and which alloy is most important?
5. What is the most widely used building material today, and how is it made?
6. Name the three fossil fuels and indicate which one is the most important mining product in the world.
   - ⚲ Why are no periods of history called the Brass Age or the Aluminum Age?

II. SECONDARY INDUSTRIES

Primary industries do not change the form of natural resources. For example, they produce grains of wheat and live beef cattle, not sacks of flour and hamburgers. **Secondary industries**, however, take **raw materials** (natural resources that have been extracted by primary industries) and change them into a useful form. Secondary industries are of two types: construction and manufacturing.

PRECIOUS GEMS

On every continent, precious gems are popular adornments and symbols of wealth. Because of their small size and great value, gems were once a form of currency, especially when long caravans journeyed to distant lands.

Asians value gems mostly for their weight, so they polish the large stones and keep them in their original irregular shape. Westerners, on the other hand, cut the gems to enhance their color and symmetry. Lapidaries (gem cutters) chip slivers from the stone to leave flat surfaces called facets. The facets reflect light, making the gem sparkle. The largest diamond ever discovered originally weighed 3,024.75 carats (1 carat = 200 mg, or 0.007 oz.). The queen of England had it cut into nine large diamonds for inclusion in the British crown jewels.

Different countries have become famous for certain gems. Turquoise, prized for its sky-blue color, is popular in the western United States. The Chinese have carved jade for almost three thousand years. Australia is the largest producer of rainbow-like opals. Emeralds, second only to rubies in value, are mined primarily in Colombia. Rubies and sapphires come from the mines of Burma. Diamonds, the most popular of all gems, are excavated in South Africa, where in 1867 a salesman discovered them when he noticed some children playing with "pretty stones."

The two kinds of gems are organic (products of plants and animals) and inorganic (minerals). The organic gems include pearls (from oysters), amber (from fossilized tree resin), jet (from fossilized driftwood), coral (from the skeletons of tiny sea animals), and ivory (from tusks of elephants and other animals). Most inorganic gems apparently formed as volcanic lava forced its way upward through small cracks in the earth and superheated the minerals nearby. Rubies and sapphires came from aluminum oxide, and diamonds came from carbon. Man has tried to produce artificial gems by simulating the heat and pressure of volcanoes, but the value of such stones is not as high as that of natural gems.

The Bible includes many references to gems. The twelve stones on Aaron's breastplate (Exod. 39) may have led to the sixteenth-century tradition of birthstones for each month. Europeans mistakenly believed that gems were magical and brought good luck. Revelation 21 tells us that God will build the foundation of the New Jerusalem with twelve layers of different gems.

CONSTRUCTION

Mankind has used a variety of natural resources in construction. Cain built the first city, but the Bible does not say what materials he used (Gen. 4:17). The first great structure mentioned in Scripture is the Tower of Babel, made of brick and mortar. Egyptians used cut stone to build the pyramids, and the Romans used cement to build great coliseums. In the 1850s, engineers learned how to reinforce concrete with steel, making possible modern dams, bridges, and skyscrapers. You will see specific examples of these in later chapters.

Construction of infrastructure, such as this bridge in Charleston, S.C., is critical to modern nations.

MANUFACTURING

For most of human history, people made their clothes, bowls, and tools at home. The word *manufacture* originally meant "to make by hand" (*manus-*, "hand"; *factus*, "to make"). As cities grew, some individuals specialized in making certain products. Cities had bakers, cobblers, tailors, candle makers, and other specialists. In the past two centuries, however, "cottage industries" were overshadowed by large factories. **Manufacturing** now refers to big businesses and machines that turn raw materials into new products on a massive scale.

INDUSTRIAL REVOLUTION

Discoveries and inventions between 1750 and 1850 made modern industries possible. That period of radical change, known as the **Industrial Revolution**, began in the textile industry of Britain. Earlier, individuals had raised their own sources of wool and flax and turned them into clothes by hand with simple tools. Many hours of work went into the production of just a few yards of finished cloth. Finally, inventors developed machines that simplified and quickened production. When the steam engine came along to power the machines, the revolution took off, spreading to other countries.

The invention of textile machines in Britain sparked the Industrial Revolution.

Industry experienced a "second revolution" in the second half of the nineteenth century. Exciting discoveries in chemistry, physics, and biology made that revolution possible. The application of science to industry is called **technology**. The key technological breakthrough of the nineteenth century was the harnessing of electricity. Gasoline engines, telegraphs, and telephones were also invented. These inventions gave industries new freedom to place factories anywhere they wanted rather than locating them near rivers. By the twentieth century, modern technology had spawned whole new industries, such as the automobile and airplane industries.

In the second half of the twentieth century, manufacturing entered a third period of revolution called variously the Computer Age, the Electronics Age, or the Information Age. New high-tech industries, such as computer-chip manufacturing, use the most advanced discoveries of science and engineering. Robotics and computers have made industries so efficient that fewer people are needed to work in factories producing basic manufactured goods. Most people are free to find jobs outside the farm and factory in our *postindustrial society*.

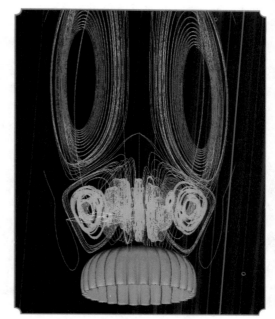

Computer technology has revolutionized manufacturing. This computer image shows air flow around a newly designed parachute.

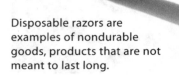

Disposable razors are examples of nondurable goods, products that are not meant to last long.

Automobiles are examples of durable goods, products that are meant to last for several years.

DURABLE AND NONDURABLE MANUFACTURING

Manufacturing industries are subdivided into two types, according to the lifespan of their products. **Nondurable manufacturing** makes products that generally last less than a year. Such products include food, chemicals, fossil fuels (petrochemicals), tobacco products, wood pulp (paper), and many other consumable products.

Durable manufacturing makes products that last more than a year, including most of the products needed for building homes, furniture, machines, and other equipment. Most durable products come from five sources: lumber, stone, clay, glass, and metals. Many of these industries take the products of other secondary industries and further improve them. For example, automobile manufacturers shape steel from steel industries and combine it with textiles, plastic, and rubber.

SECTION QUIZ

1. What are the two types of secondary industries? How are they similar?

2. Explain the difference between raw materials and natural resources.

3. What do we call the changes in industry from 1750 to 1850? What industry was the first to experience these changes?

4. What is technology? Give an example of a high-tech industry.

⚬ Identify the three revolutions in industry. What changes did each of them bring to daily life?

III. TERTIARY INDUSTRIES

As countries develop, they move from mainly primary industries (meeting basic needs) to secondary industries (construction and manufacturing). The more developed a country becomes, more of its workers move into a third type of industry. For example, only about 212,000 American adults are now miners, fewer than a million Americans work on farms, and the number of people employed in manufacturing has continued to drop. Because of advances in technology, workers in these primary and secondary industries are able to provide all of the country's needs for food, construction materials, and manufactured products. The rest of America's workers—about 80 percent—are employed in what are called **tertiary industries**, also known as *service* industries. *Services* are generally intangible, meaning that they cannot be seen or touched. Such jobs as teaching, advertising, repairing products, cleaning offices, and driving trucks are service jobs. In contrast, primary and secondary industries produce *goods* (products that can be seen and touched). All industries either produce goods or provide services.

ALTERNATIVE SOURCES OF ENERGY

Man has always looked for new ways to produce more with less energy. Modern industry would have been impossible without the development of fossil fuels. But fossil fuels are a nonrenewable resource that will run out some day. Countries also worry about the pollution caused by fossil fuels.

Fossil Fuels. The most remarkable event in the history of energy was the harnessing of steam in the eighteenth century. Early steam engines used coal, but most engines now use petroleum. In 1884 scientists learned how to turn steam into a new type of energy—electricity. Coal, petroleum, or natural gas heats water to make steam; the steam turns wheels, called turbines, to generate electricity. Fossil fuels still provide 84.5 percent of the energy in the United States.

Nuclear Fuel. World War II spawned the next great innovation in energy—nuclear fuel. Splitting atoms can create enough heat to drive steam turbines to make electricity. This resource promised to solve all of man's energy needs because atoms are everywhere. In practice, nuclear power has serious drawbacks. Nuclear fission uses dangerous, radioactive minerals. Government officials have failed to contain costs or to dispose of radioactive waste properly. In the late 1980s industrial nations decided to stop building new nuclear power plants. Properly employed and wisely built and operated, however, nuclear reactors hold great promise for inexpensive and safe energy production.

Renewable Resources. Before the Arab nations cut off their supply of oil to the United States in 1973, causing an energy crisis, 98.5 percent of the energy needs in the United States were met with oil, coal, and natural gas. After the crisis, the government began studying renewable resources, such as water and sunlight. Renewable fuels have a virtually unlimited supply and produce relatively little pollution. Modern technology is making great strides in reducing the cost of developing renewable energy.

Hydroelectricity. The most important source of renewable energy is moving water. The Romans invented the first water wheel two thousand years ago. The same year scientists learned to make electricity from steam, they also learned to turn turbines with dammed water. The United States has now dammed most of its major rivers to take full advantage of the country's potential for hydroelectricity.

Biofuel. Plants have been used for fuel ever since Adam first built a fire. America has begun experimenting with waste products from farms and city garbage. Over a hundred electric power plants are fueled with municipal wastes, 40 percent of which is paper and its derivatives. In addition, over a thousand power facilities burn wood to generate electricity, mostly in the Northeast and Northwest.

Geothermal. In some places, geothermal energy (heat from the earth) can produce enough steam to drive turbines or to heat houses. The United States accounts for most of the world's geothermal power, and most of that is produced at one installation located about sixty miles north of San Francisco. Geothermal energy is among the most polluting, releasing gases and corrosive chemicals.

Solar. The sun is the greatest source of energy in our solar system. But scientists have not yet found an economical way to harness that energy. The cost of heating water directly by the sun is three times the current rate for conventional sources. The cost of converting sunlight directly to electricity on metal chips (solar cells) is almost ten times the cost of using fossil fuels. In isolated areas, solar heat is sometimes the best choice, but solar energy has a long way to go.

Wind. One of the major untapped resources is wind. The Arabs introduced the windmill to Europe in the twelfth century. Modern windmills have been built in several windy areas of the world. Bowling Green, Ohio, is one U.S. city that has done so. Experts estimate that as much as 20 percent of U.S. electrical needs could be supplied by wind. But in most cases wind generators would take up too much area to be practical.

Renewable sources of energy are still too expensive to compete with fossil fuels. But costs of nonrenewable resources are climbing, and these resources will not last forever. Oil reserves may last another century, and coal another 250 years. One thing is certain: industries in a free market will buy the least expensive energy resource, whatever it is.

Service industries are the vital link between goods and the people who need them. Goods would be useless if they just sat in the fields, at the mines, or at the factories. Service workers are involved at every step of human activity. The U.S. Department of Labor recognizes five categories of service jobs: infrastructure, trade, finance, general services, and government.

INFRASTRUCTURE

Infrastructure refers to the basic energy and equipment needs of all industries and is divided into three types: utilities, transportation, and communication.

UTILITIES

Utilities provide electricity, gas, water, trash collection, and sewage-disposal services. Governments own most utilities, or they control the prices that utilities can charge.

Electric and gas utilities produce the energy that runs modern industries and heats homes. About 90 percent of the world's energy comes from fossil fuels, followed by water (hydroelectricity), uranium (nuclear fuel), and wind. Most energy is converted into electricity. The United States is the world's leading producer and consumer of electricity.

TRANSPORTATION

Industries have three basic choices when transporting products and people: water, land, and air. These modes of transportation have undergone major changes in the last two centuries.

Water Transportation—Mankind has used water for cheap transportation throughout history. Noah's descendants built the first great civilizations along the mighty rivers of the world. But river routes have some obvious limitations. Shallow water limits the distance boats can travel, and rivers are often far from mineral resources. In the nineteenth century, industrial nations attempted to overcome these limitations by building a vast network of canals. Railroads eventually became more important, but flat-bottomed barges are still common on waterways. They carry almost 10 percent of all U.S. freight, particularly coal and metal ores.

The ocean is another vital means of world transportation. Petroleum-powered ships transport everything from avocados to zinc. Some ships have large holds (open cargo areas below deck) to carry

This commercial crude oil supertanker, riding high in the water because it is empty, can transport more than half a million tons of crude oil.

Traffic congestion is one result of Americans' love affair with the car.

Although railroads have lost their status as the prime movers of freight in the United States, they are still a critical part of U.S. transportation, especially intermodal trains such as the one shown here.

bulky materials, such as grain, coal, and ores. Other ships carry manufactured goods in twenty-foot-long containers, which can be loaded and unloaded quickly and pulled as trailers by trucks when on land. A new class of one-thousand-foot-long superfreighters is transforming the shipping industry. A small crew of fifteen men can handle up to six thousand containers on a superfreighter. Oil supertankers are the largest ships ever built.

Land Transportation—Merchants need ways to carry goods across land. Trade by caravan has a long history because it is relatively easy to travel across flat plains. The invention of the steam engine revolutionized land transportation. In the last half of the nineteenth century, steam locomotives began carrying large quantities of goods at amazing speeds across continents. Railroads provide reliable, year-round transportation and still account for a significant amount of inland freight tonnage.

The invention of gasoline and diesel engines introduced a new mode of transportation. After World War II, cars and trucks outpaced railroads in importance. More than two-thirds of U.S. freight tonnage travels on trucks and other commercial vehicles. In many instances today, imports arrive in the country in containers by ocean freighter, are unloaded in an intermodal (more than one form of transportation) terminal, and then loaded onto either tractor-trailer trucks or intermodal freight trains for transportation across the country.

More dramatic is the almost complete reliance on cars for human transportation. Americans own more passenger cars than any other nation. They also have the lowest ratio of persons per car. This fact has led to problems of increased demand for petroleum-based fuels, overcrowding on highways, increased wear on those highways, and higher numbers of accidents and traffic deaths.

The United States has more paved roads than any other country, and new roads are being paved every day. However, paved roads are also becoming more common in small, densely populated countries such as Holland.

Air Transportation—Airplanes are the fastest form of transportation on earth, and they are least limited by geographic features. The fastest passenger plane in the world was the *Concorde*, a supersonic transport (SST) built by England and France. It could fly 1,550 miles per hour, or twice the speed of sound. Such aircraft made once-popular ocean liners obsolete, but their use was discontinued in 2004, just thirty-five years after the first flight in 1969, because of low (10 percent capacity) ridership.

Because of its great expense, air travel is practical only for transporting people and small cargo, such as mail. The industry is highly susceptible to fluctuations in fuel prices. The United States, however, leads the world in commercial aviation. Its passenger planes fly nearly ten times more passenger-miles than any other country. (One passenger-mile represents one passenger transported one mile.) The United States also has the largest number of airports in the world.

The Concorde made its last flight in 2004, thirty-five years after it debuted.

Common Transportation Statistics				
Country	Railroad Miles	Passenger Cars (millions)	Airplane Passenger Miles (billions)	Airports
Australia	33,827	9.840	32.9	294
Bangladesh	1,681	0.065	2.4	15
Brazil	18,276	11.630	14.2	665
Canada	30,250	16.860	29.5	507
China	44,675	6.500	13.8	351
Egypt	3,146	1.700	5.0	71
France	18,342	28.100	46.8	273
Germany	28,671	43.770	65.6	328
India	39,289	5.060	8.6	232
Israel	398	1.470	8.8	28
Japan	14,650	53.540	63.8	141
Mexico	10,957	11.000	9.4	231
Russia	54,157	21.230	10.9	471
S. Africa	12,969	3.970	9.9	143
United States	141,509	221.820	190.1	5,131

A textbook publisher uses a web press to mass produce its materials.

COMMUNICATION

Communication is a form of transportation, not of goods or people, but of ideas and information. Communication industries can be divided into two broad categories, based on the medium used to pass on information: print media and electronic media.

Print Media—Written language has been around for a long time, perhaps since Adam's day. Until two hundred years ago, private couriers carried most of the world's *personal communication*, such as letters and packages. Since then, national governments have taken over most of the world's postal services. The Universal Postal Union, established in 1875, regulates international mail to ensure that it is delivered. The United Nations now operates this agency.

In the early days, the primary means of mass communication were speeches and lectures given in one place to a large audience. The invention of the printing press in 1456 enabled individuals to share ideas and discoveries with the masses. The **publishing industry** prints three major forms of publications: books, newspapers, and magazines.

European monarchs feared the power of publishers and strictly controlled what they could write. After gaining independence in 1783, the United States became one of the first countries to guarantee freedom of the press. Steam engines made it possible to print "penny papers" quickly and cheaply in the early nineteenth century, making daily information available to even the poorest citizen.

Electronic Media—In earlier times, people came up with some ingenious methods of rapid, long-distance communication, including flags and smoke signals. In the 1830s, Samuel Morse discovered a whole new medium for communicating ideas—electricity. Sending messages through electronic impulses is called **telecommunications**, which includes the telephone, radio, and television industries.

The telephone was patented in 1876 by the American inventor Alexander Graham Bell. It allowed people to talk directly rather than in Morse code. In 1920, the Radio Corporation of America (RCA) began the first commercial radio broadcasts. Regularly scheduled television broadcasts began in London sixteen years later. Radio and television became the dominant mass media of the world. Unlike print media, they transmit information (sound and pictures) that even illiterate adults and young children can enjoy. The United States has more telephones, radios, and televisions than any other country.

The "space age" brought radical changes to personal and mass communications. Since Russia launched the first satellite in 1957, more than 4,600 satellites have been positioned in space. Signals can be transmitted instantly around the world without cable connections. Computer modems allow people at any corner of the globe to exchange any form of media—text, sound, and pictures—with a keystroke. E-mail, instant messaging, and the Internet have dramatically reduced the time needed for communicating messages, news, and ideas. Cell phones have further reduced the relative size of the world in terms of communication ability. On the other

Common Communication Statistics

Country	Internet Users (M)	Telephones (Mainline/ Cell) (M)	Radio Stations (AM/FM/SW)	Television Stations
Australia	9.47	10.8/14.4	262/345/1	104
Bangladesh	0.24	.74/1.4	12/12/2	15
Brazil	14.30	38.8/46.4	1365/582/161	138
Canada	16.11	19.9/13.2	245/582/6	80
China	94.00	263.0/269.0	369/259/45	3240
Egypt	2.70	8.7/5.8	42/14/3	98
France	21.90	34.0/42.0	41/3500/2	584
Germany	39.00	54.4/64.8	51/787/4	373
India	18.50	48.9/26.2	153/91/68	562
Italy	18.50	26.6/55.9	100/4600/9	358
Japan	57.20	71.2/87.0	215/89/21	211
Mexico	10.03	15.9/28.1	850/545/15	236
Russia	6.00	35.5/17.6	420/447/56	7306
United Kingdom	25.00	34.9/49.7	219/431/3	228
United States	159.00	81.5/158.7	4854/8950/18	1500+

hand, approximately two-thirds of the people of the world have never made a phone call!

TRADE

Someone needs to sell the products of primary and secondary industries. This is the job of trade industries. They buy and sell natural resources and manufactured goods. **Wholesale businesses** buy goods from producers in large quantities to sell in smaller quantities to **retail businesses**, which sell goods directly to consumers. A notable exception is Wal-Mart, which is so large and which controls so much of the world consumer market that it can buy goods directly from the producers in huge quantities and therefore at very low prices. Wal-Mart then sells directly to consumers through its Wal-Mart and Sam's Club chains. Eliminating the middleman (the wholesalers) allows Wal-Mart to charge lower prices.

FINANCE

Modern industry would have been impossible without the rise of modern banking. Bankers, insurance companies, real estate agents, and investment firms help people to buy property, goods, and services. Finance industries make money available to help start and fuel the growth of other industries.

GENERAL SERVICES

Many other tertiary industries sell "support" services. They repair machines and also keep people healthy and happy while they do their work. They include maids, mechanics, nurses, teachers, zookeepers, engineers, lawyers, researchers, computer programmers and repair technicians, and amusement park attendants.

GOVERNMENT

The fifth form of tertiary industry is government. Most government employees, such as police officers, work for cities and states. The national government employs soldiers, lawmakers, judges, and *bureaucrats* (government officials or clerks who carry out the daily function of government).

SECTION QUIZ

1. What is another name for tertiary industries?
2. List the five kinds of tertiary industries.
3. What vehicle is most common for transporting
   a. freight to other countries?
   b. freight within the United States?
   c. people within the United States?
4. What do we call the industry that prints information for mass communication?
5. What are the three types of telecommunications industries?
   - Are department stores, such as Wal-Mart, retail or wholesale businesses?

Alexander Graham Bell revolutionized communication with his invention of the telephone.

IV. THE WEALTH OF NATIONS

The earth's resources are neither unlimited nor evenly divided among the nations. Each country must make difficult choices about the best way to develop and distribute its resources, goods, and services. The study of the process by which people and countries make such choices is called **economics**.

WHO MAKES THE CHOICES

The Creator owns all of the earth's resources (Ps. 24:1; 50:10). Mankind is merely His steward, placed in charge of the creation to use and develop its resources for His glory (see Gen. 1:28). Every system for making economic choices should be evaluated in light of that fact. The governments of the world generally have economic systems that can be classified as capitalist, socialist, or mixed economies.

CAPITALISM

The money and equipment (buildings, tools, computers, vehicles, etc.) necessary to build industries are called **capital**. Most Western countries follow a system of **capitalism**. Private individuals or corporations build most industries, risking their own capital by making investments in hopes of making a profit.

Anyone can start a business and attempt to profit financially. Another name for such an economy (in its ideal form) is a **free market** because businesses freely compete in the marketplace for buyers with little interference from the government. People who take risks to start businesses are called *entrepreneurs*. In 2005, the wealthiest capitalists in the world were Ingvar Kamprad, the Swedish founder of the IKEA retail furniture chain, who had a net worth of $53 billion, and Bill Gates, the American founder of Microsoft, whose net worth was an estimated $47 billion.

Both workers and capital are essential ingredients for a business in a free market economy.

SOCIALISM

During the nineteenth century, opponents of capitalism developed an alternative system called **socialism**. Under socialism, the government owns the major industries and promises to make production decisions for the welfare of society. In such a *command economy*, the government determines which industries are developed, where they are built, and what they produce. In socialist economies, few businessmen are willing to take risks with capital because much of the profit goes to the government in the form of high taxes. The most extreme form of socialism is called **communism**, under which the government owns everything.

The number of socialist governments mushroomed in the first half of the twentieth century, but many socialist leaders ended up making choices to enrich themselves at the expense of their own people. Making choices to benefit the group proved just as wrong as making choices for selfish interests. Both systems ignore God and assume that an elite is better able to assess what is best for the masses of people than are the individuals themselves. Between

1989 and 1991, socialist governments fell like dominoes in Eastern Europe and the Soviet Union. Socialist countries that have not fallen nonetheless experience problems that are inherent to such an economy.

MIXED ECONOMIES

Most of those countries whose socialist economies collapsed adopted a *mixed economy* that attempted to combine elements of capitalism and socialism. Private citizens can own property and businesses, but the government closely regulates their choices. In spite of socialism's poor record, even some leaders in capitalist countries have sought to move toward mixed economies.

HOW COUNTRIES MEASURE WEALTH

Most people think of wealth as the ownership of things, such as cattle, land, and money. But real **wealth** is the ability to *produce* new things. Consider the biblical example of Jacob. He was wealthy, not because of the size of his flocks and herds, but because the animals produced plenty of offspring each year to feed and clothe his growing family. The more a country produces each year, the more things its people can eat and enjoy that year and the better prepared they can be to face the next year.

The most common measurement of a country's wealth is the **gross domestic product (GDP)**. The GDP is the monetary value of all the goods and services produced for sale within a country's borders over the course of a year. Economists total the value of the products produced by all of the primary, secondary, and tertiary industries. Look at the definition of GDP again. It is the *gross* (total) value of all *products* (goods and services) made by *domestic* (home, or inside the country) workers in one year.

The total GDP means very little, however, until it is compared to the number of workers who produced those products. A more meaningful measurement is **per capita GDP** (the average value of products produced by each person in the country). This measurement shows how much each person is producing each year. In other words, it shows the average worker's *productivity*.

Examine the chart comparing the productivity of Bangladesh and Luxembourg. The GDP of Bangladesh is much greater than that of Luxembourg, so, at first glance, Bangladesh seems to be more productive. After you consider the number of people who produce the goods, however, you can see the low productivity of Bangladesh's industries. Bangladesh has more than three hundred times as many people as Luxembourg, but each Luxembourger produces goods and services valued almost thirty times greater than that produced by a Bangladeshi.

A high per capita GDP does not always mean that a country has a lot of industry or that the average worker makes a lot of money. Several rich countries, such as the United Arab Emirates and Qatar, have a high per capita GDP because primary industries ship valuable exports (oil, in their case), but rich sheiks and bureaucrats pocket the money. The average citizen receives little benefit from the oil sales. Timor-Leste (formerly East Timor) has the world's lowest per capita GDP at $400.

Countries with the Highest GDPs in July 2006

Country	GDP ($B)
1. United States*	$12,360
2. China	$8,859
3. Japan*	$4,018
4. India	$3,611
5. Germany*	$2,504
6. United Kingdom*	$1,830
7. France*	$1,816
8. Italy*	$1,698
9. Russia*	$1,589
10. Brazil	$1,556
11. Canada*	$1,114
12. Mexico	$1,067
13. Spain	$1,029
14. South Korea	$965
15. Indonesia	$866

*Member of G-8 (group of eight countries that produce more than ¾ of the world's manufacturing value)

GDP vs. per Capita GDP

Country	Population	GDP	Per Capita GDP
Bangladesh	144,320,000	$275.7B	$2,000
Luxembourg	468,600	$27.27B	$58,900

Countries with the Highest per Capita GDPs

Country	Per Capita GDP
1. Luxembourg	$58,900
2. United States	$40,100
3. Norway	$40,000
4. Switzerland	$33,800
5. Denmark	$32,200
6. Ireland	$31,900
7. Iceland	$31,900
8. Canada	$31,500
9. Austria	$31,300
10. Australia	$30,700
11. Belgium	$30,600
12. United Kingdom	$29,600
13. Netherlands	$29,500
14. Japan	$29,400
15. Finland	$29,000

HOW COUNTRIES DISTRIBUTE WEALTH AMONG THEMSELVES

Socialist countries view the world as a pie with a limited supply of wealth that must be cut into equal pieces to feed everyone. In theory, they imitate Robin Hood, who stole from the rich and gave to the poor. In reality, however, the world's supply of wealth is unlimited. Industrial countries do not steal to become rich; they make new wealth that did not exist before. For example, they turn iron ore into automobiles and silicon into computer chips. Their industries just keep making bigger pies and more of them.

DEVELOPED AND DEVELOPING COUNTRIES

The effective use of raw materials, labor, and capital is called **development**. Economists actually have a way to measure the value that manufacturers add to raw materials. If the original metals in a sports car are worth $500 and the final car is worth $30,500, then the **value added** is $30,000. The United States is responsible for nearly one-third of the world's value added by manufacture (more than $1 trillion each year).

Development translates into power. Countries with productive economies can afford to buy weapons and influence neighbors with their money. Eight countries produce more than three-fourths of all value added by manufacture. The leaders of this **Group of 8 (G-8)** meet in a different country each year to resolve economic and political disputes. They met in Scotland in 2005 and in Russia in 2006.

G-8 members are **developed countries**, which have a wide range of industries that take full advantage of their people's skills. Most citizens enjoy the financial benefits of such development as reflected in a high per capita GDP.

China and several other big nations are not included in the G-8. They have high national GDPs and many factories, but they are considered **developing countries**. Their GDPs are high because of their large population, but their per capita GDPs are very low. Developing countries have not yet taken full advantage of their people's skills.

DIVISION OF LABOR

The best evidence of a nation's development is its *division of labor*, which is highly sophisticated in developed nations. Rather than everyone working on subsistence farms, workers can choose from among hundreds of different occupations. Most jobs are in tertiary, or service, industries. Developing nations, on the other hand, have relatively few jobs available in service industries. The chart shows an example of the difference between the labor force in Bangladesh, Luxembourg, and the United States.

The division between developed and developing countries is not always so clear-cut. Brazil, which has a growing number of industrial and service industries, does not really belong in the same category as poor, agricultural Bangladesh. The world's poorest countries—with a per capita GDP around $3,000 or less—belong in a separate category of "underdeveloped" or "least developed" countries. Unfortunately, these countries have little promise of development in the next few decades. Many of those countries are not underdeveloped because they lack resources but because they have

> ### Through Christian Eyes
>
> Traditionally, Christians have sent missionaries primarily to underdeveloped countries. What roles may missionaries legitimately play in helping these nations become developed countries? What benefits may these efforts produce for world evangelism?

Comparison of Division of Labor			
Country	Agricultural Labor	Industrial Labor	Service Labor
Bangladesh	63.0%	11.0%	26.0%
Luxembourg	0.5%	16.3%	83.1%
United States	0.9%	19.7%	79.4%

unstable governments or cultural habits that discourage initiative and progress.

THE HOPE OF PROSPERITY

What makes some countries rich and others poor? This is not an easy question to answer. Possessing natural resources is not essential to riches. Japan's industries have thrived even though its islands lack natural resources. On the other hand, the Democratic Republic of Congo's mines are rich in resources, but its per capita GDP is among the lowest in the world.

Far more important factors in developing wealth are labor and government. People are a resource, not a drain on the economy. The more hard workers a country has, the more possibilities it has for creating new wealth. Hard work includes a willingness to study, to learn, and to try new things, even if it means taking risks. The Bible clearly states that stealing, cheating, and mistreating others diminish wealth, but God blesses hard work.

> *Wealth gotten by vanity shall be diminished: but he that gathereth by labour shall increase.*
> (Prov. 13:11)

Proverbs also states that the Lord blesses righteous living. The word *righteousness* means "following a rule or standard." The main factor in wealth is God, who blesses those who live according to the standard of His Word and judges those who do not. The question of the wealth of nations, which has puzzled economists for centuries, is best answered this way.

> *Righteousness exalteth a nation: but sin is a reproach to any people.*
> (Prov. 14:34)

National progress and wealth are also dependent on a stable government. People are more willing to work hard, take risks, and invest in business if they are free and have a government that encourages such efforts and works to protect them from exploitation or external attacks.

For a government to be fair and stable, it must be good. Repeatedly in Proverbs, God states that rulers who obey His law will enjoy stability and peace (Prov. 16:12; 20:28; 25:5; 28:2; 29:4, 14). So why do wicked people and countries sometimes seem to prosper? The Lord exalts whom He will. Babylon was "a golden cup in the Lord's hand" (Jer. 51:7), destroying Jerusalem in 586 BC and carrying the Jews away as captives. But the ill-gotten wealth of the wicked Babylonians was fleeting. God eventually judged that empire for its sin. No nation that rejects God's Word will escape divine judgment in the end.

> *Blessed is the nation whose God is the Lord.*
> (Ps. 33:12)

Although "the love of money is the root of all evil" (1 Tim. 6:10), money itself is not evil. Wealth—and the ability to enjoy it—is a gift of God (Eccles. 5:18-20). The Lord gave mankind resources to serve God and others, and through that service find joy and fulfillment. True wealth is found in heaven, not on earth (Matt. 6:19-20).

How Countries Wage Trade Wars

Some countries have tried to achieve **economic self-sufficiency**, the ability to produce everything they need without buying or selling from other countries. In 1961, the Communist leader in Albania isolated his country in every way possible. As a result, Albania became the poorest country in Europe. In contrast, the world's wealthiest nations are also the biggest trading nations.

God meant for people to trade. For example, Israel under Solomon enjoyed extensive trade with the surrounding nations (1 Kings 10). Throughout history, nations have depended on trade to acquire from others the raw materials that they lack. The United States, though rich in resources, must import 100 percent of its bauxite, manganese, and graphite. It also must import most of its industrial diamonds (98%), platinum (88%), tungsten (84%), chromium (82%), tin (81%), and nickel (64%). Without these metals, assembly lines for airplanes and other critical industries would come to a halt. Efforts to ensure trade promote peace among nations.

Trade is essential for more than exchanging raw materials. Every industry needs a **market**—people or businesses to buy its products. **Exports** are the primary and secondary goods that a country ships to other countries. **Imports** are all of the goods that a country receives from other countries. Countries measure international trade in terms of the monetary value of exports and imports. The difference between these two values is called the *balance of trade.*

Occasionally, countries have disputes over trade. Sometimes those conflicts lead to war, but countries have other weapons at their disposal. **Tariffs** are taxes on imports and exports. In theory, if the United States places a high tariff on Japanese automobiles, sales of Japanese cars drop and domestic sales increase. (In reality, sometimes consumers are willing to pay the higher prices for the foreign-made products, so domestic sales continue to languish.) Another weapon is an **embargo** (ban on importing or exporting certain products or trading with a particular country). Arab nations used an oil embargo in the 1970s to drive up the price of oil and to hurt the U.S. economy. (Oil prices affect practically all other prices because fuel oil is used in the production and distribution processes.)

Section Quiz

1. What measurement shows the value of all the goods and services produced within a country in one year?
2. What is another name for money that is invested in business equipment?
3. Explain the main difference between capitalism and socialism.
4. What is another name for the least developed countries?
5. What term is used for the people who want to buy a product?
6. What are import and export taxes called?
   - In what sense is every nation a "developing country"?

FREE TRADE VS. FAIR TRADE

Suppose that your father has just lost his job making jackets because of foreign competition. Meanwhile, your friends are rushing to the mall because a retail store is having a fabulous sale on jackets, the labels of which read "Made in China." How do you resolve this tension? There are two possibilities. **Protectionism** is the belief that the government should restrict foreign imports because they take away jobs. The main way of achieving this goal is to place high tariffs (import taxes) on the foreign goods, making them more expensive than similar domestic goods. On the other hand, **free trade** (imposing no or only low tariffs) allows retailers the freedom to sell any products their customers want.

The United States government has taken different sides on this heated issue at different times in its history. When the British Parliament began restricting free trade, colonial leaders staged the Boston Tea Party. But after the colonies won independence, trade wars between the state governments killed trade and threatened economic disaster. So the authors of the Constitution dropped all barriers to trade between states (called *domestic trade*). Since then, protectionist debates have raged in Congress over *foreign trade*. This issue, in part, precipitated the Civil War, with the North favoring high restrictive tariffs and the South supporting free trade.

Protectionism reached its height in the 1920s. The United States imposed high tariffs to protect its industries from European industries, which were rebuilding after the ravages of World War I. The tariffs seriously curtailed international trade and hurt the economies of both European countries and the United States. Since World War II, free trade has become popular among capitalist nations. They held several rounds of talks to draw up rules for trade, which became known as the **General Agreement on Tariffs and Trade (GATT)**. Tariffs fell from 40 percent to 5 percent, and the volume of worldwide trade ballooned.

Countries with common interests have been negotiating *regional free trade agreements*, which drop trade restrictions within a region but keep a wall of protective tariffs against outsiders. The earliest and most far-reaching regional agreement was the European Union (EU), whose roots go back to 1951. Its members have torn down trade barriers within Western Europe while maintaining barriers to Eastern Europe and Asia. The Association of Southeast Asian Nations (ASEAN) was formed in 1967. In 1993, Mexico joined Canada and the United States in the North American Free Trade Agreement (NAFTA).

But Americans became increasingly disillusioned with low tariffs. Most businessmen were willing to compete in a free market—but not if the foreigners had unfair advantages such as those in the following list. Supporters of *fair trade* argued that the United States was losing jobs and exports because of the following practices.

1. Unfair labor practices: Some countries allow cheap labor, child labor, and prison or slave labor.

2. Unfair government policies: Governments of some developed nations gave businesses tax breaks and subsidies (financial assistance). Governments of less developed nations imposed few costly regulations.

3. Unfair pricing: Businesses in some developed countries sometimes dumped products at below-cost prices to drive American companies out of business.

4. Piracy: The theft of ideas and products, copies of designer clothes with false labels, and unlicensed copies of music, computer programs, and books.

In 1987, the United States and 117 other countries entered a new round of GATT negotiations to find a way to stop such practices. Seven years later, they established the **World Trade Organization (WTO)**, a permanent body with one representative for every nation. The WTO replaced GATT. Individual countries no longer had the final say in their trade policies. In essence, free trade turned into "managed free trade" under the direction of international bureaucrats.

In 2005, the U.S. Senate approved the Central American Free Trade Agreement (CAFTA) with five Central American countries (Guatemala, El Salvador, Honduras, Costa Rica, and Nicaragua) and the Dominican Republic.

Can You:
Define These Terms?

industry
primary industry
subsistence farmer
cash crop
commercial farmer
nomadic herding
natural resources
aquaculture
mineral
metal
bauxite
alloy
fossil fuel
coal
petroleum
natural gas
secondary industry
raw material
manufacturing
Industrial Revolution
technology
nondurable manufacturing
durable manufacturing
tertiary industry
infrastructure
mass communication
publishing industry
telecommunications
wholesale business
retail business
economics
capital
capitalism
free market
socialism
communism
Gross Domestic Product (GDP)
per capita GDP
development
value added
Group of 8 (G–8)
developed country
developing country
economic self-sufficiency
market
export
import
tariff
embargo
protectionism
free trade
General Agreement on
    Tariffs and Trade (GATT)
World Trade Organization (WTO)

CHAPTER REVIEW

HOW MUCH DO YOU REMEMBER?

1. Label each of the following as primary, secondary, or tertiary industries.
    a. a local drug store
    b. a peach orchard
    c. a toaster factory
    d. a petroleum refinery
    e. a hot dog stand at a ball game
    f. a copper mine
    g. a local fire department
    h. a commercial airline company

2. What three fertilizers are most important for crops?

3. List the three fossil fuels. In what form is each found?

4. Name five products taken from petroleum.

5. Give the leading product in each category (ranked by tons).
    a. precious metals
    b. common metals
    c. building materials
    d. fertilizer
    e. fossil fuels

6. How did railroads change transportation? Why have passenger trains declined?

7. Give three examples of mass communication.

8. Why does China have a high GDP but a low per capita GDP?

9. What is the most important factor in the wealth of a nation: raw materials, capital, or labor?

WHAT DO YOU THINK?

1. Why is concrete such a useful building material?

2. How would your life be different if God had not made petroleum?

3. What technology was not around when you were younger?

4. What is the most common industry in your area?

5. Why are some countries poor even though they have valuable raw materials?

6. Read Exodus 34:21. Explain why this command was difficult to obey. What was God teaching about man's first priority in life?

7. Name the occupations of five adult friends or relatives. Tell whether their jobs are part of a primary, secondary, or tertiary industry.

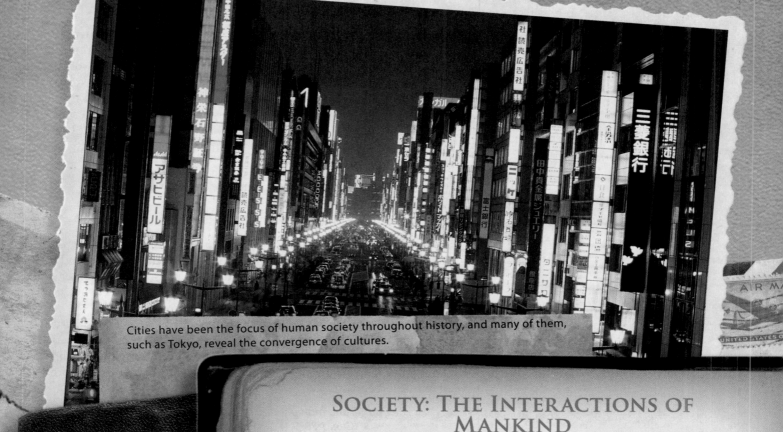

Cities have been the focus of human society throughout history, and many of them, such as Tokyo, reveal the convergence of cultures.

SOCIETY: THE INTERACTIONS OF MANKIND

I. CULTURE: THE WAYS OF SOCIETY
  A. LANGUAGE—THE FOUNDATION OF CULTURE
  B. REGIONS—THE LOCATIONS OF CULTURE
  C. INSTITUTIONS—THE TRANSMISSION OF CULTURE

II. DEMOGRAPHY: THE STATISTICS OF SOCIETY
  A. VITAL STATISTICS
  B. COMMUNITY STATISTICS

III. POLITICS: THE GOVERNANCE OF SOCIETY
  A. DUTIES OF GOVERNMENT
  B. TYPES OF GOVERNMENT
  C. RELATIONS AMONG GOVERNMENTS

A man's life consisteth not in the abundance of the things
which he possesseth.
(Luke 12:15)

So far, you have studied the physical world and how people meet their physical needs. But the unseen spiritual world is far more important to study if you are to understand man's place in the world. The physical world and all of its riches will pass away, but the spiritual world will endure forever.

The Lord made Adam in His image and gave him an eternal soul. His main purpose in life was to glorify God and to enjoy Him forever. However, he was not supposed to serve God by himself; he would need the help of other people.

It is not good that the man should be alone; I will make him
an help meet for him.
(Gen. 2:18)

In all earthly relationships, people are to reflect the image of their Creator, who is Father and King. Geography includes the study of **society**, the relationships among human beings. God has an explicit purpose for society, which is an outward manifestation of the unseen spiritual world.

The development of society is an integral part of man's duty to subdue the earth. The Lord told the first couple, Adam and Eve, to fill the earth with people and to have dominion over society for God's glory. The Lord repeated this **Creation Mandate** to Noah and all of his descendants.

Be fruitful, and multiply, and replenish the earth.
(Gen. 1:28; 9:1)

I. CULTURE: THE WAYS OF SOCIETY

When people hear the word *culture*, they usually think of daily life—clothing, food, sports, customs, music, literature, art, and crafts. But **culture** involves much more. It is society's total "way of life," including all of its traditions and institutions. *Traditions* are the customs or usages that society passes down from one generation to the next. *Institutions* are the formal organizations by which society transmits traditions.

LANGUAGE—THE FOUNDATION OF CULTURE

No one is born with culture. It is taught, and language is the primary instrument for transmitting culture. The ability to speak and reason distinguishes man from the animal world. Man's speech imitates his Maker, Who communicates through both His written Word, the Bible, and His living Word, Jesus Christ (Heb. 1:1–2).

After the Flood, the descendants of Noah had one language and one culture. God commanded them to spread over the earth, but they wanted to stay together in a single society. So they moved down from the mountains of Ararat to build a city on the fertile plain of the Euphrates River (Gen. 11:1–4). The people began building a worship center to promote their wicked, man-centered culture. God said,

*Behold, the people is one, and they have all one language;
. . . and now nothing will be restrained from them, which
they have imagined to do. Go to, let us go down, and there
confound their language, that they may not understand one
another's speech.*
(Gen. 11:6–7)

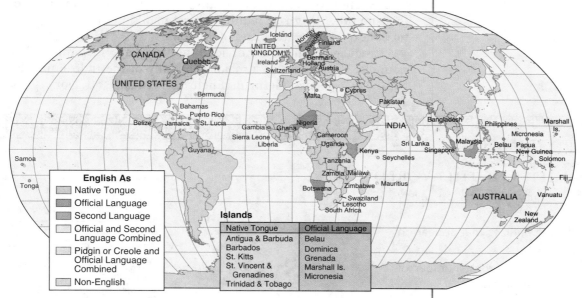

English-Speaking Nations

Babel's man-centered system of thinking is a manifestation of
the philosophy that has come to be known as **humanism**. Humanism is the belief that human thought and values (rather than religious
thoughts or values) should be the central features of culture and that
humans can on their own solve all of their problems. Humanists ignore man's basic problem, which is not conflict among humans but
spiritual conflict with God. All humans face the wrath of God and
will be cast into an everlasting hell unless they are reconciled to their
Creator. God visited the city at Babel and confused their language.
The end result was that they obeyed the divine command to scatter,
which they were determined to ignore (Gen. 9:1, 7; 11:4, 7–8).

God did not scatter people randomly. The descendants of Ham,
Shem, and Japheth spread abroad "after their families, after their
tongues, in their lands, after their nations" (Gen 10:5, 20, 31). Each
family spoke a common language and traveled as a unit. Those families became the founders of the ancient culture regions. (Genesis 10
is a catalog of these regions.)

SPOKEN LANGUAGES

What God did at Babel was not the end of the confusing of
human language. Ever since Babel, wherever mountains, oceans,
and deserts have prevented people from talking to one another,
new languages and cultures have developed. Approximately sixty-
six hundred languages are spoken in the world today. Agreeing on a
total is difficult, however. Speech patterns within a single language
often vary considerably, in which case each speech pattern is called
a **dialect**. But sometimes different languages are so similar that they
are mutually understandable. For example, speakers of Portuguese
can understand Spanish with little difficulty.

Through Christian Eyes

When God confused human language
at Babel, was He judging the human
race or showing it mercy? (Be sure to
read Acts 17:26–27 before you answer.)

Most-Spoken Languages

Language	Speakers (M)
Mandarin Chinese	885
Spanish	332
English	322
Arabic	235
Bengali	189
Hindi	122
Portuguese	170
Russian	170
Japanese	125
German	98

Most linguists recognize ten major **language families**, groups of languages that share many common characteristics. Ninety-nine percent of all people speak a language under one of the ten major families, the most prominent of which is the Indo-European family. Indo-Europeans account for half of the world's total population. Linguists believe that the Indo-European family originated in a region somewhere between India and Europe. The modern boundaries of this and other language families reflect mankind's fascinating history of exploration, wars, and migration.

Language families are divided into language subfamilies. For example, "Germanic" is a major subfamily of the Indo-European family. It includes German, English, Swedish, and Norwegian.

LET'S GO EXPLORING

LANGUAGE FAMILIES OF THE WORLD

1. What language family appears on every continent?

2. List all the language families that appear on the continent of Africa.

3. Which continent has the largest number of language families? How many?

4. Look at the eight culture regions on the map (Africa, Asia, Central Eurasia, Europe, Latin America, the Middle East, North America, and Oceania). List what appears to be the main language family in each region.

Look at the climate map on pp. 38–39 and the vegetation map on pp. 42–43. What climates and land features are most often associated with "other" languages? Why?

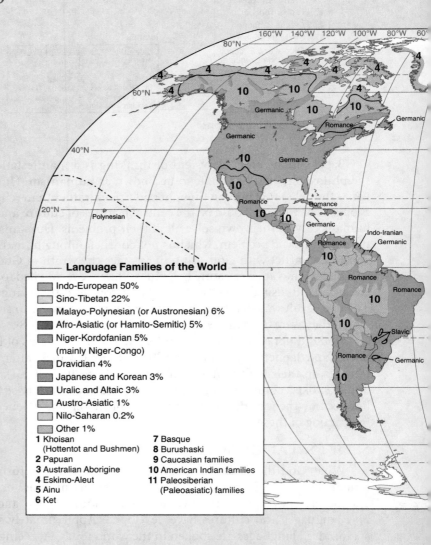

Language Families of the World

- ☐ Indo-European 50%
- ☐ Sino-Tibetan 22%
- ☐ Malayo-Polynesian (or Austronesian) 6%
- ☐ Afro-Asiatic (or Hamito-Semitic) 5%
- ☐ Niger-Kordofanian 5% (mainly Niger-Congo)
- ☐ Dravidian 4%
- ☐ Japanese and Korean 3%
- ☐ Uralic and Altaic 3%
- ☐ Austro-Asiatic 1%
- ☐ Nilo-Saharan 0.2%
- ☐ Other 1%

1 Khoisan (Hottentot and Bushmen)	7 Basque
2 Papuan	8 Burushaski
3 Australian Aborigine	9 Caucasian families
4 Eskimo-Aleut	10 American Indian families
5 Ainu	11 Paleosiberian (Paleoasiatic) families
6 Ket	

Another major subfamily is the "Romance" languages, which descended from Latin, the language of the ancient Romans. It includes Spanish, French, and Italian.

WRITTEN LANGUAGES

Primitive societies rely on word of mouth to transmit culture. But advanced societies have written languages to keep more accurate and complete records. Writing allows the rapid spread of culture. Before 1900, less than 10 percent of the world's population was literate. Now around 75 percent of the world's people are literate. Most developed countries have a literacy rate of greater than 95 percent.

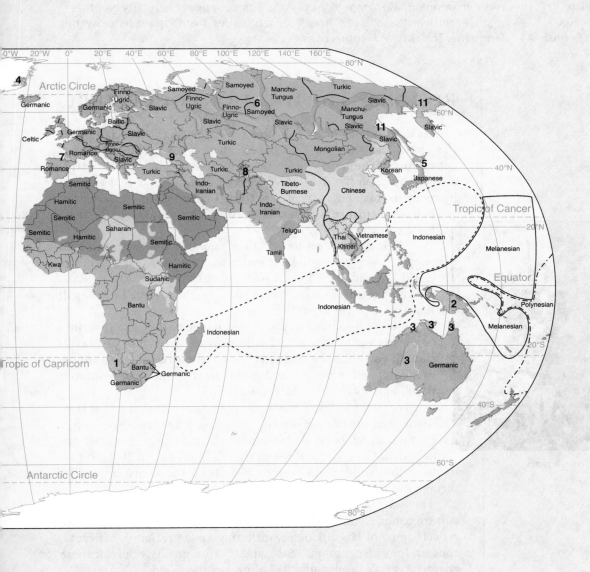

ENGLISH—THE "LINGUA FRANCA" OF THE WORLD

The phrase *lingua franca* is Latin for "Frankish language." It originally referred to the language used by the court of the Frankish emperor Charlemagne (742?–814). The word has come to mean a common language that is used by people of different nations in business, science, and politics. Since the Tower of Babel, many different languages have been used in international relations, but the one that has come closest to becoming the *lingua franca* of the world is English.

Three other languages have more *native speakers* than English—Mandarin, Hindi, and Spanish. But English is the leading second language of the world, learned by more than 157 million people. The countries colored purple on the map (p. 79) expect nearly all of their students to study English in public school. More than forty countries have also made English the official language used in government meetings and documents. India, which has sixteen major languages, each spoken by more than one million people, has made English an "associate official" language. The United Nations uses two main languages for its primary documents—English and French.

Native peoples in many British colonies learned a simplified version of English for work and trade. These *pidgin languages* were a colorful combination of local words and English words with a basic grammar. In some cases, pidgin became the native language of the people and is called creole. The words for many items sold by English-speaking nations, such as *telephone, jeans,* and *cigarette,* appear in nearly all other languages, from Japanese to Swahili.

Colombian woman

Scottish man

Filipino girl

REGIONS—THE LOCATIONS OF CULTURE

As descendants of Adam spread over the earth (especially after the Flood and the Tower of Babel), they developed many different cultures. The term *culture* refers to not only human society as a whole but also the distinctive ways of doing things that are easily recognizable and associated with definable regions or groups of people. A **culture region** is a human society that shares the same basic culture.

Maps make it easier to study complex information about people, just as they make it easier to study physical relief. The world is divided into eight main culture regions: Africa, Asia, Central Eurasia, Europe, Latin America, the Middle East, North America, and Oceania.

Although individual countries change names, grow, shrink, or cease to exist, the world culture regions remain fairly constant. If you learn the characteristics of these regions, you will be well equipped to understand events in your lifetime, no matter what happens to individual countries.

The boundaries of the world regions are similar to the continents but are not necessarily the same. The main exception is Eurasia, which is divided into four distinct culture regions, two of which, Central Eurasia and the Middle East, sit at the crossroads of the world. Both regions have been the focus of conflict throughout history.

The units of this textbook are organized according to the world culture regions. Although sin has marred God's image, every culture reflects some of His attributes, including an appreciation of beauty, concern for order, a moral sense, and creative genius. Look for these characteristics as you study the cultures of the world.

Within each world region are many **subregions** that display increasingly similar characteristics. Northern America, for example, consists of two large subregions, the United States and Canada. Subregions are further divided into even smaller subregions within the chapters.

SECTION QUIZ

1. What is culture?
2. Name the eight culture regions of the world.
3. Why is language the foundation of culture?
4. What is a language family?
5. Which language family has the most speakers?

INSTITUTIONS—THE TRANSMISSION OF CULTURE

Every society has many institutions that transmit culture. The proper goal of all institutions is to help people glorify God, but Adam's sin separated man from God and marred every relationship among mankind. Ever since, society has struggled to subdue not only the earth but also the evil in human hearts.

We can determine how well society is accomplishing God's purposes by studying cultural institutions. Because God has put in every heart a knowledge of both the spiritual world and of man's obligations to the Creator (Rom. 1:19–20; 2:14–15), man is without excuse.

But human institutions have diverged from their purpose of glorifying God to two extremes: glorifying the group or glorifying the individual. Although world culture regions have many differences, Eastern institutions generally value the group, and Western institutions generally value the individual.

Students can learn their nation's culture by learning to read and write.

THE FAMILY

The foundation of society is the family. The Lord instituted the home in the Garden of Eden before sin ever entered the world. He created Eve to be Adam's helper in the work of dominion (Gen. 2:18). At their marriage, the Lord gave them the pattern of a godly home.

> *Therefore shall a man leave his father and his mother, and shall cleave unto his wife: and they shall be one flesh.*
> *(Gen. 2:24)*

Family life teaches traits that both parents and children need—how to obey, how to serve, how to lead, and how to love. Parents also pass on wisdom to their children. The apostle Paul instructed fathers to bring up their children "in the nurture and admonition of the Lord" (Eph. 6:4).

Every society honors the central role of the family. Western societies focus on the **nuclear family**—a man, his wife, and their children. Eastern societies typically focus on the **extended family**—the nuclear family plus grandparents, uncles, aunts, and cousins. Every balanced society honors elders, nurtures children, and emphasizes the central role of the parents.

Extended families are typical in the Orient.

Fallen societies, however, have taken family responsibilities to extremes. Eastern cultures often worship ancestors, and some husbands seek more than one wife (*polygamy*). In contrast, Western cultures tend to overemphasize the rights of individuals, leading to broken families—aborted and illegitimate children in the name of women's rights, and divorce in the name of human rights.

RELIGION

Religion is a people's beliefs regarding the supernatural person or power that has created and sustained the universe. It also entails a system of practices used to show reverence to that person or power.

Practically, religion is what gives a people its sense of purpose in life. It provides a culture with both a set of beliefs as well as a formal code of conduct that regulates how people should live and worship. Religion—or the rejection of religion—guides all other expressions of culture, including holidays, dress, and even food preparation.

The world's cultures, however, have fallen from the worship of the one true God into different forms of idolatry. Eastern cultures tend to worship the state or the group. You might remember the story of Nebuchadnezzar, who built a golden idol and demanded that all of his subjects worship him. Many Eastern cultures, such as Islamic nations, still have an "official religion" that their society expects its members to follow. Communist nations developed "cults of personality" that worship the ruler as the savior of the people. For example, North Korea exalts the founder of communism there, Kim Il Sung, in a religion called Juche (also known as Kimilsungism).

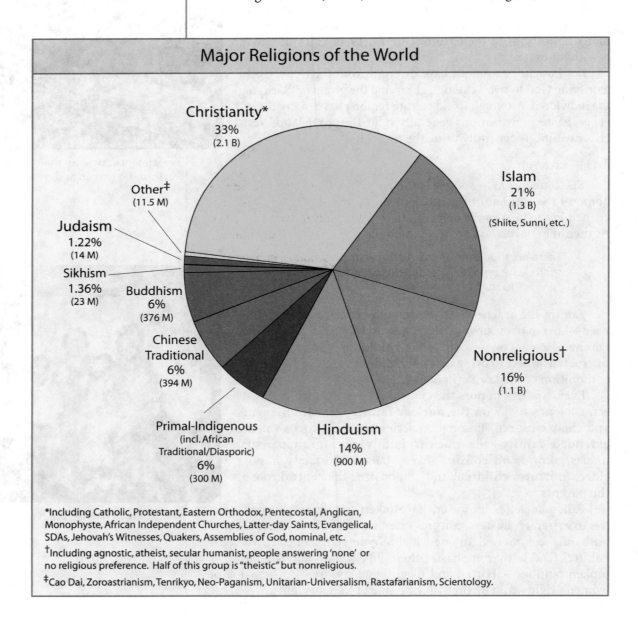

Major Religions of the World

Christianity*
33%
(2.1 B)

Islam
21%
(1.3 B)

(Shiite, Sunni, etc.)

Other‡
(11.5 M)

Judaism
1.22%
(14 M)

Sikhism
1.36%
(23 M)

Buddhism
6%
(376 M)

Chinese
Traditional
6%
(394 M)

Nonreligious†
16%
(1.1 B)

Primal-Indigenous
(incl. African
Traditional/Diasporic)
6%
(300 M)

Hinduism
14%
(900 M)

*Including Catholic, Protestant, Eastern Orthodox, Pentecostal, Anglican, Monophyste, African Independent Churches, Latter-day Saints, Evangelical, SDAs, Jehovah's Witnesses, Quakers, Assemblies of God, nominal, etc.

†Including agnostic, atheist, secular humanist, people answering 'none' or no religious preference. Half of this group is "theistic" but nonreligious.

‡Cao Dai, Zoroastrianism, Tenrikyo, Neo-Paganism, Unitarian-Universalism, Rastafarianism, Scientology.

Christianity, Islam, and Hinduism are the three largest religions in the world.

Muslim mosque

Hindu temple

Protestant church

Western cultures, on the other hand, tend more toward religious liberty. (For example, the ancient Greeks chastised Alexander the Great when he made himself a god to solidify his rule over the conquered Persians.) Western societies allow freedom of worship as long as each religion obeys general public laws. Unfortunately, Western governments also tend toward radical individualism, which leads to a failure to govern the conduct of their people by moral standards of right and wrong. Too often such governments allow every man to do as he chooses.

With so many religions in the world, many people wonder how they can know which one is true. Christianity alone offers satisfying

THE GREAT COMMISSION

Some young Christians ask themselves, "Does God want me to be a missionary?" Several special feature boxes in this book survey different types of missionary service and show how a knowledge of geography prepares Christians to serve God, whether by becoming or supporting a missionary.

In one sense, every Christian is supposed to be a missionary. Every Christian has the responsibility to fulfill the Great Commission (Matt. 28:18–20) and to maintain a good testimony (Col. 4:5–6). However, Christians often differentiate *home missions* (missions in one's own country) and *foreign missions*. According to Acts 1:8, the first Christian missionaries began at home in Jerusalem and Judea and then reached out to their neighbor Samaria and on to the farthest parts of the world.

Ye shall be witnesses unto me both in Jerusalem, and in all Judaea, and in Samaria, and unto the uttermost part of the earth.

Knowledge of geography is essential to missions work. Most of the unevangelized population of the world—billions of Muslims, Hindus, Buddhists, and people of countless other religions—live in what is known as the "10/40 window." That term designates the area between West Africa and East Asia and between 10 degrees north latitude and 40 degrees south latitude. Keep the 10/40 window in mind as you study the various

countries of the world this year. Mission boards also use geographic knowledge in determining where to locate their missionaries to achieve the greatest results. How might you use *your* knowledge of geography to fulfill the Great Commission?

Even high school students can take short-term mission trips to help fulfill the Great Commission.

Ten Largest Countries (Area)	
Country	Square miles
1. Russia	6.59M
2. Canada	3.84M
3. China	3.69M
4. United States	3.67M
5. Brazil	3.30M
6. Australia	2.96M
7. India	1.22M
8. Argentina	1.07M
9. Kazakhstan	1.05M
10. Sudan	0.96M

and consistent answers to mankind's most troubling problems. Humans are sinners who owe God an infinite debt because of their rebellion. But God sent His Son to pay for this debt by dying at Calvary for the sin of the world. Since Jesus was a man, He was able to stand in the place of sinful humans. Since He was God, He was able to pay the infinite debt they owed. As proof that God had accepted this sacrifice, Jesus was raised from the dead three days later. His Resurrection was real. He showed Himself to hundreds of His followers, as the New Testament records in several places. Because God is a loving and compassionate God, He longs for all people everywhere to believe this good news and thus receive the free gift of eternal life. To this day the marching orders for Christianity are the words of the risen Christ: "Go ye therefore, and teach all nations" (Matt. 28:19).

For those who are already followers of Jesus Christ, it is tempting at times to question whether other religions may be true. But all true Christians will learn to respond to such temptations with the apostle Peter's words to Christ: "Lord, to whom shall we go? thou hast the words of eternal life. And we believe and are sure that thou art that Christ, the Son of the living God" (John 6:68–69).

THE NATION

After God divided the languages at Babel and scattered the people, nations arose to transmit culture. A **nation** is a large group of people with a common history and language who have developed a strong sense of identity. Even after a nation loses control of its homeland, it often retains its identity. For example, Israel remained a nation even after foreigners drove the Hebrews out of the Promised Land. Today, we often call the Kurdish people of the Middle East a "nation," although they are divided among five separate countries.

Definition of Terms—According to Acts 17:26, God has directed the settling of all the ethnic groups, or nations, of the world:

> [God] hath made of one blood all nations of men for to dwell on all the face of the earth, and hath determined the times before appointed, and the bounds of their habitation.

The Greek word translated "nation" is *ethnos*, from which we get the word *ethnic*. The English word *nation* comes from a Latin root meaning "born." Both of these words share the idea of a "common birth."

Nation is often confused with related words. *Nation* refers primarily to people, but *country* refers to the land of the people, and *state* refers to the institution that governs the people. A *tribe* is a large group of people who share a common ancestor and is usually governed by elders. Conflicts occur when political boundaries separate peoples of a nation, as happened often to the Polish and the Balkan nations.

A **nation-state** is a nation of people that has established its own government, or state. When one nation conquers other nations beyond its borders, it creates an **empire**. Governments that rule over many nations are called *multinational states*.

Political Maps—A *political map* shows the boundaries that a state has drawn around its people regardless of differences in culture. The world is divided into 193 states. Each state has *sovereignty*, the unlimited authority to run affairs within its own borders. Sovereign states come in all shapes and sizes. The smallest is Vatican City, situated on 108.7 acres inside the city of Rome, Italy. The largest state is Russia, which spans two continents and encompasses about one hundred ethnic groups.

A few territories that claim independence and run their own governments are not officially recognized by most other states. The Chinese island of Taiwan is the best example. Although Taiwan has run its own affairs for more than fifty years and has one of the biggest economies in the world, China refuses to allow it a seat in the United Nations, and most nations have sided with China.

Political boundaries are a fundamental feature of culture maps because they mark the limit of a state's authority over the lives of people. People in two neighboring countries may share many culture traits, but they follow completely different laws. Some political boundaries follow the twists and turns of **natural boundaries**, such as rivers and mountains. Other **geometric boundaries** connect geometric points or follow lines of latitude or longitude. Most of the U.S. border with Canada is a geometric boundary drawn along the forty-ninth parallel (49° N). On the other hand, the border of Texas and Mexico follows primarily the Rio Grande.

As you study nations, look for the political boundaries that are unstable. Many boundaries cut across natural features, languages, religions, ethnic groups, or climates. To keep its borders intact, each state must win both the loyalty of its own people and the respect of its neighbors.

Disagreements over the limits of state authority breed the worst kind of violence in the drama of human history—war. At any time, as many as thirty or forty states are at war. When people within a state's borders fight their own government, it is called a **civil war**. The most common goals of a civil war are to replace the ruler or to separate from the state. *International* wars occur when independent states fight each other.

Ten Largest Countries (Population)	
Country	**Population**
1. China	1,300,000,000
2. India	1,087,000,000
3. United States	294,000,000
4. Indonesia	238,000,000
5. Brazil	179,000,000
6. Pakistan	159,000,000
7. Russia	144,000,000
8. Bangladesh	141,000,000
9. Nigeria	137,000,000
10. Japan	128,000,000

SECTION QUIZ

1. What is the basic difference between Eastern and Western institutions?

2. What is a nuclear family?

3. What is an extended family?

4. What are the five major religious groups?

5. Name two common types of political boundaries.

◌̇ Which of the world's 193 states shares borders with the most other states?

II. DEMOGRAPHY: THE STATISTICS OF SOCIETY

The study of human populations and their characteristics is called **demography**. Societies use three basic methods to gather demographic information: vital statistics, censuses, and surveys. **Vital statistics** are official records of births, marriages, divorces, and deaths. **Censuses** are official government counts of the entire population within the nation's boundaries. **Surveys** are counts of small samples of the total population. Surveyors and census takers collect information about age, marriage, family size, education, and so on.

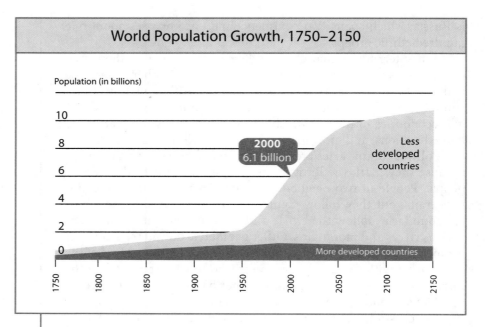

World Population Growth, 1750–2150

Population (in billions)

10

8

6

4

2

0

2000
6.1 billion

Less developed countries

More developed countries

1750 1800 1850 1900 1950 2000 2050 2100 2150

VITAL STATISTICS

The word *vital* means "related to life." Vital statistics are the "life signs" of a society. Like a doctor taking a pulse, nations seek statistics about the life and health of their people. The greatest enemy of every society is the pall of death. The two basic vital statistics are (1) the rate of natural increase and (2) life expectancy.

NATURAL INCREASE

Countries measure population increase by comparing the number of births to the number of deaths each year. The number of children born per one thousand people is called the **crude birthrate**. The United States has a crude birthrate of 14.1 (14.1 live births for every 1,000 people). If new babies were the only factor in population growth, the population would increase by 1.4 percent each year. But demographers must also calculate the number of people who die each year per 1,000 people, called the **crude death rate**. The U.S. crude death rate is 8.2. Subtracting the number of deaths from the number of births (14 – 8) gives the **rate of natural increase**. It is 6 per 1,000 or 0.6 percent.

Humanists are discouraged by high death rates and high growth rates. Their ultimate goal is to end human suffering and to limit the growth of humans on the earth. They want to decrease the world's growth rate, which is now about 1.14 percent, to match the low rate in Western societies. (The U.S. growth rate is 0.92 percent.) In fact, the population in some Western nations is decreasing.

But the Bible gives a completely different perspective on birth and death. Suffering and death are essential to God's design for this fallen world (Gen. 3:16), and bearing children is a sign of God's blessing, as families obey God's Creation Mandate. In the midst of sorrow and death, children offer hope of new life. (See Psalm 127.)

LIFE EXPECTANCY

Before the Flood, people lived long lives; Methuselah, for example, lived a record 969 years. But after the Flood, **life expectancy** (the number of years a person can expect to live) declined rapidly. By Moses' day, life expectancy had fallen to seventy years.

The days of our years are threescore years and ten; and if by reason of strength they be fourscore years, yet is their strength labour and sorrow; for it is soon cut off, and we fly away.
(Ps. 90:10)

Around 1650, however, the growth in world population began to increase. Over the next two hundred years, the world's population doubled (from five hundred million to one billion). Eighty years later, the population doubled again. By 1975, the world population had reached four billion and was adding nearly one billion people every decade. It now stands at nearly six and a half billion.

Advances in technology and medicine have done much to increase world population. Better crops and new vaccinations have practically eliminated the effects of malnutrition and some common diseases that once took countless lives. Life expectancy in the United States in 1901 was forty-nine years; by the turn of the century it was seventy-seven years. Today it is about 77.6 years. The statistics are even better for women, who usually outlive men by about 5.4 years.

One measure of national development is increasing life expectancy, which includes lower infant mortality and a longer average life span.

Population Growth Rate by Continent

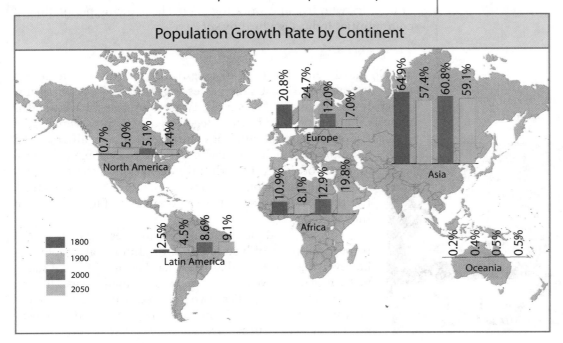

Legend:
- 1800
- 1900
- 2000
- 2050

North America: 0.7%, 5.0%, 5.1%, 4.4%

Latin America: 2.5%, 4.5%, 8.6%, 9.1%

Europe: 20.8%, 24.7%, 12.0%, 7.0%

Africa: 10.9%, 8.1%, 12.9%, 19.8%

Asia: 64.9%, 57.4%, 60.8%, 59.1%

Oceania: 0.2%, 0.4%, 0.5%, 0.5%

Urban overcrowding and mountainous terrain make living in Bolivia's cities an ordeal.

World's Largest Metropolitan Areas

Metro. area	Population
1. Tokyo, Japan	34,200,000
2. Mexico City	22,800,000
3. Seoul, South Korea	22,300,000
4. New York, N.Y.	21,900,000
5. São Paulo, Brazil	20,200,000
6. Mumbai, India	19,850,000
7. Delhi, India	19,700,000
8. Shanghai, China	18,150,000
9. Los Angeles, CA	18,000,000
10. Osaka, Japan	16,800,000

Vancouver, Canada, presents an orderly, inviting urban atmosphere.

Health improvements are most apparent in the declining death rate among children, called **infant mortality**. Infant mortality is measured by comparing the number of live births to the number of infants who die in their first year. Before the Industrial Revolution, nearly half of all babies died before they reached their first birthday. Today, the world infant mortality rate is 50.11 (a little more than 50 infants per 1,000 live births die before their first birthday). Infant mortality in the United States is only 6.5. Singapore has the lowest rate at 2.29. This achievement is the result of numerous factors, including better nutrition, better prenatal care, improved medicines, and advances in technology that allow earlier detection and treatment of formerly fatal health problems.

Despite modern advances, however, science still faces many obstacles in man's quest to increase life expectancy. About 3,500 years ago, Moses managed to live 120 years. The first person on record to surpass that age was Madame Jeanne Calment of Arles, France, who died in 1997 at age 122.

SECTION QUIZ

1. What do we call the study of human populations and their characteristics?

2. What two statistics are used to compute the rate of natural increase of a population?

3. What are the main reasons for recent increases in life expectancy?

COMMUNITY STATISTICS

Vital statistics help us to understand the life of a typical family in each nation. Nations are also interested in communities—groups of families who live and work together. The growing population of communities indicates a healthy society.

URBANIZATION

No hard and fast rule distinguishes among the different types of communities. Usage varies regarding what constitutes a city, town, or village. For simplicity, demographers have divided populated areas into two broad categories: *urban areas*, which have a large number of buildings and people in a small area, and *rural areas*, which have few buildings and people in a large area. According to the arbitrary definition of the U.S. Census Bureau, rural communities have a population of less than five thousand, and cities have a population of more than five thousand.

The size and number of communities have increased throughout most of history. Since the Industrial Revolution, however, the move to urban areas has become a virtual stampede, as people have left their farms and small villages to seek opportunities in big cities. Two hundred years ago, 95 percent of Americans lived on farms, but now fewer than 5 percent do. The growth of urban areas at the expense of rural areas is called **urbanization**. More than 80 percent of Americans, and 49.2 percent of the world population, live in an urban area.

The rise of large cities during the twentieth century was amazing. In 1900, only twelve cities had a population of more than one million. Today, over four hundred cities fit that category, and more are added almost every year. Another trend affecting urbanization is the tendency of many Americans to prefer living in the **suburbs**, an area between urban and rural areas that offers proximity to urban benefits but without the attending problems.

Cities in developing countries are growing rapidly and will soon overtake older, established cities in developed countries. By the year 2020, no U.S. cities are likely to remain on the list of the largest urban areas in the world.

El Salvador has the highest population density in the Western Hemisphere.

POPULATION DENSITY

Crowding has been a serious problem since early in history. Abraham and Lot were forced to separate because their herds and servants had become so large that "the land was not able to bear them" (Gen. 13:6). The land can support only so many farms and herds. Daniel Boone and other pioneers on the American frontier moved steadily westward in search of "elbow room." Even in modern industrial cities, where people can buy their basic needs from afar, crowding is still a concern. City leaders must work hard to provide adequate services such as sanitation, hospitals and emergency medical services, and police and fire protection.

Population density is the average number of people who live on each square mile (or kilometer) of land. For example, the average density in Egypt is about 168 Egyptians on every square mile of land.

THOMAS MALTHUS ON OVERPOPULATION

Many people in the eighteenth century believed that man could make his society perfect. Thomas Malthus (1766–1834) attacked this idealistic view in a new economic theory based on the harsh realities at that time in Britain. In *An Essay of the Principle of Population As It Affects the Future Improvement of Society* (1798), he argued that man will never escape misery and poverty because food supplies could not keep up with the population increase. The only checks on population growth were war, famine, disease, and self-restraint.

Because of that idea, the people of that day began to believe that if the world population did not stop growing, widespread famine would soon prevail as agriculture ceased to provide enough food. People came to view mankind's growth as its own worst enemy. Economists began to discourage charity and to justify subsistence wages for labor.

Great Britain soon discovered that Malthus's predictions were not entirely accurate. He had not treated the facts very scientifically. Neither was he aware of all of the changes that the Industrial Revolution was bringing. Before he died, a new wave of economic optimism swept Britain. But whenever the economy periodically declines, Malthus's theory again becomes popular. Today, many "gloom and doom" Malthusian societies are prophesying the end of mankind unless we take drastic measures to curb the rising world population, especially in India and China. But the problem is not as grave as they say, and sins such as abortion and euthanasia ("mercy killing") are certainly not the solutions.

Malthus believed that poverty and famine, such as are widely evident in many parts of Africa, were caused by overpopulation. In reality, people are a country's greatest natural resource.

Terracing steep land, such as this in Portugal, makes hilly or mountainous land arable and is an example of good stewardship.

The primary purpose of government—at the local, state or provincial, and national levels—is to protect its citizens.

France has about the same population as Egypt, but its density is 276 people per square mile because it has only one-half the area of Egypt.

Population density is a fairly good measure of crowding, but people are not spread evenly across the landscape. They generally cluster around good farmland. Nearly all of the Egyptian people, for example, live in a narrow band of land along the banks of the Nile River and in the Nile Delta. Thousands of square miles of that desert country are virtually uninhabited.

Demographers have developed an even more accurate way to measure how dense the population is. They take into account the amount of **arable land** (land that can be used to plant crops). For example, only 2.9 percent of Egypt's 386,660 square miles of land is arable. By comparing the total population to the arable land, demographers find the **physiological density**. Egypt's physiological density is more than six thousand people per square mile. Unlike Egypt, France has 33.53 percent arable land, and its physiological density is less than one thousand. This statistic also indicates that the lower the physiological density, the easier it is for each nation to feed itself.

Humanists are worried about the increasing size of cities, the loss of wilderness, and the decline in rural societies. But the Bible has a different perspective on urbanization and population density.

God meant for the earth to be subdued. He provided Israel with walled cities in the Promised Land, and He made provisions to ensure that the land would not return to its wild state (Deut. 7:22). The ultimate destination of His people is not a wilderness but the New Jerusalem, a massive city that will cover some two thousand square miles and be filled with people.

The following chapters examine urban areas, why they arose, and what they show about human geography. Studying rural areas is just as interesting for geographers. You will discover some of the natural limitations that God has placed on human settlement and see some of the natural wonders in which every nation takes pride.

SECTION QUIZ

1. Why have rural populations decreased in most developed countries?

2. What term describes the growing trend of populations to migrate to cities?

3. What is population density?

III. POLITICS: THE GOVERNANCE OF SOCIETY

When the waters receded and Noah stepped off the ark, God instituted human *government*, the rule of man over man. He gave rulers the power of life and death for one primary purpose: restraining violence. By executing murderers, the government showed respect for the value of human life and helped deter other murders.

> *Whoso sheddeth man's blood, by man shall his blood be shed: for in the image of God made he man.*
> *(Gen. 9:6)*

After the fall of the Soviet Empire in 1991, the United States struggled to find the best way to use its leadership to promote peace and prosperity. Modern technology has greatly complicated relations among nations. The invention of planes, computers, "smart" bombs, nuclear missiles, and international terrorist organizations diminished the value of borders as protective barriers. Nations are seeking new ways to cooperate to stop international crime, espionage, terrorism, and military attack.

A few countries' governments are headed by absolute monarchs, such as Saudia Arabia's King Abdullah.

DUTIES OF GOVERNMENT

The Bible defines the duties of government. Its basic responsibility is to preserve order and protect its citizens from violence by promoting good and punishing evil, beginning with the execution of murderers (Gen. 9:6; Rom 13:1–6). To implement this obligation, governments provide justice and defense. *Justice* entails a system of laws and courts to settle disputes between citizens. *Defense* entails a police force to protect law-abiding citizens from domestic criminals and military forces to protect citizens from foreign attack. Whenever no form of governing authority exists and people are doing whatever they want, a state of **anarchy** exists.

TYPES OF GOVERNMENT

Governments can be classified many ways. The most basic way, however, is the ruler's source of power. Romans 13:1 teaches that all governments, including pagan ones, receive their ultimate authority from God.

AUTHORITARIAN GOVERNMENT

Authoritarian governments hold power by claiming an authority higher than the people they govern.

Monarchies are an authoritarian form of government. Monarchs, usually kings or queens, receive their authority by birth. An **absolute monarch** rules as he pleases. Although monarchies were far more common in the past than they are now, a few absolute monarchies still exist (e.g., Saudi Arabia and Jordan).

Another type of authoritarian government is a **dictatorship**. A dictator is a person who rules by the authority of the military. Often, as in the case of Napoleon, he rises to power with public support. Some dictatorships, however, are ruled by a small group that has forced itself on the people. Dictators usually establish their own political party and allow no opposition to their actions. Dictatorships are common in undeveloped and developing countries.

The most extreme form of authoritarian government is a **totalitarian government**. Such governments make decisions about every detail of their people's lives, allegedly for the good of the whole country. Citizens must get permission before they can change jobs, hold peaceful meetings, or even

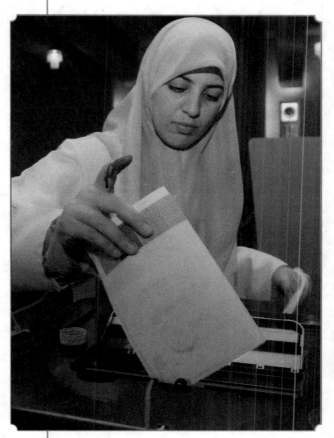

Iraqi women were finally allowed to vote in that country's first free elections in 2005.

Ten Largest Armies in the World Country	Uniformed Troops
1. China	2,250,000
2. United States	1,428,000
3. India	1,325,000
4. North Korea	1,075,000
5. Russia	960,000
6. South Korea	685,000
7. Pakistan	620,000
8. Iran	540,000
9. United Kingdom	515,000
10. Turkey	515,000

travel within the country. China is the largest country ruled by a totalitarian government. The leaders of the Chinese Communist Party also have behind them tremendous military power to back their rule. Although the people must vote, the only candidates are members of the Communist Party, and they face no opposing candidates. North Korea is perhaps the most repressive totalitarian government today.

Many authoritarian governments claim to be democracies that rule in the interest of the people, but the test of a true government "of the people" is free, fair, and regular elections. Very few countries enjoy this privilege. The people may have elections in an authoritarian government, but the leaders use their authority to limit opposition parties or to delay, manipulate, or cancel elections.

ELECTED GOVERNMENT

In contrast to authoritarian governments, elected governments rely on the consent of the people to keep their position. The word *democracy* is often used to describe elected governments. **Democracy** originally described a government in which the whole population ruled. The first *direct* or *pure democracies* arose in the ancient Greek city-states. Every adult male citizen could vote on every law and issue that came before the government. Modern nations, however, are too large to have pure democracies. Today's democracies are *indirect* or *representative democracies* in which the people elect representatives who vote on laws for them. The people have an opportunity to voice their opinions and even to run for office if they wish.

One of the most common forms of modern democracy is a limited or **constitutional monarchy**, in which the people have limited the power of the monarch by law. He or she functions more as a figurehead; the real power belongs to an elected legislature. The most powerful leader of the elected assembly supervises the writing of laws and heads the bureaucracy that executes the laws. Great Britain is an example of such a government.

The other major type of representative democracy is a **republic**. Unlike constitutional monarchies, republics elect their national leader, generally known as the president, who supervises the bureaucracy while the legislature writes laws.

Representative democracies permit the greatest degree of personal freedom of any form of government.

SECTION QUIZ

1. What is anarchy?

2. What is government's basic responsibility?

3. Where does an absolute monarch obtain his authority? a dictator? a president?

4. What is the main difference between a pure democracy and a representative democracy?

5. What are the two most common forms of modern democracies?

- Is it possible for a dictatorship to have a democratic form of government?

RELATIONS AMONG GOVERNMENTS

Every nation is concerned about its relations with other countries. The set of principles that guides a government's international relations is called its **foreign policy**. Governments have two alternatives to resolve disputes: war or negotiation.

> *What king, going to make war against another king, sitteth not down first, and consulteth whether he be able with ten thousand to meet him that cometh against him with twenty thousand? Or else, while the other is yet a great way off, he sendeth an ambassage, and desireth conditions of peace.*
> *(Luke 14:31–32)*

THE THREAT OF WAR

Nations can influence their neighbors through foreign trade and *foreign aid* (gifts of money, goods, or technology to foreign nations). But the most obvious (although not necessarily the best) way to influence neighbors is the threat of military attack.

Nations constantly evaluate their military strength and that of their potential enemies to ensure that they can defend themselves against attack. Military strength can be measured in many ways. *Active troop strength* (the number of full-time soldiers in uniform) is the most common measurement, but it can be misleading; the largest army is not necessarily the most effective army. For example, with less than fifty thousand men, Alexander the Great defeated a Persian army of more than one-quarter million men by relying on high discipline and superior tactics. The best measurement of modern military strength is national *annual defense spending* on military technology. By this measurement, the United States is now the only superpower in the world.

Powerful nations tend to vie for cultural and political leadership (hegemony) over their weaker neighbors. The powerful nations consider their weaker neighbors whom they seek to influence to be their *sphere of influence*. One cannot understand events in any of the world's culture regions without appreciating who are the "big dogs" and who are the underdogs.

Because the United States is now the world's only superpower, its sphere of influence circles the globe. It has built military bases and stationed troops in almost every region to help it "project power" for the benefit of its allies. A capitalist nation that thrives on trade, the United States believes

Greatest Military Expenditures as Percentage of GDP

Country	% of GDP
1. Jordan	14.6
2. Eritrea	13.4
3. Oman	11.4
4. Angola	10.6
5. Qatar	10.0
6. Saudi Arabia	10.0
7. Israel	8.7
8. Yemen	7.8
9. Armenia	6.5
10. Bahrain	6.3

Greatest Military Expenditures ($US)

Country	Amount (B)
1. United States	370.70
2. China	67.49
3. Japan	45.84
4. France	45.23
5. United Kingdom	42.84
6. Germany	35.06
7. Italy	28.18
8. Saudi Arabia	18.00
9. India	16.97
10. South Korea	16.18

Diplomacy and treaties, such as the one being signed by the Russian and American leaders, often prevent wars.

Flags representing the member nations fly on the grounds of the United Nations Building in New York City.

the spread of freedom and capitalism is a vital *national interest* that should guide its foreign policy. For example, President George W. Bush especially emphasized the extension of political freedom and democracy to the Muslim countries of the Middle East as part of the war against terrorism.

The first concern of U.S. foreign policy is the seven leading world powers that have the most influence on world politics. They are, by region, Russia in Central Eurasia; France, the United Kingdom, Germany, and Italy in Western Europe; and China and Japan in East Asia. Almost every other nation consults them when making foreign policy decisions.

The United States is also concerned about *militarized states*, which have a large number of soldiers and spend a large percentage of their GDP on weapons. Militarized states might be poor, but they are very dangerous. War can break out on their borders at any moment. Examples include North Korea, India, and Pakistan. (You will be studying more about militarized states as you study each cultural subregion.)

A third area of concern is the nations that oppose the role of the United States as a superpower and that reject democracy and capitalism. The most dangerous of these nations are **rogue nations** that ignore some of the most fundamental principles of international relations. They willingly use chemical weapons, terrorism, or any other means they deem necessary—even against their own people—to get their way or increase their power. The two most common types of rogue nations are Communist countries, such as China, and radical Muslim nations, such as Iran. The free nations are especially concerned that such rogue nations might provide terrorists with weapons of mass destruction, whether chemical, biological, or nuclear.

NEGOTIATING PEACE

Diplomacy is the art of negotiating agreements between nations. Formal agreements between nations are called **treaties**. To avoid war, nations can negotiate two kinds of treaties. They can either talk to their enemies and sign a *peace treaty* or make strong *military alliances* with their friends, agreeing to help each other in case of attack.

For most of its history, the United States followed Thomas Jefferson's advice to pursue "peace, commerce, and honest friendship with all nations—entangling alliances with none." But the tragedy of two world wars and the successive threats of communism and terrorism to world peace have forced it to change its foreign policy. The United States has made military alliances with more than forty countries. In the 1940s, it led the world in creating two significant *international organizations*: the North Atlantic Treaty Organization (NATO) and the United Nations (UN).

NATO is the most powerful and successful alliance in history. In 1947, the United States joined Canada and most of the free nations of Western Europe in establishing NATO to protect Western Europe from the threat of the Soviet Union. NATO's arsenal of nuclear weapons, tanks, and soldiers was so intimidating that the Soviet Union never once set foot in Western Europe, and NATO never fired a shot during the Cold War.

The **UN** was also formed in the wake of World War II. From past experience, most member nations knew that the UN would not stop war, but they wanted a neutral place where they could negotiate peaceful solutions to disputes. Representatives of the UN member nations meet in the General Assembly to vote on agreements. But the five major Allies of World War II—the United States, the United Kingdom, France, China, and the Soviet Union (now Russia)—hold the reins of power. They are the five permanent members of the **Security Council**. Any one of them can veto (reject) decisions of the General Assembly. Therefore, the UN cannot make important policies without support from these major members.

The UN has proved to be much less successful than NATO. Because of the Soviet Union's veto power, the UN was helpless to intervene in dozens of bloody wars that the Soviets supported around the world. America's military alliances and resolve, not the UN, helped contain communism and bring about the final collapse of the Soviet Empire. The UN has also proven itself weak in acting against rogue nations.

When the elder George Bush was president of the United States, he hoped that a "new world order" would emerge from the ruins of communism. But his vision did not materialize. In 1991, civil war engulfed the multinational state of Yugoslavia on Europe's southern border. The bloodshed between 1991 and 1995 was the worst in Europe since World War II. It seemed that every action taken by NATO, the UN, or the United States only worsened the situation. Eventually,

RED CROSS

The Red Cross is one of the most widely recognized volunteer organizations in the world. With a permanent presence in more than sixty countries, operations in about eighty countries, and more than 250 million members, it shows mankind's willingness to make sacrifices to relieve the sufferings of others in times of war or natural disaster.

The Red Cross headquarters is in Geneva, Switzerland. Its universally recognized symbol—a red cross on a white field—is based on the flag of Switzerland. Each nation organizes its own society, which agrees to follow the general guidelines of the headquarters. The United States has nearly one Red Cross chapter for every county. Muslim countries also have a relief agency called the Red Crescent.

Swiss businessman Jean Henri Dunant (doo-NAHN) founded the Red Cross in 1863 after he witnessed the carnage of the Battle of Solferino in 1859. At a Red Cross meeting in 1864, various nations drew up the **Geneva Convention**, a treaty establishing basic rules for how nations should treat wounded soldiers and prisoners of war. The Red Cross monitors adherence to the Geneva Convention and delivers aid packages to prisoners. Although the original focus of the Red Cross was assisting victims of war, it has expanded its activities to include collecting blood, reuniting families, assisting during natural disasters, and distributing medicine and relief goods to needy nations.

The Red Crescent (in Muslim countries) and the Red Cross (in Christian countries) provide humanitarian relief in times of war or natural disaster.

however, peace was restored, and Yugoslavia was divided into smaller states.

Yugoslavia's civil war revealed some of the serious flaws in the Enlightenment concept of the nation-state. One flaw was the two competing principles that were working against each other. According to the principle of **self-determination**, all peoples have a right to vote for the type of government they will have. However, if self-determination were taken too far, almost every sovereign country would be in danger. Few countries are true nation-states, consisting wholly of only one kind of people. If every minority voted to become independent, most nations would lose their **territorial integrity** (defensible borders).

When four ethnic minorities in Yugoslavia voted to become independent in 1990 and 1991, the Western nations recognized their independence, in spite of protests from the Serbs, the most powerful ethnic group in Yugoslavia. But when minorities in the new republics voted to break away and rejoin the Serbs, Europe refused to recognize their right to self-determination, revealing a major inconsistency.

Another flaw was that the Enlightenment failed to recognize that God in His sovereignty has established each government. People need to learn to live together despite their differences. It is foolish to believe that self-determination will bring peace. The root problem is man's sinful heart, which does not change based on where people live or how they govern. The only solution to world strife is a miraculous change of heart, which is the realm of Christ, not human kings.

SECTION QUIZ

1. What is the best measurement of the military strength of a nation?

2. List the eight world powers that have the most influence on world politics.

3. What is a rogue nation?

4. Name the most successful military alliance in history.

5. How can the five permanent members of the Security Council control the policies of the UN?

CHAPTER 4 REVIEW

HOW MUCH DO YOU REMEMBER?

1. How many culture regions are in the world? What region are you in?

2. What is the most widespread language family in the world?

3. Explain how the Enlightenment has influenced modern government.

4. Show how the rate of natural increase is derived for the United States.

5. Why has the world's population increased dramatically since 1650?

6. Explain the value of calculating physiological density.

7. What country has the largest area? the largest population?

8. What type of government do most Communist countries have?

9. Which of the following terms describe the government of the United States?
   a. elected government
   b. rogue nation
   c. republic
   d. dictatorship
   e. pure democracy

WHAT DO YOU THINK?

1. Was there written language before the Flood?

2. Use a map of your state to find all of its natural and geometric boundaries.

3. Is the United States a true nation-state?

4. Why are death rates relatively high in some developed countries?

5. List as many examples as you can of specific medical advances that have increased life expectancy.

6. Consider your own city or a city near you. What advantages might attract rural people and what problems might they find?

7. Why do most rogue nations have authoritarian governments?

8. If you were president of the United States, what culture region would worry you the most? Why? Explain your answer using your knowledge of geography and politics.

Can You:

Define These Terms?

society	infant mortality
Creation Mandate	urbanization
culture	suburb
humanism	population density
dialect	arable land
language family	physiological
culture region	density
subregion	anarchy
nuclear family	absolute monarch
extended family	dictatorship
nation	totalitarian gov-
nation-state	ernment
empire	democracy
political boundary	constitutional
natural boundary	monarchy
geometric	republic
boundary	foreign policy
civil war	rogue nation
demography	diplomacy
vital statistics	treaty
census	NATO
survey	UN
crude birthrate	Security Council
crude death rate	Geneva Convention
rate of natural	self-determination
increase	territorial integrity
life expectancy	

UNIT 3

CLIMBING IN THE ALPS

Mary Mummery was the wife of Alfred Mummery, a famous mountain climber in the late nineteenth century. Female mountain climbers were not unheard of at that time, but they were often overshadowed by their male counterparts. Many men thought that women should not climb mountains. Alfred Mummery, though, went against traditional prejudices by climbing with his wife and letting her write a chapter in his book My Climbs in the Alps and Caucasus. *The following is an excerpt from her account of their climb up Teufelsgrat, a ridge on the mountain Täschhorn, in the Alps in 1880.*

The snow once more began to thin out, leaving nothing but a huge sheet of ice. To cut across would have taken days. There was clearly nothing for it but once more to regain the ridge. Burgener was of opinion that we were past the more serious towers and pinnacles, and that, if we could only reach the crest, a sure and not too lengthy road to the summit would be ours. He therefore directed our leader to make straight up the slope towards some great slabs of rock that projected through the ice. These, however, soon became too precipitous and smooth, and we were reduced, as our last chance, to cutting up a hideous ice-gully that flanked the rocks. In places snow covered the ice, and, the gully being bent and narrow, it afforded more or less precarious footing. Burgener's injunctions were constant, "Keep where the snow is thickest." But the snow soon dwindled down till it nowhere exceeded an inch or so; still, as long as the beat of the axe could hew out a step, we advanced steadily. At length, however, the cheery chip of the axe ceased, and in response to Burgener's query came the reply, "Es giebt gar kein Eis."[1] To the right and to the left the smooth slabs of the rock-gully were but thinly glazed, and above this again was a thin coating of loose snow. The wall of rock on the right suggested, however, some possibility of continuing the ascent, and to this our leader made his way and climbed a short distance, when it became so ice-glazed and precipitous that he was brought to a stand. It was even doubtful whether he could descend, and it was evident that his position was critical in the extreme. Luckily, he had for the moment fairly reliable footing.[2]

[1]"There is no ice at all."

[2]Excerpted from Alfred F. Mummery, *My Climbs in the Alps and Caucasus*, in *Dead Reckoning*: *Great Adventure Writing from the Golden Age of Exploration, 1800–1900,* Helen Whybrow, ed. New York: W. W. Norton & Company, 2003.

EUROPE AND RUSSIA

A COMMON HISTORY

Spanning two continents, Europe and Russia appear to be a mass of diverse cultures. Every country seems to have its own language, customs, traditions, and rich history. Despite the differences within these regions, Europe and Russia have some common, unifying themes, particularly history and religion.

Europe is a continent rich in history. The Mediterranean coast was home to the earliest European empires. The Greeks built a prosperous civilization, and Alexander the Great spread Greek culture throughout the lands he conquered. Though Rome's empire did not encompass as much territory as Alexander's, Rome controlled much of Europe for over 500 years, providing unity to diverse lands. The Roman Empire spread Greek and Roman culture farther than ever before, influencing lands as far away as the British Isles. Another development during the Roman Empire was the birth of Christianity, which garnered a strong following across the empire.

When Rome fell, barbarian tribes spread throughout Europe to fill the vacuum. Over time, these tribes became states and formed the basis of modern Europe. Christianity also developed and took the form of the Roman Catholic Church. The Middle Ages were years of struggle between kings and popes. Rulers of nation-states also fought one another, as each state sought to increase its land and influence. In spite of all the warfare, travel and trade continued and aspects of the culture unified.

Russia's history traditionally began about 862, when Rurik gained control of Novgorod. In 988, a Russian ruler accepted Eastern Orthodoxy as the faith of his people. Russia was separated from Europe for some time when the Golden Horde of the Mongols ruled Russia. But by the end of the fifteenth century, Moscow led Russia away from the authority of the Mongols.

In the fourteenth century, the Renaissance brought a rebirth of learning. Some of the greatest works of art and literature were created during this time. On the heels of the Renaissance came the Reformation. The Reformation clearly defined the Protestant doctrine of justification by faith alone. Conflict over this issue as well as the supremacy of Scripture (over Roman Catholic tradition) divided Western Europe into Protestant and Roman Catholic areas. Russia was not substantially affected by the Reformation.

After the Reformation, the next few centuries brought many wars and new discoveries. Under Peter the Great, Russia focused on becoming more European than Asian and began to take a greater role in European politics. The spread of science and technology had a unifying effect; many of the

same inventions could be seen in the major cities throughout the regions. The desire for empire also spread throughout these regions. Russia fulfilled its desire for empire primarily by moving east. Western Europe spread throughout the world with colonies in Africa, Asia, Australia, and the Americas.

Wars in Europe and Russia during this time were motivated by politics, not religion. Throughout the eighteenth, nineteenth, and twentieth centuries, the major nations sought to gain land and prestige. The last major war involving these nations was World War II. The Cold War that followed was eventually won by the West.

The effects of globalization on post-Cold War Europe and Russia have brought these two regions closer through trade and diplomacy. Religion has also shifted from its earlier days. More and more Russians and Europeans are abandoning Christianity for secularism. Another religious concern is the growing population of Muslims throughout Europe.

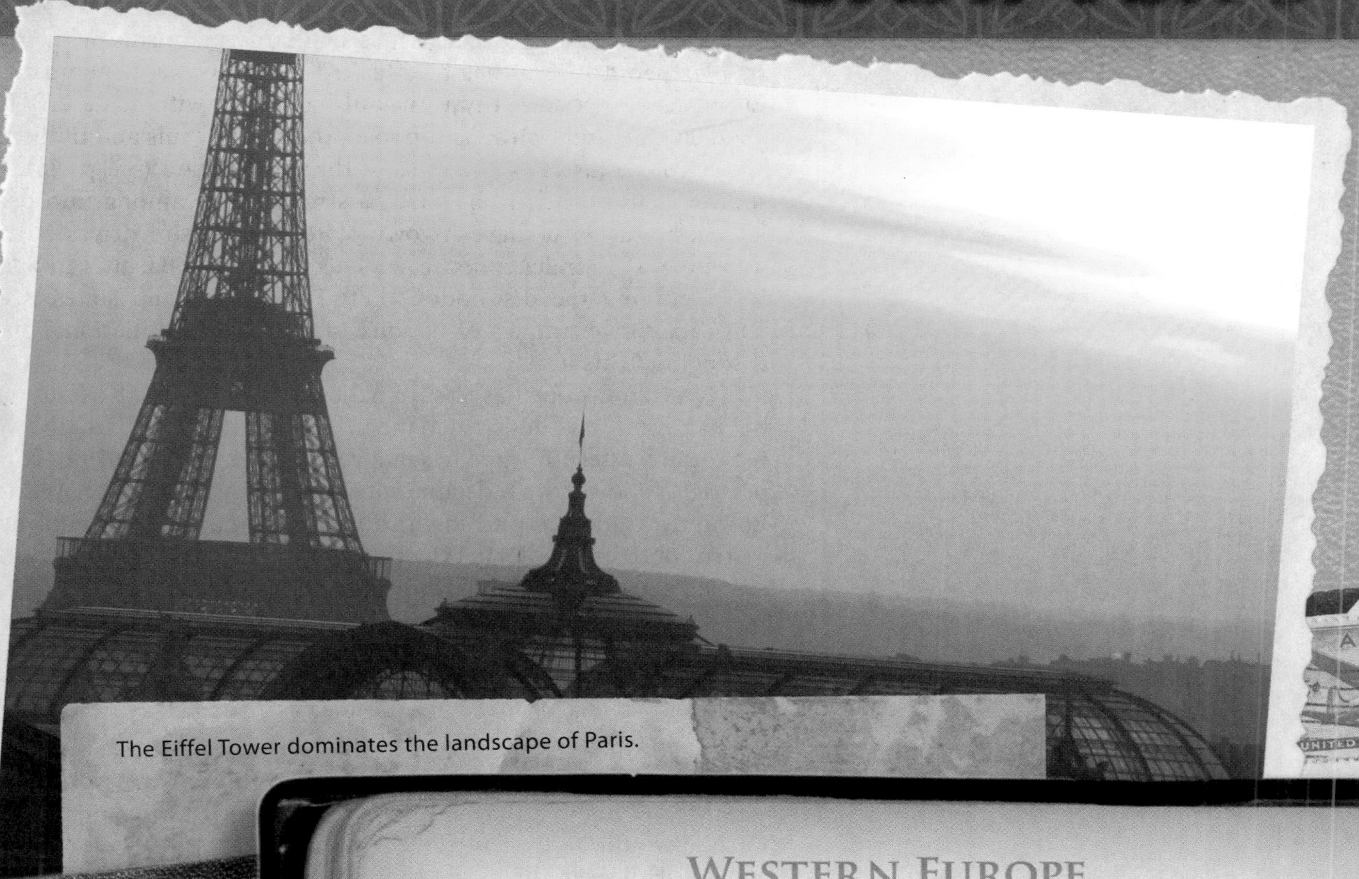

The Eiffel Tower dominates the landscape of Paris.

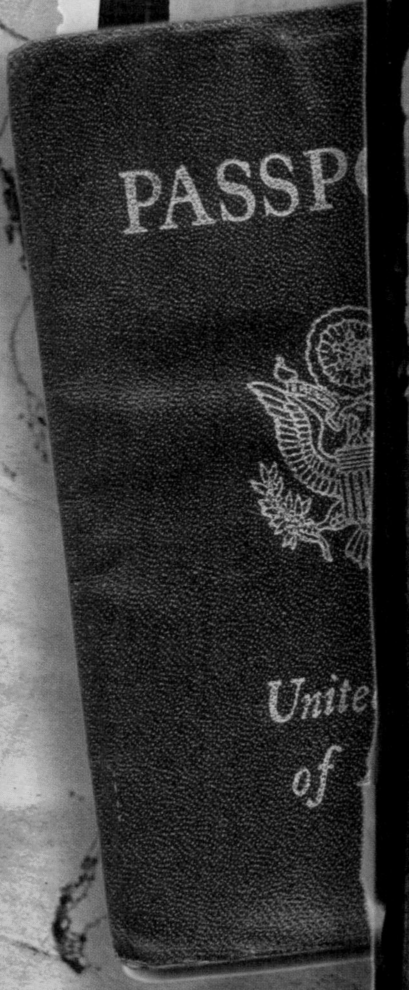

PASSPO

United
of

WESTERN EUROPE

AIR MA

UNITED STATES O

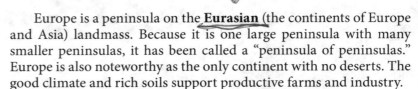

Europe is a peninsula on the **Eurasian** (the continents of Europe and Asia) landmass. Because it is one large peninsula with many smaller peninsulas, it has been called a "peninsula of peninsulas." Europe is also noteworthy as the only continent with no deserts. The good climate and rich soils support productive farms and industry.

Europe illustrates the idea of the nation-state (see p. 86). For several centuries, there has been a strong desire among Europeans for every nation to have its own state. This desire drives current movements for independence, such as that of the Basques in Spain. Remembering the distinctions between nations and states, see if you can spot examples of nations, states, and multinational states throughout this unit.

Western Europe has less than 5 percent of the earth's landmass, but its people have dominated much of world history. Virtually every nation in western Europe has enjoyed a golden age of influence and prestige, followed by a decline into relative insignificance. Western European traditions and institutions are found on every continent. Three continents—North America, South America, and Australia—are peopled by descendants of western Europeans.

I. NORTHERN EUROPE

Northern Europe consists of the British Isles and Scandinavia. With the exception of Ireland, northern Europe is primarily Protestant. Looking at a map, one might assume that most of northern Europe would be extremely cold because of its distance from the equator. However, this is not the case. Coming from off the coast of Canada, the **North Atlantic Drift** warms northern Europe so that even the harbors of Norway are kept ice free.

UNITED KINGDOM

Great Britain, the largest island in Europe, lies at the heart of the United Kingdom. The United Kingdom also includes land on the neighboring island of Ireland as well as numerous smaller islands surrounding Great Britain. The United Kingdom sits astride northern Europe's major water routes. Off the east coast lies the North Sea, the main route to the peninsulas of Scandinavia. Between Great Britain and Ireland lies the choppy Irish Sea. South of Great Britain is the English Channel, a narrow body of water between the island and the European mainland. In the past, merchant ships had to pass through this channel to reach the ports in northern Europe.

The United Kingdom has four political divisions—England in southern Great Britain, Wales in western Great Britain, Scotland in northern Great Britain, and Northern Ireland. In 1707, the kingdoms in Great Britain were officially united, with one parliament, forming the United Kingdom. In 1801 the entire island of Ireland was brought into the United Kingdom, but most of Ireland became its own nation in 1921. At that time, Northen Ireland voted to remain in the United Kingdom. You will sometimes hear the United Kingdom loosely called Great Britain or just Britain.

ENGLAND

England is the largest division of the United Kingdom. England's agricultural heartland is the rolling plains and hills of southern

---

British English

Sometimes speaking the same language does not ensure communication. The Standard English of Great Britain is quite different from the Standard English in America. To the British, gasoline is petrol, and raising the hood of a car is looking under the bonnet. The trunk of a car is the boot. Here are a few more examples.

American Word	British Word
cookies	biscuits
biscuits	scones
truck	lorry
sink	basin
closet	cupboard
candy	sweets
dessert	pudding
elevator	lift
horn	hooter
radio	wireless
drugstore	chemist

England. The United Kingdom is among the world's top ten producers of flax fiber, hops, sheep, green peas, carrots, sugar beets, and raspberries. The **River Thames** (TEMZ) flows through the center of this region. The largest city on the Thames is **London**. Off the southeast coast of England, the English Channel separates Great Britain from the continent. The narrowest point in the channel, at only twenty-one miles wide, is called the **Strait of Dover**. The turbulent channel has been called England's "first line of defense" against enemies from the mainland.

Downs are another feature of southeast England. These chalk hills cannot support trees, but they have plenty of grass for cattle and sheep. Two parallel ranges of rolling hills run along the interior.

"Angles' Land"

Early England had its share of invaders. Among them were the Jutes, Angles, and Saxons. The name England, in fact, is from two Old English words meaning "Angles' land."

GEOGRAPHER'S CORNER

TIME ZONES AND THE INTERNATIONAL DATE LINE

Travelers frequently must adjust their time when traveling. The world is divided into twenty-four standard **time zones**, roughly following meridians (see p. 7). When convenient, though, the time zones diverge from the meridians. The prime meridian (0°) passes through Greenwich, England, where standard time is based. When traveling east, a traveler *adds* one hour for each time zone he crosses. When traveling west, a traveler *subtracts* one hour.

Travelers must make another kind of adjustment at the **International Date Line**, an imaginary line in the Pacific Ocean where time on the east side is one day behind time on the west side. When crossing the line from west to east, a traveler "loses" one day on his calendar. Traveling west *adds* a day.

Calculating time changes is fairly simple. Find Moscow on the map. It is three time zones east of Greenwich. If you are in Moscow and need to know the standard time in London, you simply subtract three hours.

What would happen if you flew from Honolulu, Hawaii, to Auckland, New Zealand? The flight takes nine hours fifteen minutes. Suppose it were 8:00 a.m. Tuesday when you left Honolulu. The time of arrival would be 5:15 p.m. if you stayed in the same time zone, but since you are traveling west, you would subtract an hour for each time zone you entered. A quarter after five in the afternoon on Tuesday in Honolulu would be 3:15 p.m. two time zones to the west in Auckland. But because you cross the date line, you must add a day. Therefore, it would be 3:15 p.m. on

Wednesday. Use the map to answer the following questions.

1. Sydney, Australia, lies how many time zones east of London?

2. If it is 1:00 a.m. in Athens, Greece, what time is it in Tokyo?

3. If it were 6:00 p.m. on Sunday in Tokyo, Japan, what time and day would it be in Honolulu?

4. If it were 3:00 a.m. on Monday in the Cocos Islands, what time and day would it be in New York City?

💡 You are on a flight from Chicago, Illinois, to Tokyo, Japan. The flight takes about 13 hours. If it is 9:00 a.m. on Friday when you leave Chicago, what time will you arrive in Tokyo?

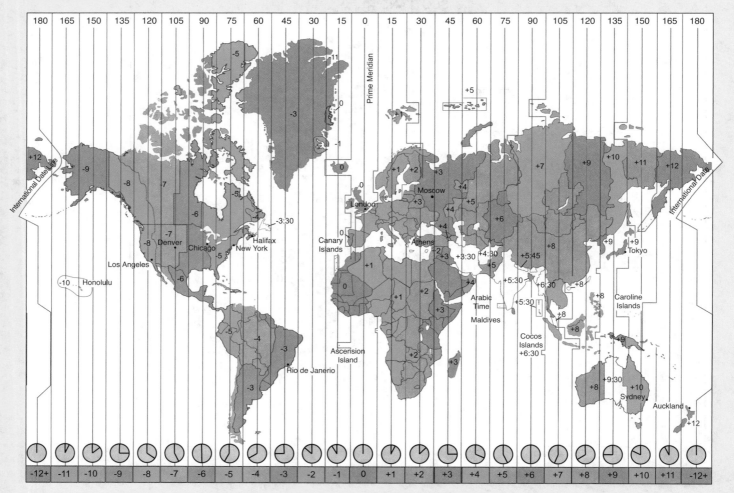

	Western Europe Fast Facts						
Flag	Country	Capital	Area (sq. mi.)	Pop. (M)	Pop. Density (per sq. mi.)	Per Capita GDP ($US)	Life Span
	Andorra	Andorra la Vella	181	0.07	390	$26,800	84
	Austria	Vienna	32,382	8.18	253	$31,300	79
	Belgium	Brussels	11,787	10.36	879	$30,600	79
	Denmark	Copenhagen	16,639	5.43	327	$32,200	78
	Finland	Helsinki	130,559	5.22	40	$29,000	78
	France	Paris	211,210	60.66	287	$28,700	80
	Germany	Berlin	137,847	82.43	598	$28,700	79
	Greece	Athens	50,942	10.67	209	$21,300	79
	Iceland	Reykjavík	39,769	0.30	8	$31,900	80
	Ireland	Dublin	27,135	4.02	148	$31,900	78
	Italy	Rome	116,306	58.10	500	$27,700	80
	Liechtenstein	Vaduz	62	0.03	484	$25,000	80
	Luxembourg	Luxembourg	999	0.47	469	$58,900	79
	Malta	Valletta	122	0.40	3,279	$18,200	79
	Monaco	Monaco	0.75	0.03	40,000	$27,000	80
	Netherlands	Amsterdam	16,033	16.41	1023	$29,500	79
	Norway	Oslo	125,182	4.59	37	$40,000	79
	Portugal	Lisbon	35,672	10.57	296	$17,900	78
	San Marino	San Marino	24	0.03	1250	$34,600	82
	Spain	Madrid	194,897	40.34	207	$23,300	80
	Sweden	Stockholm	173,732	9.00	52	$28,400	80
	Switzerland	Bern	15,942	7.49	470	$33,800	80
	United Kingdom	London	94,526	60.44	639	$29,600	78
	Vatican City	Vatican City	0.17	0.001	NA	NA	NA

CITIES: LONDON

The capital of the United Kingdom is London, one of Europe's oldest cities. Its rich history traces back two thousand years, when the Romans established a trading post named Londonium in AD 43. Today, with over seven and a half million people in the city proper, London is the largest city in Western Europe.

One reason that London became such a great city is its strategic location along the River Thames. The Thames is a tidal river. Oceangoing ships can easily navigate the fifty miles upstream to unload at some of the world's best ports. The Port of London Authority supervises some forty miles of wharves along the Thames.

The city grew in a haphazard fashion on the Thames. Old London still retains the original layout—a tangle of unplanned streets that is a driver's nightmare. From the old center, the city extends outward in every direction for up to twenty miles. In the midst of the jumble, there are many green parks. The largest parks, called royal parks, were once owned

At the corner of the Palace of Westminster is Big Ben.

by the monarchs but are now open to public use.

Along the Thames are the Palace of Westminster, where the two Houses of Parliament meet, and Westminster Abbey, where the British monarchs are crowned. Close to this area is Buckingham Palace. Since the days of Queen Victoria, the country's longest-reigning monarch, this palace at the west end of London has been the primary residence of British monarchs. A royal standard is flown to indicate when the monarch is in residence.

After World War II, the government halted the city's expansion by establishing a Green Belt, an area around the city that is protected from development by legislation. Though London's Green Belt is the largest, there are thirteen other Green Belts throughout the United Kingdom.

The South Downs run near the channel, and the North Downs run just south of the Thames.

South-central England lies west of the downs. The ancient kingdom of Wessex was once in this area. It divided its kingdom into shires, which is evident in the names of some of its counties (e.g., Hampshire [HAMP shuhr]). A range of limestone hills called the Cotswolds adds scenic beauty to this region.

Several good ports lie on the coast in south-central England. The deep Bristol Channel, an arm of the Atlantic Ocean, extends into the western side of Great Britain. The important port of Bristol lies on the River Avon, which flows into the channel. East of Bristol, visitors can examine the prehistoric ruins at Stonehenge. Some people think Stonehenge was used for occult rites, but it may also have been a "farmer's almanac" to guide planting and harvesting of crops.

Unlike south-central England, southwestern England consists of a low plateau with scattered granite highlands. Two national parks, Dartmoor and Exmoor, protect **moors**. A moor is a wasteland on a high, treeless plateau. The land cannot be cultivated, although a tangle of low shrubs does

Stonehenge dates back to 1400 BC.

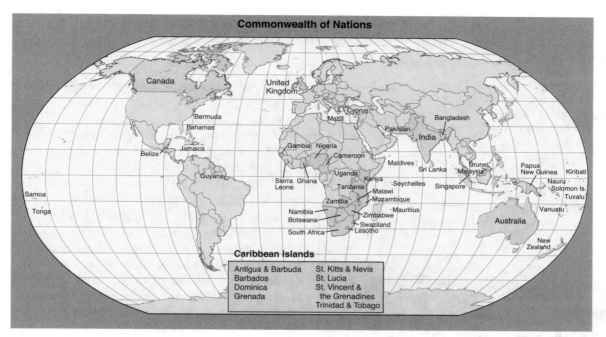

Commonwealth of Nations

Canada
United Kingdom
Bermuda
Bahamas
Belize
Jamaica
Guyana
Samoa
Tonga
Cyprus
Malta
Gambia
Nigeria
Cameroon
Sierra Leone
Ghana
Uganda
Kenya
Tanzania
Malawi
Mozambique
Zambia
Namibia
Botswana
Zimbabwe
Mauritius
Swaziland
South Africa
Lesotho
Bangladesh
Pakistan
India
Maldives
Sri Lanka
Seychelles
Singapore
Brunei
Malaysia
Papua New Guinea
Kiribati
Nauru
Solomon Is.
Tuvalu
Vanuatu
Australia
New Zealand

Caribbean Islands

Antigua & Barbuda	St. Kitts & Nevis
Barbados	St. Lucia
Dominica	St. Vincent &
Grenada	the Grenadines
	Trinidad & Tobago

grow on it. Because fields of heather are so common, moors are often called heaths. Moors also have patches of peat bog or sphagnum moss. Most moors are farther north in the uplands of Scotland. Lizard Point is the southern extreme of Great Britain, and Land's End is its western extreme.

Central England is the home of the Industrial Revolution. The Industrial Revolution started here in the eighteenth century for several reasons: easy access to iron and coal, productive farms that produced flax and wool for textiles, plentiful rivers for transportation, colonies that supplied raw materials from around the world, and political freedom that encouraged new ideas and inventions.

Northern England includes all the counties north of the River Trent and has some of England's most beautiful scenery. **The Pennines** (PEN eyenz), a mountain system extending south from Scotland to the Midlands, form the backbone of England. Sherwood Forest—the fabled haunt of Robin Hood—is located at the southern tip of the Pennines, around Nottingham.

Manchester, located at the foot of the Pennines, is the third-largest metropolitan area in the British Isles. It was once the textile capital of

Commonwealth of Nations

The **Commonwealth of Nations** was formed in 1931 to facilitate the conversion of the British Empire into an association of free and equal countries. Today, the Commonwealth consists of over fifty countries encompassing about 30% of the world's population and about 25% of its land area. Most of the countries were once part of the British Empire, and the British monarch retains a symbolic role in the Commonwealth. Mozambique is the only member that was not ruled by the United Kingdom at some time. The Commonwealth promotes democracy, human rights, and economic development among its members.

WINDSOR CASTLE

Windsor Castle has the distinct privilege of being the oldest royal residence in continuous habitation in the world. It is also the largest in the world. William the Conqueror built the original structures in 1070, overlooking the Thames. Today, the castle is nearly one mile in circumference.

The additions and reconstructions have left no trace of the original castle, but parts of each succeeding project remain. Henry II built the Round Tower in 1170, and Henry III built two towers fifty years later. George IV, who commissioned the architect Wyatville, is responsible for the appearance of most of the rest of the castle.

Prince of Wales

The heir of the British throne uses the title "Prince of Wales." Edward I of England conquered Wales in the late thirteenth century. In 1301, Edward gave the title, Prince of Wales, to his son, Edward II. It has been used by most of the heirs to the British throne since then.

The Pennines

Hadrian's Wall, completed in AD 136, protected Roman England from the northern barbarians. Seventy-four miles long and twenty feet high, it is the largest Roman ruin in Britain.

the world. West of Manchester on a major estuary of the Irish Sea is Liverpool, England's second-biggest port (after London).

WALES

Wales occupies a broad peninsula on the western side of England. The climate of the country is mild and wet, similar to that of England, but less than 10 percent of the land is arable. Dairy cattle and sheep graze the grassy but treeless uplands. Wales is mostly mountainous except for a narrow coastal plain in the south. Snowdonia is the northern range and includes Snowdon (SNOHD n), the tallest mountain in Wales. The central range is the Cambrian Mountains, and the southern range is the Brecon Beacons.

Another geographical feature is the Rhondda Valley in southern Wales. Coal mines began operating in the Rhondda Valley during the Industrial Revolution, and for many years the Welsh economy was dependent on the coal industry. However, the coal has been exhausted, and the country has been forced to find alternative incomes. Cardiff, the capital, and Swansea are the main ports on the south coast.

One in five people still speak the Celtic dialect of Wales, along with the main language—English. Outsiders find the complex Welsh language hard to pronounce and spell, however, because it has so many double consonants. Wales joined the Anglican Church when it was first founded, but the Welsh remained open to the preaching of nonconformists, who refused Anglican rule.

SCOTLAND

Scotland lies north of England. It is known for green **glens** (narrow valleys carved by glaciers) and blue **lochs** (LOKS; deep, narrow lakes carved by glaciers). The Scots, descendants of the Celts, held off many invaders who tried to take their rugged and isolated homeland. Though part of the United Kingdom, Scots have preserved a culture distinctly their own.

Scotland's border with England's Pennines is called the Southern Uplands. It consists of barren hilltops, fertile slopes, and foggy moors. The range that divides Scotland from England is the Cheviot Hills and is crowned by Hadrian's Wall, which Rome built to stop raids from the unconquered Scots north of Britannia.

North of the border, a belt of lowlands stretches across central Scotland. The flat lands and relatively fertile soil make it Scotland's most populated area. About 75 percent of the Scottish people are crowded around Glasgow, Scotland's largest city, in the west and Edinburgh, Scotland's capital, in the east.

North of the populous lowlands are the Grampian Mountains, the principal range of the Scottish Highlands. They include **Ben Nevis**, the highest mountain in the British Isles (4,406 ft.). North of this mountain system is a deep valley, called Glen More or the Great Glen. The Caledonian Canal cuts through this valley and includes the waters of Loch Ness. Beyond the Great Glen are more highlands and the Hebrides Islands, where isolated people still speak a Celtic dialect.

The discovery of oil and natural gas in the North Sea has brought many jobs and economic development to the nearby area. The city of Aberdeen on the east coast is known as the "oil capital of Europe." The United Kingdom ranks fourth worldwide in the production of natural gas. As a result of this newfound wealth, independence from the United Kingdom seems economically beneficial for Scotland for the first time. In 1997, Parliament granted Scotland its own parliament with limited self-government and taxing authority.

NORTHERN IRELAND

Northern Ireland, also called Ulster (UL stuhr), is on the island of **Ireland**, the second-largest island in the British Isles. This Protestant country, first populated by Protestants from Britain in the early seventeenth century, shares the island with Catholic Ireland. Northern Ireland consists of six counties on the northeast corner of the island. It is a land of rugged coasts and rolling hills. Many crystal lakes, called **loughs** (LOKS), dot the interior. Lough Neagh is the largest freshwater lake in the British Isles. It covers over 150 square miles and is also the center of Northern Ireland, with five counties bordering it. The plentiful lakes and rivers provide fishermen with salmon and sea trout. Among the region's many bays are the excellent harbors of Londonderry and Belfast.

Belfast, the capital and largest city, is an industrial city once famed for shipbuilding. Belfast shipyards built many warships and ocean liners, including the *Titanic*. Aircraft construction is now an important part of the economy. The textile mills are known for their fine Irish linen.

IRELAND

Ireland's thin, rocky soil was apparently caused by massive glaciers—the same forces that scraped New England. Although farther north than New England, Ireland's climate is much warmer because of the North Atlantic Drift, which carries warm water from the Gulf Stream. Ireland is consistently humid; about half of the time the weather is overcast. Westerly winds dump regular rains on the green countryside of the Emerald Isle.

A rim of mountains surrounds the coast of Ireland. Ireland ranks sixth in the production of zinc, found in the mountains west of Dundalk. The River Shannon, which flows through the rolling plain in the center of Ireland, is even longer than the Thames. The grasslands support cattle and horses. In the central and western parts of the island are many bogs, where the water sits without access to the ocean. Here, partly decayed mosses have been compressed to form thick layers of peat. Since Ireland lacks coal, many people burn peat for heating and cooking.

The Republic of Ireland covers five-sixths of the island of Ireland. Over 90 percent of the population is Roman Catholic. Most Irishmen speak English, though they do so with a brogue

The IRA

Most descendants of the British settlers in Northern Ireland are still Protestants, evenly divided between Anglicans and Presbyterians. They are loyal to the British monarch. The Catholic minority, on the other hand, would like to see Ulster reunited with Ireland. A radical group known as the **Irish Republican Army** (IRA) fought the longest and deadliest campaign of terrorism in modern European history. From the 1950s to 2005, when the organization officially disarmed, the IRA set off over ten thousand bombs and killed over three thousand people. Their goal was to force the British Parliament to surrender control of Ulster.

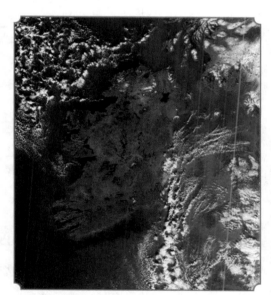

Ireland is often called the "Emerald Isle."

Giant's Causeway

According to legend, Irish giant Finn McCool (Fingal) made a pier, or causeway, out of rock so that he could walk across the Irish Sea from Ireland to Scotland. Around thirty-seven thousand columns, some of them twenty feet high, descend into the ocean on the coast of Northern Ireland. Similar columns rise up out of the sea in Scotland. The rocks are basalt, formed from lava. When the lava cooled, it cracked into prism-shaped pillars having four to eight sides.

(BROHG), or soft accent. Gaelic (GAY lik), also called Irish, is their ancient Celtic language. The constitution calls it the "first official language," and street signs and official documents must be bilingual. However, only one-quarter of the people speak Gaelic with some proficiency.

The history of English-Irish relations has been tragic. Over the centuries England instituted harsh measures discriminating against the Catholics, including a law that once prevented them from buying or inheriting land. Ireland was joined to the United Kingdom in 1801. However, in 1921, the Anglo-Irish Treaty was negotiated, creating an Irish Free State, and in 1949, the Republic of Ireland cut all ties with Britain.

For centuries Ireland was a land of poor farmers. Their young men left the farms and went to the cities seeking jobs. They often continued on, emigrating to other countries to find a "better life." Then, in the 1990s, there was a great turnaround. Ireland became known as "the Celtic Tiger" for its rapid economic progress. Today many young people of Irish ancestry are returning to Ireland, where there are many good factory jobs and desirable living conditions. Well-known exports include fine Waterford crystal.

SCANDINAVIA

Scandinavia is the Land of the Midnight Sun. There are five countries in Scandinavia: Norway, Sweden, Finland, Denmark, and Iceland. Iceland and Finland are republics, while the other three Scandinavian nations have constitutional monarchies. Parts of Scandinavia lie above the Arctic Circle, where the sun never sets for over two months each summer and where it never rises for two months each winter. During the sun's absence, the northern lights (*aurora borealis*) are visible. Norway's view is especially famous. Vacationers in Hammerfest, Norway, can see the midnight sun hanging over the Arctic Ocean.

The people are called Scandinavians from an ancient center of the Norsemen called Scandia. During the Middle Ages, the Scandinavians converted to Christianity, but they never had close ties to Rome. When Martin Luther sparked the Reformation in the sixteenth century, they became Protestants. Today, over 90 percent of all Scandinavians are Lutherans. Unfortunately, as is true in most of Europe, many Nordic people no longer attend services except for baptisms and religious holidays. In 2000, Sweden ended state control of the Lutheran church in the country.

NORWAY

Scandinavia is known for its peninsulas. Norway and Sweden share the largest peninsula, the **Scandinavian Peninsula**, with Norway facing the North Sea. Norway's mainland coastline stretches for more than sixteen hundred miles. The coast is splintered by numerous **fjords** (FYORDZ)—long, narrow bays carved by glaciers and filled with sea water. Other major fjords around the world are in Alaska, Patagonia, and New Zealand; but the most famous are in Norway. Norway's longest fjord, **Sogne** (SAWNG nuh) **Fjord**, cuts 127 miles inland.

Including long fjords, numerous small islands, and minor indentations, the full length of Norway's shore stretches 15,626 miles, or more than halfway around the world. Norway includes about 50,000 islands. Many streams drop into the fjords to create beautiful waterfalls. Norway has five of the world's ten highest waterfalls.

One of the many fjords in Norway

Norway's important cities lie on the coast, where the ocean moderates the climate. Most Norwegian cities also take advantage of fjords as natural harbors. Oslo Fjord and the surrounding area is the largest lowland in the country and contains most of the arable land.

A high plateau covers most of Norway. Glaciers cover many mountains and have scraped the rocky surface. About one-quarter of Norway is forested, and only 3 percent is arable. Nordic, or cross-country, skiing was developed in this wasteland. Skiing is a national sport.

The plateau includes several mountain ranges. The Kölen (CHUHL uhn) Mountains form Norway's border with Sweden. **Galdhøpiggen** (GAHL HUH[R] PIG uhn; 8,100 ft.), the highest peak in Scandinavia, rises in the south. Jostedals Glacier to the west of this peak is the largest glacier in continental Europe, covering 188 square miles.

Bergen, the principal port, lies on the southwest coast. Norway's fishing industry ranks as the greatest in the West. The large merchant fleet, which is one of the world's largest, transports goods around the world.

Norway's cultural center is its capital, Oslo. Oslo refines oil from large deposits in the North Sea. Oil exports have helped make Norway rich. It enjoys one of the world's highest standards of living. Norway's children are required to attend ten years of education.

Norway has a 37.5-hour workweek. Workers are primarily involved in service industries, which make up a large portion of the country's economy. Only 1.4% of the workforce is involved in oil industries, but they produce 12.3% of the annual GDP. Norway is the third-largest exporter of oil in the world.

SWEDEN

Sweden is the largest Scandinavian country and the fourth-largest country in Europe. About one-third of Sweden is lowland plains in the south. A mild climate and fertile soil make it Sweden's best agricultural region. Sweden ranks fifth worldwide for the production of mixed grains and eighth for the production of oats. A low plateau in the center of the plain has poor, rocky soil that is useful for dairy cattle.

Stockholm, the nation's capital, is the largest city in Scandinavia. The city covers fourteen islands and is connected by fifty bridges. While the North Atlantic Drift keeps nearly all of Norway's harbors ice-free year-round, many ports on the Baltic Sea, including Stockholm, freeze in winter. Ships enter only with the help of icebreakers.

Most of Sweden's western border is shared with Norway. In the south, however, the west coast lies along the Skagerrak (SKAG uh RAK) and Kattegat (KAT ih GAT), two arms of the North Sea. Göteborg (YUH tuh BAWR ee) is the second-largest city in Sweden. Ice-free year-round, Göteborg has become Sweden's leading port. The Göta (YUH tuh) Canal provides the eastern ports with a year-round trade route through the interior lakes of Vänern and Vättern.

Sweden's sparsely populated Northland is considered the last frontier of Europe. Mountains line the border with Norway, and rugged hills cover the rest of the region. Rivers flow southeast through deep gorges that broaden into valleys near the Gulf of Bothnia. Great forests of pine and spruce cover these hills and provide timber for the pulp and sawmills on the coast. Sweden is a major exporter of timber products.

The port city of Göteborg has been influential to the growth of Sweden since its founding in the seventeenth century.

Sweden joined the European Union in 1995, but it does not use the euro. The country has one of the highest life expentancies in the world while having one of the lowest birth rates. The decline in the population growth rate, in Sweden as well as in other European countries, has caused concerns regarding the "graying" of the population and the economic challenges that may result.

Almost 70 percent of Sweden's GDP is based on services. Almost 80 percent of the workforce is unionized. Its industries have a reputation for quality, high-tech engineering and metallurgy. They make everything from ball bearings to surgical instruments. Sweden is also a major producer of automobiles, including Volvos and Saabs.

Sweden's welfare state set the example for all other Nordic countries by providing "cradle to grave" benefits, including most major expenses from childbirth to burial. The "Swedish model" was a mixed economy that allowed businesses to stay in private hands, but the state taxed and regulated businesses heavily. It also adopted one of the highest income taxes in the world. In the 1990s, the people began to see the damage this system can do to private enterprise. But change is slow in coming.

FINLAND

Finland has been independent only since 1917. Prior to that time, the Finns spent a century under Russian control and seven centuries under Swedish control. Unlike the rest of Scandinavia, Finland's language and physical features are related to those of northern Russia. The difficult Finnish language is not Germanic, or even Indo-European, but Uralic. To improve their ability to trade, many Finns are learning English or German.

Finns work hard to keep their environment one of the cleanest in the world. Their love of nature is reflected in their favorite recreational activities of fishing, hunting, and camping. However, relaxing in a hot sauna is the national pastime. Every apartment complex has a sauna, and so do many homes.

Finland's only access to the ocean is the Baltic Sea. It has a long coastline along the Gulf of Bothnia. Most of Finland's population clusters in the southern coastal lowlands, which enjoy the mildest climate and the best farmland. Less than one-tenth of Finland's land is arable, but Finland's farms are self-sufficient. The ports freeze during the long winters, but the shipbuilding industry builds over half of the world's icebreakers to keep the ports open. Helsinki is the nation's capital, main seaport, and largest city. The city often hosts peace talks between warring nations.

A few Laplanders continue to herd reindeer in the Arctic.

Finland has been called the "Land of Ten Thousand Lakes" because of its southern interior. Like Minnesota, Finland has many glacial lakes, perhaps one hundred thousand. Thick forests cover three-fourths of Finland, and timber products account for 70 percent of its exports. The shimmering lakes and rivers are called "white coal" because the running water produces cheap hydroelectricity to run the mills and other industries.

Northern Finland contains the heart of **Lapland**, which extends into Sweden, Norway, and Russia. The regional capital is Rovaniemi. The **Lapps**, who call themselves Sami, have tended reindeer in this region for thousands of years. In summer, they take the reindeer north to feed on the moss and lichen of the tundra. In the winter, they return south to the forests. But since many Lapps have moved to villages to work as fishermen or lumberjacks, the Lapps' nomadic customs and culture are fading.

DENMARK

Denmark has been an independent country since 950 and even ruled England from 1013 to 1042. Its islands and mainland peninsula lie farther south than the rest of Scandinavia, making its winters less severe. Lacking mineral resources, the country depends heavily on agriculture and trade. Firm believers in welfare, the Danes pay one of the highest tax rates in the world. After taxes and duties are added to a new car, its cost triples!

The **Jutland Peninsula** extends northward from Germany and accounts for about 70 percent of Denmark's land area. Dunes along the west coast protect the peninsula from winds off the North Sea. A rocky plain covers the far north, and a sandy plain covers the southwest. Low hills roll gently across the rest of the peninsula. Farmers grow barley and raise both beef and dairy cattle. About half of Denmark's people live on ninety islands east of Jutland. Hills cover the islands, as on Jutland, but the deep soils are more fertile.

The capital city, Copenhagen, is on Denmark's largest island, Zeeland. Copenhagen houses one-quarter of the country's population and is the largest metropolitan area in Scandinavia. The name Copenhagen means "merchant's harbor," and it is indeed a strategic port. The Danes are known for elegant design and fine quality in their exported furniture, machinery, and silverware.

Denmark's overseas territories have included Iceland, **Greenland**, and the Faeroe Islands, a group of seventeen inhabited islands north of Scotland. Denmark granted Iceland independence in 1918 but retained the other islands. The Faeroe Islands and Greenland are now self-ruling provinces within the kingdom of Denmark.

Greenland is the largest island in the world, fifty times larger than Denmark and thirteen hundred miles west of Denmark in North America. Vikings deceptively named the island Greenland to attract settlers. In reality, 84 percent lies under an ice cap that averages almost a mile thick. Colonists settled on the southwest coast, the island's warmest region. In the fifteenth century, the entire colony perished, but the Danes resettled in the eighteenth century. Today, Greenlanders are a mixture of Eskimo and Danish ancestry. More than one-third are employed in the fishing industry.

Greenland is more icy than green, and Iceland, to the southeast, is greener.

ICELAND

About 650 miles west of Norway is the "Land of Fire and Ice." Large glaciers glide down the active volcanoes on Iceland. The glacier-carved fjords are reminiscent of Norway, but not the island's two hundred volcanoes, one of which erupts about every five years. Surtsey, an island off the south coast, was created by an undersea volcano in 1963. **Mount Hekla** (4,892 ft.) was once thought to conceal the gates of hell.

As elsewhere in Scandinavia, the North Atlantic Drift flows around Iceland, warming the southern coast. Temperatures similar to those in New York City keep the ports open all year.

Icelanders are proud of their heritage. The **Althing** (AHL thing), its national assembly founded in 930, is the oldest parliamentary assembly still in existence in the world. The Icelandic language is the only Scandinavian tongue that remains essentially unchanged from the Viking era. Without too much difficulty, Icelanders can read the medieval chronicles of their Viking ancestors. Desiring to keep their language pure, a special committee creates new Icelandic words for such things as telephones and computers instead of adopting foreign words.

Iceland's fjords harbor almost all the population and the island's 1 percent of arable land. The main crop is hay for the sheep, which in turn provide food and clothing. Potatoes and turnips also withstand the cool climate. Iceland's fishing fleet is one of the world's most modern. Nearly 80 percent of Iceland's exports are fish products.

The capital, Reykjavik (RAY kyuh VEEK), houses half the population. Geothermal energy provides heat for hot water, heated outdoor swimming pools, greenhouses, and 70 percent of the homes. The greenhouses enable Icelanders to grow flowers, tomatoes, and fruit during the long winters.

Iceland is known for its rugged beauty. The barren interior plateau is twenty-five hundred feet above sea level. The plateau has the largest glacier in Europe, **Vatnajökull** (VAHT nah YUH koot ul). This glacier has more ice than all the other glaciers of Europe combined. Glacial lakes dot the region, and glacier-fed rivers create beautiful waterfalls.

Iceland has more hot springs than any other country in the world. The English word *geyser* comes from Iceland's most spectacular hot spring, the Great Geysir, which spews water almost two hundred feet high.

Mount Hekla is the most active volcano in Iceland.

SECTION QUIZ

1. What river lies at the heart of Southern England?
2. What is the "backbone of England"?
3. What is Gaelic?
4. What peninsula contains both Norway and Sweden?
5. Greenland belongs to which country?
   - ☿ Why might geographers exclude Finland from Scandinavia? Why might they exclude Iceland?

II. CONTINENTAL EUROPE

Continental Europe refers to the main landmass of Western Europe, as opposed to the islands and peninsulas. Much of the continent is a wide coastal lowland with a marine-west-coast climate. The countries on this continent have greatly influenced the history and culture of the world. The Reformation divided the continent. Today

European Union

The **European Union** (EU), an organization of twenty-seven countries, seeks to form a single European community that can compete on the world stage economically and politically. Each country in the EU relinquishes some of its sovereignty when it joins the EU. The EU was formed in 1992 with the Maastricht Treaty, but early forms of cooperation existed before 1992. Since 1951, economic organizations existed among major European powers. In 1967, the unity of these countries was advanced through the creation of a European Parliament. The Maastricht Treaty expanded these developments with more interaction between the governments of the countries. The EU introduced the euro (€) in 2002 as a common currency. The EU is divided between those who use the euro (e.g., France) and those who do not (e.g., United Kingdom). In the early twenty-first century, the EU proposed a new constitution that would strengthen the EU considerably but diminish the sovereignty of the member countries. Support, however, has not been strong in some key countries. Consequently, the future of the EU is uncertain.

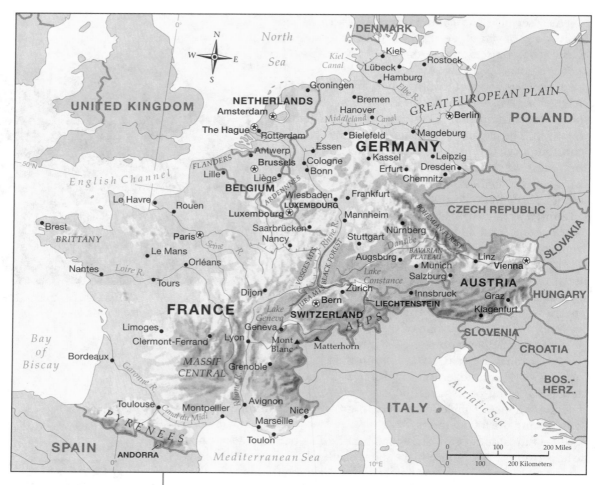

Roman Catholicism dominates the south and west, and Protestant denominations are prominent in the north.

FRANCE

France is the largest country in Europe (by landmass). Over four-fifths of the people are Roman Catholic. France has few Protestants and Jews but has a growing Muslim population. Since 1815, France has gone through four kings and five republics. It has been a parliamentary republic since 1870. The present constitution was passed in 1958. Today, France retains only a small portion of its once mighty empire that spanned four continents.

Generally, northern France is lower and flatter than the southern regions. The Great European Plain extends across the north of the European continent, from France to Russia. Three of the five major French rivers flow through northern France. On the **Seine** (SAYN) **River** lies the capital of France, Paris. With almost ten million people, Paris is the third-largest city in Europe and the second-largest in Western Europe.

The plains around Paris produce wheat, barley, and sugar beets. France leads the world in sugar beet production. It also leads Europe in wheat and exceeds the United States in barley. The plains of

The Arc de Triomphe in Paris memorializes Napoleon's brilliant victory at the Battle of Austerlitz (1805), when he crushed a combined Austrian and Russian army.

northern France continue northeast of Paris, along the border with Belgium. The plains also extend south of Paris to the basin of the **Loire River** (luh WAHR), the longest river in France. The fertile river valley produces grapes and vegetables. The cities of Orléans and Tours lie on the Loire River.

The far western province of France is a peninsula called Brittany. The north coast on the English Channel is rocky and rugged, but the south coast on the Bay of Biscay has fine beaches and major fishing villages. Bretons (BRET ns), the inhabitants of Brittany, are descendants of the Celts. The Bretons are trying to preserve their language, similar to Welsh, and some desire independence. East of Brittany is the historic **Normandy** region, which runs along the coast to the Seine River. This region is famous for the Allied invasion of France during World War II on June 6, 1945.

Three provinces lie on a broad plateau in east central France. The provinces are Alsace (al SAYCE), Lorraine, and Franche-Comté (FRAHNSH con-TAY). The plateau of Alsace-Lorraine touches the border of Germany and has been a disputed region between the two countries in the past. The Vosges Mountains at the edge of the plateau offer forest products as well as important deposits of iron ore. Steel centers process the ore at Nancy, the key industrial city in Lorraine. East beyond the Vosges (VOHZH) Mountains, the plateau drops off into the Rhine River valley. Alsace includes France's part of the valley and offers good farmland. The people speak Alsatian (al SAY shun), a Germanic language.

The Jura Mountains lie south of the Alsace-Lorraine plateau along the Swiss border. The low Jura Mountains are the dominant feature in the province of Franche-Comté. Few mountains rise above the timberline, which is around 5,300 feet. The Jurassic period in

The Pyrenees are a natural boundary between France and Spain. Few passes cross these mountains.

Mont-Saint-Michel

Off the coast of France in the English Channel is an unusual little isle called Mont-Saint-Michel (MAWNT SAN mee-SHEL). A Celtic temple once stood on the rock, and Benedictine monks later built an abbey that became a center of learning. King Philip II built the current fortress in the thirteenth century.

What makes Mont-Saint-Michel so unusual is its "moat." During high tides, the raging ocean fills the mile of land that separates the isle from the coast, but the waters recede when the tide goes out. The island was a perfect fortress, which withstood all assaults during the Hundred Years War and during the religious wars of the Reformation. Since 1875, a mile-long dike has connected the rock with the mainland.

The causeway has created problems, however. Because it did not allow water to flow freely around the island, the bay was filling with silt. In 2006, the French began a project to restore the area to its historic state. The project included replacing the dike with a bridge for pedestrians and a shuttle.

In addition to the abbey at the summit, Mont-Saint-Michel includes crypts, cellars, dungeons, a guardhouse, and the Hall of Knights. The knights of the Order of Saint Michel, formed in 1469, successfully defended the fortress against all attacks.

Montserrat (4,054 ft.), meaning "serrated mountain," is an apt name for this fantastic peak in the foothills of the Pryrenees. On its slope is a popular shrine to Our Lady of Montserrat, the patron saint of Catalonia.

evolutionary geology is named after the Jura Mountains, which display "Jurassic" dinosaur fossils.

Southern France has a complex geography of mountains, rivers, and lowlands. All three main regions in southern France have mountains exceeding ten thousand feet. But they each have lowland valleys and coastal plains as well, where large populations thrive.

Southeast France is a favorite vacation spot. The Alps divide France from Italy, and the border has been disputed between the two countries. **Mont Blanc** (MAWNT BLANGK) is the highest mountain in the Alps at 15,771 feet. It lies near the Italian and Swiss borders. Nearby is the deepest cave in the world, the Jean Bernard Cave, which reaches depths of about one mile below the surface.

The water from the snowcapped Alps drains west into the Rhone River, which flows south into the Mediterranean Sea. The valley and adjacent coasts are unique in Continental Europe because of the mediterranean climate. The region is a major producer of grapes and wine. Lyon (lee OHN), the third-largest city in France, lies in the Rhone River valley. This valley, which cuts deep into France, was historically the main overland route between mediterranean Europe and Northern Europe. Near the mouth of the Rhone River is the oldest and second-largest city in France: Marseille (mahr SAY). Between the Rhone River and Italy lies the French Riviera, Europe's answer to Hawaii as a vacation paradise.

The Alps descend into the Mediterranean Sea and form the island of **Corsica**. Corsica's mountains rise to 8,878 feet at Monte Cinto. Corsicans speak a unique language similar to Italian, and they are trying to preserve it. Corsica's beaches are favorite French resorts. The island's most famous native was Napoleon, whom the British called the Corsican Ogre.

The capitals of the four central provinces, Toulouse (too LOOZ), Limoges (lee MOHZH), Clermont-Ferrand, and Montpellier (mohn pel YAY), lie at the corners of the **Massif** (ma SEEF) **Central**. This mountainous plateau in south-central France has poor soils that make the region useful only for grazing livestock.

Toulouse is an important transportation center on the Garonne River (gah RAWN), which flows into the Atlantic. The Garonne is important because of the **Canal du Midi**, which completes a link between the Atlantic Ocean and the Mediterranean Sea. By sailing up this canal and the Garonne, French vessels can bypass the long trip around the Spanish peninsula.

The **Pyrenees** (PEER uh NEEZ) **Mountains** rise south of Toulouse and form the border with Spain. The region boasts many deep caves, including the Cave of Pierre-St. Martin. These caves descend three times deeper than the deepest caves in North America. The Basques also live in the area. Having one of France's minority languages, the Basques are working hard to keep their language alive.

The two provinces of southwest France are mostly lowlands. The region is called Aquitainian Lowlands. The Lascaux (la SKOH) Cave is famous for its prehistoric cave paintings. Bordeaux (bore DOH), the main city, lies near the mouth of the Garonne River. The fertile river valley produces grapes and corn.

THE LOW COUNTRIES

The Low Countries are so named because they lie entirely on coastal lowlands and low plateaus. The Low Countries are located at the crossroads of Western Europe, between the French and the Germans. Because these countries are small in area and are situated on desirable plains, they are some of the most densely populated countries in Continental Europe.

THE NETHERLANDS

The Netherlands has fought a great battle against the sea. Sand dunes twenty feet high protect the inland regions from the North Sea. Much of the land farther inland is below sea level. The Dutch have built strong walls of stone and earth, called **dikes**, to hold back the seawater. Big electric generators pump out the water to keep the

HIGH-TECH DUTCH DIKES

The Dutch and dikes go together. The Dutch have been building them for centuries. However, two daring projects in the twentieth century have far surpassed any previous attempt to capture land from the sea.

The first challenge was to control the floods along the Zuider Zee (zide-uhr ZAY; Southern Sea), an arm of the North Sea that reaches into the heart of the country. Storm surges in the North Sea would sometimes fill this inlet and flood the coast. In 1931 the Dutch completed a nineteen-mile-long dam called the "Enclosing Dike," which crossed the Southern Sea. Rivers slowly turned the enclosed portion of the sea into a freshwater lake called IJsselmeer (EYE suhl meer; Inner Lake). The portion beyond the dam became known as the Wadden Zee (VAHD-en zay; Outer Sea).

The next challenge was to drain parts of the IJsselmeer to obtain more land for housing and farming. Build-

ing the dikes, draining the water, and preparing the land for settlement took many years. Now, four large polders exist that a few years ago were covered by the salt waters of the Zuider Zee. The Flevoland Polder, the largest, covers over one hundred thousand acres.

Another great project was to protect Zeeland, farther south, from sea storms that might break dikes and flood homes. As much as the Dutch liked their new freshwater lake farther north, they did not want another one. If they did that to all of their estuaries, they would lose bird migrations as well as the shrimp, mussels, and eels used for food. Conservationists thus persuaded the Dutch to undertake an even greater engineering feat.

Land Reclaimed from the Sea

The Oosterschelde Barrier allows 80 percent of the normal tides to flow through the barrier, but the gates can be shut during storms to keep out the squalls.

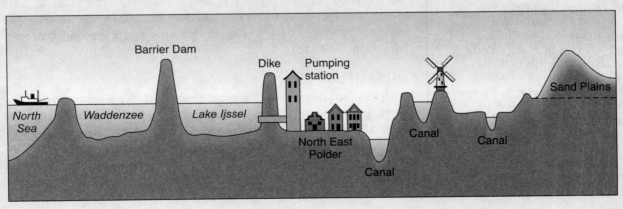

The Netherlands or Holland?

The name Holland is sometimes used for the entire country of the Netherlands, but it is only part of the country. The terms to describe the people can be very confusing also. The people of the Netherlands call themselves Nederlanders or Hollanders, but the English call them the Dutch. Their language is also called Dutch. Adding to the confusion, the Kingdom of the Netherlands once included all three Low Countries.

The new name for the modern economic union of the Low Countries, Benelux, is not so confusing. Can you guess where they got this name?

Abraham Kuyper

The Netherlands has not always been in such a state of religious decline. During the late nineteenth and early twentieth centuries, a man named Abraham Kuyper (1837–1920) challenged the way Christians thought about their lives. Converted while a pastor in the Dutch Reformed Church, Kuyper advocated the idea that the Christian faith should shape every aspect of a believer's life. He founded the Free University of Amsterdam to train Christian leaders with this worldview. He later led conservative Christians to separate from the Dutch Reformed Church and form a more conservative denomination in 1886. Believing that every area of society should be influenced for Christ, Kuyper undertook a life of politics along with his pastoral ministry. His political life reached its height when he became prime minister of the Netherlands from 1901 to 1905. Despite Kuyper's fervent activity and evident desire to see the Netherlands serve Christ, the country has embraced a blatantly ungodly stance. Historians continue to debate the causes for this startling decline.

land inside dry. At one time, windmills were used to generate power, but only a few windmills still operate.

Parcels of land reclaimed from the sea are **polders**. The polder region of the Netherlands covers a wide strip of territory behind the dunes and dikes. Polders have good fertile soil, and tulips and daffodils are important cash crops, but living on polders presents many dangers. The Dutch must wage a ceaseless battle against the sea, constantly pumping out rainwater and maintaining the dikes.

Two of the Netherlands's twelve provinces form the region of Holland, which contains 40 percent of the population and all three of the nation's largest cities. Amsterdam, the capital and largest city, is on a polder in the province of North Holland. The same tolerance that made the Netherlands a refuge for Protestants in Catholic Europe has secularized the nation today. The **World Council of Churches** (WCC) is among the international organizations headquartered in Amsterdam. The WCC has become the leading voice for undermining true Christianity and for breaking down barriers between religions, a movement called **ecumenism** (EK yuh muh NIZ uhm).

Though there is no official religion, the monarch traditionally belongs to the Dutch Reformed Church. Just over 10 percent of the people are Dutch Reformed, about 30 percent are Catholic, just over 5 percent are Muslim, and over 40 percent have no religion at all.

The province of South Holland includes both Rotterdam and **The Hague** (HAYG). Amsterdam has been called the capital since Napoleon moved it there, but the national government of the constitutional monarchy meets in The Hague. One of Europe's busiest ports, Rotterdam lies in the delta of the busiest river on the continent, the **Rhine River**. The Rhine River is one of the most important rivers in Europe and flows through or on the border of six countries. Rotterdam is also a major industrial town with oil refineries and steel manufacturing.

The two northern provinces, Friesland (FREEZ lund) and Groningen (GROH ning uhn) lie in the polder region. The dunes rise as a chain of offshore islands. The Netherlands controls the West Frisian (FRIZH un) Islands, but Germany owns the East Frisian Islands. Frisian is the language of Friesland. Like Dutch, Frisian is a Germanic language. Large deposits in this area make the Netherlands the world's eighth-largest producer of natural gas.

Three other polder provinces lie immediately east and south of Holland. The most important is Zeeland to the south. This region is a series of islands and peninsulas in the delta of the Rhine River. The great Oosterschelde Barrier has enabled the Dutch to convert some of this marshy area into productive ground.

The five provinces along the eastern border are slightly above sea level and do not have polders. However, these sand plains do not have fertile soil either. Fertilizers are used to make them productive. The eastern provinces have some salt deposits, and there are some coal mines in the Ardennes.

BELGIUM

Belgium has one of the most developed free market economies. Perhaps the country's best-known product is Belgian chocolate, and several of its products are named for the capital: Brussels lace, Brussels carpet, and Brussels sprouts. **Brussels** is the largest city in the country. Many international organizations are headquartered in Brussels, including the Parliament of the European Union and NATO, the defensive alliance for Western Europe.

The nation is divided into two regions, with three official languages—Dutch, French, and German. **Flanders** in the north, much like the Netherlands, is a region of polders and sand plains where people speak Dutch. The people are called Flemings; Belgian Dutch was once known as Flemish. Antwerp, the largest city in Flanders, is one of the busiest ports in the world and a major center for the cutting and setting of diamonds. The Flemish school of painting is also world famous.

The northern lowlands of Flanders give way to a low plateau in central Belgium. In the far south is a series of rolling hills called the **Ardennes** (ahr DEN). The forest of the Ardennes covers southern Belgium and much of Luxembourg, extending into France.

Belgium's southern district is called **Wallonia**. The Ardennes is dotted by many villages and hiking trails; most of the cities are on the Meuse River system, which begins in France and flows through central Belgium. The people, called Walloons, speak French. The Flemings and Walloons have had difficulty creating a united country, and a split is sometimes debated. Steel was once the chief industry in the south, but crude steel is now imported and the steel plants have moved to the northern ports in Flanders. Liège (lee AYZH), the largest city of Wallonia, continues to produce guns and glassware.

LUXEMBOURG

Luxembourg is one of Europe's oldest countries, dating back to 963. Luxembourg is also one of the few remaining duchies. A **duchy** is a country ruled by a duke, and the Grand Duke is Luxembourg's hereditary monarch. The official title of the constitutional monarchy is the Grand Duchy of Luxembourg. The capital is also called Luxembourg.

All but 3 percent of the people are Catholic, and most people speak all three official languages. Letzeburgesch, the local dialect of German, is used commonly. German is used in elementary school, while French is used in high school. Although villages still huddle around medieval castles, Luxembourg is now one of the world's most industrialized countries. It has the highest GDP per capita of any country in the world.

Luxembourg plays a leading role in Europe today. Its small size and central location make it a prime neutral location for international endeavors. It is an international financial and banking center. It hosts both the secretariat (administrative staff) of the European Parliament and the European Court of Justice.

GERMANY

Germany is the birthplace of the Reformation. Martin Luther was born in northern Germany, studied in its schools, was converted, and spent the rest of his life preaching to and teaching the German people. Protestant leaders, including Luther, used the printing press to spread the ideas of the Reformation around the world. Today, about one-third of the German people are Protestants. Most Lutherans live in the northern plains, while Germans in the southern uplands are Roman Catholics. This division is even reflected in their languages. They speak different dialects of German: High German and Low German.

North Atlantic Treaty Organization

The **North Atlantic Treaty Organization** (NATO) was formed in 1949. Because it includes countries close to the North Atlantic, NATO includes more countries than those in Europe. NATO's original purpose was to counter the agressiveness of the Soviet Union. Since the Cold War, though, NATO has developed into a peacekeeping organization, contributing troops to conflicts in Darfur, Iraq, Afghanistan, and the Balkans. Notable additions to NATO since the Cold War have been several countries from Eastern Europe. The twenty-six countries of NATO have pledged to come to each other's aid in the case of an attack on any of them.

Parts of Luxembourg seem to belong to a different time.

Protestantism

Protestantism is a major group in what is broadly defined as Christianity. Finding its roots in the Protestant Reformation of the sixteenth century, Protestantism "protested" against some of the doctrines and practices of the Roman Catholic Church. Among other things, Protestantism's historic beliefs have included the authority of Scripture over tradition, salvation by grace alone through faith alone in Christ alone, and a renunciation of the authority of the pope. Protestantism is characterized by denominations such as Lutherans, Anglicans, Presbyterians, Baptists, Methodists, Pentecostals, and many more.

Germans tore down the Berlin Wall in November 1989.

Berlin is the heart of Germany, both ancient and modern. With over four million people, it is the fourth-largest city in Western Europe. The city was founded on the Spree River, a tributary of the Elbe (EL buh) River, in the thirteenth century.

After World War II, Berlin lay in ruins—isolated in the midst of Soviet-occupied territory. The peace agreement allowed the Allies in the West—the United States, Great Britain, and France—to occupy the western part of Berlin. Refugees escaping the Communists flooded into West Berlin, prompting the Soviets to build a wall around it in 1961. The **Berlin Wall** became a hated symbol of the division caused by the Cold War.

The first chancellor of West Germany, Konrad Adenauer (AD n ow ur; 1949–63), utilized free-market ideas, the natural waterways and strong ports of the land, and funds from the Marshall Plan to create the *Wirtschaftswunder* (VIRT shahfts vun duh), meaning "economic miracle." He rebuilt German industry and revived the German economy. By 1955 the nation was producing more goods than it had before the war, despite the loss of East Germany.

Meanwhile, East Germany fell further and further behind. Its communistic government greatly hindered economic development.

As the 1980s drew to a close, protests started all across Eastern Europe and could not be stopped. In October 1989 East Germany's Communist leader resigned and was later placed under house arrest. Protesters, joined by the wall's guards, tore down the Berlin Wall in November. The two Germanies united into one nation on October 3, 1990.

Germany's northern plains are part of the Great European Plain that stretches from France to Russia. The deciduous forests of France and the Low Countries give way to a mixture of broadleaf trees and evergreens in Germany, especially as you move east and south into the interior of the continent. The Elbe River and its tributaries flow through the heart of eastern Germany. Upriver from Magdeburg is the town of Wittenberg, where Martin Luther posted his ninety-five theses. By using the northern dialect, High German, Luther's Bible helped to establish the standard for the German language.

The northern plains in western Germany cover five states. Two of them are city-states—Bremen and Hamburg. Hamburg, located downstream from Berlin on the Elbe River, is the main seaport and the third-largest city in Germany. Another important harbor lies on the north coast at Kiel (KEEL). The important **Kiel Canal** directly links the North Sea with the Baltic Sea. This gives German vessels a shortcut to avoid going around Denmark's Jutland Peninsula.

The people of the plains, whether east or west, produce the same products. The western plains in particular have some of the best soil in Europe, formed by a thick layer of **loess**, a fine-grained soil deposited by the wind. Germany ranks as the world's third-largest producer of rye, sugar beets, and hogs, and the second-largest producer of barley. Germany also ranks sixth in wheat production and seventh in potato production. Germany's northern plains have the largest concentration of cities and industry in the nation. Germany is now the most populous country in all of Europe. Diverse industries and great wealth make Germany potentially the most powerful and influential country on the continent.

Farthest west is Germany's most important river, the Rhine River, which flows through several important regions of Germany before it winds west into the Netherlands. At the lower end of the river, where the Ruhr (ROOR) River flows into the Rhine, is an industrial megalopolis called the **Ruhr**, the largest industrial region in Europe and perhaps in the whole world. The Ruhr, centered on the city of Essen, is one of the most crowded regions in Europe. The coal mines in this "smokestack region" make Germany the world's seventh-largest coal producer.

Farther up the Rhine River are the major river ports of Cologne (kuh LOHN) and Bonn. Bonn served as the capital of West Germany while Germany was divided; but after the fall of communism, the government decided to move the capital back to Berlin. Cologne is the largest city in this industrial district, even larger than Bonn, with almost two million people.

Germany has made up for its lack of important minerals by importing or synthesizing man-made materials. By importing iron from Sweden, Germany has become the top-ranking producer of

Religions of Europe

- Lutheran
- Calvinist
- Methodist
- Church of England
- Roman Catholic
- Eastern Orthodox
- Non-Christian

LET'S GO EXPLORING

LAND USE OF WESTERN EUROPE

1. Besides manufacturing, what are the two most common ways land is used in Continental Europe?

2. What kind of agriculture is most common on the southern peninsulas of Europe?

3. How is agriculture in the Alps different from the surrounding areas?

4. Where is the center of forestry in Europe?

☿ What would you expect to be the greatest regional difference in Western European culture: between the north and the south or between the east and the west?

Commercial Farming
- Mixed Commercial Farming
- Fruit, Specialized Horticulture
- Mediterranean Farming
- Dairy Farming

Nonfarming
- Manufacturing and Trade
- Nomadic Herding
- Forestry
- Limited Activity

- ⊢⊣ Iron
- ▢ Chromium
- Z Zinc
- ◆ Coal
- ⊤ Petroleum

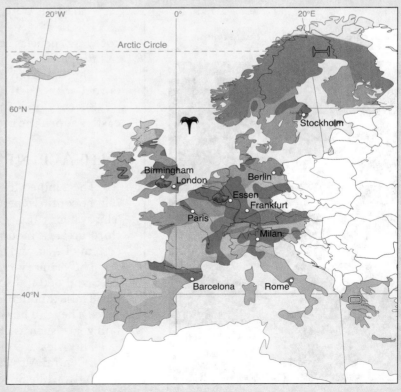

Neuschwanstein Castle

One of Europe's most-photographed medieval castles rises beneath the snowy peaks of the Bavarian Alps. Neuschwanstein (NOOSH vahn stine) Castle has such a fairy-tale appearance that Walt Disney modeled the castle at Disney World after it. Neuschwanstein Castle is actually not a medieval castle at all, but a nineteenth-century palace made to look like an enchanted castle of old. The castle is one of three built by the Mad King of Bavaria, Ludwig II.

Obsessed with German mythology, the king ordered lavish paintings for every room to depict his favorite scenes from Wagnerian operas, Arthurian legend, and ancient history. Every room is splendidly furnished and decorated. The king's bed is so ornate that fifteen men spent over four years carving it. The Mad King moved into the palace in 1886, only to drown himself a few months later.

The Black Forest covers 2,320 square miles, almost 1,500,000 acres.

crude steel in Western Europe. Germany also leads Western Europe in refined copper and refined lead.

The provinces of Southern Germany lie on hilly plateaus. Germany's plateaus are part of a wider system of plateaus that begins with the Massif Central of France and stretches through the low Jura Mountains and Ardennes eastward through Germany into the Czech Republic. The whole system is sometimes called the **Central Uplands**.

The rivers in Germany's Central Uplands flow into two major rivers: the Rhine in the west and the Danube in the east. Four of the south's five provinces lie mostly in the drainage basin of the Rhine. The main tributary of the Rhine in southern Germany is the Main. The Main flows past Frankfurt, the banking center of Germany and home of Germany's stock exchange.

The **Black Forest** along the French border is the best-known feature in the southwest. Mountains rise east of the Rhine. Dark forests of spruce and fir cover the mountains, which contain the headwaters of the Danube River. Lumber mills and granite quarries provide work. Tourists come to health resorts at the mineral springs near Baden-Baden or to obtain the handcrafted toys and cuckoo clocks.

The largest state in Germany, Bavaria lies in the southeast. Bavaria was a duchy throughout the Middle Ages, but Napoleon made it a kingdom in 1805. After the unification of Germany in 1871, Bavaria became a state. Bavaria contains Grosser Arber (4,780 ft.), the highest peak in the Bohemian Forest (known locally as the Bavarian Forest) along the Czech border.

Dairy cattle roam the hills of Bavaria. Hops, used in beer making, are a major cash crop. Munich is the center of the beer industry, celebrated at the annual festival called Oktoberfest. With almost two million people, Munich is the fifth-largest city in Germany. Its great collection of baroque, rococo, and neoclassical architecture makes it one of the finest cities in Europe.

The **Bavarian Alps** stretch along Germany's entire southern border with Austria, not far south of Munich. The range reaches 9,718 feet on the Zugspitze, a popular skiing area. Several famous castles adorn the area.

The Alpine Region

The Alpine Mountain system forms a great snowy barrier severing the southern peninsulas of Europe from the rest of the continent. The system runs from France all the way to Albania. It forms the third-greatest mountain system in the world (after the Himalayan system of Asia and the Western Cordillera of the Americas).

The primary range in the system is the **Alps**, up to 160 miles deep and 660 miles long, which curves across Italy's northern border. These mountains display the splendor of God's creation in many ways. They are home to golden eagles, marmots, and exotic mountain goats, such as chamois and ibex.

The Alps are grouped into three main divisions: the Western Alps, Central Alps, and Eastern Alps. The Western Alps lie in France and Italy, while Switzerland contains the Central Alps. The Eastern

Alps spread south from Germany across Austria and into Eastern Europe. Few passes cross this barrier, and they can be dangerous, especially in winter.

SWITZERLAND

The rugged Jura Mountains of France and Germany cross over into the northern border of Switzerland. Rhine Falls in this area is the most powerful falls in Europe. The second-largest city in Switzerland, Basel (BAH zuhl), is located in the Rhine River valley. Basel contains part of the vital canal system that links Germany's Rhine River and France's Rhone River.

The **Swiss Plateau**, or Mittelland, lies between the Jura Mountains in the north and the Swiss Alps in the south. The average altitude is 1,902 feet. The Jura Mountains protect the plateau from cold northern winds, while a warm, dry wind, called a **foehn** (FUHRN), blows from the Alps in the south. Although the winds keep the climate mild, they can cause sudden avalanches.

Glaciers apparently gouged out several long, narrow lake basins on the plateau. The two largest are Lakes Constance and Geneva, at each end of the plateau. The country's two most important rivers—the Rhine and the Rhone—flow from these lakes, respectively. Other large lakes include Lake Neuchâtel (NOO shuh TEL), Lake Lucerne, and Lake Zurich. Lake Geneva borders France, and the Rhone River flows west from the lake into France. All of the Mittelland except Lake Geneva drains into Germany's Rhine River.

Switzerland's sixth-largest city, Geneva, lies on the lake. As you might expect, the people speak French. The Red Cross is one of several international organizations that have made their headquarters in Geneva.

German, spoken by about 70 percent of the people, is one of four official languages. The people speak Schwyzerdütsch, or Swiss German, at home and in public. But standard German is used in the schools, churches, and the media.

Bern, the capital of Switzerland, is on the Aare (AHR uh) River, a tributary of the Rhine. Emmentaler, or Swiss, cheese originated near here. Throughout Switzerland, some watch companies still have their headquarters in the villages that first manufactured the precision watches for which Switzerland is famous. The largest city in Switzerland is Zurich, located at the northern tip of Lake Zurich. Unlike French Geneva, the citizens of Zurich speak German. Zurich is the hub of international investment and gold trade.

The Alps cover 60 percent of Switzerland, but less than 10 percent of the population lives there. The **Swiss Alps**, or Central Alps, stretch across southern Switzerland. It has four principal ranges. The first major range, the Bernese Alps, lies between the Swiss capital, Bern, and the upper Rhone River. Visitors to the resort of Interlaken enjoy the highest waterfall in the Alps, the Giessbach, which spills 1,982 feet down the mountainside.

The other three major ranges in the Swiss Alps lie farther south along the Italian border. The Pennine Alps in the west include both Monte Rosa (15,203 ft.) and the **Matterhorn** (14,692 ft.). Monte Rosa is the highest mountain in Switzerland, but the Matterhorn is more famous because of its rare triple-cirque peak. The

Swiss Banking

Switzerland is famous around the world for its banks. These banks are considered the safest in the world, and laws ensure utmost secrecy. This secrecy has sometimes created controversy, such as that created over the discovery that Nazis had stolen gold and hidden it in Swiss banks.

St. Bernard Dogs

St. Bernard Pass, between Mont Blanc and the Matterhorn, links France and Italy. Armies and merchants have crossed this pass for hundreds of years. It is named for the monastery at the pass, which bred the St. Bernard dogs to rescue travelers lost in the snow.

The triple-cirque Matterhorn pierces the sky.

peak forms a three-sided pyramid with steep bowl-shaped basins (or cirques) on each side.

East of the Matterhorn are the Lepontine (li PAHN TINE) Alps. Italy is easy to reach from this canton of Ticino, but the Alps separate the people from the rest of Switzerland. Engineers have bored through the Alps here to make some of the longest highway tunnels in the world. The St. Gotthard highway tunnel is over ten miles long, and the Simplon railway tunnel is over twelve miles long. People in this area speak Italian. Italians constitute about 10 percent of the Swiss population.

The Rhaetian (REE shun) Alps cover southeast Switzerland. In addition to pockets of Italians, Romansch-speaking people live in the small communities of this canton. Less than 1 percent of the Swiss people speak this quaint language, similar to ancient Latin.

Switzerland is divided into **cantons**. The cantons were once Catholic Church districts, like parishes, but they became self-governing districts. These cantons eventually joined together into the country of Switzerland. In 1515 Switzerland adopted a policy of neutrality regarding Europe's wars. France violated this neutrality in 1798 by invading Switzerland. Swiss neutrality was guaranteed by the victorious countries following Napoleon's defeat in 1815. Since this time, the Swiss have refused to join organizations that could jeopardize their neutrality. The Swiss government is one of the most democratic in the world. The cantons are united as a federal republic, but the people can demand a popular vote on any issue by submitting a petition with sufficient signatures. At one time, people in each canton met in an open-air assembly, called a *Landsgemeinde*, to conduct government by a show of hands. Today five cantons still elect their magistrates in this way.

LIECHTENSTEIN

Between Switzerland and Austria is the tiny principality of Liechtenstein (LIK tun s[H]TINE), located on the east side of the Rhine. A prince from Vienna first bought land in the area in 1699, and his descendants—the von Liechtensteins—have ruled ever since. The prince now serves under a constitutional monarchy.

Liechtenstein uses Swiss currency and lets the Swiss represent them internationally. Like Switzerland, it has remained neutral in wars and has not even had an army since 1868. The official language is German, but most people speak a dialect called Alemannic (AL uh MAN ik). About 87 percent of the people are Catholic.

Before 1950, Liechtenstein was primarily a farming country. Today, only 10 percent of the people farm. Now highly industrialized, it has one of the highest standards of living in the world. Over five thousand businesses have headquarters in Liechtenstein because of its reasonable tax rates. The government earns a large portion of its money from the sale of beautiful postage stamps.

AUSTRIA

Austria adopted a strict policy of neutrality in the Cold War because of its precarious position between the East and the West. Austria maintains close cultural and economic ties to Eastern Europe. Austrians speak German, and over seventy percent of them are Catholic. Most people live in the north, where the **Danube River** winds through the foothills of the Alps.

With almost two million people, **Vienna**, Austria's capital, is the largest city in the country. Vienna is known for baroque architecture and its outstanding musicians, including Franz Haydn, Wolfgang Mozart, Franz Schubert, and Johann Strauss. Strauss even named a waltz "The Blue Danube." Concerts, festivals, and operas are performed regularly all over Austria, enjoyed by tourists and natives alike. Vienna is also home to the headquarters of the Organization of Petroleum Exporting Countries (OPEC) and the International Atomic Energy Agency.

The Alps dominate southern Austria. Most people in this region live in the mountain valleys. Austria's forested mountains and valleys make it the leading exporter of wood in continental Europe. Austria's mines make it the world's fourth-largest producer of tungsten. The main city in the western panhandle is Innsbruck. It stands on the Inn River, a tributary of the Danube that forms most of Austria's northwestern border with Germany.

The highest and most famous mountain in Austria is Grossglockner (GROHS GLAHK nur; 12,461 ft.), located southeast of Innsbruck. It lies in a central Alpine range called the Hohe Tauern, the hub of the many other ranges in Austria. The primary mountain pass that German invaders and merchants have used to reach Italy is **Brenner Pass**, south of Innsbruck. It is the lowest major pass through the Central Alps, and warm foehns keep it open all year long. Several roads, railroads, bridges, and tunnels now cross Brenner Pass, linking Innsbruck and northern Italy (South Tyrol).

The Danube River is the pride of Vienna.

SECTION QUIZ

1. What is France's largest city, longest river, and highest mountain?
2. What does the Netherlands do to reclaim land?
3. What city in the Low Countries is home to the headquarters of the European Union?
4. What is the best-known feature of southwest Germany?
5. What river dominates the most populated region of Austria?
- ☼ Why do you think the Low Countries have been at the center of efforts to unite Europe, while the Alpine countries have traditionally stayed out of European politics?

III. MEDITERRANEAN EUROPE

Mediterranean Europe consists of three large peninsulas jutting into the Mediterranean Sea. The sea offers food, provides harbors, and moderates the climate. Mediterranean Europe has a subtropical location and a mild climate with mild, rainy winters and hot, dry summers. Farms must adapt to winter rains and summer drought. Because of the easy access to trade, this region was the cradle of Western civilization, which eventually spread across the globe.

IBERIAN PENINSULA

The **Iberian Peninsula** contains the modern countries of Spain, Andorra, and Portugal. The waters of the Atlantic Ocean

Lipizzaner Horses

One of the highlights of tours in Vienna is a stop at a majestic hall, decorated with ivory and gold and lighted with chandeliers. But tourists don't come to see the architecture. All eyes are turned to events on the dirt floor. The hall has been the home of the Spanish Riding School for over 250 years. The world-famous performers are a troupe of Lipizzaner (LIP it SAH nur) horses, "dancing horses," whose performances are unmatched for their combination of grace and strength.

The Spanish Riding School has been training the Lipizzaners for over four hundred years. It usually takes six or seven years before a horse and rider are ready to perform. They move as one, while the orchestra plays the great music of Vienna. The horses perform several ballet movements, such as a *capriole*, in which they take a flying leap in the air. They stand on their hind legs in a pose called the *levade*. Only the very strongest horses can complete a *courbette*. The horse hops into the air and completes three or more leaps without touching its forelegs to the ground.

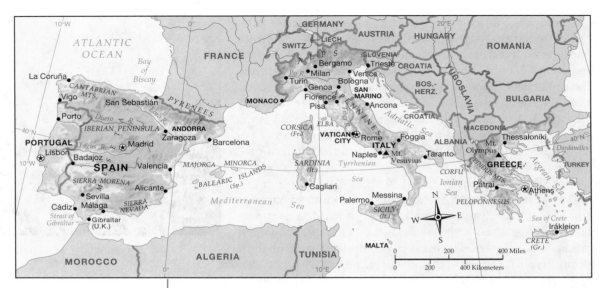

and Mediterranean Sea surround almost 90 percent of the peninsula. The short land border on the north runs through the rugged Pyrenees Mountains.

SPAIN

Over 80 percent of the Iberian Peninsula lies in Spain. Spain's main provinces were united in 1469 when Isabella I, queen of Castile, married Ferdinand II of Aragon. Most Spaniards are Roman Catholic, and Castilian Spanish is the primary language of business and government.

In 1936 the country was engulfed in a bloody civil war when Spain's military revolted against the country's newly formed Republican government. The fascist victor, Francisco Franco, ruled as a dictator from 1939 to 1973. After Franco's death, Juan Carlos became king of Spain. He pushed democratic reforms, and in 1978 Spain adopted a constitution. The government began to increase local control by allowing the election of regional parliaments. In an attempt to bolster the country's economy, Spain joined the European Economic Community (now the EU) in 1986.

The capital city of Spain, **Madrid**, perched on top of a plateau rising over 2,000 feet, is the highest capital in Europe and the most populous among Europe's mediterranean nations. Madrid is uncomfortably hot in summer and freezing cold in winter. During August, the Spanish government actually relocates to a cooler location on the north coast.

A high plateau radiates from Madrid across most of interior Spain. The plateau is called the **Meseta**, meaning "Tableland." The Meseta, sprinkled with rocky hills and mountains, is the heartland of Spain. Although the higher elevations are forested, most of the plateau supports only small shrubs and flowering plants. The hot, dry summers, bitterly cold winters, and poor soils make farming difficult. The medieval ruins and small villages of the Meseta are celebrated in Spain's greatest novel, Cervantes's humorous *Don Quixote de la Mancha.*

Spain's largest river, the **Tagus** (TAY gus), cuts the Meseta in half as it flows west to the Atlantic through Portugal. Madrid lies on a tributary of the Tagus upstream from the historic city of Toledo. North of the Tagus, the Meseta stretches to the Pyrenees Mountains.

Escorial

Escorial (eh SKOR ee AHL) was the royal residence of Spanish kings, located twenty-five miles north of Madrid in the foothills of the Sierra de Guadarrama. In addition to the walled palace, the grounds include a monastery, a domed church, and a college.

Philip II ordered the complex of buildings to be built after a battle against the French in 1557 destroyed the local church. Completed in 1584, the buildings had an austere design that reflected Philip's own self-denial. Constructed of granite from a nearby quarry, the exterior of the church is largely unadorned. However, its interior is highly decorated by Spanish and Italian artists. Escorial is a massive structure, with 1,250 doors and 2,500 windows. The royal residence became a symbol of national unity in the difficult times Spain was facing.

Escorial continued to serve as the royal residence until the nineteenth century. Philip II and many other Spanish kings are buried there. Today, the complex includes a museum that houses valuable collections of books and artwork.

To the south, the Meseta reaches the Sierra Morena. Near Portugal, this mountain range contains Spain's primary mineral resources.

The mountains of the Sierra Nevada rise in the far south. This part of Spain is separated from North Africa by the narrow eight-mile-wide **Strait of Gibraltar**. This makes Spain a land bridge between Africa and Europe.

Two rivers, the Ebro and Guadalquivir, flow from the Meseta into fertile lowland basins. Most of Spain's olives come from these basins. In the north, the Ebro River drains east to the Mediterranean. The broad plain of the Ebro Basin includes the province of Aragon. The river delta is well suited for growing rice, a Spanish staple.

In the south, the Guadalquivir River flows west to the Atlantic just beyond Gibraltar. The whitewashed houses and narrow, shaded streets of Seville (say VEE yuh), Spain's fourth-largest city, make it the epitome of what foreigners think Spain is like. Cádiz is an Atlantic port sixty miles downstream from Seville. Founded by Phoenician traders in 1100 BC, the city claims to be the oldest continuously inhabited city in Europe.

Several ancient ports were established on the narrow coastal plain along Spain's Mediterranean coast. In these fertile lowlands, farmers diverted rivers to irrigate their crops. Spain leads the world in the production of olives. It ranks in the top ten for the production of a number of items, including almonds, grapes, strawberries, apricots, lettuce, cauliflower, lemons and limes, oranges, tomatoes, watermelons, oats, and rye.

The seaport and resort city of Alicante, known for its bright skies, was built on the site of the Roman city of Lucentum, or "City of Light." Valencia is located about midway up the coast. Located on the Turia River about three miles from the Mediterranean, it is the third-largest city in Spain. Valencia's rows of white houses reflect its long period of Moorish occupation.

Located in the northeast corner of Spain, **Barcelona** has been an important seaport throughout Spain's history. Today it is Spain's most important manufacturing and trading center. During the Spanish Civil War, Barcelona was a stronghold of opposition to Franco's Nationalists. The people of this region speak Catalan, similar to Provençal, used across the border in France. When Franco forbade the speaking of Catalan, the fiercely independent people continued to use it during soccer matches to cheer for their local team. Today, **Catalonia** is one of three regions of Spain in which there is a second official language. The people here, who think of themselves as Catalonians first and Spaniards second, would like independence.

The mountainous north is the only part of Spain that receives adequate rainfall. Its marine-west-coast climate benefits from the moist winds that blow off the Atlantic. The poor-quality soil does not support crops; however, the rain provides adequate pastureland. The pastures and woodlands in this region support thriving dairy and paper industries.

In the summer, Spaniards flock to the cool mountains and the northern beaches. The forested mountain slopes are broken by short, swift rivers that flow into the Atlantic. Although these rivers are not navigable, they are harnessed to generate electricity. The river mouths provide harbors for fishing fleets.

The **Cantabrian Mountains** rise from the northern and northwestern edge of the Meseta and run parallel to the Atlantic. In the far west, the people speak Galician, a Portuguese dialect. The **Basques**

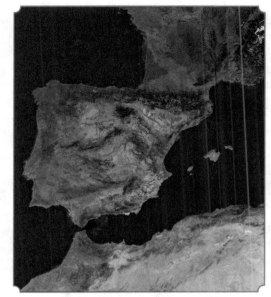

Viewed from space, the narrow Strait of Gibraltar is a striking feature of the earth's surface.

Basques

There are three small Spanish provinces in "Basque Country": Álava, Vizcaya, and Guipúzcoa. But the heart of their ancient land was Navarre, on the border with France. More than two million Basques live in Spain, and over one-half million live across the border in France. Not much is known about their origins, and their language, Euskara, is unrelated to any known language. The fiercely independent Basques have clung to their way of life despite foreign invaders.

Many Basques make their living from the sea. The adventurous Basques were the first Europeans to hunt whales in the Bay of Biscay during the sixteenth century. Two centuries ago the whales disappeared, so now the Basques fish for tuna and cod instead.

Euskara is very difficult and has several dialects. The first "unified Basque" Bible was not translated until 1995. Most Basques speak Spanish, and only a minority speak Basque. But the Basque speakers are a vocal minority, and many want independence from Spain. A terrorist group, called ETA, began a campaign of bombings and political assassinations in 1968. They have killed over eight hundred people.

Roman Catholicism

Roman Catholicism is the largest religion in the world with over one billion members. It is led by the bishop of Rome, who is called the pope. The headquarters of this religion is the country of Vatican City (many times referred to as simply the Vatican). Roman Catholicism bears a similarity to Protestantism but differs in significant ways. Among other differences, Roman Catholicism holds that the church's tradition has equal authority with Scripture and that salvation is attained by grace through the seven sacraments and other meritorious works. It also holds to the supremacy of the pope over the church as the "vicar [or substitute] of Christ." Although Roman Catholicism does not appear to be divided, within the religion there are a vast number of movements, orders, and beliefs.

The great port at Lisbon is prone to floods and other disasters. Its greatest tragedy was an earthquake in 1755 that leveled the city and killed sixty thousand inhabitants.

(BASKS) live in the eastern Cantabrian Mountains near the port of Bilbao. This area provided iron during the early Industrial Revolution. Today Bilbao is densely populated as a result of industrial development. To the east, the towering Pyrenees rise to over eleven thousand feet and form the formidable barrier between Spain and France.

ANDORRA

Nestled high in the Pyrenees Mountains, Andorra lies between Spain and France. Its name may have come from an old Moorish word meaning "thickly wooded place," but it is indeed a mixture of Spain and France. The official language is Catalan, and both French francs and Spanish pesetas were legal tender until the euro was adopted.

Isolated by steep mountains in their fertile valleys, the Andorrans lived as farmers and shepherds when Charlemagne, according to tradition, granted them independence in exchange for help in fighting the Moors. When roads to Spain and France opened in the 1950s, tourism developed. Today, tourists come to view historic sites and to buy Andorra's rare postage stamps. The low tax rate also lures bargain hunters for Swiss watches or Japanese cameras.

PORTUGAL

The country of Portugal lies on the west coast of the Iberian Peninsula. This small country once ruled one-half of the known world. During the sixteenth century, Portugal's empire included Brazil, much of India, and colonies in Africa, the East Indies, and China. Today only three small terrirories remain from the once great Portuguese empire.

The Spanish Meseta extends into Portugal almost to the coast. North of the Tagus, the climate is cool and rainy. This populous region supports many small farms that produce grapes, olives, and grains. Deposits of tungsten in this area enable Portugal to rank as the fifth-highest producer of this mineral worldwide.

South of the Tagus River, the climate is warmer and the terrain less rugged. Forests of cork oak trees in this region produce large quantities of cork for export. Wealthy landowners have large farms in the area. Because of the forests and large farms, the population is small.

With a metropolitan population of almost three million, **Lisbon** is Portugal's capital and largest city. Lisbon's harbor, at the mouth of the Tagus River, is one of the finest natural harbors in the world.

The official language is Portuguese, and most people are Roman Catholic.

The government at Lisbon has not always been stable. From 1928 to 1968, a dictator denied the people basic civil rights. In 1974, a military group seized control of the government and vowed to restore democracy. Two years later Portugal held its first free elections in more than fifty years. The standard of living improved as some state-owned industries were privatized. The country's future growth is now tied to the growth of the European Union, which it joined in 1986.

Porto is Portugal's second-largest city, and it stands at the mouth of the second-most important river, the Duero River. Like Lisbon, it is a canning center for sardines, but it is also famous for port wine. The beautiful beaches from Porto south to Lisbon have earned this coast the name Silver Coast. Men from Porto and the fishing villages along the coastal plain fish for tuna, sardines, and cod. Dried cod, called bacalhau, is one of the nation's favorite foods. The Portuguese claim that a good cook can prepare it 365 different ways, one for each day of the year.

ITALIAN PENINSULA

ITALY

Italy occupies a long and narrow boot-shaped peninsula. The Alps form the top of the boot, while its toe stretches almost to Africa. Although Italy usually has a sunny and mild climate, its extremes are exceptional. Winter is cold in the north, while the *sirocco* (winds) may bring to the south the intense heat of the Sahara. The name *Italy* comes from the ancient Romans, who referred to the southern part of the peninsula as Italia, meaning "grazing land."

Italy's coastline stretches for 4,722 miles and is known more for its beautiful beaches and resorts than its natural harbors. Nearly three-fourths of the country's land is either hilly or mountainous. Areas isolated by the mountains have their own unique customs, dialects, and cuisine. The main lowland areas lie along the west coast and on the boot heel.

The Alps form the northern border of Italy. Lake Garda and Lake Como are two of the large alpine lakes that attract many tourists. People who live along the Austrian border speak German rather than Italian.

The **Apennine** (AP uh NINE) **Mountains** stretch the length of the Italian peninsula. The highest peak, Corno Grande, reaches only 9,554 feet, and its once-thick forests have been indiscriminately cleared for crops, resulting in serious erosion. Though lower and less picturesque than the Alps, the Apennines form the backbone of Italy and separate northern Italy from the Italian peninsula.

The **Po River** is the longest river in Italy. From its origin in Italy's northwest corner, the Po flows east until it empties into the Adriatic. The broad plain of the Po is the largest in Mediterranean Europe. The Alps and the Apennines on either side of the valley provoke rains, which wash soil and minerals into the drainage basin. The resulting good soils make this

Portions of eastern Tuscany lie in the Apennines.

Venice

Unlike most cities, Venice is built on over one hundred low islands in a swampy lagoon of the Adriatic Sea. The people do not ride in cars and busses over paved streets. Instead, they ride in motorboats or in gondolas (long black boats). The seaside buildings are built on piles of mud and supported by debris, logs, and rocks. Many of these foundations were built during the Renaissance. Approximately four hundred foot-bridges cross the 150 canals, and a major road links the city to the mainland.

The sea, which once contributed to Venice's greatness, now poses a threat to its existence. Experts are working on ways to save the foundations of Venice's buildings, which are slowly eroding under the constant washing of seawater and the vibrations from motorboats. In the twentieth century, authorities noticed that the entire city was sinking about one inch every five years. They forbade drawing water from Venice's underground wells, and the sinking temporarily stopped.

Mount Vesuvius

Mount Vesuvius (vih SOO vee us) (4,190 ft.), mainland Europe's only active volcano, is about seven miles southwest of Naples. Tourists hike thirty minutes to the volcano's top. It has erupted eighty times since its most famous eruption in AD 79. The famous eruption buried the ancient Roman cities of Pompeii and Herculaneum. Volcanic ash and mud preserved the ruins of these cities.

The elevation of Mt. Vesuvius changes with each major eruption—a low of 3,668 feet in 1906 compared to its current elevation at 4,202 feet.

valley the most heavily cultivated part of Italy. Vegetables, grapes, and grains such as wheat, corn, and barley are grown here.

Large ships navigate inland on the Po as far as Turin. The region from Turin to Milan is the industrial center of Italy. Large power plants on the upper reaches of the Po provide electricity for factories producing cars, chemicals, and candy. Milan, Italy's second-largest city, is also a banking center and contains the world-famous opera house La Scala. North of the Po River Delta, the Adriatic Coastal Plain extends to the eastern border. Venice is the most famous city in this area.

A wide coastal plain lies along the west coast of the Italian Peninsula. The coastal plains rise into foothills as they move inland toward the mountains. The southern regions are the most populous with the cities of Rome and Naples. The northern region, Tuscany, contains the cities of Pisa and Florence.

Rome, the capital, stands along the Tiber River, surrounded by seven steep hills. Rome blends the ancient and the modern. Each year thousands of tourists flock to the "Eternal City" to view the antiquities which testify of Rome's past greatness. The city boasts the Colosseum, the remains of luxurious Roman baths, and the foundations of opulent palaces built for Roman emperors. Today these antiquities exist in the midst of modern office buildings and dawn-to-dusk traffic jams.

Although a parliamentary republic was established in 1946, competing interests in the country have prevented the government from forming a lasting coalition. Over fifty governments rose and fell in the first fifty years after World War II. Recently, leaders in the rich north have even called for independence from the poorer south, which wants the government to increase socialist programs that would redistribute the nation's wealth.

The heel of the boot is called **Apulia** (uh POOL yuh). This region is cut off from the rest of Italy by the Apennines. Most of Apulia is a plateau which ends in steep cliffs that drop into the Adriatic Sea. Italy produces about one-fifth of the world's olives, mostly on large estates in Apulia and Sicily. Bari and Taranto are the main ports and support a large fishing industry.

Italy controls several islands in the Mediterranean Sea. The large islands of Sicily and Sardinia are very important. **Sicily,** the most populated island in the Mediterranean Sea, is situated just two miles from mainland Italy's toe. Mount Etna, Europe's highest volcano, rises

The Mafia

Sicily is also known for the Mafia, an organized crime ring that profits from illegal operations such as gambling, selling drugs, and providing protection for legitimate businesses. The Mafia began when Sicilians grew disgruntled with the harsh foreign rulers (Greeks, Romans, Arabs, and Normans), who had taken Sicily for its strategic position between Italy and Africa. In exchange for votes, the government has often "overlooked" the Mafia's criminal activities. A strict code of silence, called the *omerta*, has made it difficult for authorities to fight the ruthless and violent Mafia.

to a height of 10,902 feet on the east coast of Sicily. The fertile volcanic soils surrounding Mount Etna encourage farming, but the rough terrain covering 80 percent of the island provides only limited arable land. Sicily was a primary setting for the imaginative journey of Homer's *Odyssey*. It also was the biblical site of Syracuse, where Paul spent three days on his way to Rome (Acts 28:12).

The island of **Sardinia** is located about one hundred miles off Italy's west coast and nine miles south of the French island of Corsica. Its mountainous terrain makes for a strikingly beautiful and sparsely populated island. Some consider Sardinia's beaches the finest in the Mediterranean, especially the exclusive Costa Smeralda (Emerald Coast). Tourist attractions on these islands include many historic sites.

MONACO

Monaco is a tiny principality on the French Riviera about ten miles from the Italian border. Much of Monaco is built on cliffs overlooking the sea.

Italians from Genoa first ruled the area in the twelfth century and built a fort in 1215. Since 1308, the Italian prince has descended from the Grimaldi family. Although the prince of Monaco has an Italian ancestry, he speaks French. The official language is French, most of the citizens are French, and France is their main trade partner. In 1918, the prince signed a treaty permitting France to annex Monaco if Monaco ever lacks a male heir to the throne. The mixed French and Italian peoples of Monaco are known as Monégasques.

The palace and fortress is called Monaco-Ville. To the west lies the industrial area of Fontvieille, while to the east lies the secluded harbor and port area of La Condamine. Beyond the port lies Monte Carlo, an area famous for its luxury hotels, shops, beaches, and gambling casinos.

SAN MARINO

San Marino is located in the central Apennines. **Mount Titano** (ti TAHN oh; 2,424 ft.) lies at the heart of the country. The people speak Italian and are Roman Catholic. Grapes, leather, and cheese are the main products. According to tradition, a Christian stonecutter named Marinus and his followers used this mountain refuge to escape religious persecution by Emperor Diocletian in AD 301. San Marino remained independent during the unification of Italy, and it now claims to be the world's oldest republic.

VATICAN CITY

The pope leads the Roman Catholic Church from Vatican City, sometimes referred to as the Holy See. The tiny country, completely surrounded by the city of Rome, obtained independence by the Treaty of Lateran in 1929. With less than one thousand people and an area of only one-sixth of a square mile, it is the smallest country in the world. Most of those who work in the country live in Rome.

Ministates Near Italy

Four small countries lie in or near Italy. These countries share Italy's mediterranean climate and are popular tourist destinations. All include historic sites, medieval buildings, and museums. Their economies depend on tourism and their rare and valuable postage stamps. Some of these ministates also have limited agriculture similar to adjacent regions of Italy.

Collectors prize stamps from Monaco, San Marino, Liechtenstein, Malta, and other ministates.

St. Peter's Basilica is almost the same height as the Great Pyramid at Giza.

Vatican City also has its own bank, post office, newspaper, and even a rarely used jail. The Vatican's radio station broadcasts in forty different languages. Its unique police force consists of Swiss guards whose sole duty is to protect the pope. These brightly costumed guards patrol with swords and halberds.

MALTA

The country of Malta is located about sixty miles south of Sicily in the Mediterranean Sea. The country consists of the two islands of Gozo and Malta as well as a few smaller islands. On Malta, a series of low hills dominates the terrain. Gozo is primarily a flat island with rocky soil and few rivers. Farmers struggle to grow grapes, onions, potatoes, wheat, and flowers. Most islanders work in the dockyards.

Around AD 60 the apostle Paul was shipwrecked on Malta (Acts 27:27–28:11) in the bay which now bears his name. Legend has it that Paul converted the entire population to Christianity during his stay on the island. Today most Maltese are Roman Catholic, and Catholic doctrine is required teaching in the public schools.

Malta's harbors and its location in the Mediterranean Sea have given the country tactical importance. Malta was long held by the British as a naval base, but the British colony gained its independence in 1964. Though the British navy has departed, English remains an official language together with Maltese.

GREECE

Greece occupies the southern tip of the Balkan Peninsula that juts out of Europe at the eastern end of the Mediterranean. Greece's terrain is mostly rough and mountainous, but about 30 percent of the country has arable soil. Farmers must work hard to get anything to grow in the rocky soil. In the country's many mountainous regions, the population is sparse, with most people residing in small villages. The largest and most productive farms are located either along the coast or on interior plains where irrigation is common.

The ancient Roman province of Achaia occupied the heart of Greece around the city of Athens. The mainland portion is Central Greece. Achaia also included a large peninsula in the south, called the **Peloponnesus** (PEL uh puh NEE sus).

Today, small villages are scattered across Central Greece. Farmers grow cotton or raise sheep and goats on the hillsides. Lamb is a central feature in many Greek dishes, such as gyros. Goat's milk is used to make a cheese called feta.

Athens sits on a plain in southeastern Greece. About a third of the country resides here, a city which sprawls over 165 square miles. One-half of the nation's industry takes place in the city, and the pollution is very harmful, both to the people and to the ancient ruins. With its nearby port, Piraeus, Athens is the commercial center of Greece.

The Peloponnesus is the large, hand-shaped peninsula in southern Greece. Though rugged, it is less mountainous than Central Greece. Crops including citrus fruits, grapes, and olives grow mainly on the coastal plains.

The Parthenon crowns the Acropolis at Athens. Even in ruins, it has moved generations of Western poets.

The ruins of Mycenae stand near the northeast end of the peninsula. Mycenae was the first civilization on mainland Europe—the center of culture recounted in Homer's epic Greek poem the *Iliad*.

On the mainland north of Central Greece is Thessaly, a valley coveted by cities in Achaia and people farther north. Its importance arises from the fertile farmland, which produces most of the wheat grown in Greece. The valley is ringed by mountains. The highest and most famous is Mount Olympus (9,570 ft.) at the north end of the valley. The Pindus Mountains border the valley on the west and rise to over eight thousand feet. Modern Greece took Thessaly from the Ottoman Turks in 1881.

North of Thessaly is a region of Greece known as **Macedonia**. It is one part of a larger historical region where Alexander the Great rose to power. It is now divided between Greece, Bulgaria, and the modern nation of Macedonia. The Macedonian region of Greece stretches along Greece's northern border east to a three-fingered peninsula on the Aegean coast, called Khalkidhiki Peninsula. The coastal plain of Macedonia is Greece's most productive agricultural area. Major crops for Greece include maize, sugar beets, olives, cotton, rice, and wheat. Another major crop, tobacco, is sold in Europe.

Macedonia's excellent seaport, Thessaloníki, is the second-largest city in Greece. It was named after a sister of Alexander the Great. The apostle Paul preached in three cities of Macedonia, including Thessaloníki (Acts 16:9–17:13).

Throughout its history, Greece has had trouble with the territories that lie on its outer edges. The ancient kingdom of Epirus lay west of Macedonia in the Pindus Mountains, and Thrace lay east on the coastal plain that touches the Black Sea. Greece took Epirus and much of Macedonia from Turkey during the Balkan War of 1912. It received part of Thrace from Turkey in 1919 after World War I. The eastern half of Thrace remains in Turkish hands. A small minority of Albanians still live in Epirus, Slavs live in Macedonia, and a large number of Turks live in Thrace. The nations of Albania, Macedonia, Bulgaria, and Turkey still covet these lands.

About one-fifth of Greece's territory consists of over 500 islands—166 of which are inhabited. Ever since Greece obtained independence,

THE OLYMPICS

The Olympics are an international symbol of athletic excellence. Although originating in Greece, the modern Olympics were first held in Athens in 1896. Today, the Olympic games draw thousands of competitors from over 180 countries. The Olympic games are split into the Summer Olympics, with categories such as gymnastics, swimming, and track and field, and the Winter Olympics, with categories such as skating, skiing, and bobsledding. The Olympics alternate between the Winter and Summer Olympics every two years. The fiercely competitive athletes are motivated by both a desire for a gold medal and a love for their country. Citizens of various countries cheer their athletes on. Perhaps you have cheered your country's athletes on during an Olympics.

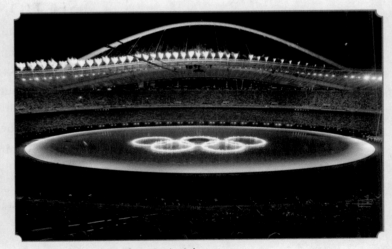

Opening of the 2004 Olympics in Athens

Eastern Orthodoxy

The Eastern churches, led by Constantinople (modern-day Istanbul, Turkey), followed an increasingly different path from the Western churches, led by Rome. The Eastern churches finally broke from Rome in 1054, when the pope demanded that they acknowledge his supreme authority. The two churches refused to cooperate until 1965, when they agreed to restore friendly relations. The Eastern churches became known as the Eastern Orthodox churches.

Although **Eastern Orthodoxy** shares much in common with Roman Catholicism, they have serious differences. A few major differences include the authority of the pope, dates for celebrating Easter, and the ability of lower order priests to marry. Eastern Orthodoxy differs even more significantly from Protestantism. Eastern Orthodoxy holds that tradition is of equal authority with Scripture and rejects that salvation is by grace alone through faith alone in Christ alone. Eastern Orthodoxy differs from both Roman Catholicism and Protestantism in its belief that man is born basically good.

Throughout the last thousand years, the Greeks have rallied to the Orthodox Church, especially when the Ottoman Turks overran the Balkans. Nearly 100 percent of the Greek people belong to the Greek Orthodox Church. Like the other Eastern Orthodox churches, Greece has its own independent church leader, called a primate, who resides in Athens.

it has fought to regain control of all the islands off Turkey. The Greeks have a name for their goal—the Megali Idea, meaning "Great Idea." Only a couple of islands in the northeast are still held by Turkey, and the eastern island of Cyprus is an independent country divided between Greeks and a Turkish minority.

The island of **Crete** lies southeast of mainland Greece at the south end of the Aegean Sea. The largest of the Greek isles, it is known as the "Great Island." Mountains rise sharply from the sea along the south shore and provide a scenic backdrop to the cities and beautiful beaches in the north. The most interesting tourist stop is the ruins of the ancient Minoan capital, Knossos, apparently destroyed by a volcano.

The **Ionian Islands** lie off the west coast of Greece in the Ionian Sea. These fertile islands receive more rainfall than the rest of Greece. The main crops include figs, citrus fruits, olives, and grapes. Ithaca, the island home of Odysseus in Homer's *Odyssey*, is a popular destination. The island of Corfu is strategically located at the north end of the chain near Italy and Albania. It has changed hands many times. This beautiful island, the second-largest in the chain, is known for its wildflowers.

The majority of Greece's islands are **Aegean Islands** in the sparkling Aegean Sea. These rocky and sparsely inhabited islands are divided into three groups. The Cyclades, a group of 220 islands owned by Greece since its independence, form a circle in the Aegean Sea. The group includes the island Thíra (or Santorini). Its huge volcanic crater indicates that the island once exploded in the largest eruption in history, perhaps accounting for the demise of Minoan civilization.

The Sporades stretch across the center of the Aegean to the Turkish coast. Throughout the Aegean, islanders fish for mackerel and harvest sponges. Greece obtained the last of these islands in 1913 as a result of the Balkan Wars.

The Dodecanese ("twelve islands") lie southeast of the Cyclades off the coast of Turkey. The largest Dodecanese island is **Rhodes**. It is blessed with streams and natural harbors, where ancient ships could anchor for the night (Acts 21:1). Rhodes made a massive bronze statue of the sun god Helios in the fifth century BC that was as tall as the Statue of Liberty. This statue, called the Colossus of Rhodes, was one of the Seven Wonders of the Ancient World.

SECTION QUIZ

1. What peninsula contains Spain and Portugal?

2. What mountainous plateau covers most of Spain, including the capital, Madrid?

3. What mountain range forms the backbone of the Italian Peninsula?

4. What is the smallest country in the world?

5. What peninsula contains such famous sites as Mycenae and Olympia?

⚬ Compare and contrast Mediterranean Europe and Continental Europe.

CHAPTER 5 REVIEW

HOW MUCH DO YOU REMEMBER?

1. What are the two largest cities in Western Europe?
2. List the peninsulas of Western Europe.
3. Contrast Protestantism and Roman Catholicism.
4. Contrast Roman Catholicism and Eastern Orthodoxy.
5. What two nations have the highest population densities in Western Europe?

WHAT DO YOU THINK?

1. Do the British Isles and Scandinavia belong in the same culture region? Why or why not?
2. Many of the countries of Western Europe have rivers. How do the rivers in Western European countries contribute to their prosperity?
3. What effect do the Alps have on European culture and geography?
4. Of the following list, which are nations and which are states?
   a. France
   b. Basque
   c. Scot
   d. Germany
   e. Andorra
   f. Greece
   g. Swiss
   h. Malta
   i. Belgian
   j. Lapp
5. What are two cultural geographic reasons that Western Europe has been so influential in world history?

Can You:
Define These Terms?

Eurasia	polder
downs	World Council
time zones	of Churches
international	ecumenism
date line	North Atlantic
Commonwealth	Treaty Orga-
of Nations	nization
moor	duchy
glen	Protestantism
loch	loess
lough	foehn
fjord	canton
European Union	Roman Catholicism
dike	Eastern Orthodoxy

Locate These Places?

North Atlantic Drift	Alps
River Thames	Swiss Plateau
Strait of Dover	Swiss Alps
The Pennines	Matterhorn
Ben Nevis	Danube River
Ireland	Brenner Pass
Scandinavian	Iberian Peninsula
Peninsula	Meseta
Sogne Fjord	Tagus River
Galdhøpiggen	Strait of Gibraltar
Jutland Peninsula	Cantabrian
Greenland	Mountains
Mount Hekla	Apennine
Vatnajökull	Mountains
Seine River	Po River
Loire River	Apulia
Mont Blanc	Mount Vesuvius
Corsica	Sicily
Massif Central	Sardinia
Pyrenees Moun-	Mount Titano
tains	Peloponnesus
Rhine River	Macedonia
Ardennes	Crete
Central Uplands	Ionian Islands
Black Forest	Aegean Islands
Bavarian Alps	Rhodes

Explain the Significance?

England	Brussels
London	Flanders
Wales	Wallonia
Scotland	Berlin
Northern Ireland	Berlin Wall
Irish Republi-	Kiel Canal
can Army	Ruhr
Scandinavia	Vienna
Stockholm	Madrid
Lapland	Barcelona
Lapps	Catalonia
Althing	Basques
Normandy	Lisbon
Canal du Midi	Athens
The Hague	

CHAPTER 6

As seen in Ukraine's Orange Revolution, Eastern Europe has struggled in recent decades to secure freedom.

EASTERN EUROPE

I. BALTIC REGION
  A. POLAND
  B. BALTIC STATES

II. THE CARPATHIANS
  A. CZECH REPUBLIC
  B. SLOVAKIA
  C. HUNGARY

III. THE WESTERN BALKANS
  A. SLOVENIA
  B. CROATIA
  C. BOSNIA AND HERZEGOVINA
  D. MONTENEGRO
  E. ALBANIA

IV. THE EASTERN BALKANS
  A. MACEDONIA
  B. SERBIA
  C. BULGARIA
  D. ROMANIA

V. THE EASTERN PLAINS
  A. MOLDOVA
  B. UKRAINE
  C. BELARUS

PASSPO

United
of

After our study of Western Europe's pleasant climate, rich soils, and bustling cities, we turn to Eastern Europe. This region is quite unlike Western Europe. For much of the twentieth century, this area was under the control of the Soviet Union. As a result, it generally lacks the material prosperity that is characteristic of Western European nations.

Since the collapse of communism in 1989, some countries have made great strides in establishing themselves politically and economically. Others have degenerated into civil war. Sadly, as is common among all of fallen humanity, the peoples of Eastern Europe continue to look to human government for security rather than to the Lord.

> *It is better to trust in the Lord than to put confidence in princes.*
> (Ps. 118:9)

Eastern Europe is appropriately called a **shatter belt**. The size, shape, and number of countries are constantly changing. The borders of some countries have shifted back and forth, reflecting the

	Eastern Europe Fast Facts						
Flag	Country	Capital	Area (sq. mi.)	Pop. (M)	Pop. Density (per sq. mi.)	Per Capita GDP ($US)	Life Span
	Albania	Tiranë	12,000	3.56	296.9	$4,900	77.2
	Belarus	Minsk	80,155	10.30	128.5	$6,800	68.7
	Bosnia and Herzegovina	Sarajevo	19,741	4.03	203.9	$6,500	77.8
	Bulgaria	Sofia	42,823	7.45	173.9	$8,200	72.0
	Croatia	Zagreb	21,831	4.50	205.9	$11,200	74.5
	Czech Republic	Prague	30,450	10.24	336.3	$16,800	76.0
	Estonia	Tallinn	17,461	1.33	76.3	$14,300	71.8
	Hungary	Budapest	35,919	10.01	278.6	$14,900	72.4
	Latvia	Riga	24,938	2.29	91.8	$11,500	71.1
	Lithuania	Vilnius	25,174	3.60	142.8	$12,500	74.0
	Macedonia	Skopje	9,781	2.05	209.1	$7,100	73.7
	Moldova	Chişinău	13,067	4.46	341.0	$1,900	65.2
	Montenegro	Podgorica	5,416	0.63	116.4	$3,800	74.7
	Poland	Warsaw	120,728	38.64	320.0	$12,000	74.7
	Romania	Bucharest	91,699	23.33	254.4	$7,700	71.4
	Serbia	Belgrade	34,116	9.40	275.4	$4,400	74.0
	Slovakia	Bratislava	18,859	5.43	288.0	$14,500	74.5
	Slovenia	Ljubljana	7,828	2.01	256.9	$19,600	76.1
	Ukraine	Kyiv	233,090	47.43	203.5	$6,300	70.0

fortunes of their powerful neighbors. Each time a nation has revolted against its conquerors and set up a new country, it has been conquered again and divided among the victors. Some countries have even disappeared from political maps for a period of time.

I. BALTIC REGION

Four nations in Eastern Europe—Poland, Lithuania, Latvia, and Estonia—have ports on the Baltic Sea. The latter three countries are known as the **Baltic States**. The dominant land feature of all four countries is the Northern European Plain, which rolls across northern Europe from France to Russia. Numerous rivers drain this agricultural belt.

The warm marine-west-coast climate of Western Europe gradually gives way to a colder climate in the heart of the Eurasian continent. The term for this type of cold, wet climate is a *humid continental* climate. Precipitation averages between twenty and thirty inches a year. Summer temperatures often reach the eighties, and freezing temperatures endure through much of the winter.

POLAND

Poland lies almost entirely within the Northern European Plain. Unfortunately, the Polish people have suffered from a lack of natural barriers. The Poles, who account for 97 percent of Poland's population, are descendants of the western Slavs, who migrated into Europe from Asia over two thousand years ago. The Slavic language evolved into a dozen languages.

The Poles were among the first Slavic tribes to convert to Christianity. In the great division of 1054 between the Eastern Orthodox and Roman Catholic (western) Churches, Poland sided with Rome. Later, during the Reformation, Protestantism showed strength initially, but Catholicism eventually prevailed.

The eighteenth century found Poland caught between three growing empires—Prussia, Austria, and Russia. In a series of three agreements, the foreign emperors agreed to divide up Poland's territories. In 1795 Poland ceased to exist as an independent country. After World War I, President Woodrow Wilson of the United States insisted that the Poles be given their own nation again.

Farmers in Poland have tilled the land of the Northern European Plain for centuries.

Then came Hitler's German armies in World War II. The Soviet armies that "liberated" Poland from the Germans were not much better. The country became part of the "**Soviet bloc**," a string of semi-independent countries in the Iron Curtain. Puppet rulers, like puppets on strings, took orders from the Soviets.

The "year of surprises"—1989—showed the world just how unpopular the Soviet system was among the people. In a few remarkable months, all the countries within the Soviet bloc cast off communism and threw open their borders to the West. Poland started the movement in April 1989, when it legalized a labor union called Solidarity and a few months later held the first free elections in Eastern Europe in forty years. Today, Poland is transitioning slowly to a free-market economy. Poland joined the North Atlantic Treaty Organization (NATO) in 1999 and the European Union (EU) in 2004.

WARSAW

With a population over two million, **Warsaw** is Poland's largest city. This historic city has seen many conquerors. The last invaders, the Nazis, leveled the city in 1944 during the sixty-three-day Warsaw Uprising, killing over one-quarter million of the city's inhabitants. In an unusual gesture of kindness, the Soviets restored the quaint buildings of Old Warsaw after the war, using old photographs and written accounts. The rest of the city now has a modern appearance, with plain rectangular apartments and high-rise buildings. A monument remains in Castle Square honoring Sigismund III Vasa, the king who first moved the capital to Warsaw in 1596.

CENTRAL PLAINS

Larger than either Italy or the United Kingdom, Poland has played a central role in the history of Europe. The best farmland and most of the nation's major cities lie on the Central Plains. Warsaw lies on the **Vistula** (VIS chuh luh) **River**, the major artery of shipping through the Central Plains. Poland's farms rank second worldwide in rye, sixth in potatoes, seventh in oats, and eighth in hogs. Poland's sausages are world renowned.

Few people live on the plains near the coast, where glaciers have left many lakes and rocky moraines. The Masurian Lakeland lies east of the Vistula on the coastal plains, and the Pomeranian Lakeland lies in the west. These lakes, nestled among low hills, are popular among campers. The Great Poland Lakeland is located west of Warsaw.

Near the mouth of the Vistula is Gdańsk (formerly Danzig), Poland's largest port and once its most populous city. The hard-working shipbuilders of Gdańsk formed Solidarity, the first trade union in the Iron Curtain. **Lech Walesa**, the head of the union, demanded changes in the 1980s that helped to bring about the end of communism in Eastern Europe. He later became the first president of free Poland, introducing many reforms to the economy.

Gdańsk, formerly called Danzig, has been an important trade center on the Baltic Sea for one thousand years. For centuries Gdańsk was a German city, a fact reflected in the town's early architecture.

SOUTHERN UPLANDS

The Polish plains rise into a series of hills and scattered mountains in southern Poland. Mines produce zinc, lead, and sulfur; Poland ranks ninth worldwide in copper and fifth in silver production. A coal field that crosses the border with the Czech Republic is the largest source of coal in Europe outside the German Ruhr.

GEOGRAPHER'S CORNER

CITY PLANNING MODELS

Few cities in the world were planned. Instead, their layout reflects the events of their history. As businesses grew and as people moved into the city, the city spread out and developed. Today, city planners in every country are attempting to foresee future growth and decline so that they can avoid problems of congested roads, pollution, or abandoned neighborhoods.

Like scientists, city planners use models to help them summarize and analyze complex information. Most city models break down the city into at least five components. The central business district (CBD) refers to the original skyscrapers and office buildings, where property value is at a premium.

Cities have changed rapidly with the rise of suburbs and high-tech industries, such as e-commerce, that allow people to work on computers at home. Examine these three models of cities typical in the early twentieth century and then answer the questions.

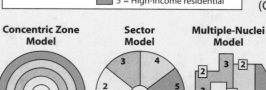

1 = Business
2 = Industrial
3 = Low-income residential
4 = Middle-income residential
5 = High-income residential

Concentric Zone Model   Sector Model   Multiple-Nuclei Model

1. What type of building is near the CBD in every model?
2. What type of housing is near industry in every model?
3. Which model appears the least planned?
4. Which model appears to show development along roads?
- Which model is most similar to a city near you? How is your city different from any of these models?

Galicia—Southeastern Poland consists of hills and low mountains, rising into the Carpathian Mountains on the border. Farms cover the uplands, although they are not as productive as farms on the Central Plains.

This region, drained by the upper Vistula River, is known as Western Galicia. (The Soviet Union took Eastern Galicia away from Poland during World War II.) **Kraków** (KRAK ou), the third-largest city in Poland, is located on the upper Vistula River. Kraków was the first capital of Poland. Here King Casimir the Great (ruled 1333–70) built the magnificent Wawel Castle on a rocky hill above the Vistula River. Kraków was the only major city in Poland that escaped destruction during World War II. Tourists still enjoy visiting the city because of its fine castles and medieval architecture.

Today many foreigners visit a rail center thirty-three miles west of Kraków, called **Auschwitz** (OUSH vits) (*Oświęcim* in Polish). Auschwitz was the largest of several Nazi "death camps" where the Nazis killed over 2.5 million Jews and Poles, whom Hitler considered "inferior races." Many Jews had lived in Poland, a haven for oppressed peoples who were forced to flee other countries in Europe. In 1933, on the eve of Hitler's rise to power in Germany, the Jewish population of Poland was about three million—the largest concentration of Jews in Europe. In 1950, this number had decreased to about forty-five thousand. (Some survivors of the Holocaust left Poland when the national state of Israel was founded in 1948.)

Silesia—The Sudeten Mountains lie on the southwest border of Poland. Waters from the Sudeten Mountains flow into the **Oder River**, which flows west and then north along the German border into the Baltic Sea. The industrial city of Wroclaw, located on the upper Oder, processes minerals from the mountains.

The region drained by the Oder River is known as **Silesia** (sigh LEE zhuh). Many emperors have fought over this valuable piece of property. Frederick the Great's invasion in 1740 sparked a major war fought on three continents. (Americans called it the French and Indian War.) Until World War II, most of the Silesian people were Germans. When the Soviets gave this land to Poland in return for the land it took from eastern Poland, over three million Germans left their homes in Silesia, and many Poles resettled there.

BALTIC STATES

Located on the Northern European Plain, the Baltic States have low rolling hills with many shallow lakes and swamps. Besides rye, farmers grow potatoes or raise dairy cattle.

The Baltic States have a rich heritage, which they celebrate with annual festivals that display traditional dress and recall the glorious deeds of the past. After centuries of occupation by foreigners, they received independence after World War I. But in 1944, the Baltic States were incorporated into the Soviet Union. Recalling their independent spirit, they were the first of the fifteen republics in the Soviet Union to declare independence. Their bravery helped to hasten the breakup of the Soviet Union.

While the Baltic States were a part of the Soviet Union, the Soviets invested a great deal of time and resources into strengthening the economies and transportation networks of these states. After the Baltic States achieved their independence, they retained the infrastructure that the Soviets had built.

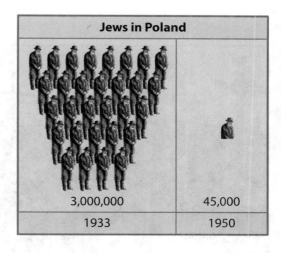

Jews in Poland

3,000,000	45,000
1933	1950

Baltic States

LITHUANIA

Lithuania is the largest of the Baltic States and the farthest from Russia's capital. Over 50 percent of Lithuania is cultivated land, and almost a third is forest. The country is mostly flat, but the eastern portion is more hilly. Eighty percent of its people are ethnic Lithuanians. Poles and Russians each make up about 6 percent of the population.

About 80 percent of the people are Roman Catholic. While Lithuania was part of the Soviet Union, devout Roman Catholics opposed the Soviet Union's atheistic government by setting up crosses on a place called the **Hill of Crosses**. Although the Soviet authorities destroyed the crosses numerous times, the Lithuanians continued to replace them. The Hill of Crosses provides an excellent example of the Lithuanians' religious fervor and nationalistic spirit.

The Lithuanians showed their resistance to the Soviets through their dedication to the Hill of Crosses.

Lithuania has the oldest documented history among the Baltic States. Tacitus (c. 55–c. 120) mentioned that this Baltic region sold amber to the Romans. Lithuania united with Poland in the twelfth century when its king converted to Catholicism and married the heir to the Polish throne. Russia later ruled Lithuania after the partitioning of the kingdom of Poland, except for the brief respite between World Wars I and II. Today it is struggling to establish a free republic.

Lithuania joined both NATO and the EU in 2004. Its trade has shifted from a focus on Russia to a focus on Western Europe. The country benefits from Klaipėda, its major warm-water port on the Baltic. Its industries include machinery, fabrics, transportation equipment, and paper products. Lithuania's two most abundant crops are potatoes and wheat.

LATVIA

Latvia is the middle Baltic State. Its landscape includes plains and forests with few hills. Latvia has over twelve thousand rivers, but few are very long. The Daugava River flowing through the country divides the north and east from the south and west. The Daugava has been used very effectively for hydroelectric power. There are also over three thousand lakes throughout the country. Riga is the capital and major city of Latvia.

About 58 percent of the people are ethnic Latvians, who are similar to Lithuanians, and about 30 percent are Russians who immigrated during the Soviet era. Latvian is the official language. It is an Indo-European language instead of a **Cyrillic** (suh RIL ik) language like Russian. Russian is still widely used since it was the official language during the Soviet era. However, recent laws require candidates for citizenship to pass a Latvian language examination. As a result, tensions between Russia and Latvia have increased.

Latvia became a member of both NATO and the EU in 2004, and its trade reflects this shift towards the West. Potatoes, sugar beets, wheat, and barley are the most abundant crops, and Latvia's major industries include transportation, agriculture, and electronics.

ESTONIA

Estonia is the northernmost of the three Baltic States. It is bordered by the Baltic Sea on its north and west shores, and most of its eastern border is taken up by Lake Pskov. The mainland has marshes, lowlands, and few hills but is rich in oil shale, which provides much of Estonia's energy needs. The major port and capital city, Tallinn, lies on the northern coast. The Baltic Sea moderates the climate of the port, which averages 25°F in the winter and 58°F in the summer. Estonia's fifteen hundred islands make up 10 percent of its land area. The two largest, Saaremaa and Hiiumaa, have cities.

Estonia has much in common with Scandinavia. The people speak Estonian, a Finnic language, and many people understand Finnish. Though controlled successively by Germany, Denmark, Sweden, Poland, and Russia, Estonia has kept a separate identity. Today, ethnic Estonians compose almost 70 percent of the population, and ethnic Russians make another quarter. The Estonian government has also made learning the Estonian language a requirement for citizenship, heightening tensions between the ethnic Estonian majority and the sizeable ethnic Russian minority.

Electronics, telecommunications, and engineering make up the bulk of the country's industry. The major agricultural products are barley, potatoes, and wheat. Estonia joined NATO and the EU in 2004, and it aims to incorporate the euro as the national currency.

Section Quiz

1. Why is Eastern Europe considered a shatter belt?
2. What are Poland's two most important rivers?
3. What two regions of Poland lie in the hills along the southern mountains?
4. Name the Baltic States. Which state is strongly Roman Catholic?
5. What are the two largest islands of Estonia?

- Why have two of the Baltic States enacted laws requiring a knowledge of each country's native language for citizenship? What are the benefits and disadvantages of these requirements?

Piatra Craiului is a mountain in the Romanian portion of the Carpathian Mountains.

II. The Carpathians

The Alps are the dominant mountain system in Western Europe, cutting the region in half. But they die out in Austria. The **Carpathian Mountains** (kar PAY thee uhn) pick up on the east side of the Danube River, becoming the dominant system in Eastern Europe. They divide the northern plains from the south.

There are many subranges within the Carpathian system. The highest subrange, the **Tatra Mountains**, rises in the far north along the border of Poland and Slovakia. The Tatra range is the continental divide, separating the rivers that flow north into the Baltic Sea and the rivers that flow south and east into the Black Sea. Most people on the Carpathian Divide live in the river valleys, not in the mountains. Three landlocked nations share parts of the Carpathians—the Czech Republic, Slovakia, and Hungary.

The Nizke Tatry (Low Tatra) National Park is located in Slovakia.

The dominance of the Soviet Union had a lasting effect on the religious life of these three nations. Before World War II, these countries had a strong Roman Catholic presence.

The leaders of the Soviet Union, however, tried to discourage religion. As a result of Soviet influence, countries within the Iron Curtain also discouraged religion. The result is evident in the religious demographics of some Eastern European countries.

Country	Roman Catholics	Protestants	Unaffiliated
Czech Republic	26.8%	2.1%	59.0%
Slovakia	68.9%	10.8%	13.0%
Hungary	51.9%	18.9%	14.5%

CZECH REPUBLIC

The Czech Republic was formerly part of Czechoslovakia, a union of Czech and Slovak peoples. These two peoples, like the Poles, are Western Slavs. The Allies created Czechoslovakia after World War I when they broke up the Austria-Hungary Empire. The Allies hoped this union would give the Slavic people enough strength to defend themselves against future threats. But Czechoslovakia fell to Hitler's armies in 1939 and then to the Soviet armies in 1945. The overthrow of the Communist Party in Czechoslovakia in 1989 was so swift and peaceful that it was called the **Velvet Revolution**.

After Czechoslovakia's independence, the Czech and Slovak representatives differed over the nature and pace of economic reforms. In 1993, these differences caused the two parts of the nation to split peacefully into the nations of the Czech Republic and Slovakia in what is called the **Velvet Divorce**.

LET'S GO EXPLORING

CLIMATES OF EASTERN EUROPE

1. What climate occurs east of Europe's marine-west-coast climate?

2. Which nations have three different climates within them?

3. Which nations have a mediterranean climate?

4. For which country or countries is the climate entirely marine west coast? humid continental?

☼ What geographical feature characterizes the majority of the marine-west-coast and humid continental climates in Eastern Europe?

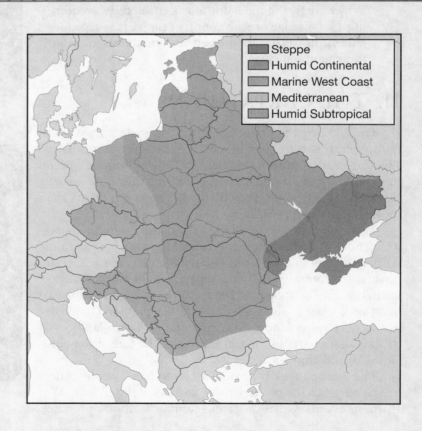

Steppe
Humid Continental
Marine West Coast
Mediterranean
Humid Subtropical

The government of the Czech Republic introduced reforms that strengthened the ecomony rapidly. To get property back into the hands of the people, leaders handed out vouchers to private citizens in an experiment called **mass privatization**. Each adult became a shareholder in the nation's various industries. After a brief period of economic hardships, the country swiftly regained its vigor. Today, the Czech Republic has one of the strongest economies in Eastern Europe. The Czech Republic joined NATO in 1999 and the EU in 2004.

BOHEMIA

The western half of the Czech Republic, called Bohemia, is a large basin ringed by highlands. Its waters drain north into Germany's Elbe River. Farmers raise cattle as well as barley, wheat, sugar beets, and potatoes. The entire country enjoys a marine-west-coast climate, similar to that of Western Europe.

Protected by the mountains, the Bohemians cultivated an independent spirit over the centuries. Today, the capital of the Czech Republic, **Prague** (PRAHG), has over one million people. Prague Castle reminds visitors that Bohemia was an independent kingdom during the Middle Ages. Known as the City of a Hundred Spires, Prague has many churches, bridges, and historical landmarks, which were spared from bomb attacks during World War II.

THE SUDETENLAND

The Bohemian Basin is ringed by the Sudeten Mountains on the northern border with Poland, and the Bohemian Mountains on the western boundary with Germany. The Bohemian range includes the famed Bohemian Forest in the west and the Erzgebirge (EHRTS guh BIER guh), meaning "Ore Mountains," in the northwest. The coal mines of the Erzgebirge make the Czech Republic a major producer of coal in the world. Uranium is also mined there.

Many Germans live in this valuable mountain region, called the Sudetenland. The Allies gave it to the Czechs after World War I to guarantee them a defensible border against Germany. But Hitler invaded in 1938, claiming a right to recover German lands. The Nazis killed or displaced many Czechs; then in retribution after World War II the Czechs forced three million Germans out of their homes. Relations between the two countries have been sour ever since.

MORAVIA

The eastern part of the Czech Republic is Moravia. About 4 percent of the Czech population is Moravian. Moravia takes its name from the Morava River, which drains south into the Danube.

SLOVAKIA

Slovakia, in the heart of the Carpathian Mountains, is separated from the Czech Republic by the White Carpathians. A spruce-fir forest carpets these mountains. The Tatra Mountains separate Poland and Slovakia. The mountains of Slovakia hold a wealth of resources, such as iron ore, copper, lead, and other metals. In the southwest, crops are grown on a plain called the **Little Alföld** (AHL fuhld). The Little Alföld extends into the northwest corner

Prague Castle, which stands on a hill overlooking the Vltava River, was the home of the kings of Bohemia. Today the president of the Czech Republic lives in a portion of the castle.

The Tatra Mountains are a major mountain range in the Carpathian Mountains.

of Hungary. Farmers in this lowland area raise wheat, cattle, and hogs. Bratislava, the capital, lies within the Little Alföld, just downstream from Vienna on the Danube River.

Although Slovakia had a slightly authoritarian government shortly after the breakup, the government is now more democratic. Slovakia joined NATO and the EU in 2004, and its economy has continued to grow. Wheat, sugar beets, and other grains are the top agricultural products of the country. Some major industries include chemicals, metal, energy, transportation, and textiles. Slovakia and the Czech Republic continue to cooperate in joint economic alliances.

HUNGARY

The Hungarians are not like their neighbors. They are descendants of Magyar tribes from the East, who invaded Central Europe in AD 896, enslaving the Slavic and Germanic peoples. They speak a Uralic language associated with the Ural Mountains, the border between Europe and Asia.

Hungary is part of a basin within a sweeping curve in the Carpathian Mountains, which reach into the north of Hungary. The country is divided by the Danube River, Europe's second-longest river. The capital of Hungary, **Budapest**, lies on the Danube River at the foot of the mountains. With more than two million people, it is the fourth-largest city in Eastern Europe.

East of the Danube, the **Great Hungarian Plain** (also known as the Great Alföld) takes dominance. This plain spreads through other countries in Eastern Europe. The Tisza River, a tributary of the Danube, runs through the middle of this plain, making it useful for both pastureland and cropland. Hungary's farmland, some of the best in all of Eastern Europe, is sufficient to meet Hungary's food demands. The chief crops are maize, wheat, beets, barley, sunflower seeds, apples, potatoes, and grapes.

Hills roll west of the Danube to the foothills of the Austrian Alps. Much of this land is used for crops. Forests cover the northeast and southwest corners of Hungary. Lake Balaton, the "Hungarian Sea," is the largest lake in the basin and a favorite vacation resort. Major products from the foothills include timber and uranium. Hungary's mines are the eighth-largest producers of bauxite in the world.

Buda + Pest = Budapest

Buda was founded on one side of the river by Romans in the second century. It became the capital of Hungary in the fifteenth century. In 1872 Buda merged with the town of Pest across the Danube, forming the present city.

SECTION QUIZ

1. What mountain system extends from the Alps across Eastern Europe?
2. What people group settled the Czech Republic and Slovakia?
3. Compare and contrast the Czech Republic and Slovakia.
4. What important plain covers a large portion of Eastern Europe?
5. How is Hungary different from all its neighbors?

III. THE WESTERN BALKANS

The **Balkan Peninsula** is a mountainous region that juts down from Europe into the eastern end of the Mediterranean. Nine countries of Eastern Europe, called the **Balkans**, lie on the peninsula. They share the peninsula with Greece and Turkey.

The Balkans' rugged ranges once isolated numerous tribes that migrated into the region, causing them to develop separate cultural identities. The terrain encouraged disunity and conflict between these peoples. The Balkans are a complex knot of two dozen separate nationalities in nine countries. The tendency of such diverse territories to break up into small, hostile nations is called **Balkanization**.

The **Dinaric** (di NEHR ik) **Alps** run down from the border of Italy along the western edge of four countries—Slovenia, Croatia, Bosnia and Herzegovina, and Montenegro—and end in northern Albania. The Dinaric Alps divide the waters that flow into the Adriatic Sea from the waters that flow east into the Great Hungarian Plain. Few good ports are available on the rugged coast of the Adriatic.

Most of the people in these four Balkan countries belong to the language group of the Southern Slavs—including Slovenes, Croats, and Serbs. But they are divided by religion and culture. The Slovenes and Croats once belonged to the Austrian Empire, and they share its Western culture, Roman alphabet, and Catholic religion. But the Serbs belonged to the Byzantine Empire and share its Eastern culture, Cyrillic alphabet, and Orthodox religion. The uniting factor between these peoples was their common enemy in the south—the Ottoman Turks, who at one time conquered all their lands. During the Cold War, these countries, with Macedonia, were part of the Communist country of Yugoslavia.

SLOVENIA

The Alps extend down from Austria and Italy into most of Slovenia. The highest peak in Slovenia is Triglav (9,396 ft.) in the Julian Alps at the northwest corner of the country. From here, the Sava River flows southeast across the country and later enters the Danube. The

Where Are the Balkans?

Many students wonder where the Balkans are and what nations make up the Balkans. To find the Balkans on a map, take a map of Europe and place your two index fingers at the top of the Adriatic Sea. Move your right finger east until you reach the Black Sea and stop. Then move both fingers down into the form of an upside-down triangle. This peninsula is the Balkan Peninsula, and all of the nations on this peninsula (except Turkey and Greece) are collectively called the Balkans.

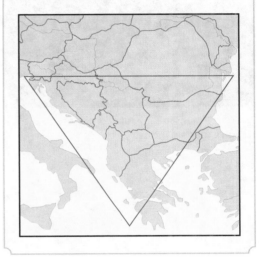

GYPSIES

One of the largest ethnic minorities in Europe is the **Gypsies**. Gypsies call themselves "Roma" and their language "Romany." This swarthy people arrived in Europe in the fourteenth century. They were mistakenly thought to be Egyptians, thus the term *gypsy*. Although the precise origin of Gypsies remains shrouded in mystery, they evidently came from northwest India a thousand years ago and have been moving ever since.

Gypsies limited their contact with the outside world and consequently preserved their own tribal language, laws, and customs. Their work reflected the life of wanderers. Some took seasonal jobs as circus performers, musicians, and acrobats. Others worked as peddlers, smiths, tinkers, woodcarvers, hangmen, undertakers, dogcatchers, or horse traders. Gypsy women, who had fewer alternatives, begged or took up fortunetelling with crystal balls and palm reading.

Gypsies earned a bad reputation because of their work. The few who were tricksters or fortunetellers made it harder for the honest majority. Even today, the verb *gyp* derives from *Gypsy* and means "to cheat." Hitler targeted Gypsies as "undesirables," and about 400,000 of them died in the Holocaust.

Today, many Gypsies have settled down and joined the modern world. Others have replaced their wagon with a camper and now follow traveling circuses. Governments throughout Europe are seeking to in-

A Gypsy girl in Warsaw, Poland

corporate the poor Gypsy population into the general populace. While Gypsies have spread to every continent, the three main tribes are in Europe. The Gitanos are in Spain, southern France, and North Africa; and the Sinti are in France and Germany. The largest tribe is the Kalderash of the Balkans.

Dinaric Alps rise south of the river. Koper is the only commercial seaport on Slovenia's tiny Adriatic coastline.

The Karst (or Kras) region, famous for its sinkholes and limestone caves, lies in the southwestern section of the country. Postojna, located east of the Italian city of Trieste, boasts the largest caverns in Europe. The name **karst** has come to refer to any exotic limestone landscape. Another tourist attraction in Slovenia is Lipica, the town for which Lipizzaner horses are named. Tourists can visit the farm where these dancing horses are still trained.

Slovenia, a democratic republic, has a president and a prime minister. The president chooses the prime minister, but the choice must be approved by the ninety-seat National Assembly, the chief legislative body. There is also a forty-seat National Council that functions as an advisory group. Slovenia was the first Yugoslavian republic to demand independence. After brief fighting in 1991, the European Union negotiated a cease-fire.

Since its independence, the mostly-Catholic Slovenia has become a leading example of free-market economics in Eastern Europe. Even while it was a part of Yugoslavia, Slovenia produced more than any other part of the country, partially because of its ties to Western Europe. Today, it has the highest per capita GDP in Eastern Europe. Wheat, watermelons, and maize are the top crops. Metallurgy, electronics, and transportation vehicles are three of the top industries. Slovenia joined the European Union and NATO in 2004 and began using the euro in 2007.

The karst caves in Slovenia contribute to the nation's tourism industry.

CROATIA

Croatian is so similar to Serbian that linguists consider it a single language called Serbo-Croatian. However, the Croats have a long history of rivalry with the Serbs. When Slovenia declared independence from Yugoslavia, Croatia followed suit. The war was much worse in Croatia. The large Serb minority in Croatia declared independence from Croatia and looked to the Yugoslav army for help. Over ten thousand people died in the fighting, until the United Nations negotiated a cease-fire and sent in thirteen thousand soldiers to keep the peace. Since 2000, Croatia has taken significant steps toward a stronger democracy.

Croatia is shaped like a boomerang. Forests cover more than a third of the country. The southern wing of Croatia includes most of **Dalmatia**. The Dalmatian Coast has large beach resorts on the mainland as well as on hundreds of islands. The mediterranean climate and the scenic backdrop of the Dinaric Alps draw many tourists. Dalmatia has been proposed as the source of the dalmatian dog breed, but this claim is disputed.

The eastern wing of Croatia lies on the Pannonian Plains, part of the Great Hungarian Plain. Low mountains roll across most of the plain. Zagreb, the capital and largest city, lies on the Sava River. The most fertile plain is Slavonia in the east along

A dry mediterranean climate is evident on the Dalmatian Coast of Croatia.

the border with Serbia. The top agricultural products for the country are maize and sugar beets. Two of the top imports for the country are cattle and pork, and the top export is refined sugar.

BOSNIA AND HERZEGOVINA

The Muslims controlled the Balkans for about five hundred years. During that time, many Slavs embraced Islam. Most of them were located in Bosnia. Croats and Serbs make up the majority of the population, but slightly less than half of the people are followers of Islam. They are sometimes listed as **Bosniaks**.

A bitter civil war erupted in 1991 after Bosnia declared independence, and the Serb minority refused to join the new nation. The fighting between Serbs, Bosniaks, and Croats dragged on until 1995, when U.S. president Bill Clinton invited the warring leaders to sit down at a military base in Dayton, Ohio, and hammer out the **Dayton Peace Accords.** The agreement, however, did not work out a complete unification. So troops (first from NATO and later, the EU) remained to enforce the fragile peace.

Bosnia consists of the northern and central portions of the country. The central portion of the country is dominated by the forested Dinaric Alps. The hilly northern portion of the country is pastureland in the northeast and forests in the northwest. The top agricultural products are maize, wheat, and a variety of vegetables.

Herzegovina consists of the southern portion of the country. The Dinaric Alps continue in this portion of the country. The wartorn capital of the country, Sarajevo, lies almost between Bosnia and Herzegovina in the south. There are a number of mining industries in the Dinaric Alps, such as steel, iron ore, coal, lead, and zinc. Industries include furniture, refining, textiles, and transportation.

MONTENEGRO

The Serbs are the most dominant Slavic people in the Balkans. After the breakup of Yugoslavia in 1991, two of the six regions, Serbia and Montenegro, united and retained the name of Yugoslavia. In 2003, the country was divided into a union of two semi-independent states, and they took the name Serbia and Montenegro.

Much poorer than Slovenia and Croatia, Serbia and Montenegro followed an authoritarian path under the leadership of Slobodan Milosevic. He won popular support by calling for a "Greater Serbia," which would include all the bordering lands where Serbs live. He played a game with the Western powers, promising to stay out of the surrounding civil wars while secretly supplying the Serb minorities. While on trial at The Hague for war crimes, Milosevic died in 2006. Later that year, Montenegro voted to become independent.

Montenegro (MON tuh NEG roh), meaning "Black Mountain," is a coastal region that goes back to the time of the Roman Empire. In the seventh century, the Slavs settled there. By the thirteenth century, the area was under the control of the Serbian Empire. With its new independence, Montenegro has the opportunity to develop independently for the first time in centuries.

The Tara River is a major river in Montenegro.

The landscape of Montenegro is mostly forested mountains. There is some land suitable for pastureland along the coast. Sheep are a major product of the region. Metallurgy, engineering, and mining are three major industries.

ALBANIA

The mountainous country of Albania lies in the west facing the Adriatic Sea. The Dinaric Alps extend into northern Albania, where they are called the North Albanian Alps. The Pindus Mountains, which are not forested like the northern mountains, extend from southern Albania into Greece. Two major industries are forestry and mining. Like Dalmatia, Albania's west coast has warm, dry summers. Durrës is the country's major port. Off the coast in the south is the Strait of Otranto, the connection to the Adriatic Sea.

The Shkodër is one of the few well-watered valleys in mountainous Albania.

Albanians are not Slavs but speak a unique Indo-European language. Albanians are divided into two groups that speak different dialects: the Gegs in the north and the Tosks in the south. The long influence of the Ottoman Empire resulted in a population that is 70 percent Muslim, the only Muslim majority in any European nation.

Albania is unique in the history of the world because the Communist leader Enver Hoxha established what he claimed was the first truly athiestic country in the world. After the Communists were finally ousted in 1992, Albania opened its doors to the world. In the years that followed, missionaries of all types poured into the country. While Islam dominates the country, Eastern Orthodoxy has an estimated 20 percent minority, and Catholicism has an estimated 10 percent minority. Other groups, such as Protestantism, have gained footholds in the country's religious life.

The economy of Albania has struggled after the fall of communism. Steps have been implemented to strengthen the economy, but the infrastructure of the country is underdeveloped. Unlike the city dwellers crammed into the capital, Tiranë, most Albanians live on small farms, raising agricultural products such as livestock, wheat, and watermelons. Agriculture makes up more than half of the GDP.

SECTION QUIZ

1. Name the mountain range that runs along the Adriatic coast in the Balkans.

2. What advantages help to explain why Slovenia is the most prosperous country in Eastern Europe?

3. Compare and contrast the Croats and the Serbs.

4. What country has the only Muslim majority in any European nation?

- Should the international community redraw nation-state boundaries to form a "Greater Croatia" and a "Greater Serbia"? What would be the benefits? What would be the disadvantages? (Refer to the map on page 141.)

IV. THE EASTERN BALKANS

Much like the western Balkans, the eastern Balkans are dominated by mountains. Macedonia is almost completely covered by mountains. Two mountain ranges dominate Bulgaria. Romania has portions of the Carpathian Mountains. Despite the prevalence of mountains, the eastern Balkans also include plains that allow many agricultural products to be grown.

MACEDONIA

Macedonia is a small landlocked country in the middle of the Balkan Peninsula. In all, 80 percent of the country is mountainous. These mountains are forested, but limited mining and grazing are possible in some portions of the mountains. Other agricultural resources include cotton, wheat, and fruit, which grow in the valley of the Vardar River. The capital, Skopje, lies in the north on the Vardar as well. The official language is Macedonian, a Southern Slavic language. Minority languages are taught in certain areas of the country along with the official language.

The historic region of Macedonia was the home of Alexander the Great. After the decline of the Ottoman Empire, the Balkan countries fought for control of this region. In the Balkan Wars of 1912 and 1913, Greece, Serbia, and Bulgaria joined together to defeat the Turks, but then they fought among themselves. The northern part went to Yugoslavia and became one of the six republics of that country.

When Macedonia declared independence after the breakup of Yugoslavia, Greece refused to let the European Union formally recognize its independence. Greece feared a movement to reunite the old lands of "Greater Macedonia." From 1946 to 1949 Macedonian guerrillas fought a bloody war against Greece. When the UN first admitted the nation, it did not grant approval for the country's new name because Greece opposes it. Until the dispute is resolved, both the United States and the United Nations officially designate Macedonia as "The Former Yugoslav Republic of Macedonia."

Macedonia experienced internal fighting in 2001. An ethnic-Albanian group calling itself the National Liberation Army (NLA) attempted to overthrow the Macedonian government. A peace treaty was signed later in 2001 that ended the NLA, but it did not eliminate the tension between the ethnic Albanians and the ethnic Macedonians.

SERBIA

The agricultural heart of Serbia is the northern plains or Pannonian Plains. This fertile farmland is part of the Great Hungarian Plain. The agricultural products of this region are sugar beets, various grains, grapes, and sheep. The region of Vojvodina covers most of the Pannonian Plains in Serbia. Serbia received this province after the breakup of the Hungarian Empire.

Belgrade, the capital since 1402, lies near the edge of the Pannonian Plains where the Sava River joins the Danube. The centrally located city has been conquered and destroyed more than thirty times. With 1.5 million people, it is the second-largest city in the Balkans.

The rest of Serbia is mountainous. The Dinaric Alps cross into the southwest, and the **Balkan Mountains** rise in the southeast

The Little Giant

Sometimes, in the providence of God, a small, seemingly insignificant country can have an enormous effect on the history of the world. Such is the case with Macedonia. Paul and Barnabas, on their first missionary journey, traveled in the area we now call Turkey, winning converts and planting churches.

Paul and Silas, on Paul's second missionary journey, intended to repeat that practice, but God intervened. Acts 16:9 records, *"And a vision appeared to Paul in the night; there stood a man of Macedonia, and prayed him, saying, Come over into Macedonia, and help us."* Responding to this "Macedonian Call," Paul and his party crossed the Aegean Sea and founded the first churches in Europe—Philippi, Thessalonica, and Berea, all in Macedonia. (Macedonia was larger in those days than it is today.) From there Christianity exploded into Athens, Corinth, Rome, and finally all of Europe. For almost eighteen centuries, Christianity heavily influenced the people of Europe. It affected their laws, architecture, educational institutions, customs, mores, and economies.

Today Christianity in Europe is in serious decline. However, Christianity is growing and thriving in Africa, South America, Central America, and many parts of Asia—places traditionally considered by European and American Christians as the unreached mission fields of the world. Perhaps the people of God need to hear the Macedonian Call once more and return to Europe with the gospel.

before crossing into Bulgaria. Between the Dinaric Alps and the Balkan Mountains lies a complex maze of minor mountain ranges. The central ranges contain some of the largest lead deposits in Europe. Forests cover the areas farthest south. Vineyards and fields of grain also make up part of the landscape of southern Serbia.

Serbia has a large province in the south, called Kosovo, next to the border of Albania. Almost 90 percent of the people are Albanians. Like Vojvodina, this ethnic region enjoyed self-rule under the Communists, but Serbia removed its special rights. Kosovo declared independence in 1992, but the rest of the world did not recognize it (except for Albania).

BULGARIA

The Bulgars probably rode into the present region of Bulgaria in the seventh century. They then settled on the western shore of the Black Sea, mixing with the Slavs, who had arrived from Poland a

The Danube River flows through Bulgaria, emptying into the Black Sea and offering commercial access to the Mediterranean Sea.

little earlier. Bulgars account for 84 percent of the people, and Turks account for another 9 percent. Eighty-three percent of Bulgarians are Bulgarian Orthodox, a branch of Eastern Orthodoxy.

Northern Bulgaria is a fertile valley along the Danube River. The river forms most of Bulgaria's northern border, but it winds up into Romania just before it enters the Black Sea. Ruse is Bulgaria's major port on the Danube. Bulgaria's main port on the Black Sea, Varna, also lies in this northern portion of the country. Farm products from the valley include barley, millet, livestock, wheat, and grapes.

Mountain ranges rise south of the plain. In central Bulgaria, the Balkan Mountains dominate the landscape, cutting across the country to the Black Sea. Sofia, the capital, lies in this range on a mountain tributary that flows into the Danube River. In the southwest, the **Rhodope** (ROD uh pee) **Mountains** dominate the countryside. These mountains reach 9,596 feet at **Mount Musala**, the highest peak in the Balkans. Between the Balkan and Rhodope Mountains in the east lies a large region of cropland. Several cities lie in this river valley.

Along with agricultural products, Bulgaria's main industries are energy and machinery. Bulgaria joined NATO in 2004 and in 2007 joined the EU.

ROMANIA

Romania is a large country at the crossroads of Eastern Europe. It shares mountain features with nations in the Carpathian region, a long border on the Danube River, and cities near the Black Sea. Although it does not share any of the Dinaric Alps or a border with Greece, Romania is still on the Balkan Peninsula. Unlike the Catholic nations of the Carpathians, its people are Eastern Orthodox.

Romania means "land of the Romans." It was the last province captured by the Roman Empire. Modern Romanians are descended from a mixture of Roman soldiers and the native peoples. Their language is the only one in Eastern Europe that developed from Latin.

Romania gained independence from communism in 1989. However, the effects of the Communists' poor stewardship continue to hinder development, and the economy has struggled. Romania joined NATO in 2004 and joined the EU in 2007. The country's efforts to join the EU have brought increased efforts to strengthen the economy. The chief agricultural products are maize, wheat, potatoes, melons, and plums. Some major industries include textiles, timber, and mining.

Transylvania

Nearly half of Romania is a section of the Carpathian Mountain system called **Transylvania**. The range extends from Slovakia into northern Romania and then curves west across the center of the country, where it is known as the **Transylvanian Alps**.

The heart of Transylvania is a hilly plateau in the west encircled by the Carpathian ranges. Hungary ruled the principality of Transylvania for much of its history; consequently, Hungarians are Romania's largest minority. Romania received Transylvania after World War I. The forested hills and gloomy castles of this region have long intrigued Western Europeans, who view Transylvania as a place of mystery and danger.

Wallachia

The Danube flows east from the Great Hungarian Plain through a break in the Carpathian Mountains called the **Iron Gate**. Steep rock walls, 530 feet apart, guard both sides of this gorge. The Danube then flows east through a broad fertile plain, shared by Romania and Bulgaria.

The populous plain below the Iron Gate is called **Wallachia** (wuh LAY kee uh). Farms produce flax, wheat, and livestock. Romania's capital, Bucharest, is located on a tributary of the Danube. It is the fifth-largest city in Eastern Europe.

In the east, the slow-moving Danube loops northward along the coast and becomes a broad swamp land before entering the Black Sea. During Communist oppression, workers were forced to build a huge canal that bypassed the swampy loop and connected the Danube directly with the seaport of Constanța. Over one hundred thousand men died constructing the Canal of Death (Canalul Morti).

Moldavia

In the east lies the Moldavian Plain. If you look at the map on page 141, you will see the Moldavian Plain and its many valleys. The plain continues east into the country of Moldova, which Romania owned until the Soviets snatched it away in World War II.

Section Quiz

1. Name the three main mountain ranges of the eastern Balkans.
2. How does the United Nations refer to Macedonia?
3. What is the highest peak of the Balkans?
4. How is Romania unique among the Eastern Balkans?
5. What are the three main regions of Romania?
* Why are two landlocked nations—the Czech Republic and Hungary—so much richer than Romania, which has a Black Sea port?

Count Dracula

Transylvania is famous for vampires, legendary spirits of the dead which leave their coffins at night and suck the blood of sleeping victims, who in turn become vampires. A garlic necklace or the sign of the cross supposedly wards off vampires, but killing one requires driving a stake through its heart. Transylvania is famous because of the most famous vampire of all, Count Dracula.

But the story is all wrong. Dracula was not a count, and he did not live in Transylvania. Vlad Tepes, a prince of Wallachia in the fifteenth century, became a hero among the local Romanians because he defied the Turks. As a reward for his bravery, Tepes was knighted into the order of Dracul. When the Turks invaded in 1462, he attacked them at night and, according to the popular accounts, impaled some twenty thousand captive Turks in a massive field of stakes.

The modern story comes from the pen of British author Bram Stoker, who never even visited Transylvania. Stoker read the story of Vlad the Impaler in a book and took a little poetic license. Even Vlad's supporters would admit that he was a cruel ruler, impaling criminals to instill fear among his own people. But Stoker's famous novel *Dracula*, published in 1897, changed Vlad's reputation forever.

Movies about vampires have created a tourism boom for Romania. But Dracula's true castle lies in ruins at Aref, Wallachia. So the government built a castle farther north at Borgo Pass, where Stoker described it, in the Carpathian Mountains of Transylvania.

Commonwealth of Independent States

V. THE EASTERN PLAINS

A huge plain extends east from the Carpathian Mountains and connects with the Northern European Plain. Together, these plains form the **Great European Plain**, which continues over one thousand miles east into Russia.

Three countries lie on the eastern plains: Moldova, Ukraine, and Belarus. Like the three Baltic States, these countries were once among the fifteen republics, or soviets, in the Soviet Union. Most of the people who settled the eastern plains are Eastern Slavs, including Ukrainians, Belarusians, and Russians.

MOLDOVA

Moldova is a hilly, landlocked country between Romania and Ukraine. Moldova is the eastern part of Romania's historic principality of Moldavia. Two-thirds of the people speak Moldovan, a language related to Romanian. It is the most densely populated country in Eastern Europe. The Soviets took control of the region during World War II, but the country gained independence along with the other Soviet republics. A minority wants to rejoin Romania.

A third of the population consists of Slavs, both Ukrainians and Russians, who live on a sliver of land east of the Dniester (NEE stuhr)

The Dniester River flows through Moldova.

River. This valuable **Transnistria** region, which is heavy in industry, once belonged to Ukraine. In 1990 the Slavs declared themselves a semi-independent republic. Fighting erupted in 1992, and Russia sent its army to restore peace. Russia's failure to remove its troops has resulted in increased tensions between the two countries.

Despite the antagonism that brought about the end of communism in 1991, Moldova became the first part of the former Soviet Union to elect a Communist as its president in 2001. Because of economic pressures, though, the new president has looked increasingly towards Western Europe.

The land of Moldova is very fertile, resulting in a predominantly agricultural economy. The major agricultural products are maize, sugar beets, wheat, and grapes. Grapes are used to produce the chief export, wine. The industries of Moldova focus mainly on agricultural-related equipment, but there are some basic manufacturing industries as well. The largest hindrance to Moldova's economy is a lack of natural resources. While Moldova produces some electricity, the country imports much of its energy resources. Consequently, parts of the country do not always have enough energy to heat their homes.

UKRAINE

After Russia, Ukraine is the most important industrial and agricultural center in the CIS. Indeed, it is the largest nation completely on the continent of Europe. After its independence in 1991, the transition to a democratic form of government proceeded slowly. The elections of 2004 and their aftermath were watched by the world. During the campaign, one candidate was poisoned; and when the election day itself was tainted with charges of fraud, large groups of Ukranians protested the results. Another election was held, and this time the opponent won in a much fairer election. This has been called the "**Orange Revolution**." Since that time, Ukraine has begun to shift its focus away from Russia and to Western Europe and the EU.

Except for two small strips of mountains, the entire country lies in the eastern plain. Low plateaus cross the center but give way to lowlands in the north and south.

NORTHERN LOWLANDS

Ukraine's northern lowlands include swamps and marshes along the border with Belarus. These waters flow into the **Dnieper** (NEE puhr) **River**, the third-longest river in Europe, which continues south through the heart of Ukraine. **Kyiv** (KEE ev), the most populous city in all of Eastern Europe, lies at the junction between the Dnieper and Desna rivers. It is the cultural center and capital of Ukraine.

CENTRAL UPLANDS

The Central Uplands cut across central Ukraine. With adequate rainfall and rich soils, these vast uplands produce many agricultural products. Ukraine ranks among the top ten producers in the world for over two dozen agricultural products. Among these are blueberries, potatoes, barley, cherries, honey, apricots, rye, cabbage, wheat, oats, and sunflower seeds.

East of the Dnieper River lies the valuable **Donets** (duh NETS) **Basin**, or Donbas. On a tributary of the Donets River is Kharkov,

Commonwealth of Independent States

After the breakup of the Soviet Union, the former republics created the **Commonwealth of Independent States (CIS)** on December 21, 1991. All of the republics eventually joined, except the Baltic States. The original emphasis of the agreement was an alliance of independent states for the purpose of promoting economic ties between them. Since the group's inception, Russia has attempted to tighten its control over the CIS republics, which it calls the "**near abroad**." Russian leaders became alarmed, though, at the willingness of some CIS members both to distance themselves from Russia and to embrace trading partners in the West. While Russia remains a major trading partner with most members, the economies of CIS members are slowly expanding beyond a reliance on Russia.

Viktor Yushchenko (far right) and Yuliya Tymoshenko (far left) led the Orange Revolution. During the presidential campaign leading up to the revolution, Yushchenko was severely poisoned, permanently disfiguring his face.

The Crimean Peninsula from space

Ukraine's third-largest city. Three other cities—Odessa, Dnipropetrovsk and Donetsk—have over one million people each. Donetsk, Ukraine's second-largest city, is a major coal-mining center, and iron ore comes from the adjoining Krivoi Rog. Ukraine ranks eleventh in the world as a producer of coal, sixth in iron ore, and third in manganese. The Communists, who built many of the region's industries, also created a pollution disaster that will take years to clean up.

SOUTHERN COASTS

Almost all of Ukraine's southern coast is a low plain. Because of the arid climate, farms must divert water from the Dnieper River. Odessa, Ukraine's largest port, lies on the coast of the Black Sea.

The most valuable southern region is the **Crimean** (KRY MEE uhn) **Peninsula**, which juts out into the Black Sea. Crimea is barely attached to Europe by a narrow 2.5-mile-wide isthmus. A long series of conquerors have held the peninsula. Russia took Crimea from the Turks in the late eighteenth century and converted it into the "jewel in the crown" of the Russian Empire.

What makes Crimea unique is the Crimean Mountains, which rise from the sea along the southern tip of the peninsula.

CHERNOBYL: WINDS OF DEATH

The rusted jungle gym sits quietly in a tangle of weeds. Beyond is the schoolhouse, a shell of concrete and broken glass. The abandoned apartment buildings and empty streets are silent. Welcome to Pripyat, Ukraine, a once thriving city of about forty-five thousand. Two miles away is V. I. Lenin Atomic Electric Generating Station in **Chernobyl** (chur NOH bul).

The nuclear accident at Chernobyl is one of the worst examples of human stewardship in modern history. The disaster struck early Saturday morning on April 26, 1986. Technicians were testing Reactor Number 4's efficiency at low power and had turned off the automatic safety precautions. After the emergency shutdown failed, it took only four seconds for the unstable uranium to explode, blowing off the top of the reactor and spewing radiation into the atmosphere. The fallout covered portions of Ukraine, Russia, and Belarus but affected Belarus the most. Winds carried radiation all over Europe, affecting everything from vegetables in France to reindeer in Lapland.

Back in Pripyat, folks knew something was very wrong—burning skin, irritated throats, dead phone lines. Soviet officials foolishly imagined they could keep a lid on news of the catastrophe. Consequently, evacuation efforts were terribly slow. There was another kind of fallout from Chernobyl as well. Chernobyl awakened nationalism among the once-loyal Ukrainians, who condemned the coverup and gross incompetence of their Soviet leaders. They eventually joined the other republics in rejecting the Soviet government.

Thirty-one people died the day of the meltdown, mostly firefighters. But at least five thousand more victims died in the years that followed, and another thirty thousand were disabled due to radiation poisoning. Most of these were troops and workers responsible for evacuation and cleanup.

Today Reactor Number 4 is entombed in concrete; and a forty-mile stretch of barbed wire, encircling the Zone of Estrangement, attempts to contain the catastrophe. The debate continues about how much fuel was released in the accident. A new cover-

ing for the reactor is also being planned. Yet with contaminated water, soil, and forests, areas of Belarus, Ukraine, and Russia face a hard future. Among the greatest tragedies of Chernobyl are children suffering from thyroid cancer, the result of exposure to radioactive iodine.

Soviet authorities constructed a structure around the remains of Reactor Number 4 to contain the radiation.

The mountains block the cold northern air and permit a pleasant mediterranean climate on the southern shore. Wealthy Russians flock to this coast, known as the "Russian Riviera." The czars even had a palace at Yalta, the best seaside resort in Crimea. Russia's main naval base in the Black Sea is Sevastopol, just west of Yalta.

The Crimea has been a sore spot between Russia and Ukraine. As a gesture of friendship, the Soviet Union gave Crimea to the Ukrainian soviet in 1954, and it passed to the independent country in 1991. But most of the natives are Russians, who would like to rejoin Russia. Both Russia and Ukraine harbor their fleets at the strategic port at Sevastopol.

BELARUS

Belarus, or "White Russia," has old ties with Russia, and those ties have continued since Belarusian independence. Alexander Lukashenko, who became president in 1994, fashioned an increasingly authoritarian government. Throughout his term in office, Belarus continued to be closely linked to Russia economically and politically. Minsk, the capital and the largest city, is the headquarters of the CIS.

Although they are related to Russians, Belarusians have their own distinctive culture and language. For many centuries they belonged to the Lithuanian Empire and its successor, the Polish-Lithuanian Empire. During the partition of Poland in the eighteenth century, Belarus fell into Russian hands. The Russian czars and later the Soviets tried to replace Belarusian with the Russian language. Today, most people, especially in the cities, speak Russian.

Most farms and cities are in the center of the country on the Northern European Plain. There are some areas of farmland in the south, but much of that area was harmed by the fallout from Chernobyl. Belarus ranks fourth in the world for the production of rye, fifth for flax, and eighth for potatoes. The far north has large forests, consisting of mixed deciduous and coniferous trees. The Belovezha Forest, a large natural preserve on the western border, is noted for the only surviving herd of wisent, or European bison.

Few people live south in the **Pinsk** (or Pripet) **Marshes**. This is the largest marshland in Europe, extending about three hundred miles on the drainage basin of the Pripyat (or Pripet) River, a tributary of the Dnieper River. The swamps and marshes yield potash for fertilizers; Belarus is second only to Canada in potash production. With environmental issues, a weak economy, and an increasingly authoritarian government, Belarus has many obstacles in its quest to become a strong, independent nation.

SECTION QUIZ

1. To what country does Moldova have the closest cultural ties?
2. What is the main river of Ukraine?
3. Why is central Ukraine so valuable to the country?
4. What is the largest marshland in Europe, and in what country is it located?
- What disputed region lies in Ukraine? Why has a final solution been so difficult to reach?

Through Christian Eyes

Christians believe that God has called them to find better, more efficient ways to manage the earth. For many years, nuclear power was considered one of the best ways to produce energy more efficiently. After the Chernobyl accident, however, many people feared that nuclear power was too dangerous and should not be pursued. Do you think nuclear power is a legitimate way to exercise good and wise dominion over God's earth?

Rye

The countries of the Great European Plain produce over 90 percent of the world's **rye**. All five top rye producers lie on the plain: Russia, Poland, Germany, Belarus, and Ukraine. Rye, a grain similar to wheat, grows well in cool climates. Two thousand years ago, Europeans learned how to grind rye into flour for bread. Rye bread is dark brown and much heavier than the wheat bread that is popular in the West. Eastern Europeans still eat a great deal of rye bread, while most rye grown in America is used to feed livestock.

CHAPTER REVIEW

Can You:
Define These Terms?

shatter belt	karst
Soviet bloc	Bosniaks
Cyrillic	"near abroad"
mass privatization	rye
Balkanization	

Locate These Places?

Vistula River	Rhodope Mountains
Oder River	
Carpathian Mountains	Mount Musala
	Transylvanian Alps
Tatra Mountains	Iron Gate
Little Alföld	Great European Plain
Great Hungarian Plain	
	Dnieper River
Balkan Peninsula	Donets Basin
Dinaric Alps	Crimean Peninsula
Balkan Mountains	Pinsk Marshes

Explain the Significance?

Baltic States	Dalmatia
Warsaw	Dayton Peace Accords
Lech Walesa	
Galicia	Transylvania
Kraków	Wallachia
Auschwitz	Transnistria
Silesia	Commonwealth of Independent States (CIS)
Hill of Crosses	
Velvet Revolution	
Velvet Divorce	"Orange Revolution"
Prague	
Budapest	Kyiv
Balkans	Chernobyl
Gypsies	Minsk

HOW MUCH DO YOU REMEMBER?

1. What two Christian religions are most common in Eastern Europe? Which of the two is associated with Western Europe?

2. Contrast the Baltic States and the Balkans.

3. List the major mountain ranges in the Balkans.

4. Give the country or countries related to the following terms.
   a. Dayton Peace Accords
   b. "Orange Revolution"
   c. Solidarity
   d. Transylvania
   e. Chernobyl
   f. Velvet Divorce
   g. Dalmatia
   h. Mount Musala
   i. Prague
   j. Hill of Crosses

5. Which Eastern European countries fit each description?
   a. coast on the Baltic Sea
   b. coast on the Adriatic Sea
   c. coast on the Black Sea
   d. landlocked

6. List the Eastern European countries that are connected with the Great European Plain.

WHAT DO YOU THINK?

1. How do the Balkans exhibit Balkanization?

2. How have the many mountains of the Balkans contributed to Balkanization?

3. Why does Russia have an interest in the countries of the Eastern Plains?

The Spasskaya (Savior's) Tower is the main gate to the Kremlin in Moscow.

RUSSIA

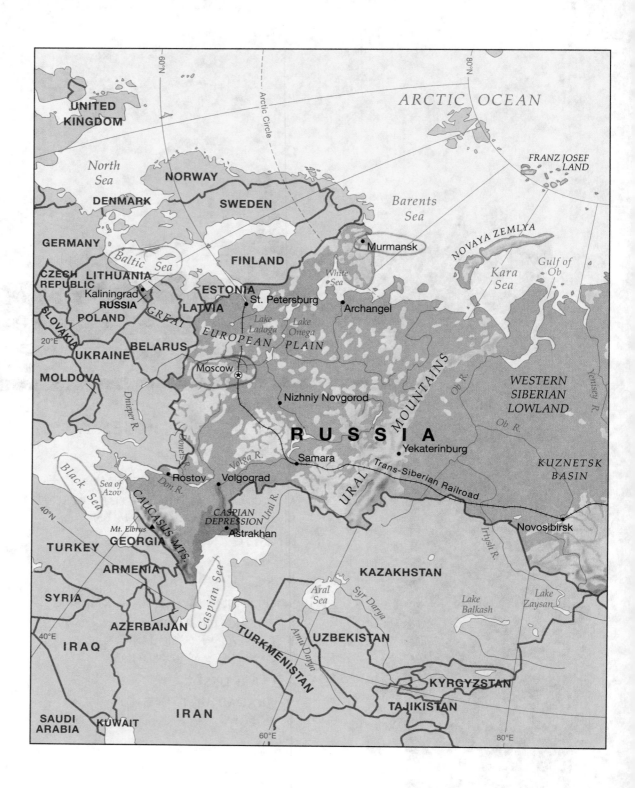

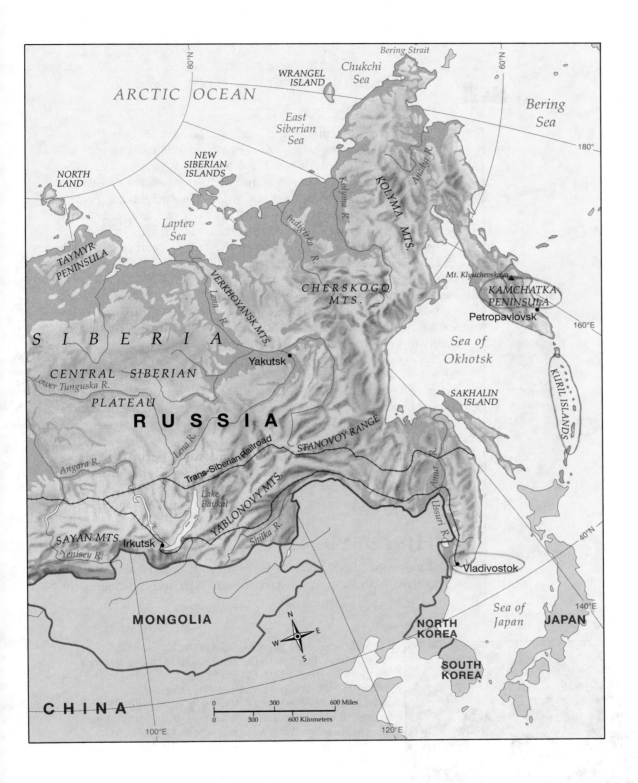

ARCTIC OCEAN

Bering Strait

WRANGEL
ISLAND

*Chukchi
Sea*

*East
Siberian
Sea*

*Bering
Sea*

NORTH
LAND

NEW
SIBERIAN
ISLANDS

*Laptev
Sea*

KOLYMA MTS.

Anadyr R.

180°

TAYMYR
PENINSULA

VERKHOYANSK MTS.

Lena R.

Indigirka R.

Kolyma R.

CHERSKOGO
MTS.

Mt. Klyuchevskaya

KAMCHATKA
PENINSULA

160°E

Petropavlovsk

S I B E R I A

Yakutsk

*Sea of
Okhotsk*

CENTRAL   SIBERIAN

Lower Tunguska R.

PLATEAU

SAKHALIN
ISLAND

KURIL ISLANDS

R U S S I A

Lena R.

STANOVOY RANGE

Angara R.

Trans-Siberian Railroad

Amur R.

*Lake
Baykal*

YABLONOVY MTS.

40°N

SAYAN MTS.

Ussuri R.

Irkutsk

Yenisey R.

Shilka R.

Vladivostok

MONGOLIA

*Sea of
Japan*

JAPAN

N

W   E

S

NORTH
KOREA

140°E

SOUTH
KOREA

CHINA

0   300   600 Miles

0   300   600 Kilometers

100°E

120°E

Russia Fast Facts						
Flag	Capital	Area (sq. mi.)	Pop. (M)	Pop. Density (per sq. mi.)	Per Capita GDP ($US)	Life Span
	Moscow	6,592,772	143.42	21.8	$9,800	67.1

With over one-tenth of the world's land area, Russia is easily the largest country on earth. From east to west, Russia is approximately 4,800 miles across. From north to south, Russia is about 1,850 miles. Russia borders fourteen countries; the only other country to join Russia in this achievement is China. These neighboring countries range from very stable to potentially explosive. Like the shatter belt in Eastern Europe, Russia is "lost" in a vast expanse of lowlands without clear natural borders, except the frigid ocean in the north and the Caucasus Mountains in the southwest.

With great size has come great opportunity. Russia has a great wealth of natural resources. Though many of these resources are found in inhospitable climates, Russia has sought to utilize these resources. Russia has several handicaps, however, that also affect its ability to use these resources properly.

Its greatest handicap is arguably its Soviet past. Russia was the largest part of the Union of Soviet Socialist Republics for most of the twentieth century. The Soviets misused many of Russia's physical and human resources. As a result, Russia has faced the dual tasks of cleaning up the mismanagement of the Soviets and managing the land well.

Despite its size, Russia has only a handful of ports that are ice-free for the whole year. This lack of warm-water ports has influenced Russian foreign policy historically. The desire for a warm-water port on the Mediterranean Sea has led Russia into many European wars.

I. HISTORY AND GOVERNMENT

Russia looks both east and west. Its culture has borrowed elements from both—the authoritarianism of Asia and the longing for

Russian Orthodoxy

Trinity Lavra of St. Sergius, located in Sergiyev Posad, has been called "the most important Russian monastery and the spiritual centre of the Russian Orthodox Church".

The dominant religion in Russia is the Russian Orthodox Church. Russian Orthodoxy is a branch of Eastern Orthodoxy (see Chapter 5). The head of the church is the patriarch of Moscow. After Peter the Great, Russian Orthodoxy enjoyed a place of special privilege as a branch of the Russian government, but this privilege brought along with it a large degree of government control. Under the Soviets, Russian Orthodoxy was variously honored and persecuted, yet it remained firmly under Soviet control. Today, Russian Orthodoxy is reasserting its role as the religion of the Russian people. Now, though, it must compete with various other religious groups. Still, Russian Orthodoxy has regained some of its former privileged status. As it has grown in influence and power, it has become increasingly aggressive against other churches.

individual rights in Europe. The Great European Plain, which has played such a major role in European history, extends into Russia and has played a decisive role there as well. The plain covers only one-fifth of Russia, but over four-fifths of the population lives there.

Like the countries of Eastern Europe, Russia has suffered under the heel of many Asian tribes, including Scythians, Huns, and Slavs. Modern Russians are descendants of the Slavs and speak a Slavic language. Russia encompasses over seventy different nationalities, but 80 percent of the people are ethnic Russians.

FROM THE CZARS TO THE PRESENT

CZARIST RUSSIA

A total of twenty-four **czars** (also spelled *tsars*) ruled Russia from 1547 to 1917. The czars and czarinas (female rulers) were **autocrats**; they had no established limits on their authority and power. During World War I under the last czar, Nicholas II, Russia experienced humiliating defeats. In the resulting confusion, **Vladimir Ilich Lenin** led the Russian Revolution in 1917 and executed the last czar the following year.

SOVIET RULE

In 1922, Lenin created the **Union of Soviet Socialist Republics (USSR)**. This union gave limited power to several "republics." Communists claimed Russia was no longer an empire but a land of equals. Joseph Stalin, Lenin's brutal successor, extended the empire deeper into Europe than any czar could have dreamed possible. After a secret agreement with Adolf Hitler, Stalin seized Moldova, Lithuania, Latvia, and Estonia in 1940, bringing the total number of Soviet republics to fifteen. After the defeat of Hitler during World War II, Stalin extended the "Iron Curtain," the area under Soviet control, to lands as far west as Germany.

After World War II, the USSR (also known as the Soviet Union) was in competition with the Western Allies. Soon the competition involved primarily the USSR and the United States. As the USSR sought to expand Communist influence throughout the world, the United States sought to limit any influence that the Soviet Union might have. Both powers built up weapon arsenals, including nuclear weapons, at an alarming rate. Both the United States and the USSR feared that the other power would attack. This period was known as the **Cold War**.

SOVIET COLLAPSE

By the 1980s the Soviet economy lagged far behind the West. Soviet premier Mikhail Gorbachev instituted the reforms *perestroika*, or "restructuring," and *glasnost*, or "openness." *Perestroika* brought more free-market policies and some private ownership of property. *Glasnost* opened the Soviet Union to the West. Instead of stabilizing the Soviet Union, these reforms only hastened its demise. The common people had tasted freedom, and they wanted more.

The whole system collapsed in 1991, as the leaders of the various republics declared independence. Boris Yeltsin, the president of the largest republic—Russia—joined the others. By December 25, Gorbachev was a ruler without a country, and he quietly resigned. In the place of the Soviet Union, Yeltsin formed the **Commonwealth**

Communist Manifesto

In the *Communist Manifesto* (1848) Karl Marx attacked the injustices of capitalism and called on the workers of the world to revolt. The workers, or proletariat, would then usher in a perfect society—all people would share their wealth in peace, brotherhood, and equality. Marx held that religion was "the opiate [drug] of the masses," designed by capitalists to enslave the workers.

Lenin, shown here addressing a crowd, led the Russian Revolution in 1917, but the Communists did not have firm control until 1920.

Even after the fall of communism, people waited in long lines to see Lenin's tomb in Red Square, Moscow.

of Independent States (CIS) to retain the economic ties among the former Soviet states.

Yeltsin's tenure was marked by political and economic turmoil, and those conditions (along with declining health) led to his resignation in 1999. His successor, Vladimir Putin, increased the power of the president and moved Russia toward a more centralized government. *second president*

A NATION IN TRANSITION

The Soviets were poor stewards of the rich resources that Russia contained. Instead of managing the land, they abused the land for their own immediate desires. This misuse has left the country in ruins, with deteriorating buildings, antiquated machinery, and polluted lakes and rivers. Even in Russia, the wealthiest of the CIS states, living conditions are poor. Some people live in areas that have been contaminated by nuclear waste from the Soviet era. Air pollution in industrial cities is also a major problem. The quality of health care in government facilities is very low.

A major concern among Russians is the strength of organized crime. Russia has the fifth highest murder rate in the world; it is more than four times the rate of the United States. The major arm of Russian organized crime is generally referred to as the "Russian Mafia." The government has increasingly given the police more power to combat organized crime. The Federal Security Service (FSB), the secret police, has been compared to its Soviet predecessor, the KGB. Putin reinforced the FSB by increasing their jurisdiction and powers.

FEDERATION GOVERNMENT

Russia is experiencing problems of **devolution**, a passing down or "de-evolution" of power. Under the Soviet Union, Moscow regulated everything. Even the train schedules in Siberia used Moscow time. With the breakup, Moscow has shifted some responsibilities to local governments. This transition, though necessary, threatens to tear Russia apart because some local areas enjoy their new powers and want more—even independence.

POLITICAL DIVISIONS

Whereas the United States has states as its main political divisions, Russia has many different names for these divisions. An **oblast** is a large region or administrative district similar to a state or province. Russia has forty-nine oblasts and one autonomous oblast. There are also ten large, sparsely populated areas, mostly in the north, that are called **okrugs** (areas). Moscow and St. Petersburg stand alone as Russia's two federal cities. Russia also has six **krais**, or territories, governed by Moscow.

Over thirty ethnic minorities have their own districts and have signed treaties with the government that give them a measure of self-rule. But the twenty-one **autonomous republics** (*autonomous* means "self-ruling") have the most population, power, and status. Since the autonomous republics were formed around ethnic groups within Russia, they are also called ethnic republics, internal republics, or Russian republics. These terms contrast them with the republics of the USSR, which were external republics or Soviet republics.

The processing facilities that the Communists built all across Russia, such as this timber plant on the Siberian frontier, were a major source of pollution.

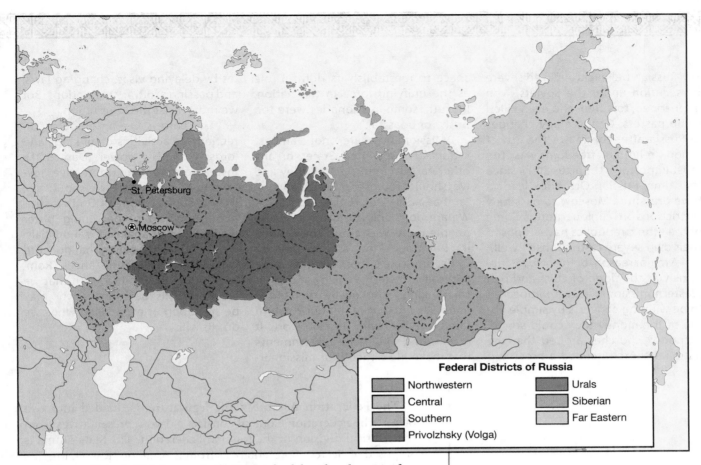

Federal Districts of Russia

- Northwestern
- Central
- Southern
- Privolzhsky (Volga)
- Urals
- Siberian
- Far Eastern

The political divisions are distinguished by the degree of autonomy that they enjoy. The autonomous republics have the most freedom, followed by the oblasts, krais, okrugs, and federal cities. The administration of these different divisions was cumbersome. To deal with this difficulty, Putin grouped the various political divisions into seven **federal districts** based on geography. These federal districts allow Moscow to govern Russia more effectively.

BRANCHES OF GOVERNMENT

The United States has had various levels of government throughout its history—each with its own clearly defined responsibilities and taxing powers. In contrast, the Russian government has generally been centralized throughout its history. The same leaders passed the laws, interpreted the laws, and enforced the laws. In 1993 the people voted for a new constitution, which separated powers among three branches of government. The new country is called the Russian Federation. The Communists still retain a substantial part of the vote, but other groups also have a large voice in the Russian Federation.

Most of the power resides in the executive branch. The executive branch is led by a president, but there is no vice president. Instead, the president chooses a premier with the consent of the State Duma. The government is run by the premier and cabinet. In the event that the president dies, the premier takes charge until the next election, which must be held within three months.

In 1996, each oblast began electing its own governor. In 2005, Putin gained the authority to appoint the governors in lieu of elections. This step was taken in response to terrorist attacks. This move by Russia's executive branch greatly increased its power.

The State Duma is the Russian Federation's lower house.

MISSIONS—AMBASSADORS FOR CHRIST

Russian believers suffered severe persecution under the Soviets, who imprisoned, tortured, and even killed some pastors. Of the many changes in Russia after the fall of the Soviet Union, religious freedom was the most important. Unfortunately, since that time, Russian Orthodox leaders have pressured Moscow to pass new restrictions on religious groups. Some of the ethnic republics have imposed their own severe restrictions as well.

A major reason for the new restrictions was the flood of cults and rich Western missionaries, who appeared to be winning converts by simple virtue of the money they could spend. Orthodox churches argued that the national church needed a breathing space to reestablish its rightful role as the unifying force in the nation. In truth, some missionaries were too pushy or boastful.

Missionaries are not ambassadors of the United States or any other earthly country. Both they and we should represent Christ and be "ambassadors" for Him (2 Cor. 5:20). We are not ministering to make the people more Western in their thinking but are seeking to win people for Christ and cause them to think more biblically. Western thinking and biblical thinking do not always go hand in hand. We must never let our Western ideas interfere with mission work. It is tempting to criticize governments that make life difficult for missionaries by delaying visas, changing laws, and passing arbitrary restrictions. But we must resist the temptation.

The Lord is like an emperor, directing the activities of all kings and lords under His power (Dan. 5:21). Instead of seeing an oppressive government as an enemy, we should see it as just another one of God's instruments. Instead of becoming bitter against God or against local officials, we can rejoice, knowing that our Lord is in control of circumstances (Rom. 8:28). All of us need to learn that we are merely His messengers, who may be spit upon or even killed while we do His will.

The **Federation Assembly**, the legislature, is divided into two houses. The Federation Council consists of two representatives from each political division in the Russian Federation. The State Duma is composed of elected representatives from throughout Russia. Russia's judicial branch of government has a **Supreme Court** that functions much like the Supreme Court of the United States. It also has a Constitutional Court that examines the constitutionality of Russia's laws.

SECTION QUIZ

1. Why has Russia sought a warm-water port throughout its history?
2. What religion is most common among ethnic Russians?
3. What was the title of those who ruled Russia for over 350 years before the Russian Revolution?
4. What kind of government did Lenin initiate?
5. What was Putin's solution about how to best administrate the various political divisions throughout Russia?

II. NORTHERN EUROPEAN RUSSIA
MOSCOW

With about fourteen million people, **Moscow** is the largest city in all of Europe. Its architecture, landmarks, galleries, and theaters display the great achievements of Russian culture.

Moscow is colder than most capitals of Europe. Its climate is determined by its location in the interior of the continent, far from the moderating influence of the oceans. During the summers, temperatures average in the sixties. Winters are harsh and snowy, with an average January temperature of less than 20°F. In most summers,

St. Basil's Cathedral is probably the most colorful landmark of Moscow.

THE KREMLIN

The Kremlin is a massive fortress at the heart of Moscow. Many **kremlins**, walled enclosures, are throughout Russia, but the one in Moscow has special significance. Its red brick walls enclose sixty-five acres. Surrounded by a moat, the Muscovite Kremlin became the greatest citadel in Europe.

The highest building in the Kremlin, the onion-domed Bell Tower of Ivan the Great, towers over 260 feet. Ivan recruited Italian architects from the West to build the Palace of Facets, completed in 1491. Both the Terem Palace and the Palace of the Patriarch were built in the seventeenth century. Workers finished the Grand Kremlin Palace in 1849 and the Armoury Palace in 1851. After the Russian Revolution, the Palace of Congresses was built in 1961.

Besides palaces, the architects also built cathedrals. Ivan the Great built the Cathedral of the Assumption, where the czars were crowned. The carved walnut throne of Ivan the Terrible, made in 1551, can still be viewed in the cathedral. Ivan the Great also built the Cathedral

of the Annunciation, whose domes are made of gold, and the Cathedral of St. Michael the Archangel, where some of the czars are buried. All three cathedrals display valuable frescoes and icons. These Russian Orthodox cathedrals formed the heart of the Kremlin, the place of royal weddings, coronations, and burials.

Outside the Kremlin is a large open area called Red Square. Once a marketplace, it now hosts parades and public entertainment. Lenin's tomb stands outside the Kremlin wall in Red Square. Also on the square is St. Basil's Cathedral, now a museum, with its ten colorful, onion-shaped domes. Ivan the Terrible built this Russian Orthodox church and then blinded the architect so that he could never design a more beautiful building. Ivan was infamous for his brutality, killing his own son in a fit of rage.

adequate rainfall reaches this far inland, but rains are unpredictable and crops often fail. Deciduous forests lie south of Moscow, with aspen, oak, and linden; but much of this has been cleared for agriculture, settlement, and industry. Evergreen trees grow in increasing numbers as you travel north of Moscow.

Moscow lies in the center of Moscow oblast. Moscow and seventeen other oblasts compose the **Central Federal District** of over thirty-seven million people, over one-quarter of Russia's population.

The Central Federal District is Russia's most important industrial area and is referred to as Central Russia. Central Russia developed around the headwaters of three important river systems: the Dnieper, Don, and Volga. These allowed easy access to trade, both north and south.

NORTHWEST RUSSIA

The northwest includes all of Russia's European holdings north of Greater Moscow. The climate permits dairy farms. The main crop is flax, which is raised both for flaxseed oil and fiber.

ST. PETERSBURG

Russia's second-largest city is **St. Petersburg**, with a population of over five million. Peter the Great hired Italian architects to design the city. The ornate buildings and waterways of St. Petersburg closely resemble those of Venice. St. Petersburg has been a major center for shipbuilding since 1704, and this industry remains an important part of Russia's economy today.

St. Petersburg displays the unusual phenomenon of "white nights." No other city of over one million people is as far north as St. Petersburg (60° N). At such a high latitude, it has virtually no sunsets from the middle of June to early July. During those days, for about five hours each day, the city has a whitish twilight instead of a sunset. In contrast, the winter nights are long and dark.

VOLGA-BALTIC WATERWAY

In spite of its great size, Russia has very few good ports with access to oceans and world trade. St. Petersburg's importance was enhanced by the completion of the **Volga-Baltic Waterway** and an interior network of railroads in the eighteenth century. Ships can reach inland to Moscow and beyond. Improved in 1964, the waterway connects several rivers in the interior, including the outlets of Lake Onega and Lake Ladoga. Located east of St. Petersburg, these two lakes are the largest in all of Europe.

KARELIA

Karelia is a flat glaciated plain north of St. Petersburg. Karelians are much like the neighboring Finns in language and culture. However, with the coming of the Russians, ethnic Karelians now constitute only a small part of the population. For sixteen years (1940–56) Karelia enjoyed a status equal to Ukraine or Russia itself as a sixteenth Soviet republic.

Lake Ladoga is the largest lake in Europe.

Icebreakers *Artica* and *Lotta* in port at Murmansk.

Russia 173

LET'S GO EXPLORING

POPULATION DENSITY OF RUSSIA

1. What is the northernmost major city in Russia?

2. Does Russia have any densely populated regions with over 250 people per square mile?

3. Where is Russia's largest concentration of people on the Pacific Coast?

4. Find the ribbon of population that ties European Russia to the Pacific. At what latitude does it lie?

What natural features explain Russia's unusual pattern of settlement in Asia above 60°N?

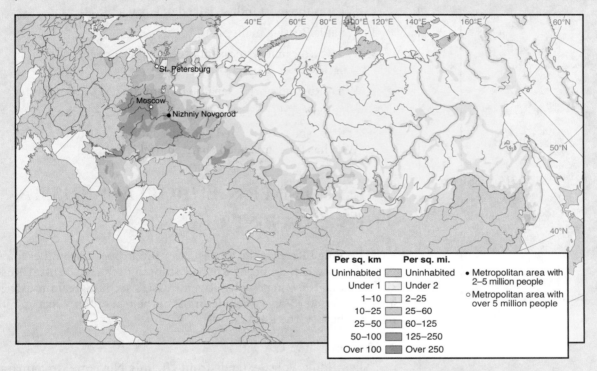

Per sq. km	Per sq. mi.
Uninhabited	Uninhabited
Under 1	Under 2
1–10	2–25
10–25	25–60
25–50	60–125
50–100	125–250
Over 100	Over 250

● Metropolitan area with 2–5 million people

○ Metropolitan area with over 5 million people

With the completion of the **White Sea–Baltic Canal** in 1939, Russia successfully linked Karelia's Arctic coast to St. Petersburg. The 141-mile canal links the White Sea to the Volga-Baltic Waterway. Ships carry timber from Karelia through the canal to St. Petersburg. Russia is the third leading producer of sawn wood in the world. The canal saves twenty-five hundred miles as compared to a journey around Scandinavia.

KOLA PENINSULA

The **Kola Peninsula** lies north of Karelia. Murmansk is the key arctic port because the currents of the Barents Sea keep the port free of ice most of the year, and icebreakers break through even when there is ice. Murmansk is north of the Arctic Circle and is the world's northernmost large city. The Barents Sea provides herring and cod, two of the world's most important commercial fishes, as well as other fish.

The Kola Peninsula is sparsely inhabited by Lapps as in Finland, but it has important mineral resources. Miners have found an assortment of metals and minerals on the peninsula. Among these

Novgorod, the First Russian City

Older even than Moscow, Novgorod was a key link at the north end of the ancient fur trade route between the Baltic Sea and the Black Sea. According to tradition, a Viking raider named Rurik gained control of Novgorod in 862, establishing the first ruling dynasty of Russia. This little nation, far from the centers of life in Europe, repulsed later attacks by Tatars from the east, Swedes from the north, and Teutonic Knights from the west. The Grand Duke of Moscow, Ivan the Great, finally conquered Novgorod in 1471. His grandson, Ivan the Terrible, became the first czar of Russia in 1547.

Russia's Western Outpost

Besides St. Petersburg, Russia has only one other port on the Baltic Sea at **Kaliningrad**, far to the west and separated from the rest of the country. Russia captured this region from Germany and has kept it as an ear in the West, where a radar system can provide early warning of attack. Kaliningrad used to be known as Königsburg but was later renamed after a Soviet official.

are phosphates, zinc, nickel, and lead. Russia is the top producer of nickel in the world. Russia also ranks fourth in producing uranium, the most important resource of the peninsula.

Vast forests and tundra stretch from the city of Archangel east across northern Russia. Among the ethnic minorities who herd reindeer in these wastelands are the Komi, a Finnic people, and the Samoyeds, whose breed of furry dogs, bred to herd reindeer, is popular in the United States.

SECTION QUIZ

1. What is the most industrial federal district in Russia?
2. What is Russia's main port?
3. What two canal systems link the northern ports with Moscow?
4. What Russian port is separated from the rest of the country?
5. Compare and contrast Karelia and the Kola Peninsula.
 ☼ St. Petersburg was called Leningrad during the Soviet era. Why has the name been changed back?

III. SOUTHERN EUROPEAN RUSSIA
THE VOLGA RIVER

The **Volga River** is the longest river in Europe, 2,193 miles long. Canals make it the hub of Russia's shipping system. Central Russia lies along the Upper Volga River. Russia's second great industrial area, the Greater Volga, includes most of the rest of the Volga and its major tributary, the Kama River.

MIDDLE VOLGA

The Middle Volga extends from Nizhniy Novgorod to Samara. **Nizhniy Novgorod** (formerly Gorki) is the third-largest city in Russia with over one and a half million people, while Samara ranks sixth with over one million people. The region is well-known for manufacturing automobiles.

Though Ivan the Terrible conquered the Tatars and tried to destroy their culture, Tatars remain the most numerous ethnic minority in Russia. Tatars compose about one-half of the population of **Tatarstan**, one of six Greater Volga republics. Their capital, Kazan, near the confluence of the Kama and Volga rivers, is the eighth-largest city in Russia.

Bashkortostan, like Tatarstan, is a key ethnic republic with a large population. Ethnic Bashkorts constitute just over one-fifth of the population, and Tatars account for one-quarter. The republic's main economic resource is oil. Russia is the second-leading producer of petroleum in the world.

LOWER VOLGA

The Lower Volga begins below Samara and flows to the Caspian Sea. **Volgograd**, called Stalingrad during the Soviet era from 1925 until 1961, has about one million people. Volgograd ranks after Moscow and St. Petersburg

An elderly Russian couple who live near the Volga River

in importance because it is Russia's southern shipping hub. It also produces much of its steel. Downriver from Volgograd is the port of Astrakhan in the Volga River delta, which allows Russia to trade with other countries on the Caspian Sea.

THE DON RIVER BASIN

The 1,224-mile-long **Don River** is second only to the Volga in importance. Flowing south through a fertile region of Russia very similar to neighboring Ukraine, it loops east and then west before emptying into the Sea of Azov. This important region includes part of the Donets Basin (also called the Donbas), Ukraine's mineral-rich eastern territory.

RUSSIA'S AGRICULTURAL HEARTLAND

The Don drainage basin consists of grasslands called **steppes** (STEPS). Rich in humus and nutrients, this productive land is called the **Black Earth** region of Russia. The semiarid climate of the steppes provides less than twenty inches of rain. Farm production soars in rainy years, but only irrigation can prevent disaster in drier years.

The Black Earth region helps to make Russia the world's fourth-largest producer of wheat. Russia also leads the world in the production of rye, oats, and barley. The abundant grains make this area the "Breadbasket of Russia."

SHIPPING

The vital port at the mouth of the Don is **Rostov** (or Rostov-on-Don). Much of the Don is shallow, but large ships sailing on the Black Sea can reach over three hundred miles upriver to the Volga-Don Canal.

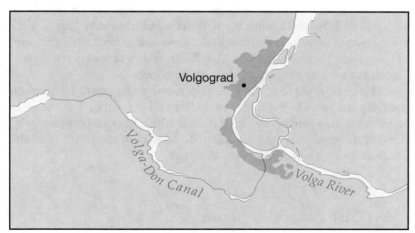

The **Volga-Don Canal** links the Don with the Volga. Completed in 1952, this sixty-three-mile-long canal with thirteen locks is Russia's final link in its European shipping system. Ships from Moscow can now reach any Russian port in Europe.

CAUCASUS MOUNTAINS

The Caucasus Mountains divide Europe from Asia between the Black Sea and the Caspian Sea. Catherine the Great conquered this area, which lies south of the Don and Volga rivers. The Russian part of the region consists of two large krais (territories) and eight autonomous

Cossacks

The steppes are famous for the **Cossacks**, fiercely independent nomads whose place in Russian lore is very similar to the Plains Indians in America. Novocherkassk near Rostov was the major city of the Cossacks.

The name *Cossack* comes from the Turkic word *Kazakh*, or "adventurer." Tracing their Slavic and Tatar origins is impossible, but their communities were independent and their elite cavalry units widely feared. The Cossacks finally fell to the Russians during the reign of Catherine the Great, an eighteenth-century czarina, whose empire extended across the Caucasus. Later czars often turned to these skilled horsemen to defend the Motherland.

This twentieth-century Cossack is posing with his weapons.

Mount Elbrus is the highest mountain in Europe.

republics. The name *Caucasian republics* refers generally to these eight republics of the Caucasus region.

The northern half of the region is lowland, part of the Great European Plain. Besides the two territories, this region includes Kalmykia. Almost half of the people are Kalmyks, a nomadic people that keep livestock and speak a Mongol language. Their religion is Tibetan Buddhism, but some have converted to Islam.

The mountains along the southern border are the highest in all of Europe. The highest of these is **Mount Elbrus** (18,510 ft.). This mountainous region is a haven for ethnic minorities and consists of seven of the eight Caucasian republics.

The greatest challenge to the Russian Federation came from a small republic called Chechnya. When the Soviet Union broke apart in 1991, the Chechens took the opportunity to secede from the Russian Federation. The czars had spent thirty years trying to subdue these people, who never willingly bowed to Moscow. Russian parents would scare their children, saying a Chechen might come and get them in the night. While Yeltsin was distracted with politics in Moscow, lawless gangsters flocked to this "refuge" in Chechnya.

In 1994 Yeltsin made a fateful decision to send in his army, but the campaign was a disaster. When Russian columns became bogged down outside the capital, Russian planes started bombing innocent civilians. Generals refused to obey orders and openly criticized the attack. The Russians eventually withdrew but invaded again in 1999 after a series of terrorist attacks in Russia and Chechnya's invasion of Dagestan. That conflict ended in 2000. Today, tensions are high in Chechnya with the region's future still in doubt.

Thirty people groups live in neighboring Dagestan. Located on the Caspian Sea, Dagestan has important oil resources, but these resources are in a sensitive area of mixed ethnic groups between volatile Chechnya in the west, Buddhist Kalmykia in the north, and the Shiite country of Azerbaijan in the south.

SECTION QUIZ

1. What is Europe's longest river?

2. Name two ethnic republics where descendants of the Tatars now live.

3. What group of people have their cultural center near the mouth of the Don River?

4. What ethnic republic in the Caucasus declared independence after the fall of the Soviet Union?

5. What is the highest mountain in Europe? In what range is it found?

☼ Why do you think so many ethnic minorities survived on the Volga, in spite of Russian conquest?

IV. Asian Russia

Russia's supply of mineral and fuel resources is the greatest in the world. Deposits of almost every industrial mineral from aluminum (bauxite) to zinc lie in Russia. Many of these resources, however, lie in remote parts of its vast Asian landmass. Compared to European Russia, Asiatic Russia is sparsely populated with very few population centers.

URAL MOUNTAINS

The **Ural Mountains** form a geographic border between the continents of Europe and Asia. The highest peak, Mount Narodnaya in the north, reaches 6,217 feet. While mineral resources lie in this part of the range, they are less developed than those farther south. The

LET'S GO EXPLORING

LAND USE OF CENTRAL EURASIA

1. What economic activity occurs north of the Arctic Circle?
2. What economic activity is most common among the nations south of Russia?
3. What is the most common economic activity along the Baltic Sea?
4. How is the economy different along the Black Sea than anywhere else in Russia?
- What does the map reveal about the agricultural conditions of eastern Russia?

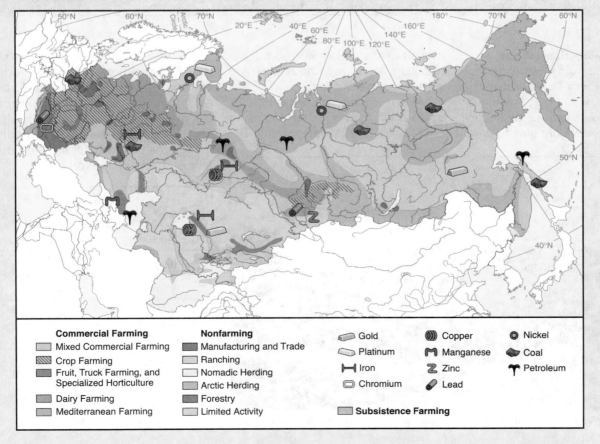

Commercial Farming
- Mixed Commercial Farming
- Crop Farming
- Fruit, Truck Farming, and Specialized Horticulture
- Dairy Farming
- Mediterranean Farming

Nonfarming
- Manufacturing and Trade
- Ranching
- Nomadic Herding
- Arctic Herding
- Forestry
- Limited Activity

Gold
Platinum
Iron
Chromium

Copper
Manganese
Zinc
Lead

Nickel
Coal
Petroleum

Subsistence Farming

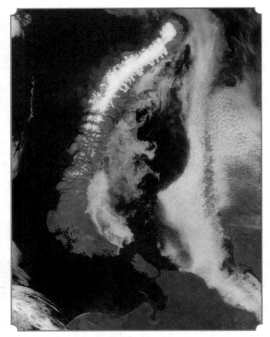

Due to its northern location and harsh environment, few people live on Novaya Zemlya.

range continues north into the Arctic Ocean to form the two large islands of the archipelago Novaya Zemlya. These two islands are the largest islands in the Eurasian Arctic. During the Soviet era, Novaya Zemlya was used as a nuclear weapons test site.

The Ural Mountains are low with several passes that enable people to cross freely. The southern Urals are more populous and have a unique culture. The most important mineral deposits in the Urals are iron ore and copper. Russia ranks sixth in copper mining and fourth in iron ore production. Mining in the Urals also enables Russia to rank among the top ten producers of potash, bauxite, and silver.

Important industrial cities have grown up near the mineral resources. **Yekaterinburg** and Chelyabinsk each have over one million people and rank as Russia's fifth- and ninth-largest cities, respectively. Yekaterinburg, named after Catherine I, the wife of Peter the Great, manufactures many products, notably turbines and ball bearings. Yekaterinburg was also the city where the last czar of Russia, Nicholas II, and his family were executed in 1918.

SIBERIA

All of Asian Russia east of the Urals is broadly termed **Siberia**. Russia's interior has no east-west mountain ranges to block cold fronts that push down from the Arctic.

Walrus and seals feed along the Arctic coast, while reindeer browse the mosses and lichens of the tundra. The polar climate keeps water and soil in a state of permafrost, that is, frozen most of the year. South of the tundra, the climate warms slightly. Wolves prowl the coniferous forests that blanket most of Siberia. The subpolar climate

TRANS-SIBERIAN RAILWAY

The **Trans-Siberian Railway**, which runs 5,778 miles from Moscow to Vladivostok on the Pacific Ocean, is the longest line in the world that has regular service. The route crosses eight time zones and requires eight days to travel.

It was built to exploit Siberia's mineral resources, which are so inaccessible and costly to bring to market.

When construction began in 1891, a rail system already joined Moscow to Chelyabinsk and Yekaterinburg. The final connection was made in 1905, including a section around the southern end of Lake Baykal. In 1916, an extension was completed that would aid troop movements to the Russia-China border. Despite Russia's lengthy railway, the United States has the most railroad tracks in the world.

Country	Length of Track (Miles)
United States	141,509
Russia	54,157
China	44,675
India	39,289
Australia	33,827
Canada	30,250

The Trans-Siberian Railway stops at Severobaykalsk, near the north end of Lake Baykal.

has freezing temperatures half the year, which drop to -60°F on occasion, and summer highs as hot as 100°F. The taiga—great coniferous forests of spruce, pine, fir, and larch—is an important source of wood products.

Southwest and southeast Siberia, where most Siberians live, have a more hospitable climate similar to that of Moscow. These populous regions are separated by Asian mountains that cross the border. The Trans-Siberian Railway links these regions, resulting in a ribbon development. Farmers grow crops on the scattered prairies, and loggers cut trees from nearby forests.

WEST SIBERIAN PLAIN

The West Siberian Plain is possibly the largest plain in the world and covers over one million square miles, amounting to about one-seventh of Russia's area. Extending from the Ural Mountains to the Yenisey River, it is a vast marshy plain drained by the Ob River and its tributaries. The Gulf of Ob and the Kara Sea in the north remain frozen, while snow melts in the south. The ice blocks the water flow, causing annual flooding along the Ob.

The Irtysh River is the main tributary of the Ob. The **Ob-Irtysh River** system ranks as the fourth-longest system in Eurasia and the seventh-longest in the world.

Novosibirsk (New Siberia), with about one and a half million people, is the largest city in Siberia. Situated on the Ob River, it has experienced phenomenal growth because of natural resources available nearby. Petroleum and natural gas deposits lie north. To the southeast lie deposits of lead, zinc, and iron ore. The region contributes to Russia's status as the fifth leading producer of coal worldwide.

CENTRAL SIBERIAN PLATEAU

The Central Siberian Plateau covers one-third of Siberia and stretches between the Yenisey and Lena rivers. It averages about two thousand feet in elevation. The lower north coast, or **Taymyr Peninsula**, is the northernmost mainland area in the world. Near the mouth of the Yenisey, miners dig nickel, cobalt, and platinum. Russia provides over 30 percent of the world's platinum; only South Africa produces more (59 percent). Diamonds come from the remote central part of the plateau.

The Trans-Siberian Railroad enters the central plateau at Krasnoyarsk, the largest city of the plateau with almost one million people, which lies on the Yenisey River.

Without railroad connections, two ethnic republics of southern Siberia—Altaya and Tuva—retain their ethnic majority. Remote Altaya is especially interesting because it is at the sensitive border between four large nations: Russia, China, Mongolia, and Kazakhstan. Altaya contains Mt. Belukha (14,783 ft.), the highest peak of the **Altai Mountains**. The mountainous republic also contains the headwaters of the Ob. There are four Altaic republics in this region of Siberia.

EAST SIBERIAN UPLAND

The East Siberian Upland is a mountain wilderness between the Lena River and the Pacific Ocean. The Lena River is the ninth-longest river in the world.

Interior—The largest Russian republic is **Sakha** (formerly Yakutia); it has the world's harshest climate of any inhabited area. It

Cold Climates

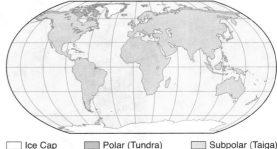

☐ Ice Cap   ■ Polar (Tundra)   ☐ Subpolar (Taiga)

Lake Baykal

Lake Baykal (or Baikal) is the deepest lake in the world and the seventh-largest lake in the world. Over one mile deep, 395 miles long, and up to fifty miles wide, it contains more water than all the Great Lakes combined.

The Baykal seal, a freshwater seal, sunbathes on the shore. Over nine hundred animal species in the lake are found nowhere else in the world. These include many unusual fish that swim near the lake's surface. The black and frigid depths are virtually lifeless and little-explored.

Over 330 rivers feed the lake, but only the Angara River drains it toward the north. The Angara provides hydro-electric power to the city of Irkutsk, an ancient trading post located on a vital pass through the mountains near the lake. The large haul of fish from the lake is loaded on trains at Irkutsk.

Lake Baykal has beautiful blue waters, like the Great Lakes in the United States, but it lacks many other advantages. It has no navigable outlet to the ocean. While the climate is better than much of the area around it, the lake surface remains frozen from January to May.

Chuvorkusky Bay is one of the many beautiful bays on Lake Baykal.

Siberian reindeer herder

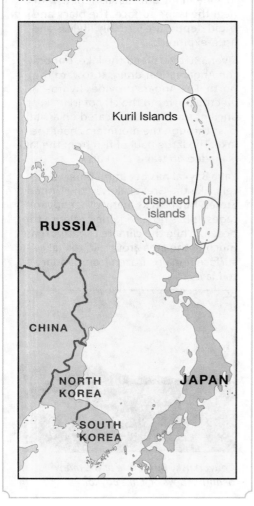

Kuril Islands

A continuing disagreement over the ownership of the Kuril Islands has prevented Russia and Japan from signing a peace treaty to World War II. The Kuril Islands were given to Russia after World War II, but Japan still claims several of the southernmost islands.

Kuril Islands

disputed islands

RUSSIA

CHINA

NORTH KOREA

JAPAN

SOUTH KOREA

contains much of the Lena and Kolyma River basins as well as the New Siberian Islands in the Arctic. Covering about 1.2 million square miles, it would be the eighth-largest country in the world if it obtained independence.

Ethnic Yakuts speak a Turkic language and constitute over one-third of the population, while Russians constitute over one-half. Yakutsk, the main city, was founded in 1632 but has grown to become the largest city of northern Siberia. The growth has come from mining in the **Yakutsk Basin** along the Lena and in the mountains. The Sakha gold fields make Russia the sixth-largest producer of gold in the world.

The Far East—Russia has more Pacific coastline than any other country. The Pacific coast has a more moderate climate and includes some farmland. The ports still freeze in winter, but some ports, such as Vladivostok, can be opened with ice breakers. Russian leaders are hopeful that its Far East will share in the booming trade of the Pacific Rim.

Russia's Far East has land within a few miles of all the great Pacific powers. Its land borders China and North Korea, while Japan is across a narrow channel from Russia's **Sakhalin Island** (SAK uh leen). The island has both coal and petroleum resources. Russia's **Kuril Islands** also extend in a chain from the Kamchatka (kam CHAT kuh) Peninsula to Japan. The United States is just across the **Bering Strait** (Alaska).

The Siberian Railway links **Vladivostok**, Russia's main Pacific port, with Russia's European ports. Russia's fishing fleet catches enough fish for Russia to rank ninth worldwide.

Two peninsulas dominate the far north coast. The Chukchi Peninsula reaches toward Alaska and divides the Bering Sea from the Chukchi Sea. The **Kamchatka Peninsula** extends south into the Pacific. Kamchatka contains twenty-nine active volcanoes, including Siberia's highest peak, snow-capped **Mount Klyuchevskaya** (15,584 ft.). Its southern end has the Russian port city of Petropavlovsk.

The Russian Empire once crossed the Pacific, including Alaska and trading centers as far south as California. The first permanent settlement in Alaska was founded in 1784. Russia did not have the means to protect these distant lands, however, and sold them to the United States in 1867. Instead, it concentrated its energies on expanding its empire in Central Asia, closer to home.

SECTION QUIZ

1. What mountain range divides Europe and Asia and forms the western border of Siberia?

2. On what group of islands did the Soviets conduct nuclear testing?

3. What are the three major geographic regions of Siberia?

4. Name the three major rivers of Siberia.

5. What is the largest city in Siberia? the main seaport?

☼ Why is Asiatic Russia so important to European Russia?

CHAPTER 7 REVIEW

HOW MUCH DO YOU REMEMBER?

1. Why are Russia's European lands more populous than its Asian lands?

2. What have been the results of the Soviets' misuse of Russia's resources?

3. Why is devolution dangerous in Russia? Why is it important?

4. Why does Russia's development have a ribbon pattern in Asia?

5. Give Russia's key port on each body of water.
   a. Arctic Ocean
   b. Baltic Sea
   c. Lower Volga
   d. Sea of Azov (Don River)
   e. Sea of Japan (Pacific Ocean)

6. What are the highest mountains and longest rivers for European and Asian Russia?

7. Give the main river, product, and city in each of the three main geographic regions of Siberia.

WHAT DO YOU THINK?

1. How would you compare the life of Russian peasants under the czars to that of Russians today?

2. Why do you think the Communist Party is still strong in Russia?

3. What is the greatest threat to freedom in Russia today?

4. Could European Russia survive without Asian Russia? Explain your answer.

5. How could Russia exercise better stewardship of its resources?

Can You:
Define These Terms?

czar	autonomous
autocrat	republic
devolution	federal district
oblast	kremlin
okrug	steppes
krai	taiga

Locate These Places?

Karelia	Lake Baykal
Kola Peninsula	Yakutsk Basin
Volga River	Sakhalin Island
Don River	Kuril Islands
Mount Elbrus	Bering Strait
Ural Mountains	Kamchatka
Siberia	Peninsula
Ob-Irtysh	Mount
Taymyr Peninsula	Klyuchevskaya
Altai Mountains	

Explain the Significance?

Vladimir Ilich Lenin	Kaliningrad
USSR	Nizhniy Novgorod
Cold War	Tatarstan
CIS	Volgograd
Federation	Black Earth
Assembly	Rostov
Supreme Court	Volga-Don Canal
Moscow	Cossacks
the Kremlin	Trans-Siberian
Central Federal	Railway
District	Novosibirsk
Peter the Great	Yekaterinburg
St. Petersburg	Sakha
Volga-Baltic	Vladivostok
Waterway	
White Sea–	
Baltic Canal	

UNIT 4

SARAH RAYMOND WRITES ABOUT CROSSING THE PLAINS

On May 1, 1865, shortly after passage of the Homestead Act opened the American West to settlers, Sarah Raymond's family—she and her father, mother, and brothers—departed from Missouri to cross the Great Plains and begin a new life. They arrived at their destination, Virginia City, Montana Territory, on September 6. Sarah kept a journal of her experience, and the following excerpt was one such entry.

Wednesday, July 26.

"Oh, the dust, the dust; it is terrible. I have never seen it half as bad; it seems to be almost knee-deep in places. We came twenty miles without stopping, and then camped for the night. We are near a fine spring of most excellent water—Barrel Spring it is called. I do not know why; there are no barrels there. When we stopped, the boys' faces were a sight; they were covered with all the dust that could stick on. One could just see the apertures where eyes, nose and mouth were through the dust; their appearance was frightful. How glad we all are to have plenty of clear cold water to wash away the dust."

(Excerpt from "Crossing the Plains, 1865," EyeWitnesstoHistory.com, http://www.eyewitnesstohistory.com/pfplains.htm)

NORTH AMERICA

ORIGINS AND MOVEMENTS

CULTURAL SNAPSHOT

When Columbus landed on San Salvador in 1492, he called the native peoples Indians, reportedly because he thought he had reached the East Indies. Later explorers also discovered people already living in other parts of the New World, from the northern coasts of modern New England and Canada to the coast of Brazil. Where had those people come from? And how did they get to the New World? Although no one can answer these questions with certainty, historians and anthropologists (people who study the origins and physical and social development of humans) have suggested the following theories.

The Overland Theory—This theory states that Asian peoples migrated across a land bridge (an exposed stretch of land called Beringia) that supposedly once spanned what today is called the Bering Sea or Bering Strait from northeastern Asia or Russia into what today is Alaska. They then moved southeastward along the Canadian Corridor into what is the western United States and into Mexico. Over a period of generations, these people fanned out across the entire continent, developing distinct tribes and languages as evidenced by the many Indian groups encountered by early explorers and settlers in the New World. This view has traditionally been the most widely proposed theory of the origins of the people of North America.

The Coastal Water Route Theory—According to this theory, Asian peoples migrated in boats, borne along by prevailing ocean currents northward along the coasts of Asia and modern Alaska and then southward along the western coasts of modern Canada and California.

The Trans-Pacific Water Route Theory—This theory states that Asian peoples in boats crossed the open Pacific Ocean directly to the New World rather than skirting the coasts.

The Combination Theory—A few theorists believe that among the first peoples of North America some used the land bridge, others sailed along the coasts, and still others sailed directly across the ocean. By one way or another, they got to the New World and established the tribes that Europeans found there hundreds of years later.

A fifth possibility points to Scripture for support. According to the Creation account, God gathered all of the water on earth together in one place and spoke dry land into existence, also apparently all in one place (Gen. 1:9–10). Then, Genesis 10:25 says, in the days of Peleg, a descendant of Noah's son Shem, "was the earth divided." Some people speculate that this phrase means that the dry land that was in one place was divided into the various continents. Proponents of the theory point to the modern map of the earth, which shows that the continents seem to fit together like the pieces of a giant puzzle. Could the division of the earth in Peleg's time have been this "continental drift" of landmasses?

Regardless of how the original inhabitants of North America got here, the countries developed as a melting pot of several different nationalities. Waves of European and Asian immigrants joined the native populations of both Canada and the United States. The slave trade further increased the diversity within the American colonies. And more recently, immigration from Latin America has surged.

In addition to movement *into* a country through immigration, people are constantly moving about *within* a country. Americans, in particular, have always been a mobile people. Settlers seeking "elbow room" moved progressively westward until they reached the Pacific coast. Today, people might relocate to find a better job. Senior citizens often retire to the Sun Belt. And many have chosen to leave the inner city for the suburbs.

Movement is an integral part of the study of culture. As you read about the various countries in the book, note how people groups have moved—and are moving even now—from country to country, region to region, or even continent to continent.

The Royal Canadian Mounted Police ("Mounties") are Canada's renowned national police force and represent the nation's British heritage and the Canadian spirit.

CANADA

I. THE MARITIME PROVINCES
   A. NEWFOUNDLAND
   B. NOVA SCOTIA
   C. NEW BRUNSWICK
   D. PRINCE EDWARD ISLAND

II. THE CENTRAL PROVINCES
   A. QUEBEC
   B. ONTARIO
   C. OTTAWA

III. THE WESTERN PROVINCES
   A. MANITOBA
   B. SASKATCHEWAN
   C. ALBERTA
   D. BRITISH COLUMBIA

IV. THE CANADIAN TERRITORIES
   A. YUKON TERRITORY
   B. NORTHWEST TERRITORIES
   C. NUNAVUT

PASSPORT

United
of

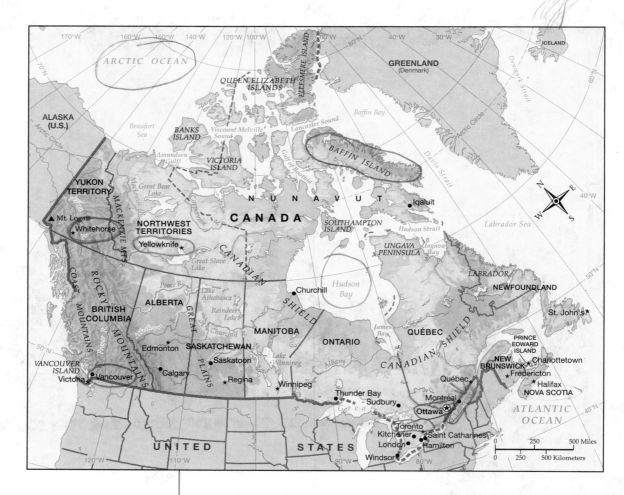

The North American continent is made up of three countries: Canada, the United States, and Mexico. Because of the vast cultural differences between Mexico and the other two countries, however, we include our study of Mexico in Latin America and focus in this unit on Canada and the United States.

Canada has the second-largest land area in the world (3,855,174 square miles). It also has the longest coastline (151,485 miles), including the coastlines of its 52,455 islands. Yet it has a relatively small population (33,390,141). This unusual combination offers Canada great benefits. Canadians are able to make a comfortable living, enjoy the blessings of both rural and urban environments, and export large quantities of raw materials.

Canada has much in common with the United States, and they are almost like brothers in many ways. Canada shares its only international border with the United States—3,987 miles along the lower forty-eight states and another 1,538 miles with Alaska. In fact, the U.S.–Canadian border is the longest unfortified border in the world. The two nations have been at peace for more than 150 years. Tourists, workers, and goods cross the borders with relative ease, although the security has been tightened since the 2001 terrorist attacks on the United States. And 90 percent of Canadians live within one hundred miles of the U.S.–Canada border.

Canada and the United States are the richest and most industrialized nations in the Western Hemisphere. They trade more goods with each other than with any other nation in the world. The United States depends on many of Canada's raw materials, such as nickel and wood pulp; and Canada buys many U.S. manufactured goods.

Both nations grew from British and French roots. Both cleared settlements in a wild frontier. Both worship primarily in churches led by Protestant preachers or Catholic priests. In both countries, significant numbers of native Indians and Eskimos still live in both the West and the cold North.

Canada also shares many geographic regions with the United States. The Canadian Atlantic coast is similar to the coast of New England. A few miles inland are the Appalachian Highlands, the northern tip of the same Appalachian Mountains that run the length of the eastern United States. The two nations share the St. Lawrence Seaway and the Great Lakes.

The interior lowlands and the Great Plains of Canada resemble the heartland of the United States. The Rocky Mountains run through both nations, as do the Pacific mountain ranges. Between those mountains are the intermountain basins. And the Northwest Territories of Canada are similar to the Alaskan wilderness of the United States.

Also like brothers, the two nations sometimes squabble, but they are still a cultural family. They sometimes disagree on international policies, such as environmental regulations, trade, and healthcare. But the common geographic and cultural bonds that link Canada and the United States like family members have only deepened with the passage of time.

I. THE MARITIME PROVINCES

Canada has ten provinces and three territories. The four smallest provinces, located in the eastern corner along the Atlantic coast, are known as the Maritime Provinces. **Maritime** means "bordering the sea." For centuries, sailors have lived in scattered villages along the coasts, depending on the sea for their livelihood, just as many of their neighbors do in New England.

NEWFOUNDLAND

The rocky island of **Newfoundland** (NOO fun lund) along with a large strip of land on the mainland form the province known as Newfoundland. In 1964, however, the province officially adopted the name "Newfoundland and Labrador" to give both parts of the province equal honor.

Canada Fast Facts

Flag	Capital	Area (sq mi.)	Pop. (M)	Pop. Density (per sq mi.)	Per Capita GDP ($US)	Life Span
🍁	Ottawa	3,855,174	33.4	10.6	$31,500	80.1

Flag	Province/ *Territory	Capital	Date of Entry to Confederation	Area (sq. mi)	Pop. (K)	Pct. Nat'l Pop.
	Newfoundland/ Labrador	St. John's	1949	156,649	517	1.6
	Nova Scotia	Halifax	1867	21,425	938	2.9
	Prince Edward Island	Charlottetown	1873	2,185	138	0.4
	New Brunswick	Fredericton	1867	28,355	751	2.4
	Quebec	Quebec City	1867	594,860	7,569	23.6
	Ontario	Toronto	1867	412,581	12,450	38.8
	Manitoba	Winnipeg	1870	250,947	1,175	3.7
	Saskatchewan	Regina	1905	251,866	995	3.1
	Alberta	Edmonton	1905	255,287	3,224	10.0
	British Columbia	Victoria	1871	365,948	4,220	13.2
	Yukon Territory	Whitehorse	1898	186,661	31	0.1
	Northwest Territories	Yellowknife	1870	1,322,910	48	0.1
	*Nunavut	Iqaluit	1999	770,000	30	0.1

The island is actually the northeastern edge of the Appalachian Mountain system, part of which lies underwater. Its rocky coasts and rolling hills are covered by stunted forests. Beautiful fjords attract many tourists to the western coast, while bird sanctuaries attract puffins and hosts of other nesting birds.

THE GRAND BANKS *location is Newfoundland*

Most Newfoundlanders live on the island. Although the climate is cool, the Gulf Stream keeps the climate from becoming too harsh. The capital, St. John's, sits beside the world-famous **Grand Banks fishing grounds**, where the cod-fishing industry reigned as king for almost five hundred years. John Cabot discovered the Grand Banks in 1497 and reported to the king of England that enough fish were

first settlement

there to feed his kingdom "till the end of time."

In just a few years, fishing boats from many parts of Western Europe were braving the icebergs, fogs, and storms to harvest fish. Cod became the most important commercial fish, but haddock, flounder, and herring were also abundant. The continental shelf off the southeast coast of Newfoundland extends far out into the Atlantic Ocean, providing a perfect fish "nursery." The comparatively shallow (averaging six hundred feet) waters receive plenty of sunlight, and the warm Gulf Stream mixes with the icy, oxygen-rich Labrador Current, encouraging explosive growth of plank-

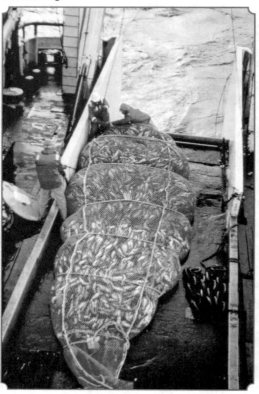

The catch from a commercial trawler (left) is as large as the entire boat holding the pre-industrial fishing catch (right), leading to overfishing.

ton and other fish food. Sadly, this thriving industry was not to last. After World War II, the number of European trawlers (large commercial fishing ships) operating on the Grand Banks increased dramatically. By 1992, fish stocks had dwindled to the point of collapse, prompting the Canadian government to impose a moratorium on cod fishing there. Human greed and misuse so damaged this natural resource that it still has not recovered.

Europeans built their first settlement in the New World in Newfoundland—a Viking outpost dating back to AD 1000. The British claimed the island in 1583, but they opposed settlement, fearing that local fishermen might become rivals to British companies. Fishermen, however, secretly built winter camps in the *coves* (small, sheltered bays) that dot the island. Fishing villages sprang up long before the first official settlements in the nineteenth century. The prosperous and independent-minded residents of Newfoundland did not join Canada until 1949. It was the last province to join the Confederation.

Mixing of Ocean Currents at the Grand Banks

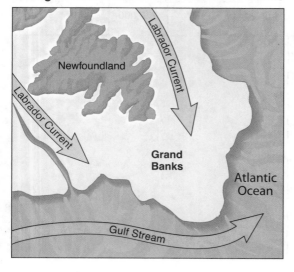

LABRADOR

The peninsula of **Labrador** on the mainland is cold year-round. The frigid Labrador Current carries Arctic water and icebergs past the coast. As air temperatures dip below -50°F in the winter, the surface of the coastal waters freezes, and freshly caught fish freeze almost instantly. Clarence Birdseye saw how this freezing kept fish edible for months and in 1915 conceived the idea of preparing frozen foods.

In spite of the cold, Labrador has stark beauty. Rocky tundra covers the north, and thick forests of spruce and pine blanket the south. During the summer, lumberjacks fell the evergreen trees and ship the logs to mills at the island city of Corner Brook to be made into newsprint. Several mountain ranges have alpine summits. Mount Caubvick, the highest peak east of the Canadian Rockies, dominates the Torngat Range in the far north. The largest herd of caribou in the world migrates to Labrador each spring to calve.

Under Labrador's rugged mountains lie zinc and one of the largest iron ore deposits in Canada. Mines near Labrador City produce more iron than any other province. Only one American state—Minnesota—produces more iron.

NOVA SCOTIA

The French settled the three southernmost Maritime Provinces, and called the region **Acadia**. They established the first French settlement in the New World, Port Royal, in 1604 on the Bay of Fundy in Nova Scotia.

Henry Wadsworth Longfellow's poem *Evangeline* helped make Acadia famous. It tells of the tragic conflict between British and French settlers. The trouble started in 1621 when Scottish colonists arrived and began claiming land that the French wanted. They fought numerous repeated wars before the Treaty of Utrecht (1713) awarded the area to Britain. But disputes continued. In 1755, the British decided to resolve the problem by forcing thousands of French Acadians from their homes and shipping them south. Some of the Acadians settled in New Orleans, where they became known as Cajuns. A few others escaped expulsion and later returned to Acadia. Today, their descendants continue to speak French and follow French ways.

Today, most Nova Scotians have a British heritage. Scottish settlers named the province Nova Scotia ("New Scotland") because of the striking geographic similarities to Scotland.

Nova Scotia is a long, narrow peninsula connected to the mainland by a twenty-mile-wide strip. Residents are never far from one of the many sandy beaches. The Canso Causeway connects the peninsula to Cape Breton Island, off the northeast corner of the peninsula. Canso Strait is the deepest water ever bridged. Nova Scotia leads the nation in its lobster and scallop catch.

Through Christian Eyes

Considering the dominion exerted by the people who fished the Grand Banks, what were the positive and negative results of their efforts? What alternatives could have helped them avoid this crisis?

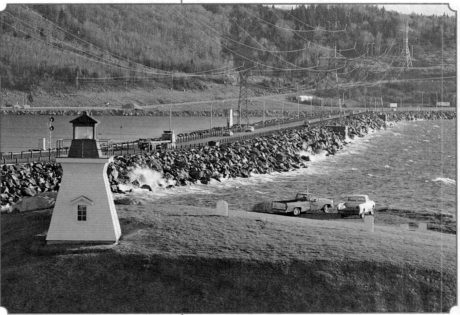

The Canso Causeway links Cape Breton Island to Nova Scotia.

The Swallowtail Lighthouse in New Brunswick shines from an island at the entrance to the Bay of Fundy.

New Brunswick Tourism & Parks, Canada.

The Atlantic Upland dominates the landscape. Coastal lowlands permit fruit growing and dairy farming. The Annapolis Valley is extensive and is the third most important fruit-growing area in Canada. Forests provide many of the Christmas trees sold each year in Canada and around the world. The capital, **Halifax**, is the largest city, port, and industrial area in the Maritime Provinces.

NEW BRUNSWICK

French Acadians make up 40 percent of New Brunswick's population and represent the second-largest French population of any province (after Quebec). The rest of New Brunswick's citizens are mainly of British or Loyalist ancestry. During the American War for Independence, approximately thirty thousand Americans who remained loyal to King George III fled to New Brunswick, the only Maritime Province that shares a border with the United States.

Most of New Brunswick is coastal lowland. Farmers in the south grow potatoes, as do their neighbors in Maine. The southwestern part of the province is Atlantic Upland, a continuation of Maine's New England Upland. The Appalachian Mountains, which extend into the northern parts of New Brunswick, are mined for lead, copper, and zinc. The forests also provide lumber.

BAY OF FUNDY

Situated between Nova Scotia and New Brunswick, the Bay of Fundy is the most famous bay of the Atlantic Ocean. It has the highest tides in the world, rising and falling as much as forty-four feet every twelve hours.

Irregularities in the shapes of the coast cause the height of tides to vary. Because the Bay of Fundy gradually narrows and gets shallower as it extends north, the bay creates a natural funnel. The tides rush farther inland here than anywhere else in the world. Visitors at Moncton, New Brunswick, at the north end of the bay, can watch a two-foot-high bore (tidal wave) flow in from many miles away.

The tides have other interesting effects along the Bay of Fundy. The tide climbs thirteen feet up over the rapids of the St. John River, making the rapids flow backwards. Visitors come from around the world to watch the St. John Reversing Falls. Another popular destination is "the Rocks." At low tide, people walk safely onto a dry beach at the foot of towering rock formations; but at high tide the ocean surrounds the rocks, which become islands. Visitors must quickly climb ladders to stay above the water.

The difference between high tide (top) and low tide (bottom) in the Bay of Fundy is dramatic.

PRINCE EDWARD ISLAND

Prince Edward Island is a tiny island in the Gulf of St. Lawrence. P.E.I., as it is affectionately called, is the smallest Canadian province, only slightly larger than the state of Delaware. Its farmland supports the highest population density of any Canadian province—about sixty-two people per square mile. Yet, because the people are so spread out, this "crowded" island is mostly rural.

Because the entire island is arable lowland, it is sometimes called Canada's Million-Acre Farm. The fertile soil has a distinct red color from rusted oxides. Leading the provinces in potato production, P.E.I. has earned the nickname "Spud Island." Beef and dairy cattle also enjoy good pastureland.

The quaint villages and sandy beaches make the scenery picturesque and inviting to tourists. Many foreigners visit the Victorian-style Green Gables House, made famous by L. M. Montgomery's novel *Anne of Green Gables.* Many residents opposed the construction of a bridge to the mainland because it threatened the island's quaint lifestyle and their individualism. Nevertheless, the bridge was completed in 1996.

A majority of the islanders have a Scottish heritage. In fact, more than half of their last names begin with "Mac." Weekend festivals feature Scottish traditions such as bagpipes and kilts.

This house at Cavendish, Prince Edward Island, inspired the novel *Anne of Green Gables.*

SECTION QUIZ

1. What two European countries competed for control of Canada?

2. Who is Canada's major trading partner?

3. Contrast Newfoundland with the provinces of Acadia.

4. Where are the highest tides in Canada?

5. Name a major product of each Maritime Province.

🔎 List all the similarities you can find between Maine and the Maritime Provinces.

II. THE CENTRAL PROVINCES

Canada lies far north of the equator, where the rays of the sun provide less warmth. Furthermore, huge inland areas lack the moderating effect of the oceans. As a result, most Canadian cities are on the southern strip of the nation, where the temperatures are less severe.

The area along the Great Lakes and the St. Lawrence River is a band of humid continental climate that escapes the frigid extremes found farther north. Summer temperatures along that band rise into the eighties, and farmland remains frost-free for about six months. The two biggest and most populous provinces—Quebec and Ontario—are in this climate on the rich southern plains and valleys. Pioneers cleared forests of pine, hemlock, sugar maple, and beech to plant their farms and to found their greatest cities.

Few people live in the harsh "northland." A solid mass of hard rock, called the **Canadian Shield**, covers most of eastern Canada. The Canadian Shield (or *Laurentian Plateau*) rims **Hudson Bay** like a giant horseshoe. The soil is thin and very poor. Apparently, glaciers scraped and wore down the mountains and hills, exposing the bedrock. The glaciers also might have dug out the thousands of lakes and marshes in the shield. Although it is poor in soil, the northland has been a blessing to miners, who exploit rich deposits of iron, copper, nickel, gold, lead, zinc, and cobalt.

A subpolar climate dominates the Canadian Shield. Needle-leaf evergreen trees, such as spruce, fir, and pine, are about the only trees that grow, and they become increasingly stunted as one travels north. These coniferous forests, called **taiga,** (TYE gah) cover most of the Central Provinces. Moose, beaver, and black bear live in the cool forests, and plenty of insects appear during the warm months. In the northernmost extremes, trees cannot grow at all and give way to tundra.

Vegetation of Northern America

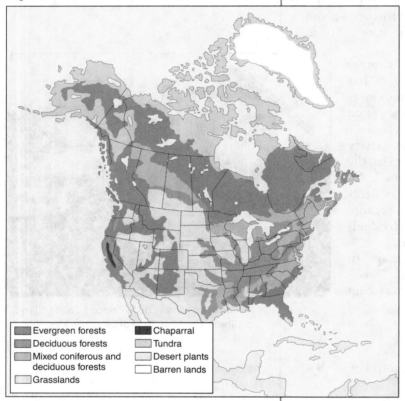

Evergreen forests
Deciduous forests
Mixed coniferous and deciduous forests
Grasslands
Chaparral
Tundra
Desert plants
Barren lands

Great variety in vegetation is evident in North America.

QUEBEC

Canada's earliest European explorers came from France. Jacques Cartier, Samuel de Champlain, and Robert de La Salle mapped the St. Lawrence and Great Lakes regions, which they called New France.

The discovery of valuable furs of beaver, mink, otter, and muskrat lured many hardy Frenchmen during the early seventeenth century. These pioneers became part of Canada's folklore, much like the free-spirited frontiersmen in the United States. They crisscrossed the interior lakes and frigid rivers, often carrying their canoes for miles on their backs.

While the French trapped furs and traded with the Huron Indians, the English explored the Hudson Bay farther north. The Hudson Bay Company, chartered in 1670, opened a thriving trade with the Algonquian Indians. As the British increased their holdings near Hudson Bay, and as the thirteen American colonies expanded, the French felt squeezed from both sides. The French and the British fought sporadically until Britain won a decisive victory in the Seven Years' War (1757–63). Tensions between the British and the French still exist in Canada today.

The heights of Old Quebec made it a good fortress for defending the St. Lawrence River.

Unlike America, which is often called a "melting pot" of peoples, Canada takes pride in its cultural "mosaic." The varied peoples who settled Canada have retained more of the distinct and colorful attributes of their Old World cultures. This mosaic is most apparent in Quebec, Canada's largest province. Eighty percent of the population of Quebec are French speaking and call themselves Quebecois (KAY beh KWAH). In 1974, Quebec made French the province's sole official language (the language used in government records and road signs).

CITIES OF THE ST. LAWRENCE VALLEY

Quebec's most productive land lies in the St. Lawrence Valley, on the southern edge of the province. The growing season is just long enough for fruits, vegetables,

SAINT LAWRENCE SEAWAY

The **St. Lawrence River** is the largest Canadian river. The French explorer Jacques Cartier, who sailed up the river in 1535, called it the River of Canada. Others have called it the Mother of Canada because it conveyed Canada's early explorers, traders, and colonists. The Saint Lawrence is a vital water route for both Canada and the United States, linking the Atlantic Ocean to the Great Lakes and the interior of the continent.

Early in Canada's history, Indians and trappers brought furs from lake areas in the north to forts on Lake Superior. The main forts were at Thunder Bay, Duluth, and Grand Portage (now a national monument in Minnesota). Large ships could sail most of the twenty-three hundred miles from Duluth to the mouth of the St. Lawrence River, but rapids and shallow water closed several stretches to ships. To make the entire seaway navigable, Canada built several canals and **locks** (a section of water with gates on both sides). Ships enter one gate, the water level is changed to match the other side, and then the ships exit the other gate.

Canadians first built canals in the most difficult spots near Montreal. They completed the Welland Canal in 1829, using several locks to bypass Niagara Falls. The last important

Ships on the St. Lawrence Seaway must pass through a lock at Montreal, Quebec.

canal, completed in 1895 at Sault Ste. Marie (SOO saint muh-REE), permitted ships to enter Lake Superior.

By the mid-1900s, when the size of ships exceeded the size of the canals, Canada and the United States joined forces on the Saint Lawrence Seaway project. They built new canals and enlarged existing ones. By 1959, oceangoing ships could again reach industrial centers on the Great Lakes. The increased shipping of grain, wood, cars, and machinery boosted the regional economy.

The seaway is not without its limitations. Ice packs close much of the waterway during the winter, and many of the newest cargo ships are too large to pass through the new locks. Despite these setbacks, the Saint Lawrence Seaway has dramatically helped both Canada and the United States.

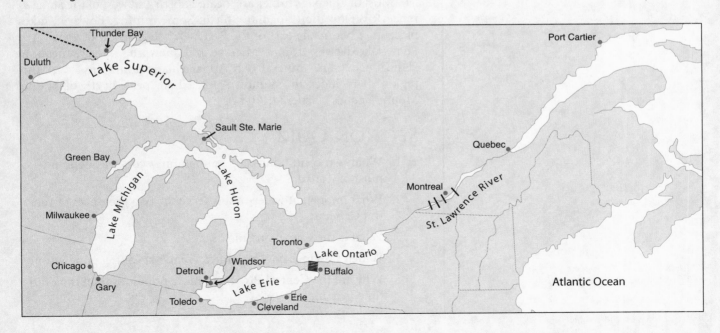

and some grains. Quebec leads the nation in dairy products and in maple syrup production. Most people in Quebec have chosen to live in this productive valley.

Quebec (Quebec City) is the capital and second largest city of the province. Founded in 1608 on a rocky bluff overlooking the St. Lawrence River, Quebec City became the cradle of French civilization in North America. There the French built the only walled city north of Mexico. By capturing Quebec in 1759, Great Britain effectively ended French rule in Canada. Today, the winding streets and beautiful old buildings give the city an old-Europe charm.

Upstream from Quebec City is **Montreal**, the largest city in the province. It sits on an island in the middle of the river. The explorer Jacques Cartier named the island Mont Réal (French for "Mount Royal") after he climbed its highest point, a 770-foot-high royal "mountain."

Located at the farthest navigable point on the St. Lawrence River, Montreal became the commercial center of the province. With more than one million inhabitants, Montreal's city proper surpasses the population of any other in the nation. Indeed, it is the second-largest French-speaking city in the world, after Paris.

Unlike Quebec City, Montreal has a large minority of English speakers. The city has French newspapers and English newspapers, French-speaking schools and English-speaking schools, and radio and television broadcasts in both languages. To get ahead in business and politics, many Canadians are **bilingual** (speak two languages).

In an effort to escape the cold winters, Montreal has built a vast underground mall, with stores, restaurants, businesses, and hotels. A subway, called the Métro, carries people throughout the city.

Hockey is the national sport. In fact, some people believe that hockey originated in Montreal. During the winter, fans fill the stadium to cheer the Montreal Canadiens, a National Hockey League team with many winning seasons.

LAND'S END

Most of Quebec's mines are located north and west of the St. Lawrence River on the Canadian Shield. Some mining, however, takes place on a peninsula east of the St. Lawrence. The Gaspé (gas PAY) Peninsula derives from a Micmac Indian word, *Gespeg*, meaning "land's end." The mineral-rich Appalachian Mountains cover this region. It includes the highest Appalachian peak north of Maine, Mount Jacques Cartier (4,190 ft.).

SECTION QUIZ

1. What two conditions keep temperatures cool throughout most of Canada?

2. What important water routes serve the two provinces of central Canada?

3. What is the Canadian Shield?

4. Which province has the largest French-speaking population?

☼ Why are the Central Provinces more populous than the Maritime Provinces?

The Great Lakes are important not only for the recreational sailing there but also as a means of moving loads of iron ore bound for steel mills.

ONTARIO

Although the province of Ontario ranks second in size, it is first in population. Canadians sometimes refer to it as the Heartland of Canada. In sharp contrast to Quebec's French heritage, Ontario's people have a strong British heritage.

NORTHERN ONTARIO

Few people live in Ontario's cold north. A narrow strip of swampy lowlands and coastal plains runs along the Hudson Bay. Although the Hudson Bay lowlands are not part of the Canadian Shield, they are just as stark and uninhabitable. A large portion of the lowlands is set aside as the Polar Bear Provincial Park. Some shipping takes place on Hudson Bay during the ice-free months, but little activity takes place during the long winter.

The Canadian Shield covers about half of Ontario. Though sparsely populated, this region has magnificent forests and one-quarter million lakes. The word *Ontario* comes from an Iroquois word meaning "shining waters." The lakes support large numbers of animals, and under the shield lie important mineral resources, making Ontario the nation's leader in gold and nickel mining.

CANADA'S POPULATION CENTERS

About 90 percent of Ontario's people live south of the Canadian Shield on a tiny finger of land between Lake Huron and Lake Ontario. It is the southernmost region in Canada. In fact, the city of Windsor lies farther south than does Boston, Massachusetts. Part of Windsor actually lies south of the closest American city, Detroit. The relatively warm climate, fertile soil, and shipping advantages of the Great Lakes Plain make this region the center of Canada's industry and population.

Dairy farms, orchards, vegetable gardens, and grain fields dot the countryside. Industries dominate the western shore of Lake Ontario, sometimes called the Golden Horseshoe. Its proximity to iron mines and ports enabled factories to thrive in the late nineteenth century. Ontario quickly became Canada's leading automobile manufacturer, just as Michigan became the leader in the United States. With the coming of the information age, computer industries have sprouted along the Golden Horseshoe.

One-half of Canada's twenty largest cities lie in the Great Lakes Plain. At the hub is **Toronto**, the capital of Ontario and the largest metropolitan area in the nation. Toronto is the nation's commercial center. Its stock exchange and banks handle more business than those in any other Canadian city. Five of Toronto's suburbs rank among the nation's twenty largest cities. Outside the Toronto metropolitan area lie the busy industrial cities of Hamilton, London, and Windsor. Ontario shares Niagara Falls with the state of New York.

The Great Lakes Plain was the last place in Canada invaded by foreign troops. During the War of 1812, the United States invaded Canada, capturing Detroit and Fort Dearborn (modern Chicago). After that war sputtered to a halt, Britain and the United States agreed to demilitarize the Great Lakes. (**Demilitarize** means to remove all forts and soldiers from a common border.) Both sides also accepted a common border of 49° N, west to the Rockies. The American invasion had another unintended result: it fostered a sense of

TORONTO

Toronto is arguably the most culturally diverse city in Canada. More than one hundred different languages are spoken there, and more than one-third of its residents speak a language other than English. More than 50 percent of its residents are nonwhites. The largest minority groups are (in descending order of number) Chinese, South Asian, black, and Filipino. Almost half of the population was born outside of Canada. The 1990s witnessed the biggest increase in immigration into the city, and each immigrant brought his or her unique culture to the Toronto metropolitan area.

The city of Toronto was founded and established by serious-minded and conservative Canadians, and their logical planning and organization of the city is evident in its well-laid-out and easily navigated streets. The downtown area is filled with towering modern skyscrapers, parks, and museums that reflect not only the city's illustrious past but also its modernity. Among its notable features, Toronto boasts the world's tallest free-standing structure (the CN Tower), the first retractable-roofed stadium (the SkyDome), the biggest museum (the Royal Ontario Museum), and Canada's largest university (the University of Toronto).

The CN Tower in Toronto rises 1,821 feet into the sky, making it the tallest self-supported structure in the world.

national identity among the divided Canadian colonies, who had joined to defend their soil against the Yankees.

OTTAWA

The national capital, **Ottawa**, is not in the Great Lakes Plain. It lies farther east, sharing the St. Lawrence River valley with Montreal and Quebec City. The Ottawa River, which flows by the city and drains into the St. Lawrence, marks the border between the provinces of Ontario and Quebec.

In 1837, colonists in Upper Canada (Quebec) and Lower Canada (Ontario) rebelled against Great Britain, demanding more democracy. After putting down the rebellions, Britain combined the two colonies into one and called it Canada. Because the British government wanted to avoid another prolonged and violent war for independence, it granted the new Province of Canada the right to govern its internal affairs. This union lasted until the **British North America Act** (1867) established a confederation of four provinces—Ontario, New Brunswick, Quebec, and Nova Scotia. Since then, six other provinces have joined the confederation. July 1 is celebrated as Canada Day.

The Dominion of Canada is modeled after the British parliamentary system. Canadians elect representatives to the House of Commons, a law-making body similar to the U.S. House of Representatives. The leader of the Commons becomes the prime minister. Like the president of the United States, the prime minister runs the executive branch of government. The Canadian

The changing of the guard occurs outside the parliament building in Ottawa, the nation's capital.

MISSIONS AND NATIONAL PRIDE

How do you feel when an American swimmer wins a gold medal in the Olympics? People in other countries feel just as proud when their athletes are honored and when their national anthem is played.

Although Canada is similar to the United States in some ways, missionaries there must make many adjustments, just as they would on any other mission field. For example, for whom should they cheer in a close race between American and Canadian Olympic swimmers? How should they respond to a hockey contest between Canadian and American teams? Their responses could greatly help—or hinder—their testimony.

When an American missionary couple finally obtain their visas and reach Canada, they must be careful not to offend nationals with their American political attitudes. They must show proper respect for the queen and become knowledgeable about Parliament. They must show an interest in Canada's national symbols: the CN Tower, not the Statue of Liberty; Butchart Gardens, not the Golden Gate Bridge; Banff National Park, not Yellowstone; the maple leaf, not the bald eagle. The missionaries must also adapt their vocabulary and greetings and be prepared to use the metric system without complaining.

In these ways, missionaries can deemphasize (without totally surrendering) their heritage to minister to foreign peoples. They seek to understand the people's beliefs and to overcome their own national pride to share the gospel. As the apostle Paul reminded the Corinthians, "I am made all things to all men, that I might by all means save some" (1 Cor. 9:22).

Roman Catholicism is the largest religious group in Canada, claiming 43 percent of the population. The next largest group (16.2 percent) is made up of people who claim no religion at all. Most other Canadians claim to be Protestants. Yet few Canadians (only 30 percent) rank religion highly in importance, few (14 percent) believe that the Bible is God's Word, and many (20–41 percent) have never read the Bible. As in America, most Protestants in Canada belong to mainline denominations. The largest denomination (9.6 percent) is the United Church of Canada, formed in 1925 by the union of several denominations. The second-largest denomination (6.9 percent) is the Anglican Church of Canada.

In spite of opposition from national church leaders and the apparent indifference of many Canadians to religion, missionaries play a crucial role in the work of Christ's kingdom in Canada.

Parliament also has a senate. Unlike the U.S. president, the prime minister chooses all 104 senators. Their job is to protect the interests of the various provinces and territories.

Under the parliamentary system, the Canadian prime minister is both the speaker in the House of Commons and the chief executive. Canada has voluntarily chosen to remain a member of the British Commonwealth and retains the British monarch as head of state. The monarch is represented in parliament by the governor general, who is appointed at the recommendation of the prime minister. Today, Parliament makes most national decisions while the roles of monarch and governor general are primarily ceremonial.

Canada has a federal system of government. Ottawa shares power with the provinces, each of which has its own unicameral (one-house) legislature and a governor called the **premier**. Like the prime minister, the premier is chosen by the legislature.

Canada has never had a civil war, but the union historically has been fragile. Because some French Canadians want a constitutional right to veto any laws that might threaten their distinctive French culture, Quebec refused to ratify the 1982 Charter of Rights and Freedoms, Canada's equivalent of the Bill of Rights. The charter made both French and English official languages, but French Canadians did not get the veto power. In 1995, Quebec almost passed a referendum to become a sovereign country. The vote failed, 49.4 percent to 50.6 percent.

Declining Christianity in Canada

The following table shows how the number of Canadians claiming to be Christians declined during the twentieth century.

Year	Percentage of professing Protestants or Catholics	Percentage professing other (or no) religion
1901	98	2
1981	90	10
1991	83	17
2001	72	28

Canada's Biblical Foundations

As in the United States, many of Canada's government buildings reflect the biblical heritage of the nation. For example, the western portal to the Peace Tower of the Parliament Buildings exhibits the inscribed words of Proverbs 29:18: "Where there is no vision, the people perish." Elsewhere are two inscriptions: "He shall have dominion also from sea to sea" (Ps. 72:8) and "Give the king thy judgments, O God, and thy righteousness unto the king's son" (Ps. 72:1).

SECTION QUIZ

1. Which province has the largest population?
2. Who is the head of state in Canada?
3. Who chooses the prime minister of Canada?
4. How many provinces are in Canada's confederation?
5. To what church do most Canadians belong?
   - ☼ Compare and contrast Quebec's regionalism with that of the American South.

III. THE WESTERN PROVINCES

The common traits shared by the United States and Canada continue into the West. In the four Western Provinces, which were settled much later than those in the East, the frontier spirit lives on.

The 4,860-mile **Trans-Canada Highway** links the East and the West. A network of railroads also crosses the continent. Only two other countries—Russia and the United States—have more rail lines than Canada. Isolated people in the far north, however, depend on airplanes for transportation.

The Central Plains of the United States extend northward into Canada's heartland, between the Canadian Shield and the Rocky Mountains. Temperatures in southern Canada are comfortable in the summer. Even so, the continental heating and cooling makes the Canadian climate somewhat harsh. Summer temperatures can climb to 100°F whereas winter nights often drop below 0°F. Because the plains lie in the rainshadow of the Rocky Mountains, rainfall is light, with most areas receiving only about fifteen inches of precipitation per year. Grasses characterize the plains' vegetation.

Because of the colder climate, Canada's frontier remained open long after the American frontier had closed. Immigrants from Germany, Poland, Russia, and eastern Canada moved in during the late nineteenth and early twentieth centuries. Early farmers struggled each year to glean crops from the rich soil before drought, insects, and untimely frosts destroyed them. "Wait until next year" became a popular saying. During the 1930s, farmers shared the misery of the Dust Bowl with America's midwestern states; Canadians call this bleak period the Dirty Thirties. Better seed and irrigation equipment have greatly improved the lot of the prairie farmer.

The Prairie Provinces have become the breadbasket of Canada. A frequent sight in these provinces are the tall grain elevators that rise from the flat landscape. These "skyscrapers of the prairie" hold mounds of wheat and barley. Canada is second only to the United States in the amount of wheat exports. Canada's barley harvest is second only to Russia's, and its flax harvest ranks first in the world.

A few people eke out a living in the northern Canadian Shield. Scattered bands of Indians struggle to survive on isolated reserves. Lakes and streams help make the taiga and tundra beautiful in the summer, but it becomes a lonely, white wilderness in winter.

The Trans-Canada Highway stretches from the Atlantic coast of Canada to the Pacific coast.

MANITOBA

Two strings of lakes straddle the center of Manitoba. The larger, Lake Winnipeg, sits in the east, and Lakes Manitoba and Winnipegosis sit in the west. Winnipeg, the province's capital and main city, sits on the Red River, which flows into Lake Winnipeg from its source in Minnesota.

Métis, descendants of French men and Indian women, once lived off the buffalo that dotted the plains. When Irish and Scottish settlers established a farming community on the Red River in 1812, the *métis* attacked them and killed their colonial leader. After the creation of the Dominion of Canada in 1867, the *métis* rebelled again. They feared that a rush of farmers would take over their land, for which they had no title. The Red River Rebellion forced Canada to grant the local people a bill of rights in 1870 and to create Canada's fifth province.

Only the southwest portion of Manitoba, the easternmost prairie province, is a prairie. Its farms lead Canada in the production of flax, buckwheat, sunflowers, and peas. But not all of the grassland is tilled. At Riding Mountain National Park, wolves, bison, and lynx continue to roam the meadows and scattered forests.

Most of Manitoba is covered by the unproductive Canadian Shield. The far northeast consists of swampy lowlands along the Hudson Bay, which it shares with Ontario. Churchill, the largest town in this desolate region, claims the title "the Polar Bear Capital of the World."

Winnipeg, Manitoba, is Canada's "Gateway to the West," much like St. Louis is the gateway to the western United States.

SASKATCHEWAN

The other two Prairie Provinces, Saskatchewan and Alberta, were settled later than Manitoba. The *métis* were the first to settle there, moving out of Manitoba and establishing farms along the North and South Saskatchewan rivers.

In the southern half of the province is the Saskatchewan Plain, a productive extension of the Interior Plains of the United States. Modern wheat farms make Saskatchewan the Northern Hemisphere's leading wheat producer. The wheat is processed in either the capital, Regina, or Saskatoon, a city farther north. From there, it is transported across the nation.

A few low hills bring variety to the flat plain. The Cypress Hills, which straddle the southwest border with Alberta, have the highest point between Labrador and the Canadian Rockies. Buffalo roam the wilderness of Prince Albert National Park, a few miles north of Saskatoon.

Northern Saskatchewan is known for its wilderness and for its uranium. Taiga and tundra cover that part of the Canadian Shield, and rich deposits of uranium

The prairies of Saskatchewan show why the province is called Canada's breadbasket.

Moraine Lake is one of the most famous lakes in Banff National Park near Calgary. Banff was the first national park in Canada.

lie under the surface. Canada is the world's leading producer of uranium, and more than half of Canada's uranium comes from Saskatchewan.

ALBERTA

West of Saskatchewan is Alberta. The Great Plains extend north over the entire province, except for the southwestern mountains and the northeastern shield. Alberta leads the continent in barley production and has the most beef cattle of any province. Edmonton is the capital and agricultural center of Alberta.

The northeastern tip of Alberta is notable for valuable oil reserves said to exceed those of Saudi Arabia. Also noteworthy is Wood Buffalo National Park, established in 1922. It features sand dunes, salt plains, boreal forests, gypsum karst formations, and river deltas at the mouth of the Peace and Athabasca rivers. Its wild herd of three thousand wood buffalo is the largest in the world.

Calgary is the gateway to the Canadian Rockies. Its growth is due partly to tourism and partly to the discovery of a major petroleum field nearby. Calgary is famous for its annual rodeo, the Calgary Stampede, held in July. Skiers flock to the nearby ski resorts in the winter. The city has also hosted the Winter Olympics.

The southwestern border of Alberta follows the Continental Divide through a succession of spectacular parks in the Canadian Rockies. The southernmost national park is Waterton Lakes, which adjoins Montana's Glacier National Park. Next is Banff, and beyond that is Jasper. Another interesting place in Alberta is Head-Smashed-In Buffalo Jump near Fort MacLeod. Visitors can see where the Plains Indians stampeded buffalo herds over the cliffs to their deaths. At a campsite below the cliffs, the Indians would then butcher the buffalo for meat.

CALGARY STAMPEDE

Rodeos in Canada? Yes, rodeos are as popular in Canada as they are in the American West. In fact, the biggest rodeo in the world is the Calgary Stampede in Calgary, Alberta, Canada. Guy Weadick organized the first Calgary Stampede in 1912. Although it is not the oldest rodeo, it has been an annual event since 1919.

Most rodeos feature the popular rough stock events, which require riders to sit on the backs of either untamed bucking broncos (horses) or Brahma bulls. Cowboys must hold on with only one hand while spurring the animal. These events, which are also called roughriding, include bull riding, bronco riding, and saddled bronco riding.

The other events are timed. Cowboys compete, both individually and in teams, in calf roping, steer wrestling, and steer roping. Cowgirls enjoy barrel racing, riding horses in tight curves around barrels. A few rodeos add milking contests, trick riding, fancy roping, and other events. The Calgary Stampede is famous for its chuck wagon races. Another favorite

The Calgary Stampede is a world-renowned rodeo.

event is open to young people in the audience—catching a greased pig.

BRITISH COLUMBIA

British Columbia is the third-largest and third most populous province. The only province on the Pacific Ocean, it is closely tied to America's Pacific Northwest.

The Rockies and the Pacific ranges cut the Pacific Northwest off from the rest of the continent. British ships did not sight its shores until 1778, but fur trade with coastal Indians quickly prospered. Americans arrived a decade later to explore the Columbia River. However, the two nations could not agree on ownership. They almost went to war in the early 1840s after American settlers began pouring into the Oregon country. Americans demanded all lands south of latitude 54°40' N; Britain claimed the lands north of the Columbia River. The two countries eventually agreed on a compromise boundary at 49° N.

Mount Robson is the highest peak in British Columbia.

WESTERN CORDILLERA

The chain of mountains that stretches from Alaska to the southern tip of South America is called the Western Cordillera. ***Cordillera*** (KOR dil YARE uh) means "a chain of mountains." The cordillera covers most of British Columbia, except for the northeastern corner, where the Peace River valley provides some agriculture on the Great Plains.

The map of North America reveals some important differences between the mountains in Canada and those in the United States. America's portion of the cordillera encompasses a one-thousand-mile-wide band of three mountain systems—the Rockies, the Sierra Nevada and Cascades, and the Coastal Ranges. In Canada, the cordillera forms a five-hundred-mile-wide band of two systems—the Rockies and the Coastal Mountains. The third U.S. system—the Coastal Ranges—disappears under the ocean off Canada's west coast.

Although logging and lead mining occur in the Canadian Rockies, and although more copper is mined there than in any other province, the biggest industry of British Columbia is tourism. Four national parks there—Yoho, Kootenay, Glacier, and Mount Revelstoke—display pristine mountain beauty. Several peaks exceed ten thousand feet. The highest peak is Mount Robson (12,972 ft.). A plateau separates the Canadian Rockies from the Coastal Mountains, which have the highest peaks in all of Canada.

PACIFIC COAST

The warm Japan Current gives the coast of British Columbia a marine-west-coast climate. The coast enjoys the most pleasant climate in Canada. Although winters are wet, temperatures generally stay above freezing. In the summer they rarely climb above 80°F. Orchards grace the valleys, and salmon fill the rivers. The tall, dense forests of Douglas fir, red cedar, and hemlock that cover the mountains make British Columbia the producer of the most lumber and other forest products in the Northern Hemisphere.

Vancouver, the largest city in British Columbia and the third-largest and fastest-growing metropolitan area in Canada, is ideally located at the mouth of the Fraser River, which empties into the Pacific Ocean north of Puget Sound. The soil of the Fraser River valley is

The flowers in the forty-nine-acre Butchart Gardens thrive in the marine-west-coast climate of Victoria, British Columbia.

the most fertile in the province. The city of Vancouver began growing rapidly in 1885, after the completion of the nation's first transcontinental railroad—the Canadian Pacific Railway (today called CP Rail). Vancouver's deep port is the busiest in the nation. Lumber, salmon, minerals, and prairie wheat pass through Vancouver to America, Japan, and the rest of the Pacific rim.

Off the west coast of British Columbia is a chain of islands that are the tops of the Coastal Range, which continues northward from Washington's Olympic Peninsula. Because the ocean has flooded this range, it is sometimes called the **Insular Mountains**. Vancouver Island is the largest insular mountain. In fact, it is the largest island off the west coast of the Americas.

British Columbia's capital, Victoria, sits on the southern edge of Vancouver Island, across from the city of Vancouver. Victoria is one of the few Canadian cities where British Canadians have been careful to keep British traditions intact. The streets and houses look much like those of British cities, and many of the people speak with a distinctly British accent. Evidence of British influence is everywhere, from the double-decker buses to the world-famous formal arrangements of Butchart Gardens. Flowered walks and ivy-covered buildings add to Victoria's charm.

SECTION QUIZ

1. Name the Prairie Provinces.
2. What is the only province on the Pacific?
3. Define *cordillera*. Which two provinces contain part of the Western Cordillera?
4. Where is Canada's mildest climate? Why is it so mild?
5. Name a product of and a national park in each Western Province.

☞ What are Canada's Coastal Mountains called after they enter the United States? Why does the name change?

IV. THE CANADIAN TERRITORIES

More than 40 percent of Canada's land is located in its northern territories, but their combined population is less than that of tiny Prince Edward Island. The obvious reason is the cold climate. Only a few Eskimos, Indians, and European Canadians brave the cold to work at reservations, trading posts, mines, and military installations.

Eskimos and Indians are the two native peoples of Canada. Indians lived south of the Arctic Circle. The Eskimos lived north of the Arctic Circle, hunting seals, walruses, and whales on the coast and caribou in the interior. Europeans called them Eskimos (possibly from French *Esquimaux* or from a Cree word meaning "eaters of raw meat"). They call themselves **Inuit**, or "real men."

When the Europeans arrived, they traded blankets, knives, guns, and other goods for fur and skins, helping them establish friendly relations. The trickle of French trappers did not upset the natives, as the rush of immigrants in America did the natives there. The large

Some Eskimos in the Arctic region live in igloos, especially when they are on hunting trips.

country had more than enough room for everyone.

The modern Indian population exceeds three hundred thousand. The Canadian government has given the Indians large tracts of land as reserves, and many Indians remain on these reserves. Unfortunately, government subsidies and little opportunity for real work have encouraged alcoholism and other evils. Some Indians move to Canadian cities, but this drastic step can be a great shock to a tribal culture.

Canada's Eskimos number about twenty-five thousand, most of whom live in northern military and mining settlements, where they hold regular jobs. A few continue to hunt and fish, mostly with the aid of modern weapons and equipment. Rifles have replaced most harpoons, and snowmobiles are as common as dogsleds. Although the traditional Eskimo way of life is almost gone, Eskimo bone carvings and other crafts have become popular.

The Al-Can Highway can be beautiful in the winter.

YUKON TERRITORY

The cold Yukon Territory, north of British Columbia and bordering Alaska, is slightly larger than California. Gold brought thousands of miners to the Klondike region in the 1890s, and mining continues to be the major activity. Today, however, lead and zinc mining have surpassed gold. The Yukon leads Canada in lead production, and it helps to make Canada the world's leading supplier of zinc.

The **Alaska Highway** (also called the Alaska-Canada Highway, or Al-Can) winds through the mountains of the Yukon to connect Dawson Creek, British Columbia, with Anchorage, Alaska. The U.S. Army blazed the first rough highway as an overland route for military supplies during World War II. A narrow central valley lies along the Yukon River. Here miners established the capital, Whitehorse, the only real city between Dawson and Anchorage. The Coastal Mountains include Canada's highest mountain, Mount Logan (19,524 ft.).

NORTHWEST TERRITORIES

This vast territory covers one-third of Canada, but only sixty thousand people live there. Nearly one-fifth of the population lives in the capital, Yellowknife. It stands beside Great Slave Lake, the deepest lake in North America. Great Bear Lake is the only lake in Canada that covers more area than the Great Slave Lake.

The **Mackenzie River**, one of the longest river systems in North America, winds northward from the Great Slave Lake through the western part of the territory to the Arctic Ocean. It is named after Sir Alexander Mackenzie, a trapper who first explored the length of the river in 1789. Most settlements in the Northwest Territory are scattered along the Mackenzie River valley. Oil companies have found petroleum in the ice-choked Mackenzie delta.

A few forests of small evergreens grow near the Mackenzie River and the southern part of the territory, but most of the land lies above

The Al-Can Highway

When the Japanese attacked Pearl Harbor, pulling the United States into World War II, the only access to Alaska from the mainland was by airplane. The U.S. government needed a land route to get supplies and equipment to its airfields and military bases in greater quantities. They persuaded Canada to donate the right of way for a road to be built by the U.S. Army Corp of Engineers at U.S. expense. After the war, ownership of the road would revert to Canada.

Construction on the road began at Dawson Creek, British Columbia, in March 1942. The 93rd, 95th, 97th, and 388th Engineer Regiments—10,607 men, including 3,695 blacks—were assigned the arduous task. The 1,522-mile-long road would follow old Indian paths through rugged, unmapped regions to link existing airfields. Critics said it could not be done and complained that black men did not have the mentality to operate heavy equipment.

But the men proved the critics wrong. They worked seven days a week, sometimes putting in twenty-hour days. In the spring and summer, they fought mosquitoes, flies, and gnats. They overcame the marshy thawed areas by building a "corduroy" road of logs laid side by side. In the winter, the men endured temperatures of -40°F for weeks at a time and struggled to move the rock-solid frozen ground. (One day the temperature was a record low of -79°.)

In June 1942, the Japanese invaded Attu and Kiska, two Alaskan islands in the Aleutians, increasing the urgency of the task. By October 25, 1943—an amazing eight months from the time they began—the engineers had achieved what critics said was impossible. They reached the city of Fairbanks, Alaska, completing the Alaska-Canada Highway. Supplies began pouring into U.S. military bases in Alaska. The Al-Can is still the only land route from the lower forty-eight American states to Alaska, and it is a monument to the soldiers' courage, stamina, and ingenuity.

Arctic cold on the Alcan highway doesn't faze these big Studebaker trucks

HUNDREDS upon hundreds of huge, multiple-drive Studebaker trucks are rumbling over the wild, rugged route of the great new 1610-mile Alaska-Canada highway. More of these big Studebakers are in service on this amazing military road than any other make of truck. And despite temperatures that often drop far below zero, Studebaker stamina is getting the cargoes of vital supplies through to our important North Pacific theater of war.

Not only on this Alcan highway that forms a land-bridge between our distant Alaska outposts and the continental United States, but also in all kinds of climates in all parts of the world, Studebaker military trucks are busy helping to tip the victory balance in favor of the United Nations. Tens of thousands of them are in service on the supply lines and at the fighting fronts. And tens of thousands more are on the way.

Studebaker engineering and craftsmanship provide Studebaker trucks in wartime with the same stand-out superiorities for which they were so widely recognized in peacetime. Through generation after generation, for more than 91 years, the men of Studebaker have made it their habit to "give more than they promise." And that is still their watchword in the manufacture of big, multiple-drive military trucks, Wright Cyclone engines for the Flying Fortress and all the other vital war matériel they are producing now.

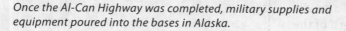
Once the Al-Can Highway was completed, military supplies and equipment poured into the bases in Alaska.

Soldiers worked under difficult conditions to complete the Al-Can Highway.

Black soldiers made a valuable contribution during the construction of the Al-Can Highway.

the timberline. Trapping, fishing, and the mining of lead and zinc are the major industries. The discovery of diamonds in 1991 northeast of Yellowknife sparked the biggest mineral rush in Canada's history, exceeding even the Klondike gold rush. More than two hundred companies have staked claims around Lac de Gras.

North of the continent is one of the earth's great **archipelagos**, or island groups. Nine of these islands exceed ten thousand square miles in area. The southern islands are flat, but the northern islands are mountainous. Barbeau Peak on Ellesmere Island is the highest peak in the archipelago (8,582 ft.). Most of the Arctic islands sit above the Arctic Circle. With few exceptions, these rocky, barren islands are uninhabited and covered by snow and ice throughout the year.

The Arctic islands and northern parts of the Canadian Shield have a polar or tundra climate. Winter temperatures often fall to −30°F or lower. Summer temperatures rarely climb above 50°F, and they stay above freezing for only about two months. Permafrost keeps large plants from growing, but small lichens and some other

FROM SEA TO SEA

Like many countries, Canada is blessed with a godly heritage. Through the course of her long history, Canada was shaped and defended by God-fearing men and women.

Many artifacts attest to that history. Canada's national motto, adopted in 1921, *A mari usque ad mare* ("From sea to sea"), is taken from Psalm 72:8: "He shall have dominion also from sea to sea, and from the river unto the ends of the earth." Consequently, Canada's national holiday was originally known as Dominion Day. The Canadian motto *Desiderantes meliorem patriam* (taken from Hebrews 11:16, "They desire a better country") is displayed on Canada's official coat of arms. Even the provincial saying of Newfoundland and Labrador bears testament to Canada's Christian heritage: "Seek ye first the kingdom of God."

One of the most powerful reminders today of Canada's Christian heritage is its national anthem. The English version sung today was written in 1908 by R. Stanley Weir in honor of the three hundredth anniversary of the founding of Quebec City. The last verse reads,

Ruler supreme, who hearest humble prayer,

Hold our dominion within thy loving care;

Help us to find, O God, in thee

A lasting, rich reward,

As waiting for the Better Day,

We ever stand on guard.

God, keep our land glorious and free!

O Canada, we stand on guard for thee.

O Canada, we stand on guard for thee.

It is important to remember that a godly history is not what makes a country right and pleasing before God. Each generation must be taught to love and fear the Lord and to live accordingly. If one generation neglects its obligation, the link is broken and so is the chain. Nevertheless, the age-old promise in Psalm 2:10–12 remains unchanged to all countries: "Be wise now therefore, O ye kings. . . . Serve the Lord with fear. . . . Blessed are all they that put their trust in him."

©2007 The Heritage Canada Foundation, www.heritagecanada.org, Reproduced with the permission of the Minister of Public Works and Government Services, 2007.

tiny plants and bushes grow in colorful profusion during summer's brief thaw.

NUNAVUT

On May 4, 1992, the Northwest Territories approved a plan to split the territory in April 1999 and to allow Inuit self-government. The new territory, *Nunavut* (Inuit for "our land"), includes most of the old territory, except for the westernmost Arctic islands and the Mackenzie River valley. Only twenty-eight small villages exist in this wide wilderness. The most populous town, Iqaluit (under 4,000), is the capital.

Nunavut includes **Baffin Island,** the largest island in the Canadian archipelago and the fifth largest island in the world. Ten thousand glaciers creep down its sides to the sea. Iqaluit is located on Baffin Island's southernmost bay, facing the Atlantic Ocean.

SECTION QUIZ

1. Distinguish the two native peoples of Canada.
2. What industry mutually benefited the Europeans and the native people?
3. Where is Canada's highest mountain?
4. Where are most settlements in the Northwest Territory?
  ⌖ How did the builders of the Al-Can Highway manage to prove their critics wrong?

CHAPTER 8 REVIEW

HOW MUCH DO YOU REMEMBER?

1. Name five geographic features shared by Canada and the United States.

2. What are the four main ethnic groups of Canadians?

3. Give three major differences between the Maritime, Central, and Western Provinces.

4. Which European country first explored and claimed the land around the St. Lawrence River?

5. What kind of government does Canada have?

6. Which province fits each description?
    a. smallest in size
    b. largest in size
    c. largest in population
    d. automobile manufacturing
    e. uranium
    f. iron
    g. potatoes
    h. flax, buckwheat, and peas
    i. butter
    j. wheat
    k. beef and oil

7. Name the two national languages of Canada.

8. Why is southern Ontario such an important region of Canada?

9. What is the largest metropolitan area in Canada?

10. Why are Canada's territories valuable despite their cold climates?

WHAT DO YOU THINK?

1. Describe the relationship between the United States and Canada.

2. What impact might Quebec's independence have on Canada? on the United States?

3. Compare and contrast the plight of the French minority in Canada to the black and Hispanic minorities in the United States.

4. Make a list of the similarities and differences between Canada and the United States. Include geography, economy, population, cities, history, and government.

Can You:
Define These Terms?

maritime	premier
taiga	cordillera
lock	Inuit
bilingual	archipelago
demilitarize	

Locate These Places?

Newfoundland	St. Lawrence River
Grand Banks	Insular Mountains
Labrador	Mackenzie River
Canadian Shield	Baffin Island
Hudson Bay	

Explain the Significance?

Acadia	Trans-Canada
Halifax	Highway
Quebec	Calgary
Montreal	Vancouver
Toronto	Alaska Highway
Ottawa	
British North	
America Act	

CHAPTER 9

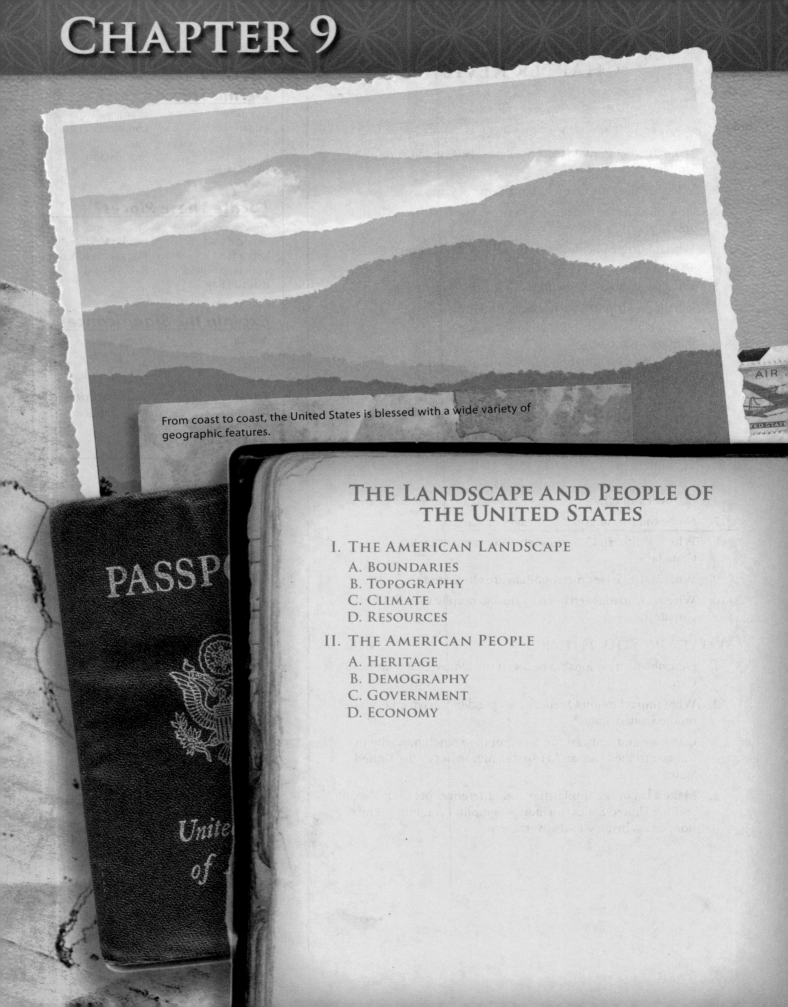

From coast to coast, the United States is blessed with a wide variety of geographic features.

THE LANDSCAPE AND PEOPLE OF THE UNITED STATES

I. THE AMERICAN LANDSCAPE
- A. BOUNDARIES
- B. TOPOGRAPHY
- C. CLIMATE
- D. RESOURCES

II. THE AMERICAN PEOPLE
- A. HERITAGE
- B. DEMOGRAPHY
- C. GOVERNMENT
- D. ECONOMY

In many ways, the United States of America is unique among the countries of the world. Its topography and climate are widely varied. It is blessed with enormous amounts and varieties of natural resources and fertile croplands. Its population is an amalgam (mixture) of prac-

America Fast Facts						
Flag	Capital	Area (sq. mi.)	Pop. (M)	Pop. Density (per sq. mi.)	Per Capita GDP ($US)	Life Span
🇺🇸	Washington, D.C.	3,718,711	296	31	$40,100	77.71

tically every people and culture on earth, each of which has made valuable contributions to the cultural landscape, yet the nation has developed its own distinct culture. It has a proud history and the freest, most stable government in existence. Its economy is the strongest on earth. And it has unequaled power and influence among the nations.

At the same time, however, the United States does not have every resource its people need and must therefore trade with other nations to obtain what it lacks. It faces problems unique to the diverse cultures in its midst. Its great economy presents both challenges and opportunities. Its government faces its own problems even as it attempts to spread freedom to the undemocratic nations of the world. And it must continually deal with devastating natural disasters and an ongoing war against Islamic terrorism.

The United States ranks third among the nations of the earth in physical size (behind only Russia and Canada). It is third in population (behind China and India). Its wealth and prosperity are attributable in part to its rich farmland, abundant resources, good climate, and hard-working people. Perhaps its greatest blessing, however, is the heritage of freedom wrought by the faith and determination of its God-fearing founders and their descendants. True freedom and economic prosperity are ultimately gifts from the Lord. God wants Christians to use their liberty not selfishly but for the good of all, and we are to be good stewards of not only our personal finances and resources but also our national wealth. As long as the United States fears and honors the one true God and uses its God-given gifts wisely, it will continue to prosper among the nations.

Blessed is the nation whose God is the Lord.
(Ps. 33:12)

I. THE AMERICAN LANDSCAPE

The land of the United States stretches from the Atlantic Ocean in the east to the Pacific Ocean in the west through the middle of the North American continent. It also includes the large peninsula of Alaska to the northwest, the islands of Hawaii farther west in the Pacific, and several territories in the Pacific and the Caribbean.

Americans are an amalgam of multiple races, religions, nationalities, and ethnicities.

From coast to coast, the geography of the United States offers a variety of majestic vistas.

The United States and Canada share the longest unfortified border of any nations on earth.

Through Christian Eyes

How should Christians respond to individual immigrants?

Unlike the U.S.–Canadian border, the U.S.–Mexican border presents the challenges of illegal aliens and the infusion of illegal drugs into the United States.

Boundaries

The United States is bounded on the north and the south by generally peaceful neighboring countries. On the north, Canada and the United States share the longest nonmilitarized border in the world. The lower forty-eight U.S. states share a 3,987-mile border with Canada. Alaska adds an additional 1,538-mile border. The main border essentially follows the St. Lawrence River from New England to Quebec and divides four of the Great Lakes. (Only Lake Michigan is completely within the United States.) It then follows the 49th parallel from Lake of the Woods in Ontario/Minnesota to the Strait of Juan de Fuca on the west coast.

Customs officials do check all traffic crossing the border, which has seventy-nine ports. Although it has been relatively easy to pass between the two countries in the past (the time required for a typical crossing is ten to twenty minutes), the terrorist attacks on the United States on September 11, 2001, forced both countries to tighten security dramatically. Nonetheless, the border remains a friendly boundary between cooperative nations.

Two hundred million people cross the border each year, an average of 300,000 daily. Fifteen percent of the crossings are commercial. The United States and Canada are great trading partners. Forty-five thousand trucks a day cross the border, most of them carrying imports or exports. The United States exports $190 billion worth of goods to Canada and imports $256 billion worth of goods from Canada every year for a total annual trade of $446 billion.

On the south, the United States is bounded by the **Rio Grande** (Spanish, "big river"); the Mexican border at California, Arizona, and southwestern New Mexico; and the Gulf of Mexico. Mexico is the second-largest trading partner of the United States, with the value of trade running $232 billion a year. The U.S.–Mexico border is also unfortified, but law enforcement is much more obvious than on the U.S.–Canada border because of the heavy traffic of illegal drugs and illegal immigrants across the border. In fact, so many illegal aliens cross the border that a group of private citizens calling themselves the Minutemen has volunteered to help patrol parts of the border, notifying the Border Patrol and Immigration and Naturalization agents whenever they observe illegal immigrants attempting to cross the border. (The U.S. government does not officially sanction or encourage such vigilante groups.) President Bush has promised to tighten border security.

Section Quiz

1. What is the world rank of the United States in physical size?

2. What is the U.S. rank in population?

3. What are the (a) northern, (b) southern, (c) eastern, and (d) western boundaries of the United States?

4. Which of the five Great Lakes is totally within the United States?

THE COMPLICATIONS OF IMMIGRATION

Since the 1990s, illegal immigration from Mexico and other Latin American countries has increased dramatically. In 2006, an estimated 9–11 million undocumented immigrants resided in the United States. Of those, about 60–70 percent were from Mexico. This situation presents great problems for the U.S. government. Health care and education costs for undocumented immigrants and their families are high. In addition, millions of tax dollars that are owed to the government by undocumented immigrants go uncollected.

It is important, however, for Americans to realize that these undocumented immigrants do not come to the U.S. to steal, cheat, or abuse others. For the most part, Mexicans and other Latin Americans are happy to work very hard in the United States in order to send money back home each week and then join their families again after a few years. The opportunity for higher paying jobs is greater in America since the dollar is much stronger than the peso. By working in the United States, they can earn more money in a shorter amount of time. Many come from impoverished conditions and seek to raise the standard of living here and back home.

Stopping illegal immigration is a daunting task, one that few politicians desire to undertake because of the emotionally charged issues involved. The issues are complicated, and there are no easy answers. First, Mexico is the second-largest trade partner of the United States, and an aggressive policy against illegal immigration could slow the flow of trade between Mexico and the United States. Second, immigrants, both legal and illegal, often provide a needed source of labor for many service-sector jobs in the United States. Dramatically reducing immigration could harm productivity in those parts of the U.S. economy. Third, the cost of constructing and maintaining a continuous, gated border would be very high. Finally, Latin Americans and Hispanics already legally living in the United States—many of whom are now voting citizens—could see such policies as a racist attack on their people and culture. Thus, the political consequences of trying to stop illegal immigration could be very costly.

President George W. Bush proposed a program that would employ new technology at border crossings while still allowing current illegal immigrants to continue working for a limited time. Still, the situation remains tenuous with no clear solution soon in sight. The question of how to solve the problem of illegal immigration remains difficult to answer.

TOPOGRAPHY

The lower forty-eight states of the United States can be divided into eight distinct topographical regions, each of which has played an important role in the historical and cultural development of the country. We discuss each of these areas in the following sections of the text, moving from east to west across the map. We then deal briefly with Alaska and Hawaii, each of which has its own unique topographical characteristics.

THE COASTAL PLAINS

The sandy plains along the coasts of the Atlantic Ocean and the Gulf of Mexico are called the **Coastal Plains.** They are three hundred feet or less in elevation and extend from Maine to Texas. The plain is very narrow in the Northeast and expands gradually as one goes south until it extends inland one hundred miles or more in the South. Some areas—such as the Everglades in Florida, the Okeefenokee Swamp in Georgia, and the Dismal Swamp in Virginia and North Carolina—have poor drainage. Other areas have fertile soil and provide numerous kinds of products, including rice, indigo, peanuts, and fruits.

Inlets that cut into the **Atlantic Coastal Plain** provide fine harbors, especially in the north. New York, Boston, and Philadelphia are famous seaports of the Atlantic coast. Good harbors are less plentiful farther south but include Wilmington, North

Much of the Coastal Plains are flat and wet, like this portion of the Gulf Coastal Plain in Louisiana.

Carolina; Charleston, South Carolina; and Savannah, Georgia. Tampa, Florida; Mobile, Alabama; New Orleans, Louisiana; and Houston and Galveston, Texas, are some of the major port cities of the **Gulf Coastal Plain**. That plain also extends inland up the Mississippi River Valley into the Midwest.

THE PIEDMONT

Farther inland from the Atlantic Ocean and beyond the Coastal Plains is an area known as the **Piedmont**. The word *piedmont* ("foothills") is appropriate because the area is the foothills of the Appalachian Mountains. The Piedmont extends from Maine to Alabama, with elevations ranging from three hundred to fifteen hundred feet. Many rivers run from the mountains through the Piedmont and the Coastal Plain and into the ocean. Where the rivers drop from the Piedmont to the Coastal Plain, there are many waterfalls, which explains why that area is called the **fall line**. Westward-moving settlers founded many cities along the fall line, where they took advantage of the powerful waterfalls to build mills and factories. The fertile ground of the Piedmont was also conducive to growing great quantities of cotton.

Waterfalls such as the Great Falls of the Potomac in Montgomery County, Maryland, are common along the fall line, where the Piedmont and the Coastal Plain meet.

THE APPALACHIAN MOUNTAINS

West of the Piedmont, the **Appalachian Mountains** extend from eastern Canada southward into northern Alabama. Several mountain groups—for example, the Smoky, Blue Ridge, Allegheny, Pocono, Catskills, Berkshire Hills, White, and Green Mountains—form the Appalachian chain. The highest peak in the chain is Mount Mitchell (6,684 feet) in North Carolina. The Appalachians form the **Eastern Continental Divide**, meaning that waters that flow down the eastern side of the mountains empty eventually into the Atlantic Ocean, and waters that flow down the western side flow into either the Great Lakes or the Mississippi River and then down to the Gulf of Mexico.

For the most part, the Appalachians are relatively low, rounded, tree-covered mountains, but they were a significant obstacle to settlement during the colonial era. After explorers discovered the Cumberland Gap—a mountain pass on the borders of what today are Virginia, Tennessee, and Kentucky—large numbers of settlers poured west of the Appalachians.

THE CENTRAL PLAINS

West of the Appalachians, settlers discovered the fertile rolling hills, forests, and prairies of the **Central Plains** stretching about a thousand miles across the heart of the country. The **Mississippi River** and its tributaries and the Great Lakes provide numerous water transportation routes. The rich soils produce abundant opportunities for raising livestock and growing corn, soybeans, wheat, and other crops.

The Great Smoky Mountains are one range in the Appalachian chain.

THE GREAT PLAINS

West of the Central Plains lies another plains region called the **Great Plains**, which begins about the one hundredth meridian and stretches to the base of the Rocky Mountains. The altitude rises gradually from about one thousand feet above sea level in the east to

Geographic Regions of the United States

Mountain
Plateau
Plain
Basin

about five thousand feet against the mountains in the west. The Great Plains are characterized by flat grasslands and a dry climate. Although the soil is rich, the dry prairie sod was long thought to be useless for farming. Irrigation, however, has brought the area, once known as the "Great American Desert," to life with fields of grain and herds of cattle.

The Rocky Mountains

The mountains that mark the western boundary of the Great Plains are the **Rocky Mountains**, the peaks of which exceed ten thousand feet. The tallest, Mount Elbert, is 14,433 feet in elevation. The Rockies presented a formidable obstacle to extensive westward settlement until the completion of the transcontinental railroad in 1869. Today, the Rockies provide mineral resources and scenic beauty. National parks and ski resorts make the region a popular vacation area.

Just as the Appalachian Mountains form the Eastern Continental Divide, the Rockies form the **Western Continental Divide**. Waters that flow down the eastern side of the mountains run eventually into the Mississippi River and to the Gulf of Mexico, whereas waters that flow down the western side run into the Pacific Ocean.

The Great Basin

Between the Rocky Mountains and the mountains along the Pacific coast is a lowland area called the **Great Basin** that includes most of Nevada and a large part of Utah. Although

Pioneers called the Great Plains the "Great American Desert," but they soon discovered that, with proper care, the plains could be a rich and fertile farmland.

For years, a major obstacle to westward movement was the Rocky Mountains, of which Grand Teton is a part.

altitudes in this intermountain region are generally five thousand feet or more, compared to the mountain ranges on either side the area is a lowland. On the north is the Columbia Plateau. To the south is the Colorado Plateau. Rivers have cut deep canyons through this region, and winds have carved unusual rock formations there.

THE PACIFIC MOUNTAIN RANGES

Along the Pacific coast of the United States is a series of mountain ranges interspersed with low valleys. The mountains are part of a system called the **Pacific Mountain Ranges** and include the Sierra Nevada along the eastern side of California; the Cascade Mountains, which run through Oregon and Washington; and the Coastal Ranges beside the Pacific shore.

The Central Valley of California and the Willamette Valley of Oregon are two of the many fertile valleys in the area. The Pacific mountains are much narrower than the Rockies, but they contain some high peaks. For example, Mount Whitney in the Sierra Nevada is the highest point in the forty-eight contiguous (adjacent or touching) states.

The Pacific mountains also contain some active volcanoes, including **Mount St. Helens** in Washington's Cascades. The largest major eruption of that volcano was in 1980, but seismic activity in the area intensified dramatically in 2004, and the volcano has had several minor eruptions since.

The fertile valleys with their mild climates and mountain streams bearing gold brought a rush of settlers to the Pacific Mountain Ranges in the 1840s and 1850s. The climate and thriving businesses continue to make the Pacific area an attractive place to settle.

El Capitan in the Yosemite Valley is part of the central Sierra Nevada range.

Mount St. Helens literally "blew its top" in 1980, and periodic seismic activity is detected there.

ALASKA

The United States is what is known as a "fragmented" state, meaning that part of its land area is separated from the rest by water or another country. Such is the case with Alaska, which is separated from the "lower forty-eight" by Canada, and Hawaii, which is separated from the mainland by the Pacific Ocean. Although Alaska is far to the north of the northwestern states, its geographic regions are a continuation of those we have mentioned in the lower forty-eight states. Coastal mountains rim the Gulf of Alaska, reaching their highest elevations in the Alaska Range. At 20,320 feet, **Mount McKinley** is the highest point in North America. In northern Alaska, the Brooks Range is the northern end of the Rocky Mountain chain. Between those two mountain groups lies an area of hills and plains drained mainly by the Yukon River.

Like the northernmost regions of Canada, Alaska has a cold climate most of the year. It is, however, an area that is rich in resources, especially oil.

Mt. McKinley in Alaska is the highest mountain in North America.

Hawaii

Finally, the westernmost state of the United States is Hawaii, a chain of volcanic islands near the center of the Pacific Ocean. The remaining active volcanoes are at the southeast end of the chain on the largest of the islands, also called Hawaii.

Rich soil covers much of these islands, and their tropical climate helps make them valuable spots for pineapple and sugar cane plantations. Some of the islands' beaches have made Hawaii a famous tourist destination. The U.S. military also uses Hawaii as its headquarters for the Pacific region.

Section Quiz

1. Into what two parts are the Coastal Plains divided?
2. What does the term *piedmont* mean?
3. In what mountain chain is the Eastern Continental Divide?
4. By what other name were the Great Plains once known?
5. What mountain is the highest in North America, and in which state is it located?
6. Which state is not only the largest in area but also twice as large as the next largest state?

Climate

Prevailing wind patterns in North America are generally from west to east across the central section of the continent. The warm **Japanese Current** flows across the northwest coast, bringing plentiful rains to that region. A cool ocean current blows by the coast of California, giving that area a mild mediterranean climate with dry, sunny summers and mild, wet winters.

These westerly winds have an important influence on the climate patterns of the United States. As they flow over the Pacific coastal mountains, they lose much of their moisture. Therefore, on the eastern side of the mountains, the winds are cooler, milder, and drier, producing arid conditions for this rainshadow area, which includes the Great Basin and the desert Southwest. Although such areas are very hot during the daytime, they lose their heat quickly at night.

After the winds pass the Great Basin, they must climb over the Rocky Mountains, losing on the western slopes of the Rockies any moisture they might have picked up. On the eastern side, the rainshadow effect once again prevails. The area of the Great Plains immediately east of the Rockies typically receives only ten to twenty inches of precipitation a year.

The temperatures of the Great Plains are affected greatly by the warming and cooling of the great landmass of the heart of the North American continent. In temperate regions, this continental effect results in wide temperature extremes, hot in summer and cold in winter. For example, temperatures might average in the 80s and 90s in summer but dip to below 0° in winter. A place at the same latitude on the west coast might have temperatures that rarely exceed 80° or go below 30°.

In the eastern United States, two basic climates predominate. The northern half is influenced by not only the

Five Largest States by Area	
State	Area (sq. mi.)
1. Alaska	591,004
2. Texas	266,807
3. California	156,537
4. Montana	145,603
5. New Mexico	121,593

Although Hawaii is known as a tourist destination, its rich soils make it an important agricultural state as well.

In March 1966, North Dakota received a blizzard that resulted in more than normal accumulation for even that cold state, nearly burying the telephone poles.

Levees broke in New Orleans following Hurricane Katrina in 2005, allowing waters from Lake Ponchartrain to ravage the below-sea-level city.

U.S. Ranking for Production of Selected Resources

The following chart shows how the United States ranks among the other countries of the world in respect to selected natural resources. Notice in how few instances the United States is actually first but how often it is in the top ten countries.

Resource	U.S. Rank
Aluminum	4
Coal	2
Copper	2
Iron ore	7
Lead	3
Natural gas	2
Oil	12
Phosphates	1
Platinum	4
Silver	7
Sulfur	1
Zinc	5

westerly flow of air across the plains but also the cold winds that sometimes dip down from Canada. The east has a generally cool, humid climate. The winters are cold, and the summers are hot. Precipitation totals range from twenty to more than forty inches a year. States around the Great Lakes also get "lake-effect snows" as the air picks up moisture as it crosses the Great Lakes. States of the Northeast are sometimes subjected to terrific storms known as "**nor'easters**," which, as their name indicates, move in from the northeast over the North Atlantic.

The South is influenced by not only the westerly flow of air across the continent and occasionally the cold Canadian air but also the warm, moist breezes from the Gulf of Mexico. Average temperatures are much milder in the South than in the North. Temperatures along the Gulf coast rarely dip below freezing. When the warm, moist air from the Gulf moves northeast and meets the cooler air moving southwest, violent thunderstorms and tornadoes occur in the summer and snowstorms in the winter, especially in the border states that divide the North from the South.

Between June and November, the southern Atlantic and Gulf coasts are susceptible to hurricanes and tropical storms that develop in the Atlantic Ocean off Africa and move across the Atlantic and through the Caribbean. The 2004 and 2005 hurricane seasons proved to be especially destructive in southwest Florida and from eastern Texas to Mississippi. Florida was hit by three major hurricanes in 2004, including Category 4 Charley; and New Orleans was hit by Category 5 (the highest level) Hurricane Katrina in 2005. A couple of days later, 80 percent of New Orleans was flooded when levees broke, allowing Lake Pontchartrain to flow into the below-sea-level city.

RESOURCES

God has graciously blessed the United States with an abundance of natural resources. Although the United States does not lead the world in the production of many of the common and necessary natural resources, it is generally among the top producers of the resources it does possess. Whatever resources it lacks, it is able to obtain through trade with other countries. Of the resources that it does possess, the United States has more than enough for its own needs and trades the excess to other nations who need them.

The key to the economic success of the United States or any other country, however, is not how many resources it has but rather how well its government creates an environment that encourages domestic production of the available resources. Other countries have more of certain resources than the United States has, but they have governments and economies that discourage the proper use and development of those resources. God has blessed the United States with a heritage of free government and broad economic freedoms that have encouraged individual and corporate initiative and genius, and those gifts have led to generally wise stewardship of natural resources.

The greatest and most valuable natural resource a country can have, however, is its people. Countries that value human life and provide governments and economies that encourage individual initiative tend to succeed economically. Conversely, societies that denigrate their people, unduly restrict or regulate their economic activities, or tax their efforts to improve themselves tend to be proportionately less successful in the use of their resources.

Another measure of a country's stewardship involves the use of its plant and animal life to produce foods and other products necessary for not only subsistence but also trading with other countries and improving the quality of life for its citizens. The United States has been very successful in doing this; its agricultural industries have been able to produce more than enough to meet U.S. needs and to "feed the world" with the surplus—and yet that production represents less than 1 percent of the U.S. GDP.

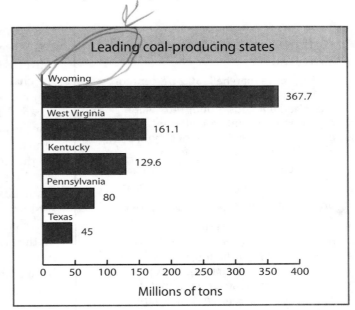

Leading coal-producing states

State	Millions of tons
Wyoming	367.7
West Virginia	161.1
Kentucky	129.6
Pennsylvania	80
Texas	45

SECTION QUIZ

1. From which direction do prevailing winds in the United States come?

2. What current brings a lot of rain to the Northwest?

3. To what type of weather feature are the U.S. Atlantic and Gulf coasts susceptible between June and November?

4. How did the city of New Orleans flood in 2005?

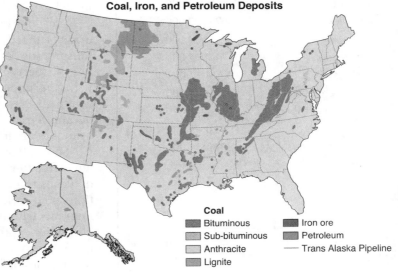

Coal, Iron, and Petroleum Deposits

Coal
- Bituminous
- Sub-bituminous
- Anthracite
- Lignite
- Iron ore
- Petroleum
- — Trans Alaska Pipeline

II. THE AMERICAN PEOPLE

Just as the word *diverse* describes the geographic variety of the United States, so it describes the American people. Very few Americans can trace their ancestry to Native American ethnicity; most are descended from immigrants who brought to their new home diverse languages, customs, and traditions. Through hard work and determination, the early settlers eventually built a strong, prosperous, and united country. They shared a respect for Christian values and a willingness to endure personal sacrifice. They were also unified by certain core values.

CORE VALUES

Core values forge a common culture and bind a people together. For Americans from the colonial period to the present, those ideals have been freedom, equality, and individualism. People have spoken and heard these words so often that they may no longer appreciate their true meaning.

FREEDOM

Freedom, or liberty, is fundamental. In times of crisis national leaders have often spoken of its importance. Patrick Henry's familiar

Leading Dairy Products–Producing States

1.	California	$3,812M
2.	Wisconsin	$2,663M
3.	New York	$1,556M
4.	Pennsylvania	$1,482M
5.	Minnesota	$1,011M
6.	Idaho	$918M
7.	New Mexico	$744M
8.	Michigan	$712M
9.	Texas	$681M
10.	Washington	$671M

Religious Affiliations of Americans

Slightly more than half (50.2 percent) of all Americans claim affiliation with an organized religious group; 140 million American represent 149 different religious bodies. The three largest bodies in the United States are as follows:

Roman Catholics	62M
Southern Baptists	20M
United Methodists	10M

Classified into broad religious groups, the American nation practices the following religions. (The first number is how many individual *members* the group claims; the second number is how many *congregations* the group has.)

Protestants	66M/222,000
Catholics *Roman Catholics*	62M/22,000
Jews *Judaism*	6M/4,000
Mormons	4M/12,000
Muslims	1.6M/1,000+
Eastern Christian, (including Orthodox)	1M/2,000
Eastern religions	150K/4,000
Unitarian Universalist	180K/1,000

The landing of the Pilgrims at Plymouth, Massachusetts, was the beginning of America's religious heritage.

words in 1775 on the eve of the Revolution frame it simply: "Why stand we here idle? What is it that gentlemen wish? What would they have? Is life so dear, or peace so sweet, as to be purchased at the price of chains and slavery? Forbid it, Almighty God! I know not what course others may take; but as for me, give me liberty or give me death!" The Preamble of the Constitution declares that one purpose for the new nation was to "secure the Blessings of Liberty to ourselves and our Posterity." The Bill of Rights, the first ten amendments added to the Constitution in 1791, further guaranteed American liberties.

To sustain the Union during its darkest moment in history, Abraham Lincoln repeated the theme in the opening words of the Gettysburg Address: "Four score and seven years ago our fathers brought forth on this continent, a new nation, conceived in Liberty. . . ." In 1941, at the brink of America's entry into World War II, Franklin Roosevelt set forth the ideal of the "Four Freedoms," which included freedoms of speech and religion, as well as "freedom from want" and "freedom from fear." To commemorate valor in that war, Ronald Reagan spoke in Normandy in 1984 for the observance of the fortieth anniversary of D-day: "We're here to mark that day in history when the Allied armies joined in battle to reclaim this continent to liberty."

Freedom has several meanings. America's first English settlers came primarily for economic opportunity. With the growth of capitalism, those in Virginia sought the rewards and challenges of economic liberty through trade. Generations that followed succeeded with the opportunities provided by profit and private property, whether in farming, commerce, or manufacturing. America quickly became a middle-class nation, in contrast to Europe's deep social divisions of aristocrats and peasants.

Soon after Jamestown, the Pilgrims and Puritans sought religious freedom in New England. The Reformation brought religious divisions to Europe, and those who dissented and suffered persecution could seek refuge in the New World. Despite later waves of immigrants with diverse faiths, tolerance eventually provided religious liberty for more colonists until the First Amendment secured religious liberty for all. The Great Awakening, the spiritual revival in the decades before the American Revolution, produced numbers of converts who sought new churches and denominations. This weakened the established churches, like the Church of England (Anglican Church), and fueled religious liberty, making a political break with England easier.

But the American ideal of religious freedom, as well as political and economic freedom, is not the same as the biblical view of liberty, which is the freedom from sin and the ability to serve God. James spoke of Scripture as the "law of liberty" (James 1:25). The New Testament also celebrates salvation as freedom from slavery, the bondage of sin. On a practical level, however, Paul did encourage Christians who were slaves to seek their freedom if they had the opportunity (1 Cor. 7:21).

Historically, the greatest meaning for freedom, from the founding fathers to today, is political liberty. This secular idea emerged during the Enlightenment. The English philosopher John Locke, along with others, focused on man's right to life, liberty, and property, rights that came from the "state of nature." Thomas Jefferson in the Declaration of Independence altered it to read "Life, Liberty, and the pursuit of Happiness." Their ideas, which were radical in an age of kings and nobles, centered on the right of "the people" to govern themselves. This commitment to democracy (the majority prevails) and a republic (rule by elected officials) put the founding fathers ahead of the times. They believed people should not be ruled by monarchs and aristocrats, whose power was determined by birth and wealth and whom they viewed as tyrannical, but by chosen leaders. Lincoln repeated this point at the end of his speech in Gettysburg: "[T]his nation, under God, shall have a new birth of freedom—and that government of the people, by the people, for the people, shall not perish from the earth."

Reagan in his 1984 speech in Normandy also reminded the world that the "men of Normandy" recognized the value of political freedom and democracy: "You all knew that some things are worth dying for. One's country is worth dying for, and democracy is worth dying for, because it's the most deeply honorable form of government ever devised by man. All of you loved liberty. All of you were willing to fight tyranny, and you knew the people of your countries were behind you." Warfare against the enemies of freedom has not only preserved America but has also united America, a land of great diversity.

EQUALITY

Another core American ideal is that of equality, a word whose meaning has changed over the centuries. In the same Declaration of Independence where he highlighted liberty, Jefferson also stated, "We hold these truths to be self-evident, that all men are created equal." Jefferson, like other writers in the Enlightenment, was simply pointing out that everyone is equally human. He was not talking about social equality; his ownership of slaves makes that clear.

Like Jefferson, Lincoln joined his discussions of equality and liberty. The opening sentence of the Gettysburg Address speaks of "a new nation, conceived in Liberty and dedicated to the proposition that all men are created equal." Lincoln had expanded the meaning of equality to include the ending of slavery.

The ideals of liberty and equality may often conflict with one another. In a society that permits freedom, some citizens will achieve more than others and inequality may result. On the other hand, if the government seeks to ensure equality by restricting some citizens' activities, then some liberty is curtailed.

INDIVIDUALISM

Likewise, another core value—individualism—may work against equality. Americans celebrate the ideal of the self-reliant individual, often at the expense of the group or society. That independent spirit contributed to a work ethic that encouraged capitalism and economic success for many but has led to some social inequality. Individualism has long been a part of Western civilization, beginning with the ancient Greeks and Romans and reinforced in the Renaissance and the Age of Reason, when philosophers declared that individuals had natural rights.

Christianity has also strengthened individualism. The Bible stresses the individual and his or her need of salvation. Luther in the Reformation dramatically shifted the focus to the individual's access to God, not through the priest or church but through Christ alone. Evangelical Christians today continue that emphasis on individual salvation rather than a social gospel that seeks to "save" society.

On the other hand, the Bible also teaches that we are to help those in need, the poor, especially widows and orphans. Not every person is able to take care of himself. Christ commands us to pay taxes, some of which may be used for social programs. Remarkably, the French observer of American society in the 1830s, Alexis de Tocqueville, observed in *Democracy in America* that religion in this country countered some of the selfishness that resulted from individualism. People of faith, he essentially argued, would generally seek the well-being of others. The American people, throughout history and even today, continue to be religious, which is unusual for an advanced, industrialized nation in the modern age. In contrast, Europe today is generally secular.

In addition to liberty, equality, and individualism, American society has another distinct quality. The United States has become the world's first universal culture, a true blend of various peoples. America's history of immigration, from the seventeenth century to the present, has brought together unprecedented numbers of different races, languages, and religions. Those cultural differences make equality more challenging, but Americans must strive to live the national motto—*E pluribus unum*, "From many, one." The Christian has an even higher mandate—Love your neighbor as yourself—a command that leaves no room for racism.

The model for unity is the universal church, the body of believers, which is one in Christ through repentance and faith in Him. Paul declares it best in Galatians 3:28: "There is neither Jew nor Greek, there is neither bond nor free, there is neither male nor female: for ye are all one in Christ Jesus."

Like the Greeks and Romans in the ancient world and the French and British in recent centuries, Americans have looked at their country as special. Puritans in New England had a mission to be "a city upon a hill," a model for the world. In the 1840s Americans celebrated "Manifest Destiny," their belief that westward expansion was divinely ordained. At the ending of World War I, Woodrow Wilson sought to make the "world safe for democracy," and at the beginning of the twenty-first century, George W. Bush sought to spread democracy globally as the answer to terrorism.

While it is normal for any nation to feel proud of its way of life, Americans must recognize that they often have failed to live up to the ideals of freedom and equality. On the other hand, they must acknowledge that any success is due only to God's grace, not American ingenuity or resourcefulness.

SECTION QUIZ

1. What are the three core values that traditionally bound Americans as a united people?

2. What historically has been the greatest meaning of *freedom*?

3. What is the model for national unity?

DEMOGRAPHY

A big part of studying geography is understanding **demographics**, the study of the characteristics of people in a particular place or a segment of that population. The goal of such study is to understand better who the people are, why they live as they do, and "what makes them tick." It includes the population count, of course, but it also includes much more.

The United States has an estimated population of 296 million. Of those, 79 percent live in **urban areas,** places with a population of 50,000 or more. This number also includes those who live in **suburbs**, areas between cities and **rural** (country) settings.

The 2000 census showed that for the first time, all fifty states increased in population, although the greatest growth has been in the southern third of the nation from the Carolinas to California, an area known as the **Sun Belt**. The increased growth there might be the result of increased numbers of retirees who move from the cooler north to the warmer climates of southern states.

The census also noted that total U.S. growth was 13.2 percent. The growth of individual states ranged from a low of 0.5 percent (North Dakota) to a phenomenal 66.3 percent (Nevada). Twelve states had a growth rate above 20 percent; only two states (West Virginia and North Dakota) had a growth rate of less than 1 percent. Most of the U.S. growth occurred in the West and the South. Only one county in the nation reported *no* growth. The most heavily populated areas continue to be the Northeast and the West Coast, although other metropolitan areas are also growing.

The growth of minority groups continued, especially among the Hispanic population. The minority populations tend to cluster in certain regions—Hispanics and Native Americans in the West and Southwest, blacks along the southeastern seaboard and in the Deep South, and Asians in the West.

The non-Anglo population is growing in all fifty states. For example, the non-white population of Texas now totals 50.2 percent of all Texans, the largest group of which are Hispanics. Such is also the case in California and New Mexico. A similar situation exists in Hawaii, where the largest minority group is Asians. Five states (Maryland, Mississippi, Georgia, New York, and Arizona) have about 40 percent minority populations. Estimates indicate that more than half of the nation's population could be minorities by 2050.

The birth rate of the United States is approximately 14 (14 live births per 1,000 people in the general population). The average life

As fewer people are needed to work on farms, populations have moved from rural to urban and suburban locations.

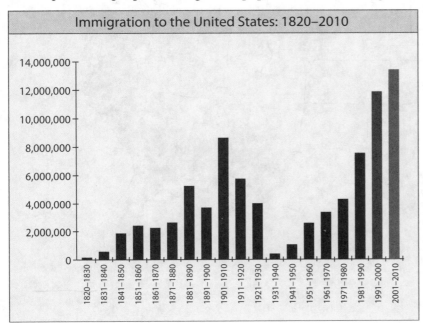

Immigration to the United States: 1820–2010

			Countries of Birth of Foreign-born U.S. Population			
Rank	1850	1880	1930	1960	1990	2000
1	Ireland 962,000	Germany 1,967,000	Italy 1,790,000	Italy 1,257,000	Mexico 4,298,000	Mexico 7,841,000
2	Germany 584,000	Ireland 1,855,000	Germany 1,609,000	Germany 990,000	China 921,000	China 1,391,000
3	Great Britain 379,000	Great Britain 918,000	United Kingdom 1,403,000	Canada 953,000	Philippines 913,000	Philippines 1,222,000
4	Canada 148,000	Canada 717,000	Canada 1,310,000	United Kingdom 833,000	Canada 745,000	India 1,007,000
5	France 54,000	Sweden 194,000	Poland 1,269,000	Poland 748,000	Cuba 737,000	Cuba 952,000
6	Switzerland 13,000	Norway 182,000	Soviet Union 1,154,000	Soviet Union 691,000	Germany 712,000	Vietnam 863,000
7	Mexico 13,000	France 107,000	Ireland 745,000	Mexico 576,000	United Kingdom 640,000	El Salvador 765,000
8	Norway 13,000	China 104,000	Mexico 641,000	Ireland 339,000	Italy 581,000	Korea 701,000
9	Holland 10,000	Switzerland 89,000	Sweden 595,000	Austria 305,000	Korea 568,000	Dominican Republic 692,000
10	Italy 4,000	Bohemia 85,000	Czechoslovakia 492,000	Hungary 245,000	Vietnam 543,000	Canada 678,000

Minority Population Concentrations

25% or more of population

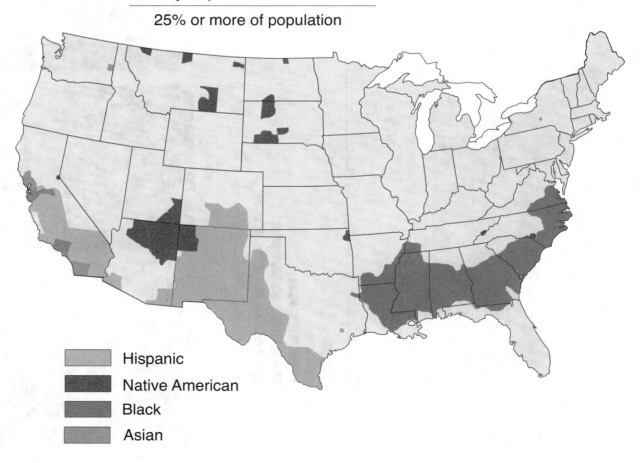

- Hispanic
- Native American
- Black
- Asian

span of an American is 77.71 years. (This is in stark contrast to both the world average of 64.33 years and that of the lowest in the world, Botswana, at 33.87 years. Japan has the highest average life span at 81.15 years.) Advances in preventative health care, better medicines, and improved technology to detect and treat physical problems earlier in life and to maintain health in old age are leading to the "graying" of the U.S. population. More people are living longer, and the average age of Americans is increasing. The number of Americans who are 65 years of age and older is expected to double by 2050.

Although this news is good from the standpoint of health, fitness, and life expectancy, it also presents potential problems for the U.S. government and economy. As the number of retirees withdrawing from the workforce (i.e., no longer paying taxes) increases and they begin to draw money from the Social Security System, the tax burden on younger Americans increases. Currently, five tax-paying workers support every retiree, but by 2030 that number is projected to have shrunk to three workers per retiree.

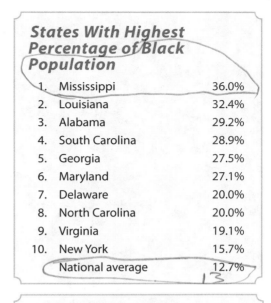

States With Highest Percentage of Black Population

1.	Mississippi	36.0%
2.	Louisiana	32.4%
3.	Alabama	29.2%
4.	South Carolina	28.9%
5.	Georgia	27.5%
6.	Maryland	27.1%
7.	Delaware	20.0%
8.	North Carolina	20.0%
9.	Virginia	19.1%
10.	New York	15.7%
	National average	12.7%

States With Highest Percentage of Hispanic Population

1.	New Mexico	45.1%
2.	Texas	37.5%
3.	California	33.1%
4.	Arizona	29.5%
5.	Nevada	21.7%
6.	Colorado	20.1%
7.	Florida	19.5%
8.	New York	15.3%
9.	New Jersey	13.3%
10.	Illinois	12.6%
	National average	14.0%

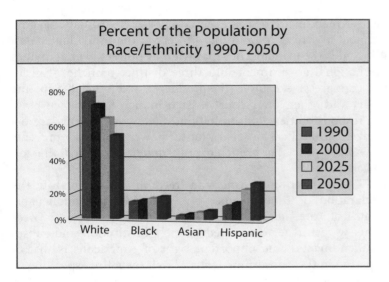

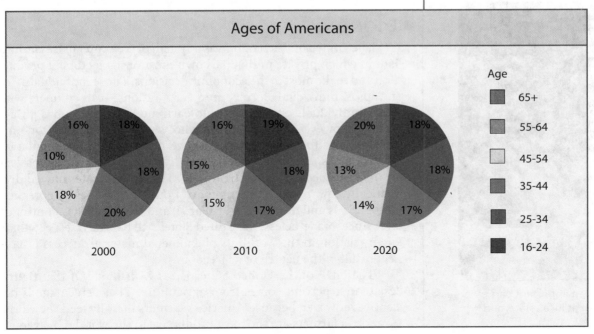

SECTION QUIZ

1. What term means the study of the characteristics of people in a particular place?
2. In which area—urban or rural—do 79 percent of Americans live?
3. What is the southern third of the United States called?
4. What is the average life expectancy in the United States?

GOVERNMENT

The United States government functions as a **federal republic**, meaning that power is shared between the national government and the governments of the fifty states. In addition are the various local governments within each state—counties, townships, boroughs, cities, etc. Each of the various governments functions under a constitution, with the U.S. Constitution being the overriding governing document or "law of the land." That document (specifically the Tenth Amendment) delegates certain powers to the national government and reserves all other powers to the individual states. It includes the principle of **separation of powers**, which divides the national government into three distinct branches: legislative (Congress), executive (the president), and judicial (Supreme Court and other lower courts). Each branch has its own powers, responsibilities, and limitations. State governments are organized similarly. The separation of powers principle prevents any elected official or branch of government from becoming too powerful.

The foundation of American freedom was set forth in the Declaration of Independence and included the "unalienable rights" of "life, liberty, and the pursuit of happiness." These rights were further delineated in the Constitution and subsequent amendments. One important right of Americans is that of participating in their government at all levels by voting, speaking or publishing their opinions, or even running for public office.

ECONOMY

The United States economy is a system of **free enterprise capitalism** in which private individuals own most of the factors of production and make most of the economic decisions. Those individuals—or groups of individuals formed into corporations—can compete with other individuals or companies to earn money. Tension has always existed, however, between those who want unrestricted economic freedom and those who advocate government control or regulation of various aspects of economic activity, usually to give themselves or their businesses favored treatment. The United States moved dramatically toward government control during the Great Depression of the 1930s and during World War II, and that trend has continued ever since. Nonetheless, the United States still has the freest economy of any nation in the world. Its phenomenal material success is a direct result of the degree of its freedom.

The GDP of the United States is $11.75 trillion. Of that figure, less than 1 percent comes from agriculture. That percentage is deceptive, however, because America's farmers literally feed the world. America's farmers are the most productive in the world. On average,

The U. S. Capitol houses the Senate and the House of Representatives.

Freedom of speech is an important part of American government at local, state, and national levels.

SHOW YOUR COLORS

The first flag used by General George Washington during the American Revolution was called the Grand Union flag and was hoisted at the siege of Boston, 1776. It had thirteen alternating red and white stripes and the British Union Jack in the upper left-hand corner (where the stars are today).

In 1777, Congress passed the first Flag Act, which specified that "the flag . . . be made of thirteen stripes, alternate red and white, that the union be thirteen stars, white in a blue field, representing a new Constellation."

Between then and 1960, several (twenty-six) laws changed the design of the flag, adding stars and arranging and rearranging those features. The current design is thirteen horizontal stripes, alternating red and white, representing the original thirteen colonies. The stars represent the individual fifty states. The colors are also symbolic. Red represents valor, or courage; white represents purity and innocence; and blue represents vigilance, perseverance, and justice.

an American farmer produces food and other related products for about 144 people.

Almost 20 percent of the GDP is industry, and an amazing 80 percent is services. The per capita GDP is $40,100. One cause of concern is the national debt, which is 65 percent of the GDP. More than 17 percent of government expenditures are payments of interest (not principal) on the national debt, only 2 percent less than is spent on national defense. The combined expenses incurred by the ongoing war on terrorism and relief for victims of an unprecedented number of natural disasters in 2004 and 2005 only exacerbate the problem,

The floor of the New York Stock Exchange, which is symbolic of the U.S. economy, is the heart of the New York City financial district known as Wall Street.

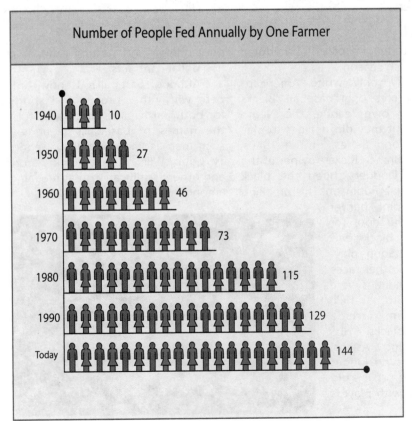

Number of People Fed Annually by One Farmer

Year	People Fed
1940	10
1950	27
1960	46
1970	73
1980	115
1990	129
Today	144

Agricultural Regions of the United States

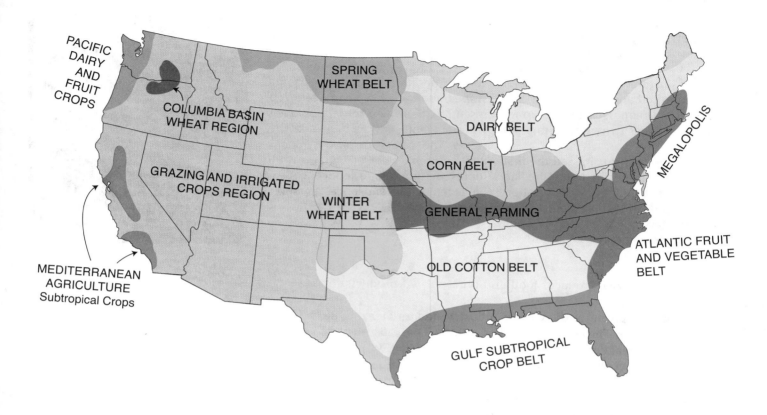

PACIFIC DAIRY AND FRUIT CROPS

COLUMBIA BASIN WHEAT REGION

SPRING WHEAT BELT

DAIRY BELT

MEGALOPOLIS

GRAZING AND IRRIGATED CROPS REGION

CORN BELT

WINTER WHEAT BELT

GENERAL FARMING

MEDITERRANEAN AGRICULTURE
Subtropical Crops

ATLANTIC FRUIT AND VEGETABLE BELT

OLD COTTON BELT

GULF SUBTROPICAL CROP BELT

AMERICA'S PASTIME: BASEBALL

Baseball has long been called "America's pastime." Alexander Cartwright invented the game in 1845 and founded the New York Knickerbocker Base Ball Club. The first recorded game was in 1846 between Cartwright's club and the New York Base Ball Club. Cartwright's team lost. Baseball was also played by soldiers during the War Between the States.

The first salaried team was the Cincinnati Red Stockings in 1869. The first professional baseball league was formed two years later as the National Association of Professional Base Ball Players, and the first formal major league, the National League, began in 1876. A rival American League was formed in 1893. These same two leagues have competed ever since.

At first, the teams played other teams in their own league and then the winners of each league played each other in the World Series. Today, some interleague play is scheduled during each season.

Initially, only white Americans played professional baseball. Blacks had their own league, the Negro League, but they did not get to play in the World Series. In the 1940s, however, Branch Rickey, owner of the Brooklyn Dodgers, hired the black player Jackie Robinson. This breaking of the color barrier opened the door for extensive black participation. Soon, players of still other races and nationalities were allowed into baseball. Today, teams include whites, blacks, Hispanics, and Asians. Baseball is no longer merely a sport; it is big business, with players demanding—and getting—multimillion dollar contracts.

Although baseball must now compete with other professional sports for both participants and spectators, the names of baseball's legends—such men as Babe Ruth, Lou Gehrig, Ty Cobb, Willy Mayes, Hank Aaron, and others—still carry great meaning among Americans today.

NATURAL TREASURES OF THE UNITED STATES

The U.S. government has sought to preserve the natural wonders of the nation for the benefit of future generations so that they can experience what the early settlers of the fledgling country saw during their westward migration. Such areas have been preserved in the form of national parks, most of which are west of the Mississippi River. The most visited national park, however, the Great Smoky Mountains National Park, is in Eastern Tennessee and western North Carolina. This national park has the largest number of people living within a day's drive. The following chapter includes photographs of several national parks. Perhaps you have visited some of them yourself. Maybe you would like to visit others in the future and enjoy firsthand the natural treasures of the United States of America. Consider conducting an in-depth study of one or more of the parks you find most interesting.

Charlie's Bunion offers phenomenal views of the rugged beauty of the Great Smoky Mountains National Park.

making it harder to pay down the national debt. Many critics say that this situation cannot be allowed to continue without potentially disastrous results to the economy.

Although the United States has a free enterprise economy, the federal government owns and controls a vast amount (nearly one-third) of the land in the nation. Fifty-five percent of the West is owned by the government, as is 36.4 percent of Alaska and Hawaii. Only 2.4 percent of government-owned land is used for military purposes. Much of the rest is national parks, forests, wilderness areas, or protected areas.

SECTION QUIZ

1. What type of government does the United States have?
2. What three branches of government guarantee separation of powers?
3. What form of economy does the United States have?
4. What sector of the economy makes up only 1 percent of U.S. GDP yet is the most productive such sector in the world?
5. What sector makes up 80 percent of U.S. GDP?
6. What percentage of western lands are owned by the federal government?
7. How are most of the federally owned lands used?

States with the Greatest Income from Agriculture

(Amounts shown are $ thousands)

Rank	State	Amount
1.	California	26,106,640
2.	Texas	12,664,912
3.	Iowa	10,833,860
4.	Nebraska	9,688,658
5.	Kansas	7,861,794
6.	Illinois	7,486,125
7.	Minnesota	7,478,126
8.	Florida	6,848,253
9.	North Carolina	6,602,899
10.	Wisconsin	6,318,908

States Containing the Most Federally Owned Lands

Rank/State		% fed. owned
1.	Nevada	91.9
2.	Alaska	66.7
3.	Utah	66.5
4.	Idaho	66.4
5.	Wyoming	50.6
6.	Arizona	50.2
7.	Oregon	49.7
8.	California	46.9
9.	Colorado	34.9
10.	New Mexico	34.1

Can You:
Define These Terms?

fall line	rural
Japanese Current	Sun Belt
nor'easter	federal republic
E pluribus unum	separation of
demographics	powers
urban areas	free enterprise
suburbs	capitalism

Locate These Places?

Rio Grande	Mississippi River
Coastal Plains	Great Plains
Atlantic Coastal	Rocky Mountains
Plain	Western Conti-
Gulf Coastal Plain	nental Divide
Piedmont	Great Basin
Appalachian	Pacific Moun-
Mountains	tain Ranges
Eastern Conti-	Mount St. Helens
nental Divide	Mount McKinley
Central Plains	

CHAPTER REVIEW

HOW MUCH DO YOU REMEMBER?

1. What countries and geographic features constitute the northern and southern boundaries of the United States?

2. What two problems confront the United States along its southern border?

3. What are some of the most famous swamps along the Atlantic Coastal Plain?

4. What geographic feature is prominent among the mountains of the Pacific Mountain Range?

5. What are the terrific storms of the Northeast called?

6. What word best describes both the American landscape and the people who live there?

7. What three core values have traditionally bound Americans as a united people?

WHAT DO YOU THINK?

1. Which do you think is a better environment for rearing a Christian family—urban, suburban, or rural—and why?

2. What challenges will affect the United States as its minority population continues to grow?

3. Do you think the separation of powers principle still works in U.S. government, or has one branch gained more power and influence than the other two? Why?

4. Why have some countries with just as many resources as—or even more than—the United States been unable to duplicate U.S. economic success?

The Statue of Liberty symbolizes the hope and opportunities of the American nation.

THE REGIONS OF THE UNITED STATES

I. THE NORTHEAST
    A. NEW ENGLAND
    B. MIDDLE ATLANTIC

II. THE SOUTH
    A. UPPER SOUTH
    B. LOWER SOUTH

III. THE MIDWEST

IV. THE PLAINS

V. THE WEST
    A. CONTINENTAL WEST
    B. OUTLYING STATES

In the previous chapter, you got a broad picture of the United States. You studied the American landscape, noting its boundaries, topographical regions, and climate. You examined the diverse peoples who make up the American population and the heritage that they share. And you looked briefly at the form of government and the economic system by which the American nation functions. In this chapter, you will take a closer look at the major geographic regions of the United States, noting each region's unique qualities and contributions to the broader American nation and the world, and will take at brief look at each state.

Each region has unique qualities, resources, activities, needs, and cultural distinctions. You will study the various regions as they are divided on the following map of the United States. Refer to the map as you read your assignments.

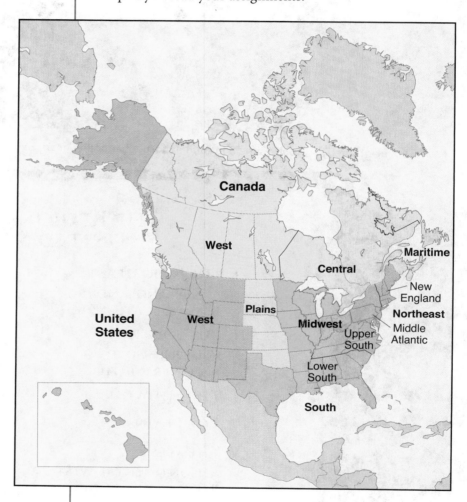

I. The Northeast

The Northeast region can be further divided into two subregions, New England and the Middle Atlantic, which are divided by a series of hills and mountains. Nine of the thirteen original colonies were in the Northeast, so the region played a critical role in the history of the United States, especially in gaining its liberty and independence. The area has abundant monuments and other historical sites that remind visitors of the region's role in history.

The Northeast is the most populated coastal region in the United States with 34 percent of the nation's total coastal population living there. Four of the ten largest metropolitan areas in the nation are located along the northeast coast, where the population density is heaviest: 641 people per square mile.

New England

The six states at the far northeast corner of the United States are very small; all six could fit inside Missouri. Yet they have played a big role in the nation from the beginning. John Cabot, an explorer who claimed the area for England in 1497, called it New England. It became the cradle of capitalism, democracy, and freedom of religion in the New World. The colonists engaged in trans-Atlantic trade from early in their history. They divided their settlements politically into **townships**, and town meetings were the basis of self-government. Because the earliest settlers in this region had come to the New

Flag	State	PO Code	Capital	Date of Statehood	Nickname	Area (sq. mi.)	Population
	Connecticut	CT	Hartford	1788	Constitution State	5,543	3,503,604
	Delaware	DE	Dover	1787	First State	2,489	830,364
	Maine	ME	Augusta	1820	Pine Tree State	35,387	1,317,25
	Maryland	MD	Annapolis	1788	Old Line State	12,407	5,558,058
	Massachusetts	MA	Boston	1788	Bay State	10,555	6,416,505
	New Hampshire	NH	Concord	1788	Granite State	9,351	1,299,500
	New Jersey	NJ	Trenton	1787	Garden State	8,722	8,698,879
	New York	NY	Albany	1788	Empire State	54,471	19,227,088
	Pennsylvania	PA	Harrisburg	1787	Keystone State	46,058	12,406,292
	Rhode Island	RI	Providence	1790	Ocean State	1,545	1,080,632
	Vermont	VT	Montpelier	1791	Green Mountain State	9,615	621,394

Northeastern Fast Facts

The rocky New England coast made lighthouses, such as this one in Massachusetts, necessary for the safety of merchant ships.

World to escape religious persecution, they emphasized freedom of worship, and Christian principles guided life in the colonies there.

The entire Northeast has a humid continental climate, but New England is not very good for farming. The winters are cold, and the growing season is short. For this reason the area relied more on commercial and manufacturing industries than on farming.

New England is divided into three types of terrain: lowlands, uplands, and mountains. The *lowlands* are a narrow strip of coastal plains. Deep harbors along the coast allowed large cities to thrive on trade and fishing. This area also produces almost half of the nation's cranberries. The **New England uplands** are a low, rocky plateau that rises above the coast. The soil in the uplands is too rocky for profitable farming, even along the stretches of coastal lowlands. Most of the good farmland is in the river valleys. Farther inland, several mountain ranges, including the **Berkshire Hills**, rise within the Appalachian Mountain chain.

LOWER NEW ENGLAND

The first New England colony was established in 1620 by the Pilgrims in what is today Massachusetts. The Mayflower Compact (a contract or agreement) laid the foundation for self-government in the colony and set precedents for the future nation. The main port that developed along the coast of Massachusetts was Boston, which became the capital and largest city of the Bay State.

Massachusetts was a focal point of the American War for Independence, the home of famous writers such as Henry David Thoreau, and at one time the whaling capital of the world. It is also famous for a number of leading political families, including the Adamses and the Kennedys.

Rhode Island, sandwiched between Massachusetts and Connecticut, was founded by Roger Williams, who named the capital Providence in recognition of the way God had provided for the colony. It was the smallest colony, but its contributions to the development of the new nation far surpassed its size. It is considered the birthplace of the Industrial Revolution in the New World because Slater's Mill in Pawtucket was the first major industry in the nation. Its owner, Samuel Slater, built a growing textile industry on the Blackstone River, and New England once produced more cloth than any other place in the world.

Most Rhode Islanders live along the coast. Their capital is the second-largest city in New England.

Connecticut was the first colony to write a constitution to describe and limit its government; hence, its nickname, "The Constitution State." The people have a high standard of living in spite of the lack of natural resources. Some famous Connecticut inventors include Samuel Colt (revolver) and Eli Whitney (cotton gin and mass production of musket parts). Connecticut was also home to Jonathan Edwards, a famous preacher of the Great Awakening. Hartford, the capital, is known as the insurance capital of the world because of the large number of insurance companies that are headquartered there. Connecticut is also the home of both Yale University and the submarine-building port of Groton.

UPPER NEW ENGLAND

Although the three states in the northern part of New England are also small, they are nonetheless larger than the lower three states. Settlement in Upper New England was hindered by the high mountains and rocky soil, which made farming and transportation difficult. Each of the states has mountains that reach above the **timber line**, the altitude at which the climate is too cold for trees. Above the timber line is the **alpine zone**, which is much like the Alps of Europe.

New Hampshire is the only Upper New England state that was one of the original colonies. The northern part of the state is dominated by the **White Mountains**, which are known for their white peaks and Christmas tree farms. In the Presidential Range of the White Mountains, the highest peaks (most of which exceed 5,000 feet in elevation) are named for presidents: Mt. Washington (the highest at 6,288 feet), Mt. Adams, Mt. Quincy Adams, Mt. Jefferson, Mt. Madison, Mt. Monroe, Mt. Pierce, and Mt. Eisenhower. Highways pass through low places in the mountains that New Englanders call **notches**. (People in other regions call them *passes* or *gaps*.)

Most people live in the southern part of the state; the industrial centers are also there, including Nashua, Manchester, and the capital, Concord. The state has only eighteen miles of coastline, and its only port, Portsmouth, is located there.

Vermont was once divided between New York and New Hampshire, but the settlers there declared their independence and set up their own government before the American Revolution. It is the only landlocked New England state and has the lowest population. Because the state lacks a seaport and good soil for farming, it must make the most of its

The construction of Slater's Mill on the Blackstone River marked the beginning of the Industrial Revolution in New England.

Jonathan Edwards is known as the preacher of the Great Awakening.

The USS *Nautilus*, the first nuclear-powered submarine, is on display in Groton, Conn., the sub capital of the world.

Picturesque Vermont was the favorite backdrop for famous painter Norman Rockwell.

natural resources, which include granite, slate, and marble. It is also famous for its maple syrup.

The **Green Mountains** run the length of the state, and river valleys form its eastern and western borders, the Connecticut River on the east and Lake Champlain on the west. Most of the state's people live in these two valleys.

Maine, the largest New England state, was once part of Massachusetts. Most of its cities are small, and most of its coastline is rocky. Although its Cadillac Mountain is only 1,500 feet in elevation, it is the highest point along the North Atlantic seaboard. Maine also includes the only national park in the Northeast.

Maine is famous for its lobsters, the most valuable seafood catch in the world. Tourists also enjoy seeing whales and puffins around the islands of Penobscot Bay. The northernmost of the **Appalachian Mountains**, the Longfellow and White mountains, are in Maine. Trees from these mountains provide most of the nation's toothpicks. The Aroostook Valley is also a productive source of potatoes.

MIDDLE ATLANTIC

The lower portion of the Northeast is composed of five states: New York, Pennsylvania, New Jersey, Maryland, and Delaware. They were settled by a diversity of nationalities, including Swedes, Finns, Dutch, Germans, Irish, and Italians.

INNER-CITY MINISTRIES

The city holds a unique place in society. It is home to business and industry as well as to a variety of cultures, races, and economic classes. Cities are also the source of "high" culture in society as seen by the many concert halls, museums, and exhibition centers. More importantly, cities serve as the nerve center for culture in general. Those who influence the life of the city will bring significant change to the surrounding area as well. Paul realized the importance of reaching the city and thus gave much effort to evangelizing in Ephesus, Corinth, and Rome—some of the largest, most influential cities in the world at the time.

Inner-city ministries, however, face inherent challenges. There is often more crime in the heart of a city than in the suburbs. There is a greater number of children with dysfunctional homes. This leads to poverty, which can lead to crime. Another problem is the perception that many

Christians have of the city. Some people, like Jonah in the Old Testament, view the city as unredeemable.

Christians should not avoid the city out of fear but rather should focus on working for change. The spiritual power available through the Holy Spirit is greater than any opposing force—human or supernatural.

The inner city presents a myriad of opportunities to minister and proclaim Christ's love, whether through politics, relief work, or personal relationships. Believers have the chance to minister to a great diversity of races and cultures. The church can help people interpret their culture. It can also function as a family for those who have been cut off from their families through immigration, relocation, or sin. Financial needs should not be ignored but should be viewed as opportunities for proclaiming the gospel. Programs could incorporate meeting basic physical needs as well as allowing people to learn devel-

opmental skills so they can provide for themselves. Such care for the poor expresses love for God (Matt. 25:34–40).

Cities have always played a significant role in the plan of God. When God gave His people the land of Canaan, He gave them a land full of cities (Deut. 6:10). When He chose the place for His glory to dwell, He chose a city, Jerusalem (1 Kings 8:1; 9:3). When He commanded Jonah to preach repentance to Assyria, He sent him to its chief city, Nineveh (Jonah 1:2). When Jesus sent His disciples to preach the gospel, He sent them first to the city of Jerusalem (Luke 24:46–47; Acts 1:8). And when the fullness of redemption is accomplished, the center of human life on earth will be a city, the New Jerusalem (Rev. 21:1–3). God's heart is in the city, and Christians should be willing to have their hearts in the city as well.

New York is the northernmost Middle Atlantic state and the most populous. Its largest city, New York City, is also the largest city in the nation. It is a megacity, or **megalopolis** (literally "great city"), an urban area made up of many different cities that are close enough to be considered a single urban area. New York City has suburbs in four states! In fact, New York is the heart of a megalopolis that runs from Boston to Washington, D.C.

The Upstate of New York is the vast area outside of the megalopolis of New York City. The area runs from the Hudson and Mohawk river valleys, which slice through the Catskills and the Adirondacks in the east, to Lake Erie and Lake Ontario in the west. The Allegheny Plateau extends westward into the interior of the state. The middle area is called the **Finger Lakes** area, where long, narrow, glacier-made lakes extend from north to south. West of the plateau is a narrow plain along the eastern coast of the two **Great Lakes** that border New York. The moderate climate makes New York a productive farming state. It ranks third in the nation in both dairy products and grape production.

The **Delaware River** flows from New York and separates two other Middle Atlantic states: Pennsylvania and New Jersey. Pennsylvania figured prominently in the nation's early history and boasts such landmarks as Independence Hall and the Liberty Bell in Philadelphia, the largest city in the state. Planned from its earliest days by Quaker William Penn, Philadelphia quickly developed into a major port city and is the fifth-largest city in the nation. Nearby are such important sites as the Gettysburg battlefield, where the bloodiest battle of the Civil War occurred; Hershey, home of the largest chocolate factory in the world; and Lancaster, where a large segment of the intriguing sect of the Amish (AH mish) live.

Northeastern Pennsylvania is rich in **anthracite**, a clean-burning form of coal. Much of that coal is used on the other end of the state in the steel mills of Pittsburgh, Pennsylvania's second-largest city. Pittsburgh is located at the confluence of the Monongahela and Allegheny rivers. Between Philadelphia and Pittsburgh is some of the richest farmland in the country. Pennsylvania ranks fourth in

The Statue of Liberty

"Give me your tired, your poor, your huddled masses yearning to breathe free. . . ."

These words are inscribed on the Statue of Liberty, which has become a symbol of the freedoms and opportunities that the United States affords to immigrants from all over the world. She is dressed in a long, flowing robe; chains of bondage lie broken at her feet; she holds a law tablet in one hand and is raising the torch of freedom in the other hand. From her crown radiate seven rays to light the way to freedom for the other nations of the world.

The statue was a gift from the people of France to commemorate America's first one hundred years of independence, which France had helped her win. It was built in France, disassembled for transport to America, and then reassembled upon arrival in New York.

Lady Liberty is the tallest statue ever built, standing 111 feet tall from toe to crown. The arm with the torch adds another 40 feet to the statue. Her nose alone is the size of a person. The statue is made of an iron framework and is covered with copper sheets, which have now turned green because of oxidation. The statue weighs 225 tons.

The Monongahela River (background) and the Allegheny River (foreground). Pittsburgh developed on the Golden Triangle where these two rivers meet, forming the Ohio River.

NIAGARA FALLS

Perhaps the most famous waterfall in North America is **Niagara Falls**. It is on the border between the United States and Canada. Goat Island divides the Niagara River, creating two separate falls, American Falls on the U.S. side of the border and Horseshoe Falls on the Canadian side. An estimated 500,000 tons (120 million gallons) of water go over the falls every minute. Observation decks are provided on both sides of the falls as well as below the American Falls. Boat tours on the river below take tourists right into the spray from the torrent.

THE AMISH

The sect known as the Amish broke from the German Mennonite Church in the 1690s to follow Jacob Amman, who believed that church members should "shun" people who had been excommunicated from the church. When they came to America in the early eighteenth century, the Amish settled in what is now Lancaster County, Pennsylvania. (Some Amish are also located in Ohio, Indiana, Illinois, Iowa, and Tennessee.)

The Amish are known for their simple lifestyle and self-sufficient communities. They live separate from the world both physically and culturally. They wear plain, unpretentious clothing, drive black or gray horse-drawn buggies, and refuse to use most modern conveniences such as electricity, and gasoline-powered tractors. They are generally farmers and rely on horse or wind power for most of their needs. They speak a unique German-English dialect called Pennsylvania Dutch (literally "Deutsch," or German). Because they do not try to gain converts to their sect and because some of their young people are rejecting their heritage, the Amish are not increasing numerically.

the nation in dairy products, fifth in grapes, and sixth in chicken eggs. The capital, Harrisburg, is situated on the Susquehanna River in the south central part of the state.

Pennsylvania's neighbor to the east is New Jersey. Most of its citizens live in the northeastern part of the state near New York City. A string of cities stretches from that area southwest to Trenton, the capital, on the Delaware River. Most of New Jersey is composed of coastal plains, including the **Pine Barrens** region, a wooded, boggy wilderness.

The moist air from the Gulf Stream gives New Jersey a humid, subtropical climate, and its soil is very fertile. Consequently, the state has developed many small farms, called **truck farms,** on which beans, tomatoes, peppers, and melons are grown, giving the state its nickname, the Garden State. It is fourth in the nation in lettuce production and tenth in greenhouse/nursery products.

Maryland and Delaware form the border between the Northeast and the South. Although they once had much in common with the Old South (i.e., before the War Between the States), they remained in the Union and have been associated with the Middle Atlantic states ever since. They share with Virginia the **Delmarva Peninsula**, the largest peninsula in the Northeast. (The name of the peninsula comes from the names of the three states that share it: *Del*aware, *Mar*yland, and Virginia [*Va.*].) The rivers of the peninsula flow into the Delaware Bay and the **Chesapeake Bay**. The Delmarva Peninsula is connected to the mainland in Virginia by the nearly eighteen-mile-long Chesapeake Bay Bridge-Tunnel.

Delaware, on the Delaware Bay, is the nation's second-smallest state (behind Rhode Island). Its largest city, Wilmington, is famous for the large number of chemical plants, including DuPont, and is known as the Chemical Capital of the World. Maryland has several large cities, all located on the Chesapeake Bay, the largest bay in the nation, which cuts the state in two. The capital, Annapolis, is the home of the U.S. Naval Academy. Baltimore, the largest city, was the first railroad center and was one end of the first telegraph line. It

An aircraft carrier navigates through a section of the Chesapeake Bay Bridge-Tunnel between Cape Charles and Virginia Beach, Va.

is also the site of Fort McHenry, which survived British attack in 1812, inspiring Francis Scott Key's poem "The Star-Spangled Banner," which became the U.S. national anthem.

Maryland's **panhandle**, the narrow strip of the state that extends deep into the continent, is only two miles wide at its narrowest point, but it extends beyond the Appalachian Mountains into the Allegheny Plateau.

SECTION QUIZ

1. Into what two subregions can the Northeast be divided?
2. What entity was the basis of self-government in New England?
3. What is the largest of the New England states?
4. Which Middle Atlantic state is known for its anthracite on one end and its steel mills on the other end?
5. What is the Delmarva Peninsula?

THE DISTRICT OF COLUMBIA

Washington, D.C., the U.S. capital, is not a part of any state. Rather, it is a district run by Congress; therefore it is called the *District of Columbia* (D.C.). The city is built on and around Capitol Hill overlooking the Potomac River. Streets of the city radiate outward, like the spokes of a bicycle wheel, from a central hub called the National Mall, which is surrounded by beautiful government buildings. The six most important such buildings are the White House, where the President lives; the Capitol, where Congress meets; the Supreme Court building; the Bureau of Engraving and Printing, which makes the nation's paper money; the Federal Bureau of Investigation (FBI) Building, which houses the government's crime-fighting bureau; and the Pentagon, which is the headquarters of the U.S. armed forces.

Washington also is home to the Smithsonian Institution, the largest museum in the nation. It includes fourteen buildings and the National Zoo. The most famous monument in the city is the Washington Monument, which honors the first president of the United States. Other memorials to presidents include the Lincoln and the Jefferson memorials and the eternal flame in Arlington National Cemetery, marking John Kennedy's grave. Numerous other memorials honor military personnel who have given their lives for the country, including the Tomb of the Unknown Soldier, the World War II Memorial, the Iwo Jima memorial, and the Vietnam Memorial. The Holocaust Memorial Museum is also in Washington, D.C.

In spite of the efforts of some people to ignore God and His Word and their influence on the nation's history, Washington is filled with such references, both subtle and overt. With all of the problems that plague the United States today—drug abuse, divorce, immorality, crime, abortion, the threats from terrorism, and others—we would be wise to heed the warning in Deuteronomy 8:11–14, 17:

Beware . . . lest when thou hast eaten and art full, and hast built goodly houses, and dwelt therein; and when thy herds and thy flocks multiply, and thy silver and thy gold is multiplied, and all that thou hast is multiplied; then thine heart be lifted up, and thou forget the Lord thy God . . . and thou say in thine heart, my power and the might of mine hand hath gotten me this wealth.

Washington, D.C., is a well-organized, well-structured city.

II. THE SOUTH

The southeastern quadrant of the United States is collectively called the South and is generally thought of as being those states south of Maryland, Delaware, and New Jersey and those from the Atlantic coast westward to Texas. The South often refers to the states that made up the Confederacy plus two border states (Kentucky and West Virginia).

Historian W. J. Cash wrote in 1941 that "the South is another land, sharply differentiated from the rest of the American nation, and exhibiting within itself a remarkable homogeneity."[1] He looked upon it as essentially a nation within a nation, not quite separate but still different enough from the rest of the country to be considered in its own right. Although his view was more true then than it is today, the South still has unique traits that set it apart from the rest of the nation. Southerners are especially noted for their unique accent, which tends to vary widely even within the South, and their general friendliness and hospitality.

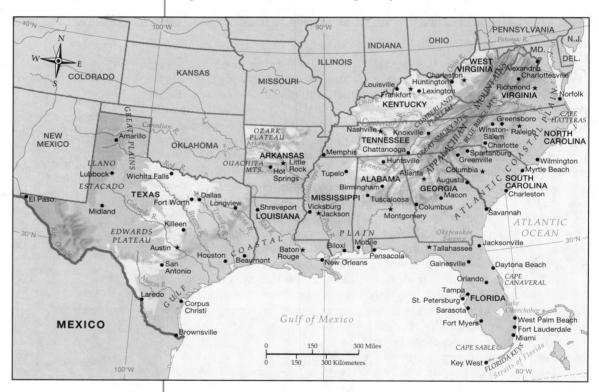

The South, which is sometimes called "Dixie," can be subdivided by several geographic features, including the Appalachian Mountains and the Mississippi River. Like the Northeast, the South also can be divided into upper and lower sections for convenience of study. Although the South has traditionally been predominantly agricultural, its diverse soils and natural resources have enabled it to become diversified industrially as well. Many tertiary industries have developed, and Southern urban areas are growing rapidly. In fact, the South is one of the most rapidly growing parts of the country.

Southern Fast Facts							
Flag	State	PO Code	Capital	Date of Statehood	Nickname	Area (sq. mi.)	Population
	Alabama	AL	Montgomery	1819	Heart of Dixie	52,423	4,530,752
	Arkansas	AR	Little Rock	1836	Natural State	53,182	2,752,629
	Florida	FL	Tallahassee	1845	Sunshine State	65,756	17,397,161
	Georgia	GA	Atlanta	1788	Peach State	59,441	8,829,383
	Kentucky	KY	Frankfort	1792	Bluegrass State	40,411	4,145,922
	Louisiana	LA	Baton Rouge	1812	Pelican State	51,843	4,515,770
	Mississippi	MS	Jackson	1817	Magnolia State	48,434	2,902,966
	North Carolina	NC	Raleigh	1789	Tar Heel State	53,821	8,541,221
	South Carolina	SC	Columbia	1788	Palmetto State	32,008	4,198,068
	Tennessee	TN	Nashville	1796	Volunteer State	42,146	5,900,962
	Texas	TX	Austin	1845	Lone Star State	268,601	22,490,022
	Virginia	VA	Richmond	1788	Old Dominion	42,777	7,459,827
	West Virginia	WV	Charleston	1863	Mountain State	24,231	1,815,354

THE UPPER SOUTH

The Upper South includes Virginia, North Carolina, West Virginia, Kentucky, Tennessee, and Arkansas. The first two states are separated from the other four by the Appalachian Mountains.

VIRGINIA

Many rivers from the mountains flow through the coastal region of Virginia and into the Chesapeake Bay. Because the ocean tides flow into and out of these rivers' mouths, the region is called the **Tidewater**. Many historically significant places, including Jamestown and the sites of numerous Civil War battles, are in the Tidewater. Virginia's largest metropolitan area is Norfolk, where the James River empties into the Chesapeake and where the busiest naval base in the nation guards water access to Washington, D.C.

Between the Tidewater and the Appalachian Mountains is the **Piedmont**, and west of the mountains is the **Shenandoah Valley**, which has been called the "breadbasket" of Virginia. The western part of the state is marked by the Appalachian Mountains.

Virginia's economy is diverse. As in many other Southern states, agriculture, which was once the leading income-producing activity, has now fallen behind other industries. Virginia still produces large amounts of

The Shenandoah Valley has been the breadbasket of Virginia throughout its history.

West Virginia is the second-leading coal-producing state.

The Cape Hatteras Lighthouse has been guiding sailors along the North Carolina coast since the mid-nineteenth century.

The Linn Cove Viaduct on the Blue Ridge Parkway provides sightseers with some beautiful views.

tobacco, corn, soybeans, peanuts, cotton, apples, and other farm products. It is also high in poultry production. The Shenandoah Valley is known for cattle and dairy products. The coastal areas are especially effective in harvesting shellfish, mainly crabs and oysters.

Virginia's mineral wealth includes coal, stone, sand, and gravel. Roanoke is a major source of railroad equipment, and several shipyards are located at Hampton Roads, Newport News, and Portsmouth. Chemicals and tourism are other major industries. Thousands of Virginians work for the national government in Washington and live in the surrounding suburbs.

WEST VIRGINIA

When Virginia seceded from the Union in 1861, the mountainous westernmost counties of Virginia did not want to secede. Instead, they held their own election, voided the Virginia vote for secession, and petitioned the U.S. Congress for admission to the Union as a separate state called Kanawha. Although the Constitution forbade the formation of a new state from an existing state, Congress agreed to admit the petitioning counties as the state of West Virginia in 1863. The area was hotly contested during the war; the town of Romney changed hands fifty-six times!

The Appalachian Mountains and rugged Allegheny Plateau cover the entire state. Most of the population and industries are in the valleys of the Ohio and Kanawha rivers, Wheeling and Parkersburg being in the Ohio Valley. The state is best known for its production of low-grade **bituminous coal**; it is second only to Wyoming in such coal production. The state, however, is working hard to diversify its economy.

NORTH CAROLINA

The terrain of North Carolina ranges from the **barrier islands** of the **Outer Banks** in the east to the Appalachian Mountains in the west. In between is the Piedmont.

North Carolina's economy was once dominated by agriculture, but other industries have grown dramatically. North Carolina is the nation's leading turkey, sweet potato, and tobacco producer, but it is also a leader in the wholesale textile trade. The **Research Triangle**, in the Raleigh-Durham area, is a world-leading center for research and development in biotechnology, pharmaceuticals, computers, and other high-tech applications.

The mountains of North Carolina include the highest mountains in the eastern United States, such as Grandfather Mountain and Mount Mitchell. Asheville is the highest major city in the eastern United States. The mountains provide hardwood for the nation-leading North Carolina furniture industry.

Also located in the North Carolina mountains is the Cherokee Indian Reservation, one of the South's "Five Civilized Tribes" of Native Americans. They had their own alphabet and system of writing. When the U.S. government forced the Indians to leave the Southeast for lands west of the Mississippi, some Cherokees fled to the mountains. Eventually, the government agreed to let them remain on a reservation established for that purpose. Each summer they present an outdoor drama, *Unto These Hills*, that tells the story of the tribe's forced removal.

KENTUCKY

Like many other Southern states, Kentucky has a variety of geographic terrains. It has mountains in the east, where it borders West Virginia, flat and fertile areas in the **Bluegrass region**, and a low plain in the far western part of the state. It is heavily coal oriented in the mountainous east (third in the nation's coal production). The edge of the rugged **Cumberland Plateau** runs down into Tennessee, dividing the eastern and central parts of that state. North of that area, however, the Bluegrass region in north-central Kentucky has the best soil in the state, and the area produces large numbers of thoroughbred horses. The northwest part of the state is known as the Western Coal Field. The far west is called the Purchase and is characterized by swamps, lakes, and flood plains.

About half of the state is classified as woodlands, and the state is third in hardwood production. The overwhelming majority (96.1 percent) of Kentucky's exports are manufactured goods, including transportation equipment, chemicals, machinery, and computer and electronic products. Agricultural products make up 2.2 percent of exports. Kentucky ranks first in the value of livestock and equine (horse) exports. Less than 1 percent of its exports are mineral resources.

Two cities of Kentucky, Louisville and Lexington, have populations of more than a quarter million each.

TENNESSEE

Literature on Tennessee invariably mentions its "three great states," referring to the fact that the state is divided into three distinct geographic regions: the mountainous East Tennessee, the Cumberland Plateau of Middle Tennessee; and the flat West Tennessee. These three regions also have their own unique political and cultural traits that make the "three states" designation even more profound. These "grand divisions" are represented by the three stars in the state flag.

The state is a parallelogram that is divided twice by the **Tennessee River**. The river forms in the east in Knoxville, at the confluence of the Holston and French Broad rivers, and flows southwest past Chattanooga and into Alabama before curving northwest and flowing into Kentucky between Middle and West Tennessee. Nashville, the capital, is on the Cumberland River. Memphis, the largest city, is on the **Mississippi River** in the southwest corner of the state.

The state motto, "Agriculture and Commerce," reflects Tennessee's diverse economy. Major agriculture products include cotton (seventh in the nation), soybeans, tobacco, cattle, dairy products, and hogs. It ranks first in the production of zinc. Aluminum is such an important product that the Aluminum Corporation of America built an entire city (Alcoa) in East Tennessee to house its workers. Other important industries include chemicals, textiles, electrical machinery, and automobiles (Saturn and Nissan). Tourism is also a big income producer for the state. Research, especially related to nuclear power and its uses, is an important focus of the U.S. Department of Energy facilities in Oak Ridge, where the first atomic bomb was developed.

The 70-foot-high Cumberland Falls in Kentucky near the Tennessee border is on the edge of the Cumberland Plateau.

Mammoth Cave

Mammoth Cave in Kentucky is reputedly the largest cave in the world. The portion of the cave that has been mapped totals more than 325 miles. Many of its long, winding passages are bare, but others have amazing formations called stalactites (forming from the ceiling downward) and stalagmites (forming from the ground upward). They often meet to form tall columns, the largest of which is 192 feet tall.

The cave became a national park in 1933, but people knew of and explored it long before that. Indians used it for hiding, protection from the elements, and as a meeting hall. Settlers mined saltpeter from it to make gunpowder.

Knoxville is on the Tennessee River, just below the confluence of the Holston and French Broad rivers.

Tennessee's neighbor across the Mississippi River is Arkansas. Mountains and forests cover half of the state. It has a smaller population than any other Southern state except West Virginia.

Arkansas has two major geographic regions. The Lowlands in the southeastern half of the state consist of the Gulf Coastal Plain and the Mississippi Flood Plain. The Ozark Plateau in the northwestern half includes the low **Ozark Mountains.** Bisecting both regions as it flows from northwest to southeast into the Mississippi River is the Arkansas River.

Like other Southern states, Arkansas has diversified its economy greatly. It is the number two producer of both chicken eggs and broilers, fifth in cotton, and ninth in soybeans. Its natural resources include oil and natural gas, bromine, bauxite (first in this resource), and lumber products. It is also a major chemical producer and the headquarters of the retail giant Wal-Mart, founded by Sam Walton.

THE LOWER SOUTH

The area designated the Lower South (sometimes called the Deep South) includes South Carolina, Georgia, Florida, Alabama, Mississippi, Louisiana, and Texas. All of those states are at least partially in the Atlantic or Gulf Coastal Plain, and that fact is reflected in the types of crops and industries that predominate there. Across the central portions of many of these states is a region called the **Black Belt** because of its dark, rich soil. Cotton once ruled the economies of the Deep South states, but they are all diversified today. Just as diverse as their economies are their demographics. The largest percentage of minorities, especially blacks, live in the Deep South, and it was the home of the civil rights movement of the 1960s.

SOUTH CAROLINA

Like other Atlantic coastal states, South Carolina has several narrow geographic regions (coastal plains, piedmont, etc.), but it can essentially be divided into the Low Country and the Upstate. The heart of the Low Country is Charleston, a major port city through which millions of dollars worth of imports and exports pass. The entire coastal region is bordered by numerous barrier-islands. The Upstate region ranges from the **fall line** (the point in parallel rivers where the elevation drops, producing waterfalls) near the capital, Columbia, to the Appalachian Mountains in the northwest corner of the state. The cities of Greenville and Spartanburg are the largest cities in the Upstate.

South Carolina is a major producer of textiles, second only to its neighbor North Carolina in that industry. It also produces more peaches than the self-styled "Peach State" of Georgia, its neighbor to the southwest. Chemical products, machinery production, and automobiles (BMW) are major industries in the state. Tourism, however, is the state's top moneymaker.

The Arthur Ravenel Bridge in Charleston, S.C., the longest cable bridge in North or South America, was opened July 16, 2005.

Middleton Place in Charleston, S.C., reveals the natural beauty cultivated by colonial planters in the Low Country.

GEORGIA

Like South Carolina, Georgia's geography ranges from swampy wetlands along the coast in the southeast to mountains in the north. In spite of the state's nickname ("The Peach State"), Georgia leads the nation in the production of peanuts and pecans, both lucrative alternatives to the soil-depleting cotton that was once a staple of Georgian agriculture. Atlanta, the state capital, lies in the Piedmont and boasts the South's highest skyscraper. It is also the headquarters of Coca-Cola, which features an interesting museum of the company.

Agriculture is still important in Georgia's economy. In addition to the other crops named, Georgia is a leader in livestock, poultry, and grape production. Although cotton is no longer the staple that it once was, Georgia is the fourth-leading cotton producer. It also produces lumber and pulpwood, and its fine marble is world famous. It is also a major auto-producing (Ford) state.

Atlanta, Georgia, demonstrates the development of major cities throughout the South.

FLORIDA

Florida is the only state with coasts on both the Atlantic Ocean and the **Gulf of Mexico**. It can be divided into three regions: the panhandle, along the northwest Gulf coast; the peninsula; and the mainly marshy area south of Lake Okeechobee, including the **Everglades** and the Florida Keys. Topography in all three areas is flat, the highest elevation in the state being only 345 feet above sea level.

The panhandle stretches 225 miles west from the peninsula, more than halfway to the Mississippi River. Tallahassee, the capital, and several tourist cities are on the panhandle. Most of the population, however, is on the peninsula. Both the largest city (Jacksonville) and the oldest city (St. Augustine) are in the northern part of the peninsula.

Both the second-largest metropolitan area—Tampa-St. Petersburg-Clearwater on the Gulf coast—and the Disney-oriented city of Orlando are located in the central area of the peninsula. Plant City, near Orlando, is famous for its vegetable and strawberry production. The Kennedy Space Center at Cape Canaveral is on the east central coast. The southern Atlantic coast from West Palm Beach to Miami is heavily populated. The southernmost point of Florida—and the United States—is Key West, the last of a chain of small islands (keys) connected by a 113-mile Overseas Highway.

The Florida Everglades is a beautiful, but forbidding, alligator- and mosquito-infested wetland.

Although Florida is famous for its tourist industry (it is a major world travel destination), it also has a thriving agricultural and industrial economy. It is first in the South in farm income and is second only to California in vegetables grown. Its major agricultural products include citrus fruit (oranges and grapefruit). Nonfarm industries include electronics, space-related products, fishing, and mining (it produces a quarter of the world's phosphates).

For years, cotton was the number one crop of the Deep South, and it remains an important, though not the major, crop in the Deep South today.

ALABAMA

More than half of this state, which is called "the Heart of Dixie," is **Gulf Coastal Plain** and is subdivided into Gulf, River, Metropolitan, and Mountain areas. The northeastern portion is hill country that includes the trailing end of the Appalachian Mountain chain. The Metropolitan area includes Birmingham, called the "Pittsburgh of the South" for its heavy steel industry, and Tuscaloosa, home to the University of Alabama. The River region is fertile cropland and is part of the Black Belt. On the Gulf at the mouth of the Alabama River is Mobile, a major port city.

Long associated with the growth of cotton, Alabama now has a diversified economy, including high-tech industries in the city of Huntsville that are associated with the National Aeronautics and Space Administration. Although cotton is still its chief crop (Alabama is tenth in cotton production), poultry products, cattle, lumber, and pulpwood are important contributors to the state's economy.

MISSISSIPPI

Almost the entire state of Mississippi is coastal plain. The Mississippi River and its tributaries dominate the area. Floodwaters from these rivers have deposited very rich soil across the vast flood plain, making the growth of cotton extremely profitable. Mississippi is third in cotton production.

The state is working hard to overcome the stigma of having historically been the poorest state in the nation. It is diversifying its economy, increasing other viable industries, both agricultural and industrial, to supplement its cotton empire. Included among its farm products are rice, soybeans, wood products, and poultry. The chemical, plastics, petroleum, and natural gas industries are also extremely important to the overall economy.

In 2005, Hurricane Katrina wreaked catastrophic damage to the gulf city of Biloxi, slowing the state's efforts to improve its economic standing among the other states.

LOUISIANA

This state, located at the mouth of the Mississippi River, is important to both the South and the nation for many reasons, not the least of which is the fact that four of the nation's ten largest ports are located there. It has been influenced by more cultures than any other Southern state. It is also a state that faces many daunting challenges.

The Mississippi Delta is a maze of waterways through which the river reaches the Gulf of Mexico southeast of New Orleans.

The entire state is coastal plain. Slow-moving, meandering streams and rivers crisscross the state as they seek an outlet into the Gulf through the **Mississippi Delta**. Swampy areas in this region are called **bayous** and are home to nearly half a million people known as **Cajuns**. Their ancestors were French refugees from an area of Maine and Canada known as Acadia. (In fact, an area of Louisiana is also called Acadia.) The Cajuns speak an interesting form of French and are famous for their unique spicy foods, including gumbo and jambalaya. Another ethnic group prominent in Louisiana is the **Creoles**, people of mixed black and European (French or Spanish) ancestry.

Key ingredients of the Louisiana economy are sweet potatoes, rice, sugar cane, soybeans, and cotton. Fishing, especially shrimp and oysters, is very important, as are muskrat and mink trapping. Louisiana leads the nation in salt production. Crude oil production at off-shore rigs in the Gulf and oil refining are also important industries for the entire nation.

Hurricane Katrina hit Louisiana in 2005, doing extensive damage to the state, especially New Orleans. Levees designed to protect the city, which is below sea level, broke, flooding 80 percent of the city. It has taken years for the city to recover and rebuild.

Because New Orleans is below sea level, when Hurricane Katrina broke through levees around Lake Ponchartrain, 80 percent of the city flooded.

TEXAS

The final state included in the South is also its largest. In fact, it is the second-largest state (by area) in the nation, trailing only Alaska, and it has more large cities that any other Southern state.

Texas is located on the U.S.–Mexico border and is so big that it shares characteristics with not only the Hispanic culture of Mexico and the American Southern culture but also the cultures of the Midwest and the Southwest. East Texas is much like other nearby Southern states, having large forests and cotton farms. On its Gulf Coastal Plain are several important port cities, including Galveston and Houston. The **Central Plains** are much like the flat, grassy plains in the states north of Texas, and the arid western part of the state resembles the neighboring states of the Southwest. The lower portion of the **Rocky Mountains** extend through that part of Texas.

Three of the nation's ten busiest ports are in Texas. (Recalling that Louisiana has four of the ten largest ports, one can readily see the importance to the nation of the seven ports of the South's Gulf region.) Texas is first in the nation in cattle and cotton production and second in hay. Its other agricultural products include poultry, wheat, and dairy products. Texas boasts three of the ten largest cities in the nation—Houston, Dallas, and San Antonio—and the industries of these and other urban areas add greatly to the Texas economy. It is the leading producer of oil and natural gas and a major producer of chemicals, machinery, and salt.

Oil pump jacks are a familiar sight in Texas.

SECTION QUIZ

1. What is the coastal region of Virginia called?
2. Which region has been called the breadbasket of Virginia?
3. What kind of coal is mined in West Virginia?
4. Which Tennessee city arose where the confluence of the Holston and French Broad rivers form the Tennessee River?
5. What is the southernmost location in the United States?
6. What is the largest state in the South and the second-largest in the nation?

III. The Midwest

The north central portion of the United States—generally encompassing the states surrounding the Great Lakes—is called the Midwest. It was referred to as "the West" from the time explorers began crossing the Appalachian Mountains. After the United States gained territories on the Pacific coast, the north central states were somewhat in the middle of the country; hence, the area became known as the Midwest.

This region is of great importance to the nation for several reasons. It is a transportation hub. It is called the "breadbasket of the nation." The states in the region were among the first to grant universal manhood suffrage, the right of every adult male to vote.

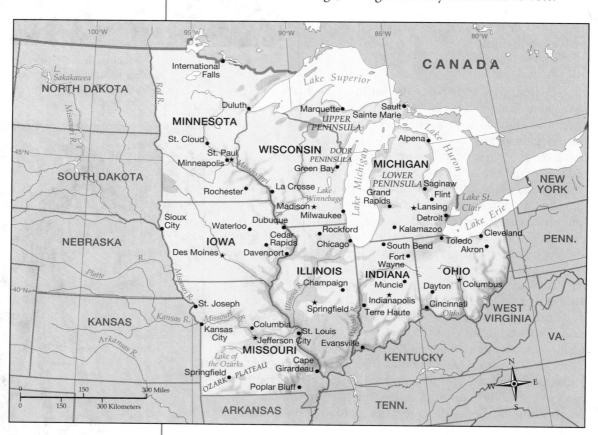

Ohio

West of Pennsylvania is Ohio. The **Ohio River** forms the state's southern border with West Virginia and Kentucky. The good farmland of the **till plains** (soil left by ancient glaciers) covers the western part of the state. The hills of the Appalachian Plateau run along the border with Pennsylvania and West Virginia and yield coal but little good farmland. Lake Erie on the northeast and Michigan on the northwest form the state's northern extent, and most of the population lives in the northern part of the state.

Ohio is considered the heart of the "rust belt," a region of declining steel industries. However, its ports on Lake Erie—Toledo and Cleveland—remain busy transporting iron and copper. The state is also the center of the glass and ceramics industry, and Akron is famous for its tires and other rubber products.

Flag	State	PO Code	Capital	Date of Statehood	Nickname	Area (sq. mi.)	Population
	Illinois	IL	Springfield	1818	Prairie State	57,918	12,713,634
	Indiana	IN	Indianapolis	1816	Hoosier State	36,420	6,237,569
	Michigan	MI	Lansing	1837	Great Lakes State	96,705	10,112,620
	Minnesota	MN	St. Paul	1858	North Star State	86,943	5,100,958
	Ohio	OH	Columbus	1803	Buckeye State	44,828	11,459,011
	Wisconsin	WI	Madison	1848	Badger State	65,499	5,509,026
	Iowa	IA	Des Moines	1846	Hawkeye State	56,276	2,954,451
	Missouri	MO	Jefferson City	1821	Show Me State	69,709	5,754,618

Table title: Midwestern Fast Facts

INDIANA

West of Ohio is Indiana, the smallest in area of the Midwestern states. Till plains cover most of the state. Southern Indiana is a hilly plateau that extends up from Kentucky. The Ohio River makes the state's southern border, and Michigan and Lake Michigan make its northern border. Evansville, the largest city in southern Indiana, is a major port on the Ohio River.

Indiana has several large industrial cities, including Gary, a port on Lake Michigan; Fort Wayne, an automotive city; and Elkhart, which leads the nation in making brass musical instruments. Indianapolis, another major city, is perhaps best known for its annual auto race, the Indianapolis 500.

ILLINOIS

Farther west is Illinois, the northern part of which is a great **prairie**, rolling plains with high grasses that spread across the western half of the Midwest. The prairie does not receive enough rainfall to support forests, but the soil is rich and productive of corn and soybeans. Associated with the farmland is the city of Moline, considered the "farm-equipment capital" of the nation. Peoria is the headquarters of Caterpillar, Inc., which makes earthmoving machines. On Lake Michigan is Chicago, the largest city in the Midwest and the transportation capital of the nation. Six major interstate highways converge there, and it is a rail and airline hub.

Southern Illinois is hilly and rocky, resembling some of the Southern states. The southernmost tip of the state, where the Ohio River meets the Mississippi River, is part of the Gulf Coastal Plain.

Indianapolis, Indiana, is the home of the annual Indy 500.

The Mackinac Bridge joins the upper and lower peninsulas of Michigan.

Wisconsin's huge farms make the state "America's Dairyland."

The Mesabi Range in Minnesota produces iron ore (taconite) in abundance.

MICHIGAN

North of Ohio and Indiana is Michigan, the largest Midwestern state and the only state with shoreline on four of the five Great Lakes. It is split in two by Lake Michigan. The lower portion, called the Lower Peninsula, is shaped like a mitten and has most of the population of the state. The entire area is covered by the Great Lakes Plain, but the best soil is in the south. The "thumb" of the mitten in the east includes the largest city of the state and the second-largest in the Midwest, Detroit. Detroit is known as the Motor City because it is the headquarters of the "Big Three" American auto makers: Ford, Daimler-Chrysler, and General Motors.

The capital, Lansing, is near the center of the "palm" of the mitten. Farther west is Battle Creek, the "cereal capital of the world." On Lake Michigan in the west is Grand Rapids, home of four of the largest Christian book publishers: Baker, Kregel, Eerdmans, and Zondervan.

The Upper Peninsula is much less densely populated and includes more wilderness area. The eastern part of the peninsula is part of the Great Lakes Plain, and the western half rises into the Superior Uplands, a plateau that continues westward into Minnesota. At the western edge of the uplands are the rugged peaks and wilderness of the Porcupine Mountains.

WISCONSIN

Wisconsin is known as "America's Dairyland" because it produces one-fourth of all the cheese produced in the United States. It also is high in production of ice cream, dried milk, and other dairy products. It has a dairy cow for every two people in the state.

Most of the state's dairy farms and cities are in the fertile Great Lakes Plain in the eastern half of the state. Milwaukee, the state's largest city, is on Lake Michigan and is famous for its breweries. The western half of the state is divided between the Superior Uplands in the north and the Driftless Area in the south. (**Drift** is deep soil deposited by glaciers. Southern Wisconsin has no drift; hence, it is "driftless.") Forestry and paper manufacturing are important industries in the northwest. Wisconsin has more than eight thousand lakes in that area. However, the poor soil there can support few farms.

MINNESOTA

The northeastern half of Minnesota is composed of the North Woods. Although the state is called the "Land of Ten Thousand Lakes," it actually has closer to fifteen thousand lakes.

Duluth is the major port on the Great Lakes. It developed into the primary port—originally for furs and later for lumber and iron ore from the **Mesabi Range**, the site of the richest iron ore–producing mines in the nation.

The Central Plains cover the rest of the state. Half of the state's population lives in the Twin Cities of Minneapolis and St. Paul, which are divided by the Mississippi

River. St. Paul is the capital. Minneapolis is the home of the massive Mall of America, which includes four hundred stores, eight theaters, and the largest indoor amusement park in the world. Minneapolis is also the headquarters of the 3M Company (Minnesota Mining and Manufacturing).

IOWA

Iowa is covered by the Central Plains but has three distinct parts. The southern and western edges are till plains. The north central region has some of the most fertile soil in the world in the Drift Prairie. The third area is the hilly Driftless Area along the northeastern border, which has no drift and poor soil. **Bluffs**, steep riverbanks, overlook the Mississippi River and are the primary nesting place for bald eagles.

Iowa, amazingly, produces 7 percent of the nation's food supply. It leads the nation in corn production, growing about one-fifth of the total. It also raises one-quarter of the nation's hogs. In fact, Iowa has four hogs for every person in the state.

Iowa enjoys commercial access to two major rivers. Sioux City is its main port on the Missouri River, and Davenport is the chief port on the Mississippi River. The capital, Des Moines, is on the Des Moines River in the middle of the state.

MISSOURI

Missouri is called the "Gateway to the West" because it was the "jumping off" point for many settlers who were heading west. St. Louis, the first major city, developed at the confluence of the Mississippi and Missouri rivers. The Gateway Arch, the largest monument in the nation, marks the spot where thousands of pioneers launched their trek into the western frontier.

Kansas City arose farther up the Missouri River at its confluence with the Kansas River. The metropolitan area includes Independence, where the Oregon Trail began. Farther north is St. Joseph, where the Pony Express route began.

Most people live in the eastern part, which is in the Central Plains. The southern half of the state, the Ozark Plateau, is sparsely populated but has the most productive lead mines in the nation. The southeastern corner of the state, called the "boot heel," is in the Gulf Coastal Plain and has soil well suited to growing cotton.

SECTION QUIZ

1. What name is given to the fertile type of soil found in western Ohio?
2. What word means rolling plains covered with high grasses?
3. What is the only state with shoreline on four of the five Great Lakes?
4. Which state is known as "America's Dairyland"?
5. What is the name of the iron ore–rich area in Minnesota?

Minneapolis can boast of having the world's largest mall, the Mall of America.

The Gateway Arch is a monument to the opening of the western frontier.

IV. The Plains

The Central Plains of the Midwest are essentially flat. Farther west, however, the **Great Plains** slope gradually upward as one moves west so that the western end at the foot of the Rockies is four thousand feet higher than the eastern end. The Great Plains are drier than the Central Plains and do not get enough rainfall to support more than grasses and squatty bushes. Early pioneers called the area the "Great American Desert," but the grasslands proved to be very fertile, requiring only steel plows and modern irrigation to grow wheat, which requires much less rain than corn. Consequently, this area became America's wheat belt. Most of the major cities in the area arose on the banks of the Missouri River and its tributaries.

Four of the states on the Great Plains border the Midwest: Kansas, Nebraska, South Dakota, and North Dakota. They tend, especially in their eastern portions, to resemble typical Midwestern towns and farms.

NORTH DAKOTA

The name of this state comes from the name that the Sioux Indians gave themselves, meaning "friends." Many tribes roamed both this state and its neighbor South Dakota.

North Dakota shares its northern border with Saskatchewan, Canada. The eastern half of North Dakota is part of the Central Plains and produces the second-largest spring wheat crop in the nation (behind only Kansas). It has the largest barley production and vies, again with Kansas, for the most sunflower seeds. It also has productive dairy farms. Agriculture remains the state's greatest source of income.

The Great Plains cover the western half of the state. That dry area includes three Indian reservations, the Badlands National Park, and numerous cattle ranches. Honey is produced in the central region of the state. Oil in the northwestern part of the state is the second-largest source of income.

Major cities in North Dakota include Fargo and Grand Forks on the Red River and Bismarck, the capital, on the Missouri River. Tourism is the third-greatest source of income for the state.

The South Dakota Badlands were named appropriately, both for the ruggedness of the terrain and the type of people who resorted there.

Plains States Fast Facts							
Flag	State	PO Code	Capital	Date of Statehood	Nickname	Area (sq. mi.)	Population
	Kansas	KS	Topeka	1861	Sunflower State	82,282	2,735,502
	Nebraska	NE	Lincoln	1867	Cornhusker State	77,358	1,747,214
	North Dakota	ND	Bismarck	1889	Peace Garden State	70,704	634,366
	Oklahoma	OK	Oklahoma City	1907	Sooner State	69,903	3,523,553
	South Dakota	SD	Pierre	1889	Coyote State	77,121	770,883

SOUTH DAKOTA

South Dakota is geographically much like the neighboring states. The southeast corner is till plain and is the location of the largest city, Sioux Falls. The Great Plains stretch across the west of the state, and the capital, Pierre, is located there. Also on the state's Great Plains are nine Indian reservations, including the site of the last battle between whites and Native Americans, Wounded Knee. The southwest corner is a remote, rugged area of knobs, spires, rock pinnacles, isolated buttes, and windswept ridges called the Badlands. The area became a hideout for outlaws and renegade Indians.

The **Black Hills** rise in the far western part of the state. This pocket of mountains towering above the Midwestern grasslands includes the highest peaks east of the Rockies. The most popular (but by no means the highest) peak is Mount Rushmore, on which the likenesses of four presidents have been carved. Deadwood is an Old West town to which prospectors came during the 1874 gold rush, sparking a war with the local Indians.

Sources of income include raising cattle and sheep and growing corn, soybeans, oats, and wheat. Meat packing and food processing are the major industries in the state. Gold is the state's most important mineral. Tourism and gambling are also sources of income.

Mount Rushmore

Mount Rushmore in the Black Hills of South Dakota is famous for the four sixty-foot-high heads that gaze from its side. It is the work of sculptor Gutzon Borglum, who began the carving in 1927 when he was sixty and spent the rest of his life creating his masterpiece. The mountain, which has become a "shrine to democracy," features the likenesses of presidents George Washington, Thomas Jefferson, Theodore Roosevelt, and Abraham Lincoln.

The sculpted heads of the presidents on Mount Rushmore took ten years to complete.

NEBRASKA

Farms cover 95 percent of the land in Nebraska, a higher proportion than in any other state. The end of the corn belt is in the eastern part of the state, which produces enough to make Nebraska the second-leading corn producer. The wheat belt slices through the southern part of the state, and Nebraska is among the top ten producers of wheat. Other major agricultural products include soybeans and hogs.

Nebraska is the only state that has a **unicameral** (one house) legislature. All other states have **bicameral** (two house) legislatures. The capital is Lincoln in the southeast corner of the state. Lincoln and Omaha, which is northeast of Lincoln on the Missouri River, are major insurance company headquarters.

KANSAS

Kansas is known as the "Sunflower State" for a good reason—it leads the nation in the production of sunflower seeds. Its most important crop, however, is winter wheat, and it leads the nation in that crop as well. The till plains in the northeast have the most fertile soil in the state. Kansas trails only Texas and Montana in total agricultural production. Major cities there include Topeka and Kansas City, which are on the Kansas River. The other major city, Wichita, is in the Osage Plains on the Arkansas River.

Although Kansas is known as a leading agricultural state, the manufacturing and services industries are actually larger income producers. Big industries include transportation equipment and computer machinery. Wichita has a major aircraft industry that produces mostly private planes. Major natural resources include oil, natural gas, and helium.

Kansas is known as "Tornado Alley" for good reason.

OKLAHOMA

The name of this state means "red man" (*okla*, "red"; *homa*, "man") and derives from the fact that the Five Civilized Tribes (Cherokee, Chickasaw, Choctaw, Creek, and Seminole) of the Southeast were forcibly relocated there in the early 1800s. Oklahoma has a larger Native American population than any other state.

In the east, Oklahoma is made up of small portions of the Gulf Coastal Plain and the Ozark Plateau, but the rest of the state is covered by the Central Plains, where the capital, Oklahoma City, is located. The elevation in that flat, treeless area is higher than even the mountains in the eastern part of the state.

Oklahoma is a great producer of wheat, hay, cattle, and hogs. The most important nonagricultural products of the state are oil and helium.

SECTION QUIZ

1. What did early pioneers mistakenly call the Great Plains?
2. In what area of South Dakota did outlaws and renegade Indians hide?
3. What percentage of the land in Nebraska is farmland?
4. What is unique about the government of Nebraska?
5. What does the name *Oklahoma* mean?

V. THE WEST

The American West is a land of extremes. It includes the highest and the lowest, the wettest and the driest, the biggest and one of the smallest, and the most and the least populated places in the nation. It also has riches beyond the early settlers' wildest dreams.

CONTINENTAL WEST

The continental West includes the Rocky Mountains, the Great Basin (a bowl-shaped area in central Nevada), the **Sierra Nevada**, and the various mountain ranges along the Pacific coast. The Rockies, however, are the largest single geographic feature of the West.

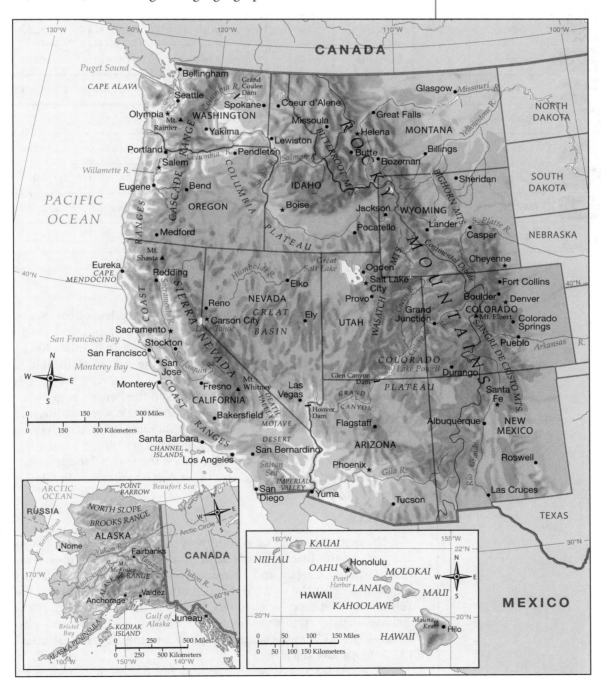

Western Fast Facts							
Flag	State	PO Code	Capital	Date of Statehood	Nickname	Area (sq. mi.)	Population
	Alaska	AK	Juneau	1959	The Last Frontier	656,424	655,435
	Arizona	AZ	Phoenix	1912	Grand Canyon State	114,006	5,743,834
	California	CA	Sacramento	1850	Golden State	163,707	35,893,799
	Colorado	CO	Denver	1876	Centennial State	104,100	4,601,403
	Hawaii	HI	Honolulu	1959	Aloha State	10,932	1,262,840
	Idaho	ID	Boise	1890	Gem State	83,574	1,393,262
	Montana	MT	Helena	1889	Treasure State	147,046	926,865
	Nevada	NV	Carson City	1864	Silver State	110,567	2,334,771
	New Mexico	NM	Santa Fe	1912	Land of Enchantment	121,598	1,903,289
	Oregon	OR	Salem	1859	Beaver State	98,386	3,594,586
	Utah	UT	Salt Lake City	1896	Beehive State	84,904	2,389,039
	Washington	WA	Olympia	1889	Evergreen State	71,302	6,203,788
	Wyoming	WY	Cheyenne	1890	Equality State	97,818	506,529

Montana

The eastern two-thirds of Montana is the treeless Great Plains, and the state's two largest cities, Great Falls and Billings, are in that region. Montana is also almost double the size of other Rocky Mountain states. The size and openness of the state explains one of its nicknames, "Big Sky Country." The western third of the state is mountainous, and the capital, Helena, lies in the Lewis Range.

Montana leads the nation in production of talc, vermiculite, and gem sapphires. It also has the only platinum mine in the country and produces gold, silver, copper, zinc, and lead. Agriculture, however, is the main income producer, and Montana is the fourth-largest wheat-producing state. Tourism is also a big industry, especially in Glacier National Park.

Wyoming

The eastern quarter of Wyoming is made up of the Great Plains and part of the Black Hills. The largest cities of the state—Cheyenne, Laramie, Casper, and Sheridan—are on the plains. The Rocky Mountains cover the western three-quarters of the state and include Yellowstone National Park, the first such park in the nation. The park includes such attractions as the geyser "Old Faithful." The state also features Grand Tetons National Park, where the largest peak soars 13,770 feet above sea level.

Most residents of Wyoming are employed directly or indirectly in farming, with cattle, hay, sugar beets, and wheat being the largest cash crops. Wyoming has larger ranches than any other state except Arizona. The largest sector of the economy, however, is mining, which makes up one-fourth of the gross state product (GSP). The most important resource is oil. The state also mines large amounts of gold, coal, and uranium. Tourism dollars flow into the state's national parks and numerous dude ranches.

IDAHO

The northern half and eastern border of Idaho are the remote mountains of the Bitterroot Range. West of the Idaho Rockies is the Columbia Plateau, which extends into neighboring Washington and Oregon. The Snake River slithers its way across the plateau, toppling 212 feet at Shoshone Falls, which is thirty feet higher than Niagara Falls. The first white residents in Idaho were missionaries to the Nez Perce Indians, Henry and Eliza Spalding, who settled at what is now Lewiston. Most of Idaho's other major cities are also located on or near the Snake River.

Say "Idaho," and many people think immediately of its top crop—potatoes. Idaho leads the nation in the production of that product, which is grown in the plateau region. But it is also a great producer of hay, wheat, dairy products, and cattle. Its natural resources include gold, silver, lead, zinc, phosphates, molybdenum, and antimony.

COLORADO

Because of Denver's reputation as the "mile-high city," many people are surprised to learn that almost half of Colorado is flat plains. The largest cities—Denver, Colorado Springs, and Pueblo—are on the plains at the *foot* of the Rockies. The plains are very fertile there, making Colorado the third-largest producer of lettuce and a major producer of cattle and potatoes.

Denver is a gateway to even higher elevations. It is the largest city in the four-state Rocky Mountain region. The federal mint at Denver produces coins and stores gold worth more than two billion dollars. The dome of the capitol there is covered with 24-carat gold leaf.

The centerpiece of Colorado, however, is the Rockies. The state has the highest mountains, including fifty-four peaks over fourteen thousand feet. Tourism in the state, much of it on its many ski slopes, is a major part of Colorado's economy. The state is also a big producer of lumber, chemicals, and computer equipment and is home to several Christian ministries and printing and publishing businesses. Although the state does not produce as much gold as it once did, it produces oil and mines a lot of silver, lead, uranium, and coal.

UTAH

The area immediately west of the Rockies is a bowl of low, rugged land called the **Great Basin**. It is surrounded by higher elevations, so water there cannot drain to any ocean. The western half of Utah is in the Great Basin. The Rockies intrude into the extreme northeastern corner of the state. The rest of the east and southeast is in the **Colorado Plateau**. Utah incorporates five national parks and seven national monuments, so tourism is a major part of its economy.

Four Corners

In only one place in the United States can you be in four states simultaneously. In the middle of the Navajo Indian Reservation is a place called the Four Corners, where the borders of Utah, Colorado, Arizona, and New Mexico meet.

Delicate Arch in Arches National Park, Utah, shows the results of massive weathering.

Carlsbad Caverns in New Mexico presents some interesting natural sculptures.

Utah is very dry and has very little land that is fit to farm, but it does produce some hay, corn, and barley. The bulk of its agricultural income comes from cattle and poultry. It is rich in copper (its top metal), gold, molybdenum, and magnesium. The state is also big in the aerospace and computer hardware and software industries. Provo is a steel center. Salt Lake City is also a major industrial center, although it is more famous as the headquarters of Mormonism.

NEW MEXICO

New Mexico includes five different geographic regions. The eastern third is part of the Great Plains. The southern two-thirds of the middle portion is the **Rio Grande Basin** whereas the northern third of the middle is part of the Rocky Mountains. The western third is primarily part of the Colorado Basin with the extreme southwestern corner being part of the **Sonoran Desert**. The heart of New Mexico, however, is the Rio Grande Valley, in which the river provides water for irrigation of crops and where the three largest cities—Santa Fe, Albuquerque, and Las Cruces—are located.

Because the state is so dry, it is not a major agricultural state, but it does produce some dairy products, hay, Piñon nuts, chili peppers, and pinewood. Most of the arable land is used for grazing and has many large ranches. It is very rich in minerals and is the leading producer of uranium, manganese, potash, salt, perlite, and other minerals. It also produces large amounts of turquoise. Albuquerque is a leading industrial center. The federal government is the largest employer, accounting for one-fourth of all jobs in the state. The Sandia and Los Alamos National Laboratories

MORMONISM

The first people to settle Utah were the Mormons. **Mormonism** is a religious sect founded by Joseph Smith in New York in 1830. Smith claimed to have been visited by an angel named Moroni, who revealed that all churches of the time were false and showed Smith writings on golden plates, which he was to translate and share with others. The result was the *Book of Mormon*. The book tells about the lost tribes of Israel, who allegedly migrated to America about 600 BC during the Babylonian Captivity. Smith called the new church that arose from these teachings the Church of Jesus Christ of Latter-day Saints. Those who followed Smith were persecuted and driven from New York, first to Ohio, then Missouri, and finally Illinois, where Smith was jailed and later killed by a mob. Brigham Young assumed leadership and led them to what is now Utah.

Mormonism differs from the fundamental doctrines of Christianity in that it (1) denies the sole authority of the Bible, making the Book of Mormon equal with the Bible; (2) denies the Trinity; (3) denies the deity of Christ, claiming that He was merely one of God's sons and that His spirit brother was Lucifer; and (4) denies the sufficiency of Christ's sacrifice on Calvary, believing that temple rituals and personal works are necessary for salvation.

One belief of Mormonism has actually been a great help to people who desire to trace their ancestral roots. The Mormons have compiled a huge database of genealogical information about millions of people.

The Mormon Temple in Salt Lake City is closed to the public because it is used for secret rites that are limited to only church members who are deemed worthy.

Although many people use that data merely as a resource for tracing their family tree, the Mormons' teaching that believers can be baptized for their dead relatives is the motivation behind the database.

engage in many types of scientific research, including top-secret military projects. Tourism at Carlsbad Caverns, White Sands, the Gila Cliff Dwellings, and other attractions also produces income for the state.

ARIZONA

The southern third of Arizona is the Sonoran Desert, the only American desert where saguaro (sah WHAR oh) cacti grow. Two-thirds of the nation's copper is mined in Arizona, mostly in mines in the Sonoran Desert. The northern two-thirds is Colorado Plateau. The eastern half of that area is the Navajo and Hopi Indian reservations. Other reservations are located in the east central and south central portions of the state. On the Colorado Plateau are the Painted Desert, the Petrified Forest, and the Meteor Crater, all of which draw large numbers of tourists. The centerpiece of the plateau, however, is the **Grand Canyon**.

Arizona is the second-largest lettuce producer and also produces a lot of cotton. But its most valuable agricultural products are cattle and dairy goods. Arizona is the nation's leading producer of copper and is a major player in the electronics and aerospace industries. The federal government owns 95 percent of the state's forests.

Arizona is fast becoming a major retirement destination. Its sunny, dry climate appeals to both retirees and those who suffer from allergies elsewhere. Phoenix is the largest city in the eight interior western states. The second-largest city in the state is Tucson.

CALIFORNIA

If California were a separate country, it would rank tenth in area, thirtieth in population, and among the top ten economies in the world. Among the fifty states, it is third in size and first in population. Geographically, it is divided into the coastal mountains, the Central Valley, the High Sierra, and the southern deserts. One desert, the Sonoran, is at the extreme southeastern end of California. Moist winds blowing inland from the Pacific lose their moisture while crossing the coastal mountains in the rainshadow effect. The Imperial Valley is in this area, but irrigation from the Colorado River has turned the desert into productive farmland. Just north of the Sonoran Desert is the south end of the Great Basin, which includes Death Valley and the Mojave Desert. Death Valley is the lowest spot on the continent—282 feet below sea level.

Running from southern California to Washington State are the Coastal Mountains. Within this region are California's largest metropolitan areas—San Diego, Los Angeles, San Francisco, Oakland, and other large and important cities.

The Central Valley includes the San Joaquin Valley in the south and the Sacramento Valley in the north, which make up the best farming region in the West. Because of the good soil and long growing season in these valleys, California is the nation's leading producer of dairy products, greenhouse/nursery products, hay, grapes, and lettuce. It ranks second in cotton and third in potatoes. It is also a great producer of cotton, poultry, and wine.

Great Salt Lake

Great Salt Lake is the largest salt lake west of the Mississippi River, with dimensions of 75 miles long, 28 miles wide, and an average of 30 feet deep (max. 35 ft.). It is the fourth-largest terminal (having no outlet) lake in the world. High temperatures and infrequent rains cause rapid evaporation. It was once much larger, but as parts of the lake dried up, it left behind dried salt flats. With a salt content of from 10 to 25 percent, it is three to five times saltier than normal ocean water, which is about 3.5 percent salt, and only slightly less salty than the Dead Sea (26–35 percent). The water in the Great Salt Lake is so salty that nothing more than brine shrimp will grow in it.

Early explorers avoided the Great Salt Lake because of its desert climate, but later settlers soon learned that it offered the flattest, easiest route to California. The first transcontinental railroad was completed at Promontory Point, Utah, north of Great Salt Lake in 1869. The Bonneville Salt Flats also became a testing ground for fast cars, and many land speed records were set there.

Salt covers boulders at the edge of Great Salt Lake.

The Pacific Coastal Mountains run right down to the ocean at some places.

Yosemite National Park offers a variety of natural beauty, including El Capitan (left), Bridal Veil Falls (right), and Half Dome (background).

Crater Lake was formed when water collected in an extinct volcano.

The Sierra Nevada ("snow-clad mountains") are in the western section of the state and include Mount Whitney, the highest U.S. mountain outside Alaska. The Cascade Mountain range extends from Oregon into northern California. The range includes a series of volcanic peaks with numerous waterfalls.

California is the home of "Silicon Valley," an area that concentrates on the development and production of computer technology. Of course, Hollywood has long been the center of the motion picture industry. Tourism is also a major moneymaker for California as people visit its many natural wonders.

NEVADA

Nevada is the heart of the dry Great Basin. It is the driest of all states, receiving less than 10 inches of rain a year. Its only major river, the Colorado, runs along its southern border. Hoover Dam was built on the Colorado River, creating Lake Mead, which now supplies water for drinking and irrigation. Nonetheless, very little agricultural development has occurred. Several parallel mountain ranges run down the Great Basin like a giant washboard. The highest of them are in the west along the California border.

Although Nevada is called the "Silver State," it leads the nation in the production of not only that metal but also gold and mercury. More than 90 percent of Nevada is owned by the federal government, including test sites for the U.S. defense industry.

Half of Nevada's employment is in the services sector. Many of those jobs are related to the state's legalized gambling, which occurs mainly in Las Vegas (the largest city), Reno, and Lake Tahoe. The state capitalizes on the human desire to get something for nothing, the hope that by some stroke of luck one will get rich.

OREGON

The western fifth of Oregon is coastal mountains. Moving eastward, another fifth of the state is the **Cascade Mountains**. Sandwiched between the two mountain ranges in the northwestern part of the state is the Willamette Valley. The south central region is part of the Great Basin. The rest of the state northward and eastward is part of the Columbia Plateau.

All of the major cities of Oregon are in the Willamette Valley, which has fertile soil and mild weather all year. This was the region about which early missionaries spoke so highly, luring settlers on the Oregon Trail in the 1840s and 1850s. The valley is a great producer of grapes, greenhouse/nursery products, hay, potatoes, beans, peppermint, cherries, and various kinds of berries.

Oregon is the leading lumber producer in the nation. This distinction has made the state a flashpoint between loggers and environmentalists. Associated industries include wood processing. Salmon fishing is also a major income producer.

WASHINGTON

The last of the forty-eight contiguous states is Washington. The eastern half of the state is part of the Columbia Plateau. The other half is split about evenly between the Coastal Mountains, which jut out into the Pacific Ocean at Olympic Peninsula, and the Cascade Mountains, with the Puget (PYOO jit) Sound Lowlands sandwiched between those mountains.

The Olympic Peninsula is sparsely populated but has several Pacific Coast Indian reservations. The peninsula gets more rain than any other place in the United States outside of Hawaii. Puget Sound is an arm of the Pacific Ocean. Its deep waters give Washington its best natural harbors. Seattle, the largest port north of San Francisco, is on Puget Sound. Its metropolitan area includes Tacoma and the capital, Olympia. The cities around Puget Sound have a large Asian population.

At the heart of the Cascade Range is **Mount Rainier**, which has twenty-five glaciers, the most outside of Alaska. South of Rainier are two volcanic mountains, Mount Adams (12,276 ft. elev.) and Mount St. Helens (8,365 ft. elev.). Mount St. Helens was 1,312 feet higher before it "blew its top" in a 1980 eruption. It remains quite active even today, with periodic rumblings being recorded from within it.

The Columbia Plateau includes Spokane, the hub of a region called the Inland Empire. This area's fertile soils make Washington the leading producer of apples, pears, and sweet cherries. The state is second in potato and grape production and third in wheat and hay. Industries include aircraft manufacturing (Boeing), computer technology (Microsoft), chemicals, and aluminum. More than half of Washington is forested, so wood products industries are also a major income source.

Outlying States

Alaska

Alaska is vast, remote, and large, being more than twice the size of Texas, the next largest state. From its southeastern islands to its western islands is a distance greater than that between Maryland and California! It is the northernmost state, touching the Arctic Ocean, and its mountains are the highest in the nation. Some of its national parks are larger than some entire states.

The state capital is Juneau, in Alaska's southeastern panhandle, a chain of islands that extend up the Pacific coast from Washington State. The waterway between those islands and the mainland is called the Inside Passage. Most of the state's people live along the Pacific coast, where the warm ocean breezes keep the temperature an average of 60 degrees. Half of the state's population lives in Anchorage.

North of Anchorage is the **Alaska Range**, the northern end of the Pacific Mountain System, which includes the Cascades and the Sierra Nevada. Denali National Park has the highest U.S. peak, **Mt. McKinley** (20,320 ft.). The range continues into the Pacific Ocean, where it becomes the chain of **Aleutian** (uh LOO shun) **Islands**, which are named for the Aleut (uh LOOT) Indians. North of the Arctic Circle is the Brooks Range, the northernmost extent of the Rocky Mountains. The North Slope, a coastal plain along the Arctic Ocean, slopes down from the Brooks Range to the ocean.

Alaska ranks last in farms and the value of farm products, but it does produce potatoes, dairy products, and greenhouse products.

The heart of the Cascade Range is Mount Rainier in Washington State.

The 800-mile-long Alaska Pipeline has supplied oil for the United States since 1977 at an average rate of one million barrels a day, meeting about one-fourth of the nation's oil need.

It is first, however, in commercial fishing, primarily salmon, crab, shrimp, halibut, herring, and cod. Anchorage and Dutch Harbor are its major ports. Lumber is also an important product. Mining of gold, which was once done extensively, has greatly diminished. Alaska's most valuable resources are oil and natural gas, which are transported via the Alaska Pipeline from the North Slope to the ice-free port of Valdez. The largest employer is local, state, and federal governments.

HAWAII

Twenty-four hundred miles from the American mainland is the fiftieth state, Hawaii. The state consists of 132 islands spread across fifteen hundred miles. The eight largest islands are sometimes called the High Islands because their elevations exceed five hundred feet.

The largest of the islands, Hawaii, is logically called the Big Island and has almost half of the state's area. It was formed by five volcanoes, two of which—**Mauna Loa** and **Kilauea**—are still active. Average temperatures are about 80 degrees along the beaches, but skiers enjoy snow-clad slopes on Mauna Kea during the winter. Trade winds bring heavy rains to the eastern side of the mountains. Hilo, the second-largest city, gets 138 inches of rain a year. Those rains help make Hawaii the nation's top producer of coffee, orchids, and macadamia nuts.

Lanai is called the "Pineapple Island." With Maui, it produces almost all of America's pineapples. Molokai, sometimes called the "Forgotten Island," is sparsely populated. Three-fourths of the state's population, however, lives on Oahu ("gathering place"). The capital and largest city, Honolulu, is on this island, which also boasts Diamond Head, a volcanic mountain, as well as Waikiki Beach and the U.S. naval base at Pearl Harbor.

The United States also has territories elsewhere in the Pacific Ocean (American Samoa and Guam) and in the Caribbean Sea (Puerto Rico and the U.S. Virgin Islands), but you will study them later when we examine those regions more carefully.

¹W. J. Cash, *The Mind of the South* (New York: A. A. Knopf, 1941).

Molten lava from Hawaii's volcanoes flows right into the sea, creating walls of steam and new land.

SECTION QUIZ

1. In which state is the geyser "Old Faithful"?

2. Which western state is the leading potato producer in the nation?

3. People of which religious group settled in Utah and today constitute the majority of citizens in that state?

4. Which desert covers the southwestern corner of New Mexico, the southern third of Arizona, and the extreme south of California?

5. Which states meet at the Four Corners?

6. Which mountain is the heart of the Cascade Range?

7. What chain of islands in Alaska are a continuation of the Alaska Range?

CHAPTER REVIEW

HOW MUCH DO YOU REMEMBER?

1. What two northeastern states were *not* among the original thirteen colonies?

2. Why were so many cities founded on the fall line?

3. Name the five major rivers of the Northeast and the major cities that are on each.

4. List the main geographic features of the (a) Upper South and (b) Lower South.

5. Why are the Great Plains so arid?

WHAT DO YOU THINK?

1. Why do you think God has blessed America with freedom and prosperity?

2. What northeastern state has no connection to the megalopolis and why?

3. Why is it good for a state's economy to diversify?

4. Is regionalism good or bad for a country?

5. Are you proud of your state? Why or why not?

6. If you could add one face to Mt. Rushmore, whose would it be and why?

Can You:
Define These Terms?

township	bayous
timber line	Cajuns
alpine zone	Creoles
notches	till plains
megalopolis	prairie
anthracite	drift
truck farms	bluffs
panhandle	unicameral
bituminous coal	bicameral
barrier islands	Mormonism

Locate These Places?

New England uplands	fall line
Berkshire Hills	Gulf of Mexico
White Mountains	Everglades
Green Mountains	Gulf Coastal Plain
Appalachian Mountains	Mississippi Delta
Finger Lakes	Central Plains
Great Lakes	Rocky Mountains
Delaware River	Ohio River
Niagara Falls	Mesabi Range
Pine Barrens	Great Plains
Delmarva Peninsula	Black Hills
Chesapeake Bay	Sierra Nevada
Tidewater	Great Basin
Piedmont	Colorado Plateau
Shenandoah Valley	Rio Grande Basin
Outer Banks	Sonoran Desert
"Research Triangle"	Grand Canyon
Bluegrass region	Great Salt Lake
Cumberland Plateau	Cascade Mountains
Tennessee River	Mount Rainier
Mississippi River	Alaska Range
Ozark Mountains	Mount McKinley
Black Belt	Aleutian Islands
	Mauna Loa
	Kilauea

UNIT 5

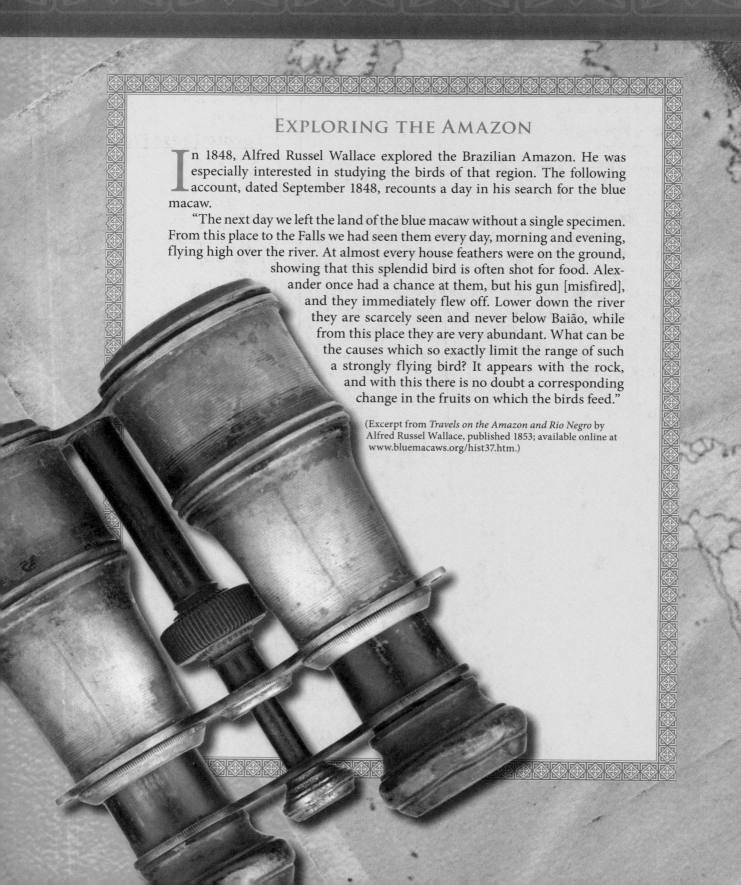

EXPLORING THE AMAZON

In 1848, Alfred Russel Wallace explored the Brazilian Amazon. He was especially interested in studying the birds of that region. The following account, dated September 1848, recounts a day in his search for the blue macaw.

"The next day we left the land of the blue macaw without a single specimen. From this place to the Falls we had seen them every day, morning and evening, flying high over the river. At almost every house feathers were on the ground, showing that this splendid bird is often shot for food. Alexander once had a chance at them, but his gun [misfired], and they immediately flew off. Lower down the river they are scarcely seen and never below Baião, while from this place they are very abundant. What can be the causes which so exactly limit the range of such a strongly flying bird? It appears with the rock, and with this there is no doubt a corresponding change in the fruits on which the birds feed."

(Excerpt from *Travels on the Amazon and Rio Negro* by Alfred Russel Wallace, published 1853; available online at www.bluemacaws.org/hist37.htm.)

LATIN AMERICA

MIDDLE AND SOUTH AMERICAN CULTURAL FOUNDATIONS

The modern cultures of Middle and South America have a rich heritage in three civilizations that dominated the region before the arrival of Europeans: the Aztecs of central Mexico, the Mayas of the Yucatán Peninsula, and the Incas of South America.

The Aztecs dominated central Mexico from their capital, Tenochtitlán, which is modern Mexico City. They developed, through the study of astronomy, a giant circular stone calendar. Their language was written as pictographs, words represented by intricate picture drawings. The Aztecs also experimented extensively with herbs to learn of their medicinal uses.

Perhaps the most startling aspect of Aztec culture, however, was its polytheistic religion, which involved human sacrifices and sometimes cannibalism. During bad times, such as periods of drought, the number of sacrifices was greater than in times of abundance. Historians estimate that 20,000 to 50,000 sacrifices occurred every year.

On the Yucatán Peninsula, the Mayas developed an advanced written language. They

Pyramid of the Niches in El Tajín, Mexico

were also gifted mathematicians and astronomers. They developed a precise solar calendar of slightly more than 365 days that was supposedly accurate to within one day every 6,000 years. The Mayans are a good example of the statement "Beauty is in the eye of the beholder." Thinking that long, backward-sloped foreheads enhanced beauty, they tied boards to their babies' heads to shape their skulls that way. They also liked the look of crossed eyes, so they hung objects close to their babies' faces, forcing them to cross their eyes to focus on the objects and thereby often producing permanently crossed eyes.

Farther south, the Incas developed an influential empire, due in part to an ingenious method of supplying their armies. They built storehouses throughout the empire and stocked them with foods that they had preserved using an early form of freeze-drying. (They left potatoes outside at night to freeze. During the daytime, when temperatures rose, the water content evaporated, leaving a pulp called *chuño*, which could be stored for up to a year. They used a similar process to preserve meat.) They also built a network of roads that made communication and control more effective. What initially helped make the empire possible, however, was later instrumental in helping invaders to destroy the civilization.

Then came the Spanish *conquistadores* in search of gold. They convinced the tribes whom the Aztecs, Mayas, and Incas had subjugated to join them in conquering their masters. Although the influence of those three empires did not disappear, it was blunted as the Spanish influence came in like a flood. With the conquistadores came Roman Catholic priests, teaching the natives that version of Christianity. The natives did not reject their old religions entirely but blended many Roman Catholic teachings with their own. Many Spaniards intermarried with the natives, producing a mixed race of people. Even today, the populations of the countries in these regions have three distinct groups of people: natives (or Indians), *mestizos* (mixed Indian and European), and Creoles (Europeans born in the New World and their unmixed offspring).

CHAPTER 11

The Maya Temple of Kukulkan, or El Castillo, at Chichen Itza, Mexico, represents the pagan worship of early inhabitants of Middle America.

MIDDLE AMERICA

I. MEXICO
   A. NORTHERN MEXICO
   B. MESA CENTRAL
   C. THE SOUTHERN TROPICS
   D. U.S.-MEXICAN RELATIONS TODAY

II. CENTRAL AMERICA
   A. GUATEMALA
   B. BELIZE
   C. EL SALVADOR
   D. HONDURAS
   E. NICARAGUA
   F. COSTA RICA
   G. PANAMA

III. THE WEST INDIES
   A. THE BAHAMAS
   B. THE GREATER ANTILLES
   C. THE LESSER ANTILLES

PASSPO

Unite
of

Canada and the United States are the main English-speaking nations of the Western Hemisphere. To the south is a different cultural region called **Latin America.** *Latin* people speak one of the languages descended from ancient Latin—Spanish, Portuguese, Italian, or French, also known as the Romance languages.

Latin America has two main subregions: Middle America and South America. **Middle America** consists of the nations and islands that lie between the United States and South America. It is what is known as a **land bridge** between North and South America. Several

Flag	Country	Capital	Area (sq. mi.)	Pop. (M)	Pop. Density (per sq. mi.)	Per Capita GDP ($US)	Life Span
	Mexico	Mexico City	761,601	106.67	139	$9,600	75.19
	Belize	Belmopan	8,866	0.28	32	$6,500	67.49
	Costa Rica	San Jose	19,575	4.03	204	$9,600	76.84
	El Salvador	San Salvador	8,260	6.74	825	$4,900	71.22
	Guatemala	Guatemala	42,042	14.66	349	$4,200	65.14
	Honduras	Tegucigalpa	43,277	6.98	161	$2,800	65.60
	Nicaragua	Managua	50,193	5.49	109	$2,300	70.33
	Panama	Panama	29,208	3.15	101	$6,900	71.94
	Bahamas	Nassau	5,380	0.30	51	$17,700	65.54
	Cuba	Havana	44,218	11.36	265	$7,000	77.23
	Dominican Republic	Santo Domingo	18,816	9.09	476	$6,300	67.26
	Haiti	Port-au-Prince	10,714	8.17	758	$1,500	52.92
	Jamaica	Kingston	4,232	2.74	644	$4,100	76.29
	Antigua & Barbuda	St. John's	171	0.06	402	$11,000	71.90
	Barbados	Bridgetown	166	0.27	1,678	$16,400	71.41
	Dominica	Roseau	290	0.06	237	$5,500	74.65
	Grenada	St. George's	133	0.08	674	$5,000	64.53
	St. Kitts & Nevis	Basseterre	104	0.03	387	$8,800	72.15
	St. Lucia	Castries	238	0.16	699	$5,400	73.61
	St. Vincent & the Grenadines	Kingstown	150	0.11	783	$2,900	73.62
	Trinidad & Tobago	Port of Spain	1,980	1.08	550	$10,500	68.91

Middle America Fast Facts

empires clashed for control of that area, which has become a colorful blend of native Indians, Europeans, Africans, and Asians. Local superstition has blended with Roman Catholicism, and local words have blended with Latin languages. Even the people's blood has mixed, creating new peoples and cultures.

Such mixing of peoples was not easy. Middle America has a violent past, stretching back to the bloody wars and human sacrifices of ancient native empires. The European conquest of the region in the fifteenth century was no less bloody. In the nineteenth century, as revolutionaries cast off their colonial powers, they tried to create prosperous democracies similar to the American republic to the north.

Over the past century and a half, the United States has tried, sometimes not too diplomatically, to use its influence to encourage democracy, peace, and prosperity among its southern neighbors. It wants the region to have governments that respect American property, thereby fostering an environment that makes free trade possible for the benefit of all participants. The nations of Middle America, however, have often interpreted such U.S. attempts as efforts to exert imperialistic control over them, creating suspicion and mistrust that hinders understanding and cooperation.

I. MEXICO

Mexico was once the crown jewel of the Spanish Empire. Its borders included much of what today is the American Southwest. In spite of its eventual loss of much of that land to the United States and

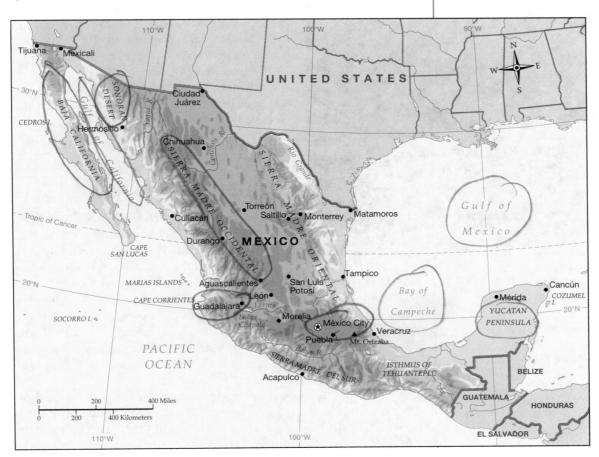

its recurring internal conflicts, Mexico remains the major force in Middle America. It has the largest Spanish-speaking population and the second-largest city in the world. Its population exceeds that of all other Middle American countries combined. Its economy is growing, and its government is becoming more stable. It epitomizes both the strengths and the weaknesses of Latin American culture.

Mexico is shaped much like a funnel, with the wide part in the north and the "spout" in the extreme south. Its entire northern border is with the United States. Its western shores are washed by the Pacific Ocean. Between the mainland and the long peninsula called **Baja** (bah hah) **California**, south of the U.S. state of California, is the **Gulf of California** (or, as the Mexicans call it, the Sea of Cortés). Mexico's eastern shores are on the Gulf of Mexico. The southern tip of the "spout" of Mexico curves north and east to form the **Yucatán** (yoo kah TAHN) **Peninsula**. Nestled between the Yucatán and the central portion of the mainland is the **Bay of Campeche** (kahm PEH cheh).

Two mountain ranges run the length of Mexico along each coast, the **Sierra Madre** (see-EH-ruh MAH-dray) **Oriental** on the east and the **Sierra Madre Occidental** on the west. The ranges join to form one range near the twentieth parallel at the **Valley of Mexico**, where Mexico City is located. That range forms the spine of the isthmus and continues into neighboring Guatemala.

The climate of Mexico ranges from desert in the north to subtropical in the south. The major population areas are in the south, although some northern border towns, such as **Tijuana** (tee WHA nah) and **Juarez** (WHA rez), are quite large. **Monterrey** (MAHN tuh RAY), an ultramodern and high-tech city, is about 150 miles south of the U.S.-Mexico border. The Mexican government is a federal republic with thirty-one state governments and one central government.

In our study of Mexico, we will begin in the northern and coastal areas and work our way southward through the central area, which is called *la Mesa Central* (MAY-suh cehn-TRAHL), and end with the tropical southern region.

NORTHERN MEXICO

The northern part of Mexico has been greatly influenced by its proximity to and contact with the United States. Its geography is much like that of the American Southwest—hot, dry, and generally flat desert. Quite often, wherever a city or town exists on the U.S. side of the border, a corresponding city or town is found on the Mexican side. Prominent examples include San Diego and Tijuana on the west coast, El Paso and Juarez in the central area, and Brownsville and Matamoros on the Gulf coast. Sometimes such cross-border towns even have the same name, as is the case with Nogales and Laredo.

An estimated one million Mexicans a year migrate to the border area in a quest for jobs in agriculture and manufacturing that abound in the border towns. Thousands of them keep going, however, and enter the United States, many of them illegally.

The poverty of many of the Mexican border towns, such as Ciudad Juarez opposite El Paso, Texas, is a stark contrast to the relative affluence found in the United States.

DESERTS, MINES, AND RANCHES OF THE NORTHERN PLATEAU

The Sierra Madre ("Mother Range") extends from the American Rockies into northern Mexico. In the upper area between the ranges lies the rugged **Northern Plateau**.

The hot, dry winds of the subtropics, which blow across the American Southwest, also blow across northern Mexico, keeping it dry year-round. Westerlies occasionally blow in from the Pacific Ocean, dropping water as they rise over the high Sierra Madre Occidental. Except for these mountains, however, all of northern Mexico is desert and semiarid grassland. The **Chihuahuan** (chee WAH wan) **Desert** covers large parts of the Northern Plateau. The state of Chihuahua—the largest state by area in Mexico—takes its name from this desert.

Irrigation permits some farming around the cities of Monterrey, Ciudad Juárez, Chihuahua, Torreón, and Saltillo. Monterrey is the most populous northern city. Chihuahua is a center for silver, lead, and zinc mining. Silver mines there and throughout Mexico make that country the world's leading producer of silver. Durango also has important iron mines.

Cattle ranching is common outside the cities. American cowboys patterned their clothing, gear, and skills after the Spanish *vaqueros* (vah KAY rohs). For the popular *charreria* (chah RAY ree ah), or Mexican rodeo, the participants—called *charros* (CHAH rohs)—dress up in fine clothes as part of the ritual.

On the western edge of the Northern Plateau rises the Sierra Madre Occidental. No paved roads cross these tree-covered mountains between the U.S. border and Durango, five hundred miles south. Only one railroad, a true feat of human engineering, winds between them. The highlight of the route is **Copper Canyon**, the Grand Canyon of Mexico. Its Basaseachic Falls is the highest in Mexico.

The Copper Canyon is a rugged area of the Sierra Madre Occidental, much of which is accessible only by train.

OIL AND TOURISM ON THE GULF

The Gulf Coastal Plain extends along the Gulf Coast from Texas all the way to the Yucatán Peninsula. Mexico's Gulf states have grown in importance since the discovery of reserves of natural gas and petroleum. The largest offshore oil field was discovered under the Bay of Campeche in the 1970s. The sale of gas and oil to the United States is Mexico's most important source of foreign currency.

The biggest port in Mexico, **Veracruz**, lies on the Gulf Coastal Plain at the gateway to Mexico City and the Mesa Central. Goods shipped from Texas and other American Gulf states must pass through Veracruz before reaching the interior. Cortés landed his invasion force there in 1519, establishing the first Spanish settlement in Mexico.

Cancún (can KOON), on the eastern tip of the Yucatán Peninsula, is a major tourist destination. It was named by the native Mayans for its many snakes, but those reptiles are no longer plentiful there. The city was built from scratch to be a resort location and is today Mexico's "showcase resort." Its white, powdery beaches are

Saguaro cacti thrive in the Sonoran Desert of northwest Mexico.

legendary. With a population approaching half a million, it—along with its Pacific Ocean counterpart, **Acapulco** (ah cah PUHL coh)—contributes greatly to the $10 billion Mexican tourist industry. Approximately 70 percent of the tourists are Americans.

GULF OF CALIFORNIA

The Gulf of California juts deep into the rugged, desert lands west of the Sierra Madre Occidental. Mexico's Pacific Northwest is nothing like America's Pacific Northwest. The **Sonoran** (soh NOH rahn) **Desert**, with its **saguaro** (sah WHA roh) **cacti**, covers much of the area.

Four states border the Gulf of California, two on the mainland and two on Baja California.

Tijuana, across the border from San Diego in Southern California, is the most popular stop for American tourists visiting Mexico. Crowds haggle in the markets for good prices on silver jewelry and other souvenirs. To the east, Mexicali sits at the southern end of California's Imperial Valley. Its elevation of thirty-three feet below sea level marks the lowest point in Mexico. As in California, irrigation from the Colorado River permits large-scale agriculture. Wheat, cotton, and sesame seeds are among the most important crops.

MESA CENTRAL

The vast **Mexican Plateau**, bordered by the two Sierra Madres, dominates the landscape of Mexico. Most of Mexico is too dry for farming. But during the rainy season in the late spring and summer, easterly trade winds from the Caribbean Sea blow over the southern end of the Mexican Plateau, bringing adequate water for crops. This region, where the mountain ranges come together, is called the Mesa Central.

Although the Mesa Central is located in the tropics, the high altitude keeps the temperatures relatively mild. The early Spanish explorers noticed the influence of altitude and gave different names to each **altitude zone.** They called the low tropical coasts the *tierra caliente* (tee-EH-rah kah-lee-EN-tay; "hot land"). The best lands on the plateaus and mountain valleys they called *tierra templada* (tem PLAH dah; "temperate land"). They divided the high mountains into the *tierra fría* (FREE ah; "cold land") of the subalpine zone, the *páramo* (PAH rah moh; "bleak plateau"), and the *tierra helada* (ay LAH dah; "frozen land") of the permanent snow cap.

The peso, available in many denominations of either coins or bills, is the Mexican monetary unit.

Thousands of small farms and villages cover the *bajío* (bah HEE oh), the flat western portion of the Mesa Central. Many subsistence farmers eke out a living on small plots, typically growing corn, beans, squash, and peppers. But more and more young Mexicans are seeking work in the *bajío*'s manufacturing cities. Guadalajara, the second-largest city in Mexico, stands on the western side of the country near Lake Chapala, Mexico's largest lake. León ranks among the twenty largest cities in Mexico. People who cannot find work in these cities move to the southeastern part of the Mesa Central, where the capital, **Mexico City**, is located.

CONQUEST OF THE AZTEC CAPITAL

The Mesa Central was the center of a series of civilizations. Ancient ruins date back to 2000 BC. Around AD 500, a mysterious early people built the first city in Middle America—Teotihuacán, the ruins of which still stand north of Mexico City. Tourists can climb the Temple of the Sun, which has a longer base than the great pyramids of the Egyptian pharaohs. The **Toltec** (TOHL tek) and later the Aztec empires dominated the Mesa Central. Tourists today can visit the temple to the rain god Quetzalcoatl (a feathered serpent), where fifteen-foot-tall stone warriors still stand guard. The **Aztecs** were especially ingenious in building their empire, including their capital, Tenochtitlán, which they built on an island in Lake Texcoco. In the center of the city was a temple to the sun god where Aztecs offered human sacrifices, cutting out the hearts of their victims.

In 1519, however, the Spanish *conquistador* (kohn KEEST ah dohr) Hernando Cortés, aided by neighboring tribes who hated the Aztecs, conquered the Aztecs. (Today, several statues honor the last Aztec chief, Cuautémoc, who vowed never to bow to the Spanish, but no statues in Mexico honor Cortés!) For the next three hundred years, Spanish *viceroys* ruled Mexico for the Spanish monarch and called their empire "New Spain." Spanish priests built missions and spread Roman Catholicism among the Indians. Spanish noblemen owned most of the land and built vast ranches, called **haciendas** (hah see EN dahs), which they ran like feudal manors. They forced the Indian **peones** (pay OH nays) to farm the land and to mine gold and copper for them. The Spaniards became wealthy; the native peoples remained poor. Even after the Spaniards left, Mexico suffered one dictator after another. Recently, however, the nation has become more stable and has begun to recover from the poverty created by centuries of abuse.

Spanish architecture is readily apparent in the haciendas that wealthy Spaniards built in Mexico.

THE SEAT OF GOVERNMENT

At the center of Mexico City is the country's main public square, the *Zócalo* (ZOH kah lo). The squares of most Spanish colonial cities are surrounded by government buildings and a church, and Mexico City is no exception. City Hall, the Metropolitan Church, and the National Palace, where the president and his cabinet live, surround the square. Nearby is the Senate, the Chamber of Deputies, and the Supreme Court of Justice. Like Washington, D.C., the capital of Mexico is a federal district run by the legislature.

History of Revolt—Mexico's history is an ongoing story of revolution, beginning with the war for independence from Spain (1810–21). From the beginning, however, the nation's leaders disagreed on states' rights and religious freedom. During the next forty years, forty presidents rose and fell. Dissatisfied opponents often took power in a **coup** (KOO)—the sudden, illegal overthrow of the government by a military officer or other government official.

Most of the early fighting took place between full-blooded Spaniards. Under the Spanish colonial system, men born in Spain (called *peninsulares*) could own estates, but Spaniards born in the colonies—called *criollos* (kree OH yohs)—were treated as second-class citizens. The inheritors of the large estates wanted to keep everything after

> ### *Through Christian Eyes*
> What does the layout of Mexican villages reveal about the role of religion in Mexican culture?

MEXICO CITY

Mexico City is the largest city in North America. Its greater metropolitan area, home to more than 22 million people, was the second largest in the world behind Tokyo (more than 32 million) in 2005, and it continues to grow. It contributes 24.1 percent of the total GDP. Nonetheless, many people suffer poverty. People who cannot find housing build makeshift homes from cardboard, old tin, and other scraps. (More than five hundred such slums exist in Mexico City.) Water, sewage, and health services are inadequate in many areas.

Yet, Mexicans take much pride in their capital city, which is the cultural center of the nation. It boasts 344 hospitals, 25,000 hotel rooms, 161 museums, 106 art galleries, 30 concert halls, and innumerable examples of Spanish colonial architecture. Although bullfighting is popular, the country's biggest spectator sport is *fútbol* (soccer). Almost every weekend, professional *fútbol* teams battle at Aztec Stadium.

At the center of Mexico City stands the largest church in the nation, the Metropolitan Church. But the most popular site among Roman Catholic pilgrims is a hill located just outside the city where they believe the Virgin Mary appeared to an Indian peasant five hundred years ago. The brown-skinned "Virgin of Guadalupe" (GWAHD uh LOOpay) is the patron saint of Mexico. Some six million people a year visit the Shrine of Our Lady of Guadalupe. Except for the Vatican, it is the most visited site in the Catholic world.

Another part of the city, the Plaza of the Three Cultures, shows how the people honor both their Indian and their Spanish heritages. Unlike the English colonists, the early Spaniards brought few women to the New World and married native Indians instead. A unique blend of these two peoples gave birth to a third culture. About 60 percent of Mexicans are mestizos (mess TEE zohs), people of mixed Spanish and Indian

The Shrine of Our Lady of Guadalupe is a famous religious location to which millions of Mexicans travel each year.

ancestry. (About 30 percent are pure Amerindian, 9 percent are white, and the remaining 1 percent are of other ethnic backgrounds.) In the Plaza of the Three Cultures, one can see Aztec ruins, a Spanish church, and a concrete office complex.

Although Mexico City has beautiful lakes and parks, it has been called the worst-located city in the world. Its teeming mass of humanity is packed, at 7,200 feet above sea level, into the broad Valley of Mexico where the Sierra Madre Oriental (east) and the Sierra Madre Occidental (west) meet. The surrounding mountains trap air pollution in the valley and create a daily health hazard. The smog is often one hundred times worse than the acceptable level. No water escapes the closed valley, making the ground spongy and the buildings unstable. (The valley is one of the most active earthquake areas in the world.) Heavy rains bring floods and turn low areas into swamps. A chain of active volcanoes borders the southern edge of the city.

Two volcanoes tower over Mexico City. The Aztecs called the taller one Popocatépetl (17,883 ft.), or "Smoking Mountain." Popo, as it is commonly called, is one of the most active volcanoes in the world, constantly spewing sulfur. Its twin is Ixtacihuatl (17,343 ft.). Farther east rises the highest peak in Middle America, called Citlaltépetl by the Aztecs or Orizaba by the Spanish. It reaches an altitude of 18,410 feet.

The volcano Popocatépetl towers over Mexico City and puffs out an occasional eruption, but residents take it all in stride.

the revolution, but the landless people believed that the lands should be broken up. A major goal of the *criollos* was land reform, the "fair" distribution of land. In a region that depends on agriculture for survival, land reform became a recurring theme of revolt and remains so today.

Finally, the overtaxed, landless ***mestizos*** (mess TEE zohs), people of mixed Spanish and Indian ancestry, and Indians revolted (1910–20). More than one million Mexicans died during the revolution, but the Liberal faction broke the power of the Conservatives, confiscated church lands, and forbade Catholic priests from entering politics. Since then, Mexico has been the only Latin American country to avoid a coup attempt, but authorities continue to battle revolutionaries in the southernmost state of Chiapas.

Reforms Since the Revolution—The Mexican government began a land-redistribution program, taking land from the wealthy and distributing it among the poor. The land grants, called ***ejidos*** (ay HEE dohs), were owned in common by the people of the village. No other nation has accomplished such a large transfer of land with relative peace.

Vicente Fox won the presidency of Mexico on the ticket of the National Action Party.

The revolutionary constitution of 1917 established a federal government similar to that in the United States. Each of Mexico's thirty-one states has its own governor and legislature. The country also has a bicameral legislature, with a Senate and a Chamber of Deputies.

But Mexico was not always a true republic. From 1929 to 1997, the Revolutionary Institutional Party (PRI) controlled the government and used its money and power to win elections. The party chose the candidate for president and most of the candidates for the legislature. The legislature had little real power to make laws. All power was vested in the president, who ruled much as a dictator for a six-year term. But he could serve for only one term before the party selected another candidate. Perhaps this blend of dictatorship and democracy is one reason Mexicans tolerated the system so long.

Demands for change increased as the PRI became corrupt and wasteful, however, and its programs failed to help the average citizen. In the late 1980s, the president began encouraging more private ownership of land and other economic reforms. But economic freedoms spurred demands for political freedom. In 1989, the opposition National Action Party (PAN) won a governorship for the first time. In 1997, a non-PRI majority was elected to the legislature. Then, in 2000, PAN elected its candidate, **Vicente Fox**, to the presidency.

SECTION QUIZ

1. What two factors make the Mesa Central the most populous part of Mexico?

2. Name three empires that have dominated the Mesa Central.

3. What are people of mixed European and Indian ancestry called?

4. Give four reasons that Mexico City is poorly located.

5. How is the federal government of Mexico different from that of the United States?

֎ Why was the "unequal distribution of land" a recurring problem in Mexico, but not in the United States?

THE SOUTHERN TROPICS

Southern Mexico has a rainy season and a dry season, rather than the four seasons that the United States has. Savannah covers the coastal areas, although it gives way to mangrove swamps in some parts. In the interior, colorful parrots, chattering monkeys, tapirs, and other exotic animals roam the lush rain forests.

POVERTY OF THE SOUTHERN HIGHLANDS

The greatest influence in the dry north has been the United States, but the greatest influence in the tropical south has been the Indian culture. Many Indians continue to live in the isolated valleys of the **Sierra Madre Del Sur,** or "Southern" Sierra Madre, which runs parallel to the southern curve of Mexico's Pacific Coast. The map on page 267 shows that the three Sierra Madre ranges join at Mexico's narrowest point, the Isthmus of Tehuantepec (tay HWAN tah pehk). From there, the range continues down the coast into Central America.

The Southern Highlands is the poorest region in the country, and one of its states, Chiapas, is the poorest state in Mexico. Many American tourists see only Acapulco, "the pearl of the Pacific," or Cancún, where tropical beaches remind them of Hawaii. But the posh resorts stand in stark contrast to the poverty of the surrounding rural areas.

The state of Michoacán (MEE chuh wah KAHN) is known for the **Tarascan** (tah RAH skan) Indians. Although they are not as famous as the Aztecs, they had a powerful empire throughout the fifteenth century. Many Tarascan Indians still carry on their traditional way of life. They fish, weave nets and baskets, and grow traditional Indian foods—corn, beans, squash, and chili peppers. The majority of the 2 percent of Mexicans who do not speak Spanish are Tarascans.

Chiapas (chee AH pahs) is the southernmost state in Mexico. A third of the people are full-blooded Indians, few of whom speak Spanish. The state broke away from Guatemala and joined the original nineteen states of Mexico in 1824. But Chiapas has become the poorest and most unstable state in Mexico. The passage of the North American Free Trade Agreement (NAFTA) in 1994 sparked a rebellion among Indian farmers, who feared they could not compete with the low prices of American grain.

Although most Indians in Chiapas claim to be Roman Catholics, they have retained many traditions from the times before Columbus. They still hold to many ancient superstitions and celebrations today.

Catholic villagers in Chiapas have driven more than thirty thousand Protestants from their homes in recent years. Local *caciques* (cah SEE kays, "party bosses") rule as small dictators. The *caciques* make their money by selling alcohol at pagan religious festivals, but Protestants refuse to participate. Although many Protestant church

The Sierra Madre del Sur rises behind the tourist city of Acapulco.

LIFE IN THE MEXICAN VILLAGE

Life in the big cities of Mexico is very modern, but the rural towns and villages still retain many of the old ways. Villages are built around a **plaza** or public square, which is the center of life in the town. A Catholic Church usually stands on one side of the plaza, which is often decorated with walks, flowers, and sometimes even a fountain.

Every week on market day, the plaza bustles with activity. Some people sell their goods from covered stalls; others sit on the pavement with their goods spread around them. Those who sit in the open might wear a *sombrero* (sohm BRAY roh), a wide-brimmed hat, as shade from the sun. People work hard during the week to have something to sell on market day. With the money they earn, they buy corn, blankets, and other items. Indians don colorful blankets, called *ponchos*, by putting their head through a hole in the center. The different designs tell which Indian group wove them.

Bullfights are popular entertainment in Mexico, but they can be very dangerous.

This public market in Mazatlan is representative of similar markets found all over Mexico.

The goods do not have price tags, so the people negotiate. One party suggests a certain number of *pesos* (PAY sohs)—the Mexican monetary unit—for an item, and the other makes a counteroffer to his liking. The verbal exchange continues until they agree on a price. In Mexico as in Spain, the people customarily stand right in your face, about twelve inches away, while they negotiate. (Americans like more space, about eighteen inches.)

Narrow streets radiate from the plaza and are lined with homes usually made of *adobe* (uh DOH bay), many of which have balconies and an interior courtyard called a *patio* (PAH tee oh), which is a place of privacy for the family. Following the Spanish custom, everyone comes home from work in the middle of the day for the main meal. After the meal, many people take a *siesta* (see AYS tah), or nap. They prefer to eat and rest during the hottest part of the day and to work in the cool of the morning and late afternoon. Because they work in late afternoon, their evening meal usually is not served until as late as 9:30 p.m.

Most meals include tortillas. The Mexican women grind corn into meal on a flat stone, mix it with water to make dough, and roll it into thin cakes. The fried cakes are called tortillas unless they are fried to crispness, in which case they are called *tostadas*. A tortilla folded to hold other food is a *taco*, a tortilla rolled around grilled meat makes a *fajita*, and a tortilla stuffed and covered with chili sauce makes an *enchilada*. Cornmeal rolled up with meat and hot chili peppers makes *tamales*. When flour is substituted for cornmeal, the stuffed flour tortilla is called a *burrito*. *Frijoles* (free HOH lays), or refried beans, are the most common supplement to the tortillas. The hotness or spiciness of Mexican foods varies throughout the regions of Mexico.

The whole town comes alive on special celebrations called *fiestas* (fee AYS tahs). On Independence Day (September 16), fireworks, special toys and decorations of tissue paper and cardboard, and mariachi music complete the festivities. The unusual fiesta of November 2 is the Day of the Dead (All Soul's Day), a celebration in memory of the dead. Children eat sugar skeletons and play with wind-up toy skeletons, while the men picnic in the cemetery. Cinco de Mayo (May 5) is also a major holiday there. Nativity scenes, snow scenes, and carols are used to celebrate the Holy Week of Christmas season. Groups representing the Holy Family travel from home to home but are refused until they reach a prearranged home. There, the children take turns trying to break the brightly decorated *piñata* (peen YAH tah) while blindfolded. When one succeeds in breaking the papier-mâché or earthenware *piñata*, all of its candy, fruit, and toys spill out for the children.

CHICHEN ITZA

Among the thirty major Mayan ruins that have been found in the jungles of the Yucatán, the most famous is Chichen Itza. That complex includes more than one hundred structures, among which are a seventy-five-foot-high pyramid, the Temple of the Warriors, the tomb of a high priest, an observatory, various wells, and the largest ball court in Middle America.

The high pyramid called the Castillo ("castle") is an engineering marvel. Each side, aligned along a point on the compass, has eighteen parts for each Mayan month. Each staircase has ninety-one steps: the steps on four sides plus the top platform equal 365 days of the Mayan year. At each equinox, the shadow of a snake appears; the shadow cast by the steps forms the body and a statue provides the head.

An entrance on the north side of the Castillo leads to two often-photographed chambers. One chamber contains an altar in the form of a reclining god, Chac Mool. The other chamber has a huge throne in the shape of a red jaguar with eyes of green jade.

The Mayas performed bloody pagan rituals. During famines, children were thrown into the seventy-five-foot-deep Well of Sacrifice to appease the rain god. Nearby stood Skull Rack and the Platforms of the Jaguars and the Eagles. There Mayas placed human heads on stakes and sacrificed still-throbbing hearts on bloody altars. Even at ball games, contestants (the losers!) were beheaded, as shown in their artwork.

Although some Mayan ruins date to before Christ, Chichen Itza does not. In fact, it did not flourish until AD 1000 and declined after 1224. The cause of the decline of the Mayas is a great mystery. Perhaps God, who especially hates child sacrifice, sent a judgment against the Mayas similar

to the judgment that fell on Judah in the time of Jeremiah.

Because they have forsaken me . . . and have filled this place with the blood of innocents; they have built also the high places of Baal, to burn their sons with fire for burnt offerings unto Baal, which I commanded not, nor spake it, neither came it into my mind: Therefore . . . I will cause them to fall by the sword before their enemies.
(Jer. 19:4–7)

members have been beaten and several pastors murdered, the gospel witness continues.

MAYAS IN THE YUCATÁN

The ancient Maya Indians built cities and massive pyramids in the southern jungles of Mexico, east of the Isthmus of Tehuantepec. The greatest concentration of Mayan ruins are on the Yucatán Peninsula. Although the great Mayan cities fell into decay long before the arrival of the Spanish, descendants of the Mayas remained on the peninsula. As Spanish dominion increased, the Mayas retreated to jungle hideouts. The Indians resented Mexican rule. Twice since Mexico became independent, the Mayas have declared the Yucatán independent.

The largest city on the peninsula today is Mérida (MEHR ih dah). Its chief product is henequen (HIN uh KWIN), a plant whose fibers sailors used to make string, twine, and rope.

U.S.-MEXICAN RELATIONS

Mexico and the United States, which share a two-thousand-mile-long border, have a long history (not always positive). The United States has greatly influenced Mexico, especially the northern area. Despite various problems, both countries have benefited greatly from their exchange of cultures and goods. In fact, the United States

Sisal fibers from the cactus-like henequen plant are hung out to dry before being processed into ropes.

is Mexico's main trading partner, and Mexico buys more American goods than any other country except Canada and Japan. Nevertheless, the relationship has been very strained at times.

Americans fought two wars against Mexico (1835–36 and 1846–48) before their boundary dispute was settled. From those wars, the United States obtained not only Texas down to the Rio Grande but also what later became California, New Mexico, and Arizona. The United States added even more territory by paying Mexico $10 million for a strip of land called the Gadsden Purchase below those southwestern territories.

The United States invaded Mexico during the Mexican revolution of 1910–20. In 1914, U.S. Marines landed on the Gulf coast to cut off arms shipments to Mexico's dictator and to help the revolutionaries. In 1916, General John Pershing led U.S. soldiers across the Texas border to track down the outlaw leader Pancho Villa (PAHN-choh VEE-yah), who had been making raids in American territory. The army withdrew the following year, as the clouds of World War I turned America's attention to Europe.

The wars, threats of war, and the Mexicans' perception of America as an arrogant bully discolored U.S.-Mexican relations for generations to follow. Signs reading, "Yanqui, go home!" have expressed the resentment that many Mexicans feel toward the United States. In turn, however, many Americans are disgruntled that so many Mexicans get into the United States illegally, allegedly taking Americans' jobs. When illegal immigrants have children in the United States, the children immediately become U.S. citizens. The parents can then begin to collect welfare and other government financial aid, putting further strains on the U.S. economy. The traffic in illicit drugs across the border is also a major point of conflict between the two peoples. In spite of these problems, the two governments have tried to work together to accomplish mutually beneficial goals, such as the enactment of NAFTA.

NAFTA AND CAFTA

In 1988, Mexico's main trading partner was the United States. But U.S.-Canadian trade was eighty times greater than U.S.-Mexican trade. Hoping to improve trade, Mexico asked to join a trade agreement with Canada and the United States. The North American Free Trade Agreement (NAFTA), signed in 1993, created the second-largest free-trade zone in the world (after the European Union).

The NAFTA negotiations stirred controversy in all three countries. Canada and the United States are industrial giants whereas Mexico is an underdeveloped nation with one-twentieth the economy of the United States. Mexico had much to offer: a potentially big market, cheap labor, and inexpensive products, such as cement and farm produce. But some Americans feared "unfair" competition from Mexican companies, which had fewer regulations on working conditions and pollution. Mexican farmers feared competition from America's cheap grain.

A similar agreement is in the process of being adopted throughout the rest of Middle America. The Central American Free Trade Agreement (CAFTA) is a treaty that has been signed by (to date) the United States and six Central American countries: Costa Rica, El Salvador, Guatemala, Honduras, Nicaragua, and the Dominican Republic. The agreement is modeled after NAFTA and is considered a steppingstone toward the development of a broader Free Trade Area of the Americas (FTAA), which would incorporate thirty-four economies.

It will be many years before we see the full impact of NAFTA, CAFTA, and, if it materializes, FTAA. Factories in the United States have begun sending many of their parts across the border to Mexican assembly plants, called maquiladoras (mah KEE lah DOR ahs). Although these jobs are not fancy, they provide Mexicans with above-average wages. Some American factories have either closed or laid off workers, but employment in the trade industry has boomed. Signatories are hoping that CAFTA will produce similar positive results for their countries.

LET'S GO EXPLORING

CLIMATES OF LATIN AMERICA

1. What is the most common climate on Mexico's northern border?

2. What three climates does Mexico share with most nations of Middle America?

3. What is the most common climate west of the highlands in Middle America?

4. What climates appear in South America but not in Middle America?

🔎 How can Mexico feed so many people even though it lacks a moderate climate?

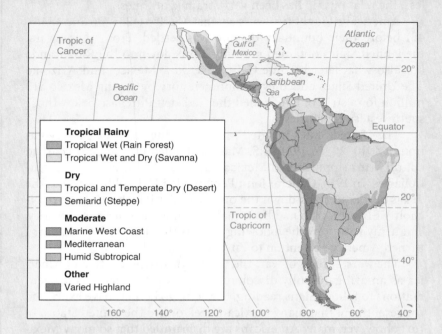

Tropic of Cancer

Atlantic Ocean

Gulf of Mexico

Pacific Ocean

Caribbean Sea

Equator

20°

20°

40°

Tropic of Capricorn

160°   140°   120°   100°   80°   60°   40°

Tropical Rainy
Tropical Wet (Rain Forest)
Tropical Wet and Dry (Savanna)

Dry
Tropical and Temperate Dry (Desert)
Semiarid (Steppe)

Moderate
Marine West Coast
Mediterranean
Humid Subtropical

Other
Varied Highland

SECTION QUIZ

1. What three mountain ranges dominate Mexico's geography?

2. List all the times that American soldiers have intervened in Mexican history.

3. What geographical features does northern Mexico share with the United States?

4. What countries are members of NAFTA?

5. What are the two largest tourist resorts in Mexico? What climate are they in?

🔎 Why would the northern states of Mexico support NAFTA but the southern states oppose it?

II. CENTRAL AMERICA

An **isthmus**, or narrow land bridge, connects Mexico with South America. Seven small countries lie in this region, known as **Central America**. Although they are strung out over one thousand miles, all seven countries would fit into Texas, with enough room left for Georgia.

Central America is very similar to southern Mexico. The mountains of the Western Cordillera continue south along the Pacific shore. The eastern coast receives more than one hundred inches of rain from trade winds blowing over the Caribbean Sea. But the Pacific Coast, which lies in the rainshadow, receives only forty inches of rain. Most people live in the comfortable *tierra templada* of the highlands.

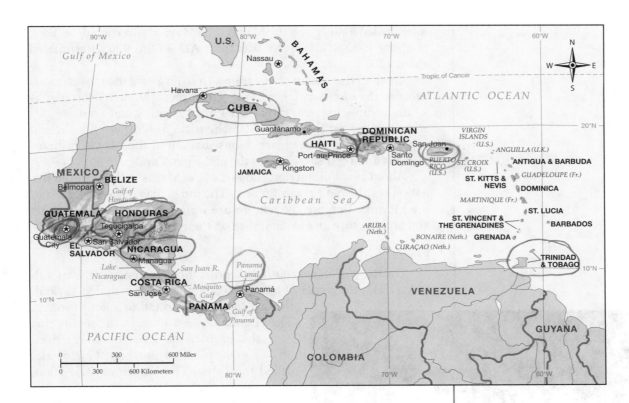

Like southern Mexico, the nations of Central America are relatively poor. The Pacific Ring of Fire poses the constant danger of earthquakes and volcanic eruptions. The fertile volcanic soils are the region's only important resource. Many Central Americans are subsistence farmers, growing just enough corn and vegetables to feed their own families.

The early European settlers introduced a new kind of farming called a **plantation economy**. Plantations require large numbers of workers to raise specialized crops, such as cotton, cacao, coffee, and bananas, all crops that require many hands to tend, gather, and ship them to foreign markets. The early Spaniards forced the Indians to clear the forests and work the plantations. Later, they brought slaves from Africa. Today, the owners hire local workers.

Central American countries share several other characteristics with Mexico. All but Belize were Spanish colonies, and their people speak Spanish. The Roman Catholic Church is predominant. Revolutions and civil strife have wracked these struggling republics, and that political instability causes economic instability.

The United States has had a profound influence in the region. American and British warships helped to keep the region free from foreign invasion during the nineteenth century. At times, the United States has supplied weapons or sent troops to restore peace. Today, although the Central American nations often resent the interference of "the Colossus of the North," they each trade with the United States more than with any other nation, including each other.

LANDS OF THE MAYA

Like southern Mexico, the four nations of northern Central America (Guatemala, Belize, El Salvador, and Honduras)

Mayas, such as these in Chichicastenango, Guatemala, live throughout Central America today.

were settled long ago by the Mayas. The **Maya** civilization dates back to about 1000 BC. Its peak was from AD 300 to 900. It crumbled about 1200.

Of all of the Indian civilizations, the Mayas are the most famous because they left written records. Until recently, their hieroglyphics and number system remained a great mystery, but accurate calendars found on the walls of Chichen Itza and other cities helped experts decipher many inscriptions that tell of the Mayas' military prowess and their sacrifices to the god Kukulcan.

About two million descendants of the Mayas still live in the five nations of the old Mayan Empire. The jungle has reclaimed most of the Mayan cities, but the nations are working to protect Mayan art and architecture and to capitalize on their tourism potential.

GUATEMALA

On the Yucatán's southern border lies Guatemala (GWAH tuh MAHL ah), the center of Maya civilization, which included Tayasal, the last Mayan city to fall to Spanish forces. The Highland Maya lived in the mountains near the Pacific; the Lowland Maya lived on the great plain of northern Guatemala, called the Petén. The Mayan capital, Tikal, and most of the population centers were in the lowlands. More than half the people of Guatemala are descendants of the Mayas, many of whom live as their ancestors in the northern plain did. The rest of the people are mestizos, called *ladinos*, who follow more Spanish traditions.

Guatemala has more people than any other Central American country and the largest city in Central America: Guatemala City, the capital. Plantations in the highlands produce coffee beans whereas the plantations on the Pacific lowlands produce sugar cane and cotton. The highlands boast the highest mountain in Central America, Volcán Tajamulco (13,845 ft.).

Guatemala is the fifth-greatest producer of coffee in the world.

After a devastating earthquake struck Guatemala in 1976, Protestant missionaries found hearts receptive to the gospel. Nearly 30 percent of the people are now Protestants in contrast to an average of 6 percent in the rest of Central America. In 1991, a Guatemalan became the first Protestant elected president in Latin American history.

Guatemala was the scene of the longest-running civil war in Central America. Some 140,000 people died in thirty-five years of bloodshed before peace was restored in 1996.

BELIZE

All of Belize (buh LEEZ) was once part of the Mayan Empire. Lowland Maya lived in the Caribbean lowlands, which extend down from the Yucatán and cover most of Belize.

Unlike the other Central American nations, Belize was settled by the British. Forsaken by the Spanish because it lacked gold, this difficult coastland was first settled by shipwrecked British sailors in 1638. The Spanish, Caribbean pirates, and Indians tried to drive the settlers away, but they did not budge. The country was called "British

Through Christian Eyes

What should Christians learn from the dramatic growth of Protestant missions in Guatemala over the past three decades?

Honduras" and remained a colony until independence in 1981, when it changed its name to Belize. Like Canada, it is a member of the British Commonwealth, and British troops protect it from Guatemala, which has claimed the country as its own.

Belize has the least population in Central America. About 49 percent of the population are mestizos, and 25 percent are Creoles. Only about 10 percent of the people are descended from the Mayas. The rest have African ancestry and are the descendants of slaves brought to work on the plantations. Those with partial African and partial European ancestry are called **mulattoes** (moo LAH tohs). Belize has the highest black population in Central America.

Belize has a distinctly British heritage, and the people speak primarily English. About 50 percent of the people are Roman Catholics and 27 percent are Protestant. Major products of the country include bananas, cacao, citrus, sugar, fish, and garment manufactures. The Mayan ruins and the Belize Barrier Reef, the world's second-longest barrier reef, make tourism a major industry.

All-terrain vehicles outnumber cars on this street in downtown Ambergris, Belize.

EL SALVADOR

Although El Salvador has a few Mayan ruins in the mountains, it is most famous for its volcanoes, more than two dozen of which rise above the central plateau—more than in any other Central American nation. Izalco, rising 7,828 feet and called the "Lighthouse of the Pacific," appeared in 1770 and remained active for almost two hundred years.

Although El Salvador has the least area of any Central American country, it is the most densely populated nation on either American continent. Its capital, San Salvador, rivals Guatemala City for bragging rights as the largest metropolitan area in Central America.

Whereas Belize touches only the Caribbean Sea, El Salvador touches only the Pacific Ocean. Most of its people live in the central plateau between the northern mountains and the coast, where they grow coffee, the nation's major crop.

The close-knit "Fourteen Families," descendants of the original Spanish landholders, have owned most of the plantations and controlled the government of El Salvador for most of its history. Bloodshed has been common. Several **juntas** (HOON tahs)—councils of military and civilian leaders—have seized power. A civil war raged from the 1970s to 1992, during which seventy-five thousand people died. Such instability has hindered economic development.

HONDURAS

The capital and largest city of Honduras, Tegucigalpa (tay GOOS ih GAHL pah), lies in the mountains that cover most of the country. Most people are peasants, or *campesinos* (kahm pay SEE nohs), who live in one-room bamboo homes called *ranchos* (RAHN chohs). Honduras is 90 percent mestizo. The northeastern region, called the Mosquito Coast, is sparsely populated tropical rain forests and grasslands that extend into Nicaragua.

The major crop of Honduras is bananas, which are grown on the north Caribbean coast. In the early twentieth century, U.S. fruit companies bought large tracts of land and provided much of the nation's income. But the companies used their money to influence

Although bananas are the major crop of Honduras, it ranks only fourteenth in world production of the fruit.

politics and to win special privileges. At times, the U.S. government used the threat of military intervention to protect U.S. companies. Because the economy—and governments—rose or fell with the price of one cash crop, Honduras earned the nickname "the banana republic" although it is not even among the top ten banana producers. That term has been used to describe any unstable Third World republic, especially one in Latin America.

Honduras has had trouble with both internal coups and its neighbors. In addition to Nicaraguan Communist insurgency, which the United States sent troops to suppress, Honduras has had border disputes with Nicaragua over the Mosquito Coast and with El Salvador over the removal of squatters. A "Soccer War" was precipitated by two highly charged soccer games between Honduras and El Salvador. Fans rioted, the violence spread, and a four-day war resulted.

NICARAGUA

Because highlands cover the central region of Nicaragua, most people live in the fertile Pacific lowlands. Lake Nicaragua, the larg-

SOCCER—THE WORLD SPORT

The most popular team sport in Middle and South America—and in the whole world, for that matter—is fútbol ("football"), or what Americans call soccer. Many cultures in history, including ancient China, have played a variety of football games. Team competitions helped to develop manly skills and bonds among future warriors. England was the first to write down modern soccer rules in 1848. The Fédération Internationale de Football Association began in 1904 with seven member nations; it now has more than 150 member nations.

Fans in countries where soccer is the major sport, such as in Europe and South America, take soccer seriously, considering their national honor to be at stake in the contests. In some instances, riots have erupted as fans expressed either joy at a victory or anger over a bad call or a defeat. Such athletic conflicts have blown into international incidents and even wars!

Every four years, the World Cup competition is held to determine the world soccer champion. After several qualifying tournaments, the thirty-two best teams compete at the World Cup site, which rotates among the cities of the world. Estimates indicate that more than one billion people listen to or watch media coverage of the final match. The members of the winning team are considered national heroes. The following table lists the winners of the World Cup.

Year	Winner	Opponent	Host country
1930	Uruguay	Argentina	Uruguay
1934	Italy	Czechoslovakia	Italy
1938	Italy	Hungary	France
(No World Cup competitions were held during or shortly after World War II.)			
1950	Uruguay	Brazil	Brazil
1954	W. Germany	Hungary	Switzerland
1958	Brazil	Sweden	Sweden
1962	Brazil	Czechoslovakia	Chile
1966	England	W. Germany	England
1970	Brazil	Italy	Mexico
1974	W. Germany	Netherlands	W. Germany
1978	Argentina	Netherlands	Argentina
1982	Italy	W. Germany	Spain
1986	Argentina	W. Germany	Mexico
1990	W. Germany	Argentina	Italy
1994	Brazil	Italy	United States
1998	France	Brazil	France
2002	Brazil	Germany	Korea/Japan
2006	Italy	France	Germany

SOUTHERN CROSSROADS OF CENTRAL AMERICA

Central America has been called the "Crossroads of the Americas." This title is especially appropriate for the three southern nations of Central America—Nicaragua, Costa Rica, and Panama—all three of which have both Pacific and Caribbean ports. All three also are linked by a railway to most of Central America. More importantly, all three control portions of the **Pan-American Highway**, an approximately 16,000-mile-long road that extends from Fairbanks, Alaska, to Puerto Montt, Chile, linking seventeen Latin American capitals.

The Pan-American Highway is not specifically designated in Canada and the United States, but it is in Mexico and Central American nations. A 54-mile stretch of highway between Panama and Colombia has not been completed. Reasons for its unfinished condition range from the need to protect the rain forest to the desire to prevent the spread of infectious diseases. A ferry has been proposed, but to date no action has been taken on the proposal.

est lake in Central America, is famed for its three volcanoes and the world's only freshwater sharks. The San Juan River flows east from the lake to the Caribbean Sea. The United States considered building a canal there in the late nineteenth century but built it in Panama instead.

Although Nicaragua is the largest country in Central America, political divisions have stifled its economic progress. The United States has been compelled to intervene several times to restore order. When Communist rebels (the Sandinista Liberation Front) took over the country in 1979, it marked the second time that a country in the Western Hemisphere was controlled by Communists. (The first was Cuba; see p. 286.) Despite their promises of land reform, the **Sandinistas** (SAHN din EES tahs) committed human rights violations and suppressed all opposition. The United States sent large amounts of money and weapons to protect Nicaragua's neighbors and supply the opposition **Contras** (COHN trahs). The Soviet Union supplied arms to the Sandinistas. The collapse of communism in Europe in 1989 left the Sandinistas without financial and military support and forced free elections, which the Sandinistas lost.

Nicaragua continues to struggle to restore and develop its economy. It is primarily an agricultural nation with almost half of its population employed in agriculture. Its main crops, typical of Central American countries, are sugar, bananas, and coffee.

COSTA RICA

The area south of Nicaragua's Mosquito Coast has long been known as Costa Rica ("Rich Coast"), and the name still fits today. Costa Rica has a pleasant climate that has helped the people attain the highest per capita GDP in Central America. The capital, San José, is high in the central plateau and has spring-like temperatures year round.

The main reason for Costa Rica's wealth is its large number of private landowners. About 95 percent of the people are direct descendants of early Spanish settlers, who developed an efficient system of small, independent farms. In contrast, other Spanish colonies relied on Indian slave labor on large plantations. In Costa Rica, however, most of the Indians fled to the mountains, leaving the Spanish to fend for themselves. Costa Rica was the first Central American country to grow coffee, and that product is its leading export today. Costa Rica was also the first country to raise bananas, its second major crop, for export.

The country is the oldest continuous democracy in Latin America. Except for a dictatorship in 1917–19 and a civil war in 1948–49, the people have freely elected their president since 1889. The country has no army. Its political stability has brought great material prosperity. It has the best education, sanitation, health care, and public services in Central America, and life expectancy is similar to that in North America.

Panama

Panama is the most developed of all the Central American nations. It has the second-highest per capita GDP in Central America, primarily because of income from the **Panama Canal** and canal-related jobs. Outside the Canal Zone, most people are subsistence farmers. The canal's presence has earned Panama the title "Crossroads of the World."

In 1907–20, the United States built the canal and received control of the zone in perpetuity (essentially forever). In 1979, the United States and Panama signed a treaty whereby Panama would get control of the canal in 1999, which it did.

Section Quiz

1. What is the most populous nation in Central America? the most densely populated?
2. Which nation was the heart of the Mayan Empire?
3. How is Belize different from the other nations of Central America?
4. What Marxist group once controlled Nicaragua?

- Why can it be said that the Panama Canal has benefited every country of Central America?

III. The West Indies

Between Florida and the northern coast of South America lie about one thousand islands and thousands of tiny *islets* (small, usually uninhabitable islands). Combined, these islands, called the **West Indies**, contain about twice as much land as Pennsylvania. They fall into three main groups: the Bahamas, the Greater Antilles (an TILL ees), and the Lesser Antilles.

Most of the West Indies lie in the tropics, and all have a mild climate. Rainfall averages about thirty inches a year, temperatures are in the 70s or 80s all year, and the vegetation is lush.

Christopher Columbus discovered the West Indies in 1492, landing first in the Bahamas and then on Cuba and Hispaniola. Because he believed the islands to be near India, he called them the Indies and the native peoples Indians. Spanish sailors soon discovered, explored, and claimed most of the other islands of the West Indies.

PANAMA CANAL

The United States keeps separate navy fleets in the Atlantic and Pacific Oceans. During the Spanish-American War, the United States experienced great difficulty in transferring battleships from one ocean to the other.

The Gatun Locks are on the the Caribbean end of the canal.

The U.S.S. *Oregon* sailed 12,000 miles around Cape Horn before it finally reached Cuba. Naval officers realized that a canal through Central America would cut the distance by two-thirds, to only 4,600 miles.

French engineers had attempted to build a canal across Panama in 1882 but gave up after seven years and twenty thousand deaths from diseases, such as yellow fever, bubonic plague, and malaria. Before Americans began construction, they drained the mosquito-infested swamps. Construction began in earnest in 1907, with the building of the Gatun Dam that created a 163-

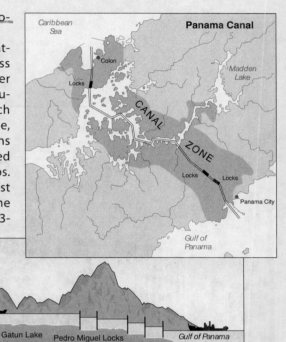

square-mile lake. Next came six pairs of locks. Finally, though plagued by landslides, American workers dug the Gaillard Cut, a channel across the continental divide. The S.S. *Ancon* made the first trial crossing in August 1914, and President Woodrow Wilson officially opened the $340-million canal on July 12, 1920.

The trip across Panama takes eight hours and costs about $32,000 per ship. Because of an unusual loop in the isthmus, a ship traveling from the Atlantic Ocean reaches the Pacific twenty-seven miles farther east than where it began! (Look at the map to see why.) About thirty-five ships take the fifty-mile trip each day.

THE BAHAMAS

The **Bahamas**, a cluster of coral islands north of the Greater Antilles, differ from the other mountainous islands of the West Indies. Because they are formed from coral rather than volcanic lava, all of the islands are low and have neither mountains nor good soils.

The Spanish did not consider the islands of value. The British, however, founded a colony there and, because of their strong navy, soon mastered the whole island chain. Several thousand British Loyalists relocated their slaves there after the American Revolution. As more African slaves were brought to the Bahamas, they became a large majority of the population.

The Bahamas are now an independent member of the British Commonwealth. As such, they enjoy the highest standard of living in Middle America. Tax breaks have attracted international banks. Fishing was once the most common occupation, but tourism provides most modern jobs. In spite of its English heritage, more of the islanders are Baptists than Anglicans or Roman Catholics.

THE GREATER ANTILLES

The Antilles islands are the crest of an underwater mountain chain. The western "range" consists of the four largest islands—Cuba, Hispaniola (his pahn YOH lah), Puerto Rico, and Jamaica. Collectively, they are called the **Greater Antilles.**

Spain used these islands as a base for exploring much of the rest of the New World and to protect their shipping routes. They built large sugar plantations and later introduced coffee, tobacco, and fruits. Most islanders on Jamaica and Hispaniola are descendants of African slaves who worked on the plantations, whereas the people of Cuba and Puerto Rico are predominantly of Spanish descent.

CUBA

With an area slightly larger than that of Tennessee, **Cuba** is the largest and most populous island in the West Indies. It has more arable land than any other country in Central America or the West Indies. Its fertile soil and central location near both Florida and Mexico made it the most influential island in the Western Hemisphere.

Cuba was once the world's third-largest producer of sugar, but it has fallen to twelfth because of droughts, declining investment, and unwise government regulation. Most sugar cane is grown on the eastern edge of the island, which receives moist trade winds. Low central mountains block this moisture from reaching the western end. The wet-and-dry climate on the west end of the island is perfect for grazing cattle and growing tobacco. Cuba is also famous for its cigars.

Cuba was one of the last Spanish holdings in Latin America. Spain lost it, however, in the **Spanish-American War** in 1898. The victorious United States soon gave up all of Cuba except a naval base at Guantanamo (gwahn TAHN uh moh) Bay, which it still operates. American politicians and businessmen greatly influenced the development of the new Cuba, but the Cubans went through a succession of governments and dictators in trying to establish a strong republican government. The island fell to rebel leader **Fidel Castro** in 1959, and he established the first Communist government in the Western Hemisphere. His main ally was the Soviet Union. The United States severed diplomatic and trade relations with Cuba.

Thousands of Cubans fled Castro's oppressive rule and came to the United States. Over the years, others have continued to risk their lives on flimsy rafts, including even automobiles converted into rafts, hoping to cross the ninety miles to freedom in Florida. Many have done so, but many more have been turned back by the U.S. Coast Guard.

Havana, the capital of Cuba, was a thriving tourist and commercial center during the heyday of republican government. It remains the largest city in the West Indies, but it has lost its elegance. While Castro amassed a personal fortune, his people sank into increasing poverty. After the Soviet Union collapsed in 1991, Cuba lost its major trade partner and source of oil. Industries closed, and cities went without power for hours at a time. In the

Cuba is filled with propaganda glorifying the Communist revolutionary Ché Gevara.

These Cubans modified an old truck into a raft and sought freedom from Castro's regime.

summer of 1994, Havana experienced its worst rioting since Castro took power. Facing up to economic realities, Castro allowed small-scale private businesses, a few private produce markets, and the foreign ownership of private property. But he failed to achieve his central goal: to reopen trade with the United States. As Castro ages, observers are speculating on the future of the people and government of Cuba.

HISPANIOLA: HAITI AND THE DOMINICAN REPUBLIC

Two countries occupy the island of **Hispaniola**. Haiti is on the west side, and the Dominican Republic is on the east side. Although the Spanish were the first settlers on the mountainous island, they gave the western third to France in 1697. France and Spain brought African slaves to both parts of the island.

Haiti—Haiti is the poorest country in the Western Hemisphere but was not always so. Before the slaves on the island revolted against France during the French Revolution, Haiti was the richest colony in the Western Hemisphere, providing most of Europe's tea and sugar cane. When Haiti was declared a republic on January 1, 1804, it became the second republic in the New World.

Unfortunately, revolutionaries had burned the plantations and devastated the countryside. Today, conflicts between rival groups keep the nation in a constant state of turmoil. Another reason for the poverty, especially food deficiency, is linked to land usage. The best land is used for cash crops for export, which limits the amount of good land for food production and produces poorer-quality crops.

Another major cause of Haiti's troubles is its religion. The one characteristic that united the slaves was **voodoo**, a strange mixture of West African spirit worship, black magic, and Roman Catholicism. At the beginning of the rebellion, voodoo priests dedicated the country to Satan, and many leaders still rely on voodoo curses and bloodshed to keep power.

Haitians have suffered under a succession of violent dictators, and such instability hinders economic growth. Like most other Latin American countries, Haiti grows such crops as coffee, rice, sugar, mangoes, and corn. What industries it has are primarily associated in some way with those crops, including refining of sugar and milling of flour. Textiles is also one of Haiti's few industries.

The people are divided into two classes: a rich minority (about 5 percent) of mulattoes and a large majority of blacks, most of whom cannot read. Educated Haitians, particularly the mulattoes, still speak French. But the majority of the people speak a mixture of French and African words called **Creole**. "Bonjour, Blanc! (Hi, White!)" is a common greeting to foreigners seen on the street.

Dominican Republic—Like Haiti, the Dominican Republic is mountainous. It boasts the highest point in the West Indies: Duarte (DWAHR tay) Peak (10,417 feet). But mountains are the only characteristic the Dominican Republic shares with Haiti. The islanders enjoy a normal life expectancy, high literacy, and a better economy.

Because of the trade restrictions that have been in place since the Castro revolution, no new cars have been imported, and Cuba is filled with 1950s-era cars.

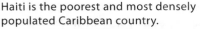

Haiti is the poorest and most densely populated Caribbean country.

In the late 1960s, the Dominican Republic, with the help of U.S. soldiers, finally set up a stable republic.

The capital, **Santo Domingo** (SAHN-toh doh-MEEN-goh), founded in 1496 by the brother of Columbus, is the oldest European-established city in the Western Hemisphere. It vies with Havana as the largest city in the West Indies.

Although agriculture represents only 11 percent of the GDP, the Dominican Republic produces a variety of crops, including coffee, rice, sugar, cotton, cacao, potatoes, and bananas. Industry is 32 percent of the GDP and includes sugar processing, nickel and gold mining, textiles, cement, and tourism.

The African slaves mixed freely with the Spanish in the Dominican Republic, so today the majority of its people are mulattoes. Spanish is spoken throughout the country, and Catholicism is the major religion. In addition, the people have developed a famous blend of the music and customs of Africa and Spain.

MEDICAL MISSIONS

For I was an hungered, and ye gave me meat: I was thirsty, and ye gave me drink: . . . naked, and ye clothed me: I was sick, and ye visited me.

(Matt. 25:35–36)

In Matthew 25:34-46, Jesus gave us an example of how to love the poor and the sick by helping them. Although some Latin American cities are very modern, others are very poor. One of the poorest nations in the world is Haiti, where only one person in a hundred has a telephone, and only one in about three hundred has a television. Without money, the people cannot afford proper medical care. Haiti has only one doctor per six thousand people, and the infant mortality rate is more than 10 percent.

The hearts of many missionaries reach out to such needy people. They are willing to forego modern conveniences to bring help. Medical missionaries view their provision of medical care as an opportunity to share the gospel. Christian doctors and nurses work patiently using substandard (by Western expectations) facilities and equipment. Like Paul in 1 Corinthians 9:22, they willingly become weak, even risking tropical diseases, to gain the weak.

To poor Haitians, even the most unfortunate American seems to live like a king. The prophet Haggai rebuked his people for living in luxury instead of building God's temple (1:4). Someday you may have an opportunity to build temples in the hearts of believers (1 Cor. 3:17). Would you be willing to build God's house by serving in a poor area such as Haiti, or will you remain in comfort at home?

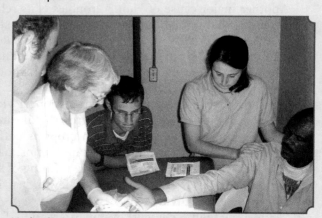

Medical missionaries serve God in foreign countries by meeting both the physical and spiritual needs of the people.

JAMAICA

The island of **Jamaica** was a Spanish colony for 150 years, until the British captured it in 1655. But it took many years for Britain to establish complete control. The Jamaican city of Port Royal became a notorious haven for pirates.

Large numbers of African slaves once worked on Jamaica's sugar plantations, and their descendants now make up about 95 percent of the population.

Most Jamaicans speak "Jamaica Talk," a colorful English dialect that mixes many old English words and African pronunciation and grammar. For example, a common greeting is, "Everyt'ing irie?" (Everything all right?)

Some Jamaicans are Roman Catholic, but far more belong to Protestant denominations. However, many Jamaicans follow Rastafarianism (RAHS tuh FAHR ee uh niz um), a mixture of African and Christian religion.

Jamaica, which became independent in 1962, has great economic potential. Plantations still produce sugar cane, and Jamaica is a center of the spice trade in the West Indies. It produces the world's finest ginger and is the leading producer of allspice. Large deposits of bauxite make the island the third-largest bauxite supplier for the aluminum industry. The stable parliamentary government helps the economy by promoting peace and tourism.

U.S. COMMONWEALTH OF PUERTO RICO

The Spanish island of **Puerto Rico** came under the control of the United States after the Spanish-American War. The people are mostly of Spanish descent. A few mestizos are the last descendants of the Arawaks (AIR uh WAHKS), who intermarried with whites. Puerto Rican farmers produce sugar cane and coffee, but manufacturing has become the island's chief source of income.

In 1951, Puerto Rico voted to become a **commonwealth** of the United States. Puerto Ricans are U.S. citizens with most of the privileges of other American citizens. They have their own constitution and elect a governor, but they cannot vote in presidential elections. They do, however, have a voice in both of the major political parties' presidential nominating conventions. Until recently, the drawback of not having the right to vote in presidential elections was balanced by their having freedom from federal taxes. An increasing number of Puerto Ricans support becoming the fifty-first state.

THE LESSER ANTILLES

The **Lesser Antilles** are a chain of smaller islands that form the eastern boundary of the Caribbean Sea. The chain curves southward from Puerto Rico to the South American coast. Tourism, fishing, and farming are the main economic activities. Tropical fruits and vegetables are common crops, and some farmers also raise sugar cane, cotton, or coffee.

The Spanish lost interest in the Lesser Antilles when they learned that the islands have no gold and silver, so the islands were left open to settlement by British, French, and Dutch colonists. The people of these islands are mostly black descendants of early slaves. Today, most of the islands remain territories of these three European countries or of the United States. Eight British islands, however, gained independence between 1962 and 1983.

LEEWARD ISLANDS

The northern islands of the Lesser Antilles, from the Virgin Islands to Dominica (DAH mih NEE cuh), are called the **Leeward Islands**. The word *leeward* refers to an island that is sheltered from prevailing winds on the open ocean. The Leeward Islands are sheltered from many tropical storms that rip through the Windward Islands farther south and east.

Just east of Puerto Rico are the most famous Leewards—the Virgin Islands. Three major islands and about a hundred islets belong to the United States, and the rest belong to Great Britain.

Most of the remaining colonies lie southeast of the Virgin Islands. Anguilla (an GWIL uh) and Montserrat (MAHNT suh RAHT) are British. The Dutch control Saba (SAY buh), St. Eustatius (yoo STAY shus), and St. Maarten (MAHR tin). Guadeloupe (GWAH duh LOOP) is the main French island. Three independent countries lie in the Leeward Islands: St. Kitts and Nevis (NEE vis), Antigua (an TEE guh) and Barbuda (bar BOO duh), and Dominica. English is the national language of all three countries, each of which has a high literacy rate. Their economies are similar to those of the Central American nations.

THE WINDWARD ISLANDS

The **Windward Islands** face the prevailing southeasterly winds that blow off the Atlantic Ocean. They suffer the full brunt of hurricanes. The chain runs from Martinique (mahr tih NEEK) to Grenada (greh NAY dah). **Martinique** is a French territory, but the other islands are former British territories that gained independence in the 1970s. **St. Lucia** (LOO shuh) is the northernmost of the three nations. Most of the middle islands are owned by **St. Vincent and the Grenadines** (GREN uh DEENZ).

The southernmost Windward nation is **Grenada**. It produces about three-fourths of the world's supply of nutmeg. A Cuban-backed Communist government took control of Grenada temporarily, but in 1983 the United States led a successful attack that drove out the Communists.

Outlying Lesser Antilles—The other islands of the Lesser Antilles are not part of the chain of Leeward and Windward Islands. Trinidad, nearly two thousand square miles in area, is the largest of the Lesser Antilles. **Trinidad and Tobago** (tuh BAY goh) became independent of Great Britain in 1962, making it the first independent nation in the Lesser Antilles. **Barbados** (bahr BAY dohs) is the only other independent nation in the Lesser Antilles. It has by far the greatest population density in the Western Hemisphere, yet its people vie with Trinidad and Tobago for the highest GDP in Middle America.

These Barbadian sailors are taking part in an Independence Day parade.

SECTION QUIZ

1. What three island groups form the West Indies?

2. What two nations share the island of Hispaniola?

3. What two island chains form the east boundary of the Caribbean Sea?

4. What is the largest island in the West Indies? the largest island in the Lesser Antilles? the most densely populated island in the Western Hemisphere?

💡 Should the United States accept Puerto Rico as a state?

CHAPTER REVIEW

11

HOW MUCH DO YOU REMEMBER?

1. What are the five altitude zones common in Latin America? Which zone has the most people?

2. Compare and contrast the federal governments of Mexico and the United States.

3. Compare and contrast the hacienda and the plantation economy.

4. Name the two large peninsulas of Mexico.

5. What is the most productive and populous region of Mexico? Why?

6. What religion is prominent throughout Latin America?

7. What role has land ownership played in Latin America's political unrest?

8. Which Central American country lacks a Spanish heritage?

9. Which Middle American countries have had a Communist government?

10. Name the four islands of the Greater Antilles.

11. Name all the Middle American nations that have been occupied by U.S. troops. Why were they sent?

12. What European nation controlled the islands of the Lesser Antilles that have since become independent?

WHAT DO YOU THINK?

1. How does Matthew 26:52 help to explain the political turmoil in Latin America? Why have the United States and Canada been more stable?

2. Should the United States try to keep out all illegal aliens from Mexico? Why or why not?

Can You:
Define These Terms?

land bridge, isthmus, saguaro cacti, plantation, altitude zone, economy, Toltec, mulattoes, Aztecs, junta, hacienda, Sandinistas, peones, Contras, coup, Hispaniola, mestizos, voodoo, ejidos, commonwealth

Locate These Places?

Latin America, Chiapas, Middle America, Central America, Baja California, Panama Canal, Bay of Compeche, West Indies, Sierra Madre Oriental, Bahamas, Greater Antilles, Sierra Madre Occidental, Cuba, Valley of Mexico, Havana, Tijuana, Santo Domingo, Juarez, Jamaica, Monterrey, Puerto Rico, Northern Plateau, Lesser Antilles, Copper Canyon, Leeward islands, Veracruz, Windward Islands, Cancún, Martinique, Acapulco, St. Lucia, Sonoran Desert, St. Vincent and the Grenadines, Mexican Plateau, Grenada, Mexico City, Trinidad and Tobago, Sierra Madre Del Sur, Barbados

Explain the Significance?

Vicente Fox, Fidel Castro, Maya civilization, Spanish-American War

CHAPTER 12

This woman represents the ancient Indian civilizations of South America, especially the Incas.

SOUTH AMERICA

PASSPO

Unite
of

Although South America is smaller than North America, it has the same wonderful diversity of geography and cultures.

When Europeans discovered South America, it was already filled with thousands of diverse Indian tribes. The Latin culture of Europe, however, eventually dominated the continent. Spanish and Portuguese explorers competed for trade rights and New World lands. To settle disputes that arose between the countries, Pope Alexander VI divided the then-known world between them, drawing a north-south line down the Atlantic Ocean. Portugal could claim lands east of that **Line of Demarcation**; Spain could claim lands west of it. After negotiations between the two countries, they signed the **Treaty of Tordesillas** (tohr day SEE yahs), which moved the line farther west, thereby giving Portugal what is now Brazil. That is why Brazil is the only Portuguese-speaking country in the Western Hemisphere. Because of geographic barriers, a key feature of this continent has been the isolation of individual countries, and these countries have had more interaction with Europe than they have with each other.

Since winning their independence in the early nineteenth century, the nations of South America have struggled to establish free, prosperous republics patterned after the United States. Unfortunately, as in Middle America, they have suffered from constant coups, wars, and revolts, problems that result because they built on social and political values of eighteenth-century Spain and Portugal. Nevertheless, South Americans have the talents and resources necessary to create thriving nations. Events at the beginning of the new millennium have given hope of a brighter future.

South America Fast Facts							
Flag	Country	Capital	Area (sq. mi.)	Pop. (M)	Pop. Density (per sq. mi.)	Per Capita GDP ($US)	Life Span
	Argentina	Buenos Aires	1,068,297	39.54	37	$12,400	75.9
	Bolivia	La Paz & Sucre	424,162	8.86	21	$2,600	65.5
	Brazil	Brasília	3,286,472	186.11	57	$8,100	71.7
	Chile	Santiago	292,257	15.99	55	$10,700	76.6
	Colombia	Bogotá	439,735	42.95	98	$6,600	71.7
	Ecuador	Quito	109,483	13.36	122	$3,700	76.2
	Guyana	Georgetown	83,000	0.77	9	$3,800	65.5
	Paraguay	Asunción	157,047	6.35	40	$4,800	74.9
	Peru	Lima	496,222	27.93	56	$5,600	69.5
	Suriname	Paramaribo	63,037	0.44	7	$4,300	69.0
	Uruguay	Montevideo	68,037	3.42	50	$14,500	76.1
	Venezuela	Caracas	352,143	25.38	72	$5,800	74.3

I. THE CARIBBEAN COUNTRIES

Two South American nations—Colombia (coh LOHM bee yah) and Venezuela (vehn uh ZWAY lah)—border the Caribbean Sea. Their peoples are a mixture of descendants from native Indians, Spanish conquerors, and African slaves. Fifty-eight percent of the people are mestizos. The rest are whites (20 percent); mulattoes (14 percent); blacks (14 percent); mixed black and Amerindian, called *zambos* (ZAHM bohs), 3 percent; and Amerindians (1 percent).

Venezuela and Colombia share many geographic features with Middle America. The Western Cordillera extends into South America, where it is known as the **Andes** (AN dees). Although Colombia

and Venezuela are located in the tropics, altitude is the major influence on climate. Most people live in the temperate *tierra templada*.

The Spanish and Portuguese colonial systems created great resentment in the colonies. The ruling *peninsulares* (peh NEEN soo LAHR ehs) from Spain treated their subjects with contempt. Their subjects included the Spanish *criollos* (cree OH yohs), or **Creoles** (CREE ohls), born in America. The Creoles became restive and finally revolted, led by the greatest hero of Latin America, **Simón Bolívar** (see-MOHN boh-LEE-vahr), "the Liberator." He was born in 1783 to a rich Creole family in Caracas, Venezuela. During a trip to Europe, he was inspired by the revolutionary fervor of the French Revolution. After a failed attempt to liberate his homeland, he fled to Haiti. Returning, he defeated the Spanish in 1819 outside the capital of New Granada (Santa Fe de Bogotá). The Battle of Boyacá (boy yah CAH) liberated Colombia but not the other divisions of New Granada. Next, Bolívar turned east and freed Venezuela. Finally, he turned south and liberated Ecuador. Bolívar then became the president and dictator of a united nation he called Gran (GRAHN, "great") Colombia. But the union broke apart a decade later.

During the sixteenth and seventeenth centuries, Cartagena was part of the Spanish Main, a series of seaports for the Spanish treasure fleet.

COLOMBIA

Like Central America, Colombia is located at the crossroads of the American continents. Its one-hundred-mile border with Panama is South America's only geographic tie to North America. In fact, the lowlands of Panama were once part of Colombia. Colombia also shares South America's two main geographic features—the Andes Mountains and the Amazon Basin.

CARIBBEAN AND PACIFIC LOWLANDS

Colombia is unique in South America because it has coasts on both the Caribbean and the Pacific. Although the Caribbean lowlands are hot, about one-fifth of the population lives there, many of the people working on plantations. Few people live on the swampy Pacific coast, where the average annual rainfall is four hundred inches.

THE MOUNTAINOUS INTERIOR

Most Colombians live in the cool valleys of the Andes Mountains. The Andes, which follow the entire west coast of South America, split into three separate ranges in Colombia, part of them stretching northward toward the Caribbean. The western range, or **Cordillera Occidental**, is the lowest of the three. Next is the **Cordillera Central**. The easternmost range, or **Cordillera Oriental**, reaches into Venezuela.

The capital of Colombia, Santa Fe de **Bogotá** (BOH guh TAH), lies in the Cordillera Oriental. A teeming city of 7.8 million people (8.5 million in the metropolitan area), Bogotá is the cultural center of the nation. As in other Latin American cities, however, rural workers live in large slums, or *turgurios* (toor GOO ree ohs).

The four other Colombian cities with populations of more than a million lie along the two river valleys between Colombia's three Andes ranges. Cartagena (cahr tuh HAY nuh) and Barranquilla

Bogotá is both the capital and the chief economic center of Colombia.

(BAHR rahn KEE yah) are near the Caribbean coast on the deepest river, the Magdalena, "the lifeline of Colombia." Oceangoing ships can travel up the river far into the interior. Major oil wells operate in the Magdalena River valley. **Medellín** (MEH deh YEEN) is in the west central area near Panama, and Cali (CAH lee) is farther to the southwest near the Pacific coast. Both cities are on the Cauca (COW cah) River. Bogotá, Medellín, and Cali form Colombia's "industrial triangle."

The Andes provide Colombia with several important products. Colombia is the world's fourth-largest coffee-producing country. It is the world's largest producer of Arabica coffee, the highest quality coffee bean.

Colombia is also rich in natural resources. It has the largest coal reserves in Latin America and the only platinum mines in South America. It is a leading producer of gold and also mines 90 percent of the world's emeralds. Those emeralds set the standard of quality for all other countries' emeralds.

Unfortunately, Colombia is also known for its export of another product—illegal drugs. Drug lords finance huge plantations to grow, produce, and refine heroin, cocaine, and marijuana. The infamous Medellín drug cartel allegedly earns $2–4 billion a year and boasts a worldwide network that rivals that of many Fortune 500 companies. Drugs now outrank coffee as Colombia's main income source. With so much money at stake, many crime networks compete for dominance, leading to great violence and the corruption or even murder of government officials.

On the east side of the Andes lies a vast wilderness, one of the largest undeveloped areas in the world. These broad grassy plains, called the **Llanos** (YAH nohs), cover 60 percent of Colombia and 30 percent of Venezuela. Most of this area is controlled by guerrillas who have driven out at least 500,000 settlers since 1990. The *llaneros* (ya NEH rohs), tough cowboys who ride the plains, are national heroes. The northernmost rivers of the Llanos flow into the Caribbean Sea, but the southern rivers flow into the Amazon River.

VENEZUELA

In 1802, Venezuela became the first Spanish colony to declare independence. Like the merchants in Boston who reacted against Britain's Stamp Act, merchants in Venezuela resisted Spanish laws restricting trade. **Caracas** (kah RAH kahs), the nation's capital, still honors the man who eventually became their liberator, Simón Bolívar, whose tomb is there.

COASTAL MOUNTAINS

In Venezuela, the Andes taper into the Caribbean Sea. The people prefer to live in the mild highlands on the coastal side of the Andes. Although it is short compared to other mountains of the Andes, Bolívar Peak exceeds sixteen thousand feet.

Near the northwest coast of Venezuela is **Lake Maracaibo** (MAH rah KYE boh), the largest lake on the continent of South America. This shallow lake connects to the Caribbean Sea by a narrow inlet, but its water is fresh. The discovery of oil fields under

---

World's Leading Coffee-Producing Countries

1. Brazil
2. Vietnam
3. Indonesia
4. Colombia
5. Mexico
6. India
7. Guatemala
8. Ethiopia
9. Uganda
10. Honduras

An earthquake destroyed Caracas in 1812, but it was quickly rebuilt and later became the center of the oil industry in Venezuela.

the lake made Venezuela the richest country on the continent. Venezuela sells most of its oil to the United States.

THE INTERIOR WILDERNESS

On the far side of the Andes, Venezuela shares the Llanos with Colombia. Waters flowing off the Andes drain into the Llanos's **Orinoco** (OH ree NO koh) **River**, the third-longest river on the continent. In one strange place near the source of the Orinoco, it splits and flows into the Amazon River system. These two great river systems are the only places in the world where flesh-eating fish called **piranha** live.

The mountains that separate the Orinoco from the Amazon are called the Guiana (gee AH nah) Highlands. This wilderness region

WHO GROWS THE BEST COFFEE BEAN?

Coffee has become the world's most popular hot beverage, and the United States leads the world in coffee consumption. The ten-minute coffee break is a common ritual. But not all coffees are the same. Even the closest of friends argue over which coffee bean is best.

According to legend, a goat herder in Ethiopia discovered coffee in the fourteenth century when his goats stayed awake all night after munching on the beans. Arab traders were the first to popularize brewed coffee. From the Arabian Peninsula, coffee plants have been transported around the world. The leading coffee-producing countries are located in or very near the tropics.

Two species of coffee plants are grown on plantations. The Arabs

Of the two major types of coffee beans, arabica beans are preferred for their flavor. Robusta beans contain almost twice as much caffeine and are often used in cheap instant coffees.

cultivated *Coffea arabica*, exporting beans from the famous coffee port of Mocha. Arabica is now grown throughout Latin America and much of Asia. The other species is *Coffea robusta*. This hardy plant thrives in the hot, rainy tropics of Africa. A robusta coffee plant produces about four pounds of beans, twice that of an arabica coffee plant.

So why doesn't everyone grow *C. robusta*, if it is so hardy and productive? The key to good coffee is *aroma*, or smell. Africa's robusta plant has a cereal-like aroma. Most coffee-drinkers prefer arabica coffee. It has two popular varieties: the Milds give off a fruity aroma mixed with the smell of flowers; the Brazils have an earthy aroma with more neutral flavors.

Although Brazil leads the world in coffee production, its beans are considered inferior to those of Colombia, Brazil's main South American competitor. The Andean soil of Colombia is much better for flavor than the soil of Brazil. Perhaps surprisingly, Vietnam is the second-leading coffee producer, and Indonesia is third. Excellent coffees are grown on the Indonesian island of Java, and sometimes coffee is even called java.

The major reason for coffee's popularity is not its aroma and flavor but the stimulant caffeine, which explains why so many people drink coffee to "get going" in the morning. Caffeine, however, is highly addictive. Withdrawal symptoms include headaches and nervousness. Mormons and conservative Muslims believe that it is sinful to drink coffee.

Angel Falls

At 3,212 feet, Angel Falls is easily the highest waterfall in the world. The upper part plummets more than half a mile straight down, and then it cascades down rocks for the remaining 564 feet.

The water issues through cracks in the side of the cliff, just below the top of a mesa. The springs merge as they fall, crashing on the rocks below and sending up blankets of mist and spray. The waters eventually reach the Atlantic Ocean via the Orinoco River.

Angel Falls is not named after its appearance, but after Jimmy Angel, an American pilot who spotted the falls in 1935 while flying over the remote Guiana Highlands. The region is still wild, but small planes offer air tours to view the falls.

contains Angel Falls and Cuquenán Falls, two of the ten highest falls in the world.

SECTION QUIZ

1. On which coast are most of Colombia's ports?
2. What are the key products of each Caribbean country?
3. What lowland wilderness do the Caribbean countries share?
4. What is the highest waterfall in the world?
- How does Colombia's geography help to explain its problems with the drug trade?

II. THE GUIANA HIGHLANDS

The **Guiana Highlands** are the rugged plateau that separates Venezuela's Caribbean coast from the Amazon Basin. Whereas Spain and Portugal controlled most of South America, three other European powers founded small colonies on the coast below the Guiana Highlands. These colonies became known as the Guianas.

The tropical climate supports rice, sugar cane, and banana plantations along the coast. In the interior, several coffee plantations operate in the highlands, and herds of cattle graze on grasslands. The European colonists imported black slaves to work on the plantations. After slavery was abolished in the nineteenth century, many blacks moved inland. The Europeans then hired laborers from India and Indonesia who brought their languages and Hindu religion.

GUYANA

The westernmost colony of the Guianas was British. It became the country of Guyana (guy AH nuh) in 1966, although the border with Venezuela was not yet settled. English is the national language of the republic, but Indian tribes in the remote rain forests still speak their own tongues. Most of the people of the country live in the flat lowlands near the coast.

Huge, block-shaped mountains, called *tepuis* (TEH pwees), rise above the highlands in the interior of Guyana. On the top are savannas. The highest *tepui*, Mount Roraima (9,219 ft.), towers above the junction between Venezuela, Guyana, and Brazil. Waters from this mountain flow south into the Amazon and north into the Orinoco.

Tepuis, such as this one, rise from the Guiana Highlands and tower over the surrounding landscape.

As in Venezuela, world-class waterfalls descend the slopes of the highlands of Guyana. They include 1,600-foot-high King George VI Falls and 350-foot-wide Kaieteur.

SURINAME

East of Guyana is a country formerly named Dutch Guiana but today called Suriname (*soo* rih NAH muh). It changed its name after receiving its independence in 1975. The Dutch brought the first coffee to South America, but the modern economy depends on bauxite (aluminum ore). Suriname has the fewest people per square mile of any nation on the continent. Its population density is similar to Canada's.

FRENCH GUIANA

French Guiana is the only part of the continent that is still under European control. It sends a representative to the French legislature in Paris. The entire territory has fewer people than Chattanooga, Tennessee. Although Cayenne (KYE en) is the major town, the most famous place in the territory is Devil's Island, an abandoned prison colony much like Alcatraz in San Francisco Bay.

SECTION QUIZ

1. What word is used for the huge, block-shaped mountains that tower above the highlands of Guyana?

2. Besides Spain and Portugal, what European nations had colonies in South America?

3. What nation has the lowest population density in South America?

4. What is the only foreign-controlled region in South America?

⚬ Why is the wildlife so unusual on the *tepuis*?

III. THE ANDEAN COUNTRIES

The Andes Mountains dwarf the mountains of North America. They form the highest mountain range in the Western Hemisphere, making them the highlight of the entire cordillera from Alaska to Chile. More than fifty peaks exceed twenty thousand feet, and at least forty of them are higher than Mount McKinley. These peaks are the highest mountains outside of Asia.

The Andes also form the longest mountain range in the world, stretching about forty-five hundred miles. These mountains divide the continent of South America. Water flowing west runs immediately into the Pacific. Water flowing east runs for many miles before it reaches the Atlantic. The Andes lie so close to the Pacific coast that in some areas the mountains slope directly down to the shore, leaving steep cliffs and jagged rocks at the water's edge. In other areas, a narrow plain lines the shore.

Because the Andean nations lie mostly in the warm and humid tropics, most of the people live high in the *tierra templada*. Isolated Indians there have been able to retain much of their culture. In sharp contrast to the Caribbean nations, four out of five people in Andean nations have some Indian heritage, either mestizo or full-blooded

River taxis are one means of getting around in Paramaribo, the capital of Suriname.

Until 1946, Devil's Island was the virtually inescapable maximum security prison that housed some of France's most notorious political and violent criminals.

Indian. Unfortunately, the Pacific Ring of Fire threatens the mountain villages.

ECUADOR

Ecuador means "equator," an apt name for the country because the equator cuts across it. Hot coastal lowlands cover about one-quarter of Ecuador, a much greater percentage than other Andean nations. As a result, Ecuador is a major exporter of bananas and cacao (a plant that is used to make chocolate, cocoa, and cocoa butter). The nation's largest city and leading commercial center is Guayaquil (GWY uh KEEL), a port city. It is the center of one of the world's largest shrimp-producing industries.

The Andes cover another one-quarter of Ecuador. Chimborazo (CHIM boh RAH zoh), Ecuador's tallest peak, is higher than Mount McKinley. More famous is **Cotopaxi** (KOH toh PAHK see), the highest active volcano in the world at 19,347 feet.

Most Ecuadorians live in the Andes. **Quito** (KEE toh), the capital and second-largest city in the nation, lies on a high and cool mountain plateau. At a monument outside Quito, one can stand with one foot in the Northern Hemisphere and the other foot in the Southern Hemisphere.

Volcanic Mount Cotopaxi towers over the surrounding landscape of Ecuador.

To the east of the Andes lies the **Amazon rain forest**, where few people lived until the discovery of oil in 1967. A pipeline across the Andes has turned Ecuador into the second-leading oil producer in South America, and oil now is Ecuador's top export. Oil spills and the resulting pollution are a continuing problem, however, as the Ecuadorians learn to be good stewards of their most valuable resource—the land.

Another hindrance to Ecuador's economic development is regional social unrest among native peoples in the Andean west. Since the late 1990s, numerous uprisings have erupted as Amerindians became frustrated by their perceived exclusion from the governing process and broken promises by government officials. As long as such instability exists and peace is threatened, the economy will remain stunted.

PERU

South of Ecuador is Peru, the largest Andean nation. The Andes ranges, which narrow to 100 miles near Quito, spread to 250 miles in Peru. Eleven peaks exceed twenty thousand feet. The highest railroad in the world crosses these mountains.

The mountains are broken by the deepest canyons in the world. Colca Canyon, which slices through the west side of the Andes into the Pacific, is twice the depth of the Grand Canyon. The second-deepest canyon, the Apurimac, cuts through the eastern side of the Andes. Its streams form the headwaters of the mighty Amazon River.

The mountainous terrain of Quito, the capital of Ecuador, differs sharply from the coastal lowlands, which tend to produce most of the country's wealth.

Peru has the highest major mines in the world. It is the largest gold producer in the world. Its zinc output is third in the world, and it is a major producer of copper.

CHILDREN OF THE SUN

A series of Indian civilizations arose along the plateaus and valleys of the Andes. The last and greatest were the **Incas**, whose name means "children of the sun." At its height, the Inca Empire controlled most of the Andes. The Incas, far from being the primitive people one might envision, were quite ingenious. They built an amazing two-thousand-mile network of stone roads, some of which are still used today; dug tunnels through mountains; built causeways over swamps; and bridged chasms with grass suspension bridges. The Inca Empire was particularly impressive because, unlike the Egyptian and Mesopotamian empires, the Incas had no waterways to provide easy transportation.

Although they had no written language, the Incas invented the *quipu* (KEE poo), a code using strings of llama wool knotted together on a rope. The meaning of each message depended on the size and number of knots and the color of the wool. Runners relayed these knot messages to and from the capital. The emperor could send a message two hundred miles in a single day.

Cusco (KOOS koh) was the sacred Inca capital. The streets were laid out in the shape of a puma, with the fortress Sacsahuaman forming the puma's head. When the Spanish *conquistador* **Francisco Pizarro** (frahn-SEES-coh pee-SAHR-oh) arrived in 1531, the empire was torn by feuds, allowing Pizarro to easily capture the Great Inca and hold

The Andes Mountains of Peru include the deepest canyons and the largest concentration of snow peaks in the world.

THE GALÁPAGOS ISLANDS

South America's most famous islands are the Galápagos (gah LAH pah GOHS) Islands, five hundred miles west of Ecuador. The Spanish named them for the huge five-hundred-pound tortoises that roamed the islands. These giants provided crews with a ready source of fresh meat and could survive in the ship's hold for a year or more without food or water.

Spanish sailors first discovered these remote islands when their ves-

sel drifted off course. The sixteen islands are dotted with volcanoes, a handful of which are still active. During the seventeenth and eighteenth centuries, English pirates buried stolen treasures on the islands. In the nineteenth century, whaling ships and seal hunters visited to pick up fresh water and supplies. Their mailbox on Santa Maria Island, where outbound whalers left letters for inbound vessels, is still in use. In 1832, the islands became a part of Ecuador.

Isolation allowed many unusual animals to flourish on the islands. Although the islands straddle the equator, the cold Peru Current keeps the weather mild and dry. Antarctic animals, such as penguins and fur seals, live alongside tropical animals, such as four-foot iguanas, flamin-

goes, and a mockingbird unknown elsewhere. Twenty-eight species of birds and nineteen species of reptiles are endemic (found nowhere else in the world). Charles Darwin used his study of Galápagos finches in 1835 to support his mistaken theory of evolution.

Most of the Galápagos Islands are too rocky and dry to support human life. However, about six thousand people live on the islands of Santa Cruz, Santa Maria, Isabela, and San Cristobal. The people living close to the coast earn a living by fishing. Although less than 4 percent of the island's land area is suited for agriculture, parts of the moist highlands produce vegetables, tropical fruits, and field crops. Coffee and cattle are among the few products exported to the mainland.

him for ransom. He promised to let him go if the people filled a royal chamber once with gold and twice with silver. When the deed was done, however, the Spanish did not keep their end of the bargain. They killed the Inca emperor but left the city intact. After plundering the gold and silver, the Spaniards forced the Incas to work in the haciendas and mines. More than a quarter million Indians still live in Cusco, making it the oldest continually inhabited city in the New World.

Old racial distinctions remain strong in Peru, partly because social values left over from the Incan Empire help maintain the divide between Indian and Hispanic populations. The upper class consists of whites, who own the coastal plantations and hold most positions of leadership. More than 40 percent of Peruvians are mestizos, who make up the middle class. They own most farms in the Andes. Mestizos usually speak an Indian language but learn Spanish to improve their social status.

The lower classes consist of Indians descended from the Incas. Most of them speak the Inca language, **Quechua** (KEH chwa), the most widely spoken native language in South America. Several English words, such as *puma* and *llama*, come from Quechua. Many Indians believe they should keep their place in society. They look down on the *cholos* (CHOH lohs)—Indians who learn Spanish and dress like mestizos.

DESERT COASTS

The high mountain barrier of the Andes has a disastrous effect on the coastal climate of South America. Easterly winds from the Atlantic Ocean drop their moisture as they cross the Andes, leaving almost no water for the rain shadow on the western side of the Andes. The problem is compounded by the **Peru Current** (also called the Humboldt Current), which flows north from the Antarctic. The cold current keeps the air cold and dry. The Sechura (seh CHOO rah) Desert lies on the north coast of Peru. Irrigation is possible farther south, where swift rivers descend from the Andes.

Pizarro established his headquarters, **Lima** (LEE mah), on one of these swift rivers, and it became the capital of Peru and the largest city of the Andean countries. The average rainfall there is only two inches per year, but a moist cloud, called *garúa*, settles on the desert city during the winter. One-quarter of Peru's people live there. It is a city of contrasts; along with beautiful Spanish architecture, it has the largest *barriadas* (BAHR ree AH dahs), or slums, on the continent.

Ruins from several ancient Indian empires dot the coastal desert. North near the modern city of Trujillo (troo HEE yoh) lies Chan Chan. Covering six square miles, it is all that remains of the powerful Chimu Empire of the twelfth century. Nearby, archeologists have found ruins of the earlier Moche Empire (AD 100–700), including burial chambers stocked with gold, silver, ceramics, and paintings.

Even more intriguing are the Nazca Lines located south of Lima. These mysterious designs, drawn by an unknown civilization in the first six centuries after Christ's birth, include condors and other animals the size of a football field. No one knew what the lines represented until pilots viewed them from the air in the twentieth century. Among the unsolved mysteries are the designs of monkeys and insects that lived, not on the Pacific, but hundreds of miles east in the Amazon forest.

Through Christian Eyes

Quechua, along with many other indigenous languages in South America, was once only spoken; it had no standard written alphabet or grammar. Throughout the last century, Christian missionaries labored to establish spelling and grammar standards. Their work demonstrated the power of the use of linguistics to spread the gospel. As Christians help create the means by which a people group is able to communicate in writing, they are able to shape that culture with the Scripture. In what specific ways do you think Christians can use linguistics to change a culture for Christ?

no deep lakes

MACHU PICCHU, LAST REFUGE OF THE INCAS

For centuries, the Inca stronghold of Machu Picchu (MAH-choo PEEK-choo) remained hidden from European eyes. Legends spoke of a mountain "city in the clouds," but adventurers were baffled by the rugged terrain and tangled vegetation. Finally, Hiram Bingham of Yale University set out to find Vilcabamba, the last refuge of the Incas who fled from Pizarro. The breathtaking ruins he found in 1911, just sixty miles northwest of Cusco, continue to amaze visitors.

Machu Picchu rises precariously between two craggy peaks. Somehow Inca craftsmen carried supplies up to the five-acre plateau, 7,875 feet in the clouds. Pure white granite temples, palaces, and dwellings served about fifteen hundred people. Without mortar or iron tools, the engineers cut stones that fit together perfectly. Earthquakes of recent centuries have not been able to topple them. The Incas hauled dirt from the valley to provide soil for vegetable gardens on the slopes.

No one knows what happened to the Incas who lived there. Perhaps they abandoned the stronghold when their last emperor died. Tradition says that seventy young ladies who served in the Sun Temple at Cusco escaped to Machu Picchu and died there. An exploration after 1911 found that the last Inca refuge, Vilcabamba, was a minor outpost deep in the Amazon rain forest, not at Machu Picchu.

LA MONTAÑA

The lowlands east of the Andes are known as *La Montaña* (mohn TAHN yuh). Water from the mountains drains into this part of the vast Amazon Basin. The city of Iquitos (ee KEE tohs) is Peru's largest port on the Amazon River. Oceangoing ships travel back and forth from the Atlantic, more than two thousand miles away.

Few people live in La Montaña. Some isolated Indian tribes continue to resist Lima's authority. Since 1978, a Communist guerilla force, called the **Shining Path**, has been fighting the government from its bases in the jungles and mountains. The Shining Path is the most deadly rebel group in Latin American history. It has killed more than twenty thousand Peruvians and destroyed $20 billion in property, including schools and hospitals.

The Shining Path uses money from the sale of coca plants to buy weapons. Coca plants are grown all along the eastern slopes of the Andes. Growing coca plants is legal, but manufacturing cocaine is not. But Indians can make forty times more money selling coca leaves rather than grain, so the temptation to ignore the law is great. President Alberto Fujimori did much in the 1990s to curb the influence of the Shining Path, improve political stability, and spur economic growth. The major leaders have been captured; and although the group is still active, their influence is mainly limited to rural areas. As a result, the country is more stable now.

SECTION QUIZ

1. What Andean nation lies on the equator?

2. What Indians built the biggest civilization in South America?

3. What is the oldest continuously inhabited city in the New World?

4. Why is Peru's coast a desert?

🔎 Why do you think Pizarro built a new capital on the coastal desert?

🔎 How can Christian linguists influence and assist cultures with no formal written language?

CAMELS OF THE WESTERN HEMISPHERE

The Indians of the New World never had the advantage of large beasts of burden—such as horses, cattle, and camels—that were essential to the Old World. The Indians of North America had only dogs, but the peoples of the Andes domesticated four small members of the camel family called lamoids.

The four "camels of the Andes" are the alpaca (al PAK uh), vicuña (vi KOO nyah), guanaco (gwuh NAH koh), and llama. Generally speaking, lamoids have small heads, long legs and necks, and large pointed ears. Unlike camels, they have no hump. The lamoids supplied the ancient Incas with wool, meat, and leather. The most useful lamoid was the large llama, which stands four feet tall at the shoulder and weighs up to three hundred pounds.

The llama is well suited for mountain life. Its lungs are used to the thin air, and its coarse, woolly hair provides plenty of warmth. It can survive on the sparse grasses and shrubs on the rocky mountain slopes. The llama can go for weeks without a drink, drawing both fluid and nourishment from the food alone.

A sure-footed pack animal, the llama easily climbs the steep trails of the high mountains. It is able to travel twenty miles per day while carrying a load of up to 130

Vicuña in Northern Chile

pounds. However, a llama knows its limits. When overburdened or exhausted, a llama will sit down and refuse to move. If forced to get up, it will hiss and spit foul saliva (like its camel cousins do).

Llamas occupied a special place in the Inca religion. An excavation of an ancient Inca city of Peru uncovered a large sacrifice table in the shape of a llama. Today the descendants of the Incas still find many uses for the llama: the hide for sandals, the hair for rope, the fat for candles, and even the droppings for fuel.

North American llama

Guanaco in Chilean Patagonia

Alpacas in Northern Chile

BOLIVIA

After Bolívar freed the region known as Upper Peru, it changed its name to Bolivia in his honor. Bolivia was once a large nation, but wars with neighbors deprived it of almost half of its territory, including access to the sea. Bounded by mountains in the west and jungles in the east, modern Bolivia is a **landlocked** nation and is called the "Tibet of South America" for that reason. This isolation has hindered the development of its trade and industry. Chile, however, has offered to help Bolivia by giving it access to the sea.

About 60 percent of Bolivians are full-blooded Indians who live in villages and work on subsistence farms and villages. Another 30 percent of Bolivians are mestizos, and the rest are of European descent. Bolivian mestizos and Bolivians of European descent speak Spanish whereas most Bolivian Indians speak either Quechua or Aymara, but all three are national languages.

Although city life in Bolivia is very modern, rural Indians suffer from primitive conditions. An estimated 70 percent of the Bolivian population lives in poverty. Dysentery, measles, tuberculosis, and whooping cough are common because the Indians cannot travel easily to doctors in the city. Consequently, Bolivians have the highest infant mortality rate and the lowest literacy rate in South America.

The nation's only important natural resources are in the mountains. Bolivia ranks fourth among the world's tin producers, but primitive mining methods hinder the mines' profitability. Farmers raise chinchillas for fur and guinea pigs for meat.

As if the problems of poverty, disease, illiteracy, and inaccessibility were not enough, Bolivia's government is unstable. In June 2005, union leaders and leftists led street demonstrations that forced President Carlos Mesa to resign after less than two years in office. He was replaced by a Supreme Court justice, but this new leader realizes that he is not really in control and that trouble could remove him from office quickly too. With such uncertainty, it is almost impossible for the nation to address its most pressing needs.

Lake Titicaca moderates the weather of the surrounding area in what otherwise would be a cold, inhospitable climate.

THE ALTIPLANO

Most of the people of Bolivia live on the **Altiplano** (ahl tee PLAH noh, "high plain"), the largest of several plains that lie between the Andes ranges. The cold and windy Altiplano, which Bolivia shares with Peru, is more than two miles above sea level and covers an area almost as large as West Virginia—twenty thousand square miles.

At the heart of the Altiplano, on the border between Peru and Bolivia, is **Lake Titicaca** (tee tee KAH kah), the second-largest lake in South America. The lake helps to moderate the cold temperatures of the Altiplano, permitting agriculture. The shores of Lake Titicaca became the center of the Tiahuanaco (TEE ah wah NAH coh) Empire, which preceded the Incas. The Incas believed that the first man and woman were created on an island in the lake.

Titicaca is the highest navigable lake in the world. Many Indian settlements dot the shore. Some Uru (OO roo) Indians actually live on the water itself, building islands from the totora reeds that grow along the water's edge. Indians also use the versatile totora for fuel, animal food, baskets, mats, houses, and boats.

A few miles southeast of Lake Titicaca is the largest city in Bolivia and, at 12,000 feet, the world's highest capital, **La Paz**, which has more than one million people. Because most government offices are located in La Paz, it is considered Bolivia's administrative capital. The legal capital, however, is Sucre (SOO kray), which is farther south in one of the many valleys of the Andes.

GEOGRAPHER'S CORNER

CROSS-SECTIONS

Topographic maps are only one way to give map-readers a three-dimensional view. Another way is cross-section diagrams, which provide a side-angle view. By exaggerating heights, they give a good overall impression of altitude and distance.

This diagram shows a 250-mile-wide area of the Andes that includes the Altiplano. Notice that the scale is different for altitude than it is for distance. Four miles in altitude equals about fifty miles of horizontal distance. Without this distortion, altitude would become almost a straight line.

Use the diagram to answer the following questions:

1. How tall is Mount Illampu?

2. Approximately how wide is the Altiplano?

3. What mountain rises above the city of Arequipa?

4. Which city has the lowest elevation?

5. Approximately how many feet above sea level is Puno?

☼ Where would you expect to find the most rainfall?

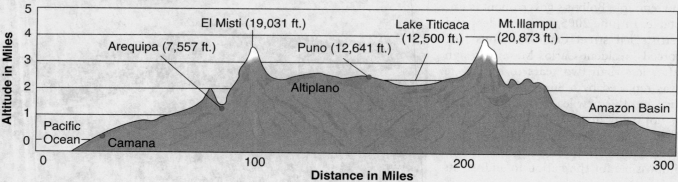

Side View of South America

Altitude in Miles / Distance in Miles

El Misti (19,031 ft.)
Arequipa (7,557 ft.)
Puno (12,641 ft.)
Lake Titicaca (12,500 ft.)
Mt. Illampu (20,873 ft.)
Altiplano
Amazon Basin
Pacific Ocean
Camana

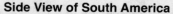

THE YUNGAS

As the Andes drop in the east, ridges and valleys abound. Bolivians call this rugged region the **Yungas** (YOON gahs). Farmers have transformed the fertile valleys to meet much of Bolivia's food needs. Santa Cruz and Cochabamba (koh chah BAHM bah) are, after La Paz, the largest cities in Bolivia.

THE EASTERN LOWLANDS

At the base of the Yungas is the **Amazon Basin**. These lowlands constitute more than half of Bolivia's land area, but few people live in the swamps and jungles.

CHILE

The Andes Mountains form a wall three thousand miles long, dividing Chile from Argentina. Yet Chile is only one hundred miles wide. This peculiar "shoestring" of land divides into three regions: the northern desert, the Central Valley, and the southern archipelago (AR kuh PEHL uh goh; a large group of islands).

THE ATACAMA DESERT

The northern twelve hundred miles of Chile is covered by the **Atacama** (ah tuh KAH mah) **Desert**, a continuation of Peru's southern desert. The climate is so dry that some places have never recorded any rainfall. The red sands, barren rock, and salt flats are mute testimony to the Atacama's reputation as the driest desert on earth.

Limited farming is possible with irrigation in the southern portions of the Atacama, where some rains fall. In spite of the harsh conditions, a few cities manage to survive. The Peru Current might hurt the climate, but it supports one of the world's three best sardine fishing grounds. The largest city in the desert is the fishing port of Antofagasta (AHN toh fah GAH stah).

People brave the scarred desert to exploit its mineral wealth. Chile has the world's only natural deposits of sodium nitrate, which is used to make explosives and fertilizer. Other countries, however, make synthetic sodium nitrate and compete with Chile for that market. Chile is second behind the United States in the production of molybdenum. Chile's primary resource, however, is copper; it is the world leader in copper production. Near the southern tip of Bolivia, Chuquicamata (CHOO kee cah MAH tah) has the world's largest open pit copper mine. Chile is also the world's sixth-largest producer of silver.

THE CENTRAL VALLEY

The **Aconcagua** (AH cohn CAH gwah) **River** marks the southern edge of the Atacama Desert. Three-fourths of all Chileans live south of that river in the Central Valley. It extends six hundred miles from Valparaíso (VAHL pah rah EE soh) to Puerto Montt (PWEHR-toh MAWNT) in the south.

The Central Valley is similar to California's lush Central Valley. Both have a mediterranean climate: westerlies bring winter rains from the Pacific Ocean. Mineral deposits in both valleys have attracted miners: southeast of Santiago (SAHN tee AH goh) is the world's largest underground copper mine, El Teniente (teh NYEHN teh, "the lieutenant or colonel"). East of the valleys are high mountains with ski resorts and spectacular scenery.

Chile's cold mountain valleys are unsuitable for large populations. Unlike other Andean nations, which have large Indian populations, most of Chile's people are Europeans or mestizos who live on the coastal lowlands. One-third of the nation lives in the capital, **Santiago**, a modern city whose metropolitan area has more than six million people.

Chile has been one of the most successful nations in South America, both economically and militarily. Chile's victory against Peru and Bolivia in the War of the Pacific (1879–83) won it possession of the mineral-rich Atacama Desert. The wealth derived from nitrates and copper has created a small but growing middle class in the Central Valley.

The poorer classes voted for **Salvador Allende** (ah YEHN day), a Marxist, for president in 1970, and he won. But his efforts to redistribute land ruined the economy and sparked a coup in 1973. General **Augusto Pinochet** (ow-GOOS-toh peen-oh-SHAY) took power and ruled with an iron fist for nearly two decades. Although Pinochet relied on secret police to keep political power, he also introduced the first free-market reforms in South America. His policies turned Chile into an economic dynamo. In 1989, Pinochet allowed the people to vote on whether to continue his military dictatorship. They chose democracy instead.

THE ARCHIPELAGO

A rugged archipelago stretches one thousand miles to the southern tip of South America. The archipelago includes some three hundred islands. Most of Chile's full-blooded Indians live there. The fierce Araucanian (ahr uh CAYN ee uhn) Indians resisted Spanish and Chilean armies for centuries, until they were defeated in 1883. Now the Indians farm or raise sheep or cattle on reservations.

Chile's archipelago is similar to Alaska's Inside Passage. Both have a mild and wet marine-west-coast climate. Forests cover the mountains and islands, but the trees are deciduous, not coniferous. Glaciers have carved deep gorges, and the ocean has flooded them to form fjords. National parks protect spectacular spots, such as pink granite pinnacles called the Torres (Towers) del Paine. A park that protects one hundred miles of fjord country was named for Bernardo O'Higgins, Chile's first president, who freed the slaves.

Below the southern tip of the continental land mass is the perilous **Strait of Magellan**, which was named for Ferdinand Magellan, whose fleet sailed through the strait and ultimately became the first to *circumnavigate* (journey around) the world. Until the construction of the Panama Canal, the strait was the main shipping route between the Atlantic and Pacific Oceans. Punta Arenas (POON-tah ah-RAY-nahs), a city of 120,000 on the strait, is the southernmost city in the world.

South of the Strait of Magellan is the large island of **Tierra del Fuego** (FWAY goh, "Land of the Fire"). Early explorers called it that because they saw many Indian campfires flickering near the shore. Oil rigs now dot the landscape, giving Chile precious petroleum.

A string of islands continues south from Tierra del Fuego toward Antarctica. The southernmost islet is Cape Horn. Nearby is Puerto Williams, the southernmost settlement (not city) in the world. The six-hundred-mile-wide **Drake Passage** separates Cape Horn from the frozen continent of Antarctica. It was named after Sir Francis Drake, the first Englishman to "round the Horn" and circumnavigate the earth.

The western half of Tierra del Fuego belongs to Chile and the eastern half to Argentina.

SECTION QUIZ

1. How has being landlocked hurt Bolivia?
2. What nation has two capitals?
3. Describe two unusual features of Lake Titicaca.
4. Name the three regions of Chile.

5. What dictator helped to bring prosperity to Chile?

🔎 Why do you think Chile has offered to help Bolivia by giving it access to the sea?

IV. THE RÍO DE LA PLATA

As you learned from reading about Chile, the southern half of South America is quite different from the tropical north. The climate is colder in the mountains and more temperate in the lowlands. Also, few pure-blooded Indians in that region survived the Spanish conquest.

The center of Spanish settlement in the east was the **Río de la Plata**, the widest **estuary, or ocean inlet,** on the Atlantic coast. The mighty Paraná (pah rah NAH) and Uruguay (oo roo GWYE) rivers flow into the Río de la Plata. These navigable rivers are the lifeblood of three nations—Argentina, Paraguay (PAH rah GWYE), and Uruguay.

The great liberator of these lands was **José de San Martín** (sahn mahr-TEEN). After winning Argentina's independence from Spain in 1813, he led his army over the Andes into Chile and surprised the Spanish garrison there. After that success, San Martín sailed to Lima and helped Bolívar free Bolivia.

ARGENTINA

With an area of more than one million square miles, Argentina is the eighth-largest country in the world. Although less populous than Mexico, Argentina has the largest number of Spanish speakers in South America. Almost all Argentines (85 percent) are of European descent; half of those are descended from Italian colonists and a third from Spanish colonists. Mestizos make up the remaining 15 percent of the population.

Argentina has the potential to become a leader in world affairs, but political strife has devastated the country from its very beginning. For fifty years after independence, merchants fought ranchers for control of the government.

Argentina enjoyed a brief "Golden Age" between 1880 and 1914, when European immigrants poured into the country. After the Great Depression, however, Argentina was plagued by a series of juntas (HOON tahs). The most famous *caudillo* (cow DEE yoh; "strongman") was **Juan Perón**, who held power 1946–55. Perón and his wife, Evita, promised to help the poor workers, but they led the country into debt and economic ruin. Nevertheless, the Peronista Party remains a strong force in the country.

THE PAMPAS

Argentina's low plains around the Río de la Plata are called the **Pampas** (PAHM pahs). Most of the nation's people, industry, and agriculture are there. The plains extend south and west across central Argentina.

The Pampas are similar to the Great Plains in the American West. A semiarid climate supports vast grasslands. The soil, among the most fertile in the world, is ideal for alfalfa, wheat, and corn. In fact, Argentina exports more corn than the United States. Cattle and sheep, which graze on huge ranches called *estancias* (eh STAHN see yahs),

Pampas grass, which grows abundantly on the Argentine Pampas, is used as an ornamental lawn decoration in the southeastern United States.

Buenos Aires, which means "fair winds," is a key to South America's international trade.

provide meat, hides, and wool for industries in the city.

Half of the people of the Pampas live in **Buenos Aires** (BWEH-nohs EYE-rehs), the nation's capital. It is the second-largest city by area on the continent and the largest by population. Buenos Aires is ideally located near the mouth of the Paraná River on the Río de la Plata. The humid subtropical climate provides much more rain than the semiarid areas in the western and southern Pampas. Winter temperatures rarely drop below freezing, even in July, the coldest month in the Southern Hemisphere.

Buenos Aires is the main industrial center of Argentina. Industries process primary products from the Pampas, including meat and leather. The nation has two other industrial cities. Rosario (roh SAHR ee oh), also on the Río de la Plata, is known for oil refineries. Córdoba (COHR doh bah), where the Pampas meet the Andes, manufactures automobiles and railroad cars.

THE ANDES BORDER

West of the Pampas lie the Andes. Steady rainfall on the eastern valleys and slopes supports several cities, including Mendoza, Salta, and San Miguel de Tucumán. But most of the Andes are remote and sparsely populated.

The Andes mountain system reaches its highest peaks in Argentina, where nine of the Western Hemisphere's ten highest peaks exist. The father of them all is Aconcagua, at 22,834 feet. Only a half dozen roads cross this rugged chain along the two-thousand-mile border with Chile.

San Martín mustered his army at Mendoza before leading them over the Andes into Chile. His history-making route to Santiago went through a pass called Uspallata Pass, or La Cumbre, south of Aconcagua. At the top of the pass stands the massive statue *Christ of the Andes*. Chile and Argentina fought over their border for many years before they finally reached a settlement in 1902. They built the statue in honor of their pledge before Christ to maintain peace. The purpose of the monument is similar to that of the Peace Garden on the border between the United States and Canada.

PATAGONIA

South of the Pampas is a high plateau called **Patagonia** (pah tah GOHN yah). It rises in step-like cliffs toward the Andes Mountains. Scenic hills and canyons resemble America's Great Basin, complete with a petrified forest. Temperatures are similar to those of Canada's cold Maritime Provinces.

The European explorers named the region Patagonia ("big feet") after the Indians, who stuffed their oversized boots with grass for insulation from the cold. Today, the Indians are gone, and most of the scattered settlers live in small coastal villages. A few inland residents raise sheep on the sparse grasses and shrubs. Their ranches are built in the canyons to protect them from the constant winds.

Gauchos, Cowboys of the South

The cowboys of Argentina, or **gauchos** (GOW chohs), are national folk heroes. Hordes of them rode the Pampas in the nineteenth century, rounding up wild horses and cattle. Today, the few who remain work on ranches.

In the early days, the gauchos spent most of their time in the saddle. They were distinguished by not only their riding skills but also their clothes, which included a wide silver belt, baggy trousers, and a brightly colored scarf. They were rovers who loved the wide open spaces and the freedom of the plains.

The gauchos hold a position in Argentine history similar to that of the Western cowboy in U.S. history.

LET'S GO EXPLORING

LAND USE OF LATIN AMERICA

1. What types of land use occur in both Central and South America?

2. Where does mediterranean farming occur?

3. What nation has the largest area of crop farming?

4. What is the most common type of land use in the Amazon Basin?

☿ Which nation has the greatest variety of land use?

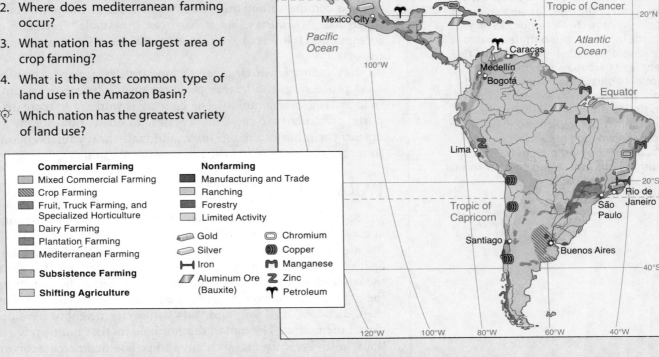

Commercial Farming
- ▦ Mixed Commercial Farming
- ▨ Crop Farming
- ▦ Fruit, Truck Farming, and Specialized Horticulture
- ▦ Dairy Farming
- ▦ Plantation Farming
- ▦ Mediterranean Farming

Subsistence Farming

Shifting Agriculture

Nonfarming
- ▦ Manufacturing and Trade
- ▦ Ranching
- ▦ Forestry
- ▦ Limited Activity

- Gold
- Silver
- Iron
- Aluminum Ore (Bauxite)
- Chromium
- Copper
- Manganese
- Zinc
- Petroleum

NORTHERN ARGENTINA

North of the Pampas, Argentina has two regions: Mesopotamia in the northeast and the Gran Chaco in the northwest.

Mesopotamia is named after the region of the Middle East that lies between two rivers. The western edge of Mesopotamia is the Paraná River; the eastern edge is the Uruguay River, at Argentina's border with Uruguay and Brazil. The climate is hot and humid.

West of the Paraná River is the **Gran Chaco**. Like the Pampas, it is flat and dry, but it is covered by shrubs and forest rather than grass. Part of the Gran Chaco, between Rosario and Tucumán (TOO cuh MAHN), is desert. The rhea, or South American ostrich, lives on the plains. The main human occupation is harvesting *quebracho* (kay BRAH choh; "ax-breaker"), a hardwood tree used for railroad ties and telephone poles. Tannin, a chemical derived from the quebracho, is used in tanning leather.

URUGUAY

The Río de la Plata is the focus of life in the tiny nation of Uruguay. **Montevideo** (MOHN teh vee DEH oh), the capital, is on this estuary. About one-half of the nation's people live in Montevideo's metropolitan area. Another one-quarter million people live in towns along the Uruguay River. Uruguay's population, like that of

The Reversal of Seasons in Different Hemispheres

An interesting geographic fact is that the Northern and Southern hemispheres have opposite seasons at any given time. When it is summer in North America, for example, the people who live south of the equator are experiencing winter. On December 25, when people in the northern United States are longing for a "white Christmas," the people of Paraguay and Uruguay are probably perspiring in summer heat! And when North Americans are raking their autumn leaves, the people of South America are planting their spring crops. Knowledge of this fact is very practical if you ever plan to travel to another hemisphere and need to know what clothes to pack.

Uruguay

Argentina, is composed of primarily European descendants (Spanish and Italian) rather than indigenous peoples. The country's location between the two giants of Brazil and Argentina has made life difficult.

INDUSTRY

Spanish is the national language of Uruguay, although Portuguese is common along the border with Brazil. The economy is very much like Argentina's, but it has been less stable. Terrorism and foreign and civil wars have plagued the tiny nation throughout its history.

Key industries of Uruguay include textiles, apparel, chemicals, meat processing, and leather production. A software-development industry is growing rapidly. The country is working to increase exports, particularly to the United States. To do so, however, its government will have to reduce its traditionally heavy intervention in the economy and increase the privatization of industry.

PARAGUAY

Spanish explorers first visited Paraguay while searching for an alternate route to the riches of Peru. **Asunción** (ah SOON see OHN), founded on the Paraguay River in 1537, became the first capital of Spain's colonies in southeastern South America. But Spain neglected the landlocked, unproductive region. Dissatisfied with Spanish rule, the people of Asunción declared their independence in 1811. Since then, dictators, civil war, and wars with every neighbor have decimated the nation. The nation did not hold its first multiparty elections until 1993. Again, such instability has hampered economic development.

About 95 percent of Paraguayans are mestizos. Most are bilingual. They speak Spanish for education, government, and commerce, but they use their native Indian tongue, **Guaraní** (gwah rah NEE), in daily life. Paraguay might be the most thoroughly bilingual nation in the world.

Like Bolivia, Paraguay is undeveloped and lacks mineral resources. Its one advantage over Bolivia is the **Paraná River**, the second-longest river system in South America. Steamboats can go up the Paraguay River, a tributary of the Paraná, to Asunción, the capital. Most of the nation's population lives along the river system.

Many Paraguayans are subsistence farmers, who make their living from the rich alluvial soils of the Paraná and Paraguay rivers. They grow barely enough crops to feed their families, cutting down forests on public lands and moving on when the soil is depleted. Most of them live in one-room ranchos, with dirt floors and no plumbing.

The Gran Chaco, west of the Paraguay River, is largely uninhabited, except for a few Guaraní Indians and Mennonites. Mennonite communities that were founded in the Chaco in 1926 now produce nearly one-half of the nation's dairy products.

SECTION QUIZ

1. What is an estuary?
2. Who liberated Argentina and Chile from Spain?

3. What is the second-largest city in South America? Why is it so big?

4. Match each area with the associated word.
   - (1) Pampas
   - (2) Paraguay
   - (3) Patagonia

   - a. Gran Chaco
   - b. plateau
   - c. gauchos

☼ Compare and contrast Bolivia and Paraguay.

V. BRAZIL

Brazil is the fifth-largest nation in the world, and the fifth-most populous. It covers half of the South American continent and contains several of the continent's key geographic areas. Its wealth of resources and vibrant culture hold the promise of a great future.

Brazil is unique among Latin American nations. It is the only nation in the Western Hemisphere that once belonged to Portugal and has Portuguese as its official language. It is also the largest Roman Catholic nation in the world. Protestant churches, however, have grown rapidly in recent years, particularly among Charismatic denominations.

ATLANTIC COAST

The Treaty of Tordesillas gave Portugal all lands east of the Line of Demarcation. Pedro Cabral's discovery of Brazil in 1500 affirmed Portugal's claim to the eastern tip of South America.

Because of the rough terrain and the hostile Indians of the interior, however, the first settlements were only along the coast. As was the case with the colonies of North America, the first European settlements in Brazil were often at harbors and tied to Atlantic trade with the Old World.

PORTUGUESE SETTLERS

Portuguese settlers built sugar plantations all along the east coast of Brazil. Within two years, **São Vicente** (SOUN vee-SEHN-teh), near the southern city of Santos, became the first colony and oldest city in Brazil. Two years later, **Recife** (reh SEE feh) was established on the northeastern tip nearest Europe.

If you look at the map of modern Brazil, you will see that Portugal settled quite a bit more of the coast than they were supposed to. In 1669, Portuguese settlers crossed the treaty line and founded Manaus (muh NOUSE) far up the Amazon River. Another group of settlers founded Pôrto Alegre on the southern coast in 1740. The westward movement required a new treaty with Spain. The Treaty of Madrid, signed in 1750, gave Portugal almost all the land of modern Brazil.

INDEPENDENCE

In 1822, **Dom Pedro,** the son of the Portuguese king, whom the king had placed in charge of Brazil, declared independence for Brazil and became its king. Brazil remained a monarchy for sixty-six years under Pedro and his son, Pedro II. Dom Pedro opened the door to thousands of European immigrants, and he freed the black slaves in 1888. However, angry slave owners, who received no money for compensation, overthrew Pedro II and declared Brazil a republic, modeling its constitution after that of the United States. The republic has been interrupted by periodic dictatorships and military rule.

Brazil shares borders with seven Spanish-speaking nations and has won a sliver of territory from each of them. It was also the first Latin American country to develop nuclear capability and the only one to send an army to Europe during World Wars I and II.

IGUAÇU FALLS

"Poor Niagara," cried the visiting wife of an American president when she first beheld Iguaçu (EE gwah SOO) Falls. Iguaçu Falls is about eighty feet higher than Niagara Falls and twice as wide, making it the widest waterfall in the world. Although Iguaçu is less powerful than Niagara on most days,

Iguaçu Falls dwarfs North America's Niagara Falls, especially during the rainy season.

the rainy season turns it into a raging torrent. Its flow has been recorded to be as high as 452,059 cubic feet per second, which more than doubles the flow at Niagara Falls.

Some 275 cataracts, separated by stony outcroppings, fall over a semicircular cliff that is 1.8 miles wide. The rushing falls plunge 237 feet into the canyons below, sending up clouds of mist in a lush jungle setting.

After the Iguaçu River flows over the Falls, it joins the Paraná twelve miles downstream. Near this point is Itaipu (ee TYE poo) Dam, the largest dam in the world. Built in 1982 to harness the mighty Paraná River, Itaipu's concrete wall is five miles long and seventy-five sto-

ries high. Brazil and Paraguay jointly constructed the amazing hydroelectric plant, which has the highest kilowatt output in the world.

The building and operation of Itaipu Dam is an example of how the people of many countries can benefit from the peaceful cooperation of countries.

MODERN COASTAL CITIES

As is typical of South America, the large cities of Brazil are very modern. Cars and buses fill the streets. Operas, plays, and orchestras entertain the people, and schools are good. Houses and apartments might be small and crowded, but they have basic appliances, such as refrigerators, toasters, and televisions.

Cities in the South—The biggest cities are in South Brazil, the nation's heartland. Most of the region enjoys a humid subtropical climate, similar to that of the southern United States. But **Rio de Janeiro** (zhah NEH roh), the nation's second-largest city and third-largest on the continent, has a pleasant tropical climate on the coastal plain. Orange groves in the area make Brazil the world's leading producer of oranges.

"Rio" is considered the most charming city of the New World. Dom Pedro made Rio de Janiero his capital, and it remains the cultural center of the nation. Its harbor is internationally acclaimed, surpassing the beauty of San Francisco Bay. Sugar Loaf, a granite dome-shaped mountain, is a famous landmark.

One recent development in this region could be seen either as a threat or as an opportunity. In the south of Brazil is a growing movement for the three southernmost states of the country to separate from Brazil and form an independent country to be called the Republic of the Pampas.

Life on the Northeast Coast—Most other major coastal cities of Brazil lie on the eastern "bulge," known as the Northeast. Eight state capitals, from São Luís to Salvador, are clustered on this crowded coast. Salvador, Fortaleza (FORT uhl AY zah), and Recife are the largest cities in the region, each with more than two million people. Recife is the major industrial city of the Northeast. Farmers from the drought-stricken interior have poured into the coastal cities to find work. Unfortunately, most of them end up in one of the cities' huge slums, called *favelas* (fah VEH lahs).

The northeast coast has a large black population, descendants of the African slaves who once worked on the sugar plantations. Whites still own and supervise most plantations, but hired workers enjoy moderately good living conditions. In addition to sugar cane, the modern plantations raise cacao, bananas, and cotton. Brazil leads the Western Hemisphere and is second worldwide in banana production. It leads the world in sugar cane production.

THE BRAZILIAN HIGHLANDS

Above the narrow coastal plain rise the **Brazilian Highlands**, a rugged plateau that dominates the east side of the continent. Near the Atlantic coast, the highlands form a steep wall-like slope called the Great Escarpment. It reaches its highest point at 9,482 feet above sea level at Pico da Bandeira (PEE-koh dah bahn-DEH-rah), just west of Vitória.

Like the Andes, the Brazilian Highlands greatly influence river drainage on the continent. Most waters flow down the highlands into two great water systems—the Amazon in the north and the Rio de la Plata in the south. One other major river, São Francisco, cuts east through the highlands. Paulo Afonso Falls, where the river drops toward the coast, is one of the world's five most powerful high falls.

Although the Brazilian Highlands lie in the tropics, the climate is not like that of the Amazon Basin. The Amazon, which straddles the equator, is rainy all year, but heavy rains fall only half the year in the highlands farther south. The Amazon always receives direct sunlight, which heats the surface and causes regular afternoon showers (by convection precipitation, which you studied in Chapter 2). But in the highlands, the direct rays of the sun shift every six months. The rainfall begins in February, when the sun shifts over the highlands. When the sun shifts back north in August, the land cools, cold air rises, and the rains cease.

CITIES IN THE SOUTH

Two hundred miles west of Rio is **São Paulo** (soun POW-loh), the second-largest city by population in Latin America (behind only Buenos Aires), exceeding even Mexico City in population. Including its metropolitan area, São Paulo is the largest South American city in area and the fifth-largest city in the world.

The *Christ the Redeemer* statue, which overlooks Rio de Janeiro, is on a 2,329-foot mountain and is 125 feet high and 92 feet wide from fingertip to fingertip.

São Paulo includes ethnic populations from all over the world. Liberdade, with more than one million inhabitants, is the largest Japanese community outside Japan. But the minorities of Brazil—including Japanese, Germans, and Arabs—now speak Portuguese and have adopted Brazilian culture.

São Paulo arose in one of the most fertile areas of the country. Plantations raise coffee, sugar cane, and cotton. São Paulo's coffee has made Brazil the world leader in coffee exports. Brazil also raises more beef cattle than any other nation, many of them raised in the dry savanna around São Paulo.

The third-largest city in Brazil, Belo Horizonte, is also located on the Brazilian Highlands in the southern heartland. It is the capital of **Minas Gerais** (MEE-nuhs zheh-RICE), one of Brazil's largest states. This highly industrialized state has the largest deposits of iron ore in the world. In fact, Brazil is the world leader in the production of iron ore. Minas Gerais has other mineral resources as well, including diamonds, manganese, and gold. Brazil produces more gold than any other nation in South America. It also produces most of the world's finest imperial topaz.

POVERTY OF THE NORTHEAST

Unlike the southern heartland, the northeast portion of the Brazilian Highlands has poor soil and long dry seasons. While the coastal cities afford decent living conditions, the interior is a virtual desert, and its people are very poor. The primary crop of that region is cassava, a root similar to a potato that can be eaten or used to make tapioca. Brazil is the world's second-leading producer of cassava (behind only Nigeria).

SECTION QUIZ

1. What country colonized Brazil?
2. What is Brazil's largest city? Which city is its cultural center?
3. Why are southern cities more prosperous than northeastern cities?
4. Brazil leads in world production of what three products from the Brazilian Highlands?
- ⚐ Why did the Spanish colonies break up after independence, but not the Portuguese colonies? What advantages has unity given Brazil?

THE AMAZON

The **Amazon River** is the greatest river system in the world. Not only does it drain the largest area, but more water flows out of the Amazon than out of the next ten largest rivers combined. The Amazon is also the longest river by some estimates. Even the lowest figures put it within 160 miles of the Nile.

The flat basin of the Amazon River is covered by a steamy rain forest, called **selva**. Spreading over one-third of the continent, it is the largest tropical rain forest in the world. The high canopy of trees supports a host of exotic animals: the anaconda, the world's longest snake; the capybara, the world's largest rodent; colorful toucans and parrots; jaguars; tapirs; and sloths. The waters teem with electric

Brasília

In an effort to move some of its population westward into the interior, Brazil built the city of **Brasília** (brah SEEL yah) in 1956. By 1960, it was a large, working city. The carefully planned, modern city was carved out of the Brazilian Highland about six hundred miles from the coast. Everything about the city, including the architecture of individual buildings, was designed to be in harmony. The economy of the new capital is slowly developing, but most people prefer to remain on the coast. The government of "the United States of Brazil" is a federal republic, with twenty-six states and the federal district of Brasília.

West of the Brazilian Highlands is the **Mato Grosso** (MAH-toh GROH-soh) **Plateau**. Swamps cover the plateau along the borders with Paraguay and Bolivia. Although it is remote, this region undoubtedly holds great potential wealth.

Every building and street in Brasília, including government buildings such as the Congress building, was planned to demonstrate architectural harmony.

eels, the razor-toothed piranha, and the ten-foot-long pirarucu. Even dolphins and sharks have appeared as far upstream as Iquitos, Peru!

Life of the Remote Indians

Few people live in the Amazon rain forest. It has a very steamy, uncomfortable climate. Temperatures hover between 75°F and 95°F throughout the year. Many areas receive more than one hundred inches of rain annually.

However, the interior began experiencing significant growth in the 1990s, mainly because of the *cerrado*, fertile savannah rich in agricultural promise. The region is flat, so it can be industrially farmed, and it has adequate rainfall. The area still needs to develop transportation to complement these opportunities.

Several small, scattered Indian tribes live deep in the forests, but they share nothing in common with the Incas. Each Indian group generally lives together in one large community structure, called a *malocas*, covered with woven palm leaves. The only significant piece of furniture is the hammock—an invention of the Amazon Indians. Sailors adopted it the world over, and hammocks are a common sight in most homes of coastal Brazilians.

Virtually all tribes practice shifting or **slash-and-burn agriculture**. They cut down a plot of forest, burn the vegetation to fertilize the soil, and then plant cassava. In most cases, they have replaced their ancient stone tools with modern steel. The women turn the cassava into flour and store it in baskets. When the soil is depleted, they cut down a new plot. Cassava is not high in nutrients, but it grows well in the poor, acidic soil. Europeans spread cassava to tropical colonies worldwide.

The Indians supplement their diet by hunting, using the longest bows in the world (some more than six feet tall). In recent centuries, the use of blowguns has spread through the western selva. In thick brush, it is easier to aim blowguns than bows to hit birds and monkeys. Using tubes eight to twelve feet long, skilled blowers can hit targets as high as 120 feet in the trees. Their poison darts fly through the air in deadly silence. The tribes make poison

The Amazon River provides a convenient water route into the interior regions of South America.

Through Christian Eyes

Is it possible for a culture to be evil? Or is it only individual humans who are sinful—making culture a neutral entity?

from the sap of the *strychnos* vine. (We get *strychnine*, an extremely poisonous chemical, from that plant.)

Missionaries have contacted most tribes of the selva and have stopped cannibalism. Although some Indians have accepted Christ and are learning to read, others remain bound by spirit worship and superstitious practices. Humanistic anthropologists are urging the Indians to retain their traditional lifestyle in harmony with nature. "Foreigners tell us to reject the missionaries and go back to our old ways," said one Yanomamo Christian. "But they do not have Christ in their hearts. Our old ways were evil. We will never go back."

MODERN DEVELOPMENT AND DEFORESTATION

As part of its program to develop the rich potential of the Amazon, the government has divided it into seven states. The largest states (in area) in Brazil are Amazonas and Pará. They share the land along the main channel of the Amazon River. **Amazonas**, with its capital of Manaus, governs the western half of the river. Pará, with its bustling capital of Belém on the coast, governs the eastern half. Pará is slightly smaller than Amazonas, but it has more than twice the population. Five other remote states include chunks of the Amazon Basin and are the least populated states of Brazil.

An increasing number of Brazilian settlers are moving into the rain forest, both legally and illegally, to exploit its riches—minerals, farmland, and lumber. The Amazon has a valuable supply of mineral resources. Pará has Brazil's second major iron ore deposit, located about 250 miles south of Belém. South America's leading bauxite and tin mines are located in the Amazon. The state of Rondônia (rohn DOHN yah), along Brazil's southern border with Bolivia, is the world's second-largest producer of tin (after China).

Farmers have attempted to grow crops in the rain forest. A few cacao and rubber plantations thrive along the banks of the Amazon. You might think that heavy rainfall would make productive soil, but the soil is actually very thin. Insects and rapid decay deprive the soil of humus. In a process called **leaching**, constant rains dissolve nutrients in the soil and carry them away.

Increasing numbers of lumberjacks are felling the forests to extract valuable hardwoods, such as mahogany and ebony. But because the trees hold the soil in place, **deforestation** is depleting the soil, rendering the land useless for future generations. Environmentalists are also concerned about the loss of these oxygen-producing forests.

SECTION QUIZ

1. What word refers to the steamy rain forest of the Amazon basin?

2. Which records does the Amazon River hold: most volume, longest river, largest rain forest, or highest waterfall?

3. What mineral products come from the Amazon Basin?

4. Why is the soil poor in the Amazon?

- ◌̣̇ Compare and contrast Brazil's settlement of the Amazon with the U.S. settlement of the West.

CHAPTER REVIEW 12

HOW MUCH DO YOU REMEMBER?

1. Match each geographic feature with its most closely associated term.

   (1) Lake Maracaibo   a. Andes Mountains
   (2) Strait of Magellan   b. estuary
   (3) Amazon River   c. Caribbean Sea
   (4) Aconcagua   d. selva
   (5) Paraná River   e. Guiana Highlands
   (6) Angel Falls   f. Tierra del Fuego
   (7) Río de la Plata   g. Paraguay River

2. Name the three plateau regions of South America.

3. Name the three major South American river systems.

4. What role did the Creoles play in the history of South America?

5. What piece of land joins North and South America?

6. What illegal drug first came from South America?

7. Why is much of South America's Pacific coast so dry?

8. What large plain lies high in the Andes?

9. What is the most fertile grassland area in South America?

10. Which countries of South America were not settled by the Spanish?

11. Why do some tropical areas have a rainy season and a dry season?

WHAT DO YOU THINK?

1. Pick a city in South America where you would like to live. Describe how your life would change if you moved there.

2. Why do environmentalists want Brazil to stop developing the selva? Should other nations have a say in Brazil's decisions?

Can You:
Define These Terms?
zambos / estuary
Creole / Pampas
Llanos / selva
piranha / slash-and-burn
tepuis / agriculture
landlocked / leaching
Altiplano / deforestation

Locate These Places?
Andes Mountains / Santiago
Cordillera Occidental / Strait of Magellan
Cordillera Central / Tierra del Fuego
Cordillera Oriental / Río de la Plata
Bogotá / Buenos Aires
Medellín / Patagonia
Caracas / Mesopotamia
Lake Maracaibo / Gran Chaco
Orinoco River / Montevideo
Guiana Highlands / Asunción
Quito / Paraná River
Lima / São Vicente
Lake Titicaca / Recife
La Paz / Rio de Janeiro
Yungas / Brazilian Highlands
Amazon Basin / São Paulo
Atacama Desert / Amazon River
Aconcagua River / Brasília
 / Mato Grosso Plateau

Explain the Significance?
Line of Demarcation / Shining Path
Treaty of Tordesillas / Salvador Allende
Simón Bolívar / Augusto Pinochet
Cotopaxi / José de San Martín
Amazon rain forest / Juan Perón
Incas / Guaraní
Cusco / Dom Pedro
Francisco Pizarro / Minas Gerais
Quechua / Amazonas
Peru Current

UNIT 6

THE AFRICAN SAFARI

One word that people readily associate with Africa is *safari*. The word originated as the Arabic verb *safar*, meaning "to make a journey," and evolved into the Swahili synonym *safari*. The first safaris were for trade—in ivory, rhinoceros horns, and slaves. They later became trips of discovery for naturalists and big-game hunters. Those usually involved large numbers of guides, interpreters, and burden bearers. More recently, as people have become more concerned for animals and the environment, safaris have been primarily for camping, photography, or just travel for travel's sake.

Perhaps the name most popularly associated with safaris in the twentieth century was Theodore Roosevelt. As soon as his presidency ended and his successor was sworn in, TR left on safari under the sponsorship of the Smithsonian Institution. He hunted big game and collected specimens for the museum. TR later wrote of his first encounter with a rhinoceros, "I pushed forward the safety of the double-barreled Holland rifle. . . . [T]he rhino saw me and jumped to his feet with the agility of a polo pony. As he rose I [shot with] the right barrel, the bullet going through both lungs. . . . Before he could get quite all the way round . . . I struck him with my left-hand barrel, the bullet entering between the neck and shoulder and piercing his heart. . . . [T]he great bull rhino . . . dropped just thirteen paces from where we stood."

Quoted from *African Game Trails* by Theodore Roosevelt. New York: Scribner, 1910.

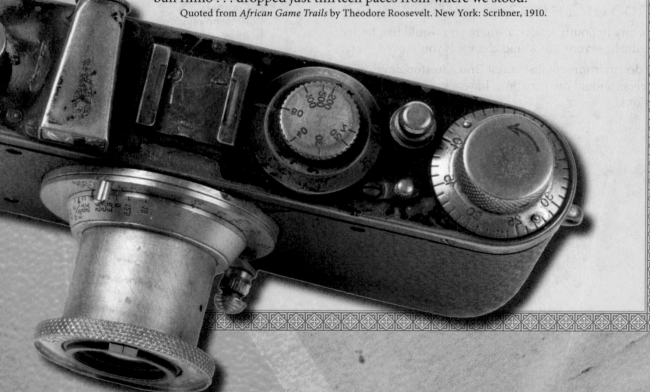

AFRICA

CHRISTIANITY AND CULTURE IN AFRICA

When you say the words *Africa* and *religion* together, people often visualize two vastly different images. Some people associate Africa with spiritual darkness, unbelief, animism, and pagan tribal religious practices. Others, however, think of a vibrant and growing body of Christian converts and a continent that is rivaled only by East Asia as the focal point of the greatest growth of the church.

Which image is more accurate? In a sense, both scenarios exist side by side.

Basically four types of organized Christianity are connected with Africa. The first was centered in the northern third of the continent. The northern coast of Africa produced such Christian fathers as Origen of Alexandria, Tertullian of Carthage, and Augustine of Hippo. In Egypt, the Coptic Christians bore witness to the saving grace of God. And Ethiopia had one of the earliest churches outside Palestine. This early Christian presence in Africa, however, was all but extinguished by the rapid spread of Islam in the region. Today, Muslims dominate North Africa from the Atlantic coast to Southwest Asia and from the Mediterranean to deep central Africa.

A second Christian presence came to Africa in the form of European missionaries, beginning with Portuguese Catholic priests in central Africa during the age of exploration (sixteenth to eighteenth centuries) and culminating in the British and American evangelical Protestant missionary movements of the late eighteenth and nineteenth centuries. During this period, such missionaries as the famed David Livingstone worked to advance the Christian church in Africa. Missionaries helped end the infamous slave trade and worked to moderate the ill effects of colonial

greed that had exploited African resources at the expense of the native Africans. Some missionaries also began promoting the development of indigenous churches in Africa.

A third Christian presence is represented by independent (i.e., native African) Christianity. These groups of believers are not associated with any particular foreign missionary activity or organizations. They either developed on their own or, having become disillusioned with some aspect of foreign missionary outreach, formed their own Africans-only churches.

Finally, Christianity is represented in Africa by a few European-only religious organizations. These churches were organized by and for European residents of Africa. Wanting to preserve their own ways of worship, they had no desire to include native Africans in their services and were not trying to evangelize them.

African tribal religions were a major obstacle to the spread of Christianity in Africa from the beginning. Animism, spirit worship, and other false religions permeated the numerous tribes in African society, prompting Christians in Europe and America to think of Africa as the Dark Continent. The people were in the darkness of sin, Satan having blinded their eyes to the truth. In addition, the Africans were in darkness regarding European ways that Westerners considered to be superior to the native African ways.

In many ways, this spiritual and intellectual darkness still affects the African culture and society today. These factors contribute to the continent's poverty, reluctance to adopt free market economics, civil strife, and political instability. Christian missionaries, however, continue to spread the good news of the grace of God and the difference He can make in the spiritual, social, and political lives of the people.

CHAPTER 13

Animals roam the Serengeti Plain in Tanzania.

SOUTHERN AND EASTERN AFRICA

I. SOUTHERN AFRICA
   A. SOUTHERN TIP OF AFRICA
   B. SOUTHWEST PLATEAU
   C. THE ZAMBEZI RIVER NATIONS
   D. INDIAN OCEAN ISLANDS

II. EASTERN AFRICA
   A. LAKES REGION
   B. THE HORN OF AFRICA
   C. SUDAN

Africa is the second-largest continent. Its size is not as important as its location, however; 80 percent of Africa's land is between the Tropic of Cancer and the Tropic of Capricorn. This position makes the climate mainly warm, and it makes the climate in most areas constant—there are no great temperature fluctuations. This position also determines the patterns of rainfall for the continent. Near the equator, there are heavy tropical rains on the west coast of Africa; this is not true in East Africa because of mountains and wind patterns.

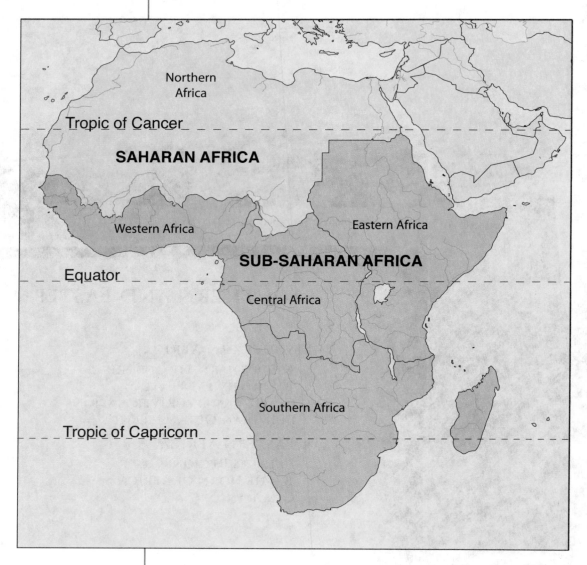

The amount of rainfall decreases as you move north or south away from the equator, and near each end of the continent there are great deserts, the Sahara in the north and the Kalahari in the south. The Sahara is perhaps the single most important geographic factor in the history of Africa, dividing the continent into two regions with very different peoples and histories. Saharan Africa shows the strong imprint of Islam, while sub-Saharan Africa's history is the history of many tribal groups. **Sub-Saharan Africa** encompasses all of the lands below the Sahara.

The rainfall pattern influences vegetation in Africa as well. While there are rain forests near the equator in the west, most of the continent is grasslands, which are usually called **savannas**. About half of Africa is covered by grasslands, and this helps to produce the great range of wildlife that has made Africa famous. When you add up the land area of all of Africa's deserts, you find that about 40 percent of the land is considered desert; however, not all of this desert land is void of plant life. Some of the desert areas are home to nomadic herders and provide adequate food for their flocks.

Africa is also home to several mighty river systems; but unlike the Mississippi, the Rhine, or the Amazon, these rivers do not permit navigation from the coast to the interior because of great falls or rapids. This is why European settlers remained along the coast in many areas. The rivers, however, do allow navigation in the interior, and they play an important role in transportation and communication within the continent.

Two other geographic features make Africa's tropical location less favorable than it might seem to be. First is the unreliable rainfall in many areas of the continent. This is related to the wind currents found in the tropics, but the long dry seasons (and the often torrential downpours when the rains finally do come) have made the life of

Southern Africa Fast Facts

Flag	Country	Capital	Area (sq. mi.)	Pop. (M)	Pop. Density (per sq. mi.)	Per Capita GDP ($US)	Life Span
	Angola	Luanda	481,354	12.13	25.2	$3,200	38.6
	Botswana	Gaborone	231,804	1.64	7.1	$10,500	33.7
	Comoros	Moroni	838	0.69	824.5	$600	62.3
	Lesotho	Maseru	11,720	2.02	172.6	$2,500	34.4
	Madagascar	Antananarivo	226,657	18.60	82.0	$900	57.3
	Malawi	Lilongwe	45,745	13.01	284.5	$600	41.7
	Mauritius	Port Louis	788	1.24	1,574.7	$13,100	72.6
	Mozambique	Maputo	309,496	19.69	63.6	$1,300	39.8
	Namibia	Windhoek	318,696	2.04	6.4	$7,000	43.4
	Seychelles	Victoria	176	0.08	463.3	$7,800	72.1
	South Africa	Pretoria	471,011	44.19	93.8	$12,000	42.7
	Swaziland	Mbabane	6,704	1.14	169.5	$5,000	32.6
	Zambia	Lusaka	290,586	11.50	39.6	$900	40.0
	Zimbabwe	Harare	150,804	12.24	81.1	$2,300	39.3

African farmers very difficult. Second is the relatively poor soil that characterizes much of the continent.

Throughout the nineteenth century, the European powers sought to increase their control of Africa. The United Kingdom outstripped the other European powers, controlling a nearly continuous path of land from Cape Town to Cairo. Not all Europeans sought an empire, though. Among the great British explorers and missionaries was David Livingstone (1813–73), who gave his life exploring the interior and striving to win lost souls to Christ. Others, like Cecil Rhodes, made fortunes at the expense of the colonies. Despite the efforts of the imperial powers, the European empires crumbled in the wake of World War II.

Post–World War II Africa was caught in the middle of another contest, between communism and democracy. Newly independent African colonies often experienced civil wars as the two political systems struggled for dominance. The collapse of Russian communism and the breakup of the Soviet Union relieved much of that tension. Today, widespread civil wars are being fought over religion and a variety of other issues. Diseases such as AIDS also hinder progress.

I. Southern Africa

The region of southern Africa is located south of the rain forests of the Congo Basin. Southern Africa also includes the large island country of Madagascar as well as a few other island countries. The most important country in southern Africa is South Africa.

Southern Tip of Africa

The southern tip of Africa consists of the countries South Africa, Lesotho, and Swaziland. Of these, South Africa is the largest and most prosperous country in the area. Lesotho is surrounded by South Africa, and three of Swaziland's four sides border South Africa.

South Africa

The Portuguese rounded the **Cape of Good Hope** in 1488. By 1652 the Dutch East India Company had set up a supply station there. In the early nineteenth century, the British took over the Dutch station and made it the capital of a British colony. Over 3.3 million people live in **Cape Town** today, making it the third-largest city in southern and eastern Africa.

The Cape—Only a small part of the Cape region is coastal lowland. The region's climate varies radically, from desert west of Cape Town to marine west coast in the east. Most of the Cape is a large plateau with a steppe climate. The **Orange River** is the longest river in South Africa, flowing through the steppe to the west coast. It cuts across the middle of the region and forms the northwestern border with neighboring Namibia. Ships on the Atlantic Ocean cannot navigate up the river because the powerful Augrabies Falls drops a total of 625 feet near the coast.

Natal—The **Drakensberg Mountains** (DRAH kuhnz BERG) rise from the coastal plain of Natal to 11,424 feet above sea level in the tiny landlocked country of Lesotho. The mountains are actually an **escarpment**, a steep rise from a plain to a plateau. Winds from the

---

Racial Diversity in South Africa

South Africa, like many other countries, is a racially diverse land. The Dutch colonists, and later the British, intermarried with the Africans. The people of mixed descent are called **Coloureds** (KUL uhrds), a recognized ethnic group that constitutes about 9% of the population of South Africa. Other ethnic groupings in South Africa are blacks (80%), whites (10%), and Indian/Asians (2.5%). The British originally brought Indian laborers on contract in the 1860s to work on sugar plantations.

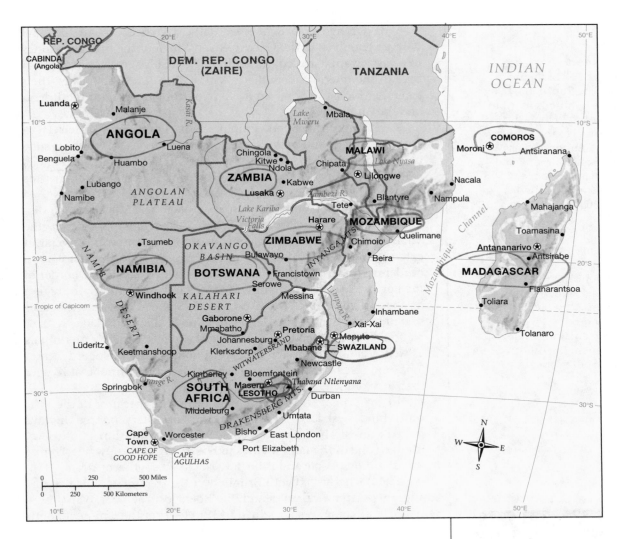

ocean give Natal a humid subtropical climate. The second-highest waterfall in the world, **Tugela Falls** (too GAY luh), takes a 3,110-foot plunge on Natal's border with Lesotho.

In Natal are the **Zulu** (ZOO loo), the most famous of the Bantu tribes. In 1818, a fierce warrior named Shaka became chief and led the Zulu against all neighboring tribes. Under Shaka, a great kingdom called Zululand emerged. When Britain annexed the southeast Zulu territory in 1843, fighting began between Britain and the Zulu. In 1879 the Zulu demolished a British regiment, but the British won the war later that year. The British policy of indirect rule permitted the Zulu to govern themselves in Natal as a British colony. Today, KwaZulu-Natal is one of nine administrative provinces in South Africa. The Zulu continue to defend their unique identity. While the other tribes support a strong central government, the Zulu leaders in the Inkatha Party desire a weak federation.

Orange Free State—The original Dutch farmers, called **Boers** (BOORS), spread out from Cape Town across the fertile coastal plain. When the British took over, many Boers fled inland. In 1836 some left for the far interior. This Great Trek ended after they crossed the Orange River. They called their new nation the Orange Free State.

The Drakensberg mountains rise high above South Africa and Lesotho.

Bantu

Many tribes settled the diverse lands of South Africa. Almost all of them are of the Bantu tribes. The **Bantu** (BAN too) peoples include hundreds of tribes across sub-Saharan Africa. Linguistic studies trace the Bantus to the Benue River in Cameroon. Whether because of drought, war, or need for more land, the Bantus began their Bantu migrations around 2000 BC and reached South Africa by AD 1000.

The largest group of Bantu in South Africa today is the Nguni, accounting for 60 percent of all the blacks. The Zulu and Xhosa (KOH suh) speak the main languages of the Nguni, but the Swazi and Ndebele are also included in this group. The other Bantus are divided among three smaller groups: 20 percent are Sotho, 4 percent are Tsonga, and 2 percent are Venda. The other 14 percent of blacks in South Africa are non-Bantus.

Mined gold is refined in machines like this one.

The Orange Free State eventually stretched east to the Vaal River, a tributary of the Orange River. Much of the plateau belongs to a vast savanna, called the **veldt**, that spreads across several countries in the interior of southern Africa. The Boers established their capital at Bloemfontein, but faced opposition from both the British and the Zulu.

Over time, the Boers simplified the grammar of their High Dutch language and incorporated words from other languages such as Zulu. The resulting language is quite different from Dutch and is called **Afrikaans** (AF ri KAHNS). Today, the Dutch South Africans call themselves **Afrikaners** (AF ri KAH nurs).

Transvaal—A number of Boers crossed the Vaal River to distance themselves further from Britain. The Transvaal ("across the Vaal") became the second independent Boer country in the veldt. It extended north to the **Limpopo River** (lim POH POH), the northern border of modern South Africa. It also reached east to the border of the Portuguese colony on the coast (Mozambique). Today, the region has been divided into several provinces. Some of the eastern border remains unsettled. A popular destination in the Transvaal is Kruger National Park, which claims to have the greatest variety of animals as well. Visitors can watch elephants, lions, giraffes, leopards, antelope, and cheetahs. Rhinos and hippos are more common at Kruger than at Serengeti, a park in Tanzania.

In 1886 prospectors struck gold near Johannesburg in the Witwatersrand District. English-speaking foreigners poured in and staked claims. The influx of people made **Johannesburg** (joh HAN is BURG) one of the largest cities in South Africa. It now boasts over seven million people and is the largest city in southern Africa.

The Boers clashed with Britain over the treatment of British immigrants. After a valiant stand, the Boers lost the Boer War (1899–1902). Four colonies later joined in 1910 to form the Union of South Africa. In 1961 the name changed to the Republic of South Africa.

After World War II, the Afrikaners gained control of the government. **Pretoria** (pri TOR ee uh), near Johannesburg and the nation's fourth-largest city, became the administrative capital of the nation to balance the legislative capital at Cape Town. These two cities are the major national capitals, while Bloemfontein is the judicial "capital."

Apartheid—About 80 percent of all South Africans are blacks. However, after winning an election in 1948, the Afrikaner minority began to institute **apartheid** (uh PART hite), a rigorous policy of racial separation. The Afrikaners contended that each race was culturally different from every other race. It was best to keep all races separate so that each could develop its own unique genius. Apartheid severely regulated life for blacks, Coloureds, and Asians. These groups could not vote in national elections and, after 1959, had no representation in the South African Parliament. Opposition groups, such as the African National Congress (ANC) and the Pan-African Congress (PAC), were banned, so the oppressed groups had no organized voice.

Under apartheid, every citizen was registered by race. Every area of life was segregated: restaurants, stores, buses, trains, and so forth. The apartheid government also forced blacks to live in reservations called "homelands." Homeland citizens had to carry identity documents at all times. If employed outside the homeland, they had to carry a passport and a pass as well. Any protest was met with swift and brutal retribution. Even children were not exempt from the government's assaults. As a result of these policies, the international community condemned apartheid. In 1973, the United Nations called apartheid "a crime against humanity."

In 1989, F. W. de Klerk became president. De Klerk responded to foreign criticism and trade embargoes by easing the apartheid restrictions. In 1990, he released the jailed ANC leader, **Nelson Mandela**. De Klerk and Mandela began negotiations to make a smooth transition away from apartheid. In 1992, a referendum proved that even most whites supported the negotiations. The negotiations between de Klerk and Mandela won each of them half of a Nobel Peace Prize in 1993. The next year, Mandela was elected president of South Africa. The old provinces were broken up into nine provinces. The number of official languages rose from two to eleven, and a new constitution went into effect in 1997.

After Mandela ended his term as president in 1999, Thabo Mbeki came into office. Mbeki was reelected for a second term in 2004. As president, he focused on improving the economic condition of the country's black population.

Although apartheid ended over a decade ago, South Africa still exhibits an uneven distribution of wealth, but the situation is improving.

Another great challenge for the new government is the lawlessness throughout the country. Immediately after apartheid ended, the crime rate increased dramatically. The poor economic conditions of those who had suffered under apartheid combined with the new freedom of mobility contributed to the high crime rate. In the last few years, the crime rate has stabilized or decreased. The murder rate, though, is still the second-highest in the world—ten times the rate in the United States.

LESOTHO

During the Zulu conquests, Chief Mosheshoe led the Basotho (or Southern Sotho) tribe to refuge in the Drakensberg Mountains. Later, the Basotho also defended the rugged terrain from the Boers and the British. Under attacks from the Boers, they asked for British help and became the protectorate of Basutoland in 1868. The kingdom gained independence in 1966. At that time Basutoland became Lesotho (luh SOH toh).

Most of the country is at a high altitude. **Thabana Ntlenyana** (tah-BAHN-uh ENT-len-YAHN-uh) in the Drakensberg Mountains is the largest mountain in southern Africa, rising to 11,424 feet. Lesotho's high plateau contains the headwaters of the Orange River. These headwaters provide water for crops and livestock. Most farmers, however, remain poor. Lesotho has made use of its water supply by exporting water to South Africa and using the water to produce electricity. Lesotho produces enough electricity to be self-sufficient and to export excess electricity to South Africa.

Lesotho is entirely surrounded by South Africa and is one of only a few nations in the world that are surrounded by another nation. As a result, Lesotho has been at the mercy of the political situation in South Africa. But in the last few years, Lesotho has been racked by its own turmoil. Shortly after a disputed election in 1998, various young army officers mutinied and threatened to cause a coup. At the Lesotho government's request, foreign troops came into the country and restored order. However, just a few months after the troops left, disorder erupted again. Elections in May 2002 brought a restructuring of the

Mandela and de Klerk worked together to end apartheid and shared the 1993 Nobel Peace Prize.

Countries with the Highest Incidences of HIV/AIDS Among the Adult Population

Country	% of Adult Pop. Infected
Swaziland	38.8%
Botswana	37.3%
Lesotho	28.9%
Zimbabwe	24.6%
South Africa	21.5%
Namibia	21.3%
Zambia	16.5%
Malawi	14.2%
Central African Republic	13.5%
Mozambique	12.2%

government and added more positions in the country's legislative body. Since that time, the country has been more stable.

SWAZILAND

The country of Swaziland (SWAH zee LAND) borders South Africa and Mozambique. From west to east, there are four major geographic sections in the country—the Highveld, the Middleveld, the Lowveld, and the Lubombo region. The Highveld, in the west, reaches an average elevation of 4,500 feet while the Lowveld reaches an average elevation of 500 to 1,000 feet. The Lubombo region is the furthest east and swells sharply from the Lowveld to an average elevation of 2,000 feet. Most of the population lives in the Middleveld, which is about 2,000 to 2,500 feet in average elevation.

Swaziland has the highest rate of HIV/AIDS among adults in the world. Almost 39 percent of the adult population is infected by the virus. The population has an average lifespan of 32.6 years.

After being ruled by the Boers and then the British, Swaziland gained independence in 1968. Most of the people are Swazi. Mbabane is the administrative capital, but the traditional royal capital is the nearby village of Lobamba. The well-watered mountains and plateaus of Swaziland offer the same good agriculture and mineral wealth as in adjacent South Africa. Sugar products, especially soft-drink concentrate, greatly contribute to Swaziland's economy. Diamonds and coal constitute a small portion of the nation's GDP.

SECTION QUIZ

1. Why is the Sahara the single most important geographic factor in the history of Africa?
2. Why are the river systems of Africa not considered navigable?
3. What famous tribe has its home in KwaZulu-Natal?
4. What was the name of the South African government's plan of segregation during the twentieth century?
5. What is the largest mountain in southern Africa? What range is it in? What country?
   - Contrast the Boers/Afrikaners and the Zulu.

SOUTHWEST PLATEAU

Three nations lie on the plateau in southwest Africa—Botswana, Namibia, and Angola. The land is hot and dry. The coast and parts of the interior are desert, and the rest is grassland.

BOTSWANA

The British protectorate of Bechuanaland became the independent nation of Botswana (bot SWAH nuh) in 1966. Botswana, a land-locked country, remains part of the British Commonwealth.

The southeast produces nickel and copper, but little development has occurred. Diamonds were discovered in Botswana in 1967, and diamonds account for 80 percent of the country's export income. The country is the largest producer of gem-quality diamonds in the world. However, a majority of the people work as farmers. Many seek jobs across the border in prosperous South Africa.

Bantus and Europeans drove the **San** (SAHN) (or Bushmen) out of South Africa and into Botswana. The San have survived as hunters and gatherers in the Kalahari Desert.

The **Kalahari Desert** (KAH luh HAHR ee), the sixth-largest desert in the world, lies on the Tropic of Capricorn, much as the Sahara lies on the Tropic of Cancer. The desert spreads across southwest and central Botswana and into neighboring Namibia and South Africa. This large desert (over 200,000 sq. mi.) covers over half of Botswana. The largest diamond mine in the world is in the northeast part of the desert at Orapa.

Northern Botswana consists of several basins with no outlet to the sea. One basin contains the Makgadikgadi Salt Pans, a large region of salt flats. The largest basin is the Okavango Basin. Rivers draining into this basin create the **Okavango Delta** (OH kuh VANG goh).

Although Botswana has a stable government and a growing economy, the country also has a tragic problem. Botswana has the second-highest rate of HIV/AIDS among adults in the world. The life expectancy there is about 34 years.

The Okavango Delta is the largest inland delta in the world.

NAMIBIA

Namibia (nuh MIB ee uh) is a country with deserts in the west and east. The barren **Namib Desert** (NAH mib) stretches eight hundred miles along the Atlantic coast. Mines provide most of the nation's resources: diamonds, zinc, lead, tin, and uranium. A cold ocean current keeps the air very dry and causes temperature inversions and thick fogs. The frequent fogs, resulting in countless shipwrecks, have given the northern shore the nickname **Skeleton Coast**. In the west, the Kalahari Desert expands into Namibia.

In spite of several rivers on its borders, Namibia is a bleak and arid land. Most people live in the arid but cooler Central Plateau between the Kalahari and Namib deserts. The plateau averages between 3,200 and 6,500 feet. Almost three-fourths of the small population raises cattle and other livestock. The main port is Walvis Bay, west of the capital, Windhoek. Walvis Bay is one of the finest ports in Africa.

The German colony of South-West Africa became a South African mandate after World War I. After decades of negotiations, UN interventions, and Communist guerilla warfare, Namibia gained independence in 1990, but the government is not yet stable. Because of South African influence, English is the official language, but Afrikaans is spoken more commonly. Eighty percent of the people are Christian, and most of those are Lutheran.

Namibia relies on South Africa for much of its economic trade. Most of its imports come from South Africa, which also receives many of Namibia's exports. The country is seeking to break away from its dependence on one country. The mining industry in Namibia produces diamonds, uranium, lead, zinc, tin, silver, and tungsten.

ANGOLA

Angola (ang GOH luh), almost twice the size of Texas, lies mainly on a series of high plateaus with altitudes averaging 6,000 feet. The Bié Plateau in the west rises to 8,800 feet. Angola's coastal plain extends from 15 to 125 miles inland. Savanna covers most of the land except for the rain forests in the far north and deserts in the southwest.

An isolated region of Angola north of the Congo River, called **Cabinda** (kuh BIN duh), has valuable petroleum reserves. Cabindans resent the fact that most of their wealth goes south to the capital. A rebel group sought independence, but Angola decimated the rebel forces in 2002.

The capital, Luanda, has 2.75 million people. Warfare has kept Angola from benefiting from its abundance of diamonds and its arable land, which once enabled the country to export large amounts of coffee. Oil is the major export today, accounting for over half of the country's GDP.

Angola is an important exception to British rule in southern Africa. Portugal had forts in the area dating to the sixteenth century. The Portuguese influence remains obvious in Angola. Portuguese is still the official language, and almost 40 percent of the people have converted to Roman Catholicism. In 1961 Angola revolted against the Portuguese, and most of the white settlers fled the country. After several years of fighting, Portugal granted Angola independence in 1975.

Angola has continued to suffer since gaining independence. It became the main battleground between Cold War superpowers in sub-Saharan Africa. The civil war claimed over half a million lives. Despite UN intervention, fighting continued even after the Cold War ended. Peace was negotiated in 2002, and the government has started to stabilize.

THE ZAMBEZI RIVER NATIONS

The **Zambezi River** (zam BEE zee) rises in southern Zambia and flows across southern Africa to the Indian Ocean. The Zambezi is the fourth-longest river in Africa and the longest in southern Africa. It runs through several southern African countries.

David Livingstone won renown after crossing the continent between 1853 and 1856. He started in Luanda, the capital of the Portuguese colony of Angola, and followed the course of the Zambezi to the far coast in Mozambique. Great Britain later claimed the lands between these two coastal colonies.

MOZAMBIQUE

Like Angola on the western coast, Mozambique (moh zum BEEK) was a large Portuguese colony on the eastern coast. Although Marxist rebel armies won the country's independence in 1975, Portuguese remains the official language. Thirty percent of the people are broadly Christians, 17 percent are Muslims, and 45 percent are animists. The country suffers from the loss of the skilled laborers who fled during the war for independence.

The Marxist rebels who won control of Mozambique did not enjoy a peaceful regime. They faced another rebel group called RENAMO (Mozambique

The Zambezi River separates Zimbabwe and Zambia. Right of the bridge in the image below is Zambia, and left of the bridge is Zimbabwe.

National Resistance). As many as one million people died in the struggle between the two factions. After the fall of communism in Europe, the UN brokered a peace agreement. The UN insisted that both sides lay down their weapons before elections could occur. Elections were finally held in 1994. Soon after that, refugees from Mozambique began returning home. It has been estimated that almost six million people returned home after the war.

Mozambique's 1,535-mile coastline on the Indian Ocean is abundant with natural harbors. The Zambezi River divides the nation. In the north is the Mozambique Plateau. A wide coastal plain covers the southern region and supports many agricultural products, including sugar, cotton, cashews, tea, and copra. Coal is mined in the west.

The long coast makes Mozambique vital to shipping and transportation. Even in ancient times, Sofala served as a port for the interior kingdom of Zimbabwe, and later, the Boers shipped goods through Maputo. Today, Mozambique serves four landlocked neighbors.

ZIMBABWE

Zimbabwe (zim BAHB wee) lies on the veldt, the savanna that covers much of southern Africa. Its average elevation is 1,000 feet above sea level. The prominent geographical feature is a ridge called the Highveld, which makes up about 25 percent of the country. The Highveld lies across the country from the southwest to the northeast. Along the Highveld is a series of hills and mountains. Zimbabwe has a wide array of mineral resources. The country produces gold, steel, nickel, and many other products. Yet 80 percent of the population lives in poverty.

On either side of the Highveld lies the Middleveld. While the Highveld averages 4,500 feet, the Middleveld plateau averages 3,500 feet. The Middleveld takes up about 40 percent of Zimbabwe. A feature of the south is the Lowveld, which reaches 600 feet at its lowest point. The Lowveld takes up about 23 percent of Zimbabwe. The two major rivers of Zimbabwe are the Zambezi at the northern border and the Limpopo at the southern borders. **Victoria Falls** lies on the Zambezi near the northwest corner. Downstream is Lake Kariba. Zimbabwe also has Mtarazi Falls, the second-highest waterfall in Africa (2,500 ft.).

In 1890 Cecil Rhodes founded Fort Victoria and Fort Salisbury, hoping to find gold and to extend British influence north of South

VICTORIA FALLS

Victoria Falls ranks among the four most spectacular waterfalls in the world. The falls drop 355 feet over a crest that spans more than one mile. The roar is audible twenty-five miles away. Even the twelve-hundred-foot-high mist is visible at that distance. The discoverer of the falls, David Livingstone, learned its native name, Mosioatunya, which means "the smoke that thunders."

Livingstone visited the falls on November 16, 1855, while on his great trek down the Zambezi River. He named it in honor of Queen Victoria of England, and the name has remained. He wrote in his diary that "scenes so lovely must have been gazed on by angels in their flight." He later described the falls as "the most wonderful sight I had witnessed in Africa."

Victoria Falls drops into a chasm on the border of Zambia and Zimbabwe.

Africa. In 1895 the British South Africa Company named the colony Rhodesia after Rhodes. The white minority maintained control, refusing to accept the idea of black rule. For a time, between 1953 and 1963, Great Britain allowed the colony to form a federation with the other two landlocked British colonies north of the Zambezi River. But the blacks in the other colonies broke away.

When Britain criticized the white population's rule in Rhodesia, the leaders declared independence in 1965. This was the first full-fledged separation by a British colony since 1776. The act was declared illegal and unconstitutional by the United Kingdom and the United Nations. Economic sanctions were put into place soon after this. Black rebels fought the white rulers until they won in 1979. After officially gaining independence on April 18, 1980, the country changed its name from Rhodesia to Zimbabwe and renamed the capital Harare. Most whites fled the country after this change of power. Since independence, Zimbabwe has had only one ruler, Robert Mugabe. Mugabe has dominated the country, rigging elections to maintain power. The United States, the European Union, and other countries have imposed sanctions against Zimbabwe.

GREAT ZIMBABWE

Zimbabwe took its name from an ancient ruin called **Great Zimbabwe**. It is the largest stone monument in Africa outside the pyramids. The ruins show evidence of the only ancient metalworking civilization south of the equator. Among the ruins were found birds carved in soapstone, which have become symbols of the nation. With no written records, the civilization that built Great Zimbabwe remains a mystery.

The ruins of Great Zimbabwe consist of three parts: a Great Enclosure on a fertile plain, a Hill Fortress overlooking the plain, and about sixty acres of lesser ruins. The granite wall of the Great Enclosure is thirty feet high, sixteen feet thick, and eight hundred feet long. It encloses platforms, passages, rooms, and two stone towers. The builders cut and fit the stones together without the benefit of mortar. Other civilizations in sub-Saharan Africa are built from mud or wood, so the stonework is unique.

The Hill Fortress stands two hundred feet above the plain. The ingenious design converts rock outcroppings and caves into rooms and pathways. The pathway to the fortress is steep and narrows to single file. One of the caves has special resonance characteristics, similar to a "whispering chamber." The voice of a person speaking in the cave resounds loud and clear inside the enclosure far below.

The Great Enclosure on the plain, as seen from the Hill Fortress at Great Zimbabwe

The BaLemba tribe in the nation of South Africa claims descent from the builders of Great Zimbabwe. According to their legends, their ancestors migrated south after King Mwali died. Their legends describe Mwali as ruling from a stone fortress and speaking unseen in thunderous tones. The legends make sense in light of these ruins, where a king could rule from the Hill Fortress and speak unseen to the Great Enclosure below, the cave making the king's voice seem like the voice of a god.

Great Zimbabwe stood in the heart of an early gold-mining region. Other valuable goods from the region included copper and ivory. Porcelain, beads, and other artifacts from Nanking, Persia, Arabia, and Indonesia have been unearthed in the Great Enclosure, showing the extent of the ancient trade.

The civilization died long before 1552, when a Portuguese historian found that the local tribes could no longer read the inscriptions. In 1867 Karl Mauch and Adam Rauch rediscovered the ruins and believed them to be the palace of the queen of Sheba from the time of Solomon. A later view was that Sofala, on the coast of Mozambique, was the biblical city of Ophir, where King Solomon obtained his gold (1 Kings 10:10–11). Arab records document Sofala as being rich in gold, which would have come from the region of Great Zimbabwe.

ZAMBIA

David Livingstone visited what is now Zambia (ZAM bee uh) in 1851, but Britain did not obtain the region until Cecil Rhodes negotiated treaties with the natives in 1891. The British named the area Northern Rhodesia, with the Zambezi River dividing it from Southern Rhodesia. Great Britain granted Northern Rhodesia independence in 1964, and the country adopted the name Zambia.

Western Zambia lies on the Angolan Plateau but supports forests. Most of the country averages about 4,000 feet above sea level. In the west are also some swamps as well as the Kafue National Park. Sharing the great copper belt with Congo in the north, Zambia is the largest producer of copper in Africa.

The Muchinga Mountains run through eastern Zambia. North of the mountains are two lakes in the Congo River drainage system. Lake Mweru is the deeper of the two. Zambia shares Lake Tanganyika with Tanzania and the Democratic Republic of the Congo. Maize and sugar cane are the largest crops in the country, yet almost three-quarters of the population lives in poverty. On top of this, 16.5 percent of the adult population lives with HIV/AIDS.

MALAWI

Almost the size of Pennsylvania, the British colony of Nyasaland was nestled along Lake Nyasa in the Great Rift Valley. Britain granted the country independence in 1964, the same year that it gave independence to Zambia. The people renamed both the nation and the lake Malawi (muh LAH wee). In 1994, the first multiparty elections were held.

Lake Malawi, the third-largest lake in Africa, is the dominant geographical characteristic of the country. The lake lies on most of the eastern border. Much of the country is on plateaus. Elevations in Malawi range from 8,500 feet in the north to 200 feet at the southern tip. Mount Mulanje rises to 10,000 feet in the south. The climate varies with the elevation and the distance from Lake Malawi.

Malawi is one of the world's poorest nations. It lacks an array of natural resources, and its remote location hinders transportation and tourism. The economy depends heavily on agriculture. Tobacco and tea are two of its most important crops. In addition, many of

MISSIONS: BIBLE COLLEGES

One of the major goals of almost any missions work is training nationals (natives of the country where the missionary is ministering). The missionary will not be around forever. When he dies or has to leave, someone must continue the work. Often, national men who desire to pastor have no place to train in preaching and studying the Bible. Because of this need, many missionaries have begun Bible colleges. Bible colleges enable nationals to receive instruction in their own language and nation.

There are many advantages to training national pastors and missionaries. One of the most important is that no cultural gap exists between the national and the people to whom he is ministering. Whereas a foreign missionary must spend time learning the culture, the national pastor already understands that culture. Bible colleges present a valuable opportunity to spread the gospel further than foreign missionaries are able.

Central Africa Bible College in Zambia seeks to reach the English-speaking parts of Africa.

Lake Malawi's tropical fish find their way to pet shops around the world. The lake is famous for its beautiful but feisty cichlids.

INDIAN OCEAN ISLANDS

Several islands lie in the Indian Ocean off the coast of Africa. France controlled each of these beautiful tropical islands at various times. Some of the people are Creoles, being of French descent mixed with African or Indian. However, there is a very cosmopolitan mixture of black Africans, Indonesians, Arab and Chinese traders, Indian laborers, and European settlers.

MADAGASCAR

Africa's largest island, Madagascar (MAD uh GAS kar), is separated from Africa's southeast coast by the Mozambique Channel. It is the fourth-largest island in the world. During the seventeenth and eighteenth centuries, pirates, such as Captain Kidd, hid there. Madagascar became a French colony in 1896 and gained its independence in 1960.

Ring-tailed lemurs are one of the many species endemic to Madagascar.

The land in Madagascar is diverse. A range of mountains parallels the east coast, leaving only a narrow coastal plain. The range reaches to 9,436 feet at the north end, and reefs block most of the east coast. To the west, the range drops gradually with long fertile valleys. The capital, Antananarivo (AN tuh NAN uh REE voh), lies on the cooler crest of the range.

The southern end of the island is desert, and many of the forested places have been cleared for agriculture. Eighty percent of the population works in agriculture, which produces over one-quarter of the country's GDP. Rice is the major crop of the country, and Madagascar ranks twentieth worldwide in the production of this crop. As the population of the island grows, more wildlife becomes endangered. This is especially unfortunate because lemurs, aye-ayes, and other species live nowhere else in the world.

The people are probably a mixture of Africans and Indonesians whose ancestors arrived about two thousand years ago. The Malagasy language, similar to Malay and Indonesian, spread throughout the island. French and Malagasy are the official languages of the country.

COMOROS

The Comoro Islands consist of four main volcanic islands and several islets northwest of Madagascar. The largest island, Grand Comore, consists of a high plateau with Mount Karthala, a volcano, at the southern end. When the Comoros (KAHM uh roze) gained independence in 1975, the island of Mayotte voted to remain part of France. Comoros still claims the island although France controls it. Most of the people are Muslims. The economy is based on agriculture, tourism, and commerce; and the main exports are cloves, vanilla, and perfume oils. The official languages are Arabic and French, but Shikomoro, a dialect of Swahili, is spoken more widely.

GEOGRAPHER'S CORNER

TRANSPORTATION ROUTES

South Africa leads Africa in the length of the tracks in its railroad system. But the limited number of railroads in the whole of Africa says nothing about their importance to the region. In fact, railroads may be more important in Africa than on any other continent. In landlocked nations where roads and cars are rare, keeping railroad lines open to the coast is a vital concern. Railroads make an easy target in the civil wars that trouble Africa.

Examine the map carefully and answer the questions.

1. Can you trace a complete railroad from Cairo to Cape Town?

2. Which nations of eastern and southern Africa appear to have no major railroads?

3. Of Africa's five culture regions, which one appears to have the largest concentration of railroads?

4. How many railroads cross from the Atlantic to the Indian Ocean? What countries do they pass through?

🔆 Outside South Africa, what port appears to be the most vital link in Africa's railroad system?

Principal Railroads of Africa

SEYCHELLES

The 115 tropical islands of the Seychelles (say SHELZ) are sprinkled in an archipelago northeast of Madagascar. About forty-one of these islands are granite mountains rising abruptly from the sea. The others are low coral islets and atolls. Mahé, the largest island, contains the capital and only town, Victoria. Ninety percent of the people live on Mahé, and most of the rest live on the nearby islands of Praslin and La Digue in the same northernmost group. The coral islands do not have any fresh water. The islands obtained independence in 1976 and have repelled attempts by rebels to overthrow the government.

The people of Seychelles are descendants of French settlers and African slaves that the French brought with them. Creole, English, and French are all official languages, but most people speak Creole. The education level is very high in the Seychelles. Eighty-eight percent of adults and 98 percent of children are literate. Almost 87 percent of the people are Catholic. Tourism and fishing are the strengths of the economy.

MAURITIUS

Mauritius (maw RISH us) is a volcanic island east of Madagascar. It is surrounded by coral reefs. Ruled in turn by the Dutch, French, and British, Mauritius opted to remain part of the British Commonwealth when it gained independence in 1968. Since independence, Mauritius has grown quickly in economic areas, such as banking, industry, and tourism.

Forty-eight percent of the population are Hindu, over 32 percent are considered broadly Christian, and about 17 percent are Muslim.

Sugar cane, the major crop of the island, tea, and molasses are exported. Both Mauritius and nearby Réunion, which voted to remain part of France, are tropical islands with booming tourist industries.

SECTION QUIZ

1. What two major deserts lie in southern Africa?
2. What river divided Northern and Southern Rhodesia? What are Northern and Southern Rhodesia called today?
3. What is the isolated region of Angola called?
4. Between what two countries is Victoria Falls located?
5. Of the four island nations, which is the largest?
   ☼ How has European imperialism left its mark on Namibia, Angola, Zimbabwe, and Seychelles?

II. EASTERN AFRICA

Africa's highest mountains and some of its most important ranges speckle the plateau in East Africa. The most impressive feature, however, is the **Great Rift Valley**. Beginning in the Middle East, this gash in the earth continues southward through East Africa. The valleys and lakes in the Great Rift Valley have been important since ancient times. East Africa shares many other features with the Middle East, located just across the Red Sea.

Another significant feature in the region is the Nile River and its tributaries, which flow west of the Great Rift Valley. The Nile is the

Eastern Africa Fast Facts

Flag	Country	Capital	Area (sq. mi.)	Pop. (M)	Pop. Density (per sq. mi.)	Per Capita GDP ($US)	Life Span
	Burundi	Bujumbura	10,745	8.09	752.9	$700	50.8
	Djibouti	Djibouti	8,880	0.49	54.8	$1,300	43.2
	Eritrea	Asmara	46,842	4.79	102.2	$1,000	59.0
	Ethiopia	Addis Ababa	435,186	74.78	171.8	$900	49.0
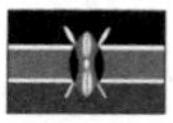	Kenya	Nairobi	224,962	34.71	154.3	$1,100	48.9
	Rwanda	Kigali	10,169	8.65	850.5	$1,500	47.3
	Somalia	Mogadishu	246,201	8.86	36.0	$600	48.5
	Sudan	Khartoum	967,499	41.24	42.6	$2,100	58.9
	Tanzania	Dar es Salaam	364,900	37.45	102.6	$700	45.6
	Uganda	Kampala	91,136	28.20	309.4	$1,800	52.7

longest river in the world. The source of this mighty river was long a mystery to Europeans. Two rivers join to form the Nile: the Blue Nile and the White Nile. In 1770 the daring Scottish explorer Robert Bruce found the source of the **Blue Nile** at the Geesh Springs in the mountains of Ethiopia. Bruce's book about his adventures sparked the modern exploration of Africa. The source of the **White Nile**, the longer of the two tributaries, lay hidden until 1862 when John Speke, a British officer, pushing ever deeper into the interior, traced the source to **Lake Victoria**. We now know that the Nile begins in Burundi on the Ruvubu River, which empties into Lake Victoria. From Lake Victoria, the water makes its way to Sudan, where it becomes the White Nile.

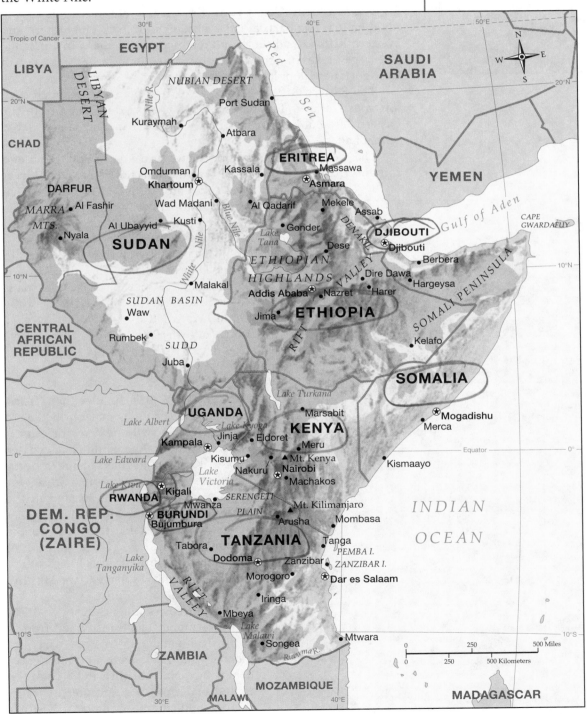

Rift Valleys of Africa

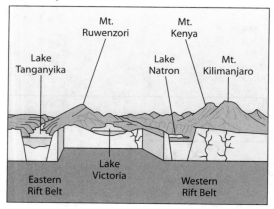

LAKES REGION

Think of wild lions, giraffes, elephants, zebras, and rhinoceroses roaming freely. If you've seen footage or photographs like this, chances are they were taken in the large nations of Kenya and Tanzania, which border the Indian Ocean south of the Horn of Africa. Although these two countries do not have a monopoly on wildlife, they are the location of many big-game safaris, Jeep tours, and wildlife documentaries. Grasses and scattered trees cover the savannas of these countries. In the west, Kenya and Tanzania share the lakes of the Great Rift Valley with three smaller countries—Uganda, Rwanda, and Burundi—where mountain gorillas roam.

The Great Rift Valley runs through the interior of this region, dividing into two parts at Lake Turkana in Kenya. The Eastern and Western Rifts extend south and rejoin at Lake Malawi in Tanzania. The largest lakes in Africa lie in this rift region. This area is a hub of transportation, population, and industry.

The Eastern Rift runs from Lake Turkana south through such towns as Nakuru, Tabora, and Mbeya. Many salt lakes lie in the Eastern Rift, but Lake Turkana is the only one included in the seven "Great Lakes."

The Western Rift runs along the western edge of East Africa and contains five great lakes. Lake Edward drains north into Lake Albert and then into the Nile River. Lake Kivu drains into Lake Tanganyika and then west into the Congo River. Lake Malawi drains south into the Zambezi River.

The land between these rifts drops to form a large basin containing the Serengeti Plain and Lake Victoria. Lake Victoria is the second-largest freshwater lake in the world. Waters from Lake Victoria flow north into the White Nile. Three countries have coastlines on this vital lake.

KENYA

Kenya is a little smaller than Texas, but its advanced cities make it the key to East Africa. The wildlife here draws tourists from all over the world. The equator crosses Kenya, and most of the country experiences hot temperatures. Most people live in the highlands located in the southwest, where the air is a little cooler and more comfortable than it is on the coastal lowlands. Forty-five percent of the people are Protestant, 33 percent are Roman Catholic, 10 percent are Muslim, and 10 percent are animists.

Since Kenya's independence in 1963, the government has transitioned from a multiparty democracy to a one-party democracy and back again to a multiparty democracy. **Nairobi** (nye ROH bee), the capital of Kenya, is the center of trade, finance, and communication for East Af-

Languages of Africa

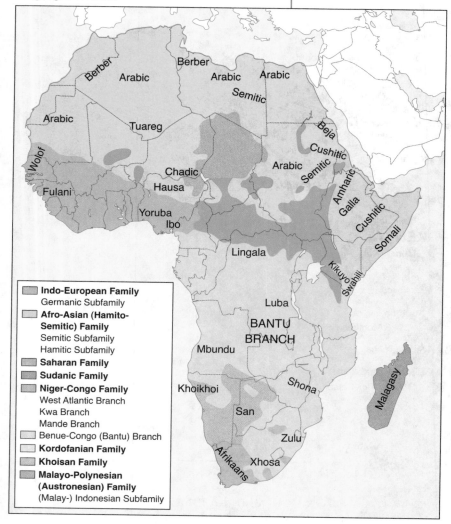

Indo-European Family
  Germanic Subfamily
Afro-Asian (Hamito-Semitic) Family
  Semitic Subfamily
  Hamitic Subfamily
Saharan Family
Sudanic Family
Niger-Congo Family
  West Atlantic Branch
  Kwa Branch
  Mande Branch
  Benue-Congo (Bantu) Branch
Kordofanian Family
Khoisan Family
Malayo-Polynesian (Austronesian) Family
  (Malay-) Indonesian Subfamily

Swahili

The people on the east coast of Africa traded frequently with Arab merchants long before the first Portuguese ships arrived. The language that developed between the coastal people and the Arabs was a hodgepodge of Arabic and Bantu languages called **Swahili** (swah HEE lee). Later, Swahili incorporated some Portuguese and English words, such as *blanketi*. English has gained some words from Swahili too, such as *safari* and *impala*.

Swahili has since become a *lingua franca* in East Africa. It is one of the two official languages of Tanzania and Kenya and is spoken by at least thirty-five million people as a first or second language. Yet even Swahili has many dialects. Missionaries who translated the Bible into Swahili developed what is now the East Africa Standard version of Swahili. Although there is talk of making Swahili the common tongue of Africa, English is more common in colleges and printed media.

rica. Kenya's economy is based on a variety of industries ranging from tourism and agriculture to mining and manufacturing.

Nairobi—Nairobi is the second-largest city in the Lakes region. Situated on a plateau at an elevation of about 5,500 feet, Nairobi has a cool climate compared to other cities near the equator. This modern city lies in its own capital district, separate from the seven provinces of Kenya. The government stationed here has been one of the more stable African governments since the country's independence from Britain in 1963. It has had only three presidents since gaining independence.

Lacking mineral resources, Kenya has built small industries. The one-half million tourists every year, however, provide far more money to the economy. The government has set aside over thirty-five parks and game reserves across the nation to protect the wildlife that draws these tourists. Nairobi National Park, on the outskirts of the capital, enables sightseers to photograph wild lions and giraffes with the skyscrapers in the background.

East Kenya—Mombasa is the largest port and capital of the Coast Province. The mangrove swamps, lagoons, and rain forests look much like coasts in West Africa, but they are interspersed with fine beaches and groves of coconut palms. The Northeastern Province lies along Kenya's border with Somalia. These hot lowlands are dry except for the Lorian Swamp. This province is the least populated in Kenya, with less than one million people.

The Eastern Province rises from the low Coast and Northeastern provinces in tiers. The grassy plains have the driest climate in the nation. The Chalbi and Dida Galgalu deserts lie east of Lake Turkana at the northern border. The main towns of Meru and Machakos lie on the higher elevations (4,000 ft.) toward the west. The province has eight national game reserves and parts of seven national parks.

West Kenya—West Kenya is dominated by high plateaus and mountains. The agricultural lands in the highlands are very fertile. The production of coffee and tea in this area is very important, since it is the only part of the national economy (other than tourism) that provides significant foreign income.

Kenya's highest peak lies in the Central Province and is just north of Nairobi. Mount Kenya (17,058 ft.) is the second-highest mountain in Africa. In the west is the Nyanza (or Lake) Province on

Over half of the world's flamingoes live in Africa. Flamingoes congregate together all along the lakes of Africa's Eastern Rift.

Lake Victoria. Kisumu, Kenya's third-largest city and the chief port on Lake Victoria, is located here.

Of Kenya's many national parks and reserves, two are quite famous. Amboseli National Park, on the southern border, offers spectacular views of Tanzania's snowcapped peak, Mount Kilimanjaro, which rises above the savanna. Masai Mara Game Reserve, Kenya's portion of the Serengeti, is home to the **Masai** (mah SYE) tribe. The nomadic Masai people are famous for their ritual dances and skills as warriors.

TANZANIA

Germany established a colony called German East Africa in the late nineteenth century, preventing Great Britain from controlling a continuous string of land along Africa's east coast. It held the colony until the British took over after World War I. The land was known as Tanganyika when it became independent in 1961. The name changed to Tanzania when the island of Zanzibar joined it in 1964. Over 120 ethnic groups live in Tanzania, and Swahili is the common language. English is also an official language, and Arabic is commonly spoken in Zanzibar.

Tanzania and the island of Zanzibar elect separate presidents. While the president of Tanzania controls foreign policy of the whole country and internal matters relating to the mainland and Mafia Island, the president of Zanzibar controls the internal matters of Zanzibar. The economy has struggled over the last few years, and steps have been taken to stimulate the economy.

Tanzania is much like Kenya. Game reserves cover one-fourth of the country. The coastal region has mangrove swamps and beaches. Dar es Salaam is the largest port. In 1996 the Parliament moved inland from Dar es Salaam to Dodoma, making Dodoma the legislative capital of the country. The executive capital remains in Dar es Salaam at present. From the first inland plateau at Morogoro, the land rises to Iringa and Dodoma. North of Dodoma is the Masai Steppe, where the Masai live and herd their cattle.

Also as in Kenya, highlands cover western Tanzania. **Mount Kilimanjaro** (kil uh mun JAHR oh) rises to 19,340 feet near the border with Kenya. This massive volcanic peak is the highest mountain in Africa. Snow falls on this mountain even though it is near the equator. West of Arusha is Serengeti National Park and Ngorongoro Crater. More wildlife is concentrated at this crater than in any other area in Africa.

Farther west lies the largest lake in all of Africa, Lake Victoria. Tanzania's main lake port, Mwanza, is located on the southern border of Lake Victoria. The best soils also lie around this lake. Farmers produce coffee, tobacco, rice, and maize. Tanzania's main port on Lake Tanganyika is the small town of Kigoma, near the border with Burundi. Four miles away at the town of Ujiji, the reporter Henry M. Stanley discovered David Livingstone, whose whereabouts had become a mystery. Their encounter on October 28, 1871, began with the now-famous words "Dr. Livingstone, I presume."

Zanzibar, Pemba, and Mafia are three large tropical islands off the coast. **Zanzibar** was once

Ngorongoro Crater

Near the Serengeti Plains, a volcanic crater, Ngorongoro Crater (en GORE on GORE oh), rises above the plains, creating a lost world bounded by rugged crater walls. The lakes in the crater provide homes for hippopotami, and the grasslands of the crater provide grazing for all the species of the Serengeti.

Mount Kilimanjaro dominates the horizon behind this portion of Amboseli National Park, Kenya.

the Arabs' largest slave-trading port in East Africa. It was also the largest producer of cloves, supplying 80 percent of the world's needs. Today, it is a resort area, and it guards its autonomy by making visitors from the mainland pass through customs. Unlike the rest of the country, Zanzibaris sometimes clamor for full independence. Most of the people who live in Zanzibar are Muslims.

UGANDA

Uganda (yoo GAHN duh) lies on a plateau averaging about 5,000 feet of elevation in the south and 3,000 feet in the north. The northeast has a volcanic range. Savanna covers the rest of the northern region, while the region around Lake Victoria in the south offers the best farmlands. The capital and main port, Kampala, lies on the northern edge of Lake Victoria. Owen Falls Dam at Jinja is a dam on Lake Victoria.

Highlands cover the southeast. The Ruwenzori Mountains, or Mountains of the Moon, are located on Uganda's western border and stretch from Lake Edward to Lake Albert. These mountains are very

SERENGETI PLAIN

The **Serengeti Plain** (SER un GET ee) has more large land animals than any other place on earth. It is also the only place left in the world where vast herds of large mammals still migrate. For these reasons, the Serengeti National Park in Tanzania is the most famous national park in all of Africa.

All five of the famous African big-game animals—lions, elephants, rhinoceroses, cape buffalos, and leopards—are now protected in the 5,700-square-mile park. Both elephants and rhinos are endangered because of poachers.

Wildebeest migrate one thousand miles north across the Serengeti every year to spend the dry season around Kenya's Masai-Mara Game Reserve. The wildebeest, or gnu, has a funny appearance, with the mane and tail of a horse, beard of a goat, and horns of an ox; but it can run fifty miles per hour. About two hundred thousand zebras often migrate with the over one million wildebeests, which provide safety in numbers. Nevertheless, danger lurks at every turn. Lions attack from the high grasses, cheetahs from rock outcroppings, leopards from trees, and huge crocodiles from the rivers and water holes.

Many other animals live on the Serengeti Plain, such as the impala,

The Serengeti Plain is home to a number of famous species of animals.

topi, eland, and the dik-dik (the smallest antelope in the world). Foxes, jackals, gazelles, giraffes, baboons, and monkeys also roam the park, while vultures, storks, and egrets soar overhead. Hyenas compete with vultures for leftovers from lion kills. Packs of wild dogs are excellent hunters, succeeding even more often than lions. Cheetahs, which reach speeds of sixty miles per hour, are the fastest animals in the world.

Is the Serengeti National Park a waste of land that could be developed? Some people may think so, but the Christian has good reasons to support the park. First, the park protects natural wildlife in its habitat. Preservation is an act of wise dominion that makes use of the natural resources God has given us. When the land is preserved, animals and plants can flourish with limited interference from humans and environmental intrusions. Humans can then admire the beauty of nature and observe the natural order God has implemented in this ecosystem.

rugged, remote, and enshrouded by clouds most of the time. Mountain gorillas draw many tourists to the area.

Uganda has been independent from Britain since 1962, but it has found little peace. A brutal dictator named Idi Amin ruled the land from 1971 to 1979, killing thousands of his opponents. After his overthrow, conditions continued to be unstable and oppressive. Yoweri Museveni, the leader of the National Resistance Army, took power in 1985. Museveni became president and was reelected for his third term in 2006. Some of the voters in Uganda, though, have been suspected of fraud.

Museveni's government has strengthened the economy of Uganda. The inflation has stabilized at a low level, and foreign investment has risen. The economy is based on agriculture and related industries. However, there is an attempt to shift from agricultural industries to construction industries.

RWANDA

Landlocked Rwanda (roo AHN duh) is almost the size of Maryland. Plateaus cover the nation, rising highest in the west. The western border follows the Great Rift Valley. In the northwest corner, Volcanoes National Park provides a home to half of the world's remaining mountain gorillas. Farther south on Rwanda's western border lies Lake Kivu. About in the center of the country is the capital, Kigali. The Kagera River forms the border on the east. Agriculture is a major part of Rwanda's economy. Forty percent of Rwanda is arable, and another 20 percent is able to support livestock. Rwanda is heavily dependent on foreign aid.

Rwanda has a high population density, with over eight hundred people per square mile. Most people speak Kinyarwanda (a Bantu language), but French and English are also official languages. According to the last survey, 56 percent of the people are Roman Catholic, 37 percent are Protestant, and 5 percent are Muslim or some other religion.

Mountain gorillas, like this young one, are at the brink of extinction.

The Hutus constitute 84 percent of all Rwandans, and most are subsistence farmers. One percent of the people belong to the Twa, a Pygmy tribe. The Tutsis (or Watusi), typically over six feet tall, were traditionally cattle herders who ruled as feudal lords over the Hutus. They now account for 15 percent of the population. In a bloody civil war in 1959, the Hutus wrested control from the ruling Tutsis. In 1962, the nation gained independence from Belgium, but tribal conflicts continued.

In 1990, the Tutsis began a civil war with the Hutus. A ceasefire was reached two years later. In 1994, following the murder of the presidents of Rwanda and Burundi, the killing began again and climaxed with one of the worst cases of genocide in recent years. Hutus began killing Tutsis and political moderates, even other Hutus. The genocide cost over 800,000 lives. With international assistance, the Tutsis managed to restore order. Rwanda has not settled on peaceful ways, though, and has engaged in wars with neighbors since that time.

BURUNDI

Like Rwanda, Burundi (boo ROON dee) is a small country with a large population. Most of Burundi is a large plateau that rises to 9,055 feet. The Ruvubu River and the Rusizi River, at the western border, flow through the country. Lake Tanganyika lies on Burundi's western border, supplying the country with over ten thousand tons of fish annually. The capital, Bujumbura, lies at the head of this lake.

Swamps along the southern coast breed deadly insects, such as the tsetse fly. Coffee is the major exported crop for both Rwanda and Burundi, but overseas trade is difficult for both landlocked nations. Burundi has natural resources, but these resources have been largely untapped.

Burundi received independence from Belgium in 1962 and has two official languages: French and Kirundi, a Bantu language. It has the same tribal divisions as Rwanda. Unlike their Rwandan counterparts, however, Burundi's Tutsi minority retained rule until losing multiparty elections in 1993. The Tutsi army officers kept power in the army and restored Tutsi control in 1996. From 2001 to 2005, the government underwent a transition period and seems to have stabilized.

SECTION QUIZ

1. What are two significant features of East Africa?
2. What city is the center of trade, finance, and communication in East Africa? What country is it located in?
3. What is Africa's highest mountain? What nation contains it?
4. What important mountain range lies on Uganda's western border?
⚬ Why are national parks important in the Lakes Region?

THE HORN OF AFRICA

On the east side of Africa, the wide Somali Peninsula jabs toward the Middle East. Because the peninsula is shaped like an animal horn, the region is often called the **Horn of Africa**. The four nations in this area are closely linked. Some of the countries in this region have been devastated by war and famine, resulting in very poor economies.

The waters of the Red Sea actually lie in part of the Great Rift Valley, which continues down into the north coast of the Horn of Africa. Many places in the Great Rift Valley are far below sea level. The hot, dry lowlands near the coast are part of the **Denakil Desert**. One spot in Eritrea plummets to 246 feet below sea level. Another spot in Ethiopia is 410 feet below sea level. But the valley falls to its lowest point down the coast in the tiny country of Djibouti. Here beside Lake Assal, the Denakil Desert sinks 509 feet below sea level. It is the lowest spot in Africa.

ETHIOPIA

In Africa, only Nigeria and Egypt have more people than Ethiopia (EE thee OH pee uh). In addition to Ethiopia's large population, its unique history and geography have given it a special place in Africa's growing sense of pride. Ethiopia is one of only two nations in Africa that no foreign nation has ever successfully colonized. The rough terrain of the Ethiopian Highlands provided refuge from advancing empires. In 1896 at the Battle of Adwa, Ethiopia became the first black African nation to win a war against a European colonial power when it defeated Italy. In the 1930s under Mussolini, Italy sought

LET'S GO EXPLORING

LAND USE OF AFRICA

1. What economic activity is most common in both East Africa and North Africa?

2. What type of farming is common on the Nile River?

3. Where can you find mediterranean agriculture?

4. What type of commercial farming is common in the Sahara?

5. What type of commercial farming is common in the Congo Basin?

◦̣- Which African country has the widest variety of economic activity?

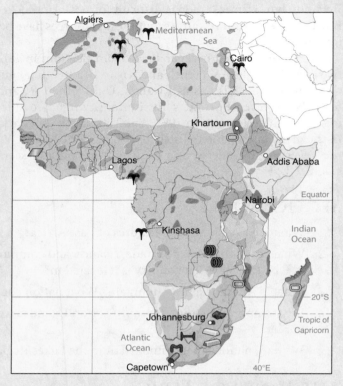

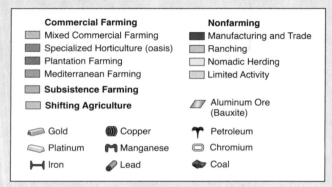

Commercial Farming	Nonfarming
Mixed Commercial Farming	Manufacturing and Trade
Specialized Horticulture (oasis)	Ranching
Plantation Farming	Nomadic Herding
Mediterranean Farming	Limited Activity
Subsistence Farming	
Shifting Agriculture	Aluminum Ore (Bauxite)

Gold	Copper	Petroleum
Platinum	Manganese	Chromium
Iron	Lead	Coal

revenge and invaded Ethiopia. The temporary conquest ended a few years later when Italy lost World War II.

Haile Selassie, the last emperor of Ethiopia, who ruled from 1930 to 1974, began developing modern industries. Discontent grew, however, because the people did not benefit equally. Several droughts and famines added to the turmoil. Marxist rebels supported by the Soviet Union overthrew Selassie, and Ethiopia endured a military rule from 1974 to 1991, when rebel groups united and overthrew the junta. Ethiopia held its first multiparty elections in 1995.

North and central Ethiopia is a rugged highland plateau. The **Ethiopian Highlands** rise to 15,158 feet at Ras Dejen in the far north. With such towering peaks, the highlands stay cool and receive large amounts of rainfall. The Blue Nile begins in Lake Tana and circles through the northern highlands before its descent west to the Sudan. Most Ethiopians live in the highlands because of the cooler climate and fertile soil. Farmers produce corn, wheat, cotton, coffee, and sugar cane. Ethiopia is the legendary home of the coffee bean, from the town of Kaffa in the southwest. Coffee is Ethiopia's top agricultural export.

Like other isolated highlands of the world, Ethiopia has a diversity of peoples—at least one hundred ethnic groups and over seventy languages. Amharic, the language of the last emperors, is the official language. Almost 40 percent of Ethiopia's people are Christian, 45 percent are Muslim, and the rest are a mix of tribal religions. Most of the Christians belong to the Ethiopian Orthodox Church, which is similar to the Copts in Egypt. The ancient language Ge'ez is used in the church services of the Ethiopian Orthodox Church, yet there has been a recent shift to using Amharic.

The capital, **Addis Ababa** (AD-is AB-uh-buh), stands on the plateau at the center of the nation. With over three million people, this city is the largest within the four nations of the Horn of Africa. The various heads of state in Africa met at Addis Ababa in 1963 and chartered the Organization of African Unity (OAU), to promote the common good of the continent. The OAU became the **African Union (AU)** in 2002, yet the headquarters of the AU remain in Addis Ababa.

This Amhara boy is a herder in the Ethiopian Highlands.

The Great Rift Valley cuts through Ethiopia south of the capital. Ethiopia has roads connecting it to all of its neighboring countries, but only one vital railroad links Addis Ababa to Djibouti through the Great Rift Valley. The part of the valley that continues southwest from the capital into Kenya contains several small salt lakes with no outlets.

The southeastern part of Ethiopia is called the **Ogaden**. This section is one of the hot, dry lowlands along the Ethiopian border. The Somalis who live in the city of Kelafo and the surrounding plains of Ogaden are Muslim. Britain allowed Emperor Selassie to annex the region in 1948; but after Somalia gained independence in 1960, Ethiopia had to fight Somalia to keep Ogaden. Even today, the Somalis still want independence. A lowland similar to Ogaden lies along the west border. Animists, speaking Nilo-Saharan languages, live in this region.

ERITREA

The geography of Eritrea (EHR ih TREE uh) is dominated by a central plateau that rises to almost 10,000 feet at Mount Soira. In the west, the elevation does not rise as high. A plain extends the length of Eritrea's coast on the Red Sea. Off the coast of Eritrea's mainland, the Dahlak Archipelago, consisting of more than 100 islands, also belongs to Eritrea.

The Denakil Desert in the south has oil, which is refined at Assab. But most of the people live in desperate poverty as a result of the long war—the longest war for independence ever fought in Africa. The people are evenly divided between Muslim seminomads, who live on the coast, and Christians (mostly Ethiopian Orthodox), who raise crops in the highlands. The economy is based largely on agriculture. Other prominent industries include ship repair and construction materials.

In 1889, Eritrea became an Italian colony. After World War II, the United Nations made Eritrea an autonomous territory under the Ethiopian crown. But when Ethiopia annexed Eritrea outright in 1952, Eritrea revolted. A bitter struggle ensued for about forty years. After Ethiopia's Marxist government collapsed in 1991, Eritrea voted to gain its independence in 1993. Eritrea has set up a stable government, but border disagreements with Ethiopia persist.

Djibouti

The little country of Djibouti (jih BOO tee), almost the size of Massachusetts, lies at a strategic spot on the coast of Africa. It guards the **Bab al-Mandeb** (BAB ul MAN-DUB), the twenty-mile-wide entrance to the Red Sea. Djibouti was once called French Somaliland, a strategic colony that France took in 1864. Djibouti received its independence in 1977. Though civil war plagued Djibouti from 1992 to 1994, the government has been generally stable since that time.

Most citizens of Djibouti live in the capital city, also named Djibouti. The capital is a convenient stop for ships sailing between the Indian Ocean and the Mediterranean Sea. International transportation is the backbone of the economy. Ethiopia relies on the railroad from Addis Ababa to ship goods, especially coffee, through this key port.

With few natural resources, rural people eke out a living raising camels on the bleak and barren landscape. Very little of the land is suitable for farming, so Djibouti relies on other countries to supply its food. The country's population is split between the Somalis and the Afars. Ninety-four percent of the people embrace Islam. French and Arabic are the official languages.

Somalia

Somalia (soh MAHL ee uh) occupies the east coast of the Horn of Africa. In ancient times, it was called Punt (or Put, as in Nahum 3:9). Italy gained control of much of Somaliland in the late nineteenth century. In 1960 the Italian and British Somaliland territories joined to form the nation of Somalia. Since then, Somalia has alienated all three of its neighbor nations by trying to annex portions where Somalis live. It invaded Ethiopia in 1977 and refused to sign a peace treaty until 1988.

Northern Somalia has many hills. Some of these reach as high as 7,000 feet above sea level. On the northwest coast of the Gulf of Aden lies the Guban, a coastal plain. Nomads herd livestock in this area. Southern Somalia is much more flat than the north. Average elevation in this area is less than 600 feet. This southern area has some arable land watered by two rivers. The rivers join and empty into the Indian Ocean at Kismayu. The capital, Mogadishu, lies near the northern end of the arable region.

The people of Somalia share the same ethnic and cultural background. The vast majority are Somalis, a black African tribe that speaks the Somali language. Somalis are Muslim and keep close ties to Saudi Arabia, which buys Somali fruit and livestock.

In spite of its ethnic unity, the region has suffered from constant internal strife between clans. In 1991 the government disintegrated, and clan warfare engulfed the south. Two years later, famine laid waste to the land. Later that year, the UN sent troops into Somalia to restore peace. However, the United States pulled its troops out after fifteen Americans died in a raid to capture one of the clan leaders. The UN withdrew in 1995, and anarchy and famine returned to

In this satellite shot, the Red Sea is the northern body of water, and the Gulf of Aden is the southern body of water. Separating them is the narrow waterway of Bab al-Mandeb.

Somalia. In 2004, a transitional government was formed, bringing some hope for the war-ravaged country.

About the same time as the government disintegrated in 1991, northwestern Somalia—former British Somaliland—declared itself an independent nation, the Somaliland Republic, but no foreign country has recognized it. Somaliland has a stronger economy than the rest of Somalia. In 2003, the region elected a president, and in 2005 it elected a legislature.

SECTION QUIZ

1. The Horn of Africa is the name for what peninsula?
2. What four nations compose the Horn of Africa?
3. What East African country was never successfully colonized by a European power?
4. What is the name of the entrance to the Red Sea?
- ☀ Have ethnic and religious differences been the primary causes of civil war in the Horn of Africa? If not, what has been the main cause?

SUDAN

Sudan (soo DAN), the largest country in Africa, shares many similarities with Egypt, its northern neighbor. Egypt controlled Sudan in ancient times. During the Middle Ages, Arabs conquered Egypt and pushed south into Sudan, bringing their religion and language with them. Most Sudanese today speak Arabic, the official language. About one-half of the population is black, and Arabs constitute nearly 40 percent of the populace. Muslims make up 70 percent of the population and are centered primarily in the north. Another quarter of Sudan's population is animist and found in the south.

Egypt regained control of Sudan in the early nineteenth century. The Sudanese threw off Egyptian rule briefly, but British and Egyptian forces combined in 1898 to subdue the rebels. Sudan gained independence in 1956, but military coups and civil war between the Muslims in the north and animists and Christians in the south hindered development for almost 50 years. The Muslims in northern Sudan were attempting to impose Islamic law, or *sharia*, in the southern highlands where the animists and Christians primarily dwell. Today, both north and south have a part in the Sudanese government.

Beginning in 2003, Sudan was also scarred by genocide in the western Darfur region. The fighting took place between two Muslim ethnic groups. A ceasefire was signed in 2004, but the fighting persisted. Diplomatic negotiations continued into 2005. The struggle in Darfur has claimed over 200,000 lives and displaced about two million.

Because of the various wars in Sudan, the country has struggled to establish its economy. The wars hindered the development of an infrastructure that could support the nation in times of peace. Sudan still has great economic potential, though, thanks to the discovery of oil in northern Sudan. The country also hopes to increase its hydroelectric power by building a new dam on the Nile. The chief crops in Sudan are grain, sorghum, millet, wheat, cotton, and gum arabic. Crop development is currently limited by a lack of irrigation.

Through Christian Eyes

The killings in the Darfur region of Sudan occurred over several years. Some groups refused to acknowledge it or label it as genocide. The influence of celebrities and human rights groups eventually drew attention to the situation, although many thousands had died by that time. What should have been the Christians' response?

NORTHERN DESERT

The land area of Sudan is equivalent to over one-quarter of the area of the United States, but large areas are desert or swamp. From Khartoum, the capital, the Nile flows north toward Egypt into the Sahara. The Libyan Desert lies to the west and the Nubian Desert to the east. Port Sudan is the only major port on the Red Sea in the northeast. The people are subsistence farmers, most of whom live along the Nile.

The Nile flows over six falls or rapids, called **cataracts** (KAT uh RAKT). The First Cataract is at Egypt's Aswan Dam, but the rest are in Sudan. The cataracts prevent ships from sailing up the river, isolating Sudan from the civilization in Egypt.

KHARTOUM

Khartoum, a center of industry in Sudan, sits in the heart of the country, where the White Nile and Blue Nile branches join to form the main Nile River. The city has two main parts. North Khartoum lies across the Blue Nile, and Omdurman is located across the White Nile. Over five and a half million people live in this metropolitan area.

CENTRAL SAVANNAS

Sudan gets its name from the Sahel, which rises in the center of the country, south of the deserts. The term *Sudan* originally referred to the entire Sahel. (Mali was called French Sudan in colonial times.) Herders raise sheep, goats, and cattle on the savannas of the Sahel. Camels provide transportation as well as milk and meat.

The El Gezira Plain lies in the central savannas between the Blue Nile and the White Nile. The Blue Nile flows from the highlands on the eastern border of Sudan, where heavy summer rains cause floods and carry silt downstream to Khartoum. The silt makes the plain the most fertile area in the country. Cotton is one of the country's chief agricultural products and a major export. The seasonal floods of the Blue Nile still affect Sudan.

SOUTHERN SUDAN

The White Nile flows to the west of the Blue Nile across southern Sudan and is called the Mountain Nile between Juba and Malakal. The White Nile does not flood because its waters spread out over a large marsh called the **Sudd**. These shallow wetlands cover an area the size of Maine, and much water is lost through evaporation. Rain forests lie along Sudan's southern border.

SECTION QUIZ

1. What is the largest country in Africa?
2. What are the two main branches of the Nile?
3. What did *Sudan* originally refer to?
4. What swampy area borders the White Nile?
 💡 How does Sudan form a transition zone between Egypt and eastern Africa?

Sudanese farmers have implemented irrigation plans in the El Gezira Plain.

Jonglei Canal

Egypt is helping Sudan build the Jonglei Canal so that the Nile will bypass the Sudd. By reducing evaporation, both countries will obtain more water for irrigation. The canal has become a hotbed of controversy, however, with some scientists pointing out the dangers of changing the natural habitats of many of the creatures in the area. Does this show a wise exercise of stewardship? Why or why not?

CHAPTER REVIEW 13

HOW MUCH DO YOU REMEMBER?

1. What geographical feature has divided Africa and, consequently, had the greatest effect on the continent?

2. Name four important rivers of southern and eastern Africa.

3. List three major deserts found in southern and eastern Africa.

4. In what country would you find each feature: Drakensberg Mountains? Ruwenzori? Serengeti Plain? Okavango Delta?

5. What waterfall makes an impressive plunge on the Zambezi River?

6. Match each feature with the country to which it is most closely related.

   1. an unusual island   a. Tanzania
   2. apartheid   b. Somalia
   3. Nile's cataracts   c. Namibia
   4. Mount Kilimanjaro   d. South Africa
   5. copper   e. Kenya
   6. Masai   f. Sudan
   7. Horn of Africa   g. Madagascar
   8. Skeleton Coast   h. Zambia

7. What two countries formed Rhodesia?

8. Who are the Afrikaners, and where did they come from?

WHAT DO YOU THINK?

1. What are the dangers of living in a southern or eastern African country?

2. Why is having an ocean port so important for a country?

3. What have been the effects of imperialism on southern and eastern Africa?

Can You:
Define These Terms?

sub-Saharan Africa	apartheid
savanna	Swahili
escarpment	cataract
Afrikaans	

Locate These Places?

Cape of Good Hope	Victoria Falls
Orange River	Great Rift Valley
Drakensberg Mountains	Blue Nile
Tugela Falls	White Nile
veldt	Lake Victoria
Limpopo River	Mount Kilimanjaro
Thabana Ntlenyana	Serengeti Plain
Kalahari Desert	Horn of Africa
Okavango Delta	Denakil Desert
Namib Desert	Ethiopian Highlands
Zambezi River	Sudd

Explain the Significance?

Cape Town	Cabinda
Zulu	Great Zimbabwe
Boers	Nairobi
Bantu	Masai
Afrikaners	Zanzibar
Johannesburg	Addis Ababa
Pretoria	African Union (AU)
Nelson Mandela	Ogaden
San	Bab al-Mandeb
Skeleton Coast	

CHAPTER 14

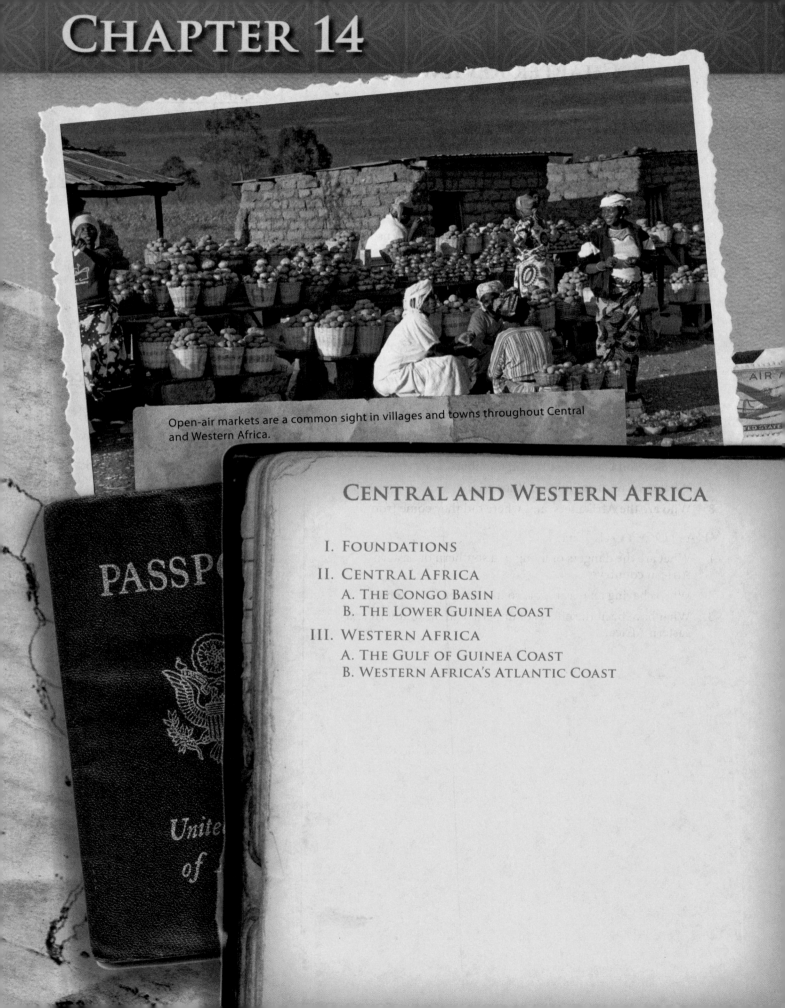

Open-air markets are a common sight in villages and towns throughout Central and Western Africa.

CENTRAL AND WESTERN AFRICA

All of the lands below the Sahara are called **sub-Saharan Africa**. As you learned in the last chapter, the environment and cultures there differ radically from the north. For example, North Africa suffers from too little rain; the nations farther south suffer from too much rain or unpredictable rains. Another obvious difference is the prevalence of the black race in sub-Saharan Africa. But many other differences also exist, as you will learn in comparing the countries in this chapter with those in northern Africa in the next chapter.

I. FOUNDATIONS

Except for a strip of the Sahel in the north (discussed in the next chapter), jungles and savannas dominate the landscape and lifestyles of the twenty nations in central and western Africa. The equator runs through the center of this region. Regular winds off the Atlantic continually dump rain along the equator, just as they do in the Amazon River Basin. A few degrees north and south of the equator, the winds shift, creating a rainy season and a dry season. A savanna rises there.

Unlike mediterranean climates and river valleys in the Sahel, tropical rain forests and dry savannas cannot generally support intensive agriculture. Typically, the people are hunters and gatherers, sometimes practicing slash-and-burn agriculture to supplement their meager existence. Their simple agriculture permits the existence of small villages, but there is not enough food to support large groups in one place.

The **village** is an important concept in understanding life in Africa. In the traditional African village, each person plays a vital role in the survival of the whole community. Having more than one wife is a sign of wealth, so polygamy is common. Young children pull weeds or sort vegetables; older children herd livestock or do household chores. At a certain age (twelve or thirteen in some cultures, fifteen to twenty in others), young men and women go through **initiation rites**. Those rites, which usually involve a multiple-step process, include hunts, dances, and ceremonies with masks, to mark their transition into adulthood. The men under age thirty-five traditionally protect the village; older men govern.

The foundation of African society is the tribal village, such as this one in Rhoumsiki, Cameroon.

Loyalty to the village extends to larger social units. Several villages that trace their descent to a common ancestor form a clan. Two or more clans, in turn, form a tribe. A headman wields the highest authority in the village. A strong tribal **chief** unites several villages, using headmen as his administrators.

Whenever people are isolated in small groups, their speech patterns diverge quickly. Dialects arise and then turn into new languages. Although Africa has only one-tenth of the people of the world, it has one-third of the languages. Strong identification with a tribe that speaks the same language or dialect is called **tribalism**. In spite of European influence, tribalism continues to be a central feature of sub-Saharan Africa. Individuals feel more allegiance to their tribe than to their nation-state.

Through Christian Eyes

What are some positive and negative aspects of tribalism?

African Animism

Religious animists believe that all things—rocks, trees, water, sun, owls, snakes, thunderstorms—have a spirit and that these spirits, not God and not man, are in charge of this world. Therefore, man is no more important than anything else—a tree or a pig, for instance. A person must perform certain religious rituals or the spirits will become angry and he will experience bad luck. There are other rituals he must perform in worship of the objects whose spirits he believes are dominant in his locality. This will please the spirits and bring him good luck.

Religious animism is practiced to some degree in every African country. African converts to Christianity often attempt to merely add Christianity to their animistic beliefs. They attend worship services, pray, sing, and give to have good luck or to avoid bad luck. Why is animism so enduring? It seems that many professing Christians in Africa have only a "head knowledge" of Christ. They believe that Jesus died and rose again, but in their hearts they are not confident that God is in control of everything. They want to be known as followers of Jesus because they believe that Jesus is God's Son. But they still live in fear of evil spirits and think that they must daily work to appease them. True Christianity, however, releases people from such fear, affirming what Christ said of Himself when He returned to heaven: "All power is given unto me in heaven and on earth" (Matt. 28:18).

Fear of demonic spirits dominates tribal religions, and Africans have developed many rituals to appease the spirits. The tribal religions of Africa follow **animism** (Latin *anima*), the worship of the "souls" of animals, rivers, trees, and other objects. Superstitious and demonic practices are still common. The shamans in Africa, called witch doctors, communicate with spirits, offer healing, and use sorcery. Sub-Saharan Africa has the largest remaining area of tribal religions in the world today.

European **colonialism** brought radical changes to life in sub-Saharan Africa, some good but some bad. The people now have a mixture of traditional ways and modern Western ways. People in the cities wear clothing reflecting both African and Western styles, and they shop in both department stores and street markets. Cities have modern hospitals, schools, industries, homes, and entertainment. In contrast, villages lack electricity and plumbing, and villagers often prefer witch doctors to medical clinics.

Imperialism in Africa After World War I

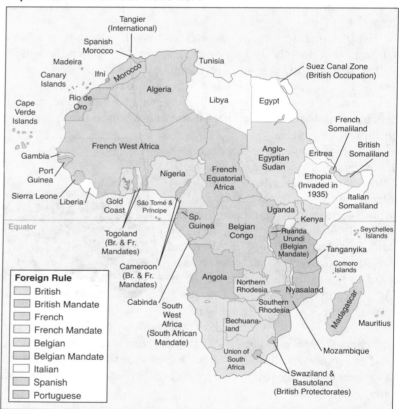

Although the people in the twenty nations of central and western Africa still speak their various tribal languages, the *official* language of each nation usually is the language of the most recent European ruler. Two of these African countries speak Portuguese, the language of the first colonial power in the region. One nation speaks Spanish. But the majority speak French and English.

Europeans introduced modern economic and political ideas and most modern industries. Plantations are now common in the rain forests near the coast. Lumbering and plantations, however, have stripped much of the rain forest. Colonialism began to break down after World War II. Independence came as early as the 1950s for some former colonies. Others did not gain their independence until the 1960s and 1970s. Many countries struggled with independence, and civil wars and coups were not uncommon. In some countries, Marxist leaders came with independence. In others, tribal strife led to political instability. Sub-Saharan Africa became a battleground between Marxists and capitalists.

Autocrats ruled their governments with an iron hand, sometimes allowing elections but not allowing competitive political parties. Today, corruption and self-advancing rulers are perhaps the greatest problems hindering the establishment of free governments in the region.

The end of the Cold War in 1989 brought new hope to this troubled land. Autocrats could no longer count on aid from Communists or from free nations that were willing to overlook the corruption because they need anti-Communist allies. In 1991, Benin became the first nation on mainland Africa ever to vote in free elections to remove from office a president and his political party.

However, the greatest benefit since the end of the Cold War has been the recent spread of the gospel. Christ offers a miraculous peace that no government can give or take away, a peace that is not disturbed by wars or economic disasters.

> *Peace I leave with you, my peace I give unto you: not as the world giveth, give I unto you. Let not your heart be troubled, neither let it be afraid.*
> *(John 14:27)*

SECTION QUIZ

1. What word is used to describe all countries south of the Sahara?

2. What is the most important concept that underlies most of African society?

3. What word means a strong attachment to a group with the same language or dialect?

4. What word means the worship of spirits believed to be present in inanimate objects?

5. What are perhaps the greatest problems facing the establishment and growth of free governments in western and central Africa?

☀ What has been this region's greatest benefit since the end of the Cold War?

II. CENTRAL AFRICA

The equator crosses the heart of Central Africa. Most of the region has a tropical wet climate, with average temperatures of 80°F and one hundred inches of rainfall each year. Mangrove swamps, with their tangled vegetation and stagnant waters, barricade the coastal lands. Where rivers or clearings break through this barrier, dense jungles line the path inland. Forest elephants, gorillas, and panthers roam these jungles, and pythons grow up to thirty-two feet long. Unlike the Amazon River, which flows through a low coastal plain and is navigable for one thousand miles, the rivers of Africa drop down from high plateaus to the coast. The frequent rapids and waterfalls prevent easy travel to the interior.

Dense jungles, wild beasts, rough waters, and, worst of all, diseases plague Africa. Snails carry the disease bilharzia, which afflicts the Nile Valley as well as tropical Africa. More serious are the diseases spread by insects, such as *Aëdes aegypti* mosquitoes, which spread jungle **yellow fever**. Although treatments and preventative vaccines are available, epidemics still occur.

The tsetse fly spreads the fatal African sleeping sickness that plagues much of Central Africa.

Range of Diseases in Africa

As it feeds on the blood of animals and humans, the tsetse fly spreads African sleeping sickness. Approximately sixty-six million people in Africa suffer from African sleeping sickness, and more

AIDS AND THE CHRISTIAN'S RESPONSE

AIDS is a global epidemic that affects about thirty million people worldwide.

Sub-Saharan Africa has the highest rate of AIDS in the world. Approximately 64 percent of the people infected with HIV/AIDS live there, even though their countries make up less than 10 percent of the world population. The first step for African countries is to recognize the problem. Because of the stigma attached to the disease, many people do not get tested and some governments refuse to acknowledge the enormity of the problem. The president of South Africa initially denied that HIV causes AIDS. Education is an important part of the battle. Some countries, such as Uganda, have implemented programs that encourage sexual abstinence outside of marriage. Unfaithfulness of even one partner can affect an entire family. Many women get HIV through an unfaithful partner. Others contract it through sexual assault. Because of the physical method of transmission, women are more likely to get HIV than are their partners. Sixty percent of sub-Saharan Africa's AIDS patients are women.

The AIDS epidemic has taken a huge toll on the labor force in sub-Saharan Africa, devastating the economies of those countries. The average life expectancy in the region has dropped to only forty-seven years.

More than twelve million children in Africa have been orphaned by AIDS. And there are many children who are infected themselves. Children can contract the disease simply by being born to an infected mother.

Certainly, Christians should be sympathetic toward those who have HIV/AIDS. Just as Christ healed the lepers of His day, Christians should be willing to minister to those from all levels of society. Could God be calling you to minister to AIDS victims in Africa?

than twenty-five thousand Africans contract it each year. The disease occurs only in Africa between the fifteenth parallels north and south of the equator. It progresses from fever to seizures and finally to delirium and coma. Death results unless the victim seeks medical help in time. Sleeping sickness killed many explorers and left others stranded by killing their packhorses or oxen. Even today, farmers cannot raise cattle or horses in the regions infested by tsetse flies.

The anopheles (uh NOFF uh LEEZ) mosquito infests many of the world's tropical areas, including most of the African continent. It spreads the dreaded killer **malaria**. For some varieties of malaria there is no known remedy. Malaria kills more than a million people a year, 90 percent of them in Africa. It is the single biggest killer of African children under the age of five.

A new epidemic spread across sub-Saharan Africa in the 1970s. The Acquired Immune Deficiency Syndrome (AIDS) destroys the body's immune system. It is most often spread by sexual contact and sometimes by drug users who share needles. More than 24.5 million Africans have been infected with the human immunodeficiency virus (HIV), which causes AIDS. Approximately 2.7 million new cases are diagnosed in Africa each year, most of them in sub-Saharan Africa. Scientists have not yet found a cure.

THE CONGO BASIN

The **Congo River** is the great river of Central Africa. The fifth-longest river worldwide, the Congo is second only to the Amazon in volume. It pours more than one million cubic feet of water into the Atlantic every second. Like the Amazon, it drains a vast region, called the **Congo Basin**, which covers all or part of five countries. Tropical rains caused by evaporation continually replenish the river.

CENTRAL AFRICAN REPUBLIC

The Central African Republic, only slightly smaller than Texas, is the only landlocked country in Central Africa. It is located almost exactly in the center of Africa on the southwest border of Sudan.

Flag	Country	Capital	Area (sq. mi.)	Pop. (M)	Pop. Density (per sq. mi.)	Per Capita GDP ($US)	Life Span
	Central African Republic	Bangui	240,533	4.30	18	$1,100	43.5
	Democratic Republic of the Congo	Kinshasa	875,520	62.66	72	$700	51.5
	Republic of the Congo	Brazzaville	131,853	3.70	28	$700	52.8
	Gabon	Libreville	103,347	1.42	14	$5,800	54.5
	Equatorial Guinea	Malabo	10,830	0.54	50	$50,200	49.5
	São Tomé and Príncipe	São Tomé	386	0.19	500	$1,200	67.3
	Cameroon	Yaoundé	183,567	16.38	96	$1,900	47.8

Central Africa Fast Facts

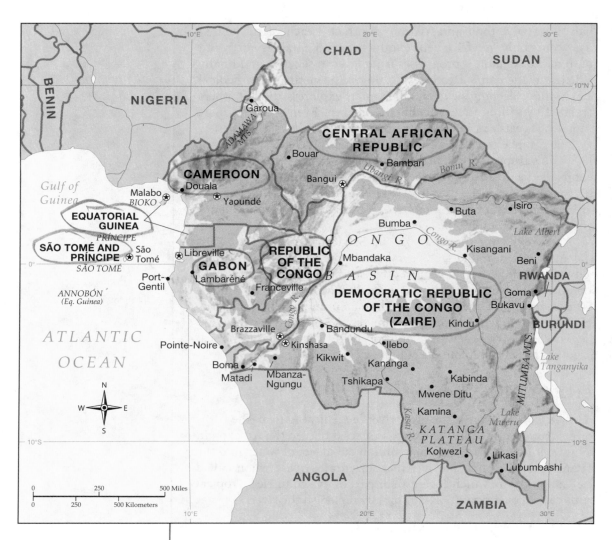

The terrain ranges from flat to rolling hills. Plateaus averaging three thousand feet in height split the nation into two drainage basins. Savannas cover the northern plateau, where water flows into the Chari River and empties into Lake Chad. Only 3.1 percent of the land is arable, and the country is often threatened with the extremes of dust storms and floods.

More than half of the people are rural farmers who raise grains, beans, yams, groundnuts, sesame seeds, and cattle for meat. Natural resources include diamonds, uranium, gold, and oil.

Seventy percent of the people practice animism. Even many people who profess Christianity are heavily influenced by animism.

The southern regions are equatorial rain forests and part of the Congo Basin. The Ubangi River forms the southern border. That populous region includes all of the main cities, including the capital, Bangui.

DEMOCRATIC REPUBLIC OF THE CONGO

Three countries share the waters of the Congo River. The largest nation in the Congo Basin, the Democratic Republic of the Congo, is the third-largest country on the continent and the largest in sub-Saharan Africa. It is a little less than one-fourth the size of the United States and straddles the equator. It shares a border on the north with the Central African Republic and a western border with the Republic of the Congo. It has only a narrow outlet to the Atlantic Ocean at the mouth of the Congo River.

The Democratic Republic of the Congo was the personal property of Leopold II, the king of Belgium, from 1885 until 1908, when he relinquished control to the Belgian government. The Belgian Congo, as it was then known, received its independence in 1960.

The country is made up of more than two hundred tribal groups. Four of those tribes make up 45 percent of the population. The largest tribes belong to the Bantu family of tribes. With such tribal diversity in the country, the government struggled for unity and stability. A military leader named **Mobutu Sese Seko** took control during a civil war that occurred after independence. He later renamed all of the country's geographic features with African names: the Congo River became the Zaire River; the country became Zaire. He even changed his own name from Desiré Mobutu to

These children attend school in a UN-sponsored refugee camp in the Democratic Republic of the Congo.

Mobutu Sese Seko. Mobutu also took over all businesses run by Europeans, but the national language remained French. A rebel leader from the eastern forests later overthrew the aging Mobutu in 1996 and restored the name Congo, but the old problems remained.

Half of the population is Roman Catholic. Twenty percent of the people are Protestants, and 10 percent are Muslims. Another 10 percent are part of syncretic sects or indigenous religions.

Rain Forest—Throughout the jungle regions of the Congo Basin, cassava is a staple crop. It is the DRC's top crop, and the DRC is the fifth-largest producer of cassava worldwide. The country has very little Atlantic coastline but enough to obtain a valuable resource—offshore oil wells.

Near the mouth of the Congo River are several rapids. The ocean port of Matadi lies just below the lower rapids. Above the rapids is **Kinshasa**, the capital. With nearly eight million people, it is by far the largest city in sub-Saharan Africa. Navigation is possible from Kinshasa upstream for over a thousand miles northeast to the city of Kisangani.

A thick rain forest lies in the northeast. Stanley (now Boyoma) Falls marks the end of navigation on the Congo River just upstream from Kisangani. This region is famous for isolated Pygmy villages. The quiet okapi, a short-necked giraffe with striped legs, also roams these dark forests.

The Congo River has a major tributary in the south, the Kasai River. The city of Ilebo lies at the farthest navigable point on this tributary. Kananga, the third-largest city in the DRC, lies on a branch of the Kasai.

Mineral Riches in the Highland Borders—Highlands mark the end of the Congo Basin along the eastern border: the Virunga Mountains in the north and the Mitumba Mountains farther south along Lake Tanganyika. The mountains produce tin but are better known as a haven for chimpanzees and the endangered mountain gorillas in Virunga National Park.

PYGMIES

The **Pygmies** are one of the most distinct peoples of Africa. Their average height is only four feet six inches, and they continue to live in the jungle by hunting and gathering food. Pygmies travel in small groups of about ten or twenty families, building villages of sticks and leaves to live in for a few months before moving on. They have no chiefs but make decisions by group discussion.

Survival depends on their intimate knowledge of the jungle. Pygmies know the life cycles of more than one thousand species of plants: they know when to gather the food and what is edible or medicinal. They also know the habits of more than three hundred animals. Women dig wild yams and gather edible leaves, nuts, berries, and mushrooms. In the rainy season, men may help the women gather caterpillars.

The men prefer, however, to gather honey and to hunt. Some tribes use crossbows and typical arrows to shoot monkeys; others use small bows and poison-tipped arrows. A group of only two or three men can hunt porcupines and four-pound Gambian rats, but large groups of men are needed to track

elephants, red hogs, and gorillas. They bring them down using iron-tipped spears. Men, women, and children may form lines to drive duikers (the smallest antelope) into nets or into groups of waiting spearmen.

Pygmy tribes live in the various countries of the Congo Basin and its borders. Each tribe speaks the Bantu languages of the settled tribe in their area. The Pygmies' ability to survive in the jungle gives them a mystique even among Africans. The settled farmers attribute supernatural powers to Pygmies, especially as diviners and healers. Welcomed in farming areas, Pygmies often help clear fields and harvest crops. In return, they receive the right to gather bananas and manioc from the fields. They also trade meat to the settled tribes for iron knives and rice.

The Italian anthropologist Mauro Campagnoli with two Bagyeli Pygmies of Cameroon.

Great mineral wealth lies in the southern tip of the nation, at the **Katanga Plateau**. Lubumbashi, the DRC's second-largest city, is the capital of the important province of Katanga. Copper is the nation's primary export. The mining city of Kolwezi is the hub of Africa's largest copper deposits. This copper belt has the third-largest copper reserves worldwide. Other mines make the DRC the world's leading producer of cobalt. Additional products include diamonds, uranium, gold, silver, and zinc.

The Democratic Republic of the Congo's vast economic potential makes it the hub of Central Africa. Unfortunately, poor leadership and frequent wars have hindered its development.

REPUBLIC OF THE CONGO

Africa has two Congos, which sometimes leads to confusion when one is trying to study the continent's geography. The "other Congo," on the west side of the Congo River, belonged to France. The capital of French Equatorial Guinea was at **Brazzaville**, across the river from Kinshasa. It is the largest city in the former French colonies. All of the French colonies in Africa became independent in 1960. This "other" Congo is simply called the Republic of the Congo, or Congo-Brazzaville.

The Congo River and its northern tributary, the **Ubangi River**, form the eastern border. Gabon forms the western border. The northeastern state of Likouala,

The Ubangi River forms part of the borders of several Central African countries.

west of the Ubangi, includes a remote swampy jungle, the largest and least-explored jungle wilderness in the world.

The population is made up of several tribal groups, including Kongo (48 percent), Sangha (20 percent), and other tribes. Most of the people live in the hills and low plateaus along the southern border. The population is almost evenly split between Christians (50 percent) and animists (48 percent). Two percent of the people are Muslims.

Subsistence agriculture is common throughout the country, although only 1 percent of the land is arable. The second-most produced agricultural product is cattle for meat. Plantations grow and export cassava, cacao, coffee, bananas, and peanuts. Although Congo-Brazzaville is not as rich as Gabon, it does produce a little petroleum. Other resources include potash, lead, zinc, uranium, copper, and phosphates.

THE LOWER GUINEA COAST

West of the Congo Basin is a region called the Lower Guinea Coast. It consists of three countries on the mainland and an island nation: Gabon, Equatorial Guinea, Cameroon, and São Tomé and Príncipe.

GABON

A country the size of Colorado, Gabon gained its independence from France in 1960. It had been part of **French Equatorial Africa**, which also included the Republic of the Congo, the Central African Republic, and Chad. The Ogooué River, which drains the country, supports a vast, wild rain forest.

Timber from Gabon's jungles, including ebony and mahogany, is an important product. Some other crops that grow in Gabon include plantains, yams, cassava, groundnuts, cacao, coffee, sugar, and palm oil. Although only 1 percent of the land is arable, about 60 percent of the work force is engaged in agriculture. Fifteen percent of the work force is engaged in various industrial-type work. Manganese, gold, uranium, and petroleum supplement the lumber profits. Other important industries include chemicals, textiles, cement, and ship repair. Income from these industries is slowly helping to improve living conditions, education, and health care.

The population is overwhelmingly of the Bantu tribes. Less than 11 percent of the people are European or of other ethnic groups. Most of the people are Christians, with estimates ranging from 50 to 75 percent of the total population.

EQUATORIAL GUINEA

Equatorial Guinea is slightly smaller than Maryland and consists of several islands and a small mainland region (often called Rio Muni) that is sandwiched between the coast of Cameroon on the north and Gabon on the east and south. The capital, Malabo, is on the island of Bioko.

Portugal first claimed the region in 1471. Spain gained control in the mid-nineteenth century, forming the only Spanish colony in sub-Saharan Africa. After Equatorial Guinea gained independence in 1968, it became the only African country with Spanish as its official language.

Central African countries, including Gabon, are major producers of coffee.

Because of its Portuguese and Spanish heritage, most of the population is nominally Christian, predominantly Roman Catholic. Some pagan practices are also present in the society.

An oil boom in 1997 produced phenomenal economic growth of 71.2 percent, but because the president of the country, his family, and his close friends control the oil industry, little of that wealth filters down to the common people. About 30 percent of the population is unemployed.

More than 95 percent of the work force is engaged in industry, which is amazing for a third world country. Only about 2.5 percent are in agriculture. In addition to oil, other industries include fishing, mining (gold, bauxite, diamonds, and tantalum), livestock, and timber. Major agricultural products include plantains, yams, coffee, cassava, bananas, and palm oil.

CAMEROON

Previously a German colony, Cameroon was divided between France and Britain after World War I. Those two European powers ruled the country until 1960. Since colonial days, Cameroon's stable, autocratic government has made steady progress. The country has built manufacturing plants and mines. The most important industrial product is petroleum, drilled in the Gulf of Guinea.

Cameroon, which is about twice the size of Oregon, has an odd shape. A sliver of land extends seven hundred miles north of the

GEOGRAPHER'S CORNER

HEALTH STATISTICS

Sub-Saharan Africa and the Sahel have some of the poorest, least-developed nations in the world. You have already studied several statistics that indicate poor development, including low per capita GDP. But why does poverty lead to high infant mortality and low life expectancy? Because people need money to buy proper food and health care.

Everyone needs a certain amount of dietary energy for the body to fight off disease. People whose energy intakes are significantly reduced are considered malnourished. Per capita calorie intake indicates the amount of dietary energy the average person receives daily in each country.

Another important ingredient in a healthy nation is medical care. Developed countries offer some kind of clinic in every small town, or at least within a short driving distance. But in poor countries, most health facilities are in the cities. Even when free care is available, rural people have difficulty reaching the facilities. Two statistics indicate the ease of getting medical care: population per physician and population per hospital bed.

Use the statistics on the accompanying chart to answer the following questions. (*Do not include the United States in your answers*; it is in the table only for purposes of comparison and contrast.)

1. The people of which African country have the highest energy intake?

2. Which countries have a per capita calorie intake below 2,000?

3. Which five countries have the greatest need for doctors?

4. Which African country has the best ratio of people per physician?

Country	Per capita calorie intake	Population per physician
Benin	2,520	17,364
Burkina Faso	2,410	25,018
Cameroon	2,260	13,514
Cape Verde Islands	3,210	5,848
Central African Republic	1,980	28,571
Democratic Republic of the Congo	1,630	14,493
Côte d'Ivoire	2,620	11,111
Equatorial Guinea	2,243	4,065
Gabon	2,610	3,456
Nigeria	2,700	3,715
São Tomé and Príncipe	2,153	2,141
United States	3,757	182

Bight of Biafra to reach the swampy shores of Lake Chad, which Cameroon shares with Nigeria and two other nations. That narrow stretch of the country separates Chad on the east from Nigeria on the west. The Adamawa Mountains rise in the northwestern half of the country along the border with Nigeria. The highest mountain in West and Central Africa is farther south near the coast. Mount Cameroon rises dramatically to 13,353 feet just west of Douala, but most of the region is a rugged plateau.

Southern Cameroon, the most populous region of the country, consists almost entirely of lowlands clothed with rain forest. The village of Debundscha is one of the wettest places in the world, receiving as much as four hundred inches of rainfall annually. Several rivers flow southwest to the Gulf of Guinea. Both the capital, Yaoundé, and the largest city, Douala, lie on these rivers.

As a result of the French colonial influence, French is the official language of Cameroon, but twenty-four major African languages are also spoken there. The tribes in Cameroon speak a number of Bantu languages. Bantu is a subgroup of the **Niger-Congo family of languages**. Most Africans south of 5° N speak a language in this group. Bantu was first spoken somewhere in the mountains of Cameroon, and it later spread as the conquering Bantu moved south. About three hundred tribal groups in Africa see themselves as Bantu, each with its own name, history, and language or dialect. The size of these tribes ranges from a few hundred people to millions.

Forty percent of the people of Cameroon profess Christianity. Another 40 percent practice indigenous religions. The remaining 20 percent are Muslims.

São Tomé is a contrast between the poverty of country villages and modern life in the cities.

SÃO TOMÉ AND PRÍNCIPE

About 150 miles off the coast of northern Gabon and Equatorial Guinea is the country of São Tomé and Príncipe. The islands of São Tomé (SOUN too-MEH) and Príncipe (PREEN see puh) are similar to the Cape Verde Islands. The islands were uninhabited until the Portuguese came in 1470. By 1500, the country was generally settled by the Portuguese. The nation gained independence from Portugal in 1975.

Seventy percent of the people are Creoles. Reflecting the Portuguese heritage, 70 percent of the people are Roman Catholic. Only about 3 percent are evangelical Christians. Almost 20 percent, however, claim no religion at all.

The two main islands and the half-dozen islets are volcanic and have good soil. The dense mountainous jungle was cleared for large plantations. The work force is engaged in primarily agricultural pursuits and fishing. Major crops include bananas, yams, cacao, copra (dried coconut), coffee, and various vegetables.

Major industries include textiles, soap, beer, timber, and fishing. Vast oil reserves

LET'S GO EXPLORING

CLIMATES IN AFRICA

1. What are the only three climates found in North Africa?

2. What two climates appear in southern Africa and nowhere else?

3. At 20° N, what is the climate on the west coast? on the east coast?

4. At the equator, what is the climate on the west coast? on the east coast?

5. At the Tropic of Capricorn, what is the climate on the west coast? on the east coast?

- Do you see a pattern in Africa's climate as you proceed north and south of the equator?

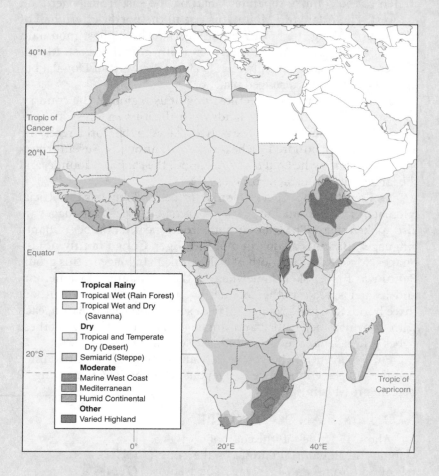

Tropical Rainy
- Tropical Wet (Rain Forest)
- Tropical Wet and Dry (Savanna)

Dry
- Tropical and Temperate Dry (Desert)
- Semiarid (Steppe)

Moderate
- Marine West Coast
- Mediterranean
- Humid Continental

Other
- Varied Highland

are thought to exist as well, and the country hopes to tap into them soon.

SECTION QUIZ

1. What is the name of the country formed from the Belgian Congo?

2. What are the only two African capitals that face each other across a river?

3. What is the main river of the Central African Republic?

- Why would the Democratic Republic of the Congo keep French as the national language?

III. WESTERN AFRICA

Thirteen countries cover the great western bulge of Africa. The largest, Nigeria, is bigger than Texas, but the others are quite small. Gambia, about the size of Connecticut, is the smallest country on the continent. All thirteen countries could fit into India. Although many Muslims live in the northern part of this region, animists and Christians make up the majority farther south. In this section, you

Western Africa Fast Facts

Flag	Country	Capital	Area (sq. mi.)	Pop. (M)	Pop. Density (per sq. mi.)	Per Capita GDP ($US)	Life Span
	Nigeria	Abuja	356,669	131.86	375	$1,000	47.1
	Benin	Porto-Novo	43,483	7.86	184	$1,100	53.0
	Togo	Lomé	21,925	5.55	264	$1,700	57.4
	Ghana	Accra	92,456	22.41	251	$2,400	58.9
	Burkina Faso	Ouagadougou	105,869	13.90	132	$1,200	48.9
	Côte d'Ivoire	Yamoussoukro	124,502	17.65	144	$1,500	48.8
	Liberia	Monrovia	43,000	3.04	82	$900	39.6
	Sierra Leone	Freetown	27,699	6.01	217	$900	40.2
	Guinea	Conakry	94,927	9.69	102	$2,200	49.5
	Guinea-Bissau	Bissau	13,946	1.44	133	$800	46.9
	Gambia	Banjul	4,363	1.64	425	$1,800	54.1
	Cape Verde	Praia	1,556	0.42	271	$6,200	70.7
	Senegal	Dakar	75,699	11.99	162	$1,700	59.2

will learn first about the countries on the southern part of the bulge, those that have a coast on the Gulf of Guinea. Later, you will read about those that are on the western part of the bulge and have coasts on the Atlantic Ocean.

THE GULF OF GUINEA·COAST

The curved coast on the southern side of Africa's bulge from Côte d'Ivoire to Gabon bounds the Gulf of Guinea. Early traders gave various parts of that coast different names based on the types of trade conducted there: the Slave Coast, the Ivory Coast, and the Gold Coast. The long, curving eastern portion of this coast was called the **Slave Coast** because so many slave ships operated from the bays called **bights** in that area. The **Bight of Benin**, an extension of the Gulf of Guinea, extends north from the Gulf of Guinea into the coasts of three nations—Nigeria, Benin, and Togo—between the Volta and Niger rivers.

NIGERIA

With more than 131 million people, Nigeria is the most populous nation in Africa. Unlike most other West African nations, Nigeria was an English colony, and English remains its official language. Nigeria

The Volta

The Volta River is a major river that empties into the Gulf of Guinea. The three main headwater streams are the Red Volta, the White Volta, and the Black Volta. Some of the headwaters flow through the interior country of Burkina Faso and then into the coastal nation of Ghana.

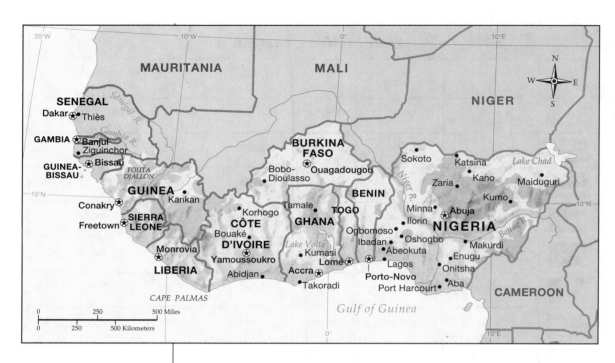

The Niger River is the lifeblood of Nigeria.

received independence from Britain in 1960, and it is an example of how Africa has struggled to rise above its troubled past.

Rivers divide the nation into three distinct geographic regions. The Niger River, the lifeline of Nigeria, flows into the country from Niger in the west and then proceeds southeastward to a point just below the center of the country. There, just south of the capital, Abuja, it is joined by the **Benue River** (BAYN way), the Niger's main tributary, which flows into Nigeria from Cameroon in the east. Thus enlarged, the Niger flows south into the Gulf of Guinea, effectively dividing the country into a northern half and two southern quarters.

A different tribe has dominated the history and culture of each of those three regions.

In 1991, Nigeria moved its capital from the southwest city of Lagos to Abuja, which is more centrally located and between the three major tribes. The leaders hope that the move will boost regional development and help them create a new national identity.

Hausaland's Muslims in the North— North of the Niger and Benue rivers rise the plateaus of the Sahel. The dominant **Hausa** tribe there is the largest ethnic group in Nigeria. About 21 percent of all Nigerians are Hausa. Unlike most other tribes, the Hausa are Muslims, and their language belongs to the Afro-Asiatic family of languages, the same family as Arabic.

The Hausa built many city-states before the arrival of the Europeans, three of which are still important cities today: Katsina, Zaria, and Kano. Kano is the largest city in the north and the fourth-largest in Nigeria. The Fulani tribe took control in the nineteenth century and intermixed with the Hausa. The Fulani account for another 9 percent of the population.

Today, most of those northern people are rural, living in traditional ways on the savanna, grazing cattle or growing crops. Two of

THE SLAVE TRADE ALONG THE SLAVE COAST

Slavery has been practiced since ancient times. Europeans enslaved Europeans, Asians enslaved Asians, and Africans enslaved Africans. God permitted the Jews to have slaves, but they had to be treated fairly. The evils of the African slave trade remain an ugly blot in history, and its bitter legacy still plagues Africa.

The slave trade flourished in Western Africa in the seventeenth and eighteenth centuries. Muslim nations controlled much of the slave trade on the west coast and in the Sahel, but Europe found slaves along the southern coast of the African bulge, an area that became known as the "Slave Coast." At first, the more powerful African tribes captured their enemies—fellow Africans—and sold them to European traders at ports. Later, as the slave trade became more profitable, Europeans went hunting in Africa's interior for slaves. The traders shipped the slaves to the Americas to labor on plantations. Many of the slaves died en route because of disease, overcrowding, and inhumane treatment.

Great Britain shared in the blame for the worldwide trade in slaves. But later it became the world's first empire to successfully abolish slavery. As a result of the untiring efforts of Christians in England, particularly the Quakers, the British Empire abolished the slave trade in 1807. The British later banned slave ownership in 1833. American ship owners from the Northeast also shared in the blame because they profited from transporting the slaves from Africa to the Caribbean and the Americas. The U.S. government outlawed the slave *trade* in 1807, but it did not abolish slavery itself until the Civil War.

The antislavery movement left an interesting legacy in two countries of West Africa. While slavery continued up and down the Slave Coast and in the interior of Africa, two places northwest of the Slave Coast became havens for freed slaves. Some reformers in Great Britain and the United States thought that they could best help freed slaves by resettling, or repatriating, them in their African homeland. Colonies were established for former slaves in what became known as Sierra Leone and Liberia. The names of the countries' capitals reflect the national origins: Freetown and Monrovia (for U.S. president James Monroe). The Guinea Highlands isolated the coastal settlements from the turmoil in the interior.

---

these crops are especially important. Nigeria is the second-leading producer worldwide of millet (a type of grain) and the third-leading producer of peanuts (also known as groundnuts).

Conflict in the region is common between Hausa Muslims and Ibo Christians, who make up about 18 percent of the population. Religious wars in 1995 led to hundreds of deaths and to the destruction of numerous Christian and Muslim villages.

Yorubaland's Christians in the Southwest—The **Yoruba** dominate the lands south and west of the Niger. The Yoruba make up about one-fifth of the population of Nigeria as well as a major portion of Benin. The entire Slave Coast (basically the coastal region between the prime meridian and 10° E longitude, from Ghana to Cameroon) was once Yoruba territory. Unlike the Hausa, the Yoruba have adopted many Western ways, and many of them have converted to Christianity. About 40 percent of Nigeria's population is nominally Christian.

Most of Nigeria's people live in the southwest. That region rises slowly from the coast through dense rain forests to the grassy Plateau of Yorubaland (2,000 ft.). The two largest cities in this region are Lagos and Ibadan, each with about 1.5 million people. **Lagos** was an important slave market and the capital of Nigeria. It is now the most important industrial center in Western and Central Africa.

To the east of Lagos lies Benin City, the former capital of the **Benin Kingdom**, one of the greatest kingdoms of Western Africa, which flourished between the thirteenth and eighteenth centuries. Its bronze and brass statues won international esteem, but the king's wealth depended on the slave trade, which declined after Europeans banned it.

Hausa
Yoruba
Ibo
are the 3 largest
ethinc tribes

Development of Nigeria's many resources has helped industries keep growing. Southwest Nigeria has the most resources of any region in the country. It has propelled Nigeria to a leading position in the production of cassava (first), cacao (fourth), and plantains (fifth). Nigeria also leads Africa in production of both hardwoods and petroleum.

Petroleum is the most important natural resource of Nigeria. Its estimated reserves are the second greatest in Africa, trailing only Libya. It provides one-fifth of U.S. oil imports. Most of Nigeria's oil comes from the Niger Delta. Unfortunately, the country's corrupt military dictatorship has allowed the profits to vanish into the pockets of government officials rather than benefiting the people. Polls of international businessmen indicate that Nigeria is either the most or the second-most corrupt country in the world. To do business in Nigeria, foreigners are almost forced to join in the bribery and fraud. Compounding the problem are attacks by rebels, who disrupt the flow of production because they are envious of the wealth the oil has brought to the Niger Delta region. In 2006, terrorism and religious violence (between Christians and Muslims) threatened Nigerian oil production. Western Africa will continue to languish until Nigeria reforms its government and defeats the rebels.

The Ibo in the Southeast—The southeastern quarter of Nigeria is called **Biafra**, named for the Bight of Biafra, which lies east of the Niger Delta and continues south into Central Africa. Most of the region is lowland, but mountains rise over six thousand feet along the southeastern border with Cameroon. The region provides palm oil, hardwood, and rubber.

In 1967, the **Biafran War** erupted as the **Ibo** people fought for an independent nation. Like the Yoruba, the Ibo have adopted Western ways and Christianity. Both tribes have a similar language in the Kwa language family, which is common across the southern coast from Liberia to Nigeria. But the Ibo still wanted independence. A terrible famine compounded the suffering of war. After a million Ibo had died, they finally surrendered in 1970. Instead of punishing the Ibo, however, the Nigerian government tried to bring reconciliation.

During the war in Biafra, starvation and malnutrition affected thousands of innocent civilians.

BENIN

To the west, between Nigeria and Togo, is Benin, formerly known as Dahomey (duh HOH mee). Its northern neighbors are Niger and Burkina Faso. About the size of Tennessee, it is one of the smallest and most densely populated countries in Africa. Benin was once part of French West Africa. Porto-Novo is its capital.

Of the country's sixty ethnic groups, the southern Fon tribe is in the majority. The Bariba are the main group in the sparsely populated northern savanna.

About two-thirds of the people of Benin practice a form of animism called **voodoo**. The rest of the people are Christians or Muslims. In 1996, voodoo was declared an official state religion, and its practitioners were even given a paid holiday. The people of Benin feel a close tie to descendants of slaves who were transported to the Caribbean islands and Brazil's northeast coast.

Eighteen percent of Benin's land is arable, producing cotton, corn, cassava, yams, beans, palm oil, and peanuts. It has small offshore oil deposits and some limestone and timber, but its main industries are textiles, cement, and construction materials. The country toyed with Marxism from 1970 to 1989, but the economy was near collapse and the government was a succession of military dictatorships. In 1991, Benin became the first Western African country to successfully transfer power from a dictatorship to a democracy. It also held free elections in 1996 and 2001. Although some irregularities were noted in the elections, Benin has made great strides toward free self-government.

TOGO

Sandwiched between Benin on the east and Ghana on the west, with a small border on the north shared with Burkina Faso, is a country that is about twice the size of Maryland. Togo is only about 50 miles wide and about 325 miles long and is essentially covered by the Togo Hills, which are tallest near the central portion of the country, and savanna in the north.

Togo was a colony of both Denmark and Germany, under which the colony became known as Togoland. Following World War I, France and Great Britain were granted control of the region. After World War II, it was under the trusteeship of the United Nations. In 1960, the portion under British control voted to become part of Ghana. The French part declared independence. Gnassingbe Eyadema seized power in 1963 and ruled through a cult of personality until his death in 2005. The dictator's son, Faure Gnassingbe, assumed control and was elected to the presidency later that year. The country is now in transition from dictatorship to democracy and a multiparty political system.

Togo is a country of bare essentials and subsistence living in tribal villages.

Forty-six percent of the land in Togo is arable, and 65 percent of the population engages in agricultural work. Major crops include yams, maize, cassava, vegetables, sorghum, coffee, cacao, and millet. Another agricultural activity of Togo is raising livestock.

Only about 5 percent of the work force engages in industrial activities. Major industries include fishing, mining (phosphates), cement, handcrafts, textiles, and beverages.

Lomé, on the coast, is the capital of Togo and the country's only seaport. Few people live in the northern savanna. Native African tribes make up 99 percent of the population with only 1 percent being non-African. Because of the overwhelming predominance of tribal groups, indigenous religious beliefs are practiced by more than half of the people. Slightly less than one-third of the people profess Christianity. The rest of the people, about one-fifth, are Muslims.

GHANA

West of Togo is Ghana. Beginning in 1471, the people of Ghana had extensive contact with European traders, first the Portuguese and then the English, Dutch, and Swedes. The abundance of gold in Ghana prompted Europeans to call it the **Gold Coast**. Initially, the Portuguese paid rent to the Ashanti Empire for their coastal base. In 1820, the British took over and made the area a colony. Britain granted independence in 1957, and the new nation took the name Ghana after the ancient African empire based in the Sahel. Mines still produce some gold, and the Ashanti people display gold treasures on festive occasions.

The independent Ghana quickly aligned itself with China and the Soviet Union. It experienced a series of military coups between 1966 and 1979, however, which prevented the stability necessary for the development of a strong economy. Military dictatorship was replaced by civilian government, but the country suffered much turmoil and bloodshed for two years. Since 1996, however, Ghana has been one of Africa's most stable governments.

Ghana's chief export is cacao; the country is the world's second-largest producer of cacao beans. Ghana, Côte d'Ivoire, Nigeria, and Cameroon combined produce 70 percent of the world's cacao. Because prices for cacao have dropped in recent years, Ghana has been destroying large quantities of cacao in an attempt to drive up the price. Ghana also is the second-largest producer of yams. It ranks fourth in the world in plantains and sixth in cassavas.

Cacao seeds (better known as "beans") are dried and used in the production of chocolate. Cacao is Ghana's chief export.

Major industries of Ghana include mining (bauxite, manganese, silver, gold, and diamonds), lumbering, light manufacturing, aluminum smelting, fishing, and ship building. More than 25 percent of the work force is employed in industry. (Perhaps surprisingly for a developing country, 39 percent of the work force is engaged in various services.)

The major river of Ghana is the Volta, which is formed by the confluence of the Black Volta and the White Volta rivers near the center of the country. From there, the Volta flows southward, through Lake Volta, to the Gulf of Guinea. Lake Volta was created when Ghana's government built Akosombo Dam. Lake Volta is one of the largest man-made lakes in the world. The dam was a controversial project, however, because it flooded approximately 740 villages, displacing about 80,000 people. Neither has the dam delivered sufficiently on the government's promises of benefits that its construction would bring to the nation. It has also hindered transportation within the country.

One of the best museums in sub-Saharan Africa is Ghana's Cape Coast Castle, where visitors can tour blood-stained slave dungeons.

Burkina Faso

Lying north of Benin, Togo, Ghana, and Côte d'Ivoire is the only landlocked country of Western Africa—Burkina Faso, a country slightly larger than Colorado. It shares an eastern border with Niger, and on the north and west is Mali. Burkina Faso lies in the Sahel but shares the Volta River with Ghana. As in the rest of the Sahel, savannas cover the land and droughts are frequent. The northern part of the country is desert.

The country was a French protectorate from 1897 to 1932. The French called it Upper Volta. In 1932, it was divided among Niger, Sudan, and Côte d'Ivoire. Then, in 1960, it gained its independence as a parliamentary democracy. In 1966, a coup toppled the government, and the country has been plagued with dictatorships and periodic coups ever since. In 1983, a Marxist leader took over, promising reforms and better living conditions. To break all connections to the colonial past, the new dictator changed the name of the country to

Burkina Faso, which means "land of upright men." In 1987, however, the military revolted, assassinated the president, and set up yet another dictatorship under the ousted president's best friend. He put down an attempted coup in 2003. Such a history of instability prevents sustained economic development and ensures continued problems.

Much of the male work force migrates to other countries for seasonal jobs, but some industries are trying to gain a foothold in the troubled country. Major industries include textiles, cotton lint, cigarettes, and agricultural processing. Most of the people are poor cattle herders and subsistence farmers, but only about 40 percent of the GDP comes from agriculture. The leading agricultural products are cattle meat, sorghum, millet, groundnuts, and maize. Natural resources include manganese, limestone, marble, phosphates, pumice, and salt.

Millet, being sold here in a market in Gaova, is a major product of Burkina Faso.

CÔTE D'IVOIRE

West of Ghana lies Côte d'Ivoire. It is bordered on the north by Burkina Faso and Mali, on the northwest by Guinea, and on the southwest by Liberia. It is slightly larger than New Mexico and has dense forests in the center and savannas in the north.

French sailors arrived on its coast in 1483 and began trading with the people of the interior for ivory. This prompted the French name for the country, Côte d'Ivoire, meaning "Ivory Coast." Formerly part of French West Africa, the country gained independence in 1960 and made Abidjan, a major port city, the capital. The capital has since been moved inland to Yamoussoukro, which boasts a presidential palace with its own crocodile lake.

In contrast to many other countries of the region, Côte d'Ivoire became a relatively stable country, and economic prosperity naturally accompanied that stability. It did not experience its first military coup until 1999. Foreign aid essentially ceased at that point, however, and the economy began to suffer. In spite of the presence of UN peacekeepers, political turmoil, disputed elections, and civil war have plagued the country ever since. Rebels, many of them Muslims, still control about half of the country.

Because they had a chance to develop during the years of stability, numerous industries continue despite the uncertainties. Industries include beverages, wood products, oil refining, truck and bus assembly, textiles, fertilizer, and ship construction and repair. Côte d'Ivoire leads the world in cocoa bean production and is number three in yam production. It also produces much rice, coffee, and plantains. Its natural resources include oil, natural gas, diamonds, manganese, iron ore, bauxite, and copper.

Unlike many African countries that reject ties with former colonial powers, Côte d'Ivoire welcomes French businessmen, teachers, and other skilled workers. Although the foreigners seem to be the richest inhabitants, the entire nation benefits from growing businesses and industries. The standard of living ranks in the top ten for all of Africa.

The people of Côte d'Ivoire are of more than sixty different tribes. Between 25 and 40 percent practice indigenous religions, 35 to 40 percent are Muslims, and 20 to 30 percent are Christians.

The Birth of Liberia

In 1822, the American Colonization Society sent a boat with freed American slaves to the Atlantic coast of Africa. They thought that they could establish the former slaves in a U.S. colony and eventually they would develop a free country of their own, thereby both improving their own lot in life and helping to solve the slavery issue in the United States. The former slaves named their country first Monrovia (later changed to Liberia based on the word *liberty*). They named their capital city Monrovia after James Monroe, a U.S. president and one of the sponsors of the effort. In 1847, the black leaders of Liberia declared independence and established a republic modeled after the United States. Even their flag is similar to that of the United States. Over forty years, more than 12,000 former slaves voluntarily relocated to Liberia. Today, descendants of freed slaves form only a small minority (only 5 percent of the population), but they have wielded the most influence. Ironically, in their constitution, they did not grant indigenous Africans equal rights with the former American and Caribbean slaves.

WESTERN AFRICA'S ATLANTIC COAST

Black Africans populate the four mainland nations of the west Atlantic coast. Lying above the equator, the region has both a wet and a dry season.

LIBERIA

Liberia is one of only two African nations never colonized by Europeans. Furthermore, it was the first black republic in Africa and the second in world history (after Haiti).

Liberia's neighbors are Côte d'Ivoire on the east, Guinea on the north, and Sierra Leone on the northwest. It is similar in size to Tennessee and is mostly plateau with dense tropical forests. Hills rise into mountains along the border with Guinea. Liberia gets about 160 inches of rain per year.

People of sixteen native tribes, each with its own language, make up 95 percent of Liberia's population. About 2.5 percent of the people are Americo-Liberians, descendents of former U.S. slaves. Another 2.5 percent are Congo People, descendants of former Caribbean slaves. About 40 percent of the people profess some form of Christianity. Missionaries have reached some of the indigenous peoples, but about 40 percent are animists. Another 20 percent are Muslims.

Seventy percent of the Liberian work force is employed in agriculture. Major crops include cassava, rice, bananas, and vegetables. Liberia is also the world's ninth-leading producer of natural rubber. Only 8 percent of the work force is engaged in industry. Major industries are rubber and palm oil processing, timber, and diamonds.

In 1980, the opposition overthrew the government and killed the president. Another coup wracked the country in 1990, sparking one of the most horrifying civil wars in history and bringing to power a man named Charles Taylor. Taylor, who did little to improve conditions in Liberia, supported revolution in neighboring Sierra Leone and lined his own coffers, bankrupting the country. Rebels forced him out in 2003. In 2005, the Liberians elected Ellen Johnson-Sirleaf, the first female president in Africa. Taylor was captured and turned over to the UN in 2006 to stand trial for war crimes.

Monrovia, the capital of Liberia, was named for U.S. president James Monroe.

Thousands of Liberians became refugees during civil war in that country.

Natural resources of Liberia include iron ore, timber, diamonds, and gold. But Liberia's flag is also important to the country's economy. Liberia collects a fee from ship owners who wish to register their ships in Liberia and fly the Liberian flag. By this means, the ship owners avoid many regulations of industrialized nations. Because of this policy, Liberia has one of the largest commercial fleets in the world. (Panama also benefits from a similar policy. Greece's registry includes numerous cruise ships, which puts that country in competition with the commercial fleets of Liberia and Panama.)

SIERRA LEONE

Northwest of Liberia is Sierra Leone, which is about half the size of Illinois. The coastal area is low-lying swamps, which give way to wooded hills and a plateau as one moves into the interior. The eastern region is mountainous. The country is bordered on the north and east by Guinea.

The first Europeans to visit there were the Portuguese, and they gave the country its name, which means "lion mountains." In 1787, however, an Englishman named Granville Sharp established Sierra Leone as a settlement for freed slaves, and the capital was appropriately called Freetown. Today, only 2 percent of the people are descended from freed slaves, and most of them live near Freetown. They follow Christianity and speak a form of English called Krio. The mostly Muslim (60 percent of the population) indigenous tribal peoples resent the prosperity, education, and influence of this small minority.

These workers are panning for diamonds near Freetown, Sierra Leone.

The British colony gained independence from Britain in 1961. Sierra Leone's independence has been marred in recent years by a bloody civil war that began in 1991 and wasted the country.

Sierra Leone is one of the leading producers of diamonds. The diamonds are found in gravel beds in the swampy rivers of the southeast. (Control of this wealth is one reason for the fighting.) Other industries include ship repairing; petroleum refining; and manufacturing of beverages, textiles, cigarettes, and shoes.

Forty-nine percent of the GDP of Sierra Leone is the result of agriculture. Sierra Leone is the world's ninth-largest producer of citrus fruit. It also produces large quantities of rice, vegetables, cassava, pulses, and coffee, although it is not a major producer of any of those products.

SECTION QUIZ

1. Which two nations were settled by freed slaves?

2. What was the main product of Côte d'Ivoire in colonial days? What is the main product today?

3. Through what two nations does the Volta River flow?

4. What are the three largest tribal groups in Nigeria?

☀ Why is the future of West Africa dependent on Nigeria's politics and economy?

GUINEA

North of Sierra Leone is Guinea, the capital of which is Conakry. That city is one of only two major ports on Africa's Atlantic coast. Guinea also shares borders with Mali and Côte d'Ivoire on the north and east, Liberia on the south, Guinea-Bissau on the northwest, and Senegal on the north. Mangrove swamps cover the coastal plain. A plateau rises near the Atlantic and continues into the interior highlands. Forests cover the hills and low mountains in the eastern half of the country. The headwaters of two great rivers—the Senegal and the Gambia—lie in Guinea's mountainous north, called Fouta Djallon.

With a third of the world's reserves of bauxite, Guinea ranks behind only Australia and Brazil in bauxite mining. Most of the bauxite comes from the north. Guinea also has deposits of iron ore, gold, uranium, and diamonds. In addition to mining, Guinea's industries include fishing, light manufacturing, and agricultural processing.

Eighty percent of the work force is engaged in agriculture. Guinea is the world's third-largest producer of citrus fruit. Other major agricultural products include rice, groundnuts, cassava, plantains, and cattle meat.

Approximately 85 percent of the population of Guinea is Muslim. Christians make up only 8 percent of the population. The remaining 7 percent practice various indigenous religions.

Guinea was formerly a French protectorate called French Guinea and later French West Africa. The country gained its independence in 1958 and promptly became the first openly Marxist government in Africa. The rulers turned their backs on France and the West and turned to the Soviet Union for support. The country has been affected by not only the failure of Communist economic policies but also the political turmoil in neighboring Sierra Leone and Liberia, illustrating once again that political instability contributes greatly to economic instability.

GUINEA-BISSAU

Guinea-Bissau (GIN ee-bih SOU), a country about half the size of South Carolina, lies on the coast between Guinea and Senegal. It is mostly lowlands with swamps, rain forests, and mangrove wetlands. It includes about twenty-five islands off the coast.

Portuguese exploration of the area began in the fifteenth century. By 1430, the Portuguese traded regularly along the coast of West Africa. Guinea-Bissau became a major center of the Portuguese slave trade. It was also one of the few regions that remained in Portuguese hands throughout Europe's competition for global empire. Portugal did not give up the colony until 1974, and then only after years of bitter fighting. Marxist leaders then kept a grip on the nation until the end of the Cold War, ensuring that it remained one of the poorest countries in the world. Between 1980 and 2003, the country experienced a series of military coups, further destabilizing the economy and hindering development.

Subsistence agriculture dominates the economy (82 percent of the work force engage in agriculture) while large deposits of bauxite and oil lie unexploited. In addition to oil and bauxite, the country's natural resources include fish, timber, phosphates, clay, granite, and limestone. Guinea-Bissau is the world's eighth-largest producer of cashew nuts. It also produces rice, pork, cattle meat, groundnuts, plantains, and various roots and tubers.

Giant ant hills are common in Guinea-Bissau.

GIMME YOUR GUINEAS

A *guinea* is a gold coin that was used in England from 1663 to 1813. It was named after the gold-rich Guinea Coast of Africa. Other kinds of "guineas" have remained in circulation.

Whereas merchants sought gold guineas, nations sought land "Guineas." France, Portugal, and Spain each got one in Africa. But the countries couldn't have the same name, especially after independence. The first independent colony, French Guinea, became simply *Guinea*. Portuguese Guinea added the name of its capital, becoming *Guinea-Bissau*. The for-mer Spanish colony took a different tack, becoming *Equatorial Guinea* because it lies on the equator.

In Southeast Asia the Dutch got a guinea. They colonized the island of *New Guinea*, which they thought looked like the "old" Guinea. To complicate matters, however, the island was later split, with half belonging to the independent nation of *Papua New Guinea* and half belonging to Indonesia. Do you know the name of Indonesia's portion of the island?

Guinea fowl were named for the Guinea Coast of Africa; however, *guinea pigs* were not. . . . But that's a different story.

Fifty-two percent of the people practice indigenous religions. Most of the rest (about 45 percent) are Muslim. Only about 5 percent are Christians.

GAMBIA

North of Guinea-Bissau and squeezed almost imperceptibly within the borders of Senegal is Africa's smallest country—Gambia. Averaging only twenty miles in width and stretching two hundred miles up the Gambia River, Gambia is about twice the size of Delaware. Mangrove swamps line the river. Banjul (pop. 46,700) is both the national capital and the country's only port. The largest city is Serekunda with a population of 344,100.

The first explorers of Gambia were the Portuguese, who were followed by the French, but Great Britain was the country that colonized Gambia (1853). In fact, Gambia was Britain's first African possession. It became a major slave center until the slave trade was abolished in 1807. It remained under the British imperial umbrella until it gained full independence in 1970. One civilian president served from 1970 to 1994, when a coup toppled him. The military dictator kept his promise to return to civilian rule in 1997. Numerous problems, including attempted coups, have plagued the country ever since, and the regime is still considered repressive.

Seventy-five percent of the work force is in agriculture. Gambia's major agricultural products are groundnuts, millet, cattle meat, rice, sorghum, and maize. Natural resources include fish, titanium, tin, zircon, silica sand, clay, and oil. Major industries are clothing, peanut processing, tourism, beverages, agricultural machinery, and wood- and metalworking.

CAPE VERDE

The Cape Verde islands consist of ten main islands and five islets and have a combined area slightly greater than that of Rhode Island. They lie four hundred miles west of the coast of Senegal. One island is a still-active volcano. The Portuguese discovered the then-uninhabited islands in 1460 and, recognizing that they were strategically located on the major trade routes, settled them with slaves, who were eventually converted to Roman Catholicism.

One of the major industries of Cape Verde is fish processing.

Today, most of the population is of mixed Portuguese-African ancestry; the rest are black Africans. Most of the people are Roman Catholics. The second-largest group is Protestant, mostly Church of the Nazarene.

Cape Verde became a province of Portugal in 1951. The people gained full Portuguese citizenship in 1961 and eventually gained complete independence in 1975. It was one of the last nations in Africa to gain independence.

Industries of the islands include food, beverages, fish processing, shoes and garments, ship repairs, and salt mining. Agricultural products include pork, pimiento, allspice, goat and cow milk, hen eggs, pulses, mangoes, and tomatoes.

The European Union and the World Bank are financing a massive expansion and improvement of Cape Verde's airport and port facilities, thus making Cape Verde one of the world's largest per capita aid recipients. The country's ongoing problems include high unemployment and poverty. Only 15 percent of the land is suitable for agriculture, meaning that the islands must import a significant amount of food. Nonetheless, unlike many other countries of Western Africa, Cape Verde has remained relatively peaceful since independence.

SENEGAL

The final country of what is considered Western Africa is Senegal, which is slightly smaller than South Dakota. The capital, Dakar, is the westernmost point of Africa.

Most of Senegal is lowlands and has a semi-desert climate. After all, much of it lies in the dry Sahel. It has suffered greatly from droughts and from an influx of refugees from its northern neighbor, Mauritania. Its advantage over Mauritania is the prominence of the Sénégal River and its tributaries.

Ninety-four percent of the Senegalese are Muslims. Most of the 5 percent who are Christians are Roman Catholics. The other 1 percent practice indigenous religions. Perhaps the greatest importance of Senegal is the diplomatic and cultural link it provides between the Islamic world in North Africa (you will read more about this in the next chapter) and black Africa to the south and west.

Many of the people of Senegal are nomadic herders, tending cattle, sheep, and goats in the north and raising food crops in the south. Seventy percent of the work force is involved in agriculture. Senegal is the world's seventh- and eighth-largest producer of groundnuts and millet, respectively. It also produces cattle and chicken meat, rice, maize, hen eggs, and cassava. Major industries include fishing, agricultural and fish processing, phosphate mining, fertilizer production, and ship construction and repair. Tourism has also increased as travelers learn of the infamous slave-hold of Maison des Esclaves off Dakar.

Both France and Portugal had trading settlements along the coast of Senegal, but France capitalized on its situation, making Senegal a part of French West Africa in 1895. In 1958, the Senegalese voted for self-government. They gained independence in 1960. With independence, Senegal experimented unsuccessfully for twenty years with socialism. Although the country was politically stable, opposition parties were illegal, the government strongly controlled the economy, and women did not enjoy equal rights. Only when the government allowed opposition, privatized industries, and granted equal property rights to women did improvements begin.

The notorious prison Maison des Esclaves, or "house of slaves," is located on Ile de Goree in Senegal.

SECTION QUIZ

1. List four culture traits that distinguish sub-Saharan Africa from North Africa.

2. What is the primary religion of Senegal, Gambia, and Guinea?

3. In the west coast region of Africa, where is animism dominant?

☀ Where was Marxism common on the west coast? Which country developed a stable, Western government? Why was there a difference?

LET'S GO EXPLORING

POPULATION DENSITY OF AFRICA

1. Which countries in Africa have two separate regions with high population density (over 250 per square mile)?

2. Which countries in Central and West Africa have a density that never rises above 25 per square mile?

3. Where is the only place in Africa that a dense population extends all the way across the Sahara Desert without a break?

4. What is the only coastal area that is completely uninhabited?

☀ What appears to be the shortest route through the Sahara from populated regions in West Africa (2–25 per square mile) to the populated regions in North Africa?

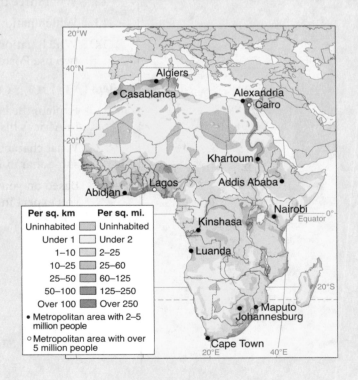

Per sq. km	Per sq. mi.
Uninhabited	Uninhabited
Under 1	Under 2
1–10	2–25
10–25	25–60
25–50	60–125
50–100	125–250
Over 100	Over 250

• Metropolitan area with 2–5 million people
○ Metropolitan area with over 5 million people

Can You:
Define These Terms?

village	autocrats
initiation rites	yellow fever
chief	malaria
tribalism	Pygmy
animism	bight
colonialism	voodoo

Locate These Places?

sub-Saharan Africa	Ubangi River
Congo River	Bight of Benin
Congo Basin	Benue River
Kinshasa	Lagos
Katanga Plateau	Biafra
Brazzaville	Gold Coast

Explain the Significance?

tsetse fly	Slave Coast
Mobutu Sese Seko	Hausa
French Equato- rial Africa	Yoruba
	Benin Kingdom
Niger-Congo family of languages	Biafran War
	Ibo

CHAPTER REVIEW

14

HOW MUCH DO YOU REMEMBER?

1. List all the nations in each coastal region.
   a. West Atlantic Coast
   b. Ivory Coast
   c. Gold Coast
   d. Slave Coast
   e. Lower Guinea Coast

2. What four European languages are national languages in West and Central Africa?

3. Which two cities served as capitals of French colonies in sub-Saharan Africa? Name the two main territories and all the modern nations that were once in each one.

4. What is the main river among the nations of West Africa? of Central Africa?

5. Name four tropical diseases that plague Africa.

6. Why was the exploration of sub-Saharan Africa difficult?

7. Why is Côte d'Ivoire one of the most developed countries in sub-Saharan Africa?

8. Which nation has the most people? the largest area?

9. What is the largest city in all of West Africa and Central Africa?

10. What nation in West Africa is landlocked? in Central Africa?

11. What nation contains most of the Likouala, the largest jungle wilderness remaining in Africa?

12. What three tribal groups dominate Nigeria?

13. Which nations have islands?

14. Which nation uses Spanish as the national language? Which two use Portuguese?

WHAT DO YOU THINK?

1. Explain the benefits and problems that village life has created in Africa's history.

2. What characteristics are common to prosperous countries in sub-Saharan Africa?

3. Based on your knowledge of South America, what climate do you expect in the nations south of Central Africa?

CHAPTER 15

The Sahara dominates life in Northern Africa.

PASSPO

United
of

NORTHERN AFRICA

I. THE SAHEL
  A. MAURITANIA
  B. MALI
  C. NIGER
  D. CHAD

II. THE MAGHREB
  A. MOROCCO
  B. ALGERIA
  C. TUNISIA

III. LIBYA AND EGYPT
  A. LIBYA
  B. EGYPT

Northern Africa Fast Facts

Flag	Country	Capital	Area (sq. mi.)	Pop. (M)	Pop. Density (per sq. mi.)	Per Capita GDP ($US)	Life Span
	Algeria	Algiers	919,590	32.93	36	$7,200	73.3
	Chad	N'Djamena	495,755	9.94	20	$1,500	47.5
	Egypt	Cairo	386,662	78.89	205	$3,900	71.3
	Libya	Tripoli	679,358	5.90	9	$11,400	76.7
	Mali	Bamako	478,767	11.72	25	$1,200	49.0
	Mauritania	Nouakchott	397,955	3.17	8	$2,200	53.1
	Morocco	Rabat	172,414	33.24	193	$4,200	70.9
	Niger	Niamey	489,191	12.52	26	$900	43.8
	Tunisia	Tunis	63,170	10.17	170	$8,300	75.1

Northern Africa is a unique region on the African continent. In many ways, the area has more in common with the Middle East than with the rest of Africa. As in the Middle East, the search for water and adherence to the Islamic faith are the central concerns of life.

The life and history of the region is dominated by the **Sahara**, the world's largest desert. It is about the same size as the United States and is the only desert in the world that spans an entire continent from shore to shore. The Arabs looked at this vast, barren expanse and called it simply "the desert," or Sahara. Annual rainfall ranges between one and five inches, and some parts are dry all year long. Average temperatures hover around 90°F but frequently exceed 120°F. Although it has few natural resources, the Sahara served as a crucial trade route throughout history.

When conquering Muslim armies arrived from Arabia in the seventh century, Islam took root in North Africa. Islam is the dominant religion, especially on the coast, where Arab armies faced little resistance. But Islam has not brought peace or prosperity. Northern Africa continues to struggle with poverty and political unrest worse than that in many neighboring countries. Muslim nations have closed their borders to Christian missionaries, who have the only solution for their thirsty land.

But whosoever drinketh of the water that I shall give him shall never thirst; but the water that I shall give him shall be in him a well of water springing up into everlasting life.
(John 4:14)

I. THE SAHEL

Between the Sahara and the jungles of central Africa lies a transitional region called the **Sahel**. This band of grass-covered plains is about three hundred miles wide. The northern part of the Sahel near the Sahara is the driest, often receiving as little as four inches of rain annually. Here the short grasses support scattered populations of Berber and Arabic nomads, who herd cattle and sheep. To the south, the grasses become more plentiful. This region sometimes receives up to twenty-four inches of rain per year. Most of the farmers are blacks, who settled the region long before Arab nomads came from the north.

Four countries—Mauritania, Mali, Niger, and Chad—are dominated by the Sahel. The Sahara covers only the northern part of these countries, and grazing lands cover much of the rest. Only the southern extremes can support crops and a large population. Unfortunately, the rain comes all at once, during the summer. Droughts often devastate the subsistence farmers, who do not have irrigation equipment. The people are so poor that children rarely attend schools. As a result, the Sahel has some of the lowest literacy rates in Africa.

The Sahel is a transitional zone in more ways than just climate and agriculture. The four countries of the Sahel display a complex mix of peoples and cultures. Mauritania, for example, has a significant Moor population (Arab and Berber mix), while the other three Sahel countries are composed of a variety of native tribal groups. Islam is a leading religion in all four countries, but its influence progressively weakens in the south and east, where there are more blacks. Mauritania is 100 percent Muslim, and Mali and Niger are 80

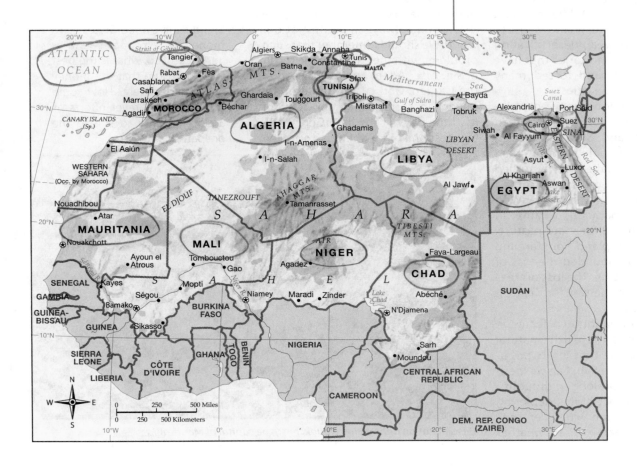

to 90 percent Muslim. Chad is only about half Muslim. Christianity and tribal religions make up the remaining percentages.

The mix of languages in the Sahel is also complex. Arabic is the official language in the westernmost country, Mauritania. It is also an official language in the easternmost country, Chad, but more than 120 native languages are also spoken there. The Arabs had less impact on the two central countries, Mali and Niger, where native black languages are common. Because these two countries were once part of French West Africa, French is the official language in both of them, and it is also an official language in Chad.

MAURITANIA

Mauritania is the only country of the Sahel that has a seacoast, which gives it access to shipping and the rich fishing waters of the Atlantic. Recently discovered offshore oil reserves are a welcome boost to the country's economy.

DESERTIFICATION OF THE SAHEL

At one time, scattered acacia, mahogany, and baobab trees made the Sahel a true savanna. But recent droughts and famines have raised fears that the Sahara is swallowing the savanna as it spreads southward. This process is called **desertification**, or desiccation. While it is hard to measure how much land is lost to the desert each year, desertification has caused food shortages that have killed thousands and forced many others to flee to the cities.

Two conditions may contribute to desertification. One is human abuse of the land. Since the 1960s, the number of people has more than doubled in the Sahel. Newly drilled wells attracted herders who settled permanently for the first time. With this increased population came an increased demand for more pasture, firewood, and cropland. Poor farming techniques compounded the loss of soil through erosion. The loss of trees and soil opened the way for the desert to invade.

Another often-ignored factor in desertification is the earth's natural cycles. During the time of its population increase, the Sahel also experienced extreme, prolonged droughts. Droughts are a fact of life, depleting soil and vegetation wherever they strike. A few years of bad weather does not necessarily mean the climate has changed, but the earth may go through times of warming and cooling. If this is the case, then no amount of human effort can stop the climate changes.

Whatever the cause of environmental change, we must recognize that God is always in control of our world. We should remember that such problems with the earth are the result of sin. After Adam and Eve sinned in the Garden, God cursed the ground, saying "in sorrow shalt thou eat of it all the days of thy life" (Gen. 3:17). Our responsibility, then, is to follow biblical mandates about hard work and good stewardship of resources. Some measures are now being taken to reduce desertification in the Sahel, such as new farming techniques and planting trees in rows to slow down wind erosion.

Should the United States send money to help poor countries in Africa? If so, what is the best way to ensure that the money is used effectively? How could Christians use relief efforts as an opportunity to spread the gospel?

Desertification approaches Nouakchott, the capital of Mauritania.

The Sahara covers most of northern Mauritania, where rainfall is rare due to the cold ocean currents. The region's only natural resource is iron ore, which comprises 40 percent of the country's exports. The nomadic people who live in this region are called Moors. They account for over two-thirds of all the people in Mauritania. The Moors once engaged in the prosperous slave trade, which was not officially outlawed until 1980.

The southern border, which is in the Sahel, is more hospitable. Black tribes farm the country's only fertile plain along the Sénégal River. However, recent drought, overgrazing, and deforestation have contributed to desertification. Many rural farmers and nomads have migrated to the capital, Nouakchott, located on the coast, living in makeshift camps and relying on foreign aid for survival.

Mauritania was not always so poor. The **Ghana Empire**, which may have risen to power as early as the fourth century, was centered in Kumbi Saleh, a city at the southeast corner of Mauritania. The empire controlled all the western trade routes across the Sahel into the thirteenth century, keeping all the gold nuggets and allowing the gold dust to continue north. The ancient capital now lies in ruins.

Today, Mauritania is governed by a military council that deposed the president in 2005. The council aims to create a democratic state. However, Mauritania continues to suffer from disagreements between ethnic groups.

MALI

Present-day Mali, which lies just east of Mauritania, stands in stark contrast with its own rich history. At one time, three great African empires—Ghana, Mali, and Songhai—occupied the region. Most early caravan routes in the western Sahara stopped at a desolate basin in the northern tip of Mali, where salts were plentiful. The salt mines of Taghaza provided traders with a valuable commodity, prized among the people of the southern rain forests, who gladly traded gold for salt.

Today, however, Mali is one of the poorest countries in the world. Because the country is mostly desert and is landlocked, 90 percent of the population is concentrated in the Sahel region in the south. Most people are engaged in subsistence farming or fishing. The main exports are cotton, rice, and livestock. Unfortunately, the country's economy is vulnerable because of constant fluctuation in the market prices for cotton.

Two major rivers, the Senegal and the Niger, flow through this region. The **Niger River** is the third-

Boats gather at a small port along the Niger River. Photo by Monique van Gaal.

largest in Africa and the most important river in the Sahel. Most ancient and modern cities of Mali lie on this river. Mali's capital, **Bamako**, is the largest city in the Sahel. Local wildlife includes wart hogs, baboons, panthers, leopards, giraffes, elephants, crocodiles, and hippopotamuses.

TIMBUKTU

Mali was once the center of the glorious **Mali Empire**, which arose when it conquered Ghana around 1200. By taking control of the gold trade, the empire increased its riches to mythic proportions. **Mansa Musa**, a leading king of Mali, gained a reputation as the richest man in the world. When he made a year-long pilgrimage to Mecca in 1324 with a caravan of sixty thousand people, he was preceded by five hundred slaves, each bearing a six-pound staff of gold, and three hundred camels, each bearing three hundred pounds of gold. His lavish gifts flooded Mecca's economy and caused gold to drop in value for over a decade.

After his trip to Mecca, Mansa Musa brought back Muslim scholars to teach the Koran and the Arabic language at new seminaries in his empire. He chose Timbuktu as the site of a new capital, and he built a large central mosque. The city soon became the key university city in all of Northern Africa, known worldwide for its learning.

Timbuktu (now spelled Tombouctou) has become the epitome of remote and mysterious civilization. Europeans had no idea where the Mali Kingdom was located or where it got its riches. The Mali people guarded all the trade routes in the north, and water routes were impossible in the disease-ridden swamps and rapids to the south at the mouth of the Niger.

No European laid eyes on Timbuktu until 1826, though many tried. The Scottish explorer Alexander Laing finally reached Timbuktu after a two-year-long odyssey. Tragically, Laing was murdered before he could return. Hoping to sneak into the city, a Frenchman named René Caillié learned Arabic as a convert to Islam. In 1827 he posed as an Arab from Egypt and joined a caravan from Senegal. He reached Timbuktu a year later, but all he found was a town of mud houses and huts, long ago fallen into decline. He returned to Paris to report his findings, which earned him a prize of ten thousand francs offered by the Paris Geographical Society.

A man enters a mosque in the ancient city of Timbuktu, where many buildings are made of mud.

NIGER

The Sahara covers two-thirds of Niger, Mali's neighbor to the east. The low **Aïr Mountains** in the north interrupt the vast sands of the desert. This "Switzerland of the desert" supplies lush vegetation in some valleys and oases. The Aïr Mountains have the largest uranium reserves in Africa, which provide mining jobs. Niger has almost no other valuable industry.

A wide savanna spans the southern border of Niger. In spite of average daily summer temperatures over 100°F, the Niger River in the southwest is the country's most attractive and populous region. The modern capital, Niamey, is on this river. Over three-fourths of the people here are subsistence farmers, who are threatened by frequent droughts common to the Sahel. In 2005, drought and locust infestation caused food shortages for nearly 2.5 million people.

Niger's living conditions are even worse than those in Mali. Niger is one of the poorest countries in the world and has the lowest per capita GDP and lowest life expectancy in the Sahel. Niger's government provides very little service to its people; all aid is received from foreign countries. Foreign aid provides for education and healthcare, especially HIV/AIDS relief.

Like Mali, Niger has an interesting history. White desert nomads, called **Tuaregs**, came from the north and took control of ancient Niger's trade routes through the mountains. The largest oasis and market town, Agadez, was their capital. Today eight percent of all Nigerians are Tuareg.

The largest African empire, **Songhai**, was born along the Niger River in the eighth century. This black kingdom grew slowly at first, until its first great ruler, Sunni Ali, took over the declining Mali empire in 1464. However, Morocco blamed Songhai for its economic decline and invaded in 1591. Morocco won easily because it was the first to use firearms in a battle on African soil. Although this defeat ended the last empire of the Sahel, a reduced Songhai kingdom remained until France invaded in the nineteenth century.

Tuareg men ride their camels through the Sahel, near the Sahara.

CHAD

Chad is one of the Sahel's most primitive countries. Roughly three times the size of California, Chad has only 166 miles of paved roads, the least in the Sahel. There are few cars, and most people walk for transportation.

The northern two-thirds of Chad is one of the driest regions in the Sahara. The far north has the highest elevations in the entire desert. Like the Aïr Mountains, the **Tibesti Mountains**, which are dormant volcanoes, rise up out of the sand. The highest Tibesti peak is Emi Koussi (11,204 ft.). The only inhabitants of this region are Arab nomads.

As in the neighboring countries, Chad's population is concentrated in the southern Sahel, away from the hot and dry Sahara. The Chari River and its tributaries, navigable only during the rainy season, provide a fertile region for agriculture. Eighty percent of the people are subsistence farmers, growing cotton and raising livestock. The Chari continues into **Lake Chad** on the western border. This lake is the most important body of water in the Sahel, and it harbors a wealth of fish. The capital, N'Djamena, lies near Lake Chad at the confluence of the Chari River and its largest tributary.

Chad has reserves of uranium and petroleum, but civil war between the Arab people of the north and the black peoples of the south kept the country from developing for nearly three decades. Libya invaded at one time, hoping to annex Chad, but was forced out

Shrinking Lake Chad

Lake Chad once had a surface area of approximately 9,600 square miles, or roughly the size of Lake Erie. Since 1963, however, Lake Chad has shrunk to one-twentieth of its former size. Two causes have been identified in this drastic change. First, because the surrounding region is susceptible to food shortages, water from Lake Chad has been used to irrigate massive areas of farmland in Chad and neighboring countries. In addition, the average rainfall has decreased since the 1960s. The lakebed is flat and shallow and is therefore naturally vulnerable to the slightest climate change. Scientists are concerned that Lake Chad will eventually disappear, and with it a vital source of water and wildlife.

A full Lake Chad in 1963, as seen from space.

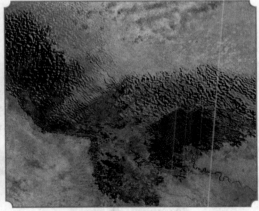
A depleted Lake Chad in 2001. The green areas indicate vegetation that has grown in the former lakebed.

by the UN. A form of peace was restored in 1990. Regional ethnic violence is still a problem, but Chad was able to begin development of its oil reserves in 2003.

Modern Chad's Christian population, the largest in the Sahel, is due in part to missionaries who arrived during the country's colonial days. At a time when many natives died while working in the Belgian Congo and others were captured and enslaved by Arabs, missionaries were able to introduce Christianity to the Sara peoples and open Bible schools. The Sara today are the most educated in the country and have gained most of the leadership positions in government and business. Their language dominates the more than one hundred language groups in Chad.

SECTION QUIZ

1. What European country controlled the four countries of the Sahel before their independence?

2. What term describes the expansion of the desert toward the savanna?

3. What country in the Sahel has been influenced the most by Islam? What country in the Sahel has the largest Christian population?

4. Through which countries of the Sahel does the Niger River flow? the Sénégal River?

☼ What was the largest empire in Africa? Explain the geographic advantages that made a large empire possible.

II. THE MAGHREB

Most of North Africa's people live along the Mediterranean Sea, for obvious reasons. The **Atlas Mountains**, a fifteen-hundred-mile chain, lies along the northwest coast of Africa. The mountains, which rise to a maximum elevation of 13,661 feet at Jebel Toubkal in Morocco, have a major impact on the weather and culture. The Arabs call the mountains the *Djezira el-Maghreb,* meaning "Island of the West," because they are a haven of life in the bleak desert. The mountain barrier blocks winds blowing off the sea, causing orographic rainfall. The water flows down to the sea, bringing mois-

Jebel Toubkal, the highest point in the Atlas Mountains

The lush Mediterranean coastline of Northern Africa, as seen in Morocco

ture to the valleys and coastal plains. Precipitation is near twenty inches annually, and this rainfall provides the only dependable water supply to support crops, livestock, and cities.

The coast enjoys a pleasant mediterranean climate and scenery comparable to southern Europe. Summers are dry but mild. Rains come in winter, with snow falling in the high mountains. Grapes, wheat, olives, and tomatoes are important crops. Northern Africa accounts for one-fifth of the world's phosphate mining.

The Arabs refer to the three countries of northwest Africa—Tunisia, Algeria, and Morocco—as the **Maghreb**, meaning the "West." The **Berbers** first settled the region over three thousand years ago. Some farmed the coastal plains and valleys, while others kept livestock on the mountainsides or at the edge of the desert. They traded with the Phoenicians, Greeks, and Romans, and major ports arose along the coast. These port cities—Tangier, Algiers, Tunis, and Tripoli—were the foundation of what later became known as the **Barbary Coast** states of Morocco, Algeria, Tunisia, and Tripoli (modern Libya).

As the Arabs spread across North Africa, they intermixed with the Berbers. The Arab-Berber ethnic group now accounts for nearly 99 percent of the population in the countries of the Maghreb. Arabic is the official language, and Islam (Sunni Muslim) is their religion. A small minority still speaks the Berber language and continues traditional Berber farming practices, folk dances, and marriage customs. France gained control of the Maghreb during the era of European colonialism, and close cultural ties to France (such as language) remain, even though the Maghreb gained independence in the mid-twentieth century.

MOROCCO

Morocco has coasts on both the Mediterranean and the Atlantic. A narrow peninsula juts out between these coasts, almost touching Europe. It is only eight miles across the **Strait of Gibraltar** to Europe. Throughout history conquerors crossed this strait, through the border town of **Tangier**, to invade either Africa or Europe. Today it is still an important shipping point between the Mediterranean and the Atlantic.

Morocco's two other major ports—**Casablanca** and Rabat—lie on the Atlantic coast. Casablanca, with nearly 3.4 million people, is the largest Northern African city outside Egypt. Casablanca is a popular tourist resort with a unique mixture of Spanish and French heritage. Rabat is the capital of Morocco. After gaining independence from France in 1956, the young Islamic country created a constitutional monarchy. The royal family claims direct descent from the prophet Muhammad. The king assumed broad powers, including the command of the army. In 1996, Morocco instituted a bicameral parliament.

Coastal lowlands provide rich farmland across northwestern Morocco. Beyond the coastal lowlands, the Atlas Mountains cover

Barbary Pirates

Pirates flourished along the Barbary Coast between the sixteenth and nineteenth centuries. Muslim raiders captured European ships and held sailors for ransom. Most countries, including the newly independent United States, paid tribute in return for protection. When the pasha of Tripoli demanded an increase in payments, the daring U.S. Navy sailed "to the shores of Tripoli" and won international respect with its victory in the Tripolitan War (1801–5). France ended piracy in these waters once and for all when it captured Algiers in 1830. This European domination lasted until the Barbary States gained independence in the mid-twentieth century.

Built by King Hassan II of Morocco, this mosque in Casablanca is the world's largest mosque outside of Mecca.

A typical market stall in the city of Marrakech, with pyramids of spices in the back. Marrakech has some of the most exotic markets in Morocco.

Cave Art Through Christian Eyes

Herodotus, a Greek historian who lived more than four centuries before Christ, described horse-drawn chariots that crossed the Sahara. Scholars scoffed at how naive Herodotus was. How could horses survive in the waterless Sahara?

In the twentieth century, however, several caves were discovered in the desert of Algeria that gave credibility to his story. Some four thousand paintings, now protected in an Algerian national park, adorn the walls of the many shelter caves at Tassili-n-Ajjer, just north of the Ahaggar Mountains. The drawings include chariots drawn by four horses. The earliest paintings, which some historians date from around 3000 BC, also show scenes of cattle, wild sheep, giraffes, and even hippos. Bones of hippos have been found as well, indicating that hippos may once have lived in this region. Obviously, hippos require standing water and do not live in the Sahara today. Apparently oases were once larger and more numerous in the Sahara, at least along some viable trade routes. Later paintings, dating after 700 BC, show camels, which are more suited to an arid climate.

The Flood would explain the source of this lost water. The land probably dried slowly after the Flood. Initially, the Sahara would have been filled with standing ponds and lakes in its basins. Herodotus was not so naive after all.

Algerian cave art shows wild cattle living in the Sahara.

most of the rest of Morocco. The mountains provide water for hydroelectric plants as well as lead and phosphates. Morocco is the world's leading exporter of phosphates.

Morocco claims a phosphate-rich area in the southwest known as the **Western Sahara**. When Spain gave up this territory in 1975, Mauritania and Morocco moved in. Algeria opposed this illegal land grab and supported the Polisario, a native independence movement. In the bitter fighting, Mauritania withdrew its claim, but Morocco then claimed the entire region. While Morocco's troops captured the coastal cities, they could not defeat the nomads in the interior. Disputes continued until the UN imposed a cease-fire in 1991. Sovereignty over the area has not yet been resolved.

Morocco also faces the challenges of economic troubles. In 2006, it instituted a free trade agreement with the United States in hopes of encouraging more foreign investment. Increased revenues will support education, create new jobs, and improve living standards.

ALGERIA

East of Morocco is Algeria, the second-largest country in Africa (after Sudan). It is approximately the size of Texas and Alaska combined. Because most of Algeria is desert, 91 percent of the population lives along the country's 620 miles of Mediterranean coastline, even though the area is prone to devastating earthquakes. The capital, Algiers, is one of the biggest cities on the Barbary Coast. The mild climate in this area supports the production of wine and citrus fruits, two of Algeria's important exports.

Palms grow at an oasis in the desert.

A hilly region called the Tell separates the coast from the Saharan plateau. Oaks, cedars, olive trees, and maquis grow in the fertile basins and plains of this area. A species of tailless apes, known as the Barbary apes, live here, along with boars, antelopes, and jackals. Barbary sheep, the only wild sheep in Africa, roam the dry mountains.

South of the Atlas Mountains are the varied features of the Sahara. When most people hear the word *Sahara*, they think of sand deserts. These wide areas of drifting, blowing sand are called **ergs**. The Grand Erg cuts a swath across central Algeria. Its sands cover thousands of square miles, with only a few large oases to break the monotony. The discovery of oil and natural gas reserves in the Grand Erg Oriental (the eastern part of the erg) has provided the government with capital for industries, such as chemicals, machinery, textiles, and cement.

Ergs cover less than 20 percent of the Sahara. Much more common are **regs**, flat desert areas covered with pebbles. The Tanezrouft Reg, on Algeria's southern border, is a monotonous gravel plain that stretches hundreds of miles. Algeria also has **hammadas** along its southern borders. A hammada is a solid mass of barren, windswept rock. The bare rock of the **Ahaggar Mountains** seems to rise out of nowhere in the middle of the Sahara.

The central land between the Atlas and Ahaggar mountains has no drainage to the sea and no permanent streams. Little vegetation grows in the desert. Coarse grasses, woody shrubs, and palm trees survive only at wadis and oases. Many oases are small and support only enough trees for a family or two, but several oases in the Sahara are large enough to support entire towns and cities. Wadis lead to shallow salt lakes called **chotts**. The chotts usually contain little or no water—just mineral deposits left behind after the water evaporates. The lowest such basin is Chott Melrhir, 131 feet below sea level.

A boat was stranded when the water dried up in this chott in Tunisia, near the Algerian border.

Present-day Algeria has been shaped by its history of foreign invasions. Arab invaders, who first arrived in the eighth century, brought their Arabic language and the religion of Islam. French colonization, which began in 1830, created the country's modern borders. The French controlled every aspect of Algerian life, and natives who resented the rule revolted in 1954. More than one-quarter million people died before Algeria was granted independence in 1962. Many French colonists returned to France. The socialist Muslim government established after independence has suffered continual terrorist violence. The most radical Islamic wing disbanded in 2000, and a truly democratic presidential election was held for the first time in 2004.

Algeria is one of the world's top five exporters of natural gas. Money from natural gas and petroleum have helped the country to industrialize and educate its citizens. Literacy has climbed from 10 percent to 70 percent. Unfortunately, unemployment is still high.

TUNISIA

Tunisia, which is slightly larger than the state of Georgia, has several geographic advantages over its desert neighbors. It supports twice the population of Libya, its large neighbor to the east, because of a pleasant climate, consistent water supply, and productive land. Tunisia's life expectancy is the second highest in Africa.

GEOGRAPHER'S CORNER

MAKING INFERENCES

At this point, you have studied many kinds of maps. You should now be able to pick up maps of completely new areas and draw inferences, or reasonable conclusions, from what you see. Look again at the map of North Africa at the beginning of this chapter. Answer each question and make the inference.

1. What African capitals lie on the Mediterranean coast? Why are they located there?

2. What Spanish islands lie off the coast of Morocco? Why are they Spanish?

3. How many nations touch Lake Chad? Why were so many borders drawn to include this lake?

4. Where are the geometric boundaries in North Africa? Why here and not in other places?

The ruins of ancient Carthage look out over the Mediterranean.

Most of the cities and farms are in the north, at the edge of the Atlas Mountains. These highlands rarely exceed two thousand feet, but it is enough elevation to cool the region and bring moisture. The average temperature in the north varies from 52°F in winter to 79°F in summer. This region produces wheat, olives, and tomatoes. Little rain falls in the southern desert, where temperatures are much hotter.

Part of Tunisia is a prominent peninsula that juts into the Mediterranean, almost cutting the sea in half. Tunis, the capital, is ideally located for trade, being only a short distance from Sicily and the Italian peninsula. Like Tangier in Morocco, Tunis has been used as a launch pad by invading armies. The ancient city of Carthage on this peninsula controlled trade passing through the western Mediterranean.

Tunisia's economy has recently seen growth in many major areas—farming, mining, tourism, and manufacturing. Heavier rainfall and more liberal economic policies contributed to an increase of 5 percent in the country's GDP by 2005.

SECTION QUIZ

1. What mountain range provides water for much of the Maghreb?

2. What geographic feature in Morocco almost reaches Europe?

3. What is the difference between ergs and regs?

4. What high mountains form hammadas in southern Algeria?

5. What is the largest city in Northern Africa outside of Egypt?

☼ What two modern cultural features of the Maghreb were introduced by Arab invaders?

III. Libya and Egypt

Libya and Egypt make up the remainder of Northern Africa and serve as a transitional area between Africa and the Middle East. They are the two most influential Northern African countries, and both have played important roles in recent world politics.

Libya

Like the other Northern African countries, Libya, which lies between Tunisia and Egypt, is primarily desert. Desert covers over 90 percent of Libya's land. Half of the country's population is urban and lives along the coastal plain, where there is a pleasant mediterranean climate. A small number of farmers and herders live in this area, surviving by raising crops or herding livestock, such as sheep. Their primary products are grains, dates, olives, and citrus fruits.

Hammadas rise from the desert in Libya.

The **Gulf of Sidra** extends south into the center of Libya. Here the desert comes right up to the coast because there are no hills to bring rain. This desert divides the Mediterranean coasts into east and west, where the people live. The waters of the Gulf are some of the warmest in the Mediterranean and are rich in tuna fish.

Since the time of the Roman Empire, the hump on Libya's eastern coast has been called Cyrenaica, after the early capital of Cyrene. In New Testament times it was the home of Simon, who carried Christ's cross (Mark 15:21), and of Lucius, a church member at Antioch (Acts 13:1). Banghazi is the main eastern city today.

The western coast is known as Tripolitania. **Tripoli**, the capital, is the largest city in Libya. It was founded by the Phoenicians and became one of the major Mediterranean ports of ancient history. It also played a role in the later Barbary Wars with the United States. Today, Tripoli is the country's largest manufacturing center.

The portion of the Sahara extending into Libya is one of the hottest regions in the world. The highest temperature ever measured—136°F—was recorded just south of Tripoli in 1922. Caravans, which have crossed the vast Sahara since ancient times, stopped at scattered oases to resupply. Libya's large oases, which lie in the west, became centers of trade. Black peoples in the south sold gold, ivory, and slaves in return for salt, cloth, and dates from the Mediterranean region. Arabs used camels to transport goods across the dry terrain, where horses or other draft animals would have perished. The sweet fruit of the date palm, which does not spoil as quickly as other fruits, provided convenient food for desert travel.

The eastern half of Libya has some of the most barren desert of the Sahara, where not even desert nomads wander. This area, called the **Libyan Desert**, extends east into Egypt and south into Sudan. Petroleum was discovered in this wasteland in 1959, just south of the Gulf of Sidra.

Libya became independent from Italy in 1951, but Colonel **Muammar Qaddafi** overthrew the new king in 1969. He removed all signs of Italian culture and instituted a military dictatorship. At one time he hoped to create a mighty new empire, attacking

Muammar Qaddafi

neighbors in Chad, Sudan, and Niger. He also funded terrorist activities around the world. The United States put a check on his work in 1986, when U.S. bombers struck several cities in retaliation. Since then, terrorist activities have decreased. After September 11, 2001, Qaddafi strongly condemned al-Qaeda terrorists. Beginning in 2003, Qaddafi agreed to end Libya's weapons programs and has made an effort to improve dealings with Western nations.

All the Barbary States have some oil in their desert regions, but Libya's deposits are the greatest. Libya's oil wealth gives it the largest per capita GDP in Africa. Libya now also has the highest life expectancy in Africa. The country has used its oil profits to develop agriculture, industries, and transportation. For example, the Great Man-Made River Project, begun in 1984, is being built to bring water underground from the Sahara to the northern farmlands. The Man-Made River is the world's largest engineering project. Further economic improvement is expected to result from the country's changing relationship with the rest of the world.

EGYPT

Egypt, one of the world's oldest and most fascinating countries, still thrives today along the Nile River. Located near the birthplace of civilization in the Middle East, Egypt seeks to maintain its rich ancient culture and heritage while surviving in the unpredictable Arab world.

Most people still associate Egypt with ancient pyramids and temples, which stand along the Nile Valley. As early as 2700 BC, Egypt was united as a state under one ruler. This began the long succession of dynasties and pharaohs who built the famous monuments. The dynastic period lasted until nearly five hundred years before Christ, when Egypt experienced a series of invasions by Persians, Greeks, Romans, and Arabs, who each brought a new culture. The Ottoman Turks controlled Egypt beginning in 1517, until an Albanian officer named Mohammed Ali won control in 1805. Ali's rule ushered in the modernization of Egypt, which included the building of modern Cairo and the completion of the Suez Canal in 1869. Unfortunately, the process drained much of Egypt's resources, and the British occupied the country until independence was granted in 1922.

Egypt has the largest population in the Arab world, and it is struggling to find its place in modern civilization. A military coup in 1952 replaced the monarchy with a republic. Gamal Abdel Nasser became one of Egypt's

The three pyramids at Giza are located just outside of Cairo.

most revered leaders, although other countries often disapproved of his policies. President Anwar Sadat succeeded Nasser in 1970 and reversed many of his policies. Most notably, he ended hostility toward Israel. In 1977, Sadat signed the Camp David Accords with

Israel's prime minister. In the Accords, Egypt agreed to recognize Israel's right to exist and Israel agreed to return the Sinai Peninsula (which it had taken during the Six-Day War of 1967) and to remove its settlers.

In 1981, President Sadat was murdered by Islamic terrorists. A large minority of radical Muslims continues to threaten the government. The current president, Hosni Mubarak, has proposed economic and political reform. In 2005, he announced an amendment that would allow multi-candidate presidential elections for the first time in the republic's history.

LIFE ALONG THE NILE

The **Nile River** is the lifeblood of Egypt. It is the longest river in the world, at 4,160 miles. Nearly all of Egypt's population lives along the river, where palm trees shade the houses and villages in the valley. The climate is hot and dry, with summer temperatures averaging 90°F in the north and reaching 110°F in the south. Only one inch or less of rain falls in the valley each year, but the delta region near the Mediterranean Sea may receive up to seven or eight inches.

VALLEY OF THE KINGS

Thebes was the great capital of Egyptian kings for fifteen hundred years, but only its ruins remain. The modern city of Luxor now stands in its place. Nearby in the desolate Valley of the Kings are more than sixty tombs of the pharoahs and their families. Most of the tombs were robbed long before archeologists explored them, but in 1922 an English archeologist chanced upon fabulous riches in the previously untouched tomb of nineteen-year-old Tutankhamen, or King Tut. The most recent discovery, that of the mummy of Queen Hatshepsut, took place in 2007.

Other reminders of the ancient kings' glory are the ruins of their temples of worship. The Temple of Karnak is the most well known of these sites. Sphinxes once lined the avenue leading to the front gateway, flanked by towers 143 feet high. Inside, a colonnade enclosed the Great Court, and the 140 pillars of the Great Hall of Pillars supported an eighty-foot-high ceiling. Huge pylons, or gateways, led into the central court and then into the inner sanctuary, where the golden statue of Amun, god of the wind and air, stood in his sacred boat. The temple complex also has temples for Amun's consort Mut and their son Khons. Also well known are the Colossi of Memnon, which guard the entrance to the temple of Amenhotep III. Each seated figure rises nearly sixty feet.

Entrances to the tombs in the Valley of the Kings

Sphinxes at the Temple of Karnak

Until the early twentieth century, the Nile flooded every year, bringing with it precious silt. The farmers channeled the floodwaters into their fields to sustain their crops of grain and cotton. The population was restricted to about ten miles on either side of the Nile, where the floodwaters could be channeled.

Beginning in 1902, new dams ended the flood patterns. The largest, **Aswan High Dam**, was finished in 1970. **Lake Nasser**, the reservoir behind the high dam, stretches southward about three hundred forty miles, entering Sudan, where it is called Lake Nubia. The dam and lake have stopped the flooding and allow year-round irrigation. About two million acres of land receive the waters automatically throughout the year. Now two or three crops can be raised in one year. However, the dam also traps the rich sediments in Lake Nasser, preventing the replenishment of soil downstream. Egyptian farmers must now rely on fertilizers.

The rural farmers are called **fellahin** (fel uh HEEN). They live in houses made of sun-dried brick and plow their fields with wooden plows pulled by buffalo. While they now have radios and other modern conveniences, they lack adequate health care. Sanitation is poor, and disease is rampant. Small worms called schistosomes live in the murky Nile and spread a disease known as bilharzia, which affects the liver and blood vessels.

The area between the Aswan High Dam and the Nile Delta is called **Upper Egypt**. Temples and tombs stand along the Nile in this region. The greatest ruins are at Thebes, which served as Egypt's capital during its early dynasties.

About one hundred miles from the Mediterranean, the Nile River splits and fans out to a width of nearly one hundred fifty miles. Early geographers noted that this region was triangular in shape like the Greek letter delta. They called it the Nile Delta, and the term *delta* became the term for alluvial deposits at the mouth of any river. The Nile Delta is also called **Lower Egypt** because it has the lowest elevation of the river.

Alexander the Great established the city of **Alexandria** near the mouth of the delta. It was the site of the huge lighthouse called the Pharos, one of the seven ancient wonders of the world, and the largest library ever compiled in the ancient world. Today, Alexandria is the second-largest city in Egypt with six million people.

Muslim conquerors moved the capital from Alexandria to **Cairo** (KYE roh), near the start of the delta. With sixteen million people, Cairo is the largest city in Africa. Cairo has become a major tourist center because of the pyramids located across the river at Giza. Like most cities, Cairo mixes prosperity and poverty. Shantytowns stand across from modern business and industrial centers.

DESERTS EAST AND WEST

Deserts cover the rest of Egypt. The Sahara hems in the Nile Valley on both sides. However, the two sides are quite different. The **Eastern Desert** is rugged and covered by barren mountains reaching almost seven thousand feet high. It is sometimes called the Arabian Desert, but it should not be confused with the larger Arabian Desert that covers the Arabian Peninsula. The nation's largest petroleum deposit lies near the villages on the Red Sea coast.

Power generated by the Aswan High Dam brought electricity to many villages for the first time.

The Western Desert or Libyan Desert is a low plateau covering two-thirds of Egypt. A few hills, salt flats, and depressions interrupt the flat sand horizons. Oases dot the vast wasteland, the largest of which is Al Kharijah. The **Qattara Depression** in the northwest drops to 436 feet below sea level. It covers an area almost as large as New Jersey. Egypt has considered digging a fifty-mile canal northward to the Mediterranean to flood the basin and create a new lake. This hydroelectric project would be more significant than the Aswan High Dam.

While most Egyptians are Muslims, a large minority of Coptic Christians live in the country, many of them in the deserts. The Coptic Church, which boasts around six and a half million members, has strong historical ties to the desert. Christianity spread throughout Egypt soon after the time of Christ, and it survived after the Arab conquest. Ancient historical sites, including monasteries, are scattered throughout the desert, especially at oases. The religion of the **Copts** is one of ritual and tradition, similar to Roman Catholicism and Eastern Orthodoxy. However, they follow the unscriptural belief that Jesus has only a divine nature, not a human nature.

SINAI PENINSULA

Although most of Egypt lies in Africa, the **Sinai Peninsula** is part of Asia. It is divided from African Egypt by the Isthmus of Suez, a bridge of land between the **Gulf of Suez** and the Mediterranean Sea. The Gulf of Suez is the western arm of the Red Sea. The **Suez Canal** cuts through the isthmus to connect these two bodies of water. Egypt's largest port, Suez, is located at the southern end of the canal. The Sinai Peninsula borders Israel to the east and was a disputed territory during the Six-Day War. The main resources of the area are petroleum and manganese.

Origins of the Coptic Church

The Coptic Church claims to have been founded by Mark, the Gospel writer. During the fifth century, the Coptic Church broke with traditional Christian doctrine by denying Christ's human nature. There were some attempts to unify Christianity and the Coptic Church, but these were unsuccessful. The Coptic Church flourished until the Muslim invasion in the seventh century. Because of Muslim pressures, many Copts converted to Islam. Under Muslim rule, the Copts were persecuted, and their numbers steadily declined. In the late-nineteenth and early-twentieth centuries, the Copts gained religious freedom and other privileges that had previously been denied, yet most Copts still feel oppressed.

Suez Canal

The Suez Canal was the longest canal in the world when it was opened in 1869. It stretches almost 120 miles from the Red Sea at Suez to the Mediterranean Sea, where a new commercial center, Port Said, was built. The canal is the shortest route between Europe and the Indian and Pacific Oceans. It is one of the busiest waterways in the world. The canal is 66 feet deep and 590 feet wide at its most narrow points, with wider spots every six miles for ships to pass. Thousands of workers took ten years to complete the job; many of them died in the arduous work of building the canal. The Suez Canal put Egypt back in the forefront of world affairs.

Interestingly, the French engineer Ferdinand de Lesseps was not the first to dig a canal here. Pharaoh Necho lost many slaves in his attempt to build the canal in the seventh century BC. King Darius of Persia conquered Egypt and completed the job around 522 BC. The Romans made improvements to the canal, but it eventually filled with silt.

A tanker travels through the Suez Canal.

AFRICAN PROBLEMS WITH "PROGRESS"

Now that you have finished reading about Africa, you may still wonder why there seems to be so little progress or improvement in quality of life. The lack of economic and political development can be somewhat explained by the problems that have plagued Africa in the past few centuries. Some problems are due to natural causes and cannot be helped; others are caused by man's broken nature.

Many of Africa's struggles are caused by the continent's geography. Much of the soil in Africa is infertile, especially in the Sahara and Sahel regions. As a result, proper nutrition is not always possible, affecting the physical well-being of all people. This in turn affects the available workforce. In addition to malnutrition, Africa has high concentrations of diseases such as malaria, typhoid, tuberculosis, and AIDS.

Africa has also suffered from outside incursions throughout its past. When European colonists first arrived, they acted as brooding protectors of the original inhabitants of the continent. Over time, with the discovery of valuable natural resources such as gold and diamonds, the colonists behaved more as owners of the land and people. The slave trade removed a portion of the population from Africa each year. These factors hindered the natural development of African culture and environment.

When colonies gained independence, they had few examples of good government on their continent. With the influence of tribalism, it was hard to find people who were interested in federal government or who did not have personal ambitions. Thus governments have been prone to corruption. The Marx-

ists promised peace and prosperity, but they delivered strife and poverty over the following decades. Religious conflict between Arab Muslims and black Christians resulted in more civil unrest. Establishing a stable government continues to be a challenge for many African nations.

Because of the political and civil unrest, foreign investors are leery of giving to Africa, even though there is great need. The mistakes of the past few years reinforce their opinion that their money may not be safe or effective amidst war and corruption. Consequently, the needs continue. The foreign aid that comes in bandages the wounds for a time but is not enough to heal the problems completely.

The Monastery of St. Catherine sits at the foot of Jebel Musa.

The mountainous Wilderness of Sinai lies at the south of the peninsula and takes its name from Mount Sinai, where Moses received the Ten Commandments (Exod. 31:18). Jewish, Christian, and Islamic traditions all identify Mount Sinai with Jebel Musa (meaning Mount of Moses, 7,497 ft.), although there is no physical proof. At the foot of Jebel Musa, Orthodox monks live in the Monastery of St. Catherine. Famous for ancient Bible manuscripts, it is also the oldest Christian monastery in the world (built c. AD 530).

Besides attracting religious pilgrims, the Wilderness of Sinai attracts divers to Ras Muhammad (Cape Muhammad). The Ras Muhammad Reef off the southern tip of the peninsula is among the greatest coral reefs in the world.

SECTION QUIZ

1. What natural resource has transformed Libya's economy?

2. What body of water divides the coast of Libya in two?

3. What is the most populous region in Egypt?

4. Which is farther north: Upper Egypt or Lower Egypt?

5. What are Egypt's peasant farmers called?

⚬ Why does Egypt have so much influence in the Arab world?

CHAPTER REVIEW

HOW MUCH DO YOU REMEMBER?

1. What climate is common on the northern coast of Africa in addition to desert? Why?

2. What two factors contribute to the process of desertification?

3. Give the modern country where each ancient empire began.
   a. Ghana Empire
   b. Mali Empire
   c. Songhai Empire

4. List three characteristics that the countries of the Sahel share with the countries of the Maghreb.

5. Why is the Sahel's population concentrated in the south of each country?

6. For each Sahel country name one distinctive feature that is different from the other three countries. Then list four characteristics that all of them share in common.

7. What were the Barbary States? What people group gave this region its name?

8. What river is the lifeblood of Egypt?

9. What Christian sect survives in Egypt?

10. What part of Egypt lies in Asia?

11. List four major sources of water in Northern Africa, either natural or man-made.

12. Which ancient empires influenced the development of the countries along the Northern African coast?

WHAT DO YOU THINK?

1. Why are missionary activities extremely limited in North Africa? How could the peoples of North Africa be reached?

2. Why do you think the Northern African countries continue to struggle with poverty and political unrest even though they are among some of the oldest civilizations in the world?

3. Why are there tensions in the Sahel countries between the peoples of the north and south? What should be done?

4. What two valuable natural resources are found in the countries along the Mediterranean? Why are relationships with these countries so important to the rest of the world?

Can You:
Define These Terms?

desertification	hammada
erg	chott
reg	fellahin

Locate These Places?

Sahara	Ahaggar Mountains
Sahel	Gulf of Sidra
Niger River	Libyan Desert
Aïr Mountains	Nile River
Tibesti Mountains	Lake Nasser
Lake Chad	Eastern Desert
Atlas Mountains	Qattara Depression
Barbary Coast	Sinai Peninsula
Strait of Gibraltar	Gulf of Suez

Explain the Significance?

Ghana Empire	Western Sahara
Bamako	Tripoli
Mali Empire	Muammar Qaddafi
Mansa Musa	Aswan High Dam
Timbuktu	Upper Egypt
Tuaregs	Lower Egypt
Songhai Empire	Alexandria
Maghreb	Cairo
Berbers	Copts
Tangier	Suez Canal
Casablanca	

UNIT 7

ENCOUNTERS WITH THE ARABS OF SAUDI ARABIA

The following excerpt describes one of many tense encounters that British adventurer Sir Richard Francis Burton had with the Arabs during his travels in the Middle East in 1852. Burton traveled posing as a Persian poet, mystic, and merchant.

"I never saw a more pugnacious assembly: a look sufficed for a quarrel. Once a Wahhabi stood in front of us, and by pointing with his finger and other insulting gestures, showed his hatred to the chibuk [a Turkish pipe], in which I was peaceably indulging. It was impossible to refrain from chastising his insolence by a polite and smiling offer of the offending pipe. This made him draw his dagger without a thought; but it was sheathed again, for we all cocked our pistols, and these gentry prefer steel to lead. . . .

"These Wahhabis were by no means pleasant companions. Most of them were followed by spare dromedaries, either unladen or carrying water-skins, fodder, fuel, and other necessaries for the march. The beasts delighted in dashing furiously through our file, which being lashed together, head and tail, was thrown each time into the greatest confusion. And whenever we were observed smoking, we were cursed aloud for Infidels and Idolaters."

Excerpt from *Dead Reckoning: Great Adventure Writing from the Golden Age of Exploration*, 1800–1900, Helen Whybrow, ed., pp. 516–17, 528.

SOUTHWEST ASIA

PROMISE AND PERIL

CULTURAL SNAPSHOT

The broad, rich culture of the region comprising the Eastern Mediterranean, the Persian Gulf, and the Caucasus/Central Asia is built on dozens of ancient civilizations, including Sumer, Akkad, Israel, Babylon, Persia, Assyria, and many others. Although vestiges of those various cultures still exist today, the region is dominated by three major religions and the cultures that flow from each of them: Judaism, Islam, and Christianity.

The first two of these three religions have their origins in the biblical Abraham. God promised Abraham an heir in his old age, but Abraham tired of waiting for God's promise and tried to achieve it himself by having a child by his wife's handmaid, Hagar. The child who was born was named Ishmael. He became the father of the modern-day people known as Arabs, who made important contributions in such fields as mathematics, astronomy, and medicine. From those people also came the religion of Islam. Over the centuries, Islam has spread beyond the Middle East to become the predominant religion of not only that area but also the Persian Gulf, the Caucasus and Central Asia, and much of Africa and southern and eastern Asia.

When Abraham's child of the promise arrived in God's perfect time, a second nation was born. Isaac became the father of the Israelites, from whom came the religion of Judaism. Judaism contributed, through the Old Testament, influential literature and a moral code (the Ten Commandments) among other things.

The culture of modern Israel is based on two key factors: Judaism and Zionism. Judaism itself is divided between Orthodox Jews, who want to adhere strictly to the religious rules, and secular Jews, who are more liberal and tend to follow Judaism only as an ethnic and racial tradition. (Secular Jews have always outnumbered Orthodox Jews.) The Zionist movement began as a reaction against the growing anti-Semitism around the world. It promoted the creation of a Jewish homeland and resulted in the founding of the state of Israel in 1948. Today, Zionists are hard-line supporters of the development and advancement of Israel. They violently oppose any accommodation of the Arabs. Zionism is central to the national self-image of Israel, and it is a lightning rod for anti-Semites around the world.

Israel also was the birthplace of Jesus Christ, Whose life, death, resurrection, and ascension produced the religion of Christianity. Christianity built upon the moral code of Judaism but raised the standards and expectations for moral and spiritual life. Simultaneously, it offered hope where Judaism offered only the hopelessness of human tradition.

Judaism, Islam, and Christianity have had an uneasy coexistence in this region, punctuated by frequent periods of tension and warfare. At the center of the controversy is Israel. Generally, the Muslims have sought the destruction of Israel. As recently as 2006, the Palestinian terrorist organization Hamas (winner of the 2006 parliamentary elections in Palestine) refused to renounce its pledge to destroy Israel. The same year, the president of Iran declared that Israel should be wiped off the map.

Throughout the conflict between Jews and Muslims, Christianity has sought not only to defend Israel's right to exist but also to broker peace between the two groups. Despite such efforts, the Christian countries of the West have been the target of Islamic terrorists (e.g., the September 11, 2001, attacks on the World Trade Center and the Pentagon; the train bombings in Spain; the bombings in the London subway system; Muslim riots in France).

Some people, considering this apparent "no-win" situation, ask, "Why bother working for peace in these regions?" As counterproductive as it might seem, this search for peace is actually commanded of believers. Psalm 122:6 commands, "Pray for the peace of Jerusalem." In doing so, we are actually praying for the return of the Prince of Peace, Who is the only One Who can bring true peace to our troubled world.

Jerusalem is the focus of three major world religions: Judaism, Islam, and Christianity.

EASTERN MEDITERRANEAN

I. TURKEY
   A. OVERVIEW
   B. POLITICS AND DEMOGRAPHY
   C. THRACE
   D. ANATOLIA

II. CYPRUS

III. THE MANDATE OF SYRIA
   A. SYRIA
   B. LEBANON

IV. THE MANDATE OF PALESTINE
   A. ISRAEL
   B. THE PALESTINIANS
   C. JORDAN

While the jagged peninsulas of southern Europe have plentiful harbors and a mild mediterranean climate, the coasts along the eastern Mediterranean Sea have few good ports, scarce water, and almost no natural resources. Yet the strategic location of this region has placed it at the center of the world stage.

The countries at the eastern edge of the Mediterranean touch three continents. Turkey is anchored in Europe, Israel borders Africa,

Eastern Mediterranean Fast Facts

Flag	Country	Capital	Area (sq. mi.)	Pop. (M)	Pop. Density (per sq. mi.)	Per Capita GDP ($US)	Life Span
	Cyprus	Nicosia	3,571	0.78	218	$20,300	77.65
	Israel	Jerusalem	8,019	6.28	783	$20,800	79.32
	Jordan	Amman	35,637	5.76	162	$4,500	78.24
	Lebanon	Beirut	4,015	3.83	953	$5,000	72.63
	Syria	Damascus	71,498	18.45	258	$3,400	70.03
	Turkey	Ankara	301,384	69.66	231	$7,400	72.36

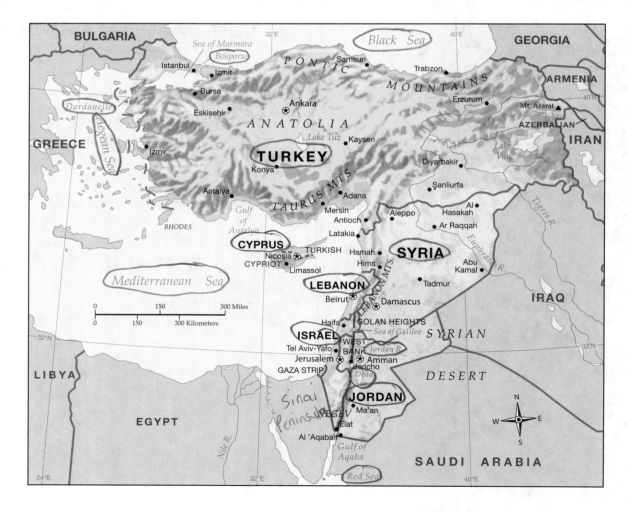

and several nations in the eastern part of the region border Asia. Ancient cultures from all three continents have mixed in the Eastern Mediterranean for thousands of years.

While a primary source of controversy in the Persian Gulf has been oil, the primary cause of trouble in the Eastern Mediterranean has been religion. Whether the issue is oil or religion, however, terrorism has been and now is the method of expression most associated with this region. Muslims overran the area long ago, but in 1948 the United Nations allowed the Jews to establish an independent state in the heart of Muslim territory. The region has been torn by strife ever since. The presence in the region of Western powers that are trying to mediate or enforce peace seems only to have added fuel to the fire of hatred between the Muslims and the Jews. The challenge that the nations of the world now face is to find a just and merciful resolution to one of the most bitter conflicts in world history. Christians should be especially concerned to work toward that end because the Lord came to teach the peoples of the earth justice and mercy (Matt. 12:17–21).

I. TURKEY

OVERVIEW

Turkey is the crossroads between Europe and Asia and the Middle East. It is part European and part Middle Eastern in its influences. Its location forms a "**chokepoint**," controlling movement of goods and peoples between the three great continents. As such, it has played a pivotal role in history. It is itself influenced by both its external and internal geography. It is often called **Asia Minor**, signifying both its size—it is much like a small continent—and its influence on history.

EXTERNAL GEOGRAPHY

Turkey is bordered on three sides by bodies of water. North of Turkey is the Black Sea. On the west is the Aegean Sea. Between the Black Sea and the Aegean are two narrow straits, the Bosporus and the Dardanelles. On the south is the Mediterranean Sea and the countries of Syria and Iraq. And on the east are the countries of Georgia, Armenia, and Iran. On the northwest, however, Turkey extends across the Bosporus into Europe, and that area borders Bulgaria and Greece's western extreme.

INTERNAL GEOGRAPHY

Turkey is slightly larger than Texas in area. It is rimmed by mountains, and its overall elevation is higher than that of any surrounding countries. Half of the land is above 3,280 feet in elevation; two-thirds of the land is above 2,625 feet. Turkey is home to the biblical **Mount Ararat**, which towers to 16,945 feet in an eastern area that juts between neighboring Armenia and Iran. The mountains of Turkey are susceptible to numerous earthquakes.

Seven major river basins are within Turkey, each originating within its borders and flowing out of the country. Two of them flow into the Caspian Sea; one flows to the Arabian Sea via the Tigris and Euphrates Rivers, the Persian Gulf, and the Gulf of Oman.

Turkey's climate is temperate. It has hot, dry summers and mild, wet winters. Conditions are more harsh in the interior region and in areas of greater elevations.

POLITICS AND DEMOGRAPHY

Although Turkey is predominantly Muslim, it has close ties to Europe. Turkey allied itself with Western Europe and the United States when it joined NATO in 1952. Like its European neighbors, Turkey has sought to become a secular (nonreligious) state. The Father of Modern Turkey, **Kemal Atatürk** (keh-MAHL at-ah-TURK), introduced this policy when he won control of Turkey in 1923. Atatürk introduced a long list of reforms, including a new non-Arabic alphabet, Western laws, the right of women to vote, a ban on polygamy ("many wives"), a ban on wearing veils and turbans, and the adoption of the West's solar calendar to replace the Muslim lunar calendar. These Western reforms remain in effect today.

Turkey has the largest population in the Middle East and the second-largest population in Europe. About half of its people live in rural areas. In spite of reforms, rural people have limited health care, and a large percentage of them remain illiterate. Much of Turkey's economy revolves around the primary industries of agriculture and mining. Even so, Turkey is slowly developing its resources.

The great hope of Turkey's secular government is its proximity to Europe. Turkey wants to trade with the rich nations of Europe and avoid the religious strife that has hurt the rest of the Middle East. The key to Turkey's hopes is membership in the European Union (EU). But Europe forced Turkey to wait for three reasons: Turkey's weak economy, its historic conflict with Greece, and its history of human rights abuses against the Kurds. In addition, some people have questioned whether Turkey is actually more Asian or Middle Eastern than European. The EU, however, has now allowed Turkey to begin the lengthy process of becoming a full member of the greater European community of nations. The next few years will determine whether Turkey is successful in achieving that long-desired goal.

To the Turks, the EU's hesitance to admit their country to full membership is evidence of prejudice. The common people have grown increasingly bitter, and religious leaders are pushing for a return to the Muslim world. A radical Islamic Party came to power in 1996, hoping to replace Turkey's civil laws with the *sharia* (shah REE ah), a law code based on a strict interpretation of the Koran, and to withdraw Turkey from NATO. But the army intervened—as it has in the past—threatening to seize power unless the Muslim leaders promised to uphold democracy and to protect the secular constitution.

THRACE

The European portion of Turkey is a small corner of the Balkan Peninsula, an area called **Thrace**. It is a hilly area with a mediterranean climate that is good for agriculture. Thrace includes **Istanbul** (is tan BULL), formerly called Constantinople, the largest city in the Middle East and the heartbeat of Turkey.

STRATEGIC STRAITS

The water passage between Thrace and Asia Minor, the main part of Turkey, is the only route from the Black Sea to the Mediterranean Sea. In making that passage, ships leaving the Black Sea first enter the narrow strait called the **Bosporus** (BOS pohr us), passing Istanbul on the European side. A bridge

Istanbul is on the European side of the Bosporus and marks the bridge between Europe and the Middle East.

spans that strait today. Next, the ships enter the small Sea of Marmara (MAR mohr ah). Finally, they enter the Aegean Sea by passing through a second strait, called the **Dardanelles** (DAHR den ELS), which the Greeks called the Hellespont. From there, the ships enter the Mediterranean. The armies of both Xerxes of Persia and Alexander the Great of Greece crossed at the Dardanelles.

THE RISE AND FALL OF THE BYZANTINE EMPIRE

For most of its history, Thrace belonged to the Greeks, not the Turks. The two peoples fought each other for centuries, and modern Turkey has had confrontations with Greece several times over the area. Indeed, Atatürk won his reputation after World War I by defending Turkey against an invading Greek army.

Thrace was the center of the last Greek Empire, which lasted more than one thousand years. It began when emperor Constantine moved the capital of the Roman Empire to Byzantium in 330, renaming the town Constantinople. When the Roman Empire split in 395, the eastern capital remained at Constantinople. After the collapse of the western Roman Empire, the empire in the east became known as the **Byzantine Empire** (after Byzantium).

After the death of Emperor Justinian (527–65), under whose leadership the empire reached its climax, the empire began to decline. Arabs and Turks encroached increasingly more on Western Europe, even as Crusaders fought to defend the empire. The final blow came in 1453, when the Turks overran the capital and renamed it Istanbul.

The Byzantine Empire, however, kept Greek civilization alive while the rest of Europe fell to barbarians, preserving both Greek literature and philosophy and Roman government and legal order. Until its fall, Constantinople was the center of the Eastern Orthodox

Byzantine Empire

THE WONDERS OF ISTANBUL

Among the many wonders in the ancient city of Istanbul are the Hagia Sophia, Topkapi Palace, and the Blue Mosque. The Hagia Sophia was the mother church of the Byzantine Empire. The interior moldings are covered with gold leaf, and the crucifix and altar are of pure gold. But the Turks turned the Hagia Sophia into a mosque. They added four minarets, and covered the mosaics of Christ and the archangels because the Koran teaches that such images are a form of idolatry. But Atatürk had the old church restored as a museum, and the mosaics have since been uncovered for visitors.

Topkapi Palace was the seat of the Ottoman Empire. Mehmet II, who conquered Constantinople, first built the palace, which includes fountains, three hundred rooms, and even secret passageways. Adding to the splendor are a wealth of diamonds, rubies, and emeralds. At first, only government officials lived in the palace, but Suleiman the Magnificent made it his home in the 1540s. The palace included rooms for a harem of four thousand women. It is now a museum.

In 1609, Sultan Ahmed I commissioned a mosque to be built across from the Hagia Sophia. It became known as the Blue Mosque because of the twenty thousand blue ceramic

The Hagia Sophia in Istanbul is an example of Byzantine architecture.

tiles decorating the interior. The unusual design includes a series of half-domes leading up to the central dome. The mosque also has six minarets, rather than the traditional four.

Church. Even today, after centuries of Muslim rule, the patriarch of the city is the most honored Orthodox leader and is reverently called the ecumenical patriarch.

SECTION QUIZ

1. What strait separates Europe and Asia?
2. What is the only non-European nation in NATO?
3. Name the region of Turkey that lies in Europe.
4. What is the largest city in the Middle East? Give two former names for this large city.

⚛ Should the European Union allow Turkey to become a member? Why or why not?

ANATOLIA

The Asian section of Turkey, what is sometimes called Asia Minor, is **Anatolia**.

Many historic cities lie on this crossroad between Asia and Europe. The ancient city of Troy once stood on the Asian side of the Dardanelles, near the Aegean. The German archeologist Heinrich Schliemann discovered the ruins of Troy in 1871, thereby proving that Homer's epic poem *The Iliad* was not a complete myth. Another ancient city is Troas, where Paul boarded ship on his first missionary journey to Europe.

Several empires arose in Anatolia, the first being the Hittite Empire (1700–1200 BC). The Hittites were experts at ironworking, which enabled them to build war chariots and to win many battles.

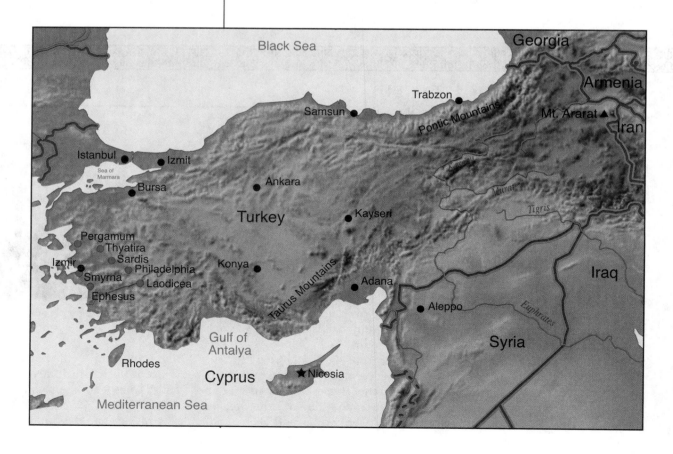

THE SEVEN CHURCHES IN THE WESTERN VALLEYS

Most of Anatolia consists of mountains and a high central plateau. But in the west, long fertile valleys drop from the plateau to the Aegean coast. This valley region has the most productive land in Turkey. The west coast has long been inhabited, and there tourists can visit many sites described in the New Testament, including the seven churches discussed in Revelation 1:11–3:22.

Ephesus used to be a major port but is now a ruin on a large peninsula near the modern city of Izmir (iz MIHR). Izmir was once called *Smyrna* (SMUR nah), which became the dominant port when the harbor at Ephesus filled with silt. Today, it has about two million people.

The other churches discussed in Revelation stood about fifty miles from Smyrna. *Sardis* (SAHR dis) was the capital of the kingdom of Lydia, but it fell to the Seljuk Turks in the fourteenth century. The fall of *Philadelphia* in 1390 completed the Ottoman Turks' conquest of Asia Minor. *Laodicea* (lay OD uh SEE uh) is adjacent to the modern town of Denizli (den iz LEE). Paul greeted the church of Laodicea in his epistle to the church in nearby Colossae (Col. 4:15–16), and it was immortalized in Revelation as the church where the Christians were "lukewarm, and neither cold nor hot" (Rev. 3:16), an apparent allusion to the nearby hot springs, which are still visible.

Pergamos (PUR guh MUS), or Pergamum, was noted for its pagan religion, which was a synthesis of at least three different religions. The people there encouraged the assimilation of many different beliefs and even had an altar dedicated to the worship of Zeus. Perhaps this is what John described as "Satan's seat." *Thyatira* (THIGH uh TY ruh) was a fortress town, designed to be a buffer zone between two warring areas, so it was always on military alert. It also was a large commercial center where many craft guilds were located. Each guild had its own pagan rituals and feast days, often involving immorality as well as pagan religious activities, and that certainly would have been a problem for believers.

Ironically, in spite of the early proliferation of Christianity in Asia Minor, today Muslims constitute 99.8 percent of the population. Although the government is officially a secular state, Islam has a firm hold on the people of Turkey, and radical Muslim leaders are continually pressing for a return to a religious state.

THE RISE OF THE OTTOMAN EMPIRE IN THE PONTIC MOUNTAINS

The **Pontic** (PAHN tik) **Mountains** stretch across northern Turkey eastward from the Dardanelles and rise along the Black Sea, leaving only a narrow coastal strip. These mountains also form the eastern border with Georgia, Armenia, and Iran. The Turkish coast along the Black Sea has no harbors for large, modern ships, although Trabzon in the east was once a port on the Silk Road. Many of the modern coastal villagers are fishermen. The coastal lowlands also have a mild mediterranean climate that enables farmers to grow corn.

Turkish tribes called Seljuks began settling in Anatolia about one thousand years after Christ. But the Crusaders weakened the power of these Seljuk Turks, and in their wake the Ottoman Turks rose to power. In 1326, the sultan of the **Ottoman Empire** captured

Ruins—such as those of the library in Ephesus and the city of Smyrna—are all that remains of the cities where the seven churches of Revelation were located in the first century.

Ottoman Empire

Bursa in the Pontic Mountains and made it his capital. The Ottomans expanded their control of Byzantine lands until they held all of Asia Minor by 1390. With the final conquest of Constantinople in 1453, the Byzantine Empire came to an end. The Turks then moved their capital to Constantinople.

The Ottoman Empire was the last of the great Muslim empires that ruled the Eastern Mediterranean. It reached its pinnacle under Suleiman the Magnificent (1520–66), when he captured Budapest, the capital of Hungary, and reached the walls of Vienna before being defeated. Over time, the Ottoman Empire declined, and several of its lands broke away. Nevertheless, the remnants of the empire survived until its final defeat in World War I. The Allied nations divided the remaining lands, intending to prepare them for eventual independence.

CAPITAL ON THE CENTRAL PLATEAU

The high Central Plateau is the most dominant feature of Asia Minor. Because the Pontic and Taurus mountains block most moisture, the plateau gets less than ten inches of rain annually. Irrigated portions are very productive, and Turkey is by far the largest producer of wheat and barley in the region. It also produces sugar beets.

Even today, a few nomadic herders roam with their flocks over the dry grasslands. The Seljuk Turks, who originally came from Central Asia, settled there in the eleventh century, bringing with them the Turkish language and Islam. Turkish remains the official language; 90 percent of the people speak it.

When Turkey became a nation in 1923, Atatürk moved the capital from Istanbul to Ankara (ANG kah rah), and it quickly became the most important city in the Central Plateau. Its population is approaching four million.

TAURUS MOUNTAINS IN THE SOUTH

The rugged **Taurus Mountains** cross southern Turkey, continuing east until they meet the Pontic Mountains near Mount Ararat, the highest mountain in Turkey. The Taurus Mountains form a barrier between the south and the rest of Turkey. Historically, the only pass between the Central Plateau and the coast was the Cilician Gates, north of modern Adana.

The Turquoise Coast—A narrow coastal plain lies on the southern coast at the foot of the Taurus Mountains. Both this area and the western valleys have a mediterranean climate and receive about twenty-five inches of precipitation annually. Farmers there grow grapes, citrus fruits, olives, tobacco, and cotton. The beautiful scenery has earned the south the title "the Turquoise Coast."

Kurds on the Southeastern Borders—The headwaters of the Tigris and Euphrates rivers are in the eastern Taurus Mountains. These rivers wind their way through the plateau, then drop into the upper Mesopotamian Plain. Most of the region is dry, except for the fertile riverbanks, which allow farmers to grow grains and fruit. Abraham once stayed in the city of Haran, near Urfa (oor FAH). The main modern cities there are Sanliurfa and Diyarbakir (dy yahr bah KEER).

Turkey's largest minority group, the Kurds, live in southeastern Turkey, near the border with Iraq and Iran. The Kurds constitute 20 percent of Turkey's population. Some Kurds have moved to cities, dropping their Kurdish language and customs; however, more than half still herd sheep in the mountains. The Persian Gulf War hindered the vital trade in that region.

Many Kurds want independence. A faction of Communist Kurds started a rebellion in 1984, which claimed the lives of more than twenty thousand people. In 1995, Turkey launched its largest military attack since World War I, driving deep within northern Iraq to wipe out rebel Kurdish bases, and atrocities were committed by both sides during the conflict. The war to oust Saddam Hussein from power in Iraq revived a desire by Turkish Kurds to unite with Iraqi Kurds below the southeastern border, but the Turkish government strongly opposed that move. The United States, only with difficulty, prevented Turkish intervention.

SECTION QUIZ

1. Give two names for the part of Turkey in Asia.
2. Name two biblical cities in Anatolia.
3. What two mountain ranges border the Central Plateau?
4. What is the typical climate of the plateau?
5. What ethnic group makes up 20 percent of the population of Turkey?
- ☀ Why are the Dardenelles and the Bosporus so important?

II. CYPRUS

The island of Cyprus is a little bigger than half the state of Connecticut. It is the third-largest island in the Mediterranean Sea (behind Sicily and Sardinia). Two forested mountain ranges cross Cyprus from east to west, rising as high as 6,406 feet, with the **Mesaoria Plain** between them. Near the center of the plain on the northern half of the island is the capital, **Nicosia** (NIK oh SEE ah).

The valley and the coasts have a typical mediterranean climate—mild, rainy, winters and hot, dry summers. Only the mountains get snow in winter. Although only about 8 percent of the land is arable, the climate supports grapefruit, lemons, oranges, grapes, and olives.

The economy of Cyprus is heavily dependent on the tourist trade, which is susceptible to erratic swings caused by political and social instability. The economy also depends on its limited agriculture and government service, which combined represent more than half of the workforce. Natural resources of Cyprus include copper, asbestos, gypsum, timber, salt, and marble.

Cyprus has a rich history. Greeks, Persians, Romans, Byzantines, Franks, and Venetians have occupied it. The Ottoman Turks ruled it from 1571 until the British gained administrative control in 1878. Although Cyprus gained its independence in 1960, the British retain two military bases on the southern and southeastern coasts of the island.

The ethnic composition of the island's population makes it a volatile, divided country. Seventy-eight percent of its inhabitants are Greek Cypriots

Nicosia is the capital of Cyprus.

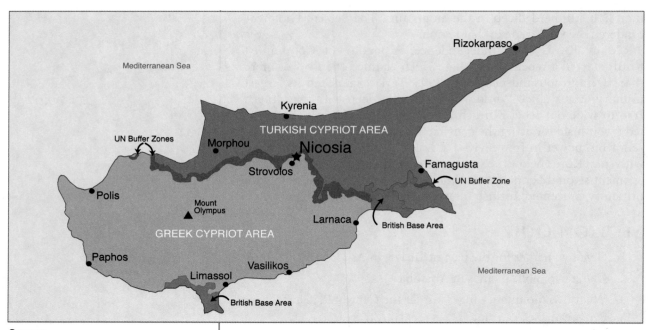

Cyprus

who follow the Greek Orthodox religion. Eighteen percent are Turkish Cypriots, who are Muslims, mostly Sunnis. The remaining 4 percent are a mixture of Christians and Jews.

After gaining independence, Cyprus tried to balance the interests of the Greek and Turkish communities to bring stability to the island. Most of the people wanted to stay united, but a few Greek Cypriots wanted to reunite with Greece and a few Turkish Cypriots wanted to **partition** (divide) the island into two countries. Fighting broke out in 1963, but the UN stepped in to restore peace. In 1974, Greece backed a coup that overthrew the president. In response, Turkey invaded the island and captured the northern one-third of the island for the Turkish Cypriots.

United Nations peacekeepers have remained in Cyprus since 1964. The UN's goal is to unite the island into one sovereign Cyprus, but events since the 1974 war have not been promising. In 1983, the northern portion declared itself the Turkish Republic of Cyprus, but only Turkey has recognized it as a legitimate government. The Greek Cypriots rejected a UN-brokered agreement in April 2004. A month later, the southern two-thirds of the island, known as the Republic of Cyprus, joined the EU. Turkey and the northern Cypriots resent the implication that the division of the island might be permanent and fear that the south and Greece will prevent Turkey's admission to the EU. The potential for war is ever present on the island.

SECTION QUIZ

1. What two rival groups live on Cyprus?
2. What is the ethnic composition of the island of Cyprus?
3. Which country supported a coup that toppled Cyprus's president?
4. Which country retaliated by invading and capturing the northern third of the island?
* Should Cyprus be partitioned permanently? Why or why not?

LET'S GO EXPLORING

LAND USE IN THE MIDDLE EAST

1. Which countries have some mediterranean agriculture?

2. Which two countries on the Arabian Peninsula have large areas of subsistence agriculture?

3. Find a continuous path of agriculture from Israel to Iran. Which countries share parts of this agricultural region, known as the Fertile Crescent?

💡 Which country in the Middle East seems to have the largest area of productive land?

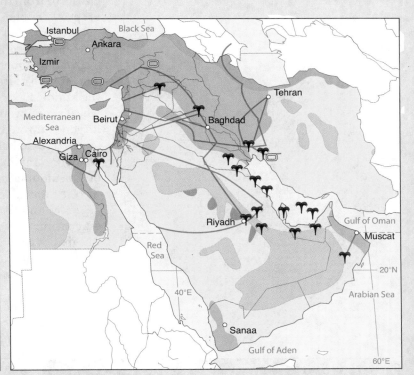

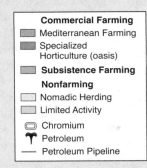

Commercial Farming
- Mediterranean Farming
- Specialized Horticulture (oasis)

Subsistence Farming

Nonfarming
- Nomadic Herding
- Limited Activity

- Chromium
- Petroleum
- Petroleum Pipeline

III. THE MANDATE OF SYRIA

The land southeast of Turkey along the eastern Mediterranean is often called the **Levant** (leh VAHNT). The lowlands and mountain ranges of the Levant have a mediterranean climate. These fertile lands contrast with the wastes of the Syrian Desert in the interior. The Levant and the river valleys of Mesopotamia form a crescent-shaped area called the **Fertile Crescent**, which has been heavily populated since Bible times. For thousands of years, merchants and marching armies have passed through this fertile land route.

The Levant belonged to Turkey until Turkey's defeat in World War I. France and Britain took over these territories, called **mandates**, which they governed in the name of the League of Nations. Their goal was to prepare the people for self-government and independence. The French mandate was called **Syria**, and two countries were born from it: Syria and Lebanon. The British mandate was called **Palestine**.

SYRIA

Syria has arable lowlands along the Mediterranean coast, which rise to the Jabal an-Nusayriyah Range. Many farming towns lie in this region, where forty inches of rain fall each year. Arvad was the most important port in Bible times (Ezek. 27:8), but today the major port is Latakia (lat uh KEE uh).

The **Syrian Desert** covers most of Syria east of the mountains. Almost uninhabited, the rocky desert plateau slopes downward and eastward from the mountains to the Euphrates River valley. The desert provides phosphates, but the most important resource is oil. Syria also gets most of its precious water from the Euphrates.

Syria's second largest city, Aleppo, lies in the north on the dry side of the mountains, near the border with Turkey. Aleppo has been a major hub of transportation since ancient times. Many railroads in the Middle East meet in Aleppo, which also is the focus of cotton and wheat growing and is known for its textile industry. It ships most of its goods through the port at Latakia.

Syria's capital and largest city, **Damascus**, is also on the arid side of the mountains but in the south. The Barada River, which flows off the mountains, made Damascus a virtual oasis. In ancient times, the city was a convenient stop for caravans traveling through the desert to and from the Euphrates. Damascus claims to be the oldest continuously inhabited city in the world. It was already a city in Abraham's time (Gen. 14:15). Later, Paul became a Christian on the road to Damascus (Acts 9). Today, shoppers at the old marketplaces (*suqs*) can still buy beautiful samples of old-fashioned textiles and metalwork.

Northeast of Damascus are the ruins of Palmyra, another major stop on the caravan route between the Mediterranean Sea and the Persian Gulf. This ancient town arose at an oasis in the Syrian Desert. Solomon first fortified "Tadmor in the wilderness" (1 Kings 9:18; 2 Chron. 8:4). The name *Tadmor* means "palm." The Greeks later called the town by the Greek word for "palm," *Palmyra*. The city was destroyed after it revolted against Roman rule in 273. The ruins have been excavated near the modern town of Tadmur.

Today, 90 percent of all Syrians are Arabs. The remaining 10 percent are a mixture of Kurds, Armenians, and other ethnic groups. Syria is 90 percent Muslim (74 percent Sunni Muslim and another 16 percent other Muslim sects). About 10 percent are Christian. Arabic is the official language.

Syria claims to be a republic, but it has been ruled by a military leader since 1963. **Hafez al-Assad** (ah SAHD) took power in a 1970 coup. Upon Assad's death, his son **Bashar al-Assad** was elected president in a one-man "race." As was the case under his father, Bashar al-Assad's government strictly controls the economy, limits personal freedoms, and suppresses opposition ruthlessly. Assad has promised changes but has failed to deliver on those promises. The U.S. government believes that Syria, like Iran, has been supporting terrorists around the world. During the U.S. invasion of Iraq in 2003, Syria provided safe haven for anti-American insurgents. Syria and Israel have disputed the Golan Heights, an area between the two countries, from which Syria allowed guerrillas to launch attacks against Israel.

LEBANON

Southwest of Syria is the country of Lebanon. Two parallel mountain ranges, called the Lebanon and Anti-Lebanon mountains, run down the length of the country. Their highest peaks are Qurnat

Syrian street vendors display their wares for potential customers.

as-Sawda (10,115 ft.) and Mount Hermon (9,232 ft.), respectively. Between the two parallel ranges lies the Bekáa Valley.

France received Lebanon as part of its mandate after World War I. In 1920, France separated Lebanon from Syria, and both remained under French control until 1946.

RUINS OF ANCIENT TYRE

The major city of ancient Lebanon was Tyre. Built on an island, it was the capital of Phoenicia until 583 BC. Tyre was a great trading center in the ancient world. King Hiram of Tyre exported cedars to Solomon (1 Kings 5), and a park preserves the last major grove of the Cedars of Lebanon near the mountain Qurnat as-Sawda. As prophesied, God brought Nebuchadnezzar against Tyre in a destructive siege (Ezek. 26). Later, Alexander the Great built a causeway to take the island in 332 BC.

RUINS OF MODERN BEIRUT

The modern capital of Lebanon is **Beirut**. With more than one million people, it is the largest city in the country. Beirut once had a thriving economy based on its resorts and its fruit crops (apples, cherries, grapes, lemons, oranges, and peaches). It was a city of splendor and was known as the "Paris of the Middle East." But that was before the civil war between Muslims and Christians.

Lebanon has the largest proportion of Christians of any Middle Eastern country. About 39 percent of the population claim to be Christians of one sort or another. Most of the Christians are called **Maronites** (MAHR uh nites, descendants of a Syrian hermit named St. Maron). The Maronites later united with the Roman Catholic Church as a separate religious community, acknowledging the pope but following their own format for religious services.

About 60 percent of Lebanese are members of several competing Muslim groups. Sunni Muslims are the largest group, with more than one million followers. Next are the more than one-half million Shiites. There are also about two hundred thousand **Druze** (DROOZ), or Druse, who broke from the Shiites and followed an eleventh-century Egyptian ruler named Al-Hakim, who claimed to be God. In 1860, the Druze massacred many Maronites, and the two groups have been bitter enemies ever since.

Warfare between Maronites, Sunnis, Shiites, and the Druze erupted in 1975. Street fighting, bombings, and the taking of European hostages became commonplace. Terrorists assassinated the Sunni prime minister and the Maronite president. The war became more complex when the Israelis moved into the Bekáa Valley in the south to reduce terrorist bases. Israel eventually carved out a "security zone" in southern Lebanon. The Syrians also moved in to extend their own authority. Once beautiful, Beirut became a pile of rubble.

In 1983, four nations (France, Britain, Italy, and the United States) sent peacekeepers to Beirut, but they could not stop the fighting. The United States withdrew after a suicide bomber drove a truck into the military barracks and killed 241 marines. Israel later withdrew its forces. When Saddam Hussein invaded Kuwait in 1990 and diverted the West's attention to the Persian Gulf, Syria took the opportunity to invade Lebanon and destroy the last Christian army, thus ending the civil war. Although the

Mount Hermon, on the border between Syria and Lebanon, is the only mountain in the region with snowcaps.

Shown here before the 1975 war, Beirut is the capital and commercial center of Lebanon.

Although the famed cedars of Lebanon are not nearly so plentiful as they once were, a cedar is nonetheless featured on the nation's flag.

peace agreements granted all four religions proportional representation in the government, many Christians refused to participate. The people have begun rebuilding their country, but peace is by no means assured. In 2005, the popular prime minister was assassinated, and the outpouring of grief led to demonstrations that forced the Syrians to withdraw their troops. Observers of the Middle East realize that Lebanon remains a powder keg.

From 1975 to 1990, the economy was badly hindered by the ongoing violence and uncertainty. Stability came in the early 1990s, however, and the economy began to recover. Today, the Lebanese economy is dominated by banking and other commercial services. It has a foundation in a free market and encourages foreign investment. Its banking industry's secrecy rivals that of the Swiss. Other growing industries include plastics, textiles, marble, cement, and wood.

SECTION QUIZ

1. What is the Fertile Crescent?
2. What desert forms the interior of the Levant?
3. What is Syria's main resource?
4. What two parallel mountain ranges run the length of Lebanon?
5. What are mandates? Give two examples of mandates in the Middle East.
   - Why does Lebanon have a larger coastal population than Syria?

IV. THE MANDATE OF PALESTINE

Palestine was the British mandate formed out of the Ottoman Empire. The British kept the mandate until 1948, when the territory became the two nations of Israel and Jordan. In modern usage, the term *Palestine* refers only to this area from the intertestamental period through 1948. In ancient times, it included all of what is now Israel, as well as the part of Jordan called Gilead.

Both Jews and Christians call this area the **Holy Land** because most of the events recorded in Scripture took place there. Abraham, Joshua, David, and Elijah walked its dirt roads. Most importantly, Christ came to this corner of the earth two thousand years ago, and there He will return at His Second Coming.

ISRAEL

Thou mayest go in unto the land which the Lord thy God giveth thee, a land that floweth with milk and honey; as the Lord God of thy fathers hath promised thee.
(Deut. 27:3)

Three issues galvanize the countries of the Middle East: Islam, oil, and Israel. Of those three issues, perhaps the most volatile is Israel. As the only non-Muslim country in the region, it is clearly the "odd man out" among the nations of the Eastern Mediterranean.

PHYSICAL GEOGRAPHY

At its widest point, Israel reaches only about seventy miles wide. Its total land area is about the same as that of Massachusetts. Moving eastward from the Mediterranean Sea, one crosses several geographic landforms in relatively quick succession to the Transjordan Highlands on the east bank of the Jordan River.

The **Coastal Plains** are two lowland areas along the Mediterranean Sea: the *Plain of Sharon* in the north and the *Plain of Philistia* in the south. As one proceeds inland from the Plain of Philistia, the land rises into an area of low hills called the **Shephelah** (shuh FAY luh). The land continues to rise east of the Shephelah into the **Lebanese Mountains**, which run north-south for the full length of Israel. The ancient capital city of **Jerusalem** is at the top of these mountains; hence, the Bible always refers to going *up* to Jerusalem, even if one is traveling from north to south.

In the extreme south lies the arid **Negev** (NEHG ehv), which, although it is desert, produces abundant crops of fruits and vegetables with the help of irrigation. It also has rich deposits of potash, bromine, and copper. Northwest of the Plain of Sharon, the **Valley of Jezreel** (also known as the Plain of Esdraelon) extends inland just north of **Mount Carmel** from the Mediterranean to the Jordan River. In the extreme north, the waters from the mountains drain into Lake Hula and then southward into the Sea of Galilee and from there into the Jordan River, which continues flowing due south and empties into the Dead Sea. Between the Dead Sea and the Central Hills is the Wilderness of Judah.

Jewish Cities on the North Coastal Plain—The coastal plain along the Mediterranean Sea has Israel's best farmland. North of Mount Carmel, the coastal plain is called Acre (AHK uhr), or Acco, named for the ancient city by that name. However, the modern city of Haifa (HY fah) has far surpassed Acco and is now the third-largest city in Israel.

The Plain of Sharon stretches south from Mount Carmel to **Tel Aviv**, Israel's largest port and second-largest city. Tel Aviv is short for Tel Aviv-Yafo, which includes the ancient port of Joppa (or Yafo)

Largest Cities of Israel	
City	**Population**
1. Jerusalem	685,000
2. Tel Aviv	348,000
3. Haifa	276,000
4. Beersheba	180,000
5. Ashqelon	104,000

THE VALLEY OF JEZREEL

The Valley of Jezreel (or Plain of Esdraelon) is mentioned as a prominent place quite often in the Bible. In the Old Testament, it is where the Midianites, Amalekites, and other heathen nations camped while preying upon Israel during the time of the judges. Bible expositors interpret it to be the site of the last great Battle of Armegeddon in the New Testament (Rev. 16:13–16). Napoleon, whose armies fought there, described it as the perfect battlefield. Later, the British general Allenby concurred.

The views of the Valley of Jezreel as seen from the Nazareth ridge (left) and Mt. Carmel (right) clearly show how Napoleon could describe it as the perfect battlefield.

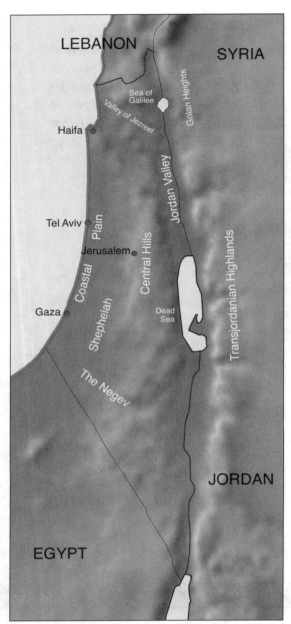

The Physical Divisions of Israel and Its Neighbors

in its city limits. Sharon is renowned for its fertility and flowers, especially the Rose of Sharon (Song of Sol. 2:1).

Independent Palestinian Cities in the Gaza Strip—The Plain of Philistia extends from Tel Aviv south to Egypt. The land is not as productive as the other coasts. In the Six-Day War, Israel won the coastal strip that is called the **Gaza** (GAH zah) **Strip**.

An Israeli soldier orders settlers to evacuate their homes in Gaza in preparation for occupation by Palestinians.

WADIS IN THE SHEPHELAH

The Shephelah is a region of low hills between the coastal plain and the mountains. Its average elevation is one thousand feet.

Wadis (WAH deez), dry stream beds that fill up with water after rainstorms, descend from the mountains and cross the Shephelah on their way to the coast. The parched ground soaks up little moisture from these infrequent torrents. In the ancient struggle between the Philistines and Judah, the main routes from the plain into the mountains of Judah followed the wadis.

MOUNTAIN SYSTEM

The Lebanon and Anti-Lebanon Mountains continue south from Lebanon. They rise less than four thousand feet in this area, but between them is the northern end of the **Great Rift Valley**, which falls below sea level. The **Jordan River** flows through this valley from its headwaters on Mount Hermon south to the **Dead Sea**. (South of the Dead Sea, the Great Rift Valley continues to the Red Sea and into East Africa.)

The mountains of Judah (or Judea) lie west of the Jordan River. The main mountain in this range is the **Mount of Olives** (2,737 ft.). The main cities of ancient Judah, including Jerusalem, lie along the top of the mountain range. Many Palestinians live in these cities today.

Israel also occupies the **Golan** (GOH lahn) **Heights**, a small part of the Anti-Lebanon Mountains northeast of the Sea of Galilee. Israel

Side View of Israel

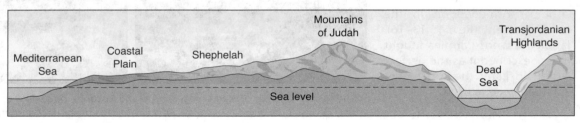

took this region from Syria during the Six-Day War, but Syria wants it back. In Bible times it was called Bashan (BAY shun), famous for its pastures and bulls (Ps. 22:12).

Mountains of Galilee—Galilee refers to the northernmost mountains of Israel. The main peaks are Mount Tabor (1,929 ft.) and Mount Meron (3,963 ft.), the highest mountain in Israel. Jesus lived most of his life in Galilee and preached in its synagogues (Mark 1:39). His childhood home, Nazareth, overlooked the Valley of Esdraelon.

This region includes the **Sea of Galilee** in the Great Rift Valley. The Jordan River pauses in this lake on its way to the Dead Sea. The lake is subject to strong winds, which swoop down from the north into the Rift Valley. Today the main town is Tiberias on the west

GEOGRAPHER'S CORNER

BIBLE GEOGRAPHY

A knowledge of geography is an invaluable tool in understanding events in the Bible because it helps one understand why some cities were so important, why Bible characters traveled the routes they did, and

The valley of Megiddo is prophesied to be the battleground of the nations.

why battles were fought where and how they were.

Perhaps the single most important factor in Israel's history was the trade routes that crossed the country. Armies and merchants generally follow well-watered lowlands. Ever since ancient times, the main route from Egypt to Mesopotamia followed the coast until it reached Mount Carmel (1,789 ft.). Because the slopes of Mount Carmel descend directly into the sea, the mountain created a barrier to travel along the coastal plain. There, the ancient trade route veered inland to the Iron Pass, at the fortress of **Megiddo** (muh GID oh). Traders

traveled east to the Jordan River before continuing north to Damascus.

The valley from Megiddo to the Jordan is the only valley through the mountains. It has two parts, divided by the narrowest spot in the valley near the town of Jezreel. The western part of the valley, from Megiddo to Jezreel, is called the **Plain of Esdraelon** (ez DRAY lon), or Valley of Megiddo. This plain will become the greatest battlefield in history, where Christ defeats the forces of Antichrist.

Beth-shan and Megiddo, guarding each end of the valley, were the most strategic cities in ancient Palestine. With Jezreel in the center of the valley, these cities controlled trade between Egypt and the Persian Gulf. Israel's enemies from the east gathered in the valley of Jezreel, where Gideon defeated them. The Philistines later controlled Beth-shan and displayed the body of King Saul on the city walls (1 Sam. 31:10). Josiah died at Megiddo, attempting to prevent an Egyptian army from using the pass on its way to Assyria (2 Kings 23:29).

These places will become important again, according to prophecy. The name *Armageddon* comes from

Har Megiddo, or Mount of Megiddo. Revelation 16:12–16 tells about vast armies that will come from all nations to a battle at Armageddon. Revelation 19:11–21 tells how Christ will be the conqueror at this battle. His clothes will be blood-stained because of a slaughter compared to the trampling of grapes.

Read the following passages about this same time period, and answer the questions, using the map for place names.

1. Where will Jesus first arrive on earth when He returns for this battle (Zech. 14:4)?

2. What will happen when His feet touch the ground (Zech. 14:1–9)?

3. What city will be surrounded by these armies from all nations (Luke 21:20–28)?

4. How far south will they be ranked (Isa. 63:1–6)? (Find the city on the map.)

🔆 How deep will the blood be from all of these troops? For what distance will this blood run (in modern units)? How far is it between the northern and southern extent of these armies, according to the map? (All answers can be found in Revelation 14:20.)

MASADA

Near the Dead Sea is a flat-topped, steep-sided mountain called Masada (mah SAH dah), which means "fortress, or stronghold." It was the setting for the stirring story of the Jewish Zealots' last stand for freedom in their revolt against Rome, and it has become a patriotic symbol for Israel, much as the Alamo is a symbol for Texas.

King Herod built a major citadel on the summit of Masada about 35 BC. A Roman garrison took over the fort in 4 BC, but the Zealots seized control in AD 66 in the revolt against Rome. After the Romans took Jerusalem in AD 70, Masada became the last holdout of the Jewish revolt. Two years later, the fifteen thousand men of the Tenth Legion, led by Silva, arrived to quell the resistance. He surrounded the mountain with eight camps and built a siege ramp on the west side. After nearly two years, Silva's men breached the walls—only to find dead bodies. Rather than be tortured by the Romans, the 960 men, women, and children had committed suicide the night before.

Israeli archaeologists took great interest in studying the site at Masada. Excavations in 1955 and 1963 by Yigael Yadin restored the wall, cisterns, and palaces. They found remains from each period: frescoes in

This view of Masada shows the ramp that the Romans built to break the seige.

the throne room of Herod's palace built on the northern cliffs; weapons and stone missiles used by the Zealots as well as fragments of scrolls of Genesis, Leviticus, Deuteronomy, Psalms, and Ezekiel; Roman coins left by a garrison stationed there until AD 111; and a Byzantine church from the fifth century.

Today, visitors can still see many of these ruins, but the frescoes have been moved to museums. Visitors can reach the twenty-acre plateau on the summit of Masada by cable cars or by climbing the siege ramp. One

other path, the Snake Path, climbs the steep eastern face on a winding route that few visitors attempt.

In 2005, a team of Israeli doctors and scientists succeeded in getting a 2000-year-old seed discovered at Masada to germinate. The seed, which the team named Methuselah because of its age, was from a date palm. The scientists nurtured it to germinate, and it grew to be nearly a foot tall and produced seven leaves. Such lab plants germinated from older seeds usually live for only a short time.

coast. During Jesus's life on earth, Capernaum at the north end was more important.

Archeologists have excavated ruins all over Israel. As cities were destroyed, new ones were built on top of their ruins, creating huge mounds called **tells**. Archeologists dig layer by layer, investigating the history of each time period. The largest tell in Israel is Hazor. Hazor was strategic because it guarded the entrance to the Jordan Valley from the northern trade route to Damascus.

West Bank—The **West Bank** is the mountain region west of the Jordan River and south of Galilee, which Jordan owned until Israel captured it during the Six-Day War. This region includes many of the famous biblical regions of Judah and Samaria.

The ten northern tribes established a new capital at Samaria. Their land included the strategic passes at Megiddo and the Valley of Jezreel, so they were often invaded by advancing empires.

THE DIVIDED CAPITAL

Jerusalem, the most populous city in Israel, sits in the mountains of Judah at the western edge of the West Bank. It has again become the heart of Israel. The Hebrew parliament, or **Knesset** (kuh NES eht), is located in the city. Israel established the first true democracy in the Middle East. The government guarantees all three great religions access to their holy sites in Jerusalem: the Temple Mount and the Wailing Wall for Jews, the Dome of the Rock mosque for Muslims, and various sites in Jerusalem and Bethlehem for Christians. The country's industries have excelled. Israel's per capita GDP exceeds that of all of its neighbors and even that of many oil-producing nations in the Middle East. Israel's health care and educational opportunities are excellent.

Jerusalem has two parts: the Old City and the New City. Israel took East Jerusalem, or the Old City, during the

The Knesset is Israel's parliament.

Six-Day War. It has small, winding streets and many ancient buildings. A wall built by Suleiman the Magnificent surrounds the Old City. The Knesset is located in West Jerusalem, the more modern part of the city. The streets are wider and the atmosphere

pulses with new life. Other buildings in the New City include the Holocaust Museum and the Shrine of the Book, where the Dead Sea Scrolls are housed. Although the capital of Israel is Jerusalem, most foreign embassies are based in Tel Aviv.

MODERN NEGEV

The Hebrew word *negev* means simply "south," and it refers to the southern part of Israel. It has three parts: historical Negev, the Wilderness of Zin, and Arabah.

Historical Negev—In the Bible, the Negev always refers to a small arid region around the towns of Beersheba and Ziklag. Because it supports marginal agriculture, it was sharply distinguished from the uninhabited wastes of the southern wilderness. In the best years, this region gets just enough moisture for some agriculture. Abraham and Isaac settled in Beersheba (Gen. 26:33), and David lived in Ziklag before he became king (1 Sam. 30:1–2). Beersheba's position as the southernmost habitable city in Israel made it proverbial in the phrase "from Dan to Beersheba" (1 Sam. 3:20).

Wilderness of Zin—The Wilderness of Zin lies south of the biblical Negev. Steep wadis cut through its rugged mountains, and several craters gouge the landscape. The largest crater, Maktesh Ramon, is called the Grand Canyon of Israel.

Arabah—East of the wilderness and south of the Great Rift Valley is a wide barren valley called the **Arabah**. The Wadi Arabah descends through the valley northward into the Dead Sea. Elat (Eloth in 1 Kings 9:26), at the south end of the valley on the Gulf of Aqaba, is Israel's only port on the Red Sea. Solomon built a fleet at Ezion-geber, next to Eloth.

Although the modern Negev is an apparent wasteland, the ingenious people have devised a method using small amounts of salt water

The Dead Sea Scrolls

In 1947, a Bedouin shepherd threw a rock into a cave. It hit a clay pot and shattered it. When the shepherd went to investigate, he discovered one of the greatest archaeological finds of the century—the Dead Sea Scrolls. Subsequent investigations of nearby caves turned up more manuscripts, more than 900 in all. Some of these are mere fragments, whereas a few are complete scrolls.

Many manuscripts date from the first century BC, making them hundreds of years older than the former oldest-known copy, the Masoretic text. They were likely recorded and preserved by a Jewish sect called the Essenes. The Dead Sea Scrolls contain every book of the Bible except Esther and Nehemiah, along with worship hymns, commentaries, and rules regulating community life. The Isaiah scroll is the only complete copy of the biblical books. The veracity of the Scripture is attested to by the remarkable accuracy the modern copies show when compared with the ancient scrolls.

Kibbutz

A **kibbutz** (kih BOOTS) is a Jewish community in which the people share everything in common. No one in the community owns private property, and all members of the kibbutz have an equal say about how the kibbutz is run. The first kibbutz began in 1909, and originally all of the communities grew crops. Since then, some have expanded into manufacturing or tourism. Kibbutz En Gev, for example, operates a popular resort on the southeast shore of the Sea of Galilee and is quite prosperous.

The plural of kibbutz is *kibbutzim* (typical of Hebrew—*cherubim, seraphim, Elohim*). Israel has more than eight hundred kibbutzim with an average of 275 members each. Each member works hard to help his community succeed. To join a kibbutz, a prospective member works on a trial basis. After a year, the community votes on whether to accept him or her as a full member.

Through Christian Eyes

What are some advantages and disadvantages of living in a kibbutz?

to grow hardy plants, such as tomatoes, peanuts, and cotton. This specialized farming, called brackish water agriculture, has allowed Israel to become a major supplier of these products to Europe.

Historical Background

Israel is the **Promised Land**, the place God gave to His chosen people and where they were to live forever. The Israelites conquered the Promised Land under Joshua and built a great nation that lasted about fifteen hundred years. But the Romans destroyed Jerusalem in AD 70, and the Israelites spent the next two thousand years dispersed in foreign lands and persecuted by all peoples. The modern state of Israel testifies to the Jews' undying dream of returning to their homeland.

This dream became a burning passion at the end of the nineteenth century with the rise of the **Zionist Movement**. Hardy pioneers began moving to Zion to build farms on the rough Palestinian frontier. At first, their numbers were few, and the Turks would not give them legal recognition of owning land. But after Palestine became a British mandate, Jewish immigrants began to pour into the area, especially during the Nazi persecution of the 1930s. Against overwhelming odds, the Jews won independence in 1948.

Since its independence, Israel has welcomed Jews from all over the world. They revived the dead Hebrew language and created words for modern items. Immigrants have come from at least one hundred nations and speak nearly as many languages. As part of the process of adapting to the new country, immigrants can take a five-month course on the nation's culture. In addition, the first job of every Israeli citizen is military service. Every adult citizen must serve: women serve two years, and men serve three. Israel is surrounded by sworn enemies. (Iran's president declared in late 2005 that his country's goal is to "wipe Israel off the face of the map.") Its very survival depends on the willingness of every citizen to defend Israel's right to exist.

Judaism

The Jews are unlike any other people in the Middle East. After the death of David's son King Solomon, the ten northern tribes broke away, but the two southern tribes remained faithful to God. Their land became known as the Kingdom of Judah, after the larger tribe. Their religion became known as **Judaism**, and the people as Jews.

Oral traditions (the *Mishnah*) became increasingly important to religious life.

A group of refugees in Galilee collected the oral traditions of Judaism into sixty-three books, called the *Talmud*. Just as Muslims have a basic creed—"There is no god but Allah, and Muhammad is His Messenger"—Jews have a basic creed, called the *Shema*, around which they have rallied: "Hear, O Israel, the Lord Our God, the Lord is One."

Despite efforts at unity, Israel is divided between Orthodox Jews and secular Jews as well as between hardliners, who oppose any compromise with Israel's enemies, and liberals, who want to take a softer approach with them. Sometimes these groups have turned to violence. Complicating this political division, Judaism also has many different branches that differ in the degree of their devotion to tradition. **Orthodox Jews** believe that the Pentateuch, or *Torah*, is God's Word given to Moses, and they strictly follow the *Talmud*. A new branch formed in the early nineteenth century as a result of Enlightenment thinking. Followers of that branch, called

Orthodox Jews follow the teachings found in the Torah and the Talmud.

Jews in a World of Goyim

The Jews worship on Saturday because the Old Testament commanded rest, a sabbath, on the seventh day of the week (Exod. 20:8–10). Today Jews worship in synagogues, meeting places developed for instruction in Hebrew and the Old Testament. The rabbi leads services consisting of readings from Scripture and chants from the siddur (prayer book). The Scripture readings are selected from the Torah (the Pentateuch, or first five books of Moses) so that the entire Torah is read each year.

Jewish boys are circumcised after birth, in accordance with Leviticus 12:3. On the Saturday after his thirteenth birthday, the boy celebrates his bar mitzvah, when he becomes a "son of the commandment." At this ceremony, he reads from the Torah and may give a speech to show his knowledge of Scripture and Jewish traditions. Afterward, the boy receives presents at a special feast. He has now entered manhood. He is fully responsible for keeping the commandments and can participate fully with the other men at worship services. Ten men are needed to form a synagogue.

The Hebrew calendar has twelve lunar months totaling 354 days. The calendar is reconciled with the solar year by adding 28 days in 7 out of every 19 years. The western dates for Jewish holidays therefore change from year to year. Rosh Hashanah is the Jewish New Year and occurs in the autumn. The main time of fasting is the Ninth of Av (second to last month) in our autumn. This fast commemorates the two destructions of the temple (in 586 BC by the Babylonians and in AD 70 by the Romans).

Ten days after the New Year is Yom Kippur, the Day of Atonement (Lev. 23:27–28). Sukkot (Tabernacles) is the harvest festival, which begins five days later (Lev. 23:34). In early winter, Hanukkah (Feast of Lights) celebrates the victory over the Syrians in 165 BC. In late winter, Purim celebrates the deliverance through Queen Esther (Esther 9:28). In the spring, during the week of Pesach or Passover (Exod. 12:24–27), Jews eat only matzah (unleavened bread). At the end of the week, each family eats the Seder (Passover meal). Fifty days later is Shavuot (First Fruits or Pentecost, Lev. 23:15–21).

Orthodox Jews carefully follow the laws of Judaism. They eat only kosher foods made according to Old Testament dietary laws. They do not eat pork and other unclean meats (Lev. 11). In prayer, Orthodox Jews wear prayer shawls and phylacteries (tefillin) strapped to their foreheads or arms (Deut. 6:8). The tefillin are small boxes containing Scripture verses.

Many Jews in Israel pray at the Wailing Wall. This wall is the last remaining part of the foundation of the temple that was destroyed in AD 70 by the Romans. Today, two Is-

lamic mosques stand on top of the temple ruins. Muslims and all other non-Jews are called *goyim* (gentiles) by the Jews. Trodden down by these gentile nations, Jews look forward to reclaiming the site and offering sacrifices to God as described in the Old Testament.

Israel Sought U.S. Diplomatic Recognition in 1948

My Dear Mr. President:

I have the honor to notify you that the state of Israel has been proclaimed as an independent republic within frontiers approved by the General Assembly of the United Nations in its Resolution of November 29, 1947, and that a provisional government has been charged to assume the rights and duties of government for preserving law and order within the boundaries of Israel, for defending the state against external aggression, and for discharging the obligations of Israel to the other nations of the world in accordance with international law. The Act of Independence will become effective at one minute after six o'clock on the evening of 14 May 1948, Washington time.

With full knowledge of the deep bond of sympathy which has existed and has been strengthened over the past thirty years between the Government of the United States and the Jewish people of Palestine, I have been authorized by the provisional government of the new state to tender this message and to express the hope that your government will recognize and will welcome Israel into the community of nations.

Very respectfully yours,

ELIAHU EPSTEIN

Agent, Provisional Government of Israel

Harry Truman was the president when the United States granted diplomatic recognition to Israel in 1948.

Reform Jews, reject many of the old traditions but believe the Old Testament is still useful as a moral code. A newer branch, known as **Conservative Jews**, broke off from the Reform Jews in the nineteenth century because they believed in keeping more of the old traditions. A liberal branch, called **Reconstructionists**, formed in the 1930s. They see Judaism not as a religion but only as a source of social identity.

THE PALESTINIANS

Jews are not the only people who claim Palestine. The Arabs are also the descendants of Abraham, through his son Ishmael. God promised to make of Ishmael a great nation (Gen. 17:15–20). The Arabs conquered Palestine in the seventh century and have lived there ever since. The Philistines of the Bible converted to Islam during the Muslim conquests. They are now known as **Palestinians**. But Palestine fell to the Ottoman Turks in 1517, and the Turks ruled the Arabs. Ironically, both the Arabs and the Zionist farmers joined the British to overthrow the Turks during World War I. In gratitude, the British government promised to safeguard the rights of the Arabs and "view with favour the establishment in Palestine of a national home for the Jewish people."

From the beginning, however, the Palestinians and the Jews have quarreled over their respective rights, especially in the Holy City of Jerusalem. After World War II, Britain turned to the United Nations to resolve the conflict. The UN proposed a plan to divide Palestine into two parts and to make Jerusalem an international city. The Jews reluctantly accepted the plan in 1948, and modern Israel was born.

The Palestinians, however, rejected the plan and refused to give up claims to any portion of Palestine. The day after Israel became independent, Arab nations began the first of four wars to drive out the Jews. In the first war, Israel conquered West Jerusalem and annexed it to their country. Thousands of Arab Palestinians were forced into exile. These refugees became a source of bitterness between the two sides, a constant "thorn in the flesh" for Israel. Another full-fledged war against Egypt in 1956 proved inconclusive.

In 1967, three Arab nations—Egypt, Syria, and Jordan—began planning a new attack on Israel, but Israel learned about their plans and struck them first. (Such action is called a **preemptive strike**.) In that **Six-Day War**, the Israelis easily routed the unprepared Arabs, capturing much land on Israel's borders, including Egypt's Sinai Peninsula, Syria's Golan Heights, and three Palestinian regions (the West Bank of the Jordan River, the Gaza Strip along the Mediterranean coast, and East Jerusalem). Egypt and Syria attacked Israel again in the **Yom Kippur War** (1973), but the Israelis narrowly won at great cost.

Ever since these wars, Israel's politics have focused on the use or disposal of the occupied territories. Two views prevail: one group believes that Israel should trade land for peace; the other group believes that the land should remain Israel's forever. Heavily armed Jewish settlers have built communities in the occupied territories and have vowed to die before they give up one inch of their "God-given" soil. According to a 2004 agreement between Israel and the Palestinian

Authority, however, Israel has committed to return to the Palestinians seven major cities in the occupied territory. In spite of these concessions, violence continues because the Palestinians do not really want land; they want the extinction of Israel as a nation.

Although Palestinians represent only about 20 percent of Israel's population, they are a majority in the Gaza Strip. Many other Palestinians live as refugees in neighboring Arab states. Two opposing Arab groups arose among Palestinians. The Arab nations created the **Palestine Liberation Organization (PLO)** in 1964 to represent all of the Palestinian Arabs. The PLO demanded a Palestinian state, refused to recognize Israel's right to exist, and engaged in numerous terrorist acts designed to destroy Israel.

Armed Palestinian militants march in protest of the existence of Israel.

The PLO leader, **Yasir Arafat**, eventually claimed to reject terrorism to win support for Palestinians in the United Nations. He envisioned a secular Palestinian state in which Jews, Muslims, and Christians could live in peace. Israel, however, refused to give in to PLO demands. In 1987, the PLO announced a violent uprising, called the *intifada*, in the occupied territories. The Israeli army was forced to initiate curfews and engage in street battles to keep order. With no end to the fighting in sight, the Israelis became disillusioned with the costly military occupation.

Yitzhak Rabin (rah BEAN), who became prime minister in 1992, decided to open negotiations with Arafat over the future of the occupied territories. Without the knowledge of their own governments or any other nation, Rabin and Arafat secretly began negotiations in Oslo, Norway. The resulting **Oslo Accord** gave guidelines for a series of compromises. Both sides hoped that early successes would encourage support for a final settlement in 1999. Both men received the Nobel Peace Prize in 1994. The first land returned to Palestinian authority was the Gaza Strip and the city of Jericho. But violence threatened the peace process at every stage. In 1995, a radical young Jew assassinated Rabin—the first Israeli leader ever to die by an assassin's bullet.

Arafat's "moderate" views were not popular among Muslim radicals, who still want to unite the Arab nations into one Islamic "fundamentalist" state and to destroy Israel. The most feared terrorist groups are **Hamas**, **Hezbollah**, and the **Islamic Jihad**, who want to destroy Israel by any means. Although Arafat had claimed to renounce violence, he did little if anything to rein in the violent activities of the militants. He died in November 2004 and was succeeded by **Mahmoud Abbas**.

In early 2006, Hamas won the Palestinian parliamentary elections but refused to renounce terrorism or their pledge to destroy Israel. In the summer of 2006, Hezbollah, allegedly supported and supplied by Syria and Iran, kidnapped several Israeli soldiers and dramatically increased rocket attacks against Israel. Israel retaliated by bombing terrorist strongholds in Gaza, Beirut, and southern Lebanon and invading Lebanon. The conflict escalated into all-out war. Only time will tell if the Palestinians and the Israelis can work in good faith to end the violence.

THE DEAD SEA

The **Dead Sea**, fifty miles long and ten miles wide, lies at the bottom of the Great Rift Valley between Israel and Jordan. The Dead Sea boasts both the lowest shoreline and the saltiest water in the world. Its shore, 1,310 feet below sea level, has a lower elevation than any other point of land on the earth. Its waters are up to eight times saltier than ocean water, and they are about 25 percent more salty than the nearest rival, the Great Salt Lake. The Jordan River supplies most of the water, but desert wadis bring additional salts.

The Dead Sea is a lake with no outlet. Since the water evaporates quickly in the dry climate, salt deposits collect around the edges. Every ton of water from the Dead Sea contains about 125 pounds of common salt, potash, bromine, and other minerals. A peninsula called *Al Lisan* ("The Tongue") divides the Dead Sea into two parts. The larger northern section reaches a depth of 1,312 feet. The southern portion averages only twenty feet deep and is shrinking due to mineral mining.

The salty sea and surrounding desert make for a harsh environment,

Salt formations cover the shores of the Dead Sea.

but life persists. Brine shrimp and a few plants and bacteria live in the water. Springs in the rugged desert hills surrounding the lake create desert oases. One such spring, En-gedi, or Spring of the Goat, creates a large waterfall. The spring takes its name from the ibex, a wild goat living in the canyons.

People have lived in the area since ancient times. Masada, a fortress, overlooks the west shore. Bedouins found the oldest known manuscripts of the Old Testament, called the Dead Sea Scrolls, in caves at Qumran on the northeast shore. The ancient cities of Sodom and Gomorrah also stood near the Dead Sea (or Salt Sea, Gen. 14:3). Many people believe that the ruins of these cities lie under the southern part of the sea. Today, people visit health resorts on the Dead Sea to float in the salty mineral water. Jordanians and Israelis are diverting so much water from the Jordan River for agriculture that the future of the Dead Sea is threatened.

En-gedi

En-gedi is where Lot was captured by the kings of Shinar, Ellasar, Elam, and others when they sacked Sodom and Gomorrah and where David hid when he was being pursued by Saul. (See Genesis 14:1, 11–13; 1 Samuel 23:29–24:1.)

JORDAN

Jordan, located east of Israel and south of Syria, is about the size of Indiana and consists mainly of uninhabited desert. Unlike some Middle Eastern desert areas, Jordan lacks petroleum. Furthermore, only 3 percent of Jordan can be farmed. Many Jordanians work abroad and send money home to their families. Adding to the difficulties are the large number of Palestinian refugees who fled to Jordan as a result of the Arab-Israeli wars. More Palestinians now live in Jordan than native Jordanians! In spite of these problems, Jordan has been one of the most stable and peaceful countries in the region. Its government is a constitutional monarchy.

The primary resources come from the Great Rift Valley. The Dead Sea contains deposits of potash, bromine, and salt. The Jordan River valley produces citrus fruits, cabbage, melons, eggplants, and cucumbers. At the south end of the Arabah lies Jordan's only port and its only major town in the Great Rift Valley, Al 'Aqabah (for which the gulf is named). The Syrian Desert, which covers the eastern half of Jordan, offers few if any resources.

Between the Great Rift Valley and the Syrian Desert is the **Transjordanian Plateau**, where most people live. The northern border of this plateau is the Yarmuk River, which runs through a wadi dividing Jordan from Syria on the north.

The Moabites and Ammonites, descendants of Lot, lived on the plateau (Gen. 19:36–38). The wadi called Arnon runs west to the middle of the Dead Sea. This wadi divided Moab in the south from Ammon in the north. **Amman** has always been the capital of the Ammonites. In ancient times, it was called Rabbah (1 Chron. 20:1) or Rabbath Ammon. Today, it has some industries, and nearby farms produce wheat, barley, grapes, olives, and nuts. But lacking oil, having little arable farmland, and being inundated with refugees, Jordan struggles with poverty. The stabilizing force was the forty-six-year reign of King Hussein, who died in 1999. His son, Abdullah II, is now king and is continuing the struggle to bring prosperity to the country.

Petra

The ancient ruins of **Petra** stand in a narrow canyon in what is now Jordan. The Edomites founded the city in the ninth century BC and took pride in the security of its easily defended entrance. However, as Isaiah and Obadiah prophetically warned, the Edomites were conquered by the Nabataeans in 300 BC. The Romans took over in AD 106 before the city fell into ruin after the rise of Palmyra. After a brief resurgence in the twelfth century, it fell into permanent ruin.

Posing as a Muslim, Swiss explorer Jakob Burckhardt discovered the ruins in 1812. The city's ruins include mysterious 130-foot-high tombs chiseled into the salmon pink cliffs.

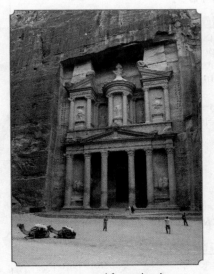

Petra, a city carved from the desert rock, is an awe-inspiring attraction in Jordan.

SECTION QUIZ

1. What three occupied territories consist mostly of Palestinians? What occupied territory once belonged to Syria?

2. What mountain interrupts the coastal plain? What city guards the pass?

3. Distinguish the modern and biblical Negev.

4. What geographic feature is common in Palestine, providing both strategic routes in the Shephelah and national boundaries on the Transjordanian Plateau?

5. Name four features of the Great Rift Valley.

⚬ What Bible cities would you like to visit in Israel? Which would be difficult to visit and why?

Can You:
Define These Terms?

choke point	Judaism
partition	Orthodox Jew
mandate	Reform Jew
Maronites	Conservative Jew
Druze	Reconstuctionist
Holy Land	Palestinian
Shephelah	preemptive strike
Negev	Six-Day War
wadi	Yom Kippur War
tell	PLO
Knesset	Oslo Accord
kibbutz	Hamas
Promised Land	Hezbollah
Zionist Movement	Islamic Jihad

Locate These Places?

Asia Minor	Coastal Plains
Mount Ararat	Lebanese
Istanbul	Mountains
Bosporus	Valley of Jezreel
Dardanelles	Mount Carmel
Pontic Mountains	Great Rift Valley
Taurus Mountains	Jordan River
Mesaoria Plain	Dead Sea
Nicosia	Mount of Olives
Levant	Golan Heights
Fertile Crescent	Sea of Galilee
Syria	Plain of Esdraelon
Palestine	Arabah
Syrian Desert	Transjordanian
Damascus	Plateau
Beirut	Petra

Explain the Significance?

Kemal Atatürk	Tel Aviv
Thrace	Gaza Strip
Byzantine Empire	Megiddo
Anatolia	West Bank
Ottoman Empire	Yasir Arafat
Hafez al-Assad	Mahmoud Abbas
Bashar al-Assad	Dead Sea
Jerusalem	Amman

CHAPTER REVIEW 16

HOW MUCH DO YOU REMEMBER?

1. The Middle East lies at the crossroads of what three continents?

2. Name the European and Asian sections of Turkey.

3. What are the two factions that divide Cyprus?

4. What language is spoken in Syria?

5. What desert surrounds Damascus?

6. Which of the four main factions in Lebanon claims to be Christian?

7. Put the following events in chronological order:
   a. King David ruled the Israelites.
   b. Muhammad founded the religion of Islam.
   c. Abram journeyed through the Fertile Crescent.
   d. The Ottoman Turks built a vast empire.
   e. Jesus Christ was born.
   f. Palestine became a British mandate.

8. What plain contains the Gaza Strip? What people live there?

9. Name the two cities that once guarded the entrance to the Plain of Esdraelon.

10. Name two lakes and a river in the Great Rift Valley.

11. In what part of Israel are the Arabah and the Wilderness of Zin?

WHAT DO YOU THINK?

1. Compare and contrast Judaism with Christianity.

2. How is Turkey different from Egypt?

3. Why is the United States allied with Turkey? What problems does this alliance create?

Islam requires prayer five times a day and permeates culture in the Persian Gulf countries.

THE PERSIAN GULF

The **Middle East**, located at the crossroads of three continents, has been the focus of world history. The descendants of Noah founded the first civilization there. The three major monotheistic religions—Judaism, Christianity, and Islam—began there. Conquering armies have swept back and forth across the ancient trade routes, bathing the land in blood. The Middle East is at once a region of wealth and poverty, of beauty and terror, of ancient ways and modern industry.

The previous chapter covered the western half of the Middle East, on the rim of the Mediterranean Sea. This chapter examines the eastern half, where the **Persian Gulf** is the center of population and trade. The gulf has been a hub of activity since ancient times, as ships have sailed through the Arabian Sea to ports in Asia and Africa. Islam was founded in this region during the Middle Ages, and it has come to dominate every aspect of life.

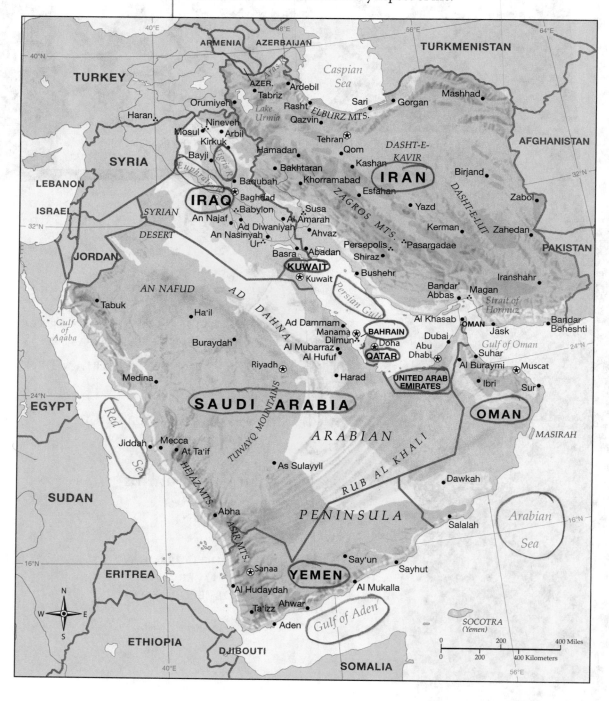

Muslims believe that Jesus was a prophet, but their founder directly attacked the deity of Jesus Christ: "Far is it removed from His transcendent majesty that He should have a son" (Surah 4:171, translated by Mohammed M. Pickhall). By rejecting the Son of God, the leaders of Islam have made themselves the enemies of the Father.

> *All men should honour the Son, even as they honour the Father. He that honoureth not the Son honoureth not the Father which hath sent him.*
> *(John 5:23)*

The great Islamic empires fell into decay long ago. The discovery of oil there in the twentieth century put the Persian Gulf back at the center of world politics, and money from oil has revolutionized life in the region. But most of the money benefits Western businesses and the Muslim rulers, while the common people continue to struggle in poverty under their harsh rulers. They envy the wealth of the West and look to their ancient cities and archeological sites as reminders of fallen glory, which they long to regain. These factors, as much as their arguments about the "decadent infidel," the West, fuel radical Islamic terrorists.

Persian Gulf Fast Facts

Flag	Country	Capital	Area (sq. mi.)	Pop. (M)	Pop. Density (per sq. mi.)	Per Capita GDP ($US)	Life Span
	Bahrain	Manama	257	0.68	2,681	$19,200	74.23
	Iran	Tehran	636,296	68.02	107	$7,700	69.96
	Iraq	Baghdad	168,754	26.07	155	$2,100	68.70
	Kuwait	Kuwait City	6,880	2.34	339	$21,300	77.03
	Oman	Muscat	82,031	3.00	37	$13,100	77.13
	Qatar	Doha	4,415	0.86	195	$23,200	73.67
	Saudi Arabia	Riyadh	756,985	26.42	35	$12,000	75.46
	United Arab Emirates	Abu Dhabi	32,000	2.56	80	$25,200	75.24
	Yemen	Sanaa	203,850	20.73	102	$800	61.75

I. SAUDI ARABIA

Saudi Arabia is the most influential country in the Middle East. Besides being the largest Middle Eastern nation, it is the greatest oil exporter in the world and sits on the largest known oil reserves on earth. But Saudi Arabia holds even greater sway in the Muslim world because it is the birthplace of Islam and home to its most holy sites.

ISLAM

Islam is a religion of works. Five basic acts, called the **Pillars of Islam**, are required of all Muslims:

1. Declare that "There is no god but Allah, and Muhammad is his messenger."
2. Pray five times a day.
3. Give alms (or the *zakat*) to the poor.
4. Fast during the month of **Ramadan**.
5. Make a pilgrimage (or *hajj*) to Mecca at least once in a lifetime.

Repeating the declaration of the first pillar is all that is required for one to become a Muslim (follower of Islam). Therefore, it was easy for the early Muslims to force conquered people to "convert." More than 1.3 billion people in the world today make this declaration. The tragic truth is that this first pillar of Islam is a direct denial of the Bible's most basic claims regarding Jesus Christ. Muhammad is not the final, greatest messenger from God. Jesus Christ is: "No man hath seen God at any time; the only begotten Son, which is in the bosom of the Father, he hath declared him" (John 1:18). As God's special messenger, Jesus taught that He was equal with the Father: "He that hath seen me hath seen the Father" (John 14:9).

Islam permeates life in most Middle Eastern countries today, even those that, like Turkey, have "secular" governments. Every city has at least one **mosque** (Islamic worship building). Criers (or loudspeakers) call the people to prayer five times daily from the *minarets* (towers) beside the mosques. Businesses stop for prayer at dawn, noon, midafternoon, sunset, and night. On Friday, the Muslim holy day, people meet at noon in the local mosque to recite their prayers together.

Declare that: "There is no god but Allah, and Muhammad is his messenger."

pilgrimage *(Hajj)* to Mecca

Islam

The Koran

Pray five times a day.

Give alms *(zakat)* to the poor.

Fast during the month of Ramadan.

HOLY CITIES ON THE WEST COAST

Saudi Arabia lies on the **Arabian Peninsula**, which juts down from the Middle East into the Arabian Sea. Two important arms of the Arabian Sea—the Persian Gulf on the east and the Red Sea on the west—lie on either side of the peninsula. Nine-tenths of the entire peninsula is desert or barren plateau, except for two semiarid regions near the coast. Saudi Arabia has no permanent rivers and no lakes. Since Saudis depend on springs or wells for water, most settlements are at oases or along the coasts.

A rare strip of highlands rises near the west coast of the peninsula, forcing monsoon winds periodically to drop precious moisture. Terracing is possible on the mountain slopes. The narrow coastal plain at the foot of the Asir Mountains in the southwest corner is the most fertile region in the country. This vital region has been inhabited since early history.

Through Christian Eyes

How should Christians in America respond to Islamic nations that are closed to the gospel?

LET'S GO EXPLORING

CLIMATES OF THE MIDDLE EAST

1. What is the most obvious contrast between the north and the south?

2. What is the predominant climate along the eastern edge of the Mediterranean Sea?

3. How many countries seem to be made up entirely of desert?

4. What climate does Iran have on the southern end of the Caspian Sea?

🔍 From what you have learned about monsoon winds, why does the entire coast of the Arabian Sea have a dry climate?

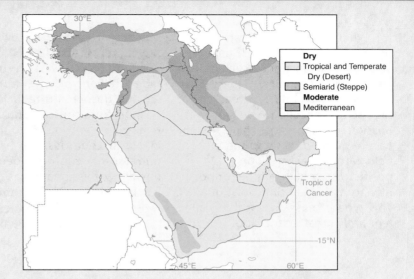

Dry	
☐	Tropical and Temperate Dry (Desert)
☐	Semiarid (Steppe)
Moderate	
☐	Mediterranean

The primary highlands in the west are the Hejaz Mountains, which run parallel to the coast. Several important cities lie in the Hejaz region. Jiddah, meaning "Bride of the Red Sea," is the largest port on the Red Sea, with 2.8 million people. It lies on the narrow coastal plain known as the *Tihamah*. Nearby in the highlands are the two holiest centers of Islam: **Mecca**, which is about fifty miles due east, and **Medina** (meh DEEN ah), which is about two hundred miles due north.

MECCA

Muhammad was born about AD 570 in Mecca, an important stop on the caravan route along the Red Sea. Forty years later, while living in a cave in the desert, he claimed to have received revelations from Allah (the Arabic word for "God"). Muhammad became the prophet of Allah and founded Islam.

The **Koran**, the Muslim holy book that records Muhammad's revelations, requires every Muslim to make at least one pilgrimage to Mecca, although exceptions are made for the ill or poor. The pilgrimage is called a *hajj*. Every year during Ramadan, two million *hajjis* (pilgrims) from around the Muslim world converge on Mecca. They buy the Koran, prayer beads, and other mementos of their visit. Assembled in the Great Mosque, they recite prayers and march around the *Kaaba*, Islam's most holy shrine. On the walls of many houses of Muslims in the Middle East, paintings commemorate the residents' *hajj*.

MEDINA

Muhammad was run out of Mecca, and he fled to Medina. It was July 16, 622, according to the Western calendar. Islam's calendar begins on this date, called the Hegira, which is 1 AH (*Anno Hegirae*, meaning "the year of the Hegira") on the Muslim calendar. Unlike the West's calendar, which is based on the 365-day solar calendar, the Muslim world

Muslim pilgrims end their *hajj* by walking around the sacred Kaaba in Mecca. People have been trampled to death in the huge crowds that gather to worship Allah.

The sheer size of The Mosque of the Prophet in Medina shows the importance of the city to Islam.

TENT MAKING

What kind of work can you do well? Many missionaries have developed skills in trades such as carpentry or mechanics. Others have studied English and can teach it for high school or college courses. These missionaries sometimes have the option of going directly to the mission field without raising support. In this position, they have a great opportunity to assist full-time missionaries. This type of missions work is called *tent making*, after the apostle Paul's practice of earning his own way by sewing tents (Acts 18:1–3).

Tent making has the disadvantage of taking time away from spreading the gospel and reducing prayer support from churches. But for Christians who want to spread the gospel in Muslim countries, they have no option. Muslim countries generally do not allow missionaries as such, but teachers and skilled technicians are welcome. Such missionaries can take comfort from Paul's example. Paul seldom received financial support from churches (Phil. 4:15).

Even if the missionary is honorably employed in his new country, he must be prepared to face serious opposition. Such missionaries should recall the Scripture passage that says that "all that will live godly in Christ Jesus shall suffer persecution" (2 Tim. 3:12). Are you willing to be a tent-making missionary somewhere in the world? Are you willing to suffer, if necessary, for the sake of the gospel?

uses a 354-day lunar calendar. The year AD 2000 was 1420 AH to Muslims.

During Muhammad's eight years in Medina, he had to drive back several attacks from Mecca. In AD 630, his army entered Mecca in triumph. Most people accepted him as the Prophet of Allah. From there, he led the Arab people on a march to conquer the world in the name of Allah. By 750, Arab armies had spread their faith as far east as the Indus River and as far west as Spain.

Muhammad died in 632 and was buried at Medina. The Prophet's Mosque over his tomb is the second most holy place for Muslims. Most pilgrims visit the mosque at Medina after they visit Mecca.

Through Christian Eyes

Compare and contrast the first three centuries of Chritianity (AD 30–313) with the first century of Islam (AD 622–750). Both religions experienced amazing growth during these years. How was the nature of their growth different?

DESERTS AND OASES OF INLAND ARABIA

The interior of the peninsula is even drier than the coast. Most of the land receives less than four inches of precipitation annually. About one-half of Saudi Arabia is tropical, and the rest is temperate, but freezing temperatures are rare. The heating and cooling of the rock and sand tend to make the climate uncomfortably hot, and temperatures over 100°F are common in the summer months. Hot, dry winds add to the discomfort.

The most desolate parts of Saudi Arabia are in the far north and the south. At least seven parts of the Arabian Desert have their own names. The most important one in the north is the An Nafud. The sands of the An Nafud eventually give way to the rocky Syrian Desert in the far north.

RUB AL KHALI

The key southern desert, the **Rub al Khali** (ROOB ahl KAH-lee), covers an area larger than California. It is the third largest desert in the world, surpassed only by the Sahara and the Gobi. The Rub al Khali is also the largest sand desert in the world. Shifting winds whip sand into dunes up to one thousand feet high. No one

An underground river makes this oasis possible—and productive.

lives there, although nomads occasionally travel across it. This uninhabited wasteland covers one-quarter of Saudi Arabia and is aptly called the **Empty Quarter**.

THE CAPITAL BOOMTOWN

Between these wastes of the An Nafud and the Empty Quarter is a large central plateau called the Nejd. This desert is not quite as harsh because of its higher elevation.

Several oases dot the plateau. **Riyadh** (ree YAHD), the capital, was built around one such oasis. In the early twentieth century, Riyadh was just a mud village. Since it became the capital of a united kingdom, however, it has become the largest city in the country, with about 4.5 million people in its metropolitan area.

Ibn-Saud (IB-en sah-OOD) conquered the desert tribes of Arabia and formed the kingdom of Saudi Arabia in the early twentieth century. To confirm his alliances, he married at least 282 women, divorcing them in turn so that he kept the Islamic requirement of no more than four wives at one time. His many descendants continue to rule Saudi Arabia with full authority. The country has no constitution. The king is bound only by Islamic law and tradition as interpreted by the **Wahhabi**, leaders of a religious sect that is noted for its strict adherence to Islamic law. Their influence is great. The Wahhabi's founder considered it his holy mission to wage *jihad* (holy war) against all other Muslim sects. It was a small step from that to waging *jihad* against non-Muslims, as has become so evident today.

Rub al Khali, also known as "the Empty Quarter," covers most of the Arabian Peninsula.

OF VEILS AND PILGRIMS

In strict Muslim societies, women must wear veils in public. Only their families are allowed to see their faces. In Saudi Arabia, they are also expected to wear a black cloak, called an *abaya* (uh BYE yuh). Even in cities where these practices are not always observed, few jobs are open to women because they are not permitted to socialize with men other than their relatives. Education for females is discouraged. They are not allowed to vote or run for office. In Saudi Arabia, they are not even allowed to drive cars. Muslim women hold the family honor in the highest regard, and they follow these cultural restrictions to ensure that they avoid any improper actions that might dishonor the family.

Men wear a turban or a *kaffiyeh* (kah FEE yeh; head scarf). Among their friends they are open and expressive, but with strangers they tend to be reserved and formal. Men often hold hands when they walk together in public as an innocent expression of friendship. But couples are forbidden to hold hands and will be arrested by the religious police, or *mutawa*.

The position and plight of Muslim women, especially those in countries with radical Muslim governments, is very oppressive, as evidenced in part by the clothing they are required to wear.

Muslims often pray and fast. They wash their face, hands, and feet and also remove their shoes before praying. Most men kneel on a prayer rug with their forehead to the ground as they recite the same prayers day after day. When they hear the call to prayer, they stop whatever they are doing, even if they are on the street. During the month of Ramadan, Muslims fast during the day, but they feast at night.

Alms and pilgrimages are also among the Five Pillars of Islam. The government collects a "voluntary tax," called *zakat*, and distributes it to the poor. The amount ranges from 2.5 percent to 10 percent. All Muslims are familiar with the currency in Saudi Arabia, the *riyal*, because they need it for their *hajj* (HAHJ) to Mecca. Men who have completed the *hajj* earn the formal title *Haji* (HAH jee), similar to *sir*. If you meet Haji Ali, you know that Ali has been to Mecca.

Bedouins

The nomads of the Arabian Desert are called **Bedouins**. Traditionally, Bedouins have lived in tents, "houses of hair" carefully woven by the women. Bedouins in Saudi Arabia make the outside of their tents from black goats' hair, but the inside is very colorful. Hand-woven curtains divide the interior, and carpets are cast on the dirt floor. The Bedouins wander between oases, seeking water for their livestock. Most Bedouins keep camels, sheep, and goats. They eat dates and dairy products and trade in village markets for pots, tools, and other household items.

Today there are about one million Bedouins, but very few of them wander all year. Many prefer the steady jobs and easier life that the oil-rich government has made available for them.

Bedouin tents are truly "mobile homes" in some of the most inhospitable areas of the world.

Non-Muslim peoples are almost outcasts in such a society, and Christian evangelism is strictly forbidden.

BLACK GOLD ON THE EAST COAST

The eastern lowlands along the Persian Gulf are mostly sand and gravel, but there are several fertile oases. The Al-Hasa Oasis, at the base of the Nejd, is fed by more than fifty springs and covers seventy square miles. The town of Al Hufuf lies in that oasis. The people grow such diverse crops as citrus fruits, rice, and wheat. Ad Dammam is the largest city on the coast, and Ras Tanura is the major port from which Saudi Arabia exports most of its oil.

The discovery of oil in 1936 created a new economy for Saudi Arabia. It has no other major resources, so the oil boom enabled the country to advance rapidly in industry, education, and health care. It currently produces about 265.3 billion barrels of oil per year. Now it must prepare new industries for the time when its oil supplies run out.

On the other hand, the oil supply should last a long time. The onshore and offshore oil wells tap the world's largest petroleum reserve. The West relies on a steady supply of relatively inexpensive oil and is concerned about the stability of the region, especially Saudi Arabia. The lavish lifestyle of the Saud family has fueled a radical antigovernment movement within the country. A civil war, an anti-West leader, or intense activity by Islamic terrorists could cut the West off from its critical oil supply. The resulting energy crisis could dwarf any previous economic disaster. For both this reason and the need to be wise stewards of our God-given resources, the West should seek alternative sources of energy.

SECTION QUIZ

1. Who founded Islam?
2. What are the two most holy cities of Islam?
3. What is another name for the Rub al Khali?
4. Who founded the Kingdom of Saudi Arabia?
5. Who are the Bedouins?
   ☼ Which Islamic pillars are unscriptural? Explain.

II. SMALL STATES ON THE ARABIAN PENINSULA

In the West, the Muslim world is sometimes called the "Arab world," although not all Muslims are Arabs. The Muslim religion began, however, on the Arabian Peninsula, and it was first spread by tribes of Arabic-speaking people called **Arabs**. The Arabs spread their language and writing as well as their religion. No matter what language they speak in daily life, all Muslims in every Muslim nation study and memorize the Koran in the original Arabic language. Translations are not permitted.

Early in the history of Islam, the center of power shifted to the populous cities farther north, leaving the Arabian Peninsula forgotten in the dust. Only a few towns thrived on the coast of the peninsula, visited by rare caravans and adventurous merchant ships. Separated by harsh deserts from the rest of the Middle East, these distant towns developed an independent spirit, resisting the later invasions of other Arabic tribes, Turks, and Europeans.

Six small coastal countries border Saudi Arabia on the east and south. Most of these lie on the Persian Gulf, but two lie farther out on the Arabian Sea. The two nations on the Arabian Sea—Yemen and Oman—do not share the wealth from the Persian Gulf oil reserves. Though they have some oil, their economies revolve around farming and trade.

YEMEN

The Arabian Peninsula rises sharply in the southwest corner. From these highlands, the rest of the peninsula slopes downward. Yemen occupies this corner. Most of its people are poor. Their meager subsistence involves farming or herding. They trade their goods at *bazaars* (open markets). Yemen has the lowest literacy rate, life expectancy, and per capita GDP in the Middle East.

Yemen has many other difficulties. Saudi Arabia still claims some of its northern border, which lies in the desert wastes of the Rub al Khali. At times, armies from the two nations have clashed.

Another problem is its history of civil war. Until 1990, Yemen was divided into two countries, North and South Yemen. South Yemen had the only Communist government in the Arab world during the Cold War, and it fought several battles with North Yemen. After the collapse of communism in Europe, South Yemen agreed to unite with North Yemen. The northern capital became the capital of the united country. Like Germany, reunified Yemen faces many challenges. For example, it must improve South Yemen's economy, which was shattered by Communist rule, and that drains the country of funds that otherwise would be used for other things.

Sanaa is the capital city of Yemen.

In 1993, Yemen became the first Arab nation to hold a multiparty general election, but the country's future is still uncertain. It especially must work to restore its image after developing a reputation as a safe haven for radical Islamists. For example, in October 2000, Islamic terrorists associated with Osama bin Laden's al-Qaeda network used an explosives-laden boat to blow a hole in the warship U.S.S. *Cole.* The goal of the terrorists is to drive out Western influence, take over the country, and set up an Islamic state.

Yemen has the highest peaks of the Arabian Peninsula. Rainfall in these highlands gives Yemen the only permanent river on the entire peninsula. Sanaa, the capital, lies in these highlands in the major agricultural area. The main cash crops are coffee and **khat** (KAHT, a shrub whose leaves are chewed in East Africa as a narcotic). Yemen is famous for mocha coffee, which is shipped from the coastal town of Mocha, west of Ta'izz.

This land on the Red Sea, once known as Sheba, was occupied long ago. The Queen of Sheba journeyed from here to visit Solomon

(1 Kings 10:1–13). Sheba once contained gold and other minerals, but they have long since been exhausted.

The Red Sea is the westernmost arm of the Arabian Sea. But before its waters enter the Arabian Sea, they pass through a narrow spot called Bab el Mandeb and then pass into the **Gulf of Aden** (AH dehn). The vital port at Aden is Yemen's main city and the former capital of South Yemen. Aden was under British control for many years.

Yemen has several islands off the eastern horn of Africa. Socotra (suh COH trah), the most important, was a major stop on the early Arab shipping routes across the Arabian Sea. Today, most islanders live by spearfishing from single-sail boats called *dhows*.

Sultanate of Oman

Oman (oh MAHN) is among the hottest countries in the world, with daytime temperatures often reaching 130°F. Most of the country is part of the Rub al Khali desert. The people wear long white robes and turbans to protect themselves against the heat, wind, and blowing sand.

Although the Portuguese captured several ports in 1507, they could not take all of Oman. Arab tribes forced the Portuguese completely out by 1650. Oman even took part of East Africa. The present line of sultans (Muslim monarchs) came to power in 1740. The government is called a **sultanate**. Because Oman's ships could not compete with modern iron vessels, however, its trade declined in the nineteenth century, and it lost its African territory in 1861. Since 1970, it has begun a major push to modernize and diversify to reduce its heavy dependence on oil. So far, the limited industry in the nation (production of *ghee*, or clarified butter; fish drying; and silver and goldsmithing) is still primitive and heavily subsidized by the government.

The mountains of Oman stand in stark contrast to the deserts of the Persian Gulf region but are just as dry.

Dhofar

Southwestern Oman, around the cities of Salalah (suh LAHL uh) and Dawkah, is a plateau called Dhofar (doh FAHR). It is known for its many frankincense trees. The plateau gets slightly more rain than the surrounding desert.

Strategic Cities on the Gulf of Oman

The main population center is a stretch of highlands that rises at the southeast corner of the Arabian Peninsula. It is the heart of Oman and one of only two places on the peninsula where mountains cause some regular rainfall. A fertile coastal strip with date palms lies at the base of the mountains. The capital, Muscat (muhs KAHT), is on that coast.

The coast is important today because of its strategic location at the entrance to the Persian Gulf. Before the Arabian Sea enters the Persian Gulf, it passes through the **Gulf of Oman**. In addition to the main territory along this gulf, Oman controls Cape Musandam, at the narrowest junction of the Gulf of Oman and the Persian Gulf. The Omani town of Al Khasab on the cape guards the strategic Strait of Hormuz (hahr MOOZ), through which all oil tankers must pass as they leave the Persian Gulf.

EMIRATES ON THE PERSIAN GULF

In the nineteenth century, various rulers on the coast of the Persian Gulf asked Great Britain to protect them from their powerful neighbors. In return, they gave Britain control of their defense and foreign affairs. When Britain withdrew from the Persian Gulf in 1971, these tiny British protectorates became independent. Since oil was discovered in the 1930s, all four minicountries on the Persian Gulf have profited greatly.

UNITED ARAB EMIRATES

Seven small states, each with its own traditions, lie along the southwestern shore of the Persian Gulf. Each is ruled by a prince, or *emir* (ih MIR), and its government is therefore called an **emirate**. During the nineteenth century, when Britain dominated the area, it enforced truces between the states to keep the naval lanes open; therefore, the area was called the Trucial (TROO see uhl) States. These states have retained sovereignty over local affairs but are now united into a single country called the United Arab Emirates (UAE). The seven emirs form the Supreme Council and appoint a president as head of state.

The UAE is the richest country in the Persian Gulf. It ranks as the fifth largest producer of oil in the world. The oil has brought riches (per capita GDP of more than $25,000), but the prosperity has drawn waves of immigrants both from neighboring Saudi Arabia and from as far away as India and Pakistan.

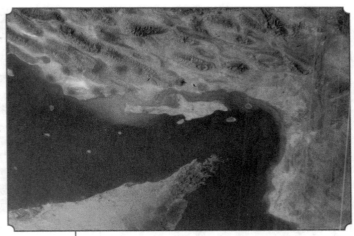

This photograph of the narrow Strait of Hormuz, taken from the space shuttle *Challenger*, shows its critical location for controlling access to and from the Persian Gulf.

Abu Dhabi is not only the capital of the United Arab Emirates but also a beautiful modern city.

United Arab Emirates

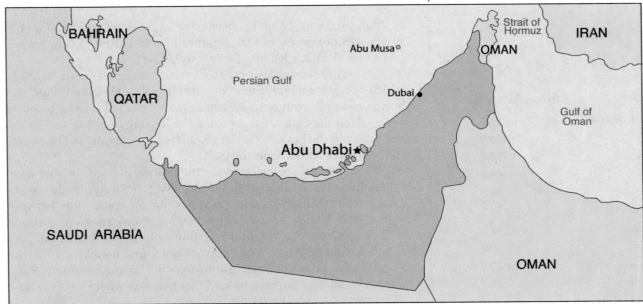

Burj Al Arab, Dubai, UAE, is 1,053 feet tall, one meter taller than the Eiffel Tower. The oblong structure about two-thirds of the way up the side of the hotel is a restaurant; behind it is a platform for landing helicopters. Cost per night: $900–3000.

Much of the wealth of the emirates is going into extravagant but aesthetic living areas such as "The Palm" of Jebel Ali. The private docks of the interior ring form a poem in Arabic, written by the governor of Dubai.

QATAR

Like the United Arab Emirates, Qatar (KAH tur) is an emirate that has grown rich from oil. The prosperity has drawn so many immigrants that more than two-thirds of the people are foreign-born. Qatar's dynasty of emirs has ruled since the nineteenth century. Before the discovery of oil, the Arab peoples supported themselves by raising camels, diving for pearls, and fishing.

Qatar is on a peninsula that extends into the Persian Gulf. Most of the peninsula is stony desert, but the southern region consists of salt flats. Since there is little water, the people distill seawater to drink. The process of **desalination** (removal of salt from saltwater) is too expensive for most countries. However, it is cheaper than importing water from hostile neighbors.

Qatar was a base for the Coalition forces in the Persian Gulf War and the main headquarters of the U.S.–led invasion of Iraq in 2003. It is also the home of the controversial Arab television network Al Jazeera, which has aired the taped messages of al-Qaeda's Osama bin Laden. Some authorities suspect that these messages contain embedded instructions for terrorist cells.

BAHRAIN

Bahrain (bah RAYN) consists of a large island and a number of small ones northwest of Qatar. Bahrain is an emirate led by a *sheik* (SHAYK), the male leader of an extended Arab family.

Many international companies have headquarters in Bahrain, which operates an oil refinery on Sitra (sih TRAH) Island. Pipelines bring crude oil from both Bahrain and Saudi Arabia. The business has enabled the country to become the leading banking and financial center in the Persian Gulf region. It is also a major port of call for U.S. warships traveling in the gulf.

Many natural springs provide the islands of Bahrain with a resource that is rare in the Middle East. The fresh water made the ancient port of Dilmun an important stop on the trade route between Sumer and India. The four-thousand-year-old ruins of Dilmun include tombs and a ziggurat like those of ancient Sumer. Copper from Magan and African ivory have been found here as well as flint weights and soapstone seals from Mohenjo-Daro (in modern Pakistan). The ancient Sumerians said that this was where Noah (whom they called Ziusudra) settled after the Flood.

World's Leading Oil-Producing Countries	
Country	**Billion barrels**
1. Saudi Arabia	265.3
2. Iraq	115.0
3. Kuwait	98.8
4. Iran	96.4
5. UAE	62.8
6. Russia	54.3
7. Venezuela	47.6
8. China	30.6
9. Libya	30.0
10. Mexico	26.9

KUWAIT

The barren land of Kuwait, at the north end of the Persian Gulf, was uninhabited until 1710, when Arab settlers found a water source at what is now the capital of Kuwait. Kuwait Bay, with its excellent harbor, soon became an important port. But its existence has been threatened by its two large neighbors, Saudi Arabia in the south and Iraq in the north.

Kuwait prospered immediately after the discovery of oil. Soon hundreds of oil wells dotted the east. In 1960, it joined Saudi Arabia and other oil-producing countries in the Organization of Petroleum Exporting Countries (**OPEC**). OPEC members decide how much oil they will produce in an attempt to control the selling price and make political statements designed to influence Western policies. This tactic proved most effective in 1973, when the availability of oil dwindled as a result of the Arab-Israeli War. Since then, however, OPEC nations have generally fought among themselves because of the glut of oil.

In August 1990, Iraq invaded Kuwait, claiming that it had exceeded OPEC production limits and that it was actually a territory of Iraq. The invasion sparked the **Persian Gulf War**, the most significant war ever fought on the Arabian Peninsula since World War I. Iraq not only seized control of the huge oil reserves of Kuwait but also threatened the safety of Saudi Arabia. The Arab nations dropped their typical opposition to Western powers and joined a grand alliance, led by the United States and Great Britain, to protect the flow of oil. The UN authorized "all necessary means" to liberate Kuwait if Iraq did not withdraw by January 15, 1991. The Coalition forces began a massive military buildup in the region with central headquarters in Saudi Arabia. When Iraq ignored the UN demand, the United States made its first official declaration of war since World War II. On January 16, the UN Coalition began five weeks of massive, around-the-clock air strikes, followed by a lightning-fast ground attack that lasted just one hundred hours before Iraq agreed to a cease-fire. The war, however, might have proven to be a Pyrrhic victory because it did not remove Saddam Hussein from power in Iraq and prompted the growth of radical Muslim organizations, including al-Qaeda, because of their resentment of a Western presence and influence in the Persian Gulf.

At the time of the Gulf War, no Gulf states had a democratic form of government. Under international pressure, however, Kuwait created a weak National Assembly in 1992. Kuwaiti men with "first-class" citizenship (13 percent of the population) were the only ones allowed to vote. But the young assembly got nothing accomplished because the leaders spent more time bickering over religious issues, such as whether to keep men and women separated at universities. Traditional views of authority and religious division will make it difficult for Kuwait to adopt full democracy.

In spite of its wealth in oil, Kuwait is heavily dependent on other countries. It imports all of its food and obtains 75 percent of its water supply from desalination and imports. Its society is divided into five

OPEC determines production levels and the prices it will charge for oil.

levels: the ruling family, Kuwaiti merchant families, former Bedouins, Arab citizens, and foreigners.

SECTION QUIZ

1. What poverty-stricken Arab country once had Communist leaders?
2. What is a sultan? An emir? A sheik?
3. What advantages does Bahrain have over the other countries of the Arabian Peninsula?
4. What factors caused the Persian Gulf War?
- ⚬ What should be the role of the United States in the Persian Gulf? Is a continual U.S. presence there necessary? Why or why not?

III. IRAQ

The **Tigris** and **Euphrates Rivers** are the most important rivers in the Middle East. They begin in the mountains of Turkey before entering Iraq. Rain and melting snow in the mountains provide a constant flow of water in spite of the low rainfall downstream—only ten inches annually. The lifeblood of Iraq, these rivers provide water for irrigation and hydroelectric projects. Also navigable, these rivers are as important to Iraq as the Mississippi River is to the United States.

The rivers flow almost parallel in Iraq for five hundred miles. Since ancient times, the land between them has been called **Mesopotamia**, meaning "land between the rivers." This well-watered plain was the home of several of the world's early civilizations, including Sumer, Babylonia, and Assyria.

Today, Iraq is one of many Arab nations that have attempted to lead the Muslim world. A ruthless dictator named **Saddam Hussein** took over the country in 1979. He proved his willingness to use any means to further his ends, including using biological and chemical warfare. The leaders of the neighboring countries feared what he might do, but many of the Arab people on the street cheered him because he "stood up to" the West. His efforts to win glory for himself and power for his nation led the country into chaos. His invasion of Kuwait sparked the Persian Gulf War, and his repeated violations of UN resolutions prompted the 2003 invasion that toppled him from power. Now Iraq is engaged in a struggle between a group who wants to establish a free, stable, democratic government and a group of holdovers from the Saddam era and Islamic terrorists who want to establish a radical Islamic state from which to launch terrorist attacks on the West.

Iraq is almost completely surrounded by land, except for a 36-mile coastline on the Persian Gulf. Its neighboring states are Turkey on the north, Syria and Jordan on the west, Saudi Arabia and Kuwait

Iraqis approved their country's new constitution in late 2005.

on the south, and Iran on the east. Its Persian Gulf access is in the southeast between Iran and Kuwait.

Iraq, which is a little more than twice the area of Idaho, may be divided into four general geographic zones: deserts, rolling uplands, northern highlands, and alluvial plain. Only about 13 percent of its land is arable.

DESERT ZONE

The Syrian Desert covers western Iraq, and the Arabian Desert sprawls across southern Iraq to the Euphrates River. Without adequate rain or rivers, a warm and dry desert climate prevails. The desert is rutted with numerous wadis, most of them dry, but they can become raging torrents in the rainy season. The desert has only a few settlements at oases, some of which produce dates from palm trees. The desert is populated by few people, mostly nomads.

Although it is sparsely populated, the vast deserts of western Iraq proved very important in the U.S.–led efforts to bring stable democracy to Iraq. That desert, especially the border with Syria, was the primary point of entry for anti-democracy insurgents battling the Western military to hinder or prevent the stabilization of the new government. U.S. military forces conducted numerous operations to close off the Syrian border, but the area is vast and hard to patrol effectively.

NORTHERN HIGHLANDS

The *northern highlands* near Turkey and in the northeast near Iran are made up of rugged mountains that range from about 3,200 feet to more than 13,000 feet. As is the case in most of the Middle East, oil is the primary resource in Iraq, especially in that Upper Mesopotamia region, where the cities of Mosul (MOH suhl) and Kirkuk (kihr KOOK) are centers of the oil industry. The area is inhabited primarily by **Kurds**.

Because half of Iraq's oil comes from the Kirkuk oil fields, it was critical to secure them early in the Iraq War.

According to Genesis 10:11, the highlands area is where the ancient city of Nineveh was located. A great empire arose in the mountains of northern Iraq. Asshur went north from Sumer and founded Nineveh, which became the capital of the **Assyrian Empire**, whose greatest leader was Sargon II. For many years, Assyria struggled with Babylon over control of the western trade routes to the Mediterranean Sea.

The high mountains in the northeast corner of Iraq are part of the range that is called the Zagros (ZAHG rohs) Mountains in Iran and the Taurus Mountains in Turkey. The Kurds have lived in that mountainous region for at least four thousand years, lost amid both ancient and modern conquerors. Kurds have long fought for an independent homeland called Kurdistan. The Kurds have suffered in all four countries where they live, but especially in Iraq. The world was shocked during the Iran-Iraq War when reports surfaced that Saddam Hussein had used chemical and biological weapons to wipe out Kurdish villages.

After the Persian Gulf War, Hussein began a campaign of slaughter against the Kurds that forced the United States and its allies to prohibit Iraqi flights north of the 36th parallel. Protected by the "no-fly zone," Iraq's Kurds built a semi-independent state with its own police, courts, and elected parliament. In some schools the forbidden Kurdish language was again taught. Foreign aid helped many villages to rebuild.

Yet the fragile Kurdish government suffered greatly from a "double embargo," unable to trade across Iraq's borders and unable to trade with the rest of Iraq. The neighboring Muslims, especially Turks, feared that Kurdish independence in Iraq would encourage revolts of Kurds in their own countries. Kurdish factions even began fighting among themselves. They united, however, to help the United States oust Saddam from power in the Iraq War.

ROLLING UPLANDS

The *rolling uplands* are located between the upper Tigris and Euphrates Rivers. The zone includes what became known during the Iraq War as the "*Sunni* (SOO nee) *Triangle*," or the "Triangle of Death," because it is heavily populated by Sunni Muslims, ardent supporters of Saddam Hussein, and because a large number of American troops were killed there trying to subdue Iraqi insurgents. The northern point of the triangle is the city of Tikrit (tih KREET), Saddam's hometown. The other points of the triangle are Ar Ramadi to the southwest of Tikrit and Baghdad to the southeast. Between Ar Ramadi and Baghdad is the insurgent stronghold of Fallujah (fah LOO jah).

The "Sunni Triangle" in Iraq

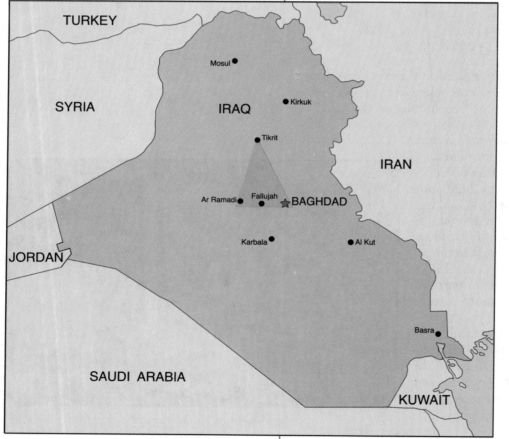

ALLUVIAL PLAIN

The final zone is the *alluvial plain* of the Tigris and Euphrates Rivers. The plain extends from just north of Baghdad through the area southeast of Baghdad, especially at the rivers' confluence, to where the rivers flow into the Persian Gulf near Basra (BAHS rah).

About three-fourths of all Iraqis live in that region, which is also known as Lower Mesopotamia. The area has always been heavily populated. Although most of the people are Arabs, their religious views differ sharply from those who live in the Sunni Triangle.

All Muslims accept the five Pillars of Islam, but they disagree over particular teachings and authority. Many wars in the Middle East can be traced to rival Muslim groups. About 80 percent of all Muslims are **Sunnis**. The name means "well-trodden path," showing their orthodoxy and conserva-

BAGHDAD

Baghdad is the capital of Iraq. With an estimated population of 5.7 million, it is also its largest city. In history, it is associated with the ancient city of Babylon and King Nebuchadnezzar and his descendants in the biblical record. (See Daniel 1–8.) The "Hanging Gardens of Babylon" were one of the seven wonders of the ancient world. In more recent history, Saddam Hussein dreamed of restoring Baghdad and Iraq to the glory it once had during those early years of empire. In fact, he saw himself as a modern Nebuchadnezzar.

The modern city of Baghdad experienced a boom in development and modernization in 1970 as a result of the influx of oil income. Divided by the Tigris River, the city's two halves are linked by eleven bridges. Many of the modern buildings, especially government buildings erected under Saddam and the many palaces he built for himself, were destroyed by the war that removed Saddam from power. Other areas of the city have been badly damaged by the ongoing war against anti-American insurgents, but most Iraqis dream of a coming time of peace when they can restore their city to its former glory and beauty.

Apart from recent wars, Baghdad is famous to many Westerners as the setting of *The Thousand and One Nights*, a collection of popular tales such as "Sinbad the Sailor," "Ali Baba and the Forty Thieves," and "Aladdin and His Magic Lamp."

tive, pragmatic position. They follow the caliphs, the appointed successors to Muhammad. Most Arabs in Saudi Arabia are Sunnis.

Shiites (SHEE ites) compose most of the remaining Muslim factions. Shiah (another word for Shiites) honor the *imam*, the hereditary successor of Muhammad. The imam claims to be a divine manifestation and qualified to interpret the holy writings. Shiites are outspoken, but they argue with Sunnis over who is the rightful heir of Muhammad. Only four countries have Shiite majorities: Iran, Iraq, Bahrain, and Azerbaijan.

The two great rivers of Iraq join in the far south to form the **Shatt al Arab**, which continues about one hundred miles through marshy lowlands before it empties into the Persian Gulf. Many Shiites live in the swamps and cities of the Shatt al Arab. After the Persian Gulf War, the Shiites rebelled against Hussein and his Sunni government. The UN cease-fire enforced a no-fly zone south of the 32nd parallel. But Hussein used ground troops to massacre the rebels. In 1992, he completed a 351-mile canal to drain the swamps, hoping to destroy the Shiite way of life and eliminate their hideout.

Ruins in that zone remind us that it has an ancient history. Iraq is very familiar with the stories of ancient civilizations, and it considers itself the heir of these empires. The Bible recounts the founding of the first cities after the Flood in that location. The civilization that developed in the plains of Shinar became known as **Sumer** (Gen. 10:9–10). North of Shinar near modern Baghdad are the ruins of an even greater civilization—the Babylonian Empire. Under Nebuchadnezzar, Babylon reached the pinnacle of ancient glory (Dan. 2:31–45). The walls of the city, which stretched about twenty-eight miles, were the thickest city walls ever made. Nebuchadnezzar also made the Hanging Gardens, one of the seven wonders of the ancient world.

SECTION QUIZ

1. What two major rivers flow through Iraq and into the Persian Gulf?

Behistun Rock

Along the caravan road between Ecbatana and Babylon is a high cliff that displays one of the greatest treasures from the ancient world. Behistun Rock is five hundred feet high. Darius ordered an account written there in stone, for all to read, of how he took the throne and organized the realm into satrapies (provinces). The inscription is important because it holds the key to reading the undeciphered letters of the ancient Babylonian language. Darius had the account of his accomplishments inscribed in three languages: Babylonian, Old Persian, and Elamite. The Behistun Rock ranks with the Rosetta Stone, which was used to unlock the mysteries of ancient Egyptian hieroglyphics.

2. What is the fertile region between those rivers called?

3. What cultural group dominates the population of northern Iraq?

4. Name the two ancient empires that arose in Iraq and the greatest leader of each.

5. What is Iraq's capital?

☼ Why would God have left out Assyria when he summarized world history in Daniel 2:31–45?

IV. IRAN

GEOGRAPHIC OVERVIEW

In area, Iran is the second largest country in the Persian Gulf (behind only Saudi Arabia). It is a little larger than Alaska and has numerous neighboring countries. On the north, Iran borders Armenia, Azerbaijan, the Caspian Sea, and Turkmenistan. On the west, about one-fourth of Iran borders Turkey and the rest borders Iraq. On the east, two-thirds of Iran borders Afghanistan and the rest borders Pakistan. And on the south, Iran is washed by the waters of the Persian Gulf and the Gulf of Oman.

The climate of Iran is mostly arid and semiarid. The narrow plain along the Caspian Sea, however, is subtropical. The terrain ranges from a rugged, mountainous rim to a high central basin to narrow plains along the coasts. The combined factors of climate and terrain make only about 10 percent of the land arable. The lowest elevation (92 feet) is along the Caspian Sea; the highest elevation (18,605 feet) is Qolleh-ye Damavand in the Elburz Mountains, south of the Caspian Sea.

THE ZAGROS MOUNTAINS

Iran is an ancient kingdom. Its people are not Arabs but Persians. The ancient **Persian Empire** included all of modern Iran. In fact, Iran was called Persia until 1935. The name *Persia* originally referred to a small region in the southern **Zagros Mountains**. The rugged mountains cover most of the western third of Iran, extending along southern and western Iran and into northern Iraq. They offer a cooler climate than do the plains of Iraq. Major sources of income in the mountains are agriculture and livestock.

THE ELBURZ MOUNTAINS

Along the northern border of Iran run the **Elburz** (ehl BOORZ) **Mountains**, which connect the Caucasus Mountains on the west with the Hindu Kush to the east in Afghanistan. Like these neighboring mountain ranges, the Elburz Mountains are high, rising to 18,376 feet at Mount Demavend near Tehran.

Tehran is the capital and largest city of Iran. With more than twelve million people in its metropolitan area, it is also the largest city in the whole Persian Gulf region. Until the rise of the caravan route in the thirteenth century, however, it was only a small town.

The rugged, snow-topped Zagros Mountains provide a natural boundary between Iran and Iraq.

It did not become the capital until 1788. Most sections of the city were built since 1910, and many of them have a distinctly European flavor. The official language is Farsi (FAHR see, Persian), an Indo-European language.

THE KHUZESTAN PLAIN

The Khuzestan (KOO sih STAHN) Plain is an extension of the fertile plains of Mesopotamia. The plain shares the same climate as Mesopotamia and contains Iran's major oil-producing area. It was the home of the Elamites in Bible times (see Ezra 4:9 and Acts 2:9) and the focus of fighting during the Iran-Iraq War (1980–88).

In the winter, the Persian kings moved to the Khuzestan Plain in the southwestern corner of Iran. The winter capital, Susa (or Shushan, as the Bible calls it), appears in Nehemiah 1:1 and Daniel 8:2. It is also the setting for the book of Esther. To help the movement of soldiers and messengers, the Persians constructed a Royal Road from Susa all the way to the Aegean Sea.

THE EASTERN DESERTS

Eastern Iran is desert. The Dasht-e-Kavir and the Dasht-e-Lut together cover thirty-eight thousand square miles of the barren Plateau of Iran. The plateau averages three thousand feet in elevation and consists of barren rocky hills and large salt flats. Most cities stand on the western edge. The border city of Zabol (zah BOHL) lies beyond the plateau in the Rigestan Desert.

RELIGIOUS OVERVIEW

Zarathustra (ZAHR ah THOO strah, *Zoroaster* in Greek) founded the ancient religion of the Persian Empire, **Zoroastrianism** (ZOHR oh AS tree uh nihz um). The Arabs defeated the last Zoroastrian forces in AD 635 near Baghdad. However, the religion is still practiced by a persecuted minority in the plateau cities of Kerman and Yazd (and in India, where adherents are called Parsis). Their sacred book is the *Avesta* (uh VES tuh), and they worship the god Ahura Mazda.

Like many other false religions, Zoroastrians destroy the dead. They do not want reminders of death and the grave. To such religions, cemeteries are grim reminders of the consequences of Adam's sin. Whereas some religions promote cremation, Zoroastrians put the corpses on Towers of Silence, where vultures strip off the flesh within a few hours. As much as false religions try to hide the fact, however, death comes to all men, and even death glorifies the true God.

> *And as it is appointed unto men once to die, but after this the judgment: so Christ was once offered to bear the sins of many.*
> *(Heb. 9:27–28)*

The official religion of Iran, however, is the Shiite branch of Islam, which about 90 percent of all Iranians follow. The Sunni minority has a difficult time in the country.

Iran has been stepping up its persecution of Christians in recent years. It has forbidden the sale of Bibles in bookstores and barred Muslims from attending church services. Only two Christian churches can hold services, and those services must be conducted in Farsi. In 1993, the Iranian parliament required all citizens to make public their religious affiliation. The government has used

Esther and the Persians

Iran (formerly Persia) provides the setting for the biblical book of Esther, a book that includes danger, excitement, a beautiful woman, political intrigue, and a satisfying ending as the "bad guy" in the story gets his just deserts. Esther, a Jewish woman, became the wife of the Persian king. A high-ranking assistant to the king tried to use his power, position, and influence with the king to exterminate the Jews. The new queen risked her own life to save the lives of her people—and succeeded. You can read the whole exciting story in your Bible!

Persepolis

Persepolis was the largest and greatest Persian capital. About twenty-five miles east of modern Shiraz, the ruins still dwarf visitors. The Audience Hall of Darius held ten thousand people, and Xerxes built the even larger Hall of a Hundred Columns. The gold, silver, ivory, and marble have long since been removed, but many fine relief sculptures remain. Naqsh-i Rustam, a cliff near Persepolis, contains four royal tombs cut into the rock, including that of Darius.

The ruins of Persepolis remind us of the fleeting nature of individual and national fame.

Baha'i houses of worship, such as this one in Iran, look much different from the typical mosque.

this information to remove Christians from government jobs, such as teaching and civil service. Converts from Islam are threatened with torture unless they deny their new faith in Christ. Since the 1979 revolution, the number of Christians in Iran has dropped from 310,000 to less than 100,000.

Baha'ism (bah HIGH iz um) is a religion based on the writings of two renegade Shiites, the Bab and Bahaullah. In 1844, the Bab predicted the imminent coming of an imam who would bring truth and justice. The government executed the Bab in Tabriz in 1850 and imprisoned his disciple Bahaullah in the Black Pit in Tehran, where Bahaullah came to view himself as the predicted imam. He was later exiled—first to Baghdad (Iraq), then to Istanbul (Turkey), and finally to Acre (Israel).

In spite of bitter persecution, about 350,000 Baha'is remain in Iran. Baha'ists have spread to Africa, India, and the United States and have their international headquarters in Haifa, Israel. Baha'ists promote the unity of all religions, and they offer no salvation from sin. In contrast to the one true God of biblical Christianity, the god of Baha'ism is unknowable.

> *And we know that the Son of God is come, and hath given us an understanding, that we may know him that is true, and we are in him that is true, even in his Son Jesus Christ. This is the true God, and eternal life.*
> (1 John 5:20)

Another Muslim minority that started in Persia is the Sufis, the mystics of Islam. **Sufism** (SOO fihz um) teaches that nothing exists except God. Although they are not orthodox Muslims, Sufis are at least peaceful. No countries are predominantly Sufi, but Sufi influence is felt throughout Islam (much as the New Age cult has spread throughout Christian lands).

RECENT DEVELOPMENTS

Because of its oil resources, Iran became a relatively successful industrial nation and a U.S. ally in the mid-twentieth century. At that time, Iran was headed by a hereditary leader, or **shah**, Reza Shah Pahlavi. But radical Muslim sects began stirring up strife and violence in the 1970s. Fanatical Shiite Muslims opposed the shah's attempts to modernize the country and to adopt a Western-style government. In seeking to thwart that opposition, the shah's regime sometimes resorted to harsh measures, which the Shiites denounced forcefully. In 1979, Iranian revolutionaries led by the religious leader Ayatollah Ruholla Khomeini overthrew the shah. (*Ayatollah* [EYE yuh TOHL ah] is the highest title of honor that a Shiite Muslim can hold.) The Iranian Shiites instituted an "Islamic Republic" in which ancient religious law, or *sharia* (shah REE ah), was to guide the state. They also stormed the American embassy and kidnapped 77 hostages, which they held captive for 444 days.

The Iranians viewed their revolution as a first step toward worldwide change. Khomeini said, "We will export our revolution to the four corners of the world because our revolution is Islamic; and the struggle will continue until the cry of 'There is no god but Allah, and Muhammad is the messenger of Allah' prevails throughout the world." Until the attacks on the United States by the al-Qaeda terrorist network, Iran's extremism was the most visible expression of a movement that has infected many other Muslim nations. Other groups have begun to echo the Iranian call for "pure" Islamic states untainted by contacts with the "corrupt" ways of the West, and other Muslim states, including Pakistan and Saudi Arabia, have adopted some measure of sharia.

The West sometimes gets the false impression that all Islamic nations are Arabic and that they all think alike. Two main contestants for the "voice of Islam" are Iran and Iraq. They have had a long history of dispute, dating back to troubles between ancient Persia and Babylon. After the revolution in Iran in 1979, Saddam Hussein feared the spread of radical Shiites in his country, and he saw an opportunity to seize some of the disputed, oil-rich territories on his border. In 1980, he launched a massive invasion of Iran, expecting to win in three weeks. Instead, the **Iran-Iraq War** dragged on for eight years, during which Saddam resorted to chemical weapons and bombing of cities to break Iran, but he gained nothing. More than three hundred thousand people died in the fighting, but neither country made any important gains.

Iran remained silent while the Western allies crushed Iraq during the Persian Gulf War. After the war, however, Iran began to reassert itself. With its oil-based economy booming, Iran continued stockpiling billions of dollars worth of modern tanks, planes, submarines, and missiles. It also began secretly acquiring the technology to produce its own chemical and nuclear weapons. In 1992, its troops occupied three islands in the Persian Gulf that it had been sharing with the United Arab Emirates: Abu Musa and the Greater and Smaller Tunbs (TOON ehbs). The dispute continues.

Iran's radical Islamic leaders continue to trouble the world. They openly defied efforts of the United Nations to prevent Iran from developing nuclear weapons. Their president also reiterated clearly their desire to "wipe Israel from the face of the map." They strongly oppose U.S. efforts to establish a secular and democratic government in neighboring Iraq and allegedly sent large numbers of people into Iraq to influence that process. Iran remains a potentially explosive element in Persian Gulf and Middle Eastern affairs.

Portraits of three of Iran's former ruling ayatollahs grin at residents from the wall of a building.

SECTION QUIZ

1. Which mountain range contains two ancient capitals of Persia?

2. During what season did the Persian kings go to the palace in Susa on the Khuzestan Plain? Why?

3. What ancient religion is still practiced in small pockets on the plateau of Iran?

4. What mountains cross Iran in the north?

5. Iran is the only country of the Persian Gulf that has an official language other than Arabic. What is it?

◌̣ Why was Persepolis a good location for the capital of an empire?

Can You:
Define These Terms?

Pillars of Islam	OPEC
Ramadan	Sunnis
mosque	Shiites
Koran	Zoroastrianism
Bedouin	Baha'ism
khat	Sufism
sultanate	shah
emirate	Ayatollah
desalination	sharia

Locate These Places?

Persian Gulf	Tigris River
Arabian Peninsula	Euphrates River
Rub al Khali	Mesopotamia
Empty Quarter	Shatt al Arab
Gulf of Aden	Zagros Mountains
Gulf of Oman	Elburz Mountains

Explain the Significance?

Middle East	Kurds
Mecca	Assyrian Empire
Medina	Baghdad
Riyadh	Sumer
Ibn-Saud	Persian Empire
Wahhabi	Tehran
Arabs	Persepolis
Persian Gulf War	Iran-Iraq War
Saddam Hussein	

HOW MUCH DO YOU REMEMBER?

1. The Middle East lies at the crossroads of what three continents?

2. What language is spoken throughout most of the Persian Gulf region?

3. What are the two holiest cities of Islam?

4. What are the two main arms of the Arabian Sea?

5. Which of the six minor states on the Arabian Peninsula best fits each description?
   a. highest per capita GDP
   b. Persian Gulf War
   c. sultanate
   d. first Arab democracy
   e. frankincense of Dhofar
   f. Dilmun

6. What advantages does Bahrain have over the other Gulf States?

7. Distinguish sultan, sheik, shah, and emir.

8. Distinguish ayatollah, imam, and sufi.

9. The Tigris and Euphrates rivers empty into what body of water?

10. Why is the Muslim world divided against itself?

11. What is the holy book of Islam? of Zoroastrianism?

12. For each empire, give the main leader and the primary capital. Also give the modern location of the capital's ruins.
    a. Babylon
    b. Assyria
    c. Persia

WHAT DO YOU THINK?

1. How should Christians in America respond to Islamic nations closed to the gospel?

2. Compare and contrast what you know of the religion of Islam with true Christianity.

3. The countries that surround the Persian Gulf now profit greatly from their petroleum resources. What problems has the new wealth brought? Are these countries better off?

4. What are the three most powerful countries on the Persian Gulf? What advantages does each of them have in the struggle to become the leader of the Muslim world?

5. Is the Middle East more similar to Asia or to Europe?

This village in the Republic of Georgia shows the geographic variety of rich valleys and high mountains that are found throughout much of the Caucasus and Central Asia.

THE CAUCASUS AND CENTRAL ASIA

I. THE COUNTRIES OF THE CAUCASUS
   A. GEORGIA
   B. ARMENIA
   C. AZERBAIJAN

II. CENTRAL ASIA
   A. KAZAKHSTAN
   B. TURKMENISTAN
   C. UZBEKISTAN
   D. KYRGYZSTAN
   E. TAJIKISTAN
   F. AFGHANISTAN

Caucasus and Central Asia Fast Facts

Flag	Country	Capital	Area (sq. mi.)	Pop. (M)	Pop. Density (per sq. mi.)	Per Capita GDP ($US)	Life Span
	Afghanistan →	Kabul	250,001	29.93	120	$800	42.9
	Armenia →	Yerevan	11,506	2.98	259	$4,600	71.6
	Azerbaijan →	Baku	33,436	7.91	237	$3,800	63.4
	Georgia →	Tbilisi	26,911	4.68	174	$3,100	75.9
	Kazakhstan →	Astana	1,049,155	15.19	14	$7,800	66.6
	Kyrgyzstan →	Bishkek	76,641	5.15	67	$1,700	68.2
	Tajikistan →	Dushanbe	55,251	7.16	130	$1,100	64.6
	Turkmenistan →	Ashgabat	188,456	4.95	26	$5,700	61.4
	Uzbekistan →	Tashkent	172,742	26.85	155	$1,800	64.2

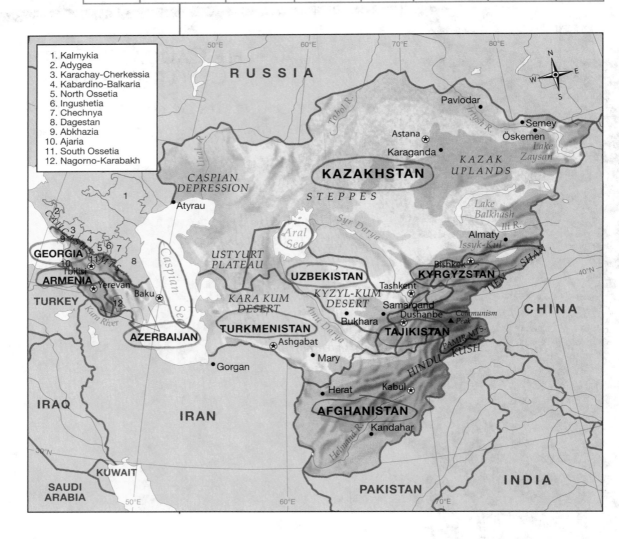

1. Kalmykia
2. Adygea
3. Karachay-Cherkessia
4. Kabardino-Balkaria
5. North Ossetia
6. Ingushetia
7. Chechnya
8. Dagestan
9. Abkhazia
10. Ajaria
11. South Ossetia
12. Nagorno-Karabakh

The nine nations of the Caucasus (KAW kuh sus) and Central Asia were once part of the Soviet Empire. Eight were republics in the Soviet Union and under Communist tyranny for more than seventy years. Russia had coveted the ninth nation, Afghanistan, for nearly a century. The Soviets backed a military coup in Afghanistan in 1978, but armed resistance forced them to send Soviet tanks the next year to prop up their puppet ruler. In spite of an international outcry, the Soviets occupied Afghanistan for ten years. The bitter fighting cost many Russian lives and precious resources, helping to bring down the whole Soviet system.

All of the nations but Afghanistan now belong to the Commonwealth of Independent States (CIS). Even after the breakup of the Soviet Union, Russian influence remained in the region, particularly in the form of economic assistance. This assistance, however, came with deadly strings attached. Nations should be wary of international commitments that require the sacrifice of national values. Such alliances can change the character of a country so that it depends upon other countries and loses its own moral character.

The countries of the Caucasus and Central Asia are heavily influenced by Islam. They are especially influenced by a particularly violent and virulent sect of Islam called Wahhabism, which insists that governments be Islamic states and that Islamic law be enforced strictly. The al-Qaeda terror network and the Taliban, who formerly ruled Afghanistan, are major players in Wahhabism. A lesser-known fact is that the ruling family of Saudi Arabia is Wahhabi, as are Muslim chaplains in the U.S. military and the U.S. prison system.

I. THE COUNTRIES OF THE CAUCASUS

The **Caucasus Mountains** lie at the crossroads between Europe, Asia, and the Middle East. The western border of the mountains runs along the Black Sea. The eastern border touches the coast of the Caspian Sea, which was settled by Asian nomads and by Muslim conquerors from the Middle East.

A complex diversity of peoples arose in the isolated valleys of the Caucasus Mountains. The people are fiercely independent and are constantly fighting among themselves. The Arabs call the Caucasus the "mountains of a thousand languages."

Many foreign empires have tried, at their own peril, to subdue the region. Modern nations also want to gain access to the vast oil deposits in the Caspian Sea. The most recent attempt to control the region was by the Soviet Union. But the three small nations in the Caucasus—Georgia, Armenia, and Azerbaijan—gained independence from the Soviet Union. The Soviets had intentionally drawn borders across ethnic lines to weaken nationalism, but lumping enemies together was a recipe for trouble, and ethnic conflicts are ongoing.

Because those countries are far beyond the main avenues of world trade and activity, the Caucasus nations have struggled to improve their economies. Ethnic conflicts have only compounded their problems. The Free World is especially concerned about the threat of nuclear weapons falling into the hands of Islamic terrorists in the Caucasus, where each country has a large Muslim population.

Villages in flat, fertile valleys against a backdrop of high, snow-topped mountains are common throughout Georgia.

GEORGIA

From about AD 1000 to 1212, Georgia, which is smaller than South Carolina, enjoyed independence and prosperity. That period carried its people through the dark intervening years of domination by Mongols, Turks, Persians, and Russians. Georgia has been trampled as the pathway in wars between many nations. Finally, the Georgians accepted annexation by Russia, which was seeking a warm-water port and additional access to the Black Sea, in return for security. In 1990, however, Georgia became the second Soviet republic to declare independence from a weakened Soviet Union.

Georgia's language is unrelated to other known languages. It also uses its own unique alphabet. Seventy percent of the people are Georgians and worship in the Georgian Orthodox Church, a type of Eastern Orthodoxy.

The Georgian economy has progressed since the country gained its independence. Although one-fourth of the GDP is still agriculture and only one-fifth is industry, more than half of the GDP involves services. Georgia is fifth in the world in production of hazelnuts, or filberts. Other major crops include tea and citrus fruits.

CENTRAL LOWLANDS

The central valley of Georgia is formed from two river basins. The Rioni River drains west into the Black Sea. The surrounding area has a mild marine-west-coast climate in which citrus fruits and grape products are grown. Georgia is the only Caucasian country with ocean ports. Those ports on the Black Sea permit greater opportunities to trade with Russia and Ukraine, Georgia's main trade partners, as well as other nations.

Tbilisi (tuh BIL eh see) has been the capital of Georgia for more than 1500 years. It is on the Kura (kuhr RAH) River, which flows southeast into Azerbaijan (AZ ur bye JAHN). Irrigation in this drier region supports tobacco and wheat. The main industries of the city involve food processing.

HIGHLAND REBELS

Mountains lie both north and south of the central valley. The south is rich with copper and manganese.

Dissatisfied Muslim minorities are concentrated in two regions on the northern borders: Abkhazia (ab KAHZ ee ah), along the Black Sea, and South Ossetia (ah SEE shah), across the border from Russia's republic of North Ossetia. Although Georgia officially is helping the United States in the war against terror, concerns remain about the Muslims living there, many of whom are suspected of being Taliban or al-Qaeda soldiers who fled Afghanistan or Chechen rebels who fled Russian offensives in Chechnya. The Russians only increase the tensions by pursuing fleeing Chechen rebels into Georgia's territory. Russia has accused the Georgians of providing safe haven for the rebels.

This Georgian shepherd tends his sheep on the grasses of the plains.

FAMOUS (OR INFAMOUS) GEORGIANS

Georgia has produced at least two famous (or infamous, depending on one's perspective) leaders. Josef Stalin, who succeeded Lenin as the dictator of the Soviet Union, was a Georgian. A little-publicized fact is that he attended Tbilisi Theological Seminary, where he studied for the priesthood, but he became an atheist and a revolutionary instead. As dictator of the Soviet Union, he was responsible for the deaths of untold millions of people.

Less blood tainted and more recent is the Georgian Eduard Shevardnadze. He was a KGB agent, Communist Party bureaucrat, Communist leader of the Soviet republic of Georgia, and foreign minister of the Soviet Union. As the first president of Georgia, he guided the country through the civil strife and uncertainties of the immediate post-Soviet years, but his popularity waned when he failed to deal with accusations of corruption and election fraud. He escaped two assassination attempts before retiring.

ARMENIA

The **Armenians** (ahr MEE nee uns) have a unique language with its own alphabet, invented in the fifth century. In the fourth century, their nation became the first in the world to officially adopt Christianity.

AN INDEPENDENT KINGDOM

Armenia's mountains, which include some of the most rugged terrain in the Caucasus, provided some degree of protection from the Greek, Persian, and Roman empires. Later, the Arabs defeated Armenia, but the country did not adopt Islam. In 884, Armenia overcame the Arabs and established a new kingdom, which lasted two centuries.

By 1639, Ottoman Turks ruled the western region of Armenia, and Persia ruled the eastern region. Russia annexed the Persian portion in 1828 and took the western portion during World War I.

Also during World War I occurred a tragedy that has ever since marred relations between Armenia and the surrounding Muslim countries. In 1915, Turkey slaughtered 1.5 million Armenians in an effort to exterminate them. When the Turks seemed to get away with that atrocity, other dictators were emboldened to pursue similar practices. For example, Hitler concluded that the world would ignore his attempted extermination of the Jews because nothing had been done following the Turks' massacre of the Armenians.

LIFE

Armenia's dry climate provides only twenty inches of rainfall annually and is conducive to farming barley, wheat, and potatoes. Copper and bauxite are the major mineral resources.

Armenia is the most densely populated nation in the Caucasus and Central Asia. A 1988 earthquake killed twenty-five thousand people and left half a million people homeless; lack of supplies hindered Armenia's rebuilding.

Armenia, with its Orthodox religion, is most threatened by its Muslim neighbor Azerbaijan. Azerbaijanis attacked Armenian minorities in

What Is a Caucasian?

The word *Caucasian* has come to refer to light-skinned peoples because of the work of anthropologist Johann Friedrich Blummenbach. Studying skulls in the 1770s, he grouped all people into one of five races. He chose the skulls of women from Georgia, in the Caucasus Mountains, as the most typical skull of the white race. However, modern theories no longer recognize the term or limit the list of races to five.

Through Christian Eyes

Is there anything that Christians can do about the atrocities committed against humanity around the world?

Mt. Ararat towers over the mountains that form the border between Armenia and Turkey.

their country even before the breakup of the Soviet Union. In response, Armenia invaded Azerbaijan to protect its ethnic brothers. These poverty-stricken nations could ill afford the war. Armenia remains close to Russia even today.

Azerbaijan

Iran (formerly Persia) has had the greatest influence over Azerbaijan. Persians controlled the region from 700 BC to AD 600 (except for the brief interruption of the Greek Empire) and from the sixteenth century to 1813 (except for a brief period under the Ottoman Turks).

The people of Azerbaijan speak Persian and practice Islam, but they are descended from Turkic peoples. Their industry and military makeup come from Russia, which controlled the region from the nineteenth century until Azerbaijan won independence. Russians constitute a 5 percent minority.

Populous Lowlands

A long plain runs southeast across the nation. The Kura River flows through this lowland valley of the Caucasus, where farmers grow cotton, grain, and tea. Some raise silkworms in the semiarid temperate climate. This area is known for its beautiful rugs and shawls.

The Kura River, which provides water for textile and chemical plants, empties into the **Caspian Sea**, the largest lake in the world. This lake provides key resources, such as fish and salt. Azerbaijan's capital, Baku (BAH koo), is the leading port. Unfortunately, rising waters have threatened the lowland city with floods.

Several other rivers also flow into the Caspian Sea, which is ninety-two feet below sea level, but no waters flow out. The resulting "deadness" makes the Caspian Sea salty, but it is not as salty as normal ocean water.

By far the most important resource of the Caspian, however, is an abundance of oil and natural gas reserves. Oil companies believe the reserves might be larger than those in the Middle East. Russia has promised to help Azerbaijan fight Armenia in return for rights to this oil. The region could become a major battleground in the twenty-first century, as nations—including China, a nearby international giant—compete for the Caspian's oil wealth. The big problem for Azerbaijan, however, is how best to get its oil and natural gas to the rest of the world. It currently must use oil pipelines across other countries—often a difficult diplomatic task. It currently crosses Russian territory.

Baku, the capital of Azerbaijan, sits on the western shore of the Caspian Sea.

Highland Minorities

Azerbaijan's highland regions have cooler climates than do the lowlands. The most important highland region lies between the Kura Valley and Armenia. The major part of this region is **Nagorno-Karabakh** (nah-GAWR-noh KAHR-uh-ванк), a territory where a large Armenian minority lives. Armenian soldiers have fought Azerbaijan for control of this territory.

Another region, called Nakhichevan (NAHK ih chuh VAHN), is separated from the rest of the country far away in the west. It, too, is sparsely populated.

SECTION QUIZ

1. Why are there so many languages and cultures in the Caucasus?

2. What did the Soviets do in the countries that they controlled in the Caucasus to weaken nationalism and ensure loyalty to the Soviet Union?

3. Why is Russia concerned about conditions in the Caucasus?

4. What gives Azerbaijan an economic advantage over the other two Caucasus nations?

⚬ Where did the sons of King Sennacherib flee after they killed their father (Isa. 37:38)?

II. CENTRAL ASIA

Central Asia is a broad term that encompasses all of the dry steppes between the Caspian Sea and western China. Deserts and high mountains separate this region from the rest of the world. In times past, fierce nomads launched raids into neighboring lands in Asia, Europe, and the Middle East. The *Huns* threatened ancient Rome in the fourth and fifth centuries after Christ. The **Turkic peoples**, who later settled most of Central Asia, conquered Turkey; and the *Mongols*, who briefly conquered Central Asia, terrorized all of Eurasia between the thirteenth and fourteenth centuries.

Central Asia was once a major trade route between the East and the West. The **Silk Road** linked the two great ancient empires: Rome and China. Europeans gladly traded gold, silver, wool, jewels, and anything else of value to the Chinese in return for silk. Eventually, European traders discovered a new water route to China that avoided Central Asia. Little is left on the dusty Silk Road except struggling cities and memories of past greatness.

In the twentieth century, the Soviets dramatically changed life in Central Asia. They forced the nomads to settle down on collective farms and to grow cotton, even though this lifestyle did not fit the dry steppes.

The new nations of Central Asia are struggling to find their place in the modern world. They suffer from a devastating shortage of water and landlocked borders that isolate them from international trade. To make matters worse, former Communist rulers continue to exercise power in Central Asia.

KAZAKHSTAN

Kazakhstan (KAH zahk STAN), the "giant" of Central Asia, is the only Central Asian nation that borders Russia. The histories of the two nations are closely linked. For years, Russian farmers settled in northern Kazakhstan. A major problem, however, is that while northern Kazakhstan is heavily Russified, the southern part is influenced more by its Turkish background. When the country was under Soviet rule, the capital was **Almaty** (ahl MAH tee) in the south, which put strong Russian authority in the heart of Kazakh territory. When the Soviet Union fell, however, Kazakhs feared that the Russians in the north would try to become part of Russia, so they moved the capital to **Astana** (uh STAH nuh) in the north, putting Kazakh authorities in the heart of the Russified area.

ASTANA, THE CROSSROAD OF KAZAKHSTAN

Astana is a prosperous modern city with a history of many names. Founded as a fortress city in 1824, it was originally known as Tselinograd. Its name was changed several times during its subsequent history. Until the 1950s, it was an insignificant mining town, but Soviet dictator Nikita Khrushchev decided to make it the center of an ambitious agriculture project. The city began to grow. In 1991, when Kazakhstan gained its independence from the former Soviet Union, the city's name was changed to Aqmola. In 1994, the Kazakh government decided to make Aqmola the national capital. The move was made, and in 1998 the city's name became Astana ("capital").

Today, Astana is a growing, thriving modern city. Its wealth comes from the diversity of its production, which includes clothing, shoes, leather goods, agricultural machinery, building materials, and dairy products. The United Nations Educational, Scientific, and Cultural Organization (UNESCO) has designated it a "City of Peace."

The Ministry of Transportation and Telecommunications, the tallest building in Astana, shows the modernity of that growing city.

Kazakhstan is Central Asia's industrial giant. Only 20 percent of its people work in agriculture, but 30 percent work in industry. The other half work in services. The country's proximity to Russia and its large minority of well-trained Russians help to explain Kazakhstan's developed economy.

The 15.19 million people of Kazakhstan are very diverse in ethnicity. Only a little more than half (53.4 percent) of them are native Kazakhs. Russians constitute the largest minority (30 percent). Ukrainians, Uzbeks, Tatars, Germans, and other ethnic groups make up the remaining 16 percent of the population. The Slavic immigrants follow the Eastern Orthodox religion, but the Kazakhs are mostly Muslim.

EUROPEANS ON THE NORTHERN STEPPES

Kazakhstan's northern steppes are good for grazing sheep and cattle. Russian and Ukrainian farmers began arriving on the northern borders in the 1730s, and Russian armies had conquered the region by the 1850s.

The move of the capital to the north in post-Soviet years sparked one of the world's most ambitious building projects as oil income was used to erect government buildings, a presidential residence, parks, and monuments.

Mines in the far northwestern steppes produce more than one-quarter of the world's chromite. Kazakhstan ranks second worldwide in chromite production.

EASTERN KAZAKH UPLANDS

The Kazakh Uplands cover the eastern lake regions around Lake Balkhash and Lake Zaysan. The climate is similar to that of the northern steppes. Karaganda and Ekibastuz are important industrial centers. Large lead mines have made Kazakhstan the second-leading smelter of lead, behind the United States.

The major industrial city at the south end of the uplands is Almaty. With 1.3 million people, it is Kazakhstan's largest city and its cultural center. Dense orchards provide one of the country's main products—fruit.

SOUTHERN AND WESTERN DESERTS

Most of the south is a desert that contains great wealth. Copper comes from Betpak-Dala, the desert north of the country's main river, Syr Darya. Uranium is mined south of the river.

In the middle of these deserts, the Syr Darya flows into the **Aral (AHR ul) Sea**. Like the Caspian Sea to the west, the Aral Sea is a salt lake with no outlet to the ocean. Although it was once the world's fourth-largest lake, extensive irrigation has reduced it to eighth in only thirty years. It was originally used to increase agricultural (especially cotton) production, but the declining waters are now leaving salt deposits as they evaporate, and crop production is actually falling as the soil quality in the area deteriorates.

Western Kazakhstan consists of lowlands on the Caspian Sea. Unlike Azerbaijan, Kazakhstan has no major cities on this salt sea. There are no Caucasus Mountains to create orographic rainfall. Instead, the region is a barren wasteland. The lowland forms a deep bowl, or *depression*, in the earth. At its lowest spot, the **Caspian Depression** is 433 feet below sea level—lower than any location in the Western Hemisphere.

Kazakhstan is a corridor between the oil-rich Caspian Sea and China. China is seeking ways to gain the fuel it needs for its expanding industrial economy and to end its dependence on long ocean routes, so Kazakhstan is of great strategic importance. Kazakhstan has granted China sole rights to exploration and exploitation of oil along its border with the Caspian.

Unwise stewardship of resources is resulting in an economic and ecological disaster in the Aral Sea, as these stranded boats demonstrate.

TURKMENISTAN

Uzbekistan (ooz BEHK ih stan) and Turkmenistan (turk mehn ih STAN) lie south of Kazakhstan. Like Kazakhstan, these two desert nations were settled by Turkic peoples, speak Turkic languages, and follow the Turkish branch of Islam, Sunni Islam.

The Turkmens account for about 85 percent of the people of modern Turkmenistan. Uzbeks constitute 5 percent and Russians 4 percent. The rest are smaller minorities such as Kazakhs, Tatars, Ukrainians, and Armenians.

Turkmenistan, which is about the size of Utah and Nevada combined, lies south of Kazakhstan and east of the Caspian Sea. Turkmenistan's most important border is on the south with Iran. It is the only former Soviet republic bordering Iran. Its major hindrance to trade, however, is its relative inaccessibility to other countries.

The Turkmens displaced the Persians about AD 900. But in the fourteenth century, they converted to Islam under the influence of Sufis from Persia. Mary became the central city. In 1924, the Soviets moved the capital west to Ashgabat.

DRYING OF THE ARAL SEA

The Aral Sea once had the fourth-largest area of any lake in the world. However, the salt water is not very deep, and the area is shrinking at an alarming rate. Since 1960 the sea has lost 40 percent of its surface area, or more than eleven thousand square miles. The remaining water is so salty that all twenty-four species of fish that used to be found in the lake have died.

The shrinkage has caused an economic disaster. Before 1960, Muynak was a bustling fishing village of ten thousand people that supplied 3 percent of the world's annual catch of pike, perch, and bream. Now the village of two hundred people sits in a desert surrounded by beached ships twenty miles from the lake.

What happened? In 1918, the Soviet government decided to raise cotton in the desert. They built the world's longest canal, the Kara-Kum Canal, in 1956 to divert water from the two rivers that feed the lake: Syr Darya and Amu Darya. As the lake dried, salt storms blew out from the dry lake bed onto the cotton farms. As a result, the salty soil needed more and more water to stay productive. From 1977 to 1987, water never even reached the lake.

The disastrous effects of these decisions offer a good example of what happens when man exercises short-sightedness and poor stewardship of God-given resources. Before putting such decisions into concrete actions, one should always consider the possible consequences or side effects, both short term and long term. If negative side effects are indicated, one must then determine if the long-term benefits outweigh the negative short-term results on either the environment or the people affected. If they do not, one must revise—or even abandon—the original planned actions to ensure proper stewardship. God was emphasizing stewardship when He taught the Israelites that they were not to use fruit trees to build war machines (Deut. 20:19). The Bible also praises Uzziah for encouraging growth in agricultural technology and soil development in Israel (2 Chron. 26:10).

These satellite photos (left 1985 and right 2001) show clearly how the Aral Sea is disappearing over time.

The left image courtesy of the Image Science & Analysis Laboratory, NASA Johnson Space Center, STS51F-36-59, http://eol.jsc.nasa.gov

The **Kara-Kum** (kah-rah KOOM) is a desert that covers 80 percent of Turkmenistan. Summer temperatures can exceed 122°F. The desert's most important resources, petroleum and natural gas, make Turkmenistan the richest Central Asian nation. It is the world's fifth-largest producer of natural gas. As in Kazakhstan, the petroleum lies along the Caspian Sea. Natural gas is found throughout the desert.

UZBEKISTAN

Uzbekistan is in the heart of Central Asia, completely surrounded by other Central Asian nations. It borders every other nation in the region. Its population is made up of Uzbeks (80 percent), Russians (5.5 percent), and small minorities of Tatars, Kazakhs, Tajiks, and Karakalpaks. It is the most populous nation in Central Asia.

When Central Asia broke from the Soviet Union, Uzbekistan hoped that the Turkic peoples of Central Asia would unite into a single nation called **Turkistan**. Uzbekistan, with its large population, had much to gain from union because it lacks wealth and trade opportunities. Not surprisingly, no other nation shared Uzbekistan's enthusiasm.

DESERT OASES

The **Kyzyl-Kum** (kih-ZIL KOOM) is a vast desert that covers 80 percent of Uzbekistan, except for a few mountains on the eastern edge. The main crop, cotton, requires irrigation. The diversion of the two rivers for irrigation has hurt Uzbekistan just as it has hurt Kazakhstan. Uzbekistan's cotton industry, the fifth-largest in the world, is in deep trouble.

Most of the Kyzyl-Kum is wilderness, but it does have a few oases and mining towns. The greatest oasis lies at **Bukhara** (BOO kah rah), north of the Amu Darya. Bukhara served as a crucial juncture of the Silk Road as caravans crossed eight hundred miles through the deserts.

Grain and spice merchants display their products for sale in this bazaar in Tashkent, Uzbekistan.

In the tenth century, Bukhara was the capital of a Muslim dynasty, the Samanids, and was second only to Mecca as an Islamic holy place. It still boasts Ulugh Beg **madrasah** (mah DRAH suh, an Islamic seminary), the oldest in Central Asia, dating from 1418. It is also the home of the largest madrasah in Central Asia, dating from 1509. Today, Bukhara is a center of Tajik culture in the middle of an Uzbek nation.

THE CROWDED FOOTHILLS

Most of Uzbekistan's population lives in the foothills of the great Asian mountain system. Its two largest cities are there.

The capital, **Tashkent**, has 2.3 million people and is the largest city in the Caucasus and Central Asia. Tashkent has a rich heritage that dates back at least to the second century BC, according to Chinese sources. Unfortunately, a 1966 earthquake destroyed most of the historic buildings. The region around Tashkent contains some of the world's greatest uranium mines.

Samarqand (SAM er KAND, sometimes spelled Samarkand) lies near the eastern border of Uzbekistan, where the Kyzyl-Kum Desert reaches the first spur of the mountains. Ancient Arab manuscripts called it "the Gem of the East." It is famous for its excellent examples of various types of architecture. Alexander the Great defeated the local tribes and destroyed the city in 329 BC, but it was rebuilt and became a leading city on the Silk Road between Rome and China. The Mongol conqueror Tamerlane, the last ruler to unite Turkistan, made Samarqand his capital in the fourteenth century.

SECTION QUIZ

1. What product ruled trade across Central Asia?
2. What desert covers most of Turkmenistan? Why is Turkmenistan the richest nation in Central Asia?
3. What is the most populous nation in Central Asia? What dream gives its poor people hope?

☿ What regions of the United States are similar to the steppes, deserts, and mountains of Central Asia? How has their history differed from that of Central Asia?

KYRGYZSTAN

Of all of the continents, only Asia has mountains that reach twenty-three thousand feet. Three of Asia's highest mountain ranges lie in the remaining three countries of Central Asia.

Kyrgyzstan (KIHR gee STAHN) is dominated by the **Tien Shan** (tee-EHN SHAHN), or the "Celestial Mountains." This northern range runs one thousand miles from Tashkent to Urumqi in China and divides Kyrgyzstan from China.

The population is made up of Kyrgyz (64.9 percent); Uzbeks (13.8 percent); Russians (12.5 percent), who hold most of the technical jobs; and Ukrainians, Germans, and other ethnic groups, which constitute smaller minorities (9.8 percent). A major problem for the country is that its boundaries divide similar ethnic groups and put dissimilar groups together, which produces a situation that is ripe for friction and conflict. Religion, of course, is a major source of that friction. While the Kyrgyz and Uzbeks are Muslims, the other groups are Orthodox.

Osh, on the edge of the Fergana Valley, is the center of Kyrgyzstan's Uzbek minority. Historically, it was where Silk Road caravans began the arduous crossing of the Pamirs into China's city of Kashgar.

The people of Kyrgyzstan are primarily involved in pastoral occupations—raising yaks (for both milk and meat), sheep, and cattle. Irrigated valleys produce wheat and a variety of fruits and vegetables. Industry is limited primarily to textiles and food processing.

TAJIKISTAN

Tajikistan (tah JEEK ih stahn) is the mountain hub of Central Asia. About the size of Iowa, it shares borders with China and Afghanistan and is only a few miles north of Pakistan.

The **Pamir** (pah MEER) **Mountains** cover the eastern half of Tajikistan. This range is sometimes called the Pamir Knot because it ties together the great ranges:

Shepherd children pose in the Pamir Mountains of southeastern Tajikistan.

Hikers come from all over the world to scale the Pamir Mountains of Tajikistan.

Families such as this eke out a living from the soil of Tajikistan.

the Tien Shan, the Hindu Kush, the Himalaya (and Karakoram), and the Kunlun.

The Pamirs have three seven-thousand-meter peaks, all of which lie on or near the northern border of Tajikistan. Communism Peak, the highest, rises to 24,457 feet (7,495 m). The other two are Lenin Peak and Korzhenevskoi Peak.

Tajiks comprise 64.9 percent of Tajikistan's people. Uzbeks form the largest minority (25 percent), but others include Russians (3.5 percent) and Kazakhs, Turkmens, Kyrgyz, and Tatars (6.6 percent).

Tajikistan is unique in Central Asia. Its language is more Iranian than Turkic. Also, most of its people are Shiite Muslims, as are most Iranians. These two similarities to Iran make Tajikistan a natural inroad for Iran in the struggle to influence Central Asia. Ironically, the two nations do not even share a border.

Tajikistan has few resources except its rivers. The world's highest and second-highest dams, Rogun Dam (1,099 feet) and Nurek Dam (984 feet), harness waterpower for industries at the capital.

In Tajikistan, male friends show mutual respect by putting their foreheads together. In contrast, women do not touch and are not touched in public.

A Tajik woman shops in the spice market in Dushanbe, Tajikistan.

AFGHANISTAN

The mountains of Afghanistan harbor more than twenty ethnic groups, including Turkic, Mongol, Arab, Aryan, and Persian peoples. The two largest, the Pushtuns and Tajiks, constitute about three-quarters of the Afghan population.

The warring tribes of this region united for the first time in 1747 under a monarchy, but rivalry among chieftains kept the country weak. In the nineteenth century, the growing Russian empire began to push south into Afghanistan and threatened Britain's empire in India, which at that time included Pakistan. The British invaded Afghanistan in 1839 to install a friendly king. But three years of bloody revolt forced the British to withdraw.

Afghanistan became a **buffer state**, a neutral state between two rivals who agreed to keep their armies out. But worries about Russia led the British into another futile war (1878–80). Eventually, the

British stayed out for good, and the world recognized Afghanistan as a sovereign nation.

Afghanistan was independent but remained weak. From 1978 to 1989, Russia waged a costly and ultimately unsuccessful campaign to set up and maintain a Communist dictatorship in Afghanistan. The United States supported the opposition to the Soviets, a coalition of Muslim tribes known collectively as the **Mujahideen** (moo JAH heh DEEN; "strugglers"). After the Soviet Union gave up its attempt to control the country and withdrew its troops, the nation broke into warring factions, and anarchy reigned. Islamic extremists known as the **Taliban** (TAL ih BAN; "seekers," or "students") eventually prevailed and restored order by enforcing rigid adherence to sharia, including such punishments as amputation of hands and arms. They also allowed Islamic terrorists to set up training camps in the country, and some of their students carried out numerous attacks against the West, including the attack on the World Trade Center and the Pentagon on September 11, 2001. Consequently, the United States invaded Afghanistan, overthrew the Taliban, and chased down terrorists who had taken refuge in the mountains along the Afghan-Pakistani border. In 2004, the Afghan people elected a democratic government, but Afghan, Pakistani, and U.S. troops continue to hunt down terrorists in the mountains bordering and extending into Pakistan.

Afghan girls are now allowed to go to school following the U.S. ouster of the Taliban from Afghanistan in 2002.

GEOGRAPHIC DIVISIONS

Geographically, Afghanistan is divided into three zones: the fertile northern plains; the rugged, earthquake-shaken central highlands (the Hindu Kush); and the desert of the southern plateaus.

The **Hindu Kush**, Persian for "Hindu Death," is a mountain barrier extending southwest from the Pamirs and across central Afghanistan. It has thirty-four seven-thousand-meter-high peaks. All of them lie in the eastern **Wakhan** (wah KAHN) **Corridor**, a narrow panhandle that Russia and Great Britain created to stretch the buffer zone to China.

Most Afghan people live in these central and eastern mountain regions. The **Pashtun** (PUSH toon) people predominate. Their domain includes the nation's largest city and capital, **Kabul** (KAH bul), which lies in one of the many mountain valleys of the Hindu Kush. Its small industries include afghans, rugs, and jewelry made from locally mined gems. Afghanistan mines more lapis lazuli, a dark blue semiprecious stone, than any other nation in the world.

The major export of Afghanistan, however, is opium. In fact, it grows poppies in such large quantities that it produces 87 percent of the world's opium. Afghan opium production generates $2.8 billion a year and represents more than 60 percent of Afghan GDP. The U.S. war against the Taliban allowed virtually unfettered cultivation of poppies. Such cultivation increased by 64 percent in 2004 and was present in all of the country's thirty-two provinces. The UN is pressuring the Afghan government to pursue rigorous eradication and prosecution programs, but that seems to be a losing battle because

GEOGRAPHER'S CORNER

RELATIVE HUMIDITY AND WIND CHILL

Statistics for temperatures in a city are not always what they may seem. Feeling hot or cold depends on more than the temperature on a thermometer. On a hot day, the body needs to cool off by releasing water through the skin into the air; and on a cold day, the body needs to bundle up to keep the skin from releasing body heat into the air.

Conditions in the air can make it more difficult to cool off or to stay warm. In the harsh interior of Central Asia, conditions make the summers unbearably hot and the winters bitterly cold. The two main factors that change the body's ability to cope with weather are relative humidity and wind chill. A high relative humidity means that the air already has as much water as it can hold. High winds create a wind chill that increases the speed at which the body loses heat. Examine these tables and answer the questions about "apparent temperature" and the temperature on the thermometer.

Wind Chill

Wind Speed (mph)	Temperature on a Thermometer (°F)													
	−30	−25	−20	−15	−10	−5	0	5	10	15	20	25	30	35
5	−36	−31	−26	−21	−15	−10	−5	−5	7	12	16	21	27	33
10	−58	−52	−46	−40	−34	−27	−15	−15	−9	−3	3	10	16	22
15	−72	−65	−58	−51	−45	−38	−25	−25	−18	−11	5	2	9	16
20	−81	−74	−67	−60	−53	−46	−31	−31	−24	−17	−10	−3	4	12
25	−88	−81	−74	−66	−59	−51	−36	−36	−29	−22	−15	−7	1	8
30	−93	−86	−79	−71	−64	−56	−41	−41	−33	−25	−18	−10	−2	6
35	−97	−89	−82	−74	−67	−58	−43	−43	−35	−27	−20	−12	−4	4
40	−100	−92	−84	−76	−69	−60	−45	−45	−37	−29	−21	−13	−5	3
45	−102	−93	−85	−78	−70	−62	−46	−46	−38	−30	−22	−14	−6	2

1. If the thermometer says 35°F, what is the apparent temperature at night if a light wind blows at 5 mph? a strong wind at 35 mph?

2. If the thermometer says 0°F, what is the apparent temperature if a light wind blows at 5 mph? a strong wind at 35 mph?

3. If the thermometer says 80°F, what is the apparent temperature on a morning with 10% humidity? 70% humidity?

4. If the thermometer says 100°F, what is the apparent temperature at noon with 10% humidity? 70% humidity?

💡 Find (a) the most dramatic single increase in temperature due to humidity and (b) the most dramatic single drop in temperature due to wind. Now find the least dramatic changes.

Heat Index

Relative Humidity (%)	Temperature on a Thermometer (°F)											
	70	75	80	85	90	95	100	105	110	115	120
0	64	69	73	78	83	87	91	95	99	103	107
10	65	70	75	80	85	90	95	100	105	111	116
20	66	72	77	82	87	93	99	105	112	120	130
30	67	73	78	84	90	96	104	113	123	135	148
40	68	74	79	86	93	101	110	123	137	151	
50	69	75	81	88	96	107	120	135	150		
60	70	76	82	90	100	114	132	149			
70	70	77	85	93	106	124	144				
80	71	78	86	97	113	136					
90	71	79	88	102	122						
100	72	80	91	108							

the industry is extremely lucrative. It is hard to convince a farmer who is making $1,700 a year growing poppies to switch to growing wheat, which brings in only $390 a year.

Kabul became important because of the thirty-three-mile **Khyber** (KYE ber) **Pass**, one hundred miles southeast of the city, which allows easy passage through the Hindu Kush. At its narrowest point, the pass is only a little more than three feet wide. Great conquerors and their armies came through the pass, including Genghis Khan and possibly Alexander the Great. A southern extension of the old Silk Road brought goods from India to Samarqand.

A semicircle of less rugged land rings the Hindu Kush borders on the north, west, and south. The northern plains support crops and livestock. In the valleys, farmers grow wheat, barley, corn, and cotton. Between the valleys, herders graze sheep and goats for milk, mutton, and wool. Many Tajiks, the other major ethnic group, live in this northern region, which borders Tajikistan. In the southwest lies the Rigestan Desert, Afghanistan's least populous region.

The country's second-largest city, Kandahar (KAHN duh HAHR), lies at the southern edge of the Hindu Kush, near the border with Pakistan. The United States made the city their base of operations in the war against the Taliban and terrorists.

SECTION QUIZ

1. What mountains cross into Kyrgyzstan? Tajikistan? Afghanistan?

2. Through what modern nation did the Silk Road pass into China?

3. Which nation speaks a language closer to Iranian than to Turkish?

4. What famous pass links Central Asia with India?

‑Ǫ‑ Why has Afghanistan had so much difficulty building a strong nation? Does it have a better chance than Tajikistan or Kyrgyzstan?

CHAPTER REVIEW
18

HOW MUCH DO YOU REMEMBER?

1. Choose three nations in this chapter and explain how the Russians have influenced their cultures.

2. List all of the nations in Central Asia and the Caucasus that fit each description.
   a. Sunni Muslim
   b. Shiite Muslim
   c. Eastern Orthodox
   d. member of CIS
   e. Russian minority over 25 percent

3. Which term in each list has the least similarity with the other terms?
   a. Kazakhstan, Uzbekistan, Turkmenistan, Turkistan
   b. Kazakhs, Uzbeks, Turkmens, Tajiks
   c. Mary, Bukhara, Astana, Samarqand
   d. Pamirs, Tien Shan, Caspian Depression, Hindu Kush
   e. Nagorno-Karabakh, Kyzyl-Kum, Kara-Kum

4. Why is the Caspian region likely to become a battleground in the future?

5. What two great challenges hinder economic development in Central Asia?

6. Which group left the longest-lasting impact on Central Asia: Huns, Turkic peoples, or Mongols?

7. Why is the cotton industry bad for Central Asia?

8. What countries in this chapter lack major mountains? In what other ways are these countries different from the ones with mountains?

9. Which nations in this chapter have no ethnic groups that represent over 50 percent of the population?

WHAT DO YOU THINK?

1. In what ways has Russian influence been beneficial in the Caucasus and Central Asia?

2. Compare and contrast the cultures of the Caucasus with the cultures of Central Asia.

3. Give reasons that the Caucasus region should be included in each region below.
   a. Europe
   b. Asia

4. What political and economic problems do you foresee in Kazakhstan's future?

5. Why is the Caspian Sea flooding while the Aral Sea is drying up? Is human activity the only culprit?

Can You:
Define These Terms?

Turkistan	buffer state
madrasah	

Locate These Places?

Caucasus Mountains	Kyzyl-Kum
	Tien Shan
Caspian Sea	Pamir Mountains
Aral Sea	Hindu Kush
Caspian Depression	Khyber Pass
Kara-Kum	

Explain the Significance?

Armenians	Tashkent
Nagorno-Karabakh	Samarqand
Central Asia	Mujahideen
Turkic peoples	Taliban
Silk Road	Wakhan Corridor
Almaty	Pashtun
Astana	Kabul
Bukhara	

UNIT 8

BICYCLING ACROSS CHINA

Over a period of two years in the early 1890s, two American college students, Tom Allen and Bill Sachtleben, traveled around the world—on bicycles. Most of the people in the countries they crossed, including China, had never seen a bicycle. The two students were mobbed in every village through which they traveled, and the Chinese government even ordered a blacksmith to make a drawing of their contraption so that the Chinese people could enjoy the benefits of such a great invention. Here is one incident, in their own words, from their travels.

The excited throng pressed in upon us. Among them was a Chinaman who could talk a little Russian, and who undertook to direct us to a comfortable inn at the far end of the city. This street parade gathered to the inn yard an overwhelming mob, and announced to the whole community that "the foreign horses" had come. It had been posted, we were told, a month before, that "two people of the new world" were coming through on "strange iron horses," and every one was requested not to molest them. By this, public curiosity was raised to the highest pitch.

[The cyclists survived the mob by going to the roof of the inn, and then it began to rain, driving the crowd indoors. But they were back in the morning as numerous as ever.]

The next morning a squad of soldiers was dispatched to raise the siege, and at the same time presents began to arrive from the various officials. . . . Fruits and teas were brought, together with meats and chickens, and even a live sheep. . . .

[When they finally took their bicycles into the street, the mob] closed in on us entirely. It was the worst jam we had ever been in. By no possibility could we mount our machines. . . . They kept shouting for us to ride, but would give us no room. [With assistance from soldiers, they finally were able to clear enough room to demonstrate some trick riding and "special maneuvers."] After refreshments in the palace, to which we were invited by the viceroy, we were counseled to leave by a rear door, and return by a round-about way to the inn, leaving the mob to wait till dark for our exit from the front.

Excerpted from Thomas Gaskell Allen Jr. and William Lewis Sachtleben, "Across Asia on a Bicycle," chap. 22 in *Dead Reckoning: Great Adventure Writing from the Golden Age of Exploration, 1800–1900*, Helen Whybrow, ed. New York: W. W. Norton & Company, 2003.

SOME EXOTIC ASIAN FOODS

CULTURAL SNAPSHOT

One of the most exotic things that the traveler to the Orient will encounter is the food. Whether it is the vast number of ways in which rice dishes are prepared, the amount and types of spices used, or the kinds of unusual foods, every country of Asia seems to offer culinary surprises for the traveler. No country illustrates this better than Japan, which is famous (or infamous!) for its many fish and seaweed dishes. Japanese restaurants are famed for their *sushi*, which many people mistakenly think is simply uncooked fish. In fact, sushi is actually a food in which raw fish may or may not be an ingredient. (Sometimes the fish is steamed or grilled.) The following explanation will make the distinction more clear.

Sushi

The most common way to make *sushi* is to cook the best grade of rice, and, while the rice is hot, add vinegar, sugar, and salt. The mixture is then fanned to cool it quickly. Vegetables or fish, chopped up and cooked, are mixed with it. It is then delicately wrapped in seaweed. It is eaten both as meals and as between-meal snacks. It is especially convenient for picnics and other outdoor events. Originally, however, the word *sushi* was used for pickled fish made by placing fish between layers of cooked rice. The rice ferments and becomes sour, giving the fish its distinctive flavor.

Some *sushi* is packed especially for convenience. Vinegared rice is placed into a square wooden box. Fish and vegetables are placed on top of the rice. Then the whole

thing is pressed into a solid mass. It is then removed from the box, and the mass is cut into small pieces. Sometimes the Japanese fix rice balls small enough to fit between the finger and thumb as a convenient snack. They were originally made for theater-goers to eat between acts and therefore are called *makunouchi*, which means "between curtains."

Fugu

Perhaps the most interesting culinary "delight" of Japanese fish eating, however, is the *fugu*, also called globefish or blowfish. Each *fugu* contains enough of the poison tetrodotoxin to kill thirty adults, and there is no known antidote. When it is properly cleaned and cooked, it is supposed to be quite safe and delicious. When it is not prepared properly, however, it can cause instantaneous death! (One must be a specially licensed chef to prepare *fugu*.) Many victims are reported every year. Yet the Japanese continue to consume *fugu*. They enjoy the "slight numbness" that the poison causes. A *fugu* meal can cost as much as $200 in a fancy restaurant, though it can be obtained for an "inexpensive" $15–20 in some places.

Through the years, the Japanese devised several alleged antidotes to the poison. One of the oldest was to drink indigo dye. Another one was to bury the patient in the earth up to his neck. Still another so-called antidote was to drink egg whites or a glassful of soapy water. For some reason, these treatments seldom seemed to work. But did the victims die from the *fugu* poisoning or the "antidote"?

The people of South Asia worship a wide variety of gods and goddesses, as is evident on the walls of this Hindu temple in India.

SOUTH ASIA

Asia is an exotic region of contrasts between wealth and poverty, high culture and demonic paganism, insurmountable peaks and broad river plains. Mountains and deserts have long isolated Asia from the West, creating distinct differences in culture and history. Because South Asia is separated from the rest of Asia by the formidable **Himalayas** on the north and by the Indian Ocean on the south, and because it is bigger than a peninsula and smaller than a continent, it is sometimes called a **subcontinent**.

The Himalayas dominate the weather system of the region. Because the cold air north of the mountains cannot rise over them to spill into South Asia, the cold temperatures do not reach into the subcontinent. As the summer heat rises in the south, a low-pressure system results, drawing warm, moist air from the Indian Ocean in the form of winds called **monsoons** (mahn SOONZ). South Asia has the strongest monsoon winds in the world. The Himalayas cause the airborne moisture to fall as rain. Eighty percent of India's total rainfall comes during the four-month monsoon season. A reverse monsoon pushes cool, dry winds across the mountains into South Asia, causing a dry season. Some islands escape the dry season because the ocean provides moisture regardless of wind direction.

The monsoon rains begin in June or July and supply the rain necessary for the agriculture on which all South Asian countries depend. If the monsoons come late or with too little rain, the plants wither and die. If the rains are early or cause floods, the rice rots. Either way, the subcontinent often experiences famine since it is largely a subsistence economy.

Because India covers three-fourths of the region, South Asia is also called the Indian subcontinent. The name is appropriate because India's influence is felt throughout the region, and several of the countries were once part of India. Today, the region includes not only India but also Pakistan, Bangladesh, Nepal, Bhutan, and the island nations of Sri Lanka and Maldives.

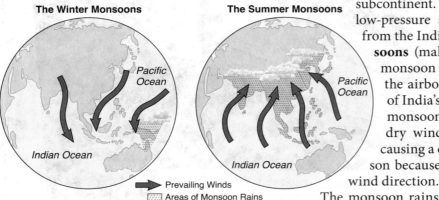

The Winter Monsoons — Pacific Ocean — Indian Ocean

The Summer Monsoons — Pacific Ocean — Indian Ocean

→ Prevailing Winds
▧ Areas of Monsoon Rains

South Asia Fast Facts

Flag	Country	Capital	Area (sq. mi.)	Pop. (M)	Pop. Density (per sq. mi.)	Per Capita GDP ($US)	Life Span
	Bangladesh	Dhaka	51,703	144.32	2,850	$2,100	62.08
	Bhutan	Thimphu	18,147	2.23	126	$1,400	54.39
	India	New Delhi	2,973,190	1,080.26	954	$3,400	64.35
	Maldives	Male	116	0.35	3,099	$3,900	64.06
	Nepal	Kathmandu	52,819	27.68	536	$1,500	59.8
	Pakistan	Islamabad	300,664	162.42	551	$2,400	63.0
	Sri Lanka	Colombo	25,332	20.07	792	$4,300	73.17

Political and religious strife characterize the crowded Indian subcontinent. **William Carey** (1761–1834) was the first modern missionary to seek to reach these exotic cultures. He translated the Bible into many of the region's languages. God used the following Scripture to motivate Carey to enlarge God's kingdom among the peoples of South Asia:

> *Enlarge the place of thy tent, and let them stretch forth the curtains of thine habitations: spare not, lengthen thy cords, and strengthen thy stakes; for thou shalt break forth on the right hand and on the left; and thy seed shall inherit the Gentiles, and make the desolate cities to be inhabited.*
> (Isa. 54:2–3)

In spite of the influence of Christianity, the region is largely unreached with the gospel.

William Carey, the first modern missionary to South Asia

I. INDIA

India, the largest country in South Asia, is also the seventh-largest country in area in the world and the second-largest in population. Its population increases by 1.5 million every month, which is equivalent to 50,000 births per day or 34.7 per minute. Of India's 1.08 billion population, only about 280 million live in cities; the rest live in small villages or in the countryside. India is predicted to overtake China as the world's most populous country by 2050.

India is often called the world's largest democracy. It is a federal republic with twenty-five states and six territories. Each state represents at least one of the major languages in India. Although Hindi is the national language, the native tongue of 30 percent of the people, English is an associate language used in commerce and diplomacy. Bengali, Urdu, Punjabi, Kashmiri, Sanskrit, and many other languages are also spoken.

MAJOR GEOGRAPHIC FEATURES

India can be envisioned as a giant triangle or an upside-down pyramid. It is bounded on the southeast by the Bay of Bengal, on the south by the Indian Ocean, and on the southwest by the Arabian Sea. Other countries provide India's border in the north: Pakistan on the northwest, China and Nepal on the north, and Bhutan and Bangladesh on the northeast. Its physical geography can be divided into several different major features or regions: mountains, rivers, a plateau, and a desert.

India is bounded by three major mountain ranges: the Himalayas on the northeast and the Eastern and Western Ghats, which run down either coast of the country.

THE HIMALAYAS

The northeastern limit of South Asia is delineated by the Himalaya Mountains, the highest mountain range on earth. The name *Himalaya* is Sanskrit for "House of Snow." It is an appropriate name for the greatest mountain range on earth. It includes **Mt. Everest** (29,028 ft.), the highest mountain in the world. (An equivalent height could be obtained by stacking the Appalachian Mountains on top of the Andes.) The Himalayas also boast most of

Mt. Everest is the highest mountain in the Himalayas and the world.

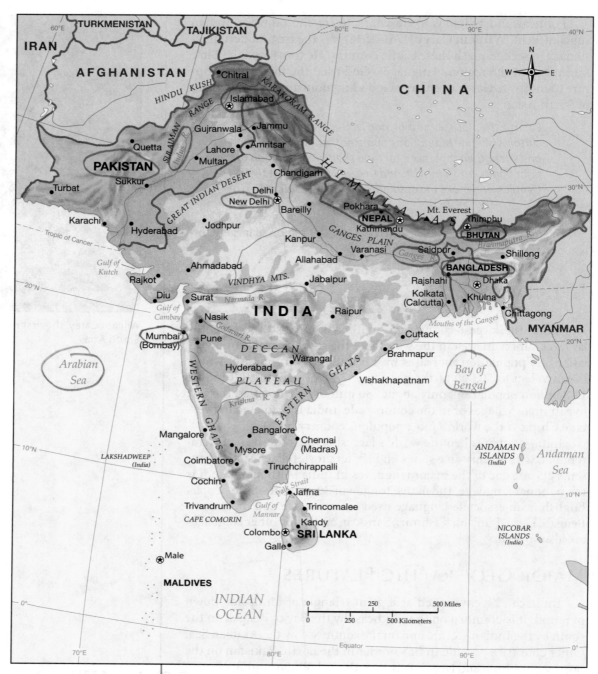

the world's highest individual mountains: 150 tower almost 23,000 feet and 10 reach more than 26,000 feet. (The next-highest mountain anywhere else is Aconcagua in the Andes of South America at 22,834 feet.) Many of the mountains are between 19,000 and 23,000 feet high, the two most famous of which are Ama Dablam (22,350 ft.), a fang-shaped peak in Nepal, and Mt. Kailas (22,027 ft.), the source of the Brahmaputra and Indus rivers in Tibet.

The *Himalayan Mountain System* forms the great mountain barrier that runs fifteen hundred miles along the south border of China. It is the only mountain barrier in the world with peaks exceeding 26,246 feet; it has fourteen of them. The Himalayas are the highest and most rugged mountains in the world, and many of them have never been climbed.

The Indus and Brahmaputra river valleys divide the Himalayan system into three distinct ranges. North of the Brahmaputra in China is the Trans-Himalaya, which contains three peaks over 22,965 feet. West of the Indus River is the **Karakoram** (KAR uh KOHR uhm), which extends three hundred miles across Kashmir to the Pamir Knot. It has 113 such peaks and four that reach 26,246 feet.

The Himalayas proper extend twelve hundred miles from the Indus River to the great eastern curve of the Brahmaputra River. The Karakoram and the Trans-Himalaya are not technically part of the range.

THE WESTERN AND THE EASTERN GHATS

The Ghats are two ranges of long, low, hardwood-covered mountains that run along the coasts of India. The **Western Ghats**, as the name indicates, run for about a thousand miles along the west coast from just north of Mumbai southward to the southernmost tip of the country. They are home to numerous rare species of plants and animals, and they contain many wildlife sanctuaries and national parks designed to protect those species. Only one break exists in the range, the Palghat Gap. The ocean side of the Western Ghats gets heavy rainfall and therefore has lush tropical vegetation and dense forests of hardwood trees. The inland side is dry.

The **Eastern Ghats** stretch for about nine hundred miles along the east coast from the Mahanadi Valley in the north, where rice cultivation is a major economic activity, to the Nilgiri Hills in the south. The word *Nilgiri* literally means "Blue Mountains." The area is famous for its production of mild Nilgiri teas. Many rivers cut through the Eastern Ghats and are used for electricity production.

THE VINDHYA MOUNTAINS

The remaining major mountain range cuts from just north of where the Western Ghats begin, inland from the Gulf of Cambay and the city of Surat, almost due east into the heart of India. Actually more like high hills (approximately 3,000 feet in elevation), the sandstone **Vindhya** (VIHN dyuh) **Mountains** have historically been the natural dividing line between northern India and southern India.

THE GANGES RIVER

Rivers also play an important role in India's geography. The northern portions of the country are delineated by the great river systems and the plains that they drain: the Indus River in the northwest, the Ganges River in the north and northeast, and the Brahmaputra in the extreme northeast.

The **Ganges** (GAN JEEZ) **River**, one of the world's longest rivers, begins in an ice cave in the Himalayas. It flows southeast more than fifteen hundred miles across north central India. It ends its journey by emptying into the Bay of Bengal from multiple mouths of a 212-mile-wide delta on the India-Bangladesh border.

The Ganges is very muddy and deposits an estimated 1.5 billion tons of sediment a year (equivalent to 4.1 million tons a day, or 170,833 an hour, or 2,847 tons a minute, or 47 tons a second)! Nonetheless, the river supplies much of the water needed to irrigate the farms in northeast India. Because its delta is so fertile, the Ganges is the most important river in India. It also holds great significance in **Hinduism**, the largest religion in India. (See the section on Hinduism, pp. 477–79.)

The Ganges Plain spreads along the river and encompasses five states and two territories. It also extends eastward up its largest

Cape Comorin is the southernmost point of the Indian mainland.

tributary, the Brahmaputra River (discussed later in this section). The Ganges Plain is the most populous region of India.

With more than 166 million people, Uttar Pradesh is the most populous state in India and contains about one-half of the course of the Ganges, including its headwaters in the Himalayas. The state's population increased by more than 25 percent in the decade 1991–2001. The state's major crop is sugar cane; India is the world's second-leading producer of sugar cane (behind only Brazil). India leads the world in production of sesame seeds and pulses (a pod-bearing plant like peas). It is the second-greatest producer of cashews (behind only Vietnam).

Three-fourths of India's vast population lives in small towns or rural villages. Uttar Pradesh is no exception. The largest city of that region, Kanpur, has only 2.72 million people, which is not many people considering the population of the entire state. Many of the people make their living by subsistence farming or in cottage industries, making simple products in their homes. Because the Indian government provided fertilizers, pesticides, and better seed to small farms, harvests improved. India now produces enough rice to feed itself, except in years that monsoon variations cause crop failures.

The rest of the Ganges flows through two states downstream from Uttar Pradesh. The more important state is West Bengal, where Bengali is the major language. Its main city near the mouth of the Ganges, **Kolkata** (kahl KAH tah, formerly Calcutta), has 15.65 million people, making it the third-largest city in India (behind Mumbai at 19.85 million and Delhi at 19.7 million). Thanks in large part to West Bengal, India produces almost one-half of the world's jute (a fibrous plant used for making rope and burlap cloth). West Bengal also produces much rice, helping make India, which produces about one-fifth of the world's rice, the second-largest rice producer in the world (behind only China).

BATHING IN THE SACRED GANGES

According to Hindu legend, the Ganges River is the goddess Ganga, who took physical form. Hindu temples line the banks of this sacred river, and stairs lead down to the water. Pilgrims believe this water is holy and cleanses their souls. Many pilgrims come for healing, and others come to die, hoping to enter paradise immediately. The smoke from cremated bodies rises above the riverbanks of the Ganges. In spite of the filth resulting from this activity and industry, Hindus use the river water for drinking, cooking, and washing. As a result, diseases such as cholera are common.

Many religions throughout history have worshiped water as a source of life and healing, as Hindus do the Ganges and ancient Egyptians did the Nile. Christianity recognizes water as a gift from God to be used wisely. God is displeased when people worship the things He has created rather than worshiping Him (Deut. 4:15–17; Rom. 1:25).

THE BRAHMAPUTRA RIVER

The headwaters of the **Brahmaputra** (BRAH muh POO truh) **River** are in Tibet. The river flows about 1,864 miles through four countries (Tibet, China, India, and Bangladesh) before joining the Ganges in the Ganges delta and emptying into the Bay of Bengal. It discharges about 725 million tons of sediment a year. It provides water and irrigation for the state of Assam in northeastern India. The rich soil aids the production of tea, the region's leading product. India is the world's leading producer of tea.

THE JUMNA RIVER

The **Jumna** (JUHM nuh) **River** is another important tributary of the Ganges in the plains. It begins west of the Ganges in the Himalayas of Uttar Pradesh but then forms the boundary between Uttar Pradesh and the central state of Haryana. **Delhi** (DEL ee), India's second-largest city, stands on the Jumna River between Uttar Pradesh and Haryana. The city is a major manufacturing center. Its suburb, **New Delhi**, is the national capital. These two cities are not part of any state but lie in the separate capital territory of Delhi.

THE INDUS RIVER

The **Indus River** flows from its headwaters in China through the states of Jammu and Kashmir and the entire length of Pakistan, emptying into the Arabian Sea. Although only a small portion of the river is within the borders of India, the valley holds great significance in history as the birthplace of one of the earliest civilizations.

THE GREAT INDIAN DESERT

Within the bounds created by the major Indian mountains and rivers about which you have read are two other geographic features: the Great Indian Desert south of the Indus River and the Deccan Plateau in central India.

Southwest of where the Indus flows through India and into Pakistan is a region called the Thar (TAHR), or the **Great Indian Desert**. Other than palm trees near springs, only small desert plants will grow without irrigation there.

The city of Ahmadabad, former capital of the state of Gujarat, is a manufacturing center with 5.6 million people. To the southwest, the Kathiawar Peninsula sticks into the Arabian Sea. A saltmarsh called the Rann of Kutch and the Gulf of Kutch are on the northwest side of the peninsula. The Gulf of Cambay is on the southeast side. The peninsula produces one-third of the world's peanuts, making India the leading producer of peanuts worldwide.

The state of **Punjab** (pun JAHB), north of the Thar, contains the Punjab Plains. These plains cross into India from northeast Pakistan and extend to meet the Ganges Plain. The Sutlej River, a tributary of the Indus River in Pakistan, drains the plains.

Most people there speak Punjabi and worship as Sikhs (SEEKS). Sikhs are followers of Guru Nanak (1469–1539), who sought to reconcile Islam with Hinduism; their religion is known as **Sikhism**. Sikhs now number more than 16 million, about 2 percent of India's population. About 80 percent of Sikhs live in Punjab, where they make up about two-thirds of the state's population. (See p. 481 for more information about Sikhism.)

A Sikh in traditional garb

THE DECCAN PLATEAU

The **Deccan** (DEK uhn) **Plateau** is the heart of the Indian peninsula. The Deccan includes eight states, parts of two others, and three territories. It is bounded on the west by the Western Ghats and on the east by the Eastern Ghats.

Mumbai (muhm BYE), formerly called Bombay, is located on the northern half of the coast. With 19.85 million people, Mumbai is the largest city in India and is the capital and major manufacturing center of the state of Maharashtra. Cotton is the major crop there; India is the world's third-largest producer of cotton.

About three-fourths of the way down the peninsula on the western coast of India is an area called the Malabar Coast. Its tropical climate makes it an ideal location for growing mangoes and bananas, and India is the world's leader in producing those fruits.

Inland, the tropical climate changes abruptly to a dry climate. The city of Mangalore on the Malabar Coast receives more than 120 inches of rain a year, but the rainfall diminishes to less than 40 inches a year at Bangalore, which is inland due east of Mangalore, almost halfway between the east and west coasts. Bangalore is a manufacturing city of more than 7.1 million people and the only inland capital of the four west Deccan states.

Much of the Deccan has a dry climate. Scattered trees punctuate the tall grasses of its savannas. Although it is semiarid, the plateau's high altitudes keep the temperatures cooler than those in the tropical lowlands.

The eastern half of the Deccan Plateau increases in elevation from the Bay of Bengal to the highlands of the Eastern Ghats. The coastal plain is somewhat wider than that in the west. The coast on the Bay of Bengal is called the **Coromandel** (kohr uh MAN dul) **Coast.** All of the major rivers of the plateau flow to that coast. Three states cover the east coast.

The Deccan has most of India's mineral resources. The largest of several deposits of iron ore and coal are in the northeast portion of the plateau. Some iron ore is exported, but India does produce its own iron and steel using its own coal to fuel the steel mills. India also mines large deposits of bauxite, manganese, and mica from that part of the plateau. Although India does have some oil, it still imports much oil.

Chennai (chuh NYE), formerly known as Madras, is India's fourth-largest city with a population of 7.6 million. It is a famous source of spices, such as turmeric and cardamon. It is India's major southeastern port, although its harbor is totally man-made. (The British took almost forty years—from 1862 to 1901—to complete it.) It is also a major rail center. Through that city flow exports of animal hides, cotton, textiles, and other products.

With Mumbai and Kolkata, Chennai was a center of the British East India Company from its inception in 1600. In fact, the city was founded by the East India Company. Expanding from these centers, the company gained control of most of India by 1763. The company relinquished rule to the British government in 1858.

DISPUTED BORDER REGIONS

India's border regions lie at the extreme edges adjacent to other nations. Some of them are remote wilderness areas. The cultures of

Many people in Mumbai live in poverty.

those areas are influenced by India's neighbor nations, especially in religious worship.

Uniting such a mixed bag of religions and peoples into one nation has not been easy, and religious violence has racked the border regions of the nation from its birth. A Hindu assassinated **Mahatma Gandhi** (muh-HAHT-muh GAHN-dee) in 1948 because Gandhi wanted to make peace with the Muslims in India. Hoping to stop the killing, the first prime minister, **Jawaharlal Nehru** (JAH-wah-HAHR-lahl NAY-roo), a close associate of Gandhi, established a "secular" federal republic in 1949. But religious fighting only increased. Since 1984, a radical Hindu party called the Bharatiya Janata Party has been trying to replace the secular state with a pure Hindu kingdom, or *Hinduvita*. That political party won more seats than any other party in 1996. For the first time since India's independence, the Congress Party of Nehru failed to win the most votes.

South of the Brahmaputra, in the eastern hills, lie five of the seven smallest states (in both area and population) in all of India. That region is the only region in India with a Christian majority. People there converted to Christianity after the days of William Carey. India has about 25 million professing Christians (2.3 percent of the total population). The wet and dry monsoons create a humid subtropical climate in this region. Instead of rain forests, deciduous trees such as maple, walnut, and birch grow in the hills, along with some tropical fruit trees and palms. However, many of the trees of the region have been cut for fuel and other needs.

The Himalayas follow the border of China from Pakistan to Myanmar (formerly called Burma). Many of India's Himalayan peoples practice the Lamaistic form of Buddhism common in neighboring Nepal and Tibet. It is the only region in India with a Buddhist majority, which is somewhat surprising because Buddhism began near the Ganges. The Himalayas cover three widely separated states of India in addition to the disputed area called **Kashmir** (kazh MIHR), which is claimed by both India and Pakistan.

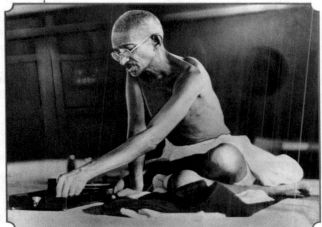
Mahatma Gandhi

Section Quiz

1. What geometric shape does India resemble?

2. What three major bodies of water border India?

3. Which mountain range forms much of India's northern border?

4. Which mountains frame the Indian peninsula?

5. Which three rivers are of greatest importance to India?

6. What geographic feature is the heart of India?

☀ What issue more than any other divides India and its neighbors?

Religions

Hinduism

More than 80 percent of the people of India are Hindus, so religious traditions greatly influence life there. For Hindus, two of the most sacred things are cattle and the Ganges. India has more cattle

Jawaharlal Nehru

Through Christian Eyes

Some people believe that the Hindu caste system is a gross violation of human rights. Others think that it is a time-honored way of managing Indian society and that those from other cultures should not be critical of it. How should a Christian evaluate the caste system?

than any other nation in the world, and they are allowed to wander unhindered wherever they choose to go. Hindus also see great spiritual significance to bathing in the Ganges.

Hindu tradition assigns people to different classes, each with its own privileges and responsibilities but also limitations. Each class, called a **caste**, strictly determines one's social status. According to the Hindu **caste system**, a Hindu must fulfill his or her role. **Brahmins** (BRAH mihns, priests and teachers) and Ksatriyas (rulers and warriors) occupy the highest castes. Merchants, skilled craftsmen (artisans), and farmers—the Vaisyas—belong to the mid-level caste. Sudras, unskilled laborers, are the lowest caste. Some despised occupations, such as tanners and garbage collectors, are considered so low that they are beneath caste. They are called "**untouchables**" and comprise approximately one-seventh of the Indian population. Today, the basic castes are divided into hundreds of subcastes, called *jatis*. A Hindu is born into the *jati* of his parents, and he must marry someone from that jati. He must also hold an appropriate occupation and can never change his caste, so the system allows for little, if any, upward mobility in society.

Hindu beliefs include **reincarnation**, the idea that every person follows an endless cycle of birth, death, and rebirth. Hindus believe that when they die, they will be reborn into another life. A Hindu accepts the caste into which he is born as the reward or punishment for his works in his past lives, and he tries to do good works so that his future lives will be better. The total effect of a person's actions is called **karma** (KAHR muh). Hindus believe that good karma might allow them to be reborn as a Brahmin or a rich man. Bad karma would cause them to be reborn into a lower caste, as an untouchable, or even as an animal.

Ultimately, the Hindu hopes to be so good that he will escape the cycle of reincarnation and become part of Brahman, the world spirit. This world spirit is not personal but rather a force that energizes the entire physical world. The view that God is nothing more than the life force throughout the world is called *pantheism*. The Bible, however, teaches that God existed before He created the universe, and He is not limited to it. God transcends creation, yet He has revealed Himself as a personal God who loves man.

Other Hindu beliefs vary greatly because Hinudism has three sets of holy books and no single founder or teacher. The first book, *Rig-Veda*, was written approximately 1200 BC and is the basis of the caste system. The *Upanishads*, written a few centuries later, teach about the Hindu gods—Brahma, Vishnu, and Shiva—as well as reincarnation and karma. The *Bhagavad-Gita*, which appeared even later, focuses on Krishna (a human manifestation of Vishnu). Some Hindus believe in one god; others believe in many gods. Many **gurus** (GOO rooz; spiritual leaders) attract followers to their own teachings. Their followers try to escape reincarnation by repeating prayers, by seeking spiritual wisdom from the gurus, by helping others, or by enduring strict discipline and self-denial (asceticism).

God's Word clearly teaches, however, that man has only one life on earth and that after death he will live eternally in either heaven or hell. If one rejects the salvation offered through Jesus

The Caste System

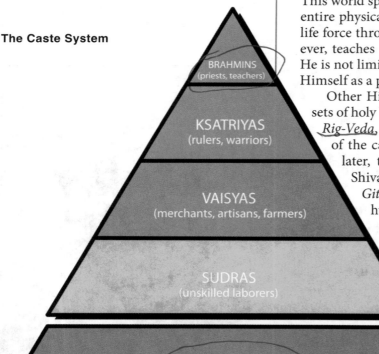

BRAHMINS
(priests, teachers)

KSATRIYAS
(rulers, warriors)

VAISYAS
(merchants, artisans, farmers)

SUDRAS
(unskilled laborers)

UNTOUCHABLES
(polluted laborers, outcasts)

Shiva

Vishnu

Christ, he or she will suffer eternally in hell. If one accepts Christ, however, he or she will live forever with Him in heaven. We are not trapped in an endless cycle of reincarnation. Regardless of social or financial standing, we all have the opportunity to find salvation in Jesus Christ.

> *And as it is appointed unto men once to die, but after this the judgment: so Christ was once offered to bear the sins of many; and unto them that look for him shall he appear the second time without sin unto salvation.*
> (Heb. 9:27–28)

ISLAM

The second-largest religion in India is Islam, with approximately 180 million adherents, comprising 13.4 percent of the population. It is the fastest-growing religion in the nation; the number of Muslims

SACRED COWS

Hindus consider cattle to be especially sacred, the symbol of all life. Cows pull plows and carts and supply milk and butter. Their manure is fuel for cooking and building material for village homes. To show thanks, Indians occasionally leave small offerings of food for the cows. They allow cattle to roam freely through India's villages and city streets, eating whatever they wish. Hindus allow the animals complete freedom because they believe them to be the reincarnation of past lives. Hindus refuse to eat beef to avoid accidentally eating a grandfather in his present incarnation.

The number of cattle in India is estimated to be more than 250 million head. (The United States has an estimated 95.8 million head.) Most of India's cows are too scrawny to serve as beef cattle, even if the Hindus did eat meat.

Taj Mahal

Shah Jahan became emperor of India in 1628 at the age of thirty-six. Tragedy struck the next year when his favorite wife, Mumtaz Mahal (meaning "chosen of the palace"), died in childbirth. She had been devoted to him through eighteen years of marriage. He grieved for two years and spent twenty-two years building a tomb in her honor. Visitors to the city of Agra in the state of Uttar Pradesh still marvel at the memorial's beautiful lines and curves.

The emperor employed twenty thousand laborers to cut the marble from a quarry, transport it two hundred miles, and raise the monument. The tomb extends 186 feet on each side, and archways rise as high as 109 feet. A great onion-shaped dome in the center adds another 120 feet. The white marble is inlaid with forty-three kinds of precious stones, including sapphires, jade, crystal, and diamonds. Quotations from the Koran, carved in black marble, decorate the tomb, which rests on an even larger red sandstone platform. At each corner of the platform are prayer towers, called minarets. The garden setting and large pools add to the beauty and serenity of the monument, which is known as the **Taj Mahal**.

The shah's son later overthrew him. When the shah died, he was buried beside his wife. After the collapse of the Mughal Empire, robbers ransacked the Taj Mahal's treasures, but it remains a symbol of one man's undying love for his wife.

increased by 36 percent between 1991 and 2001. During the same time, the majority religion, Hinduism, grew by only 20 percent. More than half of the Muslims in India live in three states. They are in the majority in only two states.

The introduction and early growth of Islam in India were primarily by violence. Arabic Muslims invaded the country in the eighth century and forced people to convert to Islam or be killed. Although relations between Muslims and people of other religious groups have never been totally peaceful, until fairly recently Muslims have chosen to tolerate or get along with the majority to avoid a backlash. With the worldwide rise of militant Islam, however, Indian Muslims have become increasingly aggressive. They are encouraged in their radicalism and militancy by the presence of Muslim-dominated governments in nearby Pakistan and Bangladesh as well as Kashmir.

Christianity

According to tradition, the apostle Thomas came to India in AD 50 and established several churches on India's west coast before being martyred. European explorers of the fifteenth century were surprised to find groups of Christians, called the St. Thomas Christians, in India. Other people believe that St. Bartholomew was the one who introduced Christianity to India. Over the years, however, the Indian churches became bound by ritual and tradition with no real understanding of the gospel. Most of the St. Thomas Christians joined the Roman Catholic Church, but some remained independent. In the nineteenth century, one group of St. Thomas Christians came under the influence of Protestant missionaries. They broke with their ritualistic church and formed the Mar Thoma Church, a more Protestant group. Combined, these two groups include about two million people.

St. Francis Xavier brought large-scale missionary activities to India in 1544. Soon thereafter, Portuguese missionaries came, as did other European missionaries, including Protestants. Today, about 30 million people, or about 2.3 percent of the total population, profess some form of Christianity. (Much of this can be traced to the seeds sown by missionary William Carey.)

SIKHISM

The religion of Sikhism arose in the early sixteenth century in the northern Indian state of Punjab when a guru named Nanak sought to combine the teachings of Hinduism and Islam. He believed that both religions taught essentially the same thing. His disciples compiled his teachings in the *Guru Granth Sahib*, which became the holy book of the Sikhs. They teach reincarnation and karma but reject the existence of original sin and Satan. Salvation, they teach, is liberation from the cycles of rebirth, at which point the soul merges with God. That state is achieved by repeating prayers, meditating, giving alms, and performing other good works.

About 16 million Indians, or 1.9 percent, profess Sikhism as their religion. About 80 percent of all Sikhs live in Punjab, making up about two-thirds of that state's population. The Sikhs there have long pressured the Indian government to recognize them as an independent nation called Khalistan. In 1984, Sikh terrorists assassinated India's prime minister, Indira Gandhi. Their ongoing terrorist activities have cost thousands of lives and caused years of fear.

JAINISM

Jainism (JYE nihz uhm) is another religion of the region and is thought to be related to both Hinduism and Buddhism. Some people classify it as a heretical version of Hinduism. Jains believe that humans can become gods, or Jina, by being "enlightened" through the worship of twenty-four Jinas who serve as inspirational bridges. Until that point, one's soul is continually reborn through reincarnation.

Jainism has even more rigorous practices than Hinduism, including the rule of no violence against any life form. For instance, Jains cannot kill any living creature and must not eat meat. Some Jains wear cloths over their mouths to avoid accidentally inhaling and killing an insect. Today there are about five million Jains in India. The religion started about 500 BC near the Ganges east of Varanasi, but today most Jains live on the west coast of India.

India has numerous other minority religions. Hinduism and all of the other competing worldviews make religion pervasive throughout the country. India has an estimated 2.4 million places of worship (temples, mosques, churches, etc.), more than the number of schools, colleges, and hospitals combined.

These followers of Jainism are wearing masks over their mouths lest they inhale—and thereby kill—a tiny insect.

India's Natural Resources and World Ranking in Production of Each

Coal	3
Chromium	3
Fishery production	3
Iron ore	4
Pig iron	5
Crude steel	8

Distribution of the Indian Labor Force

Economic Sector	Labor force %	% of GDP
Agriculture	60	17.5
Industry	17	27.9
Services	23	54.6

This photo of the homeless sleeping on the street in Pondicherry depicts a common scene in India.

GOVERNMENT AND ECONOMY

Britain increased Indian representation in the government in appreciation for India's help in World War I and continued to grant Indians an increasing role in government. The minor changes, however, caused uncertainty and unrest. The most famous leader in the protests that resulted was Mahatma Gandhi, the Father of the Nation. He led the people in nonviolent protests, or **satyagraha** (suh TYAH gruh huh), encouraging the people to destroy British power nonviolently simply by making their own goods rather than trading for them (i.e., economic self-sufficiency). One of his most famous marches was a march to the sea in 1930 to protest a salt tax. The protest resulted in more than sixty thousand imprisonments. Gandhi himself was imprisoned many times.

When Japan conquered Burma and then invaded eastern India in the early years of World War II, India joined the British cause. Britain granted the country full independence in 1947. The long British occupation had given Indians many beneficial features. It spread English among the educated, and English is still used for administrative purposes. The British also developed a vast railroad transportation network and established a strong judicial and administrative tradition.

Today, India is a federal republic: a national government, with its capital in New Delhi, that shares ruling powers with twenty-eight states and seven territories, each with its own government and capital. A president is the chief of state; a prime minister is the head of the government; and a bicameral parliament fills the legislative role. India has dozens of political parties, many of them representing religious factions, and even several Communist groups.

India has a growing economy in spite of widespread poverty and frequent natural disasters. Occupations range from subsistence farming to modern commercial agriculture and from modern industry to various service industries.

Although India is an economic powerhouse in South Asia, it faces its share of problems, all of which affect its economy in some way. It is susceptible to natural disasters, including the extremes of drought and flooding (especially during the monsoons). Such problems intensify the ever-present risks of disease. Health issues are further complicated by India's growing population, poverty, and industrial pollution.

Rice is a major crop of India.

Like religion, poverty is pervasive in India. An estimated 192 million families, many of them multigenerational, live in approximately 179 million houses. About 40 percent of Indian families live in one-room dwellings. Many thousands of Indians are homeless and live a hand-to-mouth existence. An estimated 150,000 homeless children live in Delhi alone. About 60 percent of Indians are farmers or farm workers, and those people barely make a living. Farm workers make an average income five times less than that of nonfarmers.

RUPEES AND RAJAS

If you lived in India, your money would be rupees instead of dollars. What would you buy with your rupees? Western items are readily available in the cities. You could even go to the McDonald's in New Delhi, but one thing would be different about that restaurant. It was the first McDonald's franchise with no beef on the menu. The Maharaja Mac has two "all-mutton" patties!

Although Western clothes are popular, every person's wardrobe includes some traditional Indian garments. Indian clothing tends to be brightly colored and lightweight. Indians frequently wrap lengths of cloth between their legs to make *dhotis*, or loincloths. Loose-fitting trousers are called *pajamas* and have become popular in English-speaking lands as bedtime garments. Indians also wrap cloth into hats called *turbans*.

Ladies drape lengths of cloth around them to form a long dress called a *sari*. The loose end hangs over the shoulder. Expensive saris are made of silk with borders of pure gold thread. In some regions women wear veils, bracelets, and earrings. Women also adorn themselves with a *kumkum*, a red or black powder dot in the middle of the forehead.

Several generations usually eat and sleep under one roof, especially in the villages. As a sign of respect to an elder, you would perform a *namaskar*, touching the elder's feet with your fingers. Elders usually arrange the marriages of children, and wives are expected to run the household and to serve their husbands. At one time, young girls were forced to become brides, and widows were burned on the funeral pyres of their husbands in a practice known as *suttee*. These barbaric practices have been outlawed and are not practiced openly today.

Meals are a major daily ritual. The head woman serves the food and eats only after everyone else is done. Most Indians eat meals with their fingers. The typical meal includes either rice or wheat breads, depending on where you are from. No meal would be complete without *dhal*, a porridge made from pulse (vegetables that come from seed pods such as peas, beans, and lentils). Hindus do not eat beef, but many of them eat chicken and lamb. Curries are spicy sauces made with powdered curry leaves. India's sauces can be even hotter than Mexican dishes. Other dishes include mangoes, yogurts, and other cool or sweet desserts.

Indians enjoy good poetry and music. In fact, they have about five hundred musical instruments. The oldest instruments are gongs and drums. Western audiences are familiar with

the twenty-stringed *sitar*, once used by court poets and today played at concerts across Europe and the United States.

Most Indian villagers would consider the average American visitor to be as rich as a *raja* (prince). But you must be careful how you spend your money in the marketplace. You might be buying one of the millions of Indian gods. For instance, a carving of a man riding a white elephant is likely to be the god Indra.

Indian sitar

LET'S GO EXPLORING

CLIMATES OF ASIA

1. Find the mountainous region in the center of Asia. What climate is common just south of these mountains? What climate is common just north of these mountains?

2. How many climate regions does India have? What is most common in the northeast? the west? the south?

3. What climate is most common on the islands of Southeast Asia?

4. What country has the largest area with a moderate climate? What country is second largest?

⚬ Compare and contrast the climate of China and the United States.

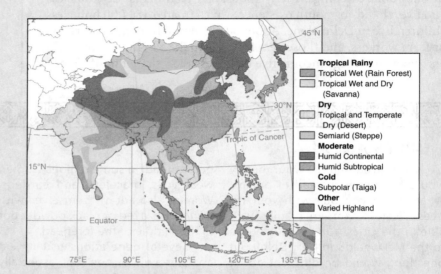

Tropical Rainy
- Tropical Wet (Rain Forest)
- Tropical Wet and Dry (Savanna)

Dry
- Tropical and Temperate Dry (Desert)
- Semiarid (Steppe)

Moderate
- Humid Continental
- Humid Subtropical

Cold
- Subpolar (Taiga)

Other
- Varied Highland

Indian Autos and the GDP

A surprising statistic concerning the Indian GDP involves the cost of road accidents to the nation. Although India has only 1 percent of the world's road vehicles, 6 percent of the world's road accidents occur there. On average, one person dies and ten more are injured in India every six minutes because of such accidents. The financial losses incurred from these accidents equal 3 percent of the GDP.

Agriculture is responsible for more than one-fifth of the GDP. Major crops include rice, wheat, cotton, jute, tea, sugar, and potatoes.

On the other hand, India's economy is rapidly becoming more diverse, with increasingly more emphasis on industry and services. Although 60 percent of the labor force is involved in agriculture, services are responsible for 51.4 percent of the GDP. The country has become heavily involved in computer software development and production and telephone customer services for U.S. companies. India's major international trading partners include China, the United States, and the United Arab Emirates.

SECTION QUIZ

1. List five major religions of India.

2. What religious belief prompts Indians to give cows free rein to do as they please?

3. Which river holds special significance to Hindus, and by what practice do they show that regard?

4. Which Indian leader promoted nonviolent protest as a means for political reform?

5. What type of government does India have?

⚬ Why do you think India has such a problem with highway accidents?

II. PAKISTAN AND BANGLADESH

The histories and cultures of India, Pakistan, and Bangladesh are very closely linked because they were all India until 1947. Britain's offer of independence for India depended on India's deciding on a system of government. When Hindu and Muslim conflicts prevented agreement, Britain separated the main Muslim regions from Hindu India to form the nation of Pakistan. One-half million people died in the conflict that followed, as Muslims and Hindus fled to their respective countries.

Pakistan (PAK ih stan) consisted of two parts: East Pakistan and West Pakistan, indicating the opposite sides of northern India. Both parts were Muslim, but they were about a thousand miles apart. The capital was in West Pakistan, but most of the people lived in East Pakistan. Communication was difficult, and the people felt little national unity. India and Pakistan went to war over Kashmir three times (1947–48; 1965; 1971). During the last war, East Pakistan, encouraged by India, sought and gained independence from West Pakistan and became known as Bangladesh (BAHN gluh DESH). Ever since, the western part has been known simply as Pakistan.

When India began testing a nuclear weapon, Pakistan responded by initiating its own nuclear weapons research. Today, both nations are nuclear powers, further increasing the regional tensions. To complicate matters, the "father" of Pakistan's nuclear program, Abdul Qadeer Khan, confessed in 2005 that he leaked nuclear secrets to Libya, Iran, and North Korea, "rogue nations" that are known for their support of terrorism. (Libya has since renounced terrorism, but only time will tell if it is committed to peaceful use of whatever nuclear information it received.)

Both Pakistan and Bangladesh also face problems common to all third-world countries: disease, poverty, unemployment, and spiritual darkness.

PAKISTAN

Pakistan is often in the news because of both its ongoing dispute with India over control of Kashmir and its support of the Western

GEOGRAPHER'S CORNER

USING OUTSIDE RESOURCES

A few facts about the world never change. Mount Everest will probably be standing when Christ returns. But dams change the flow of rivers, wars erase cities, and even mountains "change" heights with each new topographical survey.

Yet some regions experience more changes than others. By now you have learned some likely places for the next new island or new volcano. You should also have learned some likely places for the next changes in governments and national boundaries. While any government can change overnight, some countries are more unstable than others. The United States, for example, will probably remain a constitutional republic during your lifetime. But other places, such as the Indian subcontinent, may experience changes this year. An assassination, civil war, or even nuclear war could strike at any moment. Your goal this year in geography class is to gather information that will help you to understand such changes.

Here are four projects that should help you to see the value of studying geography.

1. Find any newspaper article on a country discussed in this chapter. Underline every geographic location mentioned in the article.

2. Find any magazine article on India. Explain what has changed since this textbook was written.

3. Listen to news reports until you hear a story about the Indian subcontinent. Give a brief summary of the report: the media you listened to, the time you heard it, and the topic.

🔎 Find a report about U.S. activity in the Indian subcontinent. Summarize the issues at stake, the official U.S. position, and your position as a Christian.

allies in the war against terrorism. It also has been the site of much anti-Western violence and many earthquakes.

PHYSICAL FEATURES AND SOCIETY

The Indus River valley makes up most of Pakistan. Flowing southwest from the Himalayas, the river waters a very dry region. Only those areas that can be watered from the river are suitable for agriculture. The remaining land east of the river to the border with India is part of the Great Indian Desert. Most Pakistanis live in the two provinces along the Indus River system.

The province of Punjab contains Pakistan's portion of the Punjab Plains. The province includes the capital, Islamabad (pop. 955,629), and the cities of Lahore (pop. 6.4 million) and Multan (pop. 1.5 million). The people who live in Punjab control the government, economy, and military. The region supports wheat and cotton crops.

To the south, the river flows through the province of Sind. The delta at the mouth of the Indus supports large rice crops. Karachi (kuh RAH chee), west of the delta, is the provincial capital and the nation's leading port. With a population of 14.5 million people, it is also the largest city. The province extends north beyond Hyderabad and Sukkur, areas that have major natural gas deposits.

About fifty miles downstream from Sukkur lies a ruined city now known as **Mohenjo-Daro** (moh-HEN-joh DAHR-oh). The ancient civilization that flourished there along the Indus Valley from 2500 to 1700 BC was one of the earliest on earth.

One of the world's earliest civilizations developed at Mohenjo-Daro in modern-day Pakistan.

In some nations, the remote areas offer important natural resources. Unfortunately for Pakistan, its remote regions have only minor deposits of coal and petroleum. Most of the people there herd sheep or goats.

The largest province, Baluchistan, is also the least populated. Elevations on this large plateau reach more than eight thousand feet and give some relief from tropical heat. However, the area is so arid that few plants exist there. Many of the people are nomads, leading their sheep or goats from one oasis to another. The large province includes all of the coast west of Karachi and north to the provincial capital, Quetta, and beyond.

The people of North-West Frontier Province are called Pashtuns (PUHSH toonz). They live in the mountain valleys where precipitation is adequate. The capital of the province, Peshawar, is south of Chitral and just east of the **Khyber** (KYE bur) **Pass**, the only opening for travel through the rugged and formidable Hindu Kush Mountains. When Russia invaded Afghanistan in the 1980s, many Afghan refugees crossed into Pakistan using the Khyber Pass. The region also became a haven for the Taliban and other terrorists when the United States invaded Afghanistan following the September 11, 2001, terrorist attacks on the United States.

The inhospitable terrain around the Khyber Pass on the Pakistan-Afghanistan border has long been a refuge for terrorists and criminals.

GOVERNMENT AND ECONOMY

About 97 percent of all Pakistanis are Muslims (about three-fourths of them Sunnis). The national language is Urdu, but only 10 percent of the people speak that language. The elite government officials speak English. The language spoken by the most people, however, is Punjabi (48 percent). More than ten other languages are spoken in various regions of Pakistan.

The Pakistani government is officially designated a federal republic, with a president, a prime minister, a bicameral parliament, and, like India, dozens of political parties. In reality, however, it is a modified military dictatorship ruled by General Pervez Musharraf. Musharraf declared himself president but promised to hold elections in 2007. He made that promise, however, before the war on terror began. He has tried to walk a political tightrope, supporting the U.S. war against terror enough to satisfy the Americans while also trying to placate his largely anti-American Muslim countrymen. Pakistanis have frequently and violently persecuted Christians and protested the actions of Western governments.

The Pakistani economy is largely agricultural, with 42 percent of the labor force involved in that type of activity, which contributes more than 21 percent of the GDP. Major crops include cotton (fourth in the world), sugar cane (fifth in the world), wheat, rice, milk, beef, mutton, and various fruits and vegetables. Industry accounts for more than 25 percent (textiles/apparel, food processing, pharmaceuticals, paper products, and fertilizer) and services for more than 53 percent of the GDP. Unfortunately, Pakistan is a crossroads for both terrorism and Afghan opium and heroin.

U.S.-led coalition forces ousted the Taliban from Afghanistan and continue to search for terrorists in the mountains there.

BANGLADESH

Poor. Overpopulated. Ill-governed. These words probably best describe the tiny nation of Bangladesh. Surrounded by India, Myanmar, and the Bay of Bengal, the country is essentially the delta of the Ganges, Jamuna, and Meghna rivers. The rich delta soils hold potential for many crops, but the country's location also makes it susceptible to frequent natural disasters, including **typhoons** (tye FOONS, hurricane-like storms), **tsunamis** (soo NAH mees, sometimes called tidal waves), drought, and floods, especially during the monsoons. It is considered the poorest country in the world.

PHYSICAL FEATURES AND SOCIETY

Bangladesh is slightly smaller than Iowa, but it is one of the most densely populated countries in the world. About 6.1 million people live in Dhaka (DAH kuh), the capital. Another 2.1 million people live in Chittagong (CHIHT uh GAHNG). Bengali is the official language of this crowded country.

The rickshaw-filled streets of Dhaka are nearly impossible to cross safely on foot.

Living conditions in Bangladesh are terrible, poverty is rampant, the risk of disease is extremely high, and medical care is scarce. Since two-thirds of the people rely on agriculture for their livelihood, the limited farmland and destructive weather patterns cripple the country. Rice and jute are the main crops, but production is minimal. They cannot afford to import food, so they depend on millions of tons of food donated by other nations to stave off famines. With inadequate port facilities; inefficiently run, government-owned businesses; economic reforms that are perpetually stalled in bureaucracy; and corruption in government, Bangladesh seems to be trapped in a cycle of poverty.

Eighty-three percent of Bangladeshis are Muslim. Approximately 16 percent are Hindu. The remaining 1 percent follow a variety of tribal religions and **animism** (the belief that spirits inhabit objects in nature).

GOVERNMENT AND ECONOMY

Bangladesh is a parliamentary democracy. Its government is run by a president, a prime minister, and a unicameral parliament. The country has eight to ten political parties. Although the ruling party has sufficient numbers to push through the economic reforms necessary for improving the country, its members seem lethargic, lacking the will to do what is necessary. As a result, the country depends heavily on charitable donations from other countries to deal superficially with its problems.

Nonetheless, Bangladesh has an economy that is growing slowly. Although 63 percent of the national labor force is employed in such activities, only 20.5 percent of its GDP comes from agriculture. The 11 percent who are employed in industry contribute more than 26 percent of the GDP. The remaining 26 percent of the workers are in services, which contribute more than half of the GDP.

Perhaps surprisingly, Bangladesh is a leader in the production of some agricultural products. For example, it is the second-leading producer of jute (behind only India), third in spices (behind only India and China), fourth in rice, fifth in pulses, and tenth in tea. Its other major industries include paper, cement, cotton textiles and garments, and chemical fertilizers.

SECTION QUIZ

1. What is the major religion of both Pakistan and Bangladesh?
2. From what country did Pakistan obtain independence?
3. Which region is the object of dispute between India and Pakistan?
4. What are the major products of Pakistan? Bangladesh?
5. Which country is known for its high population density?
- ☼ What factors caused the division of Pakistan, resulting in the creation of Bangladesh?

III. NEPAL AND BHUTAN

NEPAL

The nation of Nepal (neh PAHL) is landlocked, technologically backward, poverty stricken, and prone to natural disasters, and its people are at high risk of disease. Its government is tenuous, its economy weak, and its prospects for improvements grim.

PHYSICAL FEATURES AND SOCIETY

A little larger than Arkansas, Nepal contains eight of the world's ten highest peaks, including Mt. Everest. Because of its overall altitude (even its lowest peaks are in the alpine zone), it has cool summers and severe winters. It is also susceptible to floods, landslides, droughts, and famine, depending on the timing, intensity, and duration of the monsoons.

South of the Himalayas is a strip of hills and valleys that are high enough to remain cool but low enough to be forested. Along the border with India is the Tarai, a region of tropical lowlands (only 150 feet in elevation). Crocodiles, elephants, and tigers roam the Tarai. Farmers raise sugar cane and tobacco there and wheat in the nearby hills. Corn and rice grow in both regions.

The people of Nepal are a mixture of Indian and Tibetan and speak more than eight languages, the most widely spoken (48 percent) being Nepali. Whereas some polygamous societies practice polygyny, in which the men marry more than one wife, some Tibetans practice *polyandry*, in which women marry more than one husband.

Only 45 percent of the Nepalese are literate, and Nepal is the only official Hindu state in the world, with 80.6 percent of its people being Hindus. About 11 percent are Buddhist and 4.2 percent Muslim, with other minor religions rounding out the population. It is one of the poorest societies in the world, and the people are frequently plagued by cholera, leprosy, tuberculosis, and other diseases.

Perhaps the most famous Nepalese are the Sherpas and the Gurkhas. **Sherpas** (SHUR puhz) are frequently hired as guides and porters by the approximately 150,000 foreign tourists who come to Nepal every year to climb its famous peaks. Sherpas are renowned for their strength and endurance. **Gurkhas** (GOOR kuhz) are famed for their fighting abilities. Great Britain often hired Gurkha soldiers for its army.

Sherpas are renowned for their skills as guides for mountain climbers.

GOVERNMENT AND ECONOMY

Since 1991, Nepal has been a parliamentary democracy and a constitutional monarchy in which the parliament rules under the ultimate leadership of the king. In February 2005, however, the king abolished parliament, signaling a move back to absolute monarchy. Public unrest in 2006 forced the king to recall parliament and surrender the throne. The capital is Kathmandu, with a population of 812,000. The country has at least eight political parties, including the Communist Party, which is heavily influenced by China.

The economy is one of the poorest in the world. More than 80 percent of the labor force is involved in agriculture, although it contributes only 40 percent of the GDP. Leading agricultural products include sugar cane, potatoes, and wheat. The most-produced crop is rice. Only 3 percent of the people are employed in industry, which contributes 20 percent of the GDP. Tourism is the leading moneymaker for the country, but the sometimes volatile political situation makes that income tenuous.

Armed with their trademark curved knives, called khukuris, Gurkhas developed a reputation as fierce and loyal fighters.

BHUTAN

Bhutan (boo TAN), landlocked like Nepal, is about half the size of Indiana. It is bordered by China and India, but it controls some key passes in the Himalayas. Also like Nepal, it is technologically backward and economically challenged.

PHYSICAL FEATURES AND SOCIETY

The climate of Bhutan ranges from severe cold in the Himalayas to tropical in the southern plains. Its climate is notorious for its sudden and violent thunderstorms. In fact, its very name means "Land of the Thunder Dragon." Its terrain is mostly mountainous, so it has frequent landslides, especially during the rainy season. Associated with the landslides is the problem of soil erosion. The country also has limited drinking water.

Bhutan's population is 75 percent Buddhist and 25 percent Hindu. Its literacy rate is only 42 percent. Few women are educated.

GOVERNMENT AND ECONOMY

Bhutan is officially an independent state, but in practical terms it is very closely linked to India. It remained essentially isolated until 1959, when it sought help from India to stave off threats from China. It is a monarchy ruled by a hereditary king, but its king promised to allow the country to move toward democracy. A draft constitution was completed in 2001 and a referendum on it promised, but no date for the election has been set. The nation's unicameral legislature is made up of 10 delegates representing various religious groups, 105 that represent villages, and 35 that the king appoints. No political parties are legal, but Buddhist priests and Indian merchants exert great influence on the government. The country has a treaty with India whereby Bhutan controls its own domestic affairs and India controls its foreign policy. Bhutan and the United States have no formal diplomatic relations.

Bhutan has one of the world's smallest economies, and even that is closely linked to the Indian economy. (India finances three-fourths of Bhutan's expenditures.) It is based on subsistence farming, animal husbandry, and forestry. Agricultural products include rice, corn, root crops, citrus, grains, eggs, and dairy products. Its industry is backward, and most of it is cottage industry. Major industries—such as they are—include cement, wood products, processed fruits, alcoholic beverages, and calcium carbonate. Bhutan's major trading partners are India (86 percent of Bhutan's exports) and Germany (42 percent of Bhutan's imports).

SECTION QUIZ

1. What political/religious fact makes Nepal unique?

2. Which two groups of Nepalese are famous, and for what special skills is each known?

3. What do Nepal and Bhutan have in common that make them unique among other countries of South Asia?

4. What does Bhutan's name literally mean, and why is it called that?

IV. SRI LANKA AND MALDIVES

Several islands lie off the Indian subcontinent in the Indian Ocean. Two of them are independent nations, while several others are territories. The two nations are the only South Asian nations with normal life expectancy and high literacy rates.

SRI LANKA

The island country of Sri Lanka (SREE LAHNG-kuh) lies twenty miles off the southeast coast of India. It is a little larger than West Virginia and is strategically located near the subcontinent and the shipping lanes of the Indian Ocean.

PHYSICAL FEATURES AND SOCIETY

The terrain is low, flat-to-rolling plains with mountains in the south-central interior of the island. The climate is tropical monsoon, and the natural vegetation is rain forest. The island is hit occasionally by fierce cyclones and tornadoes. Combined with the monsoons, these storms cause a great deal of soil erosion. Sri Lanka was hit by a devastating tsunami in December 2004 that left 31,000 dead, 6,300 missing, and 443,000 homeless and caused an estimated $1.5 billion in property damage.

Buddhist Sinhalese from northern India settled on the northern plains of Sri Lanka about 400 BC. Today they make up about 75 percent of the population. Tamils, Hindus from southern India, began arriving three hundred years later. They finally won the northernmost point of the island, Jaffna, from the Buddhists. Today they make up about 5 percent of the island's population.

Most Sri Lankans (69.1 percent) are Buddhists. Muslims and Hindus make up 7.6 and 7.1 percent of the population, respectively.

The island has been influenced somewhat by both Portuguese and Dutch traders, but the greatest European influence was exerted by Great Britain, which claimed the island in 1796. At that time, the island was known as Ceylon. The British controlled it until they granted it independence in 1948. The name of the island was changed to Sri Lanka in 1972. Conflicts between the Sinhalese and the Tamils, who want independence, have been ongoing for decades. The warring factions finally signed a Norwegian-brokered ceasefire in February 2002.

GOVERNMENT AND ECONOMY

Today, Sri Lanka has a republican form of government, with a president, a prime minister, and a unicameral legislature. The capital is Colombo (pop. 2.2 million). The country has twenty or more political parties, and strong influence is exerted by Buddhist priests, labor unions, and radical separatist groups.

More than one-third of the Sri Lankan work force is engaged in agriculture, producing 17.7 percent of the GDP. The largest sector of the economy, however, is services, employing 45 percent of the work force and contributing 55.2 percent of the GDP.

Rice and coconuts are the two major food crops of Sri Lanka. Plantations in the south produce the main exports of tea and rubber. Sri Lanka's tea is world famous, and its mines produce rubies and sapphires. Insurance, banking, and oil refining are other major industries. Approximately 800,000 Sri Lankans work in the Middle East and send much of their earnings back home.

MALDIVES

Maldives (mal DIVZ) is the smallest nation in Asia, not quite twice the size of Washington, D.C. Its 1,190 coral islands, arranged in 26 atolls, sprinkle the sea southwest of India over a region 475

Sri Lankan teas are world famous.

"Walking" Trees?

The banyan is a very large and interesting tree found in South Asia. The trees grow from the top down. Branches send out roots through the air until they reach the ground. Each root thickens into a new trunk and sends out more branches, which in turn grow roots. Each root becomes a new leg as the tree grows and expands across the countryside. Roots that grow down through the air are called aerial roots.

As the tree grows, it begins to look like a whole forest. The largest banyan tree has 350 large trunks and three thousand smaller ones. This record tree is in Sri Lanka.

miles long and 80 miles wide. About 200 islands are inhabited; another 80 are tourist resorts. The nation is strategically located on the Indian Ocean shipping lanes southwest of the Indian peninsula.

PHYSICAL FEATURES AND SOCIETY

The islands of Maldives have a hot, humid climate. The northeast monsoons are dry; the southwest monsoons are rainy. The terrain is flat with beaches of white sand. The highest point is only about eight feet in elevation. The islands have a limited supply of fresh water.

Almost all of the people in Maldives are Sunni Muslims, descendants of Sinhalese people from Sri Lanka, and the national language is Divehi, which is related to Sinhalese. The few minorities are from India or descended from Arab traders.

The Maldivians are an amazingly literate people, especially considering that education there is not compulsory. Ninety-nine percent of the people attend grades 1–5, 51 percent attend grades 6–10, and only 5 percent attend grades 11–12—yet literacy is an amazing 99 percent. The government spends 20 percent of its annual budget on education.

GOVERNMENT AND ECONOMY

The history of Maldives was influenced by first the Dutch and then the British. It obtained its independence from Britain in 1965 and became a republic three years later. The government operates by secular Muslim law. It has a president and a unicameral legislature of fifty representatives, forty-two elected by the people and eight appointed by the president. The same president has dominated the government since he was elected in 1978, but riots in Male (MAH lee; pop. 70,000), the capital, in 2004 forced him to pledge reforms and greater freedoms. Four political parties, including three opposition parties, were allowed in June 2005.

The economy is dominated by fishing and tourism. Tourism contributes 32.9 percent of the GDP. Agricultural products grown include coconuts, corn, and sweet potatoes. Shipping, boat building, handicrafts, and coral and sand mining are important industries.

The islands of Maldives suffered extensive damage when they were hit by a tsunami in December 2004. With aid from India, the United States, and other nations, however, the country is already making a comeback.

The islands of Maldives are flat and densely populated.

Maldives was badly damaged by the 2004 tsunami.

SECTION QUIZ

1. What island nation was first united by Great Britain?
2. What two groups were at war in Sri Lanka until they signed a ceasefire in 2002?
3. What is the majority religion in Sri Lanka?
4. What fishing nation occupies a group of coral islands near India?
5. Of what religion are almost all of the inhabitants of those islands?

CHAPTER REVIEW

HOW MUCH DO YOU REMEMBER?

1. How do the mountains along the northern borders affect the climate of South Asia?

2. Why is India called the world's largest democracy?

3. What do we call the social classes of Hindus in India? What are each of those classes?

4. What is the major religion of Pakistan?

5. What country split from Pakistan in 1971? Why?

6. What two island countries lie near India in the Indian Ocean?

7. What is considered the poorest nation in the world?

8. What mountain range contains 250 of the highest mountains in the world?

WHAT DO YOU THINK?

1. In what major ways does the religion of Hinduism differ from true Christianity? What do you think would be the best approach in witnessing to a Hindu?

2. Make a list of the problems common to the countries of South Asia. What is the root cause of these problems and the best hope for improvement?

Can You:
Define These Terms?

subcontinent	reincarnation
monsoon	karma
Hinduism	guru
Sikhism	Jainism
caste	satyagraha
caste system	typhoon
Brahmins	tsunami
untouchables	animism

Locate These Places?

Himalayas	Jumna River
Mt. Everest	Indus River
Karakoram	Great Indian Desert
Western Ghats	Deccan Plateau
Eastern Ghats	Mumbai
Vindhya Mountains	Coromandel Coast
Ganges River	Khyber Pass
Brahmaputra River	

Explain the Significance?

William Carey	Jawarharlal Nehru
Kolkata	Kashmir
Delhi	Taj Mahal
New Delhi	Mohenjo-Daro
Punjab	Sherpas
Chennai	Gurkhas
Mahatma Gandhi	

CHAPTER 20

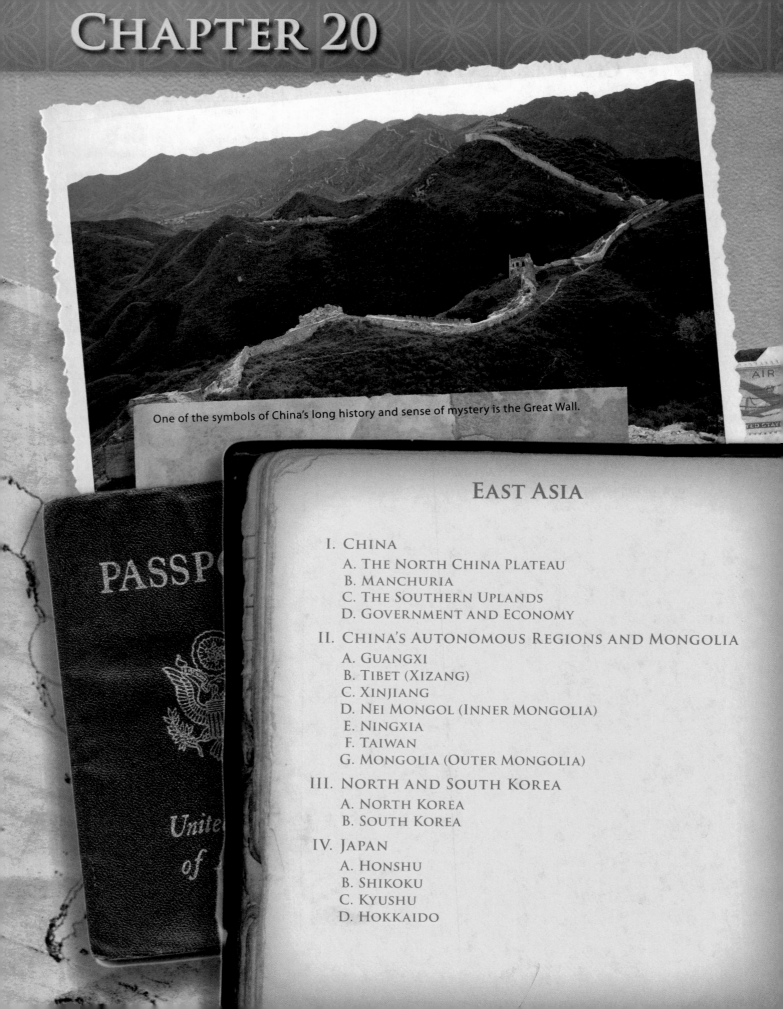

One of the symbols of China's long history and sense of mystery is the Great Wall.

EAST ASIA

Until the last few centuries, the West knew very little about the exotic lands of the Far East. The customs, religions, and even appearance of the East Asian people differed from those of Western people. Towering mountains, harsh deserts, and treacherous seas isolated the nations of East Asia from the rest of the world. Left alone, these nations built advanced civilizations that endured the test of time.

During the nineteenth and twentieth centuries, however, the ancient societies of the East came face to face with the industrialized West, which resulted in revolutionary changes to every area of life in the Far East. The nations responded in vastly different ways to the perceived threat of the West, and they are still reaping the consequences of their choices. Two nations—China and Korea—split in two, between Communist and republican governments.

Today, the countries of East Asia (with the exception of North Korea) are vibrant economic giants that compete with the best of the Western nations. Although the Far East has adopted many Western ideas about industry and government, this openness has come at a price. In the case of China, relaxed economic controls have resulted in a degree of political and personal freedom, but by Western standards the Chinese still are not free. The love of tradition has also kept much of East Asia either partially or totally closed to the gospel. Christian missionaries reached China as early as AD 735, but they seemed to have little impact. The most influential missionary in the region was Hudson Taylor (1832–1905), who organized the China Inland Mission. God used the following verse to burden Taylor to reach people beyond the coastal cities who had never heard the name of Jesus.

And this is life eternal, that they might know thee the only true God, and Jesus Christ, whom thou hast sent.
(John 17:3)

According to some estimates, China now has as many as 100 million Christians. South Korea also has a large population of Christians. However, persecution of believers and political dissidents continues. Western nations think they must address those issues carefully lest they threaten their economic interests. Along with the Middle East, East Asia promises to be a major focal point of world attention.

Geographically, East Asia is the area bounded by the Pacific Ocean on the east, Russia on the north, the Indian subcontinent and Southeast Asia on the south, and Southwest Asia on the west.

East Asia Fast Facts

Flag	Country	Capital	Area (sq. mi.)	Pop. (M)	Pop. Density (per sq. mi.)	Per Capita GDP ($US)	Life Span
	China	Beijing	3,600,927	1,313.98	365	$6,300	72.58
	North Korea	Pyongyang	46,490	23.11	497	$1,800	71.65
	South Korea	Seoul	37,911	48.85	1,288	$20,400	77.04
	Japan	Tokyo	144,689	127.46	881	$30,700	81.25

The region, which has coasts on the Yellow Sea, the East China Sea, the South China Sea, and the Pacific Ocean, is sometimes called the **Pacific Rim**.

It is a region of extremes and contrasts. Its climate ranges from tropical to subarctic. Its terrain ranges from fertile valleys to dry deserts. Its economic condition varies from modern countries similar in material wealth to the United States to the most backward, most secretive country in the world. The governments of the region range from those that allow great personal liberties to those that repress all individual freedom or initiative. Attitudes toward religion range from toleration and openness to total closure to the gospel. For these and other reasons, East Asia makes an interesting study.

I. CHINA

China is slightly smaller in area than the United States. Only Russia, Canada, and the United States surpass its immensity. Like America, it has some of its continent's richest farmlands and driest deserts. Also as in America, most of China's most populous cities are in the east. However, China has almost five times the population of the United States. Indeed, one out of six people in the world lives in China.

About 92 percent of the people in China are called **Han** (HAHN). Their language is one of the oldest in the world. Although it has many spoken dialects (e.g., Mandarin, Cantonese, Shanghiese, Fozhou, and Hokkien-Taiwanese), the written language is the same throughout China and helps to unite the nation. To improve communication,

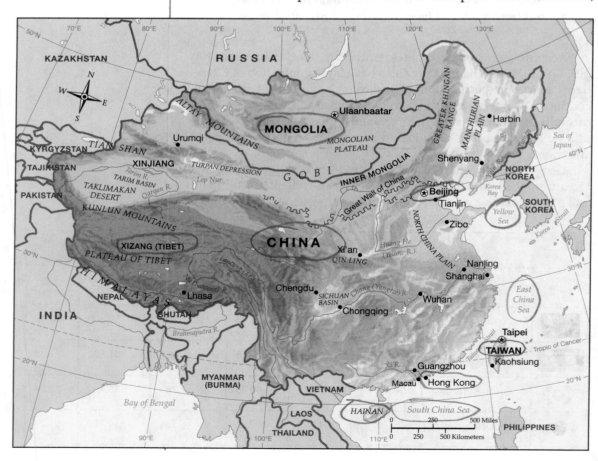

the government has made Mandarin the official language, which is now taught in all schools.

Because of its size and population, China has always dominated the Far East. The ancient Chinese viewed their land as the "Middle Kingdom"—the geographical and cultural center of the universe, surrounded by barbarians. China's recorded history of over four thousand years is longer than that of any other nation. Although China has been conquered at times, the conquerors have adopted Chinese ways and not vice versa. The Chinese have made a number of important contributions, including gunpowder, paper, printing, and the magnetic compass, although the West developed these discoveries to their full potential.

The climate of China ranges from tropical in the south to subarctic in the north. It is susceptible to frequent typhoons (about five a year), floods, droughts, earthquakes, and tsunamis. Its terrain is mostly mountainous, but it also has high plateaus, deserts (in the west), plains, deltas, and hills (mostly in the east).

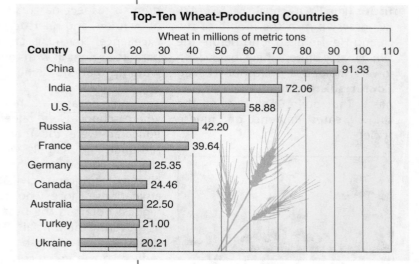

Top-Ten Wheat-Producing Countries

Country	Wheat in millions of metric tons
China	91.33
India	72.06
U.S.	58.88
Russia	42.20
France	39.64
Germany	25.35
Canada	24.46
Australia	22.50
Turkey	21.00
Ukraine	20.21

THE NORTH CHINA PLAIN

The **North China Plain** is the heart of the People's Republic of China and is sometimes called the "real" China. It extends from just north of Beijing southward to just below Shanghai and inland approximately 500 miles. The plain now supports countless villages and many of the forty-nine Chinese cities that exceed one million people. The plain also offers petroleum and coal. China is the world's leading coal producer, and it ranks fifth in petroleum.

Chinese farmers practice **intensive farming**, a form of subsistence farming in fertile areas that allows many individuals to raise crops on a small plot of land. The crops differ, however, depending on the climate. A major climate barrier is the **Qin Ling Mountains**, which run east to west across the middle of the plain, rising to 13,474 feet. The two main rivers of China, the **Huang He** (HWAHNG HEH; formerly the Yellow River) in the north and the **Chang** (CHAHNG; formerly Yangtze River) in the south, flow on either side of the range.

THE HUANG HE

The dry north is good for growing wheat, corn, and soybeans. China is among the top five producers of all these crops, and it is the leading producer of wheat. Because of the monsoons, the climate south of the Qin Ling Mountains is much wetter than the climate to the north. The people there grow rice and tobacco and raise swine. China is the world's top producer of both rice and tobacco. It is also the number one producer of cotton, apples (producing five times as many as its closest competitor in that fruit, the United States), peaches, and pears. It is among the top five producers of the following crops: grapefruit, pistachios, bananas, grapes, and pineapples. China also ranks among the top three in the production of peanuts and citrus fruits.

The Huang He flows through five of China's twenty-three provinces. According to legend, Chinese civilization began in this river

China's Sorrow

The Huang He is called "China's Sorrow." Snaking three thousand miles from the Tibetan Highlands, the river deposits precious silt along a fertile plain. Although the river's valley provides agricultural land for the Chinese, the river has also brought devastating floods that have claimed millions of lives.

The Huang He ("Yellow River") is named for the fine, yellow sand it picks up as it loops through the northern deserts. The silt-laden river then passes through a series of breathtaking gorges before it widens into the North China Plain, where the river, the muddiest in the world, deposits much of its silt. When the buildup becomes too great, China's Sorrow suddenly overflows its banks and severely floods the plains. By the time the waters subside, the river has often cut a new channel.

The Huang He has breached man-made dikes more than fifteen hundred times. Since recordkeeping began, its course has changed twenty-six times. For example, a flood in 1852 shifted its five-century-old course northward from the Yellow Sea to the Chingling Gulf. In 1938, the Chinese diverted the course back to the Yellow Sea, hoping to stop advancing Japanese armies. But in 1947 the Huang He returned to its former channel, where it has remained.

ANCIENT CHINESE PHILOSOPHERS

The Chinese philosopher **Confucius** (kun FYOO shush, ca. 551–479 BC) grew up near the mouth of the Huang He. He lived long before the Qin dynasty united China, but his followers molded a philosophy called **Confucianism** during the Han dynasty. That philosophy became the single greatest influence on Chinese society.

Confucius

Confucius taught that harmony and order would exist when men began to treat their fellow men properly. According to Confucius, "What you do not wish for yourself, do not do to others." He taught children to respect parents, citizens to obey rulers, and rulers to seek moral excellence. The focus on respect of parents fit right in with the **ancestor worship** that the Chinese traditionally practiced.

China became a "scholar's world" where schools were valued and the educated were the most admired. Although the schools were expensive and competitive, they prepared citizens for rigorous civil service examinations. Those who scored the highest obtained the best positions as government officials. That practice stabilized Chinese society and reduced government corruption.

Lao Zi (formerly spelled Lao-tzu, meaning "Old Master") lived during the fifth century BC. Though he lived before Confucius, his teachings were not developed as a complete philosophy until about 100 BC. His teachings form the basis of a religion called **Taoism** (TOW is um). Taoism presents the world as a competition between two equally matched forces called *yin* and *yang*. Yin represents the female, darkness, cold, and water; yang represents the male, light, heat, and fire. The main book of the religion is the *Tao Te Ching* (TOW TEH JIHNG). Taoists use charms, meditation, and diet to keep spiritual forces balanced. Some of them also use spells and the *I-Ching* (ee jihng), a fortunetelling book. Taoism's emphasis on the supernatural and magic is quite different from Confucianism, which emphasizes practical service to others.

Lao Zi

valley about 2200 BC but was made up of several small, warring states. Finally, in 221 BC, one of the local rulers defeated the other states and united all of China for the first time. Emperor Shih Huang Ti, the "first emperor," founded the Qin (CHIN) dynasty, from which the name *China* is derived. A **dynasty** is a series of rulers who come from the same family. Shih Huang Ti ruled with an iron fist and burned books that he feared might cause rebellion, so the government censorship so prevalent in China today is nothing new to the Chinese.

The city that is now **Xi'an** (SHEE AHN), on a tributary of the Huang He, was the capital of the Chinese dynasties for more than a thousand years, with only brief interruptions. The temples and tombs around the city include the tomb of the first emperor, which is guarded by the now-famous terra cotta army. The city was the eastern end of the Silk Road, and Marco Polo arrived there in 1275.

A life-size terra cotta army guards the tomb of the emperor in Xi'an.

THE CHANG

The southern river of the North China Plain is the Chang, which flows through four provinces. Its enormous drainage basin encompasses an area nearly the size of Mexico. At 3,880 miles long, the Chang is the world's third-largest river, the longest river in Asia, and the most important river in China. It is known as China's "main

THREE GORGES DAM

Both the Huang He and the Chang begin high on the Plateau of Tibet in Qinghai, the largest and least populated of China's provinces. As the Chang River drops down into the North China Plain, it passes through a series of three gorges, known as the Ichang Gorges. Scenic limestone cliffs rise up to two thousand feet above the rushing water.

In the 1990s, Communist China began a controversial project to dam the river and flood the gorges. After completion, which is scheduled for 2009, the **Three Gorges Dam** will generate electricity equivalent to eighteen nuclear power plants. At 1.3 miles long and 607 feet high, it will be the most powerful dam in the world, even more powerful than Itaipu (Brazil) and almost three times as power- ful as America's most powerful dam, Grand Coulee.

The project is controversial in that it involves the involuntary displacement of 1.9 million people, whose homes will be submerged by the reservoir. Several historical sites will also be lost. Some environmentalists have condemned the destruction of the beautiful scenery and the loss of habitat for the river dolphin. Outsiders have expressed concern about sewage from former factory sites that may pollute the reservoir. Upstream, the people of Chongqing are con-

The Three Gorges Dam project has been called the largest construction project since the building of the Great Wall.

cerned about buildup of sediment at the city's harbor. The cost of constructing the dam has already far exceeded its initial $17 billion estimate, and some analysts think the final cost will exceed $75 billion.

street." Ocean liners can travel seven hundred miles inland to Wuhan (pop. 2.59 million), and smaller vessels are able to navigate as far as one thousand miles inland. The Chang is one of the busiest waterways on earth and is also the deepest river in the world with depths of six hundred feet.

The upper Chang follows the western boundary of Sichuan (SEHTCH WAHN) Province, the most populous of all China's provinces. The Chang flows through the large **Sichuan Basin** before it leaves the mountains. The mountain-ringed basin contains two large cities, Chengdu (pop. 2.59 million) and Chongqing (pop. 4.87 million). The Sichuan Basin is one of the richest agricultural regions in China. Besides rice, crops of fruit, cotton, and tea grow on terraces cut from the hillsides.

Nanjing, with more than 2.87 million people, lies downstream on the Chang River, only about 150 miles from the coast. When the Ming dynasty came to power in 1368, the emperor moved the capital to Nanjing.

SHANGHAI

China's largest city, **Shanghai** (SHANG HYE; pop. 10.84 million), lies on the Huang P'u River near the mouth of the Chang. Its textile mills make cloth from the cotton of the plain, and nearby iron mines provide raw materials for heavy manufacturing. Shanghai is now a center of world trade and banking.

Downtown Shanghai is an ultramodern city.

The port at Shanghai is the fourth busiest in the world by volume and handles one-half of China's international trade. The city's growth began in 1842, when the British forced China to open it to foreigners. Shanghai took on a Western appearance as foreigners built homes, churches, and office buildings. Shanghai was the headquarters of Hudson Taylor's China Inland Mission. Today most of Shanghai's residents are factory workers who dress and eat well by Chinese standards. Communist China has declared Shanghai and several other cities special economic zones for trade. Little of the wealth being generated in such cities, however, is making it into the interior of the country. The people in the rural interior, most of whom are farmers, are as poor as ever, and some experts say they are worse off economically than they were before economic reforms began.

As a major fishing center, Shanghai contributes to China's ranking as the world-leading fish producer. China nets much of its catch through aquaculture. Farmers raise fish and shellfish in tanks, ponds, reservoirs, estuaries, and shallow bays. China's coasts offer shrimp, salmon, eel, mackerel, and sardines.

BEIJING

With a population of 7.74 million, **Beijing** (BAY ZHIHNG; formerly Peking) is China's second-largest city and the fourteenth largest in the world. Located on the North China Plain, it is only about thirty-five miles south of the Great Wall. It has served as China's capital since 1267, except for several brief periods totaling fifty-six years. For centuries, Beijing has been and still is the country's educational and cultural center. Since the Communist takeover in 1949, it has become industrialized and now produces iron, tools, and textiles.

Most of the city walls have been torn down to make way for roads. The city streets are thronged with cars, buses, and bicycles as the people commute to and from work. In the heart of Beijing is the **Forbidden City**, where the Chinese emperors once lived. To the north is the Gate of Heavenly Peace, which overlooks **Tiananmen Square**.

THE FORBIDDEN CITY

The Imperial City, a park-like area in the center of Beijing, includes the Forbidden City. Separated from the outside world by a broad moat and a wall, only the emperor and his household could enter the beautiful city. Today, however, the buildings are public museums. The presence of a Starbucks coffee shop in the Forbidden City is an indication of the economic changes that have come to China in the last decade.

Emperor Yong-le of the Ming dynasty built the Forbidden City and moved his capital to it from Nanjing in 1421. Its Dragon Throne remained the seat of the Ming emperors until 1644, when the Manchus pillaged the city. The Manchus restored it to its glory and ruled there until 1912, when rebels took over and imprisoned the last emperor in the palace, where he stayed for twelve years.

The Forbidden City has exactly 9,999 rooms. Beyond the Dragon Throne in the Hall of Supreme Harmony, two other great halls served as ceremonial chambers: the Hall of Perfect Harmony and the Hall of Preserving Harmony. The Forbidden City's palace also contained the living quarters of the Chinese emperor. In the Temple of Heaven, the emperor led religious rituals. From the main gate of the Forbidden City, Tiananmen, the emperor reviewed his troops.

A moat and a wall separate the city of Beijing from the interior of the Forbidden City.

Leaders review parades displaying the country's military might on the thirty-four-acre grounds, the largest square in the world. In 1989, Tiananmen Square became a symbol of the disaffection of the Chinese people with the Communist regime. (See the section on the government and economy of China.)

TIANJIN

Tianjin (tee an JIN), the port for Beijing, lies at the mouth of the Hai River. Tianjin (pop. 5.08 million) is at the north end of the Grand Canal, which permits inland shipping to Shanghai. When it opened in 486 BC, the canal was the longest artificial waterway in the world. More than one thousand miles long, it linked China's two largest rivers. The canal has since fallen into disrepair, although one-third of it is still open to barges.

Shanghai, Beijing, and Tianjin are China's leading industrial centers. Each is a distinct political unit called a special municipality and is not part of any province.

Chinese security forces arrest members of the banned sect Falun Gong as they meditate in Tiananmen Square in 1999, ten years after the Tiananmen Square Massacre.

THE GREAT WALL OF CHINA

Of the architectural wonders of the world, the **Great Wall** of China is certainly one of the most impressive. It was built primarily during the fourteenth to the seventeenth centuries to protect China from invasions

by the Mongols and Turkic tribes. It could not prevent invaders from scaling the wall, but it could prevent them from entering China with war horses or from escaping easily with plunder.

The wall began as several walls built in local areas of Mongolia and Manchuria in the third century BC. The bulk of the construction, however, was the joining of those walls where gaps existed. The wall is made of materials that were easily available in each region. In some places it is made of granite; in other places it is made of bricks; and in a few places it is made of double rows of logs tied together, with the space between tightly packed with soil. Because so many workers died while building the wall, it has been called the longest cemetery in the world and "the long graveyard." Contrary to popular belief, however, the dead workers were not buried within the wall but in graves nearby.

Watchtowers were constructed at intervals along the wall, and guards communicated among the towers using smoke signals. Battle forts were also constructed at strategic points along the wall, and guards assembled there if they were driven from the watchtowers. Ultimately, the wall was breached by the Manchus, who gained entry not by scaling the wall or tearing it down but by bribing a Chinese general to open the gates. Because of modern weaponry, of course, the wall is of no strategic value; it is merely a historical tourist attraction. Except in tourist areas, where preservation has been done, the wall is generally in disrepair.

The length of the entire wall is debated. The commonly cited length is 3,946 miles, but another estimate is more than 4,500 miles. A walker with a pedometer, however, calculated it as 4,163 miles. In 2006, the Chinese government ordered yet another measurement to be made.

Another debated issue about the wall is whether it can actually be seen from space. One often finds statements that it is the only man-made object that can be seen from space. The claim has been made so often that it has become an urban legend, but astronauts have attempted to locate it during their missions, and even they disagree among themselves about whether it can be seen. One astronaut thought he had found it, but what he saw was actually the Grand Canal. Because at its widest point the wall is only about the width of a city street, it is unlikely that it can be seen from space.

MANCHURIA

Because the three provinces of Manchuria—named for the **Manchus** (man CHOOS), the last foreign power to control China—are located northeast of the Great Wall, the Chinese commonly refer to them as the Northeast. The broad Manchurian Plain is an extension of the North China Plain. Crops such as soybeans, millet, corn, apples, and spring wheat grow well in the relatively short growing season with its severe winters and dry summers. The forested mountains to the north and east contain much valuable timber. Shenyang, with more than 4.11 million people, is the largest city in Manchuria and is its industrial center. Jonathan Goforth (1859–1936) was a missionary to Manchuria under the China Inland Mission.

Events of the nineteenth century humiliated the Manchu dynasty and angered many Chinese people. Defeats in the Opium Wars and the Sino-Japanese War caused much resentment of foreign intrusion in China. The Boxers, a secret society known for its ceremonial practice of shadowboxing, struck back in 1899 in a series of uprisings that became known as the Boxer Rebellion. Infuriated by anything they perceived as foreign or anti-Chinese, the Boxers even attacked Christian missionaries and Chinese converts. Many believers were killed when they would not renounce Christ. Eight foreign nations, including the United States, put down the uprising. Although the Manchus made reforms after the rebellion, the dynasty collapsed in 1912.

Manchuria has been a hotly contested region ever since. The Japanese invaded and occupied it in 1937. As the Japanese were driven out, the Communist Chinese occupied it, and it became a Communist stronghold. During the 1960s, when relations between the Soviets and the Chinese soured, the two countries massed troops along its border. Tensions were relieved once the Soviet Empire was dissolved.

THE SOUTHERN UPLANDS

Eight populous provinces lie south of the Chang River basin in southeast China. The **Southern Uplands** harbor more ethnic groups and languages than any other region in China.

Green hills and mountains characterize the Southern Uplands. Rice grows throughout the region, but the region also contributes other important resources, including sweet potatoes, tea, and sugar cane. The hills and mountains produce large quantities of tungsten, phosphates, zinc, iron ore, lead, vanadium, tin, and manganese.

China's Southern Uplands are also one of the few places in the world that produce silk. Silkworms spin a cocoon consisting of one long, light, strong thread, which the Chinese weave into silk. The worms require a warm climate and a diet of leaves from mulberry trees. For many centuries, the Chinese kept the production technique secret.

The Southern Uplands include China's southernmost province, **Hainan** (HYE NAN), which is the largest island in China. It is the source of China's natural rubber. The island also produces bananas and pepper.

The **Xi** (zih) **River** (West River) is the transportation hub of the Southern Uplands. Its volume of flow is nearly three times that of the Yellow River as a result of heavy monsoon rains. The river's delta is

China's Rank for Production of Key Resources

Resource	Rank
Aluminum	1
Zinc	1
Lead	1
Tin	1
Tungsten	1
Coal	1
Phosphates	2
Iron ore	3
Sulfur	4
Silver	4
Bauxite	4

the largest arable plain in the Southern Uplands. The deep, rich soil and the warm, moist climate make the delta extremely productive. The year-round growing season allows farmers to reap two crops a year. Tea, fruits, and sugar cane are grown there.

Located on the delta of the Xi is **Guangzhou** (gwang JOH; formerly Canton). With 4.06 million people, Guangzhou is the region's largest city. The people speak the Cantonese dialect. Westerners are familiar with Cantonese cooking, which offers a variety of steamed fresh vegetables.

Guangzhou is an important industrial and transportation center. The Xi River, railroads to the interior, and a deep-water port make it a center for international trade.

Foreign nations founded two colonies on China's southern coast. The British founded **Hong Kong**, which is about ninety miles southeast of Guangzhou. During the nineteenth century, the British forced China to cede Hong Kong Island and the tip of Kowloon Peninsula. Its deep-water port made it an ideal trading center for heavy sea traffic in the South China Sea. Business boomed under its low taxes and political freedom, and the colony grew rapidly. The colony reverted to China in 1997.

Hong Kong's economy is one of the strongest and most varied in Asia. Although it is only four hundred square miles in area (about six times the size of Washington, D.C.), its 6.94 million people make it a bustling center of trade, finance, manufacturing, and tourism. Today, Hong Kong is the twentieth-largest city in the world and the busiest port (by total containers handled) in the world. (It is the fifth-busiest port by volume.)

Hong Kong's people hope that China will keep its promise to protect Hong Kong's way of life for fifty years (the "one country, two systems" policy). For the most part, China has maintained a hands-off policy regarding the economy and internal affairs. It has attempted a few encroachments on freedoms, however, and reserves all defense and foreign policy matters for the mainland government. Christians are particularly concerned about whether Communist China will soon restrict church activities as well.

The second colony was **Macau** (muh COW), the oldest European colony in Asia, which the Portuguese founded in 1557. It lies across an estuary from Hong Kong. Its six square miles (about one-tenth the size of Washington, D.C.) consist of a small peninsula and two small islands. The backbone of Macau's economy is apparel and tourism, especially gambling, which provides 70 percent of the government's revenue. Macau reverted to China in 1999.

Hong Kong's streets are crowded, especially in the shopping district.

GOVERNMENT AND ECONOMY

China has a Communist government and only one political party—the Communists. It has a unicameral legislature called the National People's Congress, but it is a rubber stamp for the Chinese Communist Party. Yet, China has the second-largest economy in the world (behind only the United States). It leads the world in the production of many products and industries. But almost half of its work force is employed in agriculture, which contributes less than 15 percent of the GDP. Large disparities exist between the income of

Sun Yat-sen

Chiang Kai-shek

Mao Zedong

coastal populations and rural populations. And overall, the GDP lags behind many less-developed economies. How did it come to this?

Although in 1912 **Sun Yat-sen** (SOON YAHT-SEHN) had established a republican form of government and was followed by **Chiang Kai-shek** (JYAHNG KYE-SHEK), corruption and strife within the Nationalist (Kuomintang) Party caused dissension in the country. **Mao Zedong** (MOU DZUH-DONG) led the Communist Red Army in a civil war that resulted in the defeat of the Nationalist army. Chiang, his army, and the Kuomintang escaped to Taiwan, an island about one hundred miles off the coast of China in the East China Sea. Mao proclaimed the birth of the People's Republic of China (also known as Communist China or Red China) on October 1, 1949, in Tiananmen Square.

He immediately began enacting ruthless programs he thought would strengthen the economy. First, he executed more than fifty thousand wealthy landlords, abolished private property, and redistributed the land to create collective farms, or communes, on which the peasants worked as virtual slaves under government supervision. In the **Great Leap Forward** of 1958, Mao further centralized farming and industrial activity. However, bad weather, discontented workers, and unwise decisions by inept bureaucrats resulted in poor crops and widespread famine.

To eliminate opposition, both real and potential, Mao launched the **Cultural Revolution** in 1966, sending overzealous gangs of young people called the **Red Guard** throughout China in an anti-intellectual, anti-Christian rampage. Schools and universities were shut down. Millions of educated citizens died or were forcibly removed from the "corrupting" influence of the cities to be "purified" in rural communes and "re-education" camps. Schools did not reopen until 1970. Mao's programs proved to be disastrous failures.

After Mao died in 1976, his successor, **Deng Xiaoping** (DUNG SHOU PING), began to change China's direction. He vigorously pursued economic modernization. Deng encouraged students to enroll in Western universities to learn how to improve industry and economy. He also permitted some citizens to own private gardens and businesses and opened China to foreign markets.

Deng Xiaoping

In the late 1980s, Communism in Europe teetered on the brink of collapse. Chinese students began protesting in Beijing, seeking increased freedoms, especially political freedom and freedom of expression. In Tiananmen Square, they erected a thirty-foot replica of the Statue of Liberty. But on June 4, 1989, Communist tanks rolled into the square, killing perhaps five thousand people. In spite of widespread coverage of the massacre by the world media, the Communists denied that anything had happened. Thousands of protestors were imprisoned in labor camps and re-education centers. Communism had not changed.

After Tiananmen Square, however, the Communists began to institute dramatic economic reforms in the major cities. They suddenly allowed private businesses and promoted industry, especially in the high-tech computer fields. They encouraged foreign investment. They opened Chinese markets and sought greater international trade. Business and personal wealth increased dramatically. Foreign capital came pouring into China. Major cities witnessed the opening of name-brand business franchises, such as McDonald's and Wal-Mart.

But the benefits of this Western material success have not gotten beyond the major cities of the east. Rural internal areas of the country are actually worse off now than before the economic reforms because a mass migration of workers to the cities has occurred, most of them to construction jobs. And even those workers cannot enjoy the benefits of wealth because they are not permitted to remain as residents of the cities. As soon as the buildings on which they are working are completed, the workers must leave the cities, either taking similar jobs in other cities or returning to the poverty of the rural areas.

Although some Chinese economic freedoms have increased, by Western standards the people are still repressed politically and religiously. They still have no voice in their government, and only one political party is recognized. Although they have access to much more information via the Internet, the government censors that, too, the way it has always censored regular media (newspapers, television, radio, and theater).

This McDonald's in Beijing is indicative of the economic changes taking place in China.

SECTION QUIZ

1. Which geographic region is considered the heart of the "real" China?

2. What are the two major rivers of China?

3. Which two ancient Chinese philosophers' influence is felt throughout China even today?

4. Which Chinese city has the greatest population?

5. What is China's capital city?

6. China is home to which of the world's architectural wonders?

7. Which geographic region of China has more ethnic groups and languages than any other?

8. Which former British colony did China regain in 1997?

☼ Describe the disastrous reforms of Mao Zedong.

II. China's Autonomous Regions and Mongolia

China has five autonomous (self-governing) regions, twenty-three provinces (one of which is disputed), three special municipalities, and several **Special Economic Zones** and Special Administrative Regions. Each **autonomous region** offers self-rule to a minority, but these minority groups have very limited powers. China has fifty-five ethnic minorities, but only five have been given autonomous regions. The island of Taiwan has never been recognized by the Chinese Communists as an independent nation—they consider it a recalcitrant province—and the United Nations admits only China, not Taiwan, to its membership. The United States government, although having good relations with Taiwan, operates on a "one China" policy as well.

Guangxi

The autonomous region of **Guangxi** (GWAHNG ZIH) is on the coast at the Tonkin Gulf and the border with Vietnam. China's largest minority, the **Zhuang** (JWAHNG), live in Guangxi and number more than fifteen million. The Zhuang are ethnic Thai people who speak a northern Thai dialect. Many of them also speak Cantonese because they are somewhat outnumbered by the Chinese.

Tibet (Xizang)

The Plateau of **Tibet**, also known as **Xizang** (SHEE DZAHNG) rises west of China's Southern Uplands. Many high peaks are in Tibet, including Mount Everest, which it shares with Nepal. Called "the Roof of the World," Tibet has an average elevation that exceeds sixteen thousand feet.

Many of Asia's great rivers begin on the plateau and cut through parallel gorges within a space of one hundred miles, including the Indus, the Brahmaputra, the Chang, the Huang He, the Irrawaddy, and the Mekong.

Tibet is quite rugged and is one of the world's most isolated regions; consequently, Tibet is the least populated of all of China's political divisions. In fact, about five times more people live in Beijing than in all of Tibet. Only a few scattered valleys, where the climate is milder and the soil is suitable for cultivation, are habitable. The capital, **Lhasa** (LAH sah), lies in one such valley, the Tsangpo Valley.

Defended by the rugged mountains, the indigenous Tibetans enjoyed independence for most of their history. However, in 1950, Chinese Communist troops invaded Tibet and seized control. The Chinese army squelched a Tibetan rebellion in 1959, destroyed Tibetan religious shrines, and looted the temples. In 1965, much of the plateau became the autonomous region of Xizang, usually called Tibet. In 1987 and 1993, Tibetans staged violent protests against Communist rule. In response, Deng Xiaoping, the leader of the Chinese Communist Party at the time, instituted a "population transfer" policy whereby Chinese are emigrating to Tibet, threatening to make native Tibetans a minority in their own country. The Communists subsidize the settlers, building homes and setting up shops for them. The growing Chinese presence tends to muffle Tibetan dissent.

This tiny village and surrounding terrain show the harsh environs of Tibet.

Intensely religious, Tibetans follow a branch of Buddhism called Lamaism, which is led by a governmental and spiritual ruler called the **Dalai Lama** (DAH-lye LAH-mah). Tibetans worship each Dalai Lama as a reincarnation of Buddha. Before communism, the Dalai Lama ruled as a **theocrat** (one who rules by religious or divine authority) from Potala Palace in Lhasa. When the Chinese took over, he escaped to India and became head of "the Government of Tibet in Exile."

The current Dalai Lama is Tenzin Gyatso, the fourteenth Dalai Lama. He was formally recognized at age two as the reincarnation of the thirteenth Dalai Lama. Like the Roman Catholic pope, he is referred to by his followers as "His Holiness." Other terms applied to him include "Holy Lord, Gentle Glory, Compassionate, Defender of the Faith," "The Wishfulfilling Gem," and "The Presence."

XINJIANG

Xinjiang (SHIN JYANG) covers an area the size of Alaska in northwest China, making it by far the largest of China's political divisions. Like Tibet, this large autonomous region has high mountains. The Kunlun Mountains form its southern border with Tibet, and the Tien Shan (tee-EHN SHAHN), or Heavenly Mountains, cross the middle of the region.

Unlike Tibet, however, Xinjiang consists mostly of desert basins. The Tien Shan range divides the two large basins: the Tarim Basin in the south and the Junggar Basin in the north. Both basins are extremely dry because the high mountains almost completely block off any rain-bearing winds. The people of the area, the Uygurs and Kazakhs, are

The Dalai Lama is revered in Tibet as a reincarnation of Buddha.

POTALA PALACE

The title *Dalai Lama* means "Ocean of Wisdom." The ruler of Mongolia, the khan, conferred this title on the leader of the Tibetan Buddhists after the khan's own conversion in the sixth century. In 1951, Communist China occupied Tibet, which was then ruled by the fourteenth Dalai Lama. He escaped to India eight years later.

A Buddhist king of Tibet from the seventh century built the original royal residence at the city of Lhasa. His palace sits on the Potala, or "Buddha's Mountain," overlooking the city. The fifth Dalai Lama began rebuilding **Potala Palace** in 1645. The new palace far exceeded the old ruins and rose thirteen stories. When the Dalai Lama died in 1682, the monks kept his death secret until the building was finished in 1694.

The massive palace has one thousand rooms, ten thousand shrines, and twenty thousand statues. The top floor serves as a secluded place for the Dalai Lama to meditate. Other floors provide living quarters, meditation halls, libraries, storerooms, and a school for monks. The palace also contains armories, the tombs of eight Dalai Lamas, torture chambers, and the Cave of Scorpions dungeon. The palace is now a museum.

Muslims and speak Turkic languages. China fears a growing independence movement among the people of Xinjiang, especially after the independence of the former Soviet republics in Central Asia.

The **Taklimakan Desert**, which might be the driest area in Asia, occupies the Tarim Basin. The Turpan Depression in this desert is 505 feet below sea level, the second-lowest elevation in the world (after the Great Rift Valley in Israel and Africa). A string of oases along the edges of the desert once served as stations on the Silk Road. Today the region remains sparsely populated because of its harsh climate and remoteness.

The Taklimakan Desert might be the driest area in Asia.

Nei Mongol (Inner Mongolia)

The term *Mongolia* can refer to the region beyond the Great Wall of China. Inner Mongolia, or **Nei** (NAY) **Mongol**, is the part controlled by China, between the Great Wall and the country of Mongolia. Slightly smaller than Tibet, it stretches along two-thirds of the Mongolian border and southward to the Great Wall. The Gobi (GOH bee) Desert covers most of the region, but steppes (dry grasslands) mark its edges. The Chinese government has tried to increase the production of spring wheat, millet, and oats in this region. During the Middle Ages, the Mongol armies of Genghis Khan roamed throughout the Gobi. Mongols still inhabit this autonomous region. They speak a Mongol language and are traditionally Tibetan Buddhists.

Ningxia

The last of China's five autonomous regions is **Ningxia** (NIHNG shee ah), a small region that lies just inside the Great Wall where the Huang He flows into Inner Mongolia. The Hui people who live in this region have the same physical features as the Han, but they follow Islam. Of Ningxia's total population of 5.62 million, approximately one-third of the people are Huis. They are the only minority recognized for religious rather than ethnic reasons.

Taiwan

Taiwan (TYE WAHN) is an island in the South China Sea about one hundred miles off the coast of China. A mountain range reaching 13,113 feet forms the backbone of the island. The gentle western slopes descend to plains, which support most of the island's population of 22.75 million. Summer monsoons bring heavy rains and strong winds. Farmers have terraced many hills to make more land for growing rice. Chemical fertilizers and insecticides enable farmers to grow at least two crops of rice per year on the same field. Other crops include soybeans, sweet potatoes, bananas, and sugar.

Taipei, the capital of Taiwan, is a thriving modern city.

				Taiwan Fast Facts		
Flag	Capital	Area (sq. mi.)	Pop. (M)	Pop. Density (per sq. mi.)	Per Capita GDP ($US)	Life Span
	Taipei	12,456	23	1,849	$26,700	77.43

LET'S GO EXPLORING

LAND USE OF ASIA

1. Does any commercial farming take place in East Asia? If so, what kind?

2. Which two countries have the majority of the land used for subsistence farming?

3. What country is almost entirely devoted to nomadic herding?

4. What region has most of the shifting agriculture—South Asia, Southeast Asia, or East Asia?

⚙ Why is commercial farming so uncommon in Asia?

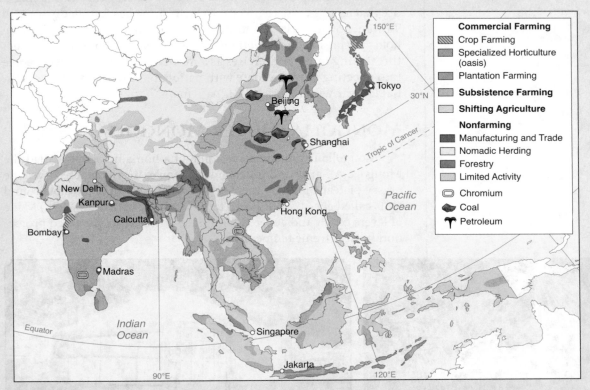

In 1949, the Chinese Nationalists led by Chiang Kai-shek fled to Taiwan and reestablished their government at **Taipei** (TYE PAY). They also claimed two tiny islands off the coast of China—**Quemoy** (kwi MOY), which is due west of central Taiwan, and **Matsu** (maht SOO), which is northwest of northern Taiwan. Situated on the north end of Taiwan, Taipei is a busy industrial center of about 2.6 million people. Taipei's history reaches back less than three hundred years, but the city museums hold many priceless treasures of China's past, brought by Chiang Kai-shek from the mainland. Operating in a free market climate, the city and the island enjoy great personal and political freedom and economic prosperity.

The Nationalists inherited the roads, factories, and irrigation projects that the Japanese developed during their rule from 1895 to 1945. The Nationalists then combined cheap Taiwanese labor with money from American investors to build one of Asia's first industrialized countries. Taiwan's manufacturing includes high-tech industries, such as computers and electronics.

The United Nations expelled Taiwan in 1971 so that Communist China could be admitted. In 1978, the United States ended diplomatic relations with Taiwan. Nevertheless, U.S. warships continue to prowl the Taiwan Strait, guarding the former ally. Although the United States does not officially recognize its status as a country, Taiwan is America's seventh-largest trading partner, and the United States is Taiwan's largest trading partner. Surprisingly, the state of Washington is, by itself, Taiwan's eighth-largest trading partner.

Although mainland China claims Taiwan, Taiwan believes that the legitimate government is in Taipei, not Beijing. Taiwan stops short of formally declaring independence for fear that China might use that as an excuse to invade. In fact, China has repeatedly warned Taiwan not to push for formal independence. Whenever Taiwan holds its presidential elections, the Chinese Communists conduct threatening military exercises as a means of intimidating the people into rejecting any candidate with nationalistic opinions. The potential for war with mainland China remains.

MONGOLIA (OUTER MONGOLIA)

Mongolia is the ancestral home of a nomadic people called the Mongols. A hardy and independent people, they wandered over the grassy plateaus grazing their herds. They lived in collapsible round tents called *gers*. (The Russian term for the structures is *yurts*.) Made of layers of felt and covered with hides, these tents provided protection from extreme temperatures.

These nomads are assembling their ger, and it will look like the photo on the right when they are finished.

Genghis Khan and his grandson Kublai Khan ruled from East Asia to Eastern Europe. The Mongols were among the most savage conquerors of all time. Skilled horsemen, they developed a system similar to the pony express, which linked the great khan in China with the outer reaches of his realm. The khan's heirs and his Mongol tribes never fully united, however, and the empire soon disintegrated.

Mongolia was controlled next by the Manchus. While China was distracted with its civil war, however, Russia stepped in to guarantee a measure of "independence" for Mongolia. The Communist Party came to power in 1924 and imposed harsh rule. As happened in other Central Asian countries, government authorities soon clamped down on Christian missionaries in Mongolia.

Mongolia's main urban center is the capital, **Ulaanbaatar** (OO lahn BAH tahr). A railroad has joined the caravan route across the six hundred miles between Ulaanbaatar and the Great Wall of China near Beijing. The capital lies in the best grazing lands of north central and northeast Mongolia. Although few nomads remain, one-half of the people still raise livestock. The large farms raise mostly sheep, but also camels, horses, cattle, and goats. Cattle and wool are the main exports.

The Gobi Desert covers over five hundred thousand square miles in Mongolia and China, making it larger than any other desert in the world except the Sahara. The desert averages four thousand feet above sea level and extends twelve hundred miles from west to east. The **Gobi Desert** is the world's coldest and most northerly desert. The soils are sandy but rarely result in sand dunes. In the 1920s Protoceratops eggs were discovered here, preserved by the dry soil. They were the first dinosaur eggs found.

Ulaanbaatar is a growing city, but it retains many of the traditional Mongolian ways, as the gers in this photo reveal.

The Junggar Basin lies between the Tien Shan and the Altai Mountains on the Mongolian border. This basin still offers a key trade route and railroad link with Central Asia. Ürümqi is the main city on the route and the capital of Xinjiang. The basin is an extension of the Gobi Desert. Mildred Cable (1879–1952) crossed the Gobi on this route several times as a missionary for the China Inland Mission, extending the mission's outreach to the most remote sections of interior China.

Mongolia Fast Facts						
Flag	Capital	Area (sq. mi.)	Pop. (M)	Pop. Density (per sq. mi.)	Per Capita GDP ($US)	Life Span
	Ulaanbaatar	604,247	2.83	5	$2,200	64.89

SECTION QUIZ

1. What region is called "The Roof of the World"?

2. Who leads the Tibetan Buddhists?

3. What is Tibet's capital?

4. What desert in the Far East contains the lowest elevation?

5. To what does the term *Mongolia* refer?

6. Which island does China claim as its own but exercise little practical control over?

7. What two other smaller islands does that island claim?

8. What is the term for the portable houses in which many Mongolians live?

☼ What arguments can be offered for and against China's claims on the island in question 6 above?

III. NORTH AND SOUTH KOREA

Korea is a peninsula that extends south from northeastern China. Mountains and hills cover most of the peninsula. The mountains provide mineral resources, and the two countries on the peninsula—North Korea and South Korea—rank among the world's top ten producers of tungsten (North Korea, fifth) and smelted zinc (South Korea, fourth). Both also produce coal, graphite (North Korea, fourth), pig iron (South Korea, ninth), and lead. South Korea is third in cadmium production as well.

Two rivers, the Yalu and the Tumen, divide the **Korean Peninsula** from China and Russia in the north. These rivers flow down from Korea's highest mountain, Mount Paektu, at the north end of the Hamgyong Mountains. South of the Hamgyongs are the Nangnim Mountains. Running down the east central portion of the peninsula are the **Taebaek Mountains**.

A minor coastal plain lies on the east coast in North Korea, but mountains dominate the eastern half of both countries. The most important coastal plain stretches along the western and southern coasts. It has most of the arable land on the peninsula, and its climate is generally humid continental. Two-thirds of all Koreans live on that plain. All of the peninsula's major cities lie in that plain, including the respective capitals.

The turbulent history of the peninsula is due in part to its unfortunate geographic position. The Korean Peninsula is a bridge between the larger, more powerful countries on every side. It has been conquered at various times by China, the Mongols, Japan, and the

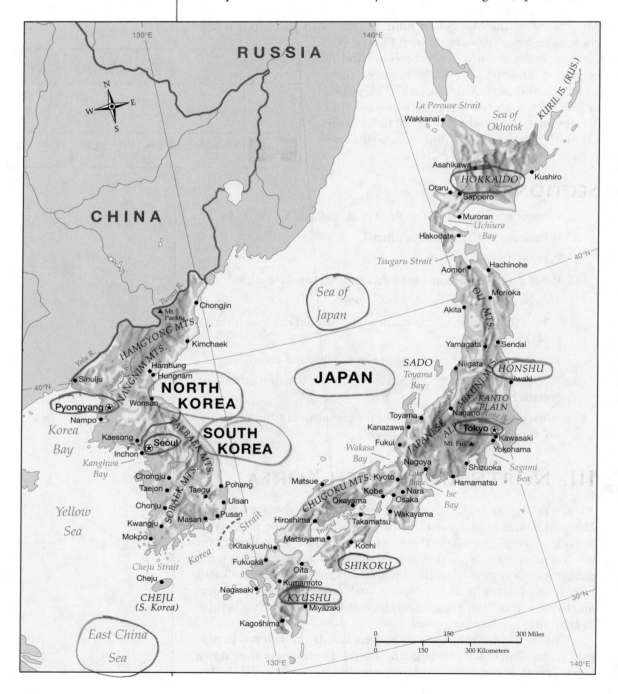

Manchus. These invaders wanted not only to expand their borders but also to protect their respective countries from attack. Within a few centuries, the Koreans drove out each wave of invaders.

In 1910, Japan took complete control of Korea and began to govern it as a colony. The Japanese initiated an extensive modernization program, building railroads and developing industries. The Korean people, however, resented Japan's repressive government. After World War II, the country was divided at the thirty-eighth parallel to facilitate the departure of the Japanese, the United States overseeing the southern half and the Soviet Union overseeing the northern half. Free elections were then supposed to be held to set Korea back on its feet as an independent nation.

NORTH KOREA

Much to the dismay of the United Nations, the Soviet Union refused to give up its territory. Instead, the Soviets established a Communist satellite called the Democratic People's Republic of Korea.

Hoping to unify the peninsula under communism, the superior North Korean army invaded South Korea in 1950. United Nations troops, most of them Americans, were rushed to the peninsula just as the Allied forces were about to be pushed into the sea at Pusan in the southeastern portion of the peninsula and in time to avert certain defeat. Eventually, the UN forces repelled the invasion and pushed the North Korean army all the way back to the Yalu River. China then came to the North Koreans' aid, launching a massive invasion that forced the UN troops back down the peninsula.

After three years of warfare, a truce was declared. The boundary between North and South Korea, the thirty-eighth parallel, is a **demilitarized zone (DMZ)**, a strip of land in which no troops or weapons are allowed. However, a peace treaty was never signed, so technically the two nations are still at war. Ever since, America has kept tens of thousands of soldiers on patrol in South Korea.

North Korea's Communist ruler, "Great Leader" **Kim Il Sung**, isolated his country from the rest of the world. The North Korean government owns all industries and farms and discourages all religion, except for worship of the state as represented by Kim Il Sung, a religion known as **Juche** (JOO chay), or Kimilsungism. (See Chapter 4.) His son, **Kim Jong Il** succeeded him and has continued his father's oppressive regime. North Koreans are required to refer to him as "the Dear Leader." Pictures of the two are everywhere in North Korea, from the sides of buildings to the front and rear interiors of every bus and streetcar in the country.

According to the *CIA World Factbook*, North Korea is "one of the world's most centrally planned and isolated economies." The capital, **Pyongyang** (pop. 3.14 million), has the only university. It is also the manufacturing center; all resources mined or produced are brought to factories there. The country has suffered food and fuel shortages every year for more than a decade, which has forced the North Korean Communists to ease their isolation somewhat by seeking foreign aid to avert famine.

Almost one-quarter of the land in North Korea is arable, and it has a temperate climate with rainfall being concentrated in the summer. The country, which is slightly smaller than Mississippi, produces vegetables, rice, potatoes, corn,

Kim Il Sung is the central focus of Juche, or Kimilsungism, and the first stop of all visitors to Pyongyang is this 65-foot statue of him.

Kim Jong Il

The "Bridge of No Return" on the DMZ is the only bridge crossing between North Korea and South Korea.

North Korea gives its military first priority when allocating resources.

Seoul is the seventh-largest city in the world in terms of population.

Korean Christianity and Missions

Christianity's growth in Korea at the end of the nineteenth century was due to the work of North American Presbyterian missionaries. There are now more than 13,000 South Korean missionaries in foreign countries. Several scholars have predicted that the majority of Christians will soon live outside of Western countries. This will provide several benefits to spreading the gospel because Asian missionaries often already know the cultures and languages of neighboring countries and thus do not have to spend as much time adjusting to the target country. They also often have access to other countries where Western missionaries cannot gain entry. The growth of majority-world missionaries (those who live among the 5.2 billion people in "developing countries") will likely direct the growth of Christianity in the coming decades.

cabbages, apples, fruit, soybeans, sweet potatoes, and beans. Yet, it cannot produce enough of these to feed its own people. Industries include military products, machines, chemicals, mining, metallurgy, textiles, and food processing. A large part of the GDP, however, is spent on the North Korean military rather than essential consumer goods.

Despite opposition from most of the rest of the world—especially the countries of East Asia—North Korea is overtly pursuing development of nuclear weapons. Kim Jong Il is firm in asserting his "right" to run his country as he pleases.

SOUTH KOREA

South Korea, also known as the Republic of Korea, is slightly larger than Indiana. The favorable climate and irrigation permit the rice fields to be double cropped. Since 1960, South Korea has undergone a rapid transformation from an agricultural society to a fast-growing industrial economy. In the 1960s, its economy was on par with those of the poorest countries of Africa and Asia. Today, it has a $1 trillion economy, the result of hard work and cooperation among business, government, and labor unions. Unlike North Korea, South Korea is free and not centralized. Farms and industries are privately owned, and there are several universities.

People flocked to the cities for employment, and four cities now exceed two and a half million people: Seoul (9.75 million), Pusan (3.72 million), Inchon (2.62 million) and Taegu (2.60 million). **Seoul** (SOHL), the country's capital and manufacturing center, is the seventh-largest city in the world and easily the largest on the Korean Peninsula. Although many of its products were once synonymous with "junk," South Korea now specializes in electronics, telecommunications equipment, automobiles, chemicals, shipbuilding, and steel. Pusan is the third-busiest seaport in the world (ranked by total containers handled).

Although South Korea has less arable land than North Korea, it has never had a problem producing more than enough food for its own people. Its main crops are rice, vegetables, watermelons, onions, and potatoes. It also produces pork, chicken, fish, eggs, and milk. It spends less than 3 percent of its GDP on the military.

After thirty-two years of military rule, South Koreans elected their first civilian government in 1993. They have a republican form of government with an elected president who appoints a prime minister. The unicameral National Assembly has 299 seats, and delegates are elected every four years. Five political parties and many labor and trade unions vie for influence in the government.

South Koreans also enjoy religious freedom. Christianity and Buddhism are the largest organized religions, with each claiming 26 percent of the population as adherents, but Christianity is growing. In fact, there are more Christian converts in South Korea than anywhere else in East Asia. The capital has the largest church in the world. Unfortunately, cults are also growing, and the Unification Church (followers of founder Sun Myung Moon, who are sometimes called Moonies) has grown very large in South Korea. Surprisingly, however, almost half of all South Koreans profess no religion at all.

South Koreans have adopted some Western customs because of their economic and political ties, but they have retained their own ancient identity. The people are ethnic Korean and speak Korean. The largest minority, the Chinese, make up only one-tenth of 1 percent of the total population.

SECTION QUIZ

1. Which mountain range forms the backbone of the east central portion of the Korean Peninsula?
2. What are the official names of North Korea and South Korea?
3. What do the letters DMZ refer to?
4. What are the names of the two Communists who have ruled North Korea?
5. What term refers to the centrality of and virtual worship of the state in North Korea?
6. What is the largest city in Korea?
* Contrast the effects of government policies in North and South Korea.

IV. JAPAN

The Japanese refer to their country as **Nippon**, which means "source of the sun." According to their mythology, the rising sun first shone on the islands of Japan. Japan is a crescent of four main islands due east of the coast of Russia and the Korean Peninsula, along with thousands of smaller islands that stretch southwest to northeast for twelve hundred miles. Like the United States, Japan has four seasons, with colder winters in the far north. Only one-half of 1 percent of the people are of ethnic origins other than Japanese (most of those being Korean).

Isolated by the 120-mile-wide Korea Strait, Japan was never invaded successfully before World War II. When Japan learned of China's advanced culture, writing, literature, and philosophy, it borrowed many Chinese ideas, including its system of government and **prefectures**, or provincial divisions.

Although the islands have few mineral resources, Japan has built a thriving industrialized nation by adopting an exemplary work ethic and importing raw materials and converting them into high-tech, high-quality goods that are in great demand. Japan leads the world in pig iron and cadmium production and is second in steel production (behind only China). Agriculturally, it is among the top five producers of strawberries, pears, and rice. Its automobiles have gained a well-deserved reputation for safety and quality of craftsmanship.

Like the Chinese, the Japanese are blinded to the gospel by their traditions. The native religion of Japan, **Shinto** (SHIHN toh), promotes the worship of many gods called *kami*, who are believed to indwell mountains, rivers, trees, and other parts of nature. Nearly all Japanese practice some Shinto ceremonies, one of the most common being offerings of flowers and cakes to appease the kami. Over time, the Japanese people have learned to follow elements of Buddhism and Confucianism too. Almost two-thirds of the Japanese

These South Korean women are dressed in traditional Korean clothing.

accept some Buddhist teaching. Estimates of the number of Christians range from 1 to 3 percent, yet conversions are rare because a new convert must break strong ties with family traditions and culture. As Christ warned,

> *A man's foes shall be they of his own household. He that*
> *loveth father or mother more than me is not worthy of me.*
> (Matt. 10:36–37)

HONSHU

Japan's population is about one-half of the United States' population, but all of its people are concentrated in an area the size of California. Narrow coastal plains lie around the mountains and support most of the population. The precious arable land (less than 12 percent) is intensely cultivated to produce some of the world's highest yields. **Honshu**, Japan's largest island, is home to more than 80 percent of the Japanese people. It contains thirty-four of the forty-seven prefectures and eight of the ten largest cities, including Tokyo.

TOKYO

With 8.12 million people, **Tokyo**, (meaning "eastern capital") is the largest city in Japan and part of the largest megalopolis in the world, with about 35 million people. **Yokohama**, Japan's second-largest city (pop. 3.52 million) and main port, is close to Tokyo. Another major city, Kawasaki, lies between them. This populous metropolitan area constitutes the Keihin Industrial Region, which produces ships, petroleum, steel, and electronic equipment. The entire industrial region is on Japan's largest lowland, the Kanto Plain, a major agricultural region that produces silk, wheat, and rice.

Tokyo is not only Japan's capital but also part of the largest megalopolis in the world.

Tokyo is a state-of-the-art financial center. It has one of the world's leading stock exchanges. Its banks and industries make Japan one of the richest nations in the world. Land in Japan, however, is scarce and expensive, and rapid growth has brought traffic and pollution problems. Nevertheless, Tokyo's crime rate is significantly lower than that of most Western cities.

In the mid-nineteenth century, Emperor Mutsuhito made one of the most amazing decisions in modern history: he attempted to transform a feudal society into an industrial giant in one generation. Mutsuhito adopted the title *Meiji*, or "enlightened rule," and set out to modernize Japan by seeking Western ideas and technology. During the Meiji Restoration, government officials went abroad to study government, education, and industry. The emperor established modern schools, modern industry, a parliament, and a modern army and navy.

But the ancient military traditions did not die. The government tried to remove Buddhist and other foreign influences in the nineteenth century. "State Shinto" stressed patriotism, the divine origin of the emperor, and the rightful world rule by the Japanese emperor. State Shinto spurred the Japanese to seek an empire in World War II.

Following Japan's defeat, the leaders abolished State Shinto and the emperor renounced all claims to divinity.

Tokyo, the national capital, was the site of another dramatic change that occurred after the war. In 1947, the Allied occupation forces, particularly the United States, helped the Japanese write and adopt a new republican constitution that transferred the emperor's power to the people. The *Kokkai*, or Diet, Japan's parliament, has two houses (the House of Councilors and the House of Representatives) and selects a prime minister. The constitution forbids waging war; however, Japan maintains armed forces for defense. The emperor is still a symbol of Japan, but he has only ceremonial duties.

KYOTO

Mountains cover about 85 percent of Japan. The loftiest peaks are found in the center of Honshu, at the Japanese Alps. Several peaks exceed ten thousand feet. The highest, **Fujiyama** (often called Mount Fuji), reaches 12,389 feet. Earthquakes are common. The Japanese Alps provide zinc and lead. Tin deposits lie in the Chugoku Mountains to the west.

Japan's third-largest city is the Osaka-Kobe metropolitan area (pop. 2.59 million), which is called the Hanshin Industrial Region. Another large city nearby is Kyoto (pop. 1.47 million). Those two cities produce pharmaceuticals, textiles, and steel. (Japan is second only to China in steel production.)

Kyoto was Japan's capital for more than one thousand years in ancient times. Warriors called **samurai** protected estates of feudal lords (*daimyo*), whose rivalries escalated into civil war. When the Yoritomo clan established itself as the country's strongest clan in 1192, the emperor granted Yoritomo the title of *shogun*, meaning "great general" of the people. Shoguns ruled Japan in the emperor's name until 1867.

Mount Fuji towers over the Japanese landscape.

OTHER INDUSTRIAL CENTERS

Honshu has three other major industrial regions. **Nagoya** is Japan's fourth-largest city at 2.18 million people, and the Chukyo Industrial Region around it produces many Japanese cars, synthetic fibers, ceramics, and aircraft. Only the United States has a greater ratio of car owners than Japan. The Hokuriku Region on the west coast extends from Niigata to Kanazawa and produces machinery and chemicals. The final industrial area is the Inland Sea Region. It lines both sides of the Inland Sea and produces rubber, trucks, and agricultural machinery. **Hiroshima** (HEER oh SHEE muh), a city of 1.14 million people and the site where the first atomic bomb was dropped, is part of that industrial area.

SHIKOKU

Shikoku, the smallest of Japan's four main islands, lies south of Honshu. With only 3 percent of the Japanese people, this mountainous and heavily forested island has only four prefectures. It has remained somewhat separate from the rest of Japan. Rice farms and villages nestled in the valleys appear as they have for more than a century. Japanese Buddhists still take pilgrimages to the island's eighty-eight sacred temples, hoping to be released from the cycle of rebirth.

Until recently, travelers had to take a ferry across the Inland Sea to reach the island. With the opening of the 7.5-mile-long Seta Ohashi Bridge, which is high enough for ships to pass under, that changed. Most people on the island live on the north shore in the area known as the Inland Sea Industrial Region.

JAPANESE CULTURE AND TRADITION

Japanese traditionally eat rice and seafoods at every meal, usually with chopsticks. Many dishes include tofu, pickled vegetables, or soy sauce. *Sukiyaki* is made with beef strips, vegetables, bean curd, and noodles. Favorite seafoods include fish, lobster, shrimp, squid, octopus, and eel. Fish are dried, cooked, or eaten raw. Raw fish is called *sashimi*. It is often served in cold, bite-sized rice cakes wrapped in seaweed. These cakes are called *sushi*.

Sushi variety platter

Traditional Japanese houses have large rooms divided by wood-and-paper sliding doors. Thick straw mats called *tatami* cover the floors, and people sit on cushions on the floor. Traditionally, men and women wore a *kimono*, a robe with long wide sleeves and a sash. These practices are changing as a result of Western influences.

The Japanese no longer have samurai warriors, with their own elaborate garb and sword. Nor do the Japanese often commit the ritual suicide called *seppuku*, or *hara-kiri*. But their lives continue to revolve around the concept of "saving face." They hold dearly to their ancient duties to the group, their elders, and their juniors. Everyone is expected to keep his or her place, and traditional rules govern every social situation. To avoid bringing shame on themselves or others, the Japanese avoid the blunt statements common among Americans.

Japanese students attend school six days a week and have short vacations in the spring and fall. Because they have no school buses, students get to school by walking, biking, or riding public buses. Schools also do not have janitors, so students help with cleanup. After-school clubs include swimming, gymnastics, English, and flower arranging. Final exams are very competitive because the students' scores determine whether they can attend college and, if so, how prestigious a school that will be. Those who do poorly must enter a trade. The exams are so stressful that some students commit suicide if they do not do as well as they think they should.

Although Japan borrowed its painting and pagoda architecture from China, Japan also has its own art forms. Haiku, a type of poetry using three short lines, is popular in America. Because good land is scarce, Japanese gardeners honor efficient use of space, such as *bonsai* (the art of growing dwarf ornamental trees). The Japanese have also perfected the art of paper folding, or origami. Another specialty is the art of flower arrangement, or *ikebana* (ee keh BAH nah).

The Japanese have borrowed much Western entertainment, especially baseball, but they have retained some of their own traditional activities, too. For example, *geisha* (GAY shah) means "artist," and geisha girls are artists of social graces. They wear traditional kimonos as they entertain patrons in restaurants with formal tea ceremonies. *Kabuki* is a theatrical performance dating from the seventeenth century. It involves lavish costumes and melodramatic scenes. The Japanese are legendary for their martial arts. *Kendo* is a type of fencing using bamboo sticks. Other such arts include *judo* (using throws), *karate* (using kicks and punches), and *aikido* (using holds). The huge and powerful *sumo* wrestlers are national heroes.

Martial arts, such as judo, are popular in Japan.

KYUSHU

Southeast of the Korean Peninsula is **Kyushu**, the southernmost and second-most-populous of Japan's main islands. The earliest settlers built Japan's first cities there. The mild climate and lush green countryside support 10 percent of Japan's population in seven prefectures. On the north coast are two cities—Fukuoka and Kitakyushu—that have a combined population of 1.39 million. The chief agricultural region in the northwest grows rice and tea. Northern coal fields produce about one-half of the coal mined in Japan.

On the west coast is the port city of Nagasaki (pop. 414,415), which is often referred to as the San Francisco of Japan. The United States dropped its second atomic bomb on Nagasaki in 1945 to end World War II.

Japan has many small islands. The United States captured the most strategic ones to use as bases for bombers during World War II. The Ryuku Islands form a curving chain of one hundred islands from Kyushu southwestward to Taiwan. Included among the Ryukus is **Okinawa**, Japan's fifth-most-populous island and the only prefecture not on one of the four main islands. The ninety-seven Bonin Islands are southeast of Japan. **Iwo Jima** is one of three Volcano Islands farther south.

HOKKAIDO

The northernmost of the four main Japanese islands is **Hokkaido** (hah KYE doh). The population is concentrated in Sapporo, a city of 1.79 million people, the fifth-largest city in Japan. Winters in Hokkaido are long and severe, and its summers are cool because of the influence of the cold Oyashio (or Kuril) Current. Surrounding waters provide a rich source of pollack and mackerel. Japan has the world's third-largest fish processing industry and the third-largest seaweed production industry.

Hokkaido compares to the American West as Japan's last frontier. Although it is the second-largest island and the largest prefecture, it has a relatively small population (only 5 percent of Japan's population) and is developed in pockets. Like the American frontier, Hokkaido has several natural resources. Lumber comes from the island's heavily forested mountains, and manganese comes from its southern peninsula. The Seikan Tunnel, the world's longest railway tunnel, transports these resources under the sea to Honshu. Hokkaido is also a recreation and vacation destination, especially for skiers.

Hokkaido also has native peoples, the Ainu, Japan's original inhabitants. The Japanese have always considered the Ainu an inferior people. Over time, the Ainu retreated north to Hokkaido. They survived by hunting, fishing,

Itsukushima Shrine

The Itsukushima (IHT soo KOO shee muh) Shrine near Hiroshima has Japan's largest *torii*, or gateway, marking a sacred Shinto site. The buildings of the shrine sit on an island in the Inland Sea, whereas the gateway stands offshore in the shallow waters of the bay. The two main supporting beams of the gateway rise fifty-three feet. The shrine dates from the twelfth century, and the magnificent gateway was added in 1875.

The sacred shrine is dedicated to three Japanese gods: Susano, Okinonushi, and Tenjin. No cemeteries defile the island, and dogs are prohibited so as not to disturb the deer. The wooded island has two pagodas, a treasury building, and the Hall of One Thousand Mats. But most of the white-and-red buildings stand on wooden platforms in the bay. The platforms make the shrine seem to float above the water. Bridges and covered walks link the buildings to one another and to the island.

Japan's high-speed trains make traveling in crowded cities a worry-free adventure.

Japanese Gardens

Japanese gardens are so famous that most public gardens in America have a section in the Japanese style. Japanese gardens often include arched footbridges, small pagodas, flowers, conifers, and ponds. Such gardens may include outdoor cafés that serve tea. These gardens are always clean, uncluttered, and carefully laid out. Tokyo has many such gardens. Two old and famous Japanese gardens are Korakuen Garden and Rikugien Garden.

One unique aspect of Japanese gardening is bonsai, the art of growing miniature trees. Grown in flowerpots or trays with carefully selected soil and fertilizer, the trees remain healthy, but their growth is stunted. Careful pruning develops branches in the desired places. A skilled bonsai gardener can shape the full-grown bonsai tree—by tying, bracing, or using copper wires—to look exactly like a normal tree, although it stands only one or two feet high. The gardener must also continually water, fertilize, prune, and shape the potted tree.

Japanese gardens are famous for their footbridges, ponds, and well-manicured walkways.

and planting small gardens. Intermarriage with the Japanese has since made full-blooded Ainu rare. Their most unusual trait is white skin. After World War II, social reforms assimilated the Ainu into the Japanese culture. As a consequence, their culture and their language—which were never fully studied—declined. The Japanese government has begun, however, to compensate the Ainu for the years of mistreatment and discrimination.

SECTION QUIZ

1. What is the religion that influences all Japanese people?

2. What is the world's largest metropolitan area?

3. Who are shoguns? samurai? Ainu?

4. What is the highest mountain in Japan?

5. Name the four main Japanese islands.

※ What factors enabled Japan to recover so quickly from World War II to become the economic giant it is today?

CHAPTER REVIEW
20

HOW MUCH DO YOU REMEMBER?

1. What are the two main rivers of China?
2. What three influences shaped the Chinese folk religions?
3. Why is the Qin Ling important?
4. Name the three special municipalities in China.
5. What key products come from the Southern Uplands of China?
6. What is China's largest autonomous region?
7. What desert dominates Mongolia?
8. Where did Chiang Kai-shek flee from Mao Zedong?
9. What is the largest city of the Korean Peninsula?
10. What are the two largest cities in Japan?
11. Which Japanese island . . .
    a. has the largest population?
    b. is the most northerly and wild?
    c. has the highest peaks?
    d. is a place for religious pilgrims?
    e. is home to the Ainu people?

WHAT DO YOU THINK?

1. Explain what is wrong with communism. Use countries in this chapter as positive and negative examples.
2. Identify the five most important differences between China and Japan.
3. Why has God allowed communism to become so powerful in China?

Can You:
Define These Terms?

intensive farming	ger
Confucianism	demilitarized
ancestor worship	zone (DMZ)
Taoism	Juche (Kimil-
dynasty	sungism)
Special Eco-	Nippon
nomic Zones	prefecture
autonomous	Shinto
regions	samurai
theocrat	

Locate These Places?

Pacific Rim	Ningxia
North China Plain	Taiwan
Qin Ling Mountains	Taipei
Huang He	Ulaanbaatar
Chang	Gobi Desert
Sichuan Basin	Korean Peninsula
Shanghai	Taebaek Mtns.
Beijing	Pyongyang
Tianjin	Seoul
Southern Uplands	Honshu
Hainan	Tokyo
Xi River	Yokohama
Guangzhou	Fujiyama
Hong Kong	Kyoto
Macau	Nagoya
Guangxi	Hiroshima
Tibet (Xizang)	Shikoku
Lhasa	Kyushu
Xinjiang	Okinawa
Taklimakan Desert	Iwo Jima
Nei Mongol	Hokkaido

Explain the Significance?

Han	Great Leap Forward
Confucius	Cultural Revolution
Lao Zi	Red Guard
Xi'an	Deng Xiaoping
Three Gorges Dam	Zhuang
Forbidden City	Dalai Lama
Tiananmen Square	Potala Palace
Great Wall	Quemoy
Manchus	Matsu
Sun Yat-sen	Kim Il Sung
Chiang Kai-shek	Kim Jong Il
Mao Zedong	

CHAPTER 21

Rice is the major food crop of Southeast Asia. Large numbers of people, such as these women tending a rice paddy in Cambodia, are employed in its production.

PASSPO

United
of

SOUTHEAST ASIA

I. INDOCHINA
  A. MYANMAR
  B. THAILAND
  C. LAOS
  D. CAMBODIA
  E. VIETNAM

II. THE MALAY ARCHIPELAGO
  A. MALAYSIA
  B. SINGAPORE
  C. BRUNEI
  D. INDONESIA
  E. THE PHILIPPINES

The region known as Southeast Asia is as large as the contiguous United States. It borders both India and China and stretches from the Indian Ocean in the west to the Pacific Ocean in the east. The countries within the region have many similarities, such as climate and resources; but they also have many contrasts, ranging from primitive tribal societies to modern, computer-driven societies.

The population centers of Southeast Asia tend to cluster around rivers, especially the fertile delta regions of the Mekong and Irrawaddy rivers, and along the narrow coastal plains where available harbor facilities make trade likely. Even steep highland areas, however, are heavily terraced to enable production of abundant crops. More than half of the total population of the region lives on islands. Dense forests, steamy jungles, and rugged mountains tend to inhibit land travel between the various countries. Most immigrants to the region are from China.

The region is part of the Pacific "ring of fire," experiencing numerous earthquakes, volcanic eruptions, and tsunamis. Because of the seasonal changes that accompany the monsoons—heavy rains and sometimes severe droughts—much of life in the region is regulated by the climate. But the rains also make possible the region's abundant crops, especially rice.

Rice can be grown in large quantities in relatively small spaces. The people of Southeast Asia rely daily on their rice production, and many more in other areas eat it regularly, too. In fact, more people of the world rely on rice than on any other staple. Five of the top ten

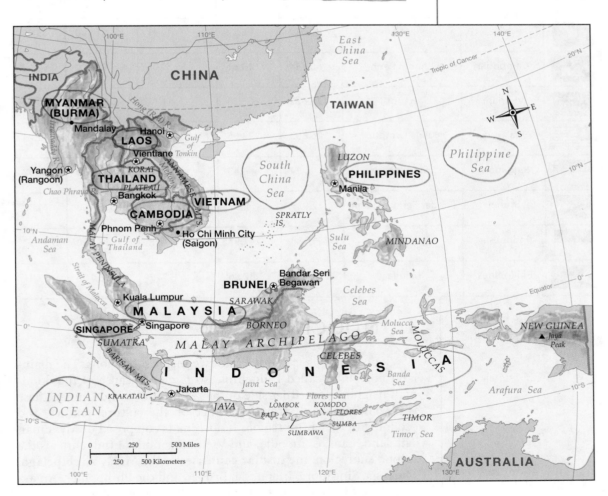

Major Countries–Rice

Consuming	Producing
1. China	1. China
2. India	2. India
3. Indonesia	3. Indonesia
4. Bangladesh	4. Bangladesh
5. Vietnam	5. Vietnam
6. Thailand	6. Thailand
7. Myanmar	7. Myanmar
8. Japan	8. Philippines
9. Philippines	9. Brazil
10. Brazil	10. Japan

rice-producing countries of the world are in Southeast Asia. (Nine of the ten are in the broader Asian region.)

Southeast Asia has also been the focus of intense competition and power struggles among European colonial powers. Of the ten Southeast Asian countries, only Thailand remained free of European colonialism. Yet Thailand was instrumental in the era of imperialism as a buffer zone between British forces in Myanmar and French forces in French Indochina (encompassing Laos, Cambodia, and Vietnam). Japan coveted the riches of the region and conquered much of it before and during World War II. In the decades following the war, all of the countries of the region gained independence from colonial powers. One positive effect of colonialism was the unifying influence exerted among various tribal groups throughout Southeast Asia, which made independence possible and practical. Today, the region is developing into an economic powerhouse, although poverty continues to abound and political instability remains a concern.

Southeast Asia Fast Facts

Flag	Country	Capital	Area (sq. mi.)	Pop. (M)	Pop. Density (per sq. mi.)	Per Capita GDP ($US)	Life Span
	Myanmar	Yangon	253,954	42.91	187	$1,800	60.70
	Thailand	Bangkok	197,595	65.44	327	$8,300	71.95
	Laos	Vientiane	89,112	6.22	71	$1,900	55.08
	Cambodia	Phnom Penh	68,154	13.61	204	$2,100	58.92
	Vietnam	Hanoi	125,622	83.54	672	$3,000	70.61
	Malaysia	Kuala Lumpur	126,853	23.95	192	$10,400	72.24
	Singapore	Singapore	264	4.43	17,042	$29,700	81.62
	Brunei	Bandar Seri Begawan	2,035	0.37	186	$23,600	74.80
	Indonesia	Jakarta	705,188	241.97	348	$3,700	69.57
	Philippines	Manila	115,124	87.86	777	$5,100	69.91

I. INDOCHINA

Southeast Asia is divided into two major subregions. The mainland portion is called **Indochina**, so named because of the dominant neighbors on either side of the region: India and China. These two countries exert strong influence on the culture, politics, and economy of the entire region. Indochina is composed of Myanmar, Thailand, Laos, Cambodia, and Vietnam. South of Indochina is the second subregion, the **insular countries** of the **Malay Archipelago**: Malaysia, Singapore, Indonesia, Brunei, and the Philippines. An **archipelago** (AHRK uh PEHL uh goh) is a large group of islands.

MYANMAR

As one moves eastward from India, the first country of Indochina one enters is Myanmar (myahn MAHR), formerly known as Burma, which is the largest country in Indochina and the second largest in Southeast Asia. Slightly smaller than Texas, it shares a border with China in the north and Laos and Thailand in the east. It has a coast on the Bay of Bengal in the southwest and the Andaman Sea in the south.

Most of the people of Myanmar live along the coastal lowlands where the rain forest offers sufficient water for rice paddies. The country ranks seventh in the production of rice. The capital, Yangon (formerly called Rangoon), and its nearly six million residents are in the lowlands of the delta of the **Irrawaddy** (IHR uh WAHD ee) **River**, which runs from the rugged eastern highlands and empties into the Andaman Sea.

The Irrawaddy River, seen here in Mandalay, is the main river of Myanmar.

More than two-thirds of the work force is employed in agriculture, which contributes more than half of the GDP. In addition to rice, Myanmar produces vegetables, sesame, groundnuts, sugar cane, hardwoods, and fish. Commercial farming is done in the lowlands. Tribal peoples in the highlands are subsistence farmers. Tragically, thanks to such farmers in the "**Golden Triangle**," where the borders of Myanmar, Laos, and Thailand meet, Myanmar ranks second in the world in production of a less desirable agricultural product: illicit opium. Only Afghanistan produces more.

Industries include food processing, clothing, wood products, copper, tin, tungsten, iron, fertilizers, cement, and pharmaceuticals. Thirteen percent of the GDP is from industry, but only 7 percent of the work force is employed in that sector.

Since Myanmar gained its independence in 1948, much of its history has been a succession of military dictatorships. Free elections were held in 1990, giving the opposition a landslide victory and control of the legislature, but the military junta refused to relinquish control and remains in power today. The regime routinely harasses and arrests those who promote democracy and human rights and is especially repressive of Christianity.

Eighty-nine percent of the people of Myanmar are Buddhists. Only 4 percent profess Christianity (3 percent Baptists, 1 percent Roman Catholics). Another 4 percent are Muslims. Other minority religions, including animism, are also practiced.

Myanmar was once the richest country in Southeast Asia, but its military regime adopted socialistic economic practices that hindered rather than promoted productivity and prosperity. Oppressive government controls, inefficient economic policies, and economic sanctions imposed by nations who oppose the regime's human rights violations have crippled the economy. Ignoring the lessons of the West and even Communist China's relaxation of socialistic economic controls, which produced the phenomenal economic growth there, the regime persists in its failed policies in spite of rampant poverty, especially in rural areas.

In Pyay, Myanmar, is an idol called the "Golden Eyeglasses Buddha."

BUDDHISM

Buddhism originated as an offshoot of Hinduism. Essentially, it is a religion that promotes the teachings of Siddhartha Gautama Buddha, who lived about five hundred years before Christ. He had experiences that prompted him to search for enlightenment and release from the sickness and sorrow of the physical world. One day, after several hours of meditation, he felt enlightened and relieved. Others gave him the name *Buddha*, meaning "Enlightened One."

Buddha began teaching others how to become enlightened. He traveled across India teaching what he called *dharma*, or saving truth. Dharma is the Middle Way of moderation between self-indulgence and self-torture. The Middle Way requires following the philosophy of the Four Noble Truths and an eight-fold path of moral principles, such as self-control, respect for life, and resisting evil. Buddha stressed the need to free oneself from desires and worldly things. He claimed that this is the way to find release from suffering. Those who succeed reach a state of complete happiness and rest called *nirvana*.

Buddhists also seek the "non-self," wherein their identity will dissolve into the larger consciousness and they will be free of the world. Jesus did not call Christians to be free from the world but to be in it (John 17:15) and a witness to it of Christ (Matt. 28:18–20).

The Bible also teaches moderation, temperance, and control of passions (Phil. 4:5; Gal. 4:22). God denounces both extremes of carnal living (1 John 2:15–17) and self-inflicted pain (Col. 2:20–23). However, none

of the Buddhist practices can bring salvation or lasting peace. Salvation comes only by trusting Jesus Christ (Acts 4:12). Buddhists see evil as a product of suffering. Thus, there is no sin, only suffering. Unless Buddhists recognize their fallen nature and live dependently upon God, they will not be able to find the peace for which they are searching.

ASEAN

Thailand was one of the original nations involved in the founding of the **Association of Southeast Asian Nations (ASEAN)** and the only member nation from Indochina. The organization was started in 1967 to promote political and economic cooperation and regional stability through consultation, consensus, and cooperation. The founding member nations were Thailand, Indonesia, Malaysia, the Philippines, and Singapore, but today all of the nations of Southeast Asia are members. The organization's Secretariat is located in Jakarta, Indonesia.

THAILAND

East of Myanmar is Thailand (TYE land), which until 1939 was known as **Siam** (sy AM). It is the only country of Southeast Asia that was never controlled by a European colonial power. It is also the strongest economic power in Indochina because it has not only abundant resources that it has developed wisely but also a sound free market economy and a generally stable (in the context of surrounding countries) government that supports that free economy. (The Thai military staged a bloodless coup in September 2006 while the prime minister was attending the opening session of the United Nations.)

A little more than twice the size of Wyoming, Thailand borders Laos, Cambodia, and Malaysia. Like Myanmar, Thailand has a major river, the Chao Phraya (CHOU prah-YAH), flowing from the northern highlands. It empties into the Gulf of Thailand near Bangkok, the capital. The river valley lies between two mountain ranges and is the most populous area of the country. Rice farming dominates the valley.

Much of Thailand's territory encompasses the Malay Peninsula, which is almost one thousand miles long. Although Myanmar shares the northern section and Malaysia owns the southern portion, Thailand has the central section for itself and therefore controls the only land route between Asia and Malaysia/Singapore. On the west side of the isthmus is the Andaman Sea; on the east is the Gulf of Thailand.

The peninsula is sparsely populated, but it is rich in mines and rubber plantations and produces teak, bamboo, and other woods.

Bangkok is Indochina's second-largest city (behind only Jakarta, Indonesia) with a population of about 8.5 million. It is a bustling modern city, and its industries include refineries, textiles, auto assembly plants, and electronic equipment.

In the middle fourteenth century, what was then known as Siam was founded as a kingdom. It switched from an absolute monarchy to a constitutional monarchy in 1932 and remains so today. Although the country has a hereditary king, its effective head is the prime minister, who is elected from among the members of the House of Representatives. The bicameral legislature has a corresponding Senate. Four political parties vie for dominance in the government.

Thailand's natural resources include tin, rubber, tungsten, tantalum, timber, lead, fish, gypsum, lignite, and fluorite. Although almost half of the work force is engaged in agriculture, less than 10 percent of the GDP is from agriculture. The remaining 90 percent of the GDP is divided almost equally between industry and services. More than a third of the work force, however, is engaged in services.

More than 94 percent of Thais are Buddhists. The next-largest religion is Islam with only 4.6 percent of the population. The greatest problem facing the government today comes from three Muslim-majority provinces in the south, which are in armed rebellion, no doubt spurred on by the spread of radical Islam around the world.

LAOS

The only landlocked country of Southeast Asia is Laos (LOUSE). It is surrounded by Myanmar and Thailand on the west, Cambodia on the south, China on the north, and Vietnam on the east. It is a largely undeveloped mountainous country. Little of its land area is

ELEPHANT ROUNDUP

Elephants, Thailand's national symbol, are used in the timber industry of the country. Workers gather many of them once a year in a big roundup that is something like a Western rodeo—but using elephants rather than horses. People from near and far come to watch the huge animals display their skills.

Opening the activities, more than one hundred elephants parade before the crowds. Their trainers, called *mahouts* (muh HOUTZ), sit proudly on the shoulders of the beasts, giving commands by nudging the beasts behind the ears with their feet.

A small group of elephants demonstrates the way wild animals are caught and trained. A few of the animals pretend to be wild. The others chase them until the mahouts rope the wild beasts by their hind legs.

In other events the elephants show off their speed, skill, and agility. Many spectators volunteer to lie on the ground and let four or five of the 8,000-lb. beasts step over them. Between races and log-lifting demonstrations, Thai dancers in colorful costumes perform traditional Thai dances.

In the most exciting event, elephants race to a line several yards away; then they stop and pick up a banana or another small article with their trunks. They return to the starting point and place the article in

Mahouts guide their elephants in demonstrating their skills at the elephant rodeo.

a small circle. They gallop back and forth picking up articles until the last article, a red flag, is returned. The first elephant to return with its red flag wins.

People live in this long, narrow boat on the Mekong River in Laos.

arable, and it rivals Myanmar as the poorest Southeast Asian country. Much of its border with Thailand is the **Mekong** (MAY KONG) **River**.

A little bigger than Utah, Laos was once much larger than it is now, but its power and influence gradually declined. It came under the control of Thailand in the seventeenth to nineteenth centuries. It was also part of French Indochina during the colonial period. In 1975, the Pathet Lao, a Communist organization, took over and closely aligned the country with Communist Vietnam. In recent years, Laos has tried to move back toward a free market economy with amazing results. But the ill effects of Communist domination are still powerful, and the country faces great difficulties. For example, its infrastructure is primitive. It has no railroads to speak of, limited telecommunications, and a poor road system. Only urban areas have electricity.

Eighty percent of the labor force is engaged in agriculture, which, dominated by rice production, contributes almost 50 percent of the GDP. The other 50 percent is about evenly divided between industry and services. In addition to rice, the country's major agricultural products include sweet potatoes, vegetables, corn, and sugar cane. Its exploited resources include copper, tin, gypsum, and timber. Other industries include food processing, garment manufacturing, and cement production.

Sixty percent of the Laotian people are Buddhists. The remaining 40 percent are animists or other indigenous religions. Only 1.5 percent profess Christianity.

CAMBODIA

South of Laos is the country of Cambodia (kam BOH dee uh). It also shares borders with Vietnam on the east and Thailand on the north and west. Its southern border is the Gulf of Thailand.

The terrain of Cambodia, which is slightly smaller than Oklahoma, is primarily low, flat plains, although it does have some mountains in the southwest and north. More than one-fifth of its soil is arable, and its natural resources include oil, natural gas, timber, gemstones, manganese, phosphates, and hydropower potential. The key term is *potential*; historically, the country has not capitalized on its great potential.

The country was under the colonial authority of France from 1863 until it gained independence in 1953. The Communist **Khmer Rouge** (kuh-MEHR ROOZH) took over in 1975 after a five-year struggle. The Communist leader, **Pol Pot**, had the idea that the solution to the country's problems was to erase all memories of colonial times and return everyone to a rural, agricultural lifestyle. In the process, the Khmer Rouge sought to eliminate all opposition by executing or starving to death an estimated 1.5 million Cambodians. Even

This collection of skulls represents the millions of Cambodians murdered in the "killing fields" under the Khmer Rouge.

the Communists in Vietnam were repulsed by such atrocities. They invaded in 1978, drove the Khmer Rouge into the countryside, and occupied Cambodia for the next ten years. The Khmer Rouge finally surrendered in 1999, and the United Nations put the leaders on trial for crimes against humanity.

Today, the country has a king who rules with a bicameral legislature composed of representatives of three recognized political parties. They are working to make Cambodia a more vibrant country that is conducive to free markets. Foreign aid toward this goal has been tied to official efforts to reduce corruption.

The prospects for improvement are bright. The GDP of Cambodia is about equally divided among each of the three sectors (agriculture, industry, and services). Although 75 percent of the work force remains in agriculture, most of it is subsistence farming. However, Cambodia can produce rice, rubber, corn, vegetables, cashews, and other products well. Its growing industries include tourism, apparel, rice milling, gem mining, and wood products. Another factor of great potential is the fact that 50 percent of the population is twenty years of age or younger.

VIETNAM

The country of Vietnam (VEE eht NAHM) can be visualized as a long, thin *S* reaching from southern China in the north to the Gulf of Thailand in the southwest. In total area it is slightly larger than New Mexico.

The northern third of the country is shaped like an inverted pyramid with the Gulf of Tonkin on the east and Laos on the west. It is bisected from northwest to southeast by the **Hong (Red) River**, which flows through the capital, **Hanoi** (ha NOY), and empties through a low, flat delta into the **Gulf of Tonkin** (TAHN kihn). The chief seaport is **Haiphong** (hye FONG) in the northern portion of the delta.

The middle of the country, which makes up a little less than one-third of the length, is a thin band of narrow coastline and central highlands running southeastward from about Vinh to about Da Nang. In this central region, the narrowest point is only thirty-one miles wide; the widest point is only about sixty miles.

The southern portion is a little more than one-third of the total length of the country. It widens and the coast, washed by the **South China Sea**, curves first southward and then south-westward near Cam Ranh. The western border in this third is Cambodia. The upper and central portion of southern Vietnam is dominated by central highlands. The lower portion is mostly flat delta, forming the mouth of the Mekong River, which flows through the heart of Cambodia. The largest city of the southern portion of the country, **Ho Chi Minh** (HOH CHEE MIHN) **City** (formerly Saigon), is at the northern reaches of the delta.

The culture of modern Vietnam reflects a variety of influences, both Western and Oriental. It became a French colony in 1858. Although the Vietnamese declared their independence at the end of World War II, they did not break free of French control until 1954, when Vietnamese rebels led by

Through Christian Eyes
What do the atrocities of the Khmer Rouge reveal about human nature?

More than two million motorcycles—and even more bicycles—jam the streets of Ho Chi Minh City.

Ho Chi Minh led the Communist defeat of the French at Dien Bien Phu as well as the South Vietnamese and American armies.

Communist **Ho Chi Minh** defeated the French forces at **Dien Bien Phu** (dyehn byehn FOO). Not everyone, however, wanted to live under communism. The United Nations proposed free elections to allow the Vietnamese to determine their country's future. Vietnamese living in the southern half of the country voted to remain free. However, when the Communists who controlled the northern half of the country refused, the UN divided the country at the 17th parallel, creating North and South Vietnam. Not willing to let the richer South remain free and separate, the North Vietnamese invaded the South, supported by a guerrilla group known as the Viet Cong. Based on the **domino theory** (the idea that if one country of Southeast Asia fell to communism, the others would soon fall too, just like dominoes), the United States sent progressively more troops to help the South. However, the Vietnam War proved to be so divisive in the United States that U.S. troops withdrew in 1975. As predicted, the South fell, and millions of people were killed, imprisoned, and persecuted. Thousands of Vietnamese known as "boat people" risked death by fleeing into the South China Sea in every imaginable kind of vessel, hoping to reach or be rescued by noncommunist countries. Many eventually managed to make it to the United States.

For the next twenty years, Vietnam struggled economically. Under international pressure to improve its human rights record, Vietnam finally began to liberalize its economic policies in 2001, and the country is making vast improvements economically. For example, exports to the United States doubled in 2002 and doubled again in 2003. In 2005, Vietnam became a member of the World Trade Organization. More than half of the work force is employed in agriculture, which contributes 21 percent of the GDP. Although four other countries produce more rice than Vietnam, that is still its top agricultural product. It ranks first in the world, however, in cashew production and third in coffee. Other products include fish, rubber, cotton, and tea. Industries such as food processing, garments, shoes, mining, cement, chemical fertilizers, and tires are contributing more than 40 percent of the GDP.

Vietnam still has a Communist government that allows no opposition party. It has a president who is elected by the unicameral National Assembly.

Vietnam is considered closed to formal missionary activity, and the influence of more than thirty years of atheistic communism is readily apparent in the people's belief systems. More than 80 percent of Vietnamese profess no religion. The largest religion is Buddhism, but only 9.3 percent of Vietnamese profess to be Buddhists. Less than 7 percent are Roman Catholics, and only about 0.5 percent are Protestants, mostly the highland Montagnards (MAHN tan YAHRDS).

SECTION QUIZ

1. Into what two areas is Southeast Asia divided?

2. The borders of which three Southeast Asian countries make up the "Golden Triangle"?

3. Which country in this region is the only one never colonized by a European power, and what is that country's former name?

4. Which river not only forms much of the border between Laos and Thailand but also flows through Cambodia and Vietnam?

5. Which religion predominates in Indochina?

💡 Did the fall of South Vietnam to communism prove or disprove the domino theory?

II. THE MALAY ARCHIPELAGO

The Malay Archipelago is the largest group of islands in the world. It begins with the lower half of the Malay Peninsula and encompasses two major groups of islands: the East Indies and the Philippines.

Most of the islands are volcanic, and mountains dominate many of them. Apart from those highland areas, all of the islands have a tropical wet climate. Some areas get as much as 200 inches of rain a year; most places get at least 100 inches.

MALAYSIA

The first country a person traveling southward from Thailand enters is Malaysia (muh LAY zhuh). Part of it is on the lower portion of the Malay Peninsula, and the rest of it is on the northern side of the island of Borneo, located to the east of the peninsula.

Like Thailand, Malaysia is a major leader among the developing countries. It is also in a strategic location along the shipping lanes of the Strait of Malacca and the southern end of the South China Sea. It is slightly larger than New Mexico.

Four-fifths of Malaysia's people live on the peninsula. The capital, **Kuala Lumpur** (KWAHL-uh loom-POOR; pop. 1.4 million), is there. A distinguishing landmark of the city is the second-tallest buildings in the world, the two Petronas Towers, each at 88 stories, or 1,483 feet. Two of Malaysia's states, Sarawak (suh RAH wAHK) and Sabah (SAH bah), are on the island of Borneo, which is about 400 miles east of the peninsula. Much of this area remains undeveloped, but its rich oil is being developed.

Sixty percent of Malaysians are Muslim. Almost 20 percent are Buddhist. A little more than 9 percent profess Christianity, many of those being Roman Catholics. The official language is Bahasa Melayu; but English, Chinese, and numerous other languages are also spoken.

Malaysia was a British colonial power in the eighteenth and nineteenth centuries and was occupied by Japan during World War II. In 1948, the Federation of Malaya was formed, and in 1957 the country gained full independence. Singapore was part of the federation until it seceded in 1965. Then Sabah and Sarawak joined the federation in 1967, forming what became known as Malaysia. The country has a constitutional monarchy ruled by the "Paramount Ruler," who is elected from among the hereditary leaders of the nine states that

This aerial view of Kuala Lumpur includes the Petronas Towers, the second-tallest buildings in the world.

make up the country. It has a bicameral parliament, with members of the lower house being elected by the people and members of the upper house being appointed by the Paramount Ruler and the state legislatures. The country has dozens of political parties.

Malaysia has experienced an economic revolution. Although it was once heavily agricultural and merely a supplier or exporter of raw materials, in the 1970s it became a major electronics manufacturer. Today, almost 60 percent of its GDP is from services, and more than 33 percent is from industry. In addition to electronics, major industries include rubber processing, oil refining, and food processing. Only 14.5 percent of its work force is now employed in agriculture, producing only a little more than 7 percent of GDP. Among its agricultural products are rubber, palm oil, cocoa, and rice.

SINGAPORE

At the southern tip of the Malay Peninsula is an island that is only a little more than three and a half times the size of Washington, D.C. But its influence far exceeds its size. Singapore (SING uh POOR) is the name of not only the island but also the country and the capital. It has been a major trade and shipping location since the time of

The Port of Singapore is the busiest seaport in the world.

Christ, and it remains the focal point of trade in the region today. In fact, it is rated as the sixth most competitive country for business in the world. It is also the busiest seaport by volume in the world.

The population of Singapore is heavily Chinese (77 percent). Native Malays make up only 14 percent of the population. Indians make up 8 percent of the population. The largest religious groups are Buddhists (43 percent) and Muslims (15 percent). Christianity is represented by about 14 percent of the population. Fifteen percent profess no religious affiliation, and the rest of the population practices a large number of other minority religions. As diverse as its religions are its languages, which include Mandarin (35 percent), English (23 percent), Malay (14 percent), Hokkien (11 percent), and numerous others, including several Chinese dialects.

The downtown business district of Singapore is a beautiful sight at night.

Singapore has taken steps to increase its amount of space by reclaiming land from the sea (resulting in a 10 percent increase in its space). Because of its lack of land, agriculture is responsible for almost none of its GDP, although it does produce rubber, copra, fruit, orchids, poultry, eggs, and ornamental fish. Its economy depends heavily on exports. A third of the GDP is industry, mostly manufacturing and construction. Singapore is the financial and high-tech hub of Southeast Asia. Two-thirds of the GDP is service oriented, and more than half of that comes from financial services and transportation/communications.

The government of Singapore is a parliamentary republic with a president and a unicameral parliament led by a prime minister. It has numerous recognized political parties.

BRUNEI

Nestled between the Malaysian states of Sabah and Sarawak on the north central coast of the island of Borneo is the tiny (a little smaller than Delaware) country of Brunei (broo NYE). It is a flat coastal plain rising to mountains in the east and hilly lowland in the west.

Brunei has been important for traders since the seventh century. In 1888, the British made it one of their protectorates to stop pirates there who were preying on British shipping. It gained independence from Britain in 1984.

Less than half a percent of the land in Brunei is arable, so only about 5 percent of its GDP comes from agriculture. It does produce some rice, fruits, vegetables, and chickens. Industry, mostly extraction and refining of oil and liquefied natural gas, makes up 45 percent of GDP. Forty-eight percent of the work force is employed in government.

That government is a constitutional sultanate. It has a legal system based on English common law, but Islamic sharia supersedes civil law in some areas. The sultan and the prime minister have hereditary positions; there are no elections. The legislature, whose members are appointed by the sultan, met for the first time in twenty years on September 25, 2004, but the sultan dismissed it a year later. The country has three small, inactive political parties.

Islam is the official religion of Brunei; 67 percent of the people of Brunei practice it. Buddhists make up 13 percent, and Christians and followers of indigenous religions make up the rest.

INDONESIA

By far the largest country of not only the Malay Archipelago but also all of Southeast Asia is Indonesia (IHN doh NEE zhuh). It is a nation of 17,508 separate islands, but only about 6,000 of them are populated. They stretch across more than three thousand miles from the Indian Ocean in the west to New Guinea and the Pacific Ocean in the east. (That is about the same distance as from New York City to Seattle, Washington.) Indonesia also has the fourth-largest population in the world (behind only China, India, and the United States).

As one might expect of such a far-flung nation, it is multi-ethnic and multilingual. Major ethnic groups include Javanese (45 percent), Sundanese (14 percent), Madurese, and coastal Malay (7.5 percent each). Other minority ethnic groups make up another 26

The World's Most Competitive Environments for Business

1. Finland
2. United States
3. Sweden
4. Denmark
5. Taiwan
6. Singapore
7. Switzerland
8. Iceland
9. Norway
10. Australia

percent. The population speaks more than 250 different languages and dialects.

The important factor that tends to unite so many different peoples of such different languages and cultures over such vast distances is religion. With 88 percent of Indonesians being Muslims, Indonesia is the largest Islamic country in the world. Radical Islamists are present in some areas of Indonesia, and leaders in the war against terrorism are keeping a wary eye on events in that area of the world.

The hub of Indonesian civilization has been the island of **Java** (JAH vuh), which is southwest of Singapore and due south of Borneo. It has been at various times under the control of Arab traders, who spread Islam throughout the islands as they sought spices and other trade items; the Netherlands, which called the region the Dutch East Indies; the Japanese in World War II; and various regional warlords, dictators, and military juntas. Today, Java is the most densely populated of Indonesia's islands, and the capital, **Jakarta** (juh KAHR tuh; pop. 8.4 million), is the tenth-largest city in the world.

Indonesia includes all or part of four of the world's eleven largest islands. Java ranks thirteenth worldwide, but four other Indonesian islands are even larger, of which New Guinea is the largest. The other three, with Java, are collectively called the Greater Sunda (SUHN duh) Islands.

The world's sixth-largest island is Sumatra (soo MAH truh), which is northwest of Java and southwest of Malaysia. It is the second-most-populated Indonesian island, and most of its people live in the eastern lowlands. Borneo, the third-largest island in the world, includes, as we have discussed already, the two Malaysian states of Sarawak and Sabah and the nation of Brunei. The eleventh-largest island in the world is Celebes (SEHL uh BEEZ) also known as Sulawesi, which is east of Borneo. And the second-largest island in the world is New Guinea, but only the western half, an area called Irian Jaya (IHR-ee-ahn JAH-yah), belongs to Indonesia.

The rest of Indonesia consists of two island chains, the first of which is the Lesser Sunda Islands east of Java, which stretch from Bali to Timor. Timor (TEE mohr) is the largest of the Lesser Sunda Islands. Rebels on the eastern half of Timor fought for and finally won independence from Indonesia in 2002. They named their new country **Timor-Leste**. Bali (BAH lee) is the most famous of the Lesser Sundas. It is a Hindu refuge in a sea of Muslims.

The second chain of islands is the **Moluccas** (muh LUHK uhz), which were at one time called the Spice Islands. This archipelago is located between the Philippines in the north, New Guinea in the east, Timor in the south, and Celebes in the west.

The Indonesian economy is recovering from a devastating tsunami that hit its westernmost islands in December 2004, killing 131,029, leaving 570,000 homeless, and doing an estimated $4.5 billion in damages. The economy is strong, however, and should recover soon.

Although 45 percent of the Indonesian work force is employed in agriculture, that sector provides only about 15 percent of the GDP.

A tsunami devastated Banda Aceh, Sumatra, Indonesia, in December 2004.

Indonesia is second in the world in coconuts and fourth in the world in coffee. Other important crops include rice, cassava (tapioca), peanuts, rubber, cocoa, copra, and palm oil. The bulk of the GDP, however, is provided by a balance of industry and services. Major industries include oil and natural gas, textiles, apparel and footwear, mining, cement, chemical fertilizers, plywood, and tourism. Indonesia's biggest trade partners are Singapore and Japan.

Indonesia is a republic with a unicameral legislature as well as a president and a vice president who are elected by the people for five-year terms. Eight political parties vie for influence in the government.

THE PHILIPPINES

The Philippine (FIHL uh PEEN) Islands lie due east of Vietnam across the South China Sea, south of Taiwan, north of the Moluccas, and west of the Philippine Sea. The 7,107 islands stretch across more than a thousand miles and make up a land area a little larger than Arizona. The two largest islands are like bookends for the other islands, Luzon on the north and Mindanao on the south.

Luzon (loo ZAHN) is the largest and most populous island. It includes both the capital, Manila (muh NIH luh; pop. 1.6 million), and the largest city of the country, Quezon City (pop. 2.5 million). Luzon and the islands around it produce rice, tobacco, sugar cane, coconuts, bananas, and mahogany. **Mindanao** (mihn dihn NOW) is the second-largest island, and its largest city is the port of Davao (dah VOW; pop. 804,000). It is a leading producer of abaca, a strong fiber used to make rope.

Only about nine hundred of the seven thousand islands between Luzon and Mindanao are inhabited. The seven largest islands produce rice, corn, and coconuts. The largest city among those islands is Cebu (say BOO; pop. 776,000), a port to which professional fishermen bring their catches.

The islands of the Philippines are in the middle of the "typhoon belt." They are usually affected by fifteen typhoons a year and are hit directly by about five or six a year. The various islands also are susceptible to landslides, volcanoes, earthquakes, and tsunamis.

The Philippine Islands were a Spanish colony from the time of their discovery by Ferdinand Magellan in 1521 until the Spanish Empire was defeated in the Spanish-American War in 1898. Japanese occupation during World War II delayed their scheduled independence, but they finally gained it in 1946. The influence of Spain is still heavily felt as more than 80 percent of the people are Roman Catholic. A little less than 10 percent are non-Catholic Christian. Only 5 percent are Muslim.

Although more than a third of the work force is employed in agriculture, that sector provides only about 15 percent of the GDP. The Philippines, however, ranks first in the world in coconut production, second in pineapples, and fourth in bananas. A little less than half of the work force is in services, but that sector provides more than

Latex harvested from rubber trees is used to produce many rubber products.

Residents of Davao participate in a holiday parade.

half of the GDP. Industry—including electronics, garments, footwear, pharmaceuticals, chemicals, wood products, oil refining, and fishing—brings in about a third of the GDP. The two major trade partners of the Philippines are Japan and the United States.

The Philippines is a republic with an elected president. It has a bicameral legislature with a House of Representatives and a Senate. A dozen or so political parties vie for influence in the government. The country's most stable period was the twenty-one-year rule of president Ferdinand Marcos, but it ended with widespread accusations of corruption in 1988. Since then, it has had several presidents and periodic coup attempts, the latest of which occurred in 2006. A vexing problem of the twenty-first century is the threat of Muslim terrorists in the southern regions of the nation.

SECTION QUIZ

1. Which two Malaysian states are located on the island of Borneo?

2. Which country in the Malaysian archipelago is the busiest seaport by volume in the world?

3. What tiny country is located on Borneo's northwest side between the two Malaysian states?

4. What is the largest country (in both area and population) in Southeast Asia?

5. What are the names of the two largest islands of the Philippines?

🔎 What religious fact about Indonesia makes it a critical player in the war on terrorism, and how might the country work to help the United States in that war?

CHAPTER REVIEW

21

HOW MUCH DO YOU REMEMBER?

1. Why are the monsoons important to Southeast Asia?

2. What crop is critical to all Southeast Asian countries?

3. What river forms the central valley of Myanmar?

4. Which three Southeast Asian countries were ruled by the French?

5. What is the major river of French Indochina?

6. Which four Southeast Asian countries are the greatest economic powers of the region?

7. What two island groups constitute the Malay Archipelago?

8. Of what three major island groups is Indonesia composed?

9. Which European country colonized the Indonesian islands?

10. Which three countries controlled the Philippines before they gained their independence?

11. Name the country that best fits each of the following descriptions: (a) largest Muslim nation; (b) Spanish heritage; (c) never colonized by a European power; (d) currently under Communist rule; (e) oil rich.

WHAT DO YOU THINK?

1. In what ways does Buddhism differ from true Christianity?

2. List the problems common to the countries of Southeast Asia. What is the greatest hope for these countries?

Can You:
Define These Terms?

Indochina	nirvana
insular countries	ASEAN
archipelago	domino theory

Locate These Places?

Malay Archipelago	Hong (Red) River
Irrawaddy River	Gulf of Tonkin
"Golden Triangle"	South China Sea
Mekong River	Moluccas

Explain the Significance?

Siam	Dien Bien Phu
Khmer Rouge	Kuala Lumpur
Pol Pot	Java
Hanoi	Jakarta
Haiphong	Timor-Leste
Ho Chi Minh City	Luzon
Ho Chi Minh	Mindanao

UNIT 9

A LITTLE GRASS SHACK

Even today, people enjoy traveling to the exotic islands of Oceania in the South Pacific. The setting of one of James Michener's novels was modeled after such an island and inspired a musical titled *South Pacific*. Hundreds of tourists visit that island every year: Bora Bora in Tahiti. The following excerpt from an article by one of those tourists hints of the legendary beauty of the place.

"I'm living it up like a Tahitian king at the Bora Bora Lagoon Resort. Actually, I'm living in higher style. The ancient Tahitian kings had no inside plumbing.

"My little grass shack is a handsome bungalow built over the most beautiful lagoon on this planet. The resort is on the island motu of Toopua, five minutes by speedboat to Vaitape, Bora Bora's main village.

"My room is an explosion of flowers. Everything is smothered in scarlet hibiscus and fragrant tiare Tahiti blossoms. I had to gently spread a mountain of flowers just to find space to sit down."

(Excerpt from *International Travel News*, January 1999; complete article available at www.findarticles.com/p/articles/mi_m3648/is_11_23/ai_61642924)

THE AUSTRALIAN AND PACIFIC REALMS

CULTURE IN THE LAND DOWN UNDER

When you think of Australia—or "the land down under," as it is often called—you might think of kangaroos, or koalas, or maybe even Tasmanian devils. But the mention of the people of the land invariably brings to mind *aborigines*.

That term basically means "those who were here from the beginning." The Aborigines were the original inhabitants of Australia, long before the arrival of the first European settlers—British convicts. Although the Aborigines had not encountered Europeans before that time, they had had extensive contact with Melanesians and Indonesians, so they were not ignorant or isolated. They were, however, primitive in contrast to how Europeans lived.

The Aborigines, who originally might have encompassed as many as 500 different clans, were hunter-gatherers. They had between 200 and 250 languages with as many as 700 dialects. Because the Australian continent is so large, most of them did not know of the existence of clans in other areas of the continent.

One thing that all Aborigines had in common was a belief that the land was sacred. The most sacred site was Uluru, or Ayers Rock, in central Australia. (More is said about this site in Chapter 22.) The Aborigines believed and taught their successive generations that with the *right* to use the land came a *duty* to care for and preserve that land. One of the most important ways they communicated this and other cultural lessons was by storytelling, especially stories that dealt with "Dreamtime," or "the time before time."

The Aborigines were experts at surviving using the available natural resources. They invented unique tools to help them survive, and they ate many things that to Westerners are usually revolting: moths, grubs, ants, termites, honeybees, cockroaches, and caterpillars. They prepared the moths by sifting them in a net to remove the heads, legs, and wings. Then they roasted the bodies in sand before eating them. Sometimes, rather than roasting them, they mashed them into a paste and baked them as cakes. The grubs they ate raw or cooked in ashes.

The coming of the Europeans, however, spelled trouble for the Aborigines and their way of life. Just as the European settlers gradually pushed the Native Americans inland from the Atlantic coast and off their ancestral lands, the Europeans in Australia dislocated the Aborigines, shrinking the areas where they were allowed to exist until there was hardly any suitable place for them. Only in recent decades has the Australian government begun to recognize the legitimacy of Aboriginal claims. Although the Aboriginal life will never return to what it was before Europeans came, the government is trying to right its wrongs in ways that will benefit both groups.

Australians today are characterized by a carefree and unrestrained lifestyle. Although Australia is nominally a Christian nation (about 70 percent of Australians identify themselves with some form of Christianity), the practical influence of religion is minimal. The emphasis on pleasure, however, is great. Perhaps British author D. H. Lawrence best described life in Australia when he wrote, "You feel free in Australia. There is great relief in the atmosphere—a relief from tension, from pressure, an absence of control of will or form. The skies open above you and the areas open around you." Although this condition might seem desirable, it is spiritually lethal.

Australia's heritage as a British penal colony has caused some consternation among Australians who would like to have a national day of celebration. Unlike the United States and France—which celebrate Independence Day and Bastille Day, respectively—Australia does not have such a celebration. Australians only half jokingly express a bit of discomfort celebrating the arrival of convicts, especially when they displaced the Aborigines. Almost as undesirable to them is the suggestion that they celebrate January 1, the date when the first parliament was seated, because they do not perceive politicians as being much better than criminals.

Because of its British heritage and its current position as part of the British Commonwealth, Australia is essentially Western in its government, economy, and policies. It faces many of the same problems that Western nations face, but it also has its own unique culture and ways of thinking.

The Sydney Opera House, on the shore of Sydney Harbor, has become a symbol of modern Australia.

AUSTRALIA AND NEW ZEALAND

I. AUSTRALIA
   A. STATES ON THE GREAT DIVIDING RANGE
   B. THE CENTRAL LOWLANDS
   C. STATES ON THE WESTERN PLATEAU

II NEW ZEALAND
   A. HISTORICAL BACKGROUND
   B. GEOGRAPHIC DIVISIONS

The rest of the textbook explores the continent of Australia, its neighbor New Zealand, and the two most remote regions of the earth—**Oceania** and Antarctica. Hidden by the broad Pacific Ocean, the many islands of Oceania were probably among the last lands settled by Noah's descendants. When the Europeans began exploring the islands in the late eighteenth century, they discovered an interesting variety of isolated peoples who had not heard the gospel. Missionaries rejoiced when those people responded openly to the gospel.

Australia and New Zealand Fast Facts

Flag	Country	Capital	Area (sq. mi.)	Pop. (M)	Pop. Density (per sq. mi.)	Per Capita GDP ($US)	Life Span
	Australia	Canberra	2,967,893	20.09	7	$30,700	80.39
	New Zealand	Wellington	103,737	4.04	39	$23,200	78.66

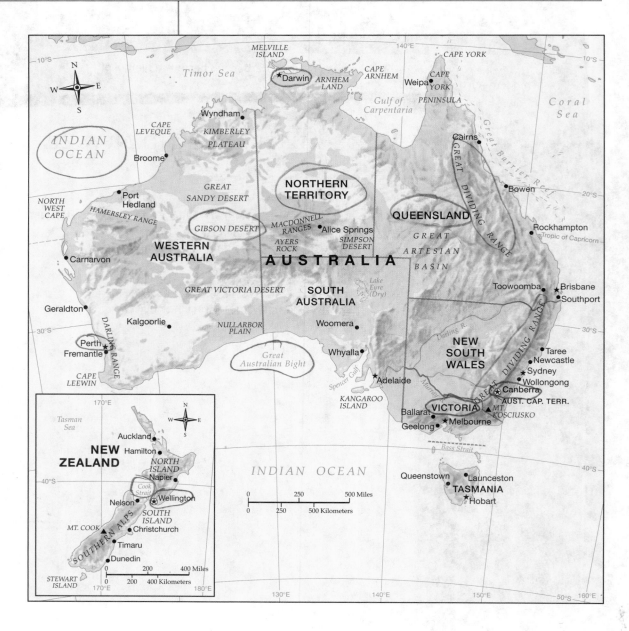

English settlers also discovered rich soil and grassland on the islands of New Zealand and on the continent of Australia. There they planted a European culture and built a society very similar to their home on the other side of the world.

I. AUSTRALIA

Australia is often referred to as "the land down under" because it lies on the opposite side of the earth from Europe and North America and in the Southern Hemisphere, where the seasons are opposite of those in the Northern Hemisphere. For example, Australian families celebrate Christmas with picnics and other outdoor activities in the middle of the hot summer.

Australia is unusual in many other ways. It is the smallest and flattest continent. Its highest peak is less than half the height of peaks on the other continents. Australia is the driest inhabited continent, with an average annual rainfall of only seventeen inches. As an "island" continent, Australia is the only inhabited continent with no land bridge to another continent.

Australia has many exotic animals that are found nowhere else. The best known are the kangaroos, which raise their young in a pouch on the mother's belly and thrive in forest and plain alike. There are many species of kangaroos, ranging in size from the tiny muskrat kangaroo to the giant red kangaroo, which grows taller than a man and can hop thirty miles per hour.

The continent is also home to some peculiar birds. It has the second- and third-largest birds in the world—the emu and the cassowary. Like the world's largest bird, the ostrich, these birds cannot fly. The beautiful lyrebird has an amazing ability to mimic as many as forty different calls. Perhaps the most famous Australian bird, however, is the kookaburra, whose fiendish "laugh" is a familiar sound in the cities.

This kangaroo family seems to be posing for the photographer.

The Kookaburra

The kookaburra is a large (up to 18 in. long) and noisy bird that lives on the islands of Australia, Tasmania, and New Guinea. It is a member of the kingfisher family. Its cry sounds like human laughter. Kookaburras are carnivores, eating large insects, small reptiles, and amphibians, but they don't drink any water, getting all they need from their food.

The Platypus

This odd creature looks as though it might have been assembled by a committee. It is a furry freshwater mammal that lays eggs and has a tail like a beaver, a bill and webbed feet like a duck, a streamlined body like an otter, and a spur on both of its hind legs that injects venom into its victims. Like a hamster, it stores food in cheek pouches until it is ready to eat it. The platypus lives in lakes and rivers on the east coast of Australia.

THE KOALA AND THE EUCALYPTUS TREE

Large forests of eucalyptus trees grow in Australia, especially along the east coast, and the koala, Australia's most-loved marsupial, dwells in them. Resembling a furry teddy bear, the koala gets all of its water and nourishment from eucalyptus leaves without ever having to descend to the ground. Fur traders once killed koalas in large numbers, but they are now protected by law.

Eucalyptus trees are also useful for medicinal and aromatic purposes. Its leaves are especially useful in treating colds, flu, bronchitis, muscle and joint stiffness, and some skin infections.

The Australian National Coat of Arms incorporates the symbols of all the states on the shield held by a kangaroo and an emu.

Australia has many unique plants, too. In all, thirteen thousand plant species grow there and nowhere else in the world. Eucalyptus trees are the most common type of tree in Australia. There are six hundred varieties, ranging from dwarfs in the dry interior to three-hundred-foot giants in the northern rain forests—the tallest hardwoods on earth. The only other important tree is the acacia, which is pictured on the national coat of arms beneath an emu and kangaroo. Early settlers called acacia trees **wattles** because they wove, or "wattled," the trees together to build frames for their mud homes. English settlers also called the tall hardwood acacia trees "gums" because the sap dulled their axes.

Australia is unique for another reason. It was the last continent to be settled by Europeans. The first British colonists did not arrive in Australia until nearly two hundred years after Jamestown was founded in Virginia. In fact, Americans were voting on the U.S. Constitution the same year that British settlers arrived in Australia.

Australia is still the most sparsely populated of the inhabited continents, and it is the only continent united under one national flag. In slightly more than two hundred years, pioneers created a thriving, industrialized nation with six proud states, each symbolized in the center of Australia's coat of arms.

Recently, however, Australia's economy has grown more slowly than those of some Asian neighbors, especially Japan and South Korea. The country's population makeup has also changed. Asian immigrants continue to increase, and about one in four Australians has a non-English-speaking heritage. Japan is now Australia's biggest trading partner, and Australia is becoming more a part of the Asian world.

STATES ON THE GREAT DIVIDING RANGE

Australia is divided into three broad geographic regions: the Great Dividing Range along the east coast; the Central Lowlands just west of the Great Dividing Range; and the Western Plateau, which is the western two-thirds of Australia.

The **Great Dividing Range** is a rugged complex of low mountains, plateaus, and hills that run parallel to the east coast of Australia. Although they are low, the mountains have played a central role in the development of the continent, much as the Appalachian Mountains influenced the history of the American colonies. Two of Australia's six states—New South Wales and Victoria—are located in eastern Australia, astride the Great Dividing Range.

The mountains influence the weather patterns of the whole continent. As winds blow off the warm ocean in the east, the moist air rises and cools over the mountains, depositing moisture by frequent rains. Several short, swift rivers flow down the eastern slope of the Great Dividing Range and empty into the ocean. The narrow coastal plains receive much more water than the vast, dry lands west of the mountains.

The first British settlements on the continent were near the rich alluvial soils of the coastal rivers. Australia's major cities and industrial areas arose on its eastern seaboard, just as America's first industries developed on the Atlantic seaboard.

NEW SOUTH WALES

Captain James Cook (1728–79), a famous British explorer, was the first European to map the east coast of Australia. He found fertile soil and one of the continent's few deep harbors at a place he named **Botany Bay**. Later, that harbor became the site of the first English settlement on the continent.

First Settlement at Sydney—At first, the king of England had little interest in this far-off land. A revolt by the American colonies

Captain James Cook was the discoverer of Australia and other islands of Oceania.

LET'S GO EXPLORING

POPULATION DENSITY OF AUSTRALIA AND NEW ZEALAND

1. How many city areas have a population density over 60 per square mile?

2. Which large city is farthest from any other?

3. What is the average population density of the interior of Australia?

4. Which island of New Zealand has the largest area of low population density (under 2 per square mile)?

🔅 Find the names of the four uninhabited regions.

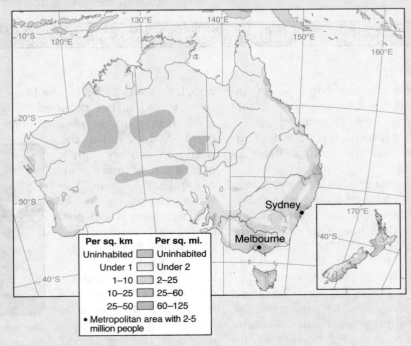

Per sq. km		Per sq. mi.
Uninhabited		Uninhabited
Under 1		Under 2
1–10		2–25
10–25		25–60
25–50		60–125

• Metropolitan area with 2-5 million people

Australian Industrial Production

Australia has a diverse economy and is a major player in world industrial production, as the following list shows.

Material	Rank
Bauxite	1
Gold	1
Manganese	1
Iron ore	2
Lead	2
Nickel	2
Uranium	2
Coal	3
Tungsten	3
Zinc	3
Aluminum	5
Copper	5

in 1776, however, changed his view. No longer able to send prisoners to a prison colony in Georgia, England needed an alternative destination.

England selected New South Wales for its new prison colony. Captain Arthur Phillip, a retired naval officer, was appointed to lead the eleven ships of the "First Fleet" and to serve as governor of the new colony. After an arduous eight-month journey, the ships anchored in Botany Bay. On January 26, 1788, the captain hoisted the British flag and formally claimed the eastern half of the continent and the island of Tasmania. The territory was called New South Wales. Each year, Australians celebrate this date as Australia Day.

Of the one-thousand-plus initial settlers, 759 were convicts sentenced to "transportation." They included men, women, and children convicted of minor offenses, such as petty theft or failure to pay their debts. In the new colony, they were given an opportunity to pay off their debts by farming. The rest of the First Fleet consisted of about two hundred British soldiers, approximately thirty wives of soldiers, and a few children.

That small settlement, called **Sydney**, became the base for the exploration and settlement of Australia. Although prison ships stopped coming in 1868, the flow of settlers never stopped. Today, Sydney is Australia's largest city, with a population of more than 4.2 million, one-fifth of the nation's population. It is also Australia's chief manufacturing center and main port.

Mother of States—Like Virginia, the first colony in America, New South Wales became a "Mother of States" in Australia. Over the years, its land was carved up into new states and territories. Although the modern state of New South Wales is only fourth in total area among Australia's six states, it remains first in industry, shipping, and agriculture. Numerous factories dot the coastal plain, manufacturing products from textiles to tractors.

Unlike their British cousins, to whom rank and privilege are still important, Australians consider themselves equals. Australia was settled by hard-working families who scratched out a rough existence in the new country. The continent offered plenty of land for

SYDNEY

For a city that began as an unpromising and inauspicious penal colony, Sydney has experienced remarkable growth. It is now the largest city and the cultural heart of Australia.

The area of what became Sydney was originally inhabited by Aborigines. James Cook discovered Botany Bay, which is now a suburb of Sydney, in 1770. In 1788, Sydney was founded as a penal colony and was named after the British Home Secretary at the time, Thomas Townshend, Lord Sydney. By 1847, however, the city had outgrown its penal colony reputation; only 3.2 percent of the population was convicts. The first of several gold rushes occurred there in 1851, bringing an influx of immigrants. Sydney began the twentieth century with a population of more than one million. Among the world's cities today, it has the second-highest percentage of immigrants.

Sydney is the capital of New South Wales and is a major tourist destination. It served as host city for the 2000 Olympics. Its residents, known as "Sydneysiders," take great pride in the most widely recognized architectural feature of their city—the Sydney Opera House.

The Sydney Opera House and the Sydney Harbor Bridge are icons of that large and beautiful metropolis.

SYDNEY OPERA HOUSE

Many consider Sydney Opera House the most beautiful building in the world. Built on a point that juts out into Sydney Harbor, the opera house looks like a huge ship that is flying into the harbor with open sails. The "sails" are high partial domes.

A Danish architect provided the winning design in a worldwide competition. The original design called for wide sails, but they proved impossible to make. The engineering problems were finally overcome after thousands of hours of computer simulations. Unfortunately, the $7 million budget blossomed to $100 million.

Queen Elizabeth presided at the formal opening on October 20, 1973.

One million ceramic tiles, specially made in Sweden to remain bright white and free of fungus, cover the concrete sails. The interior design mixes 67,000 square feet of Gothic tinted glass with space-age steel ribs and concrete fans. There are five performing halls, a theater, and two restaurants. The theater's wool curtains are the largest in the world. In addition, the

world's largest mechanical organ—consisting of 10,500 pipes—sits in one of the concert halls.

everyone. Cities were not built up; they were built out. Tall buildings and apartments are rare. Nearly three of every four Australian families own homes. The pace of life is relaxed and informal.

Blue Mountains and the Australian Alps—Within view of the coastal cities is the Great Dividing Range. The mountains west of Sydney are called the Blue Mountains. Although they look blue to residents of the city forty miles away, they are actually covered with green eucalyptus trees, which secrete a bluish oil into the air. The Blue Mountains are actually a low plateau that has been eroded by water. Visitors there enjoy exploring the Jenolan Caves, the largest cave system on the continent.

South of the Blue Mountains is another part of the Great Dividing Range, called the Australian Alps. These snow-covered mountains are much higher than the Blues. The highest range in the Australian Alps is the Snowy Mountains, where **Mount Kosciusko** (KAHZ ee US koh)—Australia's highest point—rises 7,316 feet above sea level. Covered with snow for half the year, it is the area's main attraction for skiers and hikers. It is also the site made popular by the famous poem by Australian Andrew Barton Paterson, "The Man from Snowy River."

Jumpbucks in the Interior—Just west of the mountains are fertile grasslands much like the American prairie. Wheat fields are common. But that area of Australia is most famous for its **jumpbucks** (sheep), which are everywhere—on the coast, around the mountain slopes, and in the dry interior. There are ten jumpbucks for every Australian. Australia is the world's leading producer of wool and mutton, and New South Wales is the leading producer in Australia, turning out approximately 40 percent of the nation's wool.

Australia is becoming less dependent on "the sheep's back," however, as manufacturing increases. The mines near Broken Hill on the western border of the state are major producers of silver, zinc, and lead.

The Snowy Mountain Scheme

In an effort to bring more water to the thirsty interior, the Australian government began an ambitious program in 1949 to redirect the water that rushed eastward from the mountains to the ocean. The Snowy Mountain Scheme, as the program was known, consisted of fifteen large dams and one hundred miles of tunnels. They diverted the water westward through the mountains to the farms and sheep stations in the interior.

Australian Agricultural Production

Australia has always been a leading producer of agricultural products. The following list shows Australia's world ranking in production of selected agricultural products:

Product	Rank
Lupins (like peas)	1
Mutton	1
Broad beans	4
Lentils	4
Oats	4
Beef	5
Barley	6
Peas	6
Wheat	6

Canberra—During the nineteenth century, arguments over trade and taxes hurt the six independent colonies on the continent. Late in the century, the militaristic emperor of Germany began planting colonies in the Pacific region and threatened the British colonies. The six colonies of Australia agreed to unite as a federation in 1901. As part of the settlement, the two largest states agreed to build a new seat of government midway between Sydney and Melbourne. New South Wales set aside nine hundred square miles for the capital.

The government sponsored an international competition to determine the best possible design for the new city. Of the 137 designs submitted, the design of architect Walter Griffin of Chicago won. He moved to Australia in 1913 to direct the construction of the capital. In 1927, the Australian Parliament met there for the first time. The federal government ran the Australian Capital Territory until 1989, when it was granted self-government. The capital city is named **Canberra** after the Aboriginal word *canburry*, meaning "meeting place."

Like the United States, Australia adopted a written constitution and a federal system of state governments. Like Canada, Australia has a constitutional monarchy with a parliament and claims the British monarch. The British monarch is the head of state and is represented by a governor-general in Parliament. The monarch also approves six governors, one for each state government. The Labor Party, organized in 1891, has established a socialist government that closely controls businesses, wages, and working conditions.

VICTORIA

Victoria is located on the southeast corner of Australia. In 1851, it split from New South Wales and became a separate state. The two states have been competitors ever since. Although Victoria is Australia's smallest mainland state, it is home to approximately one-fourth of Australia's population.

Nearly three-fourths of Victoria's population is located in **Melbourne**, the state capital and the nation's second-largest city. Originally, Melbourne was a prosperous mining port; however, its remote location has hurt its competition with Sydney for trade and commerce. It is too far away from world shipping routes. Nonetheless, its factories still play an important role in the Australian economy.

The city of Melbourne is the most "English" of Australia's cities. Stately buildings and beautiful parks display statues of prominent Australians. The world-renowned Victoria National Gallery is home to the finest collection of art in the nation.

Melbourne is also the sports center of Australia. The city hosts the Davis Cup tennis finals, international cricket matches, and Australia's richest horse race. Australians are able to enjoy outdoor recreation year-round in their mild climate.

Melbourne is within sight of the Great Dividing Range, which curls around Victoria's coast. The mountains near Melbourne contain great mineral wealth. In 1851, the discovery of gold at Ballarat started a gold rush, which increased the state's population sevenfold. After the rich veins of gold were mined out, the city

Melbourne, the capital of the state of Victoria, is the nation's second-largest city.

became a major railroad junction and Australia's most populous inland city.

Victoria is home to Australia's largest oil field and a major natural gas field off the coast. Coal is also mined in the state. The Latrobe Valley holds the world's largest deposit of **lignite** (brown coal). Lignite is the lowest grade of coal, however, because its high moisture produces little heat but a lot of smoke. Three vast power plants in Latrobe Valley produce nearly 90 percent of Victoria's electricity.

SECTION QUIZ

1. List six ways that Australia is an unusual continent.
2. What mountain system runs along Australia's eastern coast?
3. What is the highest peak in Australia?
4. Where did the first European settlers land in Australia? What year did they arrive?
5. What are jumpbucks?
6. What is the capital of Australia, and where is it located?
- ⚬ Why do most Australians live on the east coast?

THE CENTRAL LOWLANDS

On the other side of the Great Dividing Range is the continent's dry interior, where rain is scarce. Runoff water from the Great Dividing Range is vitally important. This low area just west of the mountains is known as the **Central Lowlands**.

LET'S GO EXPLORING

LAND USE OF AUSTRALIA AND NEW ZEALAND

1. What type of farming occurs in the tropics?
2. What is the most widespread type of land use in Australia and New Zealand?
3. What is the main commercial grain grown in Australia?
4. What two types of farming appear to be common in the Murray River basin?
- ⚬ Find the geographic names of the four main primitive hunting grounds (of the Aborigines).

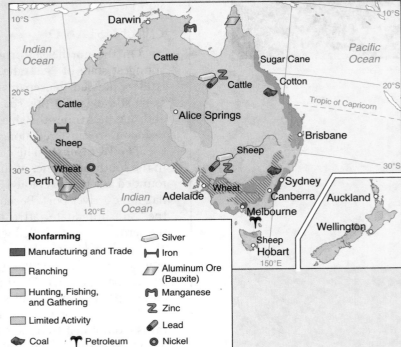
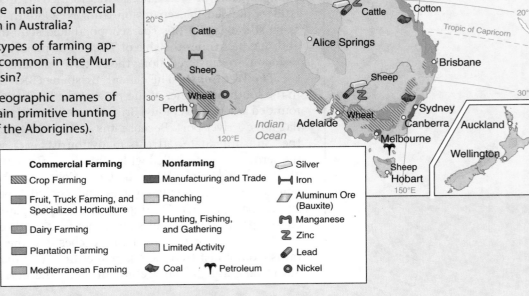

Paddle steamers ply the Murray River, Australia's longest river.

The Tasmanian Devil

The Tasmanian devil is a mammal that is now found only on the island of Tasmania, although it once also lived on the mainland of Australia. Tasmanian devils prey on small- to medium-sized animals and can devour an entire carcass, including the bones, in a very short time. (Despite what one might see in cartoons, they do not twirl around like a tornado.)

Waters flowing down the Great Dividing Range form long, leisurely rivers in the flat, inland terrain. The map on page 542 shows the three places where these rivers drain: the Gulf of Carpentaria in the tropical north, **Lake Eyre** (AYER) in the center, and the Great Australian Bight in the south.

Most rivers in the Central Lowlands dry up during the dry season. The major exception is the sixteen-hundred-mile-long **Murray River** and its tributaries, the most important water system on the continent. These rivers provide a steady supply of water for farms and pastures in the south. A large wheat crop grows in the wide plains of the Murray drainage basin. Many varieties of fruit also grow in the fertile river valley that forms the border between Victoria and New South Wales.

TASMANIA

Off the coast of Victoria is the island of **Tasmania** (taz MAYN ee uh), Australia's smallest and least populous state. Tasmania has so many apple orchards that it is sometimes called the Apple Isle. Apple trees, introduced in 1788, now produce Australia's most important fruit crop. The best orchards are located in the Huon Valley about twenty miles southwest of the capital, Hobart. In addition to exporting apples worldwide, the state also produces pears, berries, and potatoes.

The narrow Bass Strait separates Tasmania from Victoria. Like Victoria, Tasmania has low mountains and a pleasant marine-west-coast climate. Blessed with abundant rainfall, Tasmania is home to magnificent rain forests and powerful waterfalls. The fierce Tasmanian devil (a marsupial) lives in the rugged central plateau, which remains sparsely settled. Most Tasmanians inhabit the fertile coastal lowlands. The availability of cheap hydroelectric power has attracted many industries, such as pulp and paper works, a zinc refinery, and aluminum smelting. Because of its isolation, Hobart's population is small. Unlike the busy cities on the mainland, Hobart enjoys a quiet, slow pace of life.

QUEENSLAND

On the northeast corner of the continent is Queensland, the youngest state of Australia. It was formed in 1859 when Queenslanders pressed for separation from New South Wales. A frontier spirit still exists in this sparsely populated state that is nearly two-and-one-half times the size of Texas. The majority of Queensland's residents are clustered along the eastern seaboard.

The Wet Coast—The capital, **Brisbane** (BRIHZ bun), is located in the southeast corner of the state on the Brisbane River. Originally founded as a prison colony, Brisbane grew rapidly to become Australia's largest river port. Because it is so near the tropics, the capital of the "Sunshine State" attracts many tourists each winter. Brisbane's numerous parks are filled with subtropical flowers.

South of the capital is the Gold Coast, which extends to New South Wales. Spectacular waves and beautiful beaches make it a surfer's paradise. The Darling Downs, a fertile plain in the southeast corner, produces pineapples and other fruits and vegetables.

The coast north of Brisbane reaches into the tropics. Frequent rains from moist trade winds make this Australia's wettest region. Sugar cane and cotton are grown along the narrow coastal plain.

THE GREAT BARRIER REEF

Just off the northeast shore of Queensland is the largest coral formation in the world. The **Great Barrier Reef** stretches for 1,250 miles—as far north as Papua New Guinea—about

This aerial view shows part of the Great Barrier Reef near Cairns, Queensland.

the length of the entire West Coast of the United States. The "barrier" makes travel hazardous for ships sailing to the coast. Even Captain Cook, the discoverer of the reef, ran aground on it and was nearly shipwrecked. Because of the navigational hazards, numerous lighthouses were constructed, two of which are still in operation.

This underwater garden is actually 2,800–3,400 separate reefs. It includes more than 600 islands, including 300 coral cays (KEYS), 213 unvegetated cays, 43 vegetated cays, and 44 low wooded cays. Similar to tropical rain forests, the reef is home to a large variety of life forms, including more than 1,500 kinds of fish, 400 types of coral, 4,000 kinds of mollusks, and at least two endangered species, the sea cow and the large green turtle. In fact, the reef harbors more types of life than any other place on earth.

Such variety provides unique research opportunities for many types of scientists. In the 1960s, scientists began warning that the reef was disappearing. It was under attack by a poisonous starfish that devoured the polyps by the millions. Also, insecticides from farms onshore were washing into the ocean and destroying the coral. Some fertilizer companies were even mining the reef for limestone. To protect the reef, the Australian government in 1975 set aside most of it as a national park. Hundreds of thousands of people visit Queensland every year to see the reef.

Thousands of divers each year enjoy the beauty of the fish and coral on the Great Barrier Reef.

The northern tip of the east coast, Cape York Peninsula, is extremely hot and humid. Few people live in this tropical area. Climbing "tree kangaroos" feed on the leaves of the jungle canopy. Off the northeast coast of Queensland is the Great Barrier Reef. (See the boxed text for more information.)

The Dry Interior—To the west, beyond the low mountains and hills of the Great Dividing Range, the land becomes increasingly dry and grassy. Cowboys, called stockmen, live on large cattle stations (Australia's word for ranches). Some stations are the size of Delaware. More beef is produced in Queensland than in any other state. Australia exports 65 percent of the beef it produces, more than any other country in the world. Most of it is shipped to eager markets in the Far East.

Queensland also has great mineral deposits. During the gold rush of 1867, thousands of men poured into the state in search of instant wealth. Today, bauxite (aluminum ore) is mined on Cape York Peninsula, near Weipa (WEEP ah). North of Brisbane are large deposits of bituminous coal. Lead, zinc, silver, and copper are mined near the interior town of Mt. Isa (EYE zuh), Queensland's largest industrial complex.

Through Christian Eyes

To further protect the Great Barrier Reef ecosystem, the Australian government recently set apart more than nine thousand square miles in the park as a "no-fishing zone." What do you think of this idea? How does it relate to man's dominion of the earth? What are some other things that can be done to preserve the reef?

ARTESIAN WELLS

The livestock in Queensland get most of their water from a vast underground reservoir called the Great Artesian Basin. The landscape is dotted with **artesian** (ahr TEE zhun) **wells**, where water bubbles up to the surface without the need for pumps. Although the water is too salty for crops and people, cattle drink it without any problem.

As water flows west off the Great Dividing Range, some of it seeps underground into the Great Artesian Basin. This water moves through a layer of underground rock called an **aquifer** (AK wih fer, "water bearer"). The Great Artesian Basin is the largest reserve of underground water in the world.

There are two basic kinds of aquifers. The most common are *uncon-*

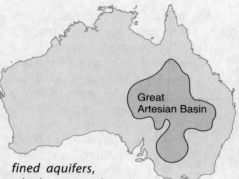

Great Artesian Basin

fined aquifers, which occur where the layer of rock above the aquifer is permeable, allowing water to seep through. Permeable layers include gravel, sand, clay, and loose rock. If a well is dug to this aquifer, the water must be pumped to the surface.

The Great Artesian Basin, on the other hand, is a *confined aquifer*. It has an impermeable layer of rock above it that traps the water and keeps it from rising to the surface. As the water pressure builds, it pushes out through breaks in the surface. Natural artesian springs result. When someone digs a hole into a confined aquifer, water pushes up to the surface, creating an artesian well.

Impermeable rock
Artesian well
Aquifer

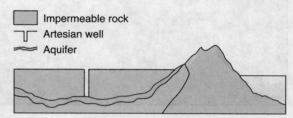

SECTION QUIZ

1. Why is runoff from the Great Dividing Range so important to the Central Lowlands?
2. What is Australia's smallest and least populous state?
3. What is the only island state in Australia?
4. What is a station?
5. What are the leading products of Queensland?
  ⚲ What is happening to the Great Barrier Reef that should concern every Australian?

STATES OF THE WESTERN PLATEAU

The western two-thirds of Australia is the dry, flat **Western Plateau**. Most of this shield is desert or semiarid grassland. The only relief is a few scattered mountain ranges. Two states, South Australia and Western Australia, and the Northern Territory were carved out of this plateau.

SOUTH AUSTRALIA

The south-central state of South Australia, colonized in 1836, was the only state not settled by convicts. It is shaped like a keystone along the waters of the **Great Australian Bight**. The state is divided into two distinct geographic regions: the populous coast and the arid interior.

The Mediterranean Coast—The coastal portion of South Australia supports 98 percent of the state's population. Much of the coast enjoys an excellent climate similar to that of the Mediterranean. Cold Antarctic currents in the Great Australian Bight keep the land dry in the summer, but steady rains fall in the winter.

Adelaide (AD el AYD), the capital, has an ideal harbor protected by Kangaroo Island from the violent willy-willies (windstorms) that blow on the Great Australian Bight. The city, which is laid out with wide streets and many parks, boasts a warm climate and a relaxed atmosphere.

East of Adelaide is some of the nation's most productive land. The Murray River system drains into this part of the state and empties into the Great Australian Bight. The lush Barossa (buh ROH suh) Valley, thirty miles northeast of Adelaide, is known for its wine. The valley was originally settled by Lutheran immigrants from Germany seeking religious freedom.

After World War II, South Australia experienced unprecedented industrial expansion. Today, the state leads the nation in lumber, shipbuilding, and smelting. Two large plants near Adelaide produce Australia's first native car, the Holden, which was introduced in 1948.

Lake Eyre

Australia's largest lake is located in the northeast corner of South Australia. **Lake Eyre** is the lowest point on the continent, fifty-two feet below sea level. Most rivers of the Central Lowlands, including the Great Artesian Basin, drain into this lake. These rivers—and the lake itself—are dry most of the time. A few times each century, heavy rains fill the rivers and lake. Within a period of two years, however, the lake returns to a barren salt bed.

1954 Holden

Holden Monaro Series II CV8

LET'S GO EXPLORING

CLIMATES OF AUSTRALIA AND NEW ZEALAND

1. Which coast has a dry climate?
2. Which coast has a tropical climate?
3. Which coast has a mediterranean climate?
4. What climate appears directly west of the Great Dividing Range?
5. What is the most widespread climate in Australia?
6. What climate is found in New Zealand?
   - What is the climate in each of the six state capitals of Australia?

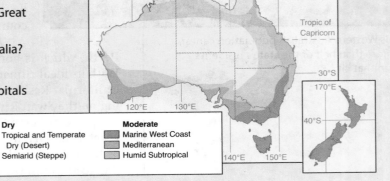

Tropical Rainy
- Tropical Wet (Rain Forest)
- Tropical Wet and Dry (Savanna)

Dry
- Tropical and Temperate Dry (Desert)
- Semiarid (Steppe)

Moderate
- Marine West Coast
- Mediterranean
- Humid Subtropical

AUSTRALIA'S TRANSCONTINENTAL RAILROAD

Early in the twentieth century, Australians envisioned a railroad that would stretch across the continent from Adelaide in the south to Darwin in the north. The first portion was completed in 1927, but it stopped in Alice Springs, almost in the middle of the continent. It took about three-quarters of a century, but the rest of the transcontinental railroad was finally completed. The inaugural trip was made in January 2004. The railroad is the longest north-south line in the world. The trip takes about 47 hours, but it facilitates getting goods from South Australia to ports in the Northern Territory and from there to the Asian markets. It also speeds Asian imports from those ports to the consumers in South Australia.

Australia also has a second transcontinental railroad that runs from Adelaide to Perth across the Nullarbor Plain. Completed in 1970, it includes the longest stretch of straight track in the world.

The inaugural trip on Australia's new north-south transcontinental railroad between Adelaide and Darwin took place in January 2004.

The Outback—The sparsely populated areas beyond the coastal cities of Australia are collectively known as the **outback**. Life is hard and lonely for the stockmen and miners who live there. They tell many tall tales about the "blowies" (flies), sandstorms, and other common features of the outback. Although every state on the continent includes part of the outback, South Australia is known as "the gateway to the outback."

The two basic activities of the outback are mining and ranching. South Australia's outback is especially famous for its mineral wealth. The discovery of opals in 1915 attracted thousands to Coober Pedy ("hole in the ground"), from which most of the world's opals come. The first "diggers" not only dug holes in search of riches but also made their homes in the ground to escape the intense heat. Even with the invention of air conditioning, many residents still prefer to live underground.

WESTERN AUSTRALIA

Western Australia is Australia's largest but most sparsely populated state. Three-fourths of the people live in the southwest corner, where good land and tall evergreen forests abound. Blessed with a mild mediterranean climate, this region has beautiful wild flowers, many of which are unique to Australia. In the spring, tourists and residents flock to the countryside to view fields ablaze with color.

Perth—The capital of Western Australia is **Perth**, which is home to more than half of the state's population. With its ideal climate, Perth is often compared to cities in Southern California. Residents enjoy swimming at sandy beaches and boating on the Swan River. West of the business section is King's Park, the pride of Perth. It includes one thousand acres of natural bush vegetation. Driving through the park provides a spectacular view of the city, with the Indian Ocean to one's back and the Darling Range ahead in the distance.

Perth is Western Australia's population center, with more than half of the state's residents living in that city.

Perth is more than one thousand miles from the nearest large city, Adelaide. Not until 1970 was a transcontinental railroad completed that connected the two coasts. It crosses the treeless Nullarbor (NUHL uh BAWR) Plain, the flattest landform on earth. The name *Nullarbor* comes from two Latin words, *nulla* and *arbor*, which mean "no tree." Engineers laid the longest stretch of straight railroad track in the world—297 miles long—in that region.

The Inhospitable Interior—The dry and inhospitable climate did little to attract early settlers to the treeless interior of Western Australia. The discovery of gold in the late nineteenth century, however, changed everything. Gold mining camps sprang up east of Perth around the town of Kalgoorlie (kal GOOR lee), along the famed "Golden Mile." Veins of rich ore were mined to a depth of four thousand feet. As the gold began running out, nickel became the major source of revenue. Bauxite is also mined in the Darling Range.

One of the richest iron ore reserves in the world was discovered in the **Hamersley Range**. Towns, mining facilities, and railroads were built to exploit these resources. The ore is moved by rail to Port Hedland on the coast. Port Hedland ships more tons of freight than any other port in Australia, except Sydney.

The central part of Western Australia is covered with deserts. The Great Victoria Desert, the Gibson Desert, and the Great Sandy Desert combine to make up the second-largest desert area in the world. The deserts gradually give way to grasslands in the northern tropics and in the south near Perth. Large cattle and sheep stations are common in those areas.

The hands on this cattle station look much like cowboys of the American West as they struggle to subdue a young cow.

NORTHERN TERRITORY

The Northern Territory is located at the heart of the desolate outback. Outside the capital of Darwin, the average population density is only one person for every five square miles of land. This territory, nearly the size of Alaska, is administered by the federal government.

The Tropical Coast—Most of the Northern Territory is located in the tropics. Tropical rain forests abound along the northern coast, gradually becoming grasslands and then desert farther inland. Trade

AYERS ROCK

The monotony of the outback is broken by the majestic **Ayers Rock**, the world's largest monolith, or freestanding rock. Jokingly referred to as the largest pebble in the world, it rises 1,134 feet above the surrounding desert. The rock forms an oval that is one and a half miles wide and four miles long. The monolith, composed of a kind of rock called conglomerate, changes color throughout the day. The early morning sun makes it look orange to deep red; it changes to violet and blue later in the day.

Erosion has cut deep gullies and basins in the rock that run from the top to the bottom. Rare desert rains create raging falls. The base of the rock is pocked with shallow caves that contain many Aboriginal paintings of scenes from the Dreamtime (see page 556). Aborigines consider this great rock sacred. They call it Uluru.

Ayers Rock cannot be missed in the flat Australian landscape.

winds bring heavy rains to the coast in the summer season, called "The Wet," but dry monsoon winds blow from the interior desert in the winter. Cyclones are common.

Nearly half the territory's population lives in Darwin, on the coast. Tourists fly to Darwin as the starting point for tours into the interior. Darwin is the only Australian city ever attacked by foreigners. During World War II, Japanese bombers based in New Guinea attacked the city.

The Interior—The primary industry in the outback is mining. Scattered mountain ranges hold considerable mineral wealth, including gold, manganese, and iron ore. The world's greatest deposit of bauxite was discovered on Arnhem Land. Australia also has the largest known reserves of uranium.

The second major industry is cattle ranching. One cattle ranch covers six thousand square miles—an area larger than the state of Connecticut. Families in the outback sometimes live fifty miles from the nearest town and fifteen miles from their nearest neighbor. Obtaining medical care is difficult. To help solve this problem, doctors make "house calls" by plane, and children attend school over two-way radio. The Royal Flying Doctor's Service and the School of the Air operate out of the central town of Alice Springs (often called "The Alice"), providing services to remote stations throughout the territory.

In the southeast corner of the Northern Territory lies the **Simpson Desert**, sometimes called the Red Center of Australia. No one, not even the hardiest stockman, lives there. Red sand is piled into waves that can rise as high as 100 feet and stretch for up to 180 miles. The red color comes from rusted iron in the sand.

Aboriginal boys are taught to be skilled hunters and fishermen.

The Aborigines—When the first British settlers landed in Australia in 1788, about five hundred tribes of dark-skinned people were scattered throughout the continent and nearby islands. These **Aborigines** (AB ohr IJ uh NEES) had migrated from Asia long ago. (The term *aborigine* refers to the earliest known settlers of a region. It comes from Latin words meaning "from the beginning.")

Although they spoke more than three hundred languages and lived in both the rain forests and the desert, the Aborigines shared the same basic culture. Each tribe was nomadic, constantly moving in search of food. Their only domestic animal was the dingo, a type of dog, and their weapons were the spear and the boomerang. One of the common foods in the bush was a fat, white grub that the Aborigines ate raw.

Like the American Indians, the Aborigines had developed a detailed knowledge of plants, animals, and natural cycles. They believed that spiritual beings created the world in an era they called the "Dreamtime." These beings became a part of nature and mankind. The superstitious religion of the Aborigines guided every aspect of their lives, including when they moved and where they camped. Their world-famous bark paintings depict scenes from their myths.

As the colonists' need for land grew, they drove the Aborigines away from the fertile river valleys and into the barren backcountry. Some were killed, and many others died as a result of diseases introduced by the white settlers. In time, the newcomers considered the Aborigines to be a passing race, to be left alone

An example of Aboriginal art near Darwin

to die out on reservations. Christian missionaries, however, had compassion and worked with the Aborigines while showing them the gospel.

About 366,500 Aborigines exist today, approximately 1.9 percent of the Australian population. In the 1960s, Australian leaders responded to the Aborigines' call for civil rights and a return of ancestral land. They gave the Aborigines control of large tracts of land in northern and central Australia. The government has kept control of all mineral rights, however, even within the Aboriginal reservations.

The land-use map on page 549 shows where Aborigines continue to live as hunters and gatherers, like their ancestors. Only a few thousand of them live that way, however. Most Aborigines work on the large sheep and cattle stations in the outback of Australia's five mainland states. Three-quarters of the Aborigines are part white and have fully adopted Western ways. On occasions called "walkabouts," some Aborigines return for a period of time to the bush life of their ancestors. Court decisions and legislation sparked by Aborigines' land claims have led to the curtailment of development by some mining companies. The full impact of such decisions is not yet known.

The Aborigines were experts at throwing many kinds of boomerangs, each for a different specific purpose.

SECTION QUIZ

1. Why do so few people live on the Western Plateau?
2. What type of climate is common on the coast of South Australia?
3. What are the two main industries in the outback?
4. What important product is mined in the Hamersley Range?
5. Who were the native people of Australia?
- ⚲ List five similarities between the Australian Aborigines and the American Indians.

II. NEW ZEALAND

New Zealand is a beautiful island country isolated from the rest of the world. Its nearest neighbor, Australia, is 1,200 miles to the west, across the stormy Tasman Sea. New Zealand has many similarities to Australia, including a British heritage and a similar history. However, New Zealand lacks the land area (it is about the size of Colorado) and mineral wealth of its continental neighbor. For its economic survival, New Zealand relies almost solely on agricultural exports. Meat, wool, and dairy products account for nearly half of what it sells abroad. New Zealand is one of the world's largest exporters of butter, cheese, and cross-bred wool.

New Zealand enjoys a marine-west-coast climate similar to that of Tasmania. Prevailing winds blow off the Tasman Sea, bringing warm, moist air that showers the islands 150 days of the year. Because clouds are so common, the native islanders called their home Aotearoa (AH oh tay ah ROH ah), or "land of the long white cloud."

Like Australia, New Zealand has unusual flora and fauna. Its variety of trees is especially noteworthy. More than 112 species live in

A boomerang must be thrown in just the right way to be effective, as this boomerang master demonstrates.

The kiwi is a flightless nocturnal bird that burrows in the ground and sniffs out its food with nostrils on the end of its beak. These endangered birds mate for life and live as long as thirty years.

the broadleaf evergreen forests that cover one-fourth of the country. The unique kauri (KOW ree) is New Zealand's largest tree. European shipbuilders once cut them down to make masts for their ships. Unfortunately, kauri take nearly one thousand years to reach their full height.

New Zealand has some unusual native animals too, most of them birds. Several flightless birds once thrived on the island. Monster birds, called moa, sometimes grew to thirteen feet in height. Their kick could kill a man, but they are now extinct. The smaller kiwi is New Zealand's national bird. About the size of a chicken, the kiwi has no wings, an extremely long beak, and feathers that look like hair. New Zealanders are nicknamed "kiwis."

HISTORICAL BACKGROUND
THE FIRST INHABITANTS

The **Maori** (MOW ree), a brown-skinned people from the islands of Polynesia north of New Zealand, were the first humans to discover the islands. They arrived on magnificent warships made of hollowed logs. At first, they lived by hunting and fishing. After the "moa hunters" hunted the moas to extinction, they learned to clear forests and plant crops. They also became brilliant woodcarvers using stone tools.

Constant wars and superstitious rituals were central to Maori life. It was not uncommon for them to eat their defeated foes. The Maori proved to be a difficult challenge for Abel Tasman, who discovered the islands in 1642 while searching for a fabled continent south of Australia. When Tasman attempted to land, the Maori killed several of his men. Tasman did not try to land again. In 1769, Captain James Cook landed and established relations with the Maori. He succeeded in mapping the coasts of the two main islands.

BRITISH SETTLERS

The first white settlers on the islands were escaped convicts from Australia and deserters from British ships. Whalers and seal hunters also built small stations along the coast to resupply their ships. Christian missionaries soon followed. English traders gave rum and guns to the Maori in return for flax, a strong fiber used for ropes. The introduction of guns led to bloody fighting among Maori tribes and between the Maori and the whites. The settlers also introduced diseases to which the Maori had no resistance, greatly reducing their population.

White settlers asked England to annex New Zealand and bring the law and order it needed so badly. On February 6, 1840, a group of Maori chiefs signed the Treaty of Waitangi in which they recognized the British monarch as their sovereign. In return, the Maori received full property rights over their land. They also agreed to sell land only to the British crown. New Zealanders celebrate the signing of the treaty each year in a holiday called National Day.

Tensions remained high on the North Island, where most of the Maori lived. Shiploads of settlers arrived and made illegal purchases. In 1845, opposition to land sales inspired a Maori uprising. This marked the start of the Land Wars. Much like the outnumbered

American Indians, the Maori put up a stiff, though hopeless, resistance. When war ended in 1872, their power was broken, and the government seized the land.

After the Maori Wars, the British colony grew rapidly. England gave it a large loan to attract one hundred thousand new settlers. The loan was also used to improve the transportation and communication systems. In 1872, the development of refrigerator ships enabled New Zealand to begin shipping meat to Europe. New Zealand has become one of the world's leading exporters of mutton. At New Zealand's request, Great Britain granted the colony dominion status in 1907.

THE GOVERNMENT TODAY

The government of New Zealand is similar to those of other independent nations that make up the British Commonwealth. The British crown is represented by a governor-general. The legislative authority is the parliament. New Zealand's parliament consists of one chamber called the House of Representatives. Every three years, members are elected to represent ninety-one general districts and four Maori districts.

Like Australia, New Zealand has a long history of government programs. In 1890, the Liberal Party began implementing a welfare system. In 1893, it became the first country to give women the right to vote. New Zealand's benevolent socialism resembled its counterparts in Europe. But by the 1980s it became obvious that the cost of welfare benefits was stifling initiative and driving businesses out of the country, so in 1985 the government began dismantling the socialist system, giving New Zealand one of the freest economies in the world.

GEOGRAPHIC DIVISIONS

NORTH ISLAND

New Zealand has two main islands and many smaller islands. **North Island** is slightly smaller than South Island, but it is home to twice as many people.

The Northern Peninsula—New Zealand has a reputation for scenic beauty and huge sheep stations. There are more than fifteen sheep for every New Zealander. More than 80 percent of the people live in cities. **Auckland**, New Zealand's largest city and chief seaport, has nearly a million people. It is located on a beautiful harbor on the northern peninsula. In addition to shipping much of the region's dairy, sheep, and timber products, this colorful city is also the country's chief industrial center. Because it has an international airport, Auckland is the point of entry and departure for New Zealand's many visitors.

In recent years, thousands of Pacific Islanders have come to Auckland seeking a better life. The city now has the largest population of Polynesians in the world. Many of the country's Maori also live in the city and the region around Auckland. The Maori population of New Zealand is relatively small (9.7 percent of the total population), but they have a powerful voice in

Auckland's harbor and center city skyline show its beauty and modernity.

the government. These Aborigines believe that their rights, established by the Treaty of Waitangi, have been violated. Some leaders are demanding compensation and a return of all government lands.

The Geothermal Center—New Zealand is on the Pacific "ring of fire," the area of greatest volcanic activity in the Pacific. The center of North Island is a volcanic plateau with some still-active volcanic peaks. Near the town of Rotorua (ROH tuh ROO uh) are hot springs, boiling mud pools, and spouting geysers. Two geysers, Pohutu and the Prince of Wales Feathers, spray hot water as high as one hundred feet into the air. A large geothermal plant nearby uses underground steam to generate substantial amounts of electricity.

Lake Taupo (taw POH), New Zealand's largest lake, is located just south of Rotorua, near the very center of the island. It fills the crater of a dormant volcano. In fact, it is the largest volcanic lake in the world. Fishermen from around the world come to fish for the large trout found there.

The Southern Hills—A series of low, rugged hills and mountains forms a V to the south and east of the island. On the slopes, sheep and beef cattle graze. New Zealanders eat the greatest amount of red meat per person in the world. (Australia is second.)

Fruit and vegetables are grown on the coastal lowlands in the east. New Zealand is the world's leading producer of *kiwifruit*, a brown, fuzzy, egg-shaped fruit with an emerald-green interior.

On the southern tip of the North Island is the city of Wellington, the capital and second-largest city in New Zealand. (The capital was moved from Auckland to the more centrally located Wellington in 1865.) Wellington is the southernmost national capital in the world. Eleven percent of New Zealand's population lives there. Its main office building, shaped in a series of stacked circles, is appropriately called the Beehive. Wellington has one of the deepest natural harbors in the world. Miles of docks receive oceangoing vessels from around the world. Ferries and hydrofoils transport people from the capital across the narrow **Cook Strait** to South Island.

Lake Taupo, New Zealand's largest lake, is ringed by volcanic mountains.

The kiwifruit contains many vitamins and minerals but is especially rich in vitamin C, a small kiwifruit having as much as a large orange.

This building, called "the Beehive," is part of the parliamentary complex of buildings that house the New Zealand government in Wellington.

SOUTH ISLAND

South Island is known for its country atmosphere and relaxed pace. Because few Maori ever settled on this island, white settlers established a distinct European lifestyle. The rugged west side of the island contrasts sharply with the plains on the east, where most people live.

The Southern Alps—The Southern Alps, a three-hundred-mile-long mountain chain, dominate the west coast. The magnificent alpine scenery includes snowfields, crevasses, and glaciers. Near the center of the chain is snowcapped **Mount Cook**, New Zealand's highest mountain, rising 12,349 feet above sea level. The Maoris called it *Aorangi*, which means "cloud piercer." Running westward to the sea are the Fox and Frans Josef glaciers. On the eastern slope is the great Tasman Glacier. Airplanes drop skiers at the heads of these glaciers, and the skiers can ski uninterrupted for stretches as long as sixteen miles. Farther south, glaciers carved a series of long valleys into the sea. These fjords create a jagged coastline similar to that of Norway. A highlight of the region is Sutherland Falls, one of the world's twenty highest waterfalls.

Rainfall is heaviest on the west slope of the mountains, averaging three hundred inches per year. The many swift rivers supply much of the country's energy needs at low cost. An underground sea cable carries surplus electricity from the South Island to the populous and industrial North Island.

The Canterbury Plains—East of the Southern Alps are the Canterbury Plains, which are dry because the prevailing westerly winds drop their moisture on the mountains before they reach the plains. Most of New Zealand's cereal grains—such as barley, wheat, and oats—are raised on these flat, fertile plains. Farther south, livestock graze on the plains and rolling hills.

About seven miles from the coast is Christchurch, the largest city on the South Island. Hydroelectric power has turned Christchurch into a major industrial center. Tourists who visit the Southern Alps come first to Christchurch. Named for a college in Oxford, England, Christchurch is well known for its parks, gardens, and British architecture. It is the most "English" of New Zealand's cities.

Mount Cook on South Island is New Zealand's tallest peak.

SECTION QUIZ

1. Why is New Zealand called "the land of the long white cloud"?

2. Who were the first people to live in New Zealand?

3. What are the two main islands of New Zealand?

4. What is New Zealand's largest city?

5. What are the two main geographic regions of South Island?

   ◌ Compare and contrast the economies of New Zealand and Australia.

CHAPTER REVIEW 22

Can You:

Define These Terms?

wattle	station
jumpbuck	aquifer
lignite	outback
artesian well	Aborigine

Locate These Places?

Oceania	Tasmania
Great Dividing Range	Great Barrier Reef
	Western Plateau
Central Lowlands	Hamersley Range
Botany Bay	Ayers Rock
Mount Kosciusko	Simpson Desert
Lake Eyre	North Island
Great Australian Bight	South Island
	Cook Strait
Murray River	Mount Cook

Explain the Significance?

Captain James Cook	Adelaide
	Perth
Canberra	Sydney
Melbourne	Maori
Brisbane	Auckland

HOW MUCH DO YOU REMEMBER?

1. Name four outstanding features of Australia that appear on its coat of arms.

2. What is Australia's tallest mountain? In what range is it located?

3. What are the three major geographic features of Australia?

4. What was the First Fleet?

5. What is Australia's largest city?

6. List ten memorable features of the outback.

7. Give the state of Australia that best fits each description.
   a. largest area
   b. largest population
   c. largest city
   d. first settled
   e. last settled
   f. island
   g. lignite
   h. opals
   i. cattle stations

8. Give the island of New Zealand that best fits each description.
   a. most populous
   b. highest peak
   c. geothermal activity
   d. Canterbury Plain

9. Describe the differences between the Aborigines and the Maori.

WHAT DO YOU THINK?

1. The land west of the Appalachians is wet, but west of the Great Dividing Range it is dry. Why the difference? (Hint: Compare currents and wind patterns.)

2. How has Australia's location as "the Land Down Under" affected its history and economy?

3. List five important similarities and five differences between Australia and New Zealand.

4. Why do you think Australia used to be called "the lucky land"?

5. Compare the histories of the Aborigines of Australia, the Maoris of New Zealand, and the American Indians of the United States.

Bora Bora in French Polynesia typifies the tropical island paradises of the Pacific.

OCEANIA: THE PACIFIC ISLANDS

I. MELANESIA
   A. PAPUA NEW GUINEA
   B. SOLOMON ISLANDS
   C. VANUATU
   D. FIJI
   E. NEW CALEDONIA

II. MICRONESIA
   A. CAROLINE ISLANDS
   B. MARIANA ISLANDS
   C. OTHER MICRONESIAN ISLANDS

III. POLYNESIA
   A. TUVALU
   B. SAMOAN ISLANDS
   C. FRENCH POLYNESIA
   D. OTHER POLYNESIAN ISLANDS

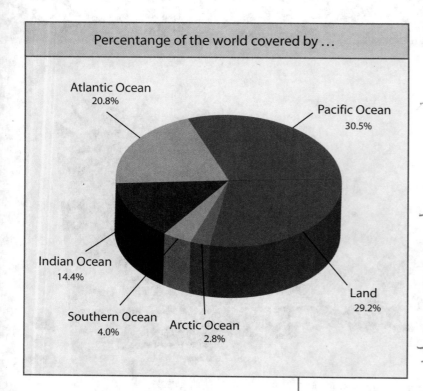

Percentage of the world covered by ...

Atlantic Ocean
20.8%

Pacific Ocean
30.5%

Indian Ocean
14.4%

Southern Ocean
4.0%

Arctic Ocean
2.8%

Land
29.2%

Although the Pacific Ocean (approx. 64 million square miles in area) is larger than all seven continents combined (approx. 57.4 million square miles in area), the 25,000 islands that are scattered across its vast expanse have less combined land area than the state of Alaska.

The first Europeans to visit the islands sent home vivid descriptions of a paradise on earth, with warm breezes, sandy beaches, friendly natives, and abundant tropical fruits. Because most of the islands lie in the humid tropics, temperatures average a balmy 80° F.

Early reports of paradise were misleading, however. Islanders faced the threat of typhoons, volcanic eruptions, and earthquakes. Disease, superstition, and tribal warfare only made matters worse.

In the past two hundred years, the islanders have been thrust into the difficult process of **acculturation**—the exposure of one group of people to the values and lifestyles of a foreign group of people and their adoption of those ways as their own. Most people on those islands still eke out a

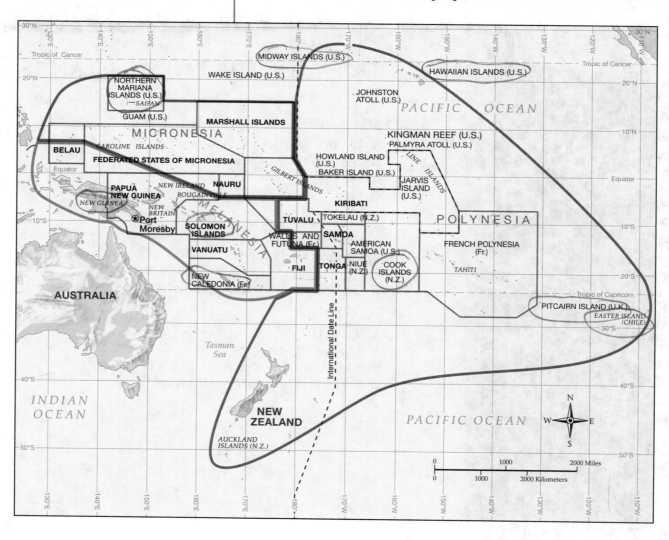

living in small villages of thatched houses. Most islands lack mineral resources, and the only major export is dried coconut meat, called **copra** (KOH prah). The people struggle to make a good living in the modern world.

Although the Pacific Islanders are poor in the world's eyes, they have been very open to evangelism. Many of them have discovered that Jesus Christ is the one real hope of paradise. "My righteousness is near; my salvation is gone forth, and mine arms shall judge the people; the isles shall wait upon me, and on mine arm shall they trust" (Isa. 51:5).

People settled the Pacific islands long before European explorers arrived. When one island became overcrowded, a group of the natives set out for another island. Because of the great distances between islands, the people developed distinct cultures, languages, and physical features.

During three voyages between 1768 and 1779, the great scientific explorer Captain James Cook filled in many empty spaces on the world map. He charted the east coast of Australia and discovered New Caledonia and the Sandwich Islands (named for the Earl of Sandwich; later named Hawaii).

Other Europeans soon followed. Traders came in search of coconut oil, sandalwood, and pearls. Next, Congregational missionaries and Roman Catholic priests came to evangelize the islanders. The missionaries provided medicine and education, and they encouraged the natives to adopt Western dress and social norms. Although many islanders still worship their ancestors and believe in animism (that spirits indwell plants and animals), the professed religion on most of the islands is Christianity.

With the rise of colonialism in the nineteenth century, foreign powers competed for control of the islands. During the 1930s, imperial Japan extended its control over many of the Pacific islands. American Marines later fought some of their bloodiest battles as they struggled to free the islands from Japanese control.

After World War II, the United Nations divided the islands among the Allied countries. They wanted to help the islands recover from their losses and develop stable governments. Most of the islands have since gained independence, although a few prefer to remain territories. For example, Guam, Wake Island, and the Midway Islands belong to the United States; New Caledonia and Wallis and Futuna belong to France; Niue and the Cook Islands belong to New Zealand; Easter Island belongs to Chile; and Pitcairn Island belongs to Great Britain.

Most of the thousands of islands of the Pacific Rim are very small. They can be divided into three broad groups: Melanesia, Micronesia, and Polynesia. We will study a few islands from each of these divisions.

Ferdinand Magellan and the Pacific Islands

During his voyage around the world in 1519–21, Ferdinand Magellan became the first European to chart the Pacific. After battling the stormy seas on the southern tip of South America, Magellan reached a calm ocean, which he called the Pacific ("peaceful"). However, for ninety-eight days his men sighted only two islands, both of which were uninhabitable. Provisions ran out, and the crew was forced to eat rats and leather. Finally, the starving men reached the tiny island of Guam in the Marianas, where they took on fresh supplies. During the next two centuries, few expeditions braved this forbidding "empty" quarter of the earth.

Although Ferdinand Magellan did not survive to complete his voyage, he is generally credited with being the first man to circumnavigate the earth, and he discovered several Pacific islands in the process.

			Pacific Island Fast Facts				
Flag	Country	Capital	Area (sq. mi.)	Pop. (M)	Pop. Density (per sq. mi.)	Per Capita GDP ($US)	Life Span
			Melanesia				
	Fiji	Suva	7,054	0.89	127	$5,900	69.53
	Papua New Guinea	Port Moresby	178,703	5.55	31	$2,200	64.93
	Solomon Islands	Honiara	10,985	0.54	49	$1,700	72.66
	Vanuatu	Port-Vila	4,710	0.21	44	$2,900	62.49
			Micronesia				
	Belau (Palau)	Koror	177	0.020	115	$9,000	70.14
	Kiribati	Bairiki	313	0.10	329	$800	61.71
	Marshall Islands	Majuro	70	0.059	844	$1,600	70.01
	Federated States of Micronesia	Palikir	271	0.11	399	$2,300	69.75
	Nauru	Yaren (District)	8.11	0.013	1,609	$5,000	62.73
			Polynesia				
	Tuvalu	Funafuti	10	0.012	1,159	$1,100	68.01
	Samoa	Apia	1,137	0.18	156	$5,600	70.72
	Tonga	Nuku'alofa	289	0.11	389	$2,300	69.53
	French Polynesia	Papeete (on Tahiti)	1,609	0.27	168	$17,500	75.90

I. MELANESIA

Melanesia (mehl uh NEE zhah) is located south of the equator, near Indonesia and Australia. The French explorer Dumont d'Urville named the region *Melanesia*, the "Black Islands," in 1831 because he was struck by the dark appearance of the land rising from the green sea. A variety of short, black-skinned peoples settled Melanesia long ago. More than twelve hundred different tribes developed, each with its own language and rituals.

Skirmishes between rival tribes were once a normal part of life. A "big man" rose to power within a tribe based on his prowess in battle. Head hunting and cannibalism (the eating of human flesh) were common practices.

The Pacific Ocean separates Melanesia from the rest of Australia's continental plate. Like the continent, these *continental islands* have a rich variety of soils, rocks, and resources. Heavy rains produce vast tropical forests. Yams and sweet potatoes grow well in the acidic soil. **Taro** (TAH roh), a potato-like root that grows up to twelve feet long, is a favorite food.

Melanesia was the last of all the Pacific islands to be visited by white Europeans. Treacherous reefs and tricky currents fill the shallow waters near the shores. Good harbors are scarce. The first missionaries did not arrive until the 1830s at Fiji (FEE jee). Even then, few missionaries attempted to reach the rugged interior.

PAPUA NEW GUINEA

Two countries occupy **New Guinea** (GIH nee), the second-largest island in the world. The western half is Irian Jaya, a province of Indonesia. The eastern half is part of Papua (POP oo uh) New Guinea, a young country that gained independence from Australia in 1975. Papua New Guinea has several other tropical islands, but 85 percent of its land area is on New Guinea. It is slightly larger than California.

RUGGED TERRAIN

The most prominent geographical feature of New Guinea is the rugged mountain system that extends the length of the island and continues into the ocean. Although New Guinea is a tropical island, a few mountains, such as the 12,793-foot Wilhelm Mountain, remain cold year-round. Steep valleys lie between the mountain ranges. Numerous large, raging rivers flow through these ranges to the ocean.

New Guinea is a land of forbidding swamps and thick jungles. Tropical rain forests cover about 75 percent of Papua New Guinea; swamps occupy much of the narrow coastland. The seven-hundred-mile Fly River—the longest river in New Guinea—flows south through an endless swamp, which is the only major flatland on the island.

The Papuan Mountains are scenic but rugged.

Taro is made from the root portion of the taro plant.

Islanders cultivate taro plants, which are the source of a favorite food in the Pacific islands.

Wildlife of New Guinea

A variety of animals flourish in the isolation of New Guinea. As in Australia, the forests host many kinds of kangaroos and other marsupials. The swamps have both salt- and freshwater crocodiles, one species of which climbs trees! The Queen Alexandria butterfly is the largest butterfly in the world—as large as a small bird. The island's most famous faunas are its 660 species of birds—more than can be found on the entire continent of North America.

Saltwater crocodiles are abundant in Papua New Guinea, especially in the Sepik River area.

Natives of Papua New Guinea take great pride in their respective tribes' elaborate facial paintings.

Papua New Guinea has several offshore islands. The largest is the Bismarck Archipelago, named after a nineteenth-century chancellor of Germany. New Britain, the largest island, is the most developed area in the country. Its capital, Rabaul, is the nation's export center. Tragically, nearby volcanoes destroyed most of the city in 1994.

COASTAL SETTLEMENT

More people live in Papua New Guinea (5.5 million in 2005) than in all the other Pacific islands combined. Many hundreds of tribes coexist, each speaking its own language. (These represent more than 10 percent of the world's languages.) Papua New Guinea has three official languages: English (although few people speak it), a creole language called Tok Pisin (tahk PIH-sin), which most people speak, and Hiri Motu (HIH-ree MOH-too), which is spoken mainly in the southern region near the capital. The tribes are divided into two main culture groups: the lowlanders on the coast and the highlanders in the interior.

The Dutch claimed the western half of New Guinea in 1828, and Great Britain claimed the southeast in 1846. But no settlers came. Interest in settlement changed when imperialist Germany laid claim to the northeast coast of New Guinea and its nearby islands in 1884. The Germans established a post at the mouth of the great Sepik River in the north. But malaria-bearing mosquitos made life difficult on the German plantations. After Germany lost World War I, their lands came under Australian supervision.

The first British settlers came in 1874 after Captain Moresby discovered a deep harbor on the south coast of New Guinea. The "settlers" actually were Protestant missionaries who hoped to preach to the local Motu people. Port Moresby is now the capital of Papua New Guinea, with modern buildings and paved roads.

CARGO CULTS

When Melanesians first faced Western culture, many of them were fascinated by its great variety of riches. They desired the goods that began to arrive by ship on their islands, but they had no idea how the goods were made or where they came from. They concluded that the goods or cargoes came from the spirit world. Late in the nineteenth century, their prophets promised a new age of plenty when tribal deities, ancient heroes, or dead ancestors would return with cargo for the Melanesians. Some leaders moved their tribes to the coasts where they built crude docks and outposts (and later airstrips) to prepare for the event. They built rows of warehouses to store the hoped-for goods. The tribes often imitated government flag-raising ceremonies and the like, hoping that such magic rites would hasten the arrival of the cargo.

These cargo cults also arose as a revolt against white colonial rule. Melanesians were often mistreated as slaves on plantations and in mines, and they never received the freedom and wealth that Europeans had. So the cult settlements refused to pay taxes, would not allow visitors, and would not work unless they were paid exorbitant wages. They abandoned their traditional wealth—gardens, pigs, and money—which they would not need in the age of plenty. These islanders expected their strange worship to bring justice, freedom, and plenty of eating, dancing, and kava (a narcotic beverage) drinking. However, because the cults threatened the white economy and government, their leaders were arrested. Most of the seventy or so cargo cults eventually died out.

Cargo cults rejected the gospel of Jesus Christ, which promises a time of eternal peace and plenty in heaven. Instead, they lusted after the vain treasures of this earth.

But godliness with contentment is great gain. For we brought nothing into this world, and it is certain we can carry nothing out. And having food and raiment let us be therewith content. But they that will be rich fall into temptation and a snare, and into many foolish and hurtful lusts, which drown men in destruction and perdition.
(1 Tim. 6:6–9)

THE GRAND VALLEY

For decades, European explorers attempted to reach the interior of New Guinea, but difficult mountain ranges, torrential rains, and disease blocked their path. Everyone assumed that no peoples could survive in such an inhospitable land. Then, in 1930, a couple of gold prospectors from Australia stumbled upon a "lost civilization" of one million souls. Hidden in the midst of the mountains of New Guinea was a Grand Valley where Melanesian Highlanders lived and fought. Because these people did not travel far from the safety of their own tribes, they thought that they were the only inhabitants on earth.

No highway system or railroads link the capital with the rest of the country. More than 96 percent of the country's 12,178 miles of roads are unpaved. Most travel is by plane or boat. Even today, few outsiders visit the remote villages. A new Highlands Highway connects some of the highland villages. The easternmost island, Bougainville, engaged in a ten-year revolution to secede from the rest of the country. Fighting ended with a truce in 1997, and a peace agreement was signed in 2001. The disarmament process continues under UN supervision. Law enforcement throughout the country is weak, and crime is a perpetual concern. Tribal warfare continues in the highlands.

THE FOUR Cs OF PAPUA NEW GUINEA'S ECONOMY

The economy of Papua New Guinea can be summarized by four products beginning with Cs: cacao, copra, coffee, and copper. The heart of the economy is subsistence agriculture, the most common crops being taro and other root crops. Eighty-five percent of the labor force is engaged in agriculture, which accounts for about 35 percent of the GDP. The country is fifth in the world in production of both taro and other roots and tubers. Most land is owned by the whole clan; individuals do not buy or sell property. Coastal tribes grow two cash crops, *cacao* and *copra*. Plantations in the high altitudes grow *coffee*, the nation's most lucrative crop. Papua New Guinea is thirty-sixth in the world in coffee production. Forty percent of the population depends directly or indirectly on coffee income for living. Unfortunately, the shortage of fertile land (only 0.46 percent is arable) encourages fighting among the highlander tribes. The country leads the world in production of game meat.

The nation is beginning to exploit its mineral resources. After the discovery of *copper* in 1965, a major mine opened on Bougainville. But in 1989 the Nasioi natives staged an uprising and closed the mine. They resented what they considered the desecration of their sacred grounds, and they did not want to be a part of the new government.

The largest gold mine outside South Africa opened in Porgera in 1991. Recently a mountain of copper was discovered at Ok Tedi near the head of Papua New Guinea's Fly River. Copper and gold account for two-thirds of the nation's exports. In 2001, mineral production represented 25 percent of the GDP. The nation is seeking to develop oil reserves too. Exxon Mobil estimates that the country has 22.5 trillion cubic feet of natural gas reserves and plans to build a pipeline from Papua New Guinea

This eruption of a volcano near Rabaul, Papua New Guinea, nearly destroyed that city.

Through Christian Eyes

Is it good to be cut off from other cultures, as the Melanesian Highlanders were? Why or why not?

Chocolate is made from beans inside the cacao pods, which grow on trees.

to Queensland, Australia. Another American company opened the country's first oil refinery in 2004 and expects to produce 30,000 barrels of oil a day, half of which will remain for domestic use. Papua New Guinea's major trading partners are Australia, Japan, China, Singapore, and New Zealand.

SECTION QUIZ

1. Define *acculturation*. Why has it been difficult for the Pacific islands?

2. What explorer first discovered Hawaii and many other Pacific islands?

3. What is the largest island in Melanesia?

4. List the four Cs of Papua New Guinea's economy.

☀ How has the large number of languages in Papua New Guinea slowed the preaching of the gospel there? What can missionaries do to remove this hindrance?

SOLOMON ISLANDS

The Spanish explorer Alvaro de Mendana first discovered the scattered Solomon Islands in 1568. In anticipation of the riches he expected to find, he named the islands after the biblical King Solomon.

Europeans never found mineral riches, but they did discover plenty of dangers. Four active volcanoes belch smoke and fire, earthquakes pose a constant threat on the seven main islands, and the hot and humid climate breeds several deadly diseases, including malaria and tuberculosis.

Between 1870 and 1911, infamous planters used bribes or force to load their ships with Solomon Islanders to work on cotton and sugar plantations in Fiji and Queensland. To end these abuses and to protect the workers, Great Britain took control of the islands in 1893.

The islands became independent in 1978, but the islanders have not yet developed a strong sense of national identity. Although English is the official language, native tribes speak ninety indigenous languages.

More than one thousand miles of ocean separate the Solomon Islands from Australia. Because of their isolation, the islands do not enjoy the same diversity of wildlife as New Guinea does. The only mammals native to the islands are some marsupials and bats (which the islanders eat). Settlers brought dogs, cattle, and rats. Unlike mammals, seabirds thrive on the islands. The frigate bird, once considered sacred, is a national emblem.

The Solomon Islands are slightly smaller than Maryland. Forests cover more than 90 percent of the land, supplying valuable wood for logging industries. In contrast, less than 1 percent of the area is arable. Islanders clear land on a few narrow coastal areas and mountain valleys to raise copra and cacao. About 75 percent of the labor force is engaged in agriculture, which provides 42 percent of the GDP.

Guadalcanal (GWAHD uhl kuh NAL) is the largest of the Solomon Islands and the second-most populous (after Malaita). The capital city of Honiara is located on a deep port at the north end of Guadalcanal. Many tourists visit battlefields on the island, which

This male frigate bird is putting on a show for a potential mate.

was the site of one of the earliest U.S. offensives in the Pacific in World War II.

VANUATU

Southeast of the Solomon Islands is **Vanuatu** (VAH noo AH too), a chain of twelve volcanic islands and some sixty smaller coral islands that together are slightly larger than Connecticut. Captain Cook named the islands New Hebrides after the Hebrides Islands in Scotland.

Several of the islands have active volcanoes. In these unstable conditions, three-fourths of the people build rural homes made of bamboo and palm leaves. Bislama, a language that combines mainly English words with Melanesian grammar, is the most widespread of the hundred different spoken languages. The subsistence economy is based on copra, cacao, coffee, fishing, and cattle raised on the slightly more than 2 percent of arable land. Sixty-five percent of the labor force is engaged in agriculture, but it provides only a little more than one-fourth of the GDP. Sixty-two percent of the GDP is service oriented.

FIJI

The Fiji archipelago has more than eight hundred scattered islands and is slightly smaller than New Jersey. Only about one hundred of its islands are inhabited. Three-fourths of the country's population lives on the large volcanic island of Viti Levu (Big Island). Suva, Fiji's capital and largest city, lies on Viti Levu's southern coast.

Before the arrival of the Europeans, warring tribes of cannibals inhabited the islands. Cannibalism ceased in 1854 when the high chief Cakobau converted to Christianity. Twenty years later, Fiji became a crown colony when Cakobau petitioned Britain for protection from the other chiefs.

Great Britain imported laborers from India to work on sugar cane plantations. Nearly half of the islanders are descendants of those Indians.

Fiji has been called "the crossroads of the South Pacific." Airplanes fly constantly in and out of the airport at Nadi, and commercial ships dock at the natural harbors at Suva and Lautoka. Sixteen

U.S. Marines invaded Guadalcanal on August 7, 1942, to drive out the Japanese.

Conversion of a Cannibal King

Only 150 years ago, many tribes of fierce warriors lived on the islands of Fiji. Often the menus of their feasts included *bokolo*, another name for roasted enemies. One cannibal chief, Cakobau, who was born in 1817, gained power on the islands. He led his people to war against enemy tribes, murdered those who displeased him, and gave cannibal feasts. During his reign, however, Christian missionaries came to Fiji to preach the gospel.

In 1854, Cakobau accepted Jesus Christ as his Savior. He changed his ways, ended cannibalism on his island, and publicly told his people that he was a Christian.

Cakobau's power grew, even though he was no longer a fierce cannibal warrior. In 1867 he became king of Fiji, and his people lived in peace on the islands. Today, most Fijians claim to be Christians. Many, however, have accepted only the form of religion. Like others around the world, these people need to accept Jesus as their Savior and ultimate king—just as King Cakobau did.

A fisherman on Fiji casts his net.

percent of Fiji's GDP comes from agricultural activities (more than 10 percent of the land is arable), with sugar cane being the major export. Seventy percent of the labor force, however, is involved in agriculture. After gaining its independence in 1970, Fiji began diversifying its economy, encouraging tourism and striving to develop the country's manufacturing and forestry. Today, 61 percent of its GDP is attributable to service industries.

When Fiji gained its independence, the government tried to balance Indian and Fijian representation. Both groups were given an equal number of representatives in the parliament. The minority voters (Europeans, Chinese, and various non-Fijian Pacific Islanders), with four representatives, held the balance of power. In 1987, the first Indian managed to gain a majority in parliament and became prime minister. That victory frightened the Fijians and led to the first coup ever to occur in the Pacific islands.

NEW CALEDONIA

James Cook discovered **New Caledonia** (KAL uh DOH nee uh) in 1774. He thought that the islands resembled Scotland; hence, the name "Caledonia," which is Latin for "Scotland."

From 1853 to 1894, the French used the islands as a penal colony. However, they later discovered that one-third of the world's nickel reserves were buried beneath the mountains of the main island. Strip

MISSIONARY AVIATION

What three things do Arctic Eskimos, Amazon Indians, and New Guinea cannibals have in common? The answer is remoteness, primitive conditions, and hostile climates. Aviator-missionaries overcome these problems by using their airplanes to move people and supplies where they could not otherwise go, and they respond quickly to medical emergencies.

One such program was started in the Chuuk (CHOOK; formerly Truk) Islands in 1997. Three missionary couples pooled their money to maintain and operate the plane transporting them from island to island.

Becoming a missionary pilot requires great dedication. The typical flight training program at a Christian college includes five years of Bible and flight training. Many mission boards require a commercial pilot's certificate, an instrument flight rating (IFR, as opposed to a merely visual flight rating, or VFR), five hundred hours of flying time, and an aircraft mechanics certificate. Boards also demand that their candidates be debt-free—perhaps the hardest challenge because flight expenses add $12,000–$20,000 to the normal college bill. Once accepted, the mission-

Missionary aviators can reach otherwise inaccessible peoples with God's Word.

ary aviator candidate must obtain financial support (typically through deputation), like any other missionary, except that he or she must raise a larger sum of money.

Missionary pilots face many challenges. Landings on small and remote airstrips can be dangerous. Dense fogs and precipitous mountains have claimed the lives of more than one missionary pilot. A pilot often must spend many days away from home. Mechanical skills are often in demand. Such busy schedules can take a toll on one's family, unless the missionary aviator makes time to provide spiritual leadership and family recreation.

Missionary aviation can also be dangerous for other reasons. For example, in April 2001, an American missionary and his wife and two children were flying over Peru when the Peruvian air force mistook them for drug smugglers and shot the plane down. The wife and her seven-month-old daughter were killed. But tragedies such as this should not discourage Christians from considering missionary aviation. God has called all His people to live lives of sacrificial service for the growth of his kingdom (Rom. 12:1–2; Matt. 28:18–20).

mines now dot more than half of the island's landscape. New Caledonia is one of the world's leading producers of nickel.

SECTION QUIZ

1. What sea bird is an emblem of the Solomon Islands?
2. Name the main Solomon island, where many American soldiers died in World War II.
3. Compare Vanuatu's economy to that of the Solomon Islands.
4. What people live in Fiji besides the native Fijians?
5. What mineral is mined on New Caledonia?

☀ Calculate the total land area of the nations in Melanesia. What percentage of this total does each nation have?

II. MICRONESIA

North of Melanesia are the small, widely scattered islands of **Micronesia** ("small islands"). Although Micronesia covers an area of ocean about the size of the continental United States, its total land area is less than that of Rhode Island.

Unlike the continental islands of Melanesia, most islands in Micronesia are **atolls** (AY tohls), rings of coral on the submerged cones of volcanoes. Because they rise only a few feet above the water, coral islands are called **low islands**. Coral sand, which lacks organic material, is a poor soil. Few plants grow well. The islanders rely on fishing to subsist. Coral islands lack fresh water, except for what they receive from rainfall. Most of the islands have little hope for a brighter future. They depend on copra, tourism, and foreign aid to survive in the modern world.

Micronesians are a little taller than Melanesians and have lighter skin and straight or woolly black hair. Only during World War II, when fighting devastated many of the islands, did Micronesia attract worldwide attention. Following the war, the United Nations gave most of the region to the United States to govern, aid, and defend. It was called the "Trust Territory of the Pacific."

The majority of those islands are now self-governed in "free association" with the United States. Under this system, the countries control their internal and foreign affairs, but the United States has promised to defend them. In return for this protection, the countries have agreed to keep out foreign military forces.

Micronesia is composed of three large island groups: the Caroline Islands, the Mariana Islands, and the Marshall Islands.

An atoll is a circular coral island that encloses a lagoon. Most of the islands of Micronesia are atolls.

CAROLINE ISLANDS

The **Caroline Islands** consist of more than 930 islands. In 1978, the Caroline Islands were divided into two groups—the Federated States of Micronesia and Belau.

FEDERATED STATES OF MICRONESIA

The Federated States of Micronesia are about four times the size of Washington, D.C., and consist of four major island groups: Kosrae, Pohnpei (formerly Ponape), the Chuuk Islands, and the Yap Islands. The 607 island states gained the status of free association with the United States in 1986.

Kosrae International Airport is a man-made runway in the water off the mountainous island.

The government buildings in the Micronesian capital of Kolonia are a mixture of traditional and modern architecture.

The waters around Chuuk are filled with sunken ships from World War II, complete with their cargoes, including this Japanese tank.

Kosrae, a high volcanic island on the eastern corner of the Carolines, is one of the few important islands among mostly coral islands in the east. Congregational missionaries have made a lasting impact there; 97 percent of the people profess Christianity. The islanders reserve Sunday strictly for going to church. The women dress modestly, and bathing suits are not permitted—even for visitors. Known for its outstanding citrus fruits, Kosrae has the potential of becoming the vegetable and fruit basket of the Pacific.

The volcanic island of Pohnpei never suffered the ravages of World War II because armies avoided its forbidding terrain and heavy rainfall. The modern city of Kolonia on Pohnpei is the capital of the Federated States.

The Chuuk Islands (formerly Truk) and the Yap Islands are predominantly volcanic. Both Chuuk and Yap were sites of Japanese bases during World War II. The U.S. bombardment of Chuuk created the best wreck-diving site in the world. More than 100 Japanese ships and planes, with their full loads of tanks, mines, and ammunition, sit on the lagoon floor.

More than 5 percent of the land is arable, and agriculture accounts for half of the GDP. Two-thirds of the labor force, however, is employed by the government.

BELAU

Poverty-stricken **Belau** (beh LOU; formerly Palau) is about two and a half times the size of Washington, D.C., but is composed of more than two hundred islands. It grows only enough food to provide for its rural population and is therefore heavily dependent on imports. Nearly two-thirds of the population lives in the capital of Koror. Half of them depend on government work for their livelihood. Another 20 percent are involved in agriculture.

SNORKELING AND SCUBA DIVING

Two of the most popular ocean sports are snorkeling and scuba diving. (SCUBA is an acronym for "self-contained underwater breathing apparatus.") People from all over the world fly to the Pacific islands to enjoy these sports. Belau's reef, one of the "seven underwater wonders of the world," offers some of the best diving anywhere. Like Australia's Great Barrier Reef, its waters are filled with coral, exotic fish, undersea caves, lava tubes, and shipwrecks.

> O Lord, how manifold are thy works! in wisdom hast thou made them all: the earth is full of thy riches. So is this great and wide sea, wherein are things creeping innumerable, both small and great beasts.
> (Ps. 104: 24–25)

Snorkeling is an easy sport that can be done in as little as a foot of water. Snorkeling requires just a mask, flippers, and a snorkel. A snorkeler floats on the surface and watches crabs, eels, schools of colorful fish, and other creatures moving on the coral floor. Scuba divers wear oxygen tanks that allow them to stay underwater for as much as an hour. But scuba equipment is expensive and requires special training to use properly.

The islands of Micronesia present many excellent opportunities for exploring underwater wonders.

MARIANA ISLANDS

The **Mariana Islands** extend 350 miles from north to south and are part of a partially submerged mountain range in the Pacific. Of the fourteen islands in the chain, only the four largest are occupied in significant numbers: Guam, Saipan, Rota, and Tinian.

Guam (GWAHM), the largest of the islands, is the most populous island in all of Micronesia with a population almost 169,000. Most of Guam's inhabitants are Japanese. The other two main ethnic groups are the Micronesians and the Chamorros (or Guamanians), the original inhabitants of the island, who speak an Indonesian language. Guam is an independently governed territory of the United States. Residents of the Marianas, however, are U.S. citizens. Tourism is the major source of income on Guam, and American military bases are the second-leading source of income.

The other islands, collectively known as the Northern Mariana Islands, are a commonwealth of the United States and are administered by the U.S. Department of the Interior. The capital of the commonwealth is Saipan.

Tinian (TIHN nee uhn), eighty miles north of Guam, is the second-most populous (approximately 4,000) of the islands but is the least developed. It was a major U.S. air base during the latter years of World War II.

The Marianas are cooler and drier than most of their neighbors. The islands' terrain varies from grasslands suitable for grazing to tropical forests. Copra, sugar, coffee, and tobacco are the chief crops.

The Mariana Islands, located southeast of Japan, were bases for the U.S. bombing missions against Japan near the end of World War II. Tinian was the base from which two B-29s dropped atomic bombs on Japan, ending the war.

MARSHALL ISLANDS

The **Marshall Islands** lie east-southeast of the Mariana Islands. They are an island group of thirty-four low-lying atolls and islands that split into two parallel chains. The islands were named for John Marshall, a British sea captain who explored them in 1788. Many of the people in the Marshalls live in poverty.

The United States used the Bikini and Eniwetok (EN ih WEE tahk) atolls from 1946 to 1958 to test nuclear bombs. The residents of Bikini, who had converted to Christianity many years earlier, vacated their islands after the military convinced them that the nuclear testing would benefit mankind. Although steps have been taken to rehabilitate the contaminated soil on these islands, the islanders are still waiting to return to their home.

Kwajalein (KWAHJ uh luhn), the largest atoll in the world, encloses a mammoth 839-square-mile lagoon. It is home to Reagan Test Site, a command and mission control center for intercontinental ballistic missiles and missile interceptors.

Kwajalein is part of the U.S. Strategic Defense initiative, which involves the research, testing, and development of missile defenses.

OTHER MICRONESIAN ISLANDS

NAURU

With an area of only 8.11 square miles, **Nauru** (nah OO roo) is the third-smallest country in the world; only Vatican City and Monaco are smaller. The oval-shaped coral island is one-tenth the size of Washington, D.C. With more than thirteen thousand people, however, it has the highest population density in the Pacific.

The nearest neighbor, East Ocean Island, lies two hundred miles away. Nauru, which used to be called Pleasant Island, has no fresh water except for rainwater, and the soil is extremely poor; none of it is arable. Yet, in stark contrast to the Marshall Islands, Nauru is prosperous and financially independent. Four-fifths of the island sits on a deposit of high-quality phosphate, an important fertilizer used by farmers around the world. The country's residents live solely off the royalties they receive from the government for the sale of phosphates. Because the phosphates will soon be depleted, however, the people of Nauru should be making plans for other sources of income.

> #### Through Christian Eyes
>
> Read Genesis 1:28, Leviticus 19:18, and Mark 12:30–31. Given these verses, what do you think of the decision to test nuclear bombs on Bikini and Eniwetok? Was it wise? Why or why not?

KIRIBATI

The **Republic of Kiribati** (KEER uh BAH tee), formerly called the Gilbert Islands, straddles both the equator and the International Date Line. Located at the juncture of Micronesia, Melanesia, and Polynesia, it contains both Micronesian and Polynesian peoples. Most islanders live in rural villages of crudely constructed houses and are heavily dependent on the sea to supplement the bananas, breadfruit, and sweet potatoes they grow. The islands are overcrowded. To help ease this problem, some inhabitants are migrating to other Pacific islands.

At low tide, one can walk from island to island in Kiribati.

SECTION QUIZ

1. What is another name for a low island? Why is soil so poor on such islands?

2. The Caroline Islands are divided into what two nations?

3. What island chain in Micronesia is a U.S. commonwealth? What island is a U.S. territory?

4. Name the largest atoll in the world.

5. What mineral compound made Nauru rich?

On which Micronesian island would you prefer to live? Why?

III. POLYNESIA

Polynesia ("many islands") encompasses a broad triangle that stretches from New Zealand in the west to Midway Island and Hawaii in the north and to Easter Island in the east.

Despite being separated by thousands of miles, the inhabitants of these islands are remarkably similar in both appearance and culture. The Polynesians have lighter colored skin and wavier hair than the inhabitants of Micronesia and Melanesia. Their different dialects are mutually understandable throughout all of Polynesia.

The beauty and natural wealth of the islands are the result of their volcanic origin. Volcanic islands, often called **high islands**, have beautiful hills and mountains. The rich volcanic ash provides fertile soil.

Polynesia has a complex system of hereditary chiefs. With the arrival of missionaries, Christianity spread quickly as the chiefs were converted. Many foreign countries vied for ownership of the islands. Three of the island groups are independent; the rest remain closely tied to their mother countries.

U.S. Marines faced heavy fighting on Tarawa, which is part of the Republic of Kiribati.

TUVALU

Although **Tuvalu** (too VAHL oo) means "cluster of eight," it consists of a 360-mile chain of nine low-lying coral atolls, one of which is uninhabited. With a total land area of only ten square miles (only one-tenth the size of Washington, D.C.), Tuvalu is the fourth-smallest nation in the world, just a little larger than Nauru. Nearly 97 percent of the adults belong to the Church of Tuvalu (a Congregationalist church).

Tuvalu, which gained its independence from Britain in 1978, is one of the most undeveloped countries in the world. The soil is poor (none of it is arable), and the islands have no mineral resources. Copra is the only major export. The country relies heavily on foreign aid from Australia, Great Britain, Japan, and New Zealand. The country began to collect fees from the foreign vessels that fish for tuna in the surrounding waters. Because young Tuvaluans lack opportunities at home, many of them seek employment on ocean vessels.

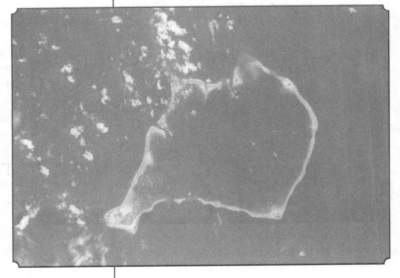
Funafuti is one of the nine atolls, eight of which are inhabited, that make up Tuvalu.

SAMOA ISLANDS

The **Samoa** (suh MOH uh) **Islands** are mostly volcanic. The soil near the coasts is fertile enough to grow bananas, taro, and cacao. Not much grows farther inland, however, because heavy rains leach the soil.

Samoans live in fales, which allow for breezes to ventilate the entire structure but also allow privacy when it is desired.

The first missionary to set foot on the islands, the Reverend John Williams of the London Missionary Society, arrived in the middle of the nineteenth century. Within a few years, Christianity completely changed Samoan culture, which had been very warlike. Much of Samoan life centers on the extended family. Some families still live in **fales** (FAH lays), framed houses that have a thatched roof and open sides. Fales remain open most of the time unless the owner lowers the coconut-leaf blinds.

The island chain has two parts. The islands west of longitude 171° W form the independent country of Samoa. The islands east of that line make up American Samoa, an unincorporated territory of the United States.

SAMOA

Samoa has two large volcanic islands, Opolu and Savaii, and seven smaller islands. Most of the people live in small villages along the coast, raising their own food on small plots of land. Samoa became the first independent Polynesian state in 1962.

AMERICAN SAMOA

Eastern Samoa, or **American Samoa**, is a United States territory that is slightly smaller than Rhode Island. As nationals, but not U.S. citizens, Samoans are able to enter the United States freely. Of the territory's seven islands, Tutuila is the largest and most populated. The capital city of Pago Pago (PAHN-GOH PAHN-GOH), located on Tutuila, overlooks one of the most beautiful harbors in the South Pacific.

Americans first used Pago Pago Bay as a refueling station for their ships in 1872. The U.S. Navy maintained a base there from 1900 to 1951.

Although American Samoa is less than one-tenth the area of Samoa, it is in much better economic shape. In 1961, the United States launched a program to bolster the economy. Many people left their villages to take industry-related jobs around Pago Pago. The local tuna canning industry continues to provide the island's primary source of income.

TONGA

Tonga (TAHNG uh) is the oldest and last remaining kingdom in the Pacific. According to tradition, the most powerful chief extended his control over all of the islands during a civil war in 1845, declaring himself King George Tupou I. Converted by Methodist missionaries, he persuaded many of his subjects to accept Christianity too. The king still wields great power in the constitutional monarchy.

The Wesleyan Free Church of Tonga has strongly influenced the nation's culture. The country's constitution strictly prohibits all trade, games, and work on Sunday. Despite a need for money from tourism, the king and others discourage it for fear the nation will lose its identity: "We will become like Hawaii, where there are no more Hawaiians," warned King Tupou IV, who was crowned in 1965.

With a population of nearly 113,000, Tonga suffers from overcrowding, especially on Tongatapu Island, where two-thirds of the people live. As arable land runs out, the people have few alternatives for making a living.

FRENCH POLYNESIA

French Polynesia includes five major island groups: the Society Islands, the Gambier and the Tubuai (Austral) Islands, the Tuamotu Archipelago, and the Marquesas Islands. About three-fourths of all French Polynesians live on the Society Islands, the largest islands in the territory.

French Polynesia is scattered over an area about the size of Western Europe. It has strong cultural, economic, and political ties to France. In 1958, the islanders voted to maintain their association with France rather than become independent. Its residents vote in French presidential elections and elect representatives to the French Parliament.

A majority of the islanders (250,000) reside on the island of **Tahiti** (tuh HEE tee)—the geographical, social, and political center of French Polynesia. Two giant volcanic mountains unite to form the island. A coral reef surrounds most of the island, giving it a protected lagoon. Chief exports include copra, pearls, and vanilla. Papeete, the capital of the territory, is a bustling port city on Tahiti. Although exports, such as black pearls, provide a modest income in French Polynesia, tourism is a big part of the economy. Because of heavy tourism, Tahiti's 130 miles of roads experience traffic jams that rival those of many Western cities.

Tahiti is often portrayed as the ideal island paradise.

MUTINY ON THE BOUNTY

The most famous mutiny in naval history occurred in the Pacific on April 28, 1789. William Bligh, commander of the HMS *Bounty*, had been sent to Tahiti to gather breadfruit and take it to Jamaica, where the British hoped to transplant breadfruit as a healthful alternative to American flour. But Bligh's harsh discipline provoked the master's mate, Fletcher Christian, to seize the ship. Bligh and eighteen loyal crewmen were set adrift on a twenty-three-foot boat. The captain managed to sail 3,618 miles in forty-eight days to Timor, where he found a ship back to England.

Meanwhile, Christian and seven fellow mutineers left Tahiti with twelve island women and six island men to find a safe island on which to hide. Sailing southeast, they decided that uninhabited, isolated Pitcairn Island would be the ideal spot. Surrounded by jagged rocks and reefs,

This tombstone on Pitcairn Island marks the resting place of the last surviving mutineer from the HMS Bounty.

the forbidding island rises steeply from the sea. After managing to land, the crew burned the ship. The colony remained undiscovered for about eighteen years, until an American sealing ship landed there in 1808. By then, only one adult male remained with the many women and children. The volcanic soil proved highly productive, but soon the two square miles of land could not support the growing population, so in the 1830s and 1850s some of the people left. In 1857, the population dropped to zero when everyone moved to Norfolk Island. After people returned, the population peaked at 233 in 1937. In 2005 the population was 47.

The inhabitants are under British jurisdiction. A supply ship comes three times a year. For medical attention, inhabitants must be transported to New Zealand, a distance of nearly 4,000 miles. Islanders make their living producing postage stamps and handcrafts and by subsistence farming and fishing.

THE MYSTERY OF EASTER ISLAND

Easter Island is an unusual volcanic island twenty-six hundred miles off the coast of Chile, far from the other inhabited islands of the Pacific. The Dutch admiral Jacob Raggeveen discovered the island on Easter, 1722. He found on the coast rows of mysterious stone heads, called *moai*. The massive heads had very long ears and flat noses. On the larger heads were red stones that looked like hats or crowns.

Most of the *moai* are ten to twenty feet tall and weigh up to fifty tons. The largest finished head is thirty-two feet high and weighs one hundred tons, but one of the unfinished heads is more than sixty feet high and weighs more than three hundred tons. How did the natives carve the *moai* out of the volcanic rock at the crater Rano Raraku, transport them to the coast, raise the heads to an upright position, and place the red stones on top?

In 1774, Captain Cook visited the island and talked to the natives. They

The people viewing the Easter Island heads indicate their immense size.

told him that their Long Ear ancestors had made the statues twenty-two generations previously—around the thirteenth century. They called their island *Rapa Nui* and considered it the navel of the world. By that time the statues had been toppled. The natives said it happened during wars with Short Ear invaders from islands far to the west.

Where did the statue-builders come from? Where did the invaders who toppled the *moai* come from? If South American legends are true, perhaps the statue builders came from Lake Titicaca. A legend from the Gambier Islands, twelve hundred miles to the west of Easter Island, may explain the origin of the tribe that toppled the statues. The legend tells of a defeated chieftain who took his tribe in two large canoes to a solitary island in the east.

Easter Island has another mystery that has not yet been explained. It is the only Pacific island with an ancient writing system. But no one has been able to decipher the rongo-rongo tablets. Many of these tablets are hidden in secret caves, along with idols and skulls. Long Ears, whose features are depicted on the *moai*, hid in these caves during the war with the Short Ears.

OTHER POLYNESIAN ISLANDS

The volcanic Hawaiian Islands are the most important islands in the Pacific because of their size and strategic location. The United States also owns the Midway Islands west-northwest of Hawaii. New Zealand is another advanced, prosperous region of Polynesia. It owns the Cook Islands, the Tokelau Islands, and Niue (NYOO ay).

SECTION QUIZ

1. Describe how Polynesia differs from the other two Pacific island regions.
2. What is the smallest country in Polynesia?
3. Why is Samoa less developed than American Samoa?
4. What is the last surviving kingdom in the Pacific?
5. What European country controls Tahiti?
- ☀ Should New Zealand and Hawaii be considered part of the Pacific island culture region? Why or why not?

CHAPTER REVIEW

HOW MUCH DO YOU REMEMBER?

1. Which is not one of the major Pacific island groups: Polynesia, Malaysia, or Melanesia?

2. Which type of island is most likely to have an abundance of mineral resources: continental island, high island, or low island?

3. Which is a major export for many Pacific islands: rubber, bananas, or copra?

4. Which activity is a result of acculturation in the Pacific: fishing, animism, or playing soccer?

5. You would be most likely to meet primitive tribal members on which island: New Guinea, Tahiti, or Guam?

6. Guadalcanal is found in which island group: Fiji, the Sandwich Islands, or the Solomon Islands?

7. Guam belongs to which island group: the Caroline Islands, the Mariana Islands, or the Marshall Islands?

8. Nauru has prospered because of which resource: copper, phosphate, or nickel?

9. Which country controls much of Polynesia: Britain, France, or Australia?

10. Which island is connected with the United States: Guam, Tuvalu, or Tahiti?

WHAT DO YOU THINK?

1. If a tribesman becomes a Christian, does he need to adopt Western styles of worship, or can he keep his tribal traditions, such as dances and music?

2. Papua New Guinea barred television broadcasts in 1986 (with fines up to $1 million for violations). The people demanded an end to the law in 1993. Do you think this kind of law is practical for Pacific countries?

3. Why did missionaries not always see true conversions to Christianity among the islanders?

4. Should Tonga and other undeveloped islands encourage tourism to bring in foreign money?

Can You:
Define These Terms?

acculturation	atoll
copra	low island
taro	high island
cargo cult	fale

Locate These Places?

New Guinea	Kwajalein
Guadalcanal	Nauru
Vanuatu	Republic of Kiribati
New Caledonia	Tuvalu
Caroline Islands	Samoa Islands
Belau	American Samoa
Mariana Islands	Tonga
Guam	French Polynesia
Tinian	Tahiti
Marshall Islands	Easter Island

Explain the Significance?

Melanesia	Polynesia
Micronesia	

CHAPTER 24

Many questions about the earth might be answered by studying undersea vents.

PASSPORT

United
of

THE LAST FRONTIERS

I. ANTARCTICA
   A. PHYSICAL GEOGRAPHY
   B. EXPLORATION
   C. INTERNATIONAL COOPERATION AND DISPUTES

II. THE OCEAN DEEP
   A. THE UNDERSEA LANDSCAPE
   B. EXPLORATION
   C. DISPUTED WATERS

III. THE HEAVENS
   A. THE TROPOSPHERE
   B. THE STRATOSPHERE, MESOSPHERE, AND THERMOSPHERE

The Lord planted in the human heart an insatiable curiosity that will never be quenched. Many places in God's vast universe remain to be studied and colonized.

> He hath made every thing beautiful in his time: also he hath set the world in their heart, so that no man can find out the work that God maketh from the beginning to the end.
> (Eccles. 3:11)

During the twentieth century, modern technology opened three new frontiers for scientific study: Antarctica, the ocean depths, and the heavens. Scientists discovered not only a wealth of new knowledge but also new areas of competition for scarce resources and military advantage. The Creation Mandate does not stop at the shores of the continents or on the beaches of Oceania. It invites man to extend his studies and to exercise his dominion over the unexplored areas of Antarctica, the undersea world, and the heavens.

I. ANTARCTICA

> The heavens are thine, the earth also is thine: as for the world and the fullness thereof, thou hast founded them. The north and the south thou hast created them.
> (Ps. 89:11–12)

At the bottom of the world is a remote region known as **Antarctica**. The Antarctic Circle, located at 66½° S latitude, marks the boundary of the region. For at least one twenty-four-hour period each year, the sun never sets in "the land of the midnight sun."

Because sunlight in Antarctica is either very slanted or nonexistent, temperatures there are extremely cold. Huge packs of permanent floating ice defied all attempts at systematic exploration until the twentieth century.

In the open seas, icebergs can be a major hazard. **Icebergs** are jagged chunks of ice that have broken off, or "calved," from a glacier as it reached the sea. Icebergs have been measured as large as two hundred miles long, sixty miles wide, and a thousand feet deep. Because more than three-fourths of an iceberg lies hidden below the water, ships may crash into the underwater portion before the crew realizes the danger is there.

South of the Antarctic Circle is the forbidding continent of Antarctica. Technically, Antarctica is surrounded by three oceans—the Atlantic, Pacific, and Indian oceans. Yet, a band of polar water circling the continent is much colder and less salty than the subtropical waters next to it. A gigantic ice pack covers this band. Pieces of the pack that break off the ice pack are called **ice floes**. The open water between floes is called a **lead**. In places, the ice extends as far as nine hundred miles from the coast.

Scientists explore ice floes in Antarctica.

In 2000, the International Hydrographic Organization designated a fifth ocean from the southernmost portions of the Atlantic, Pacific, and Indian Oceans, calling it the **Southern Ocean**. They based their decision on the fact that the waters around the continent of Antarctica have characteristics that distinguish them from all other oceans. The area lies south of 60° south latitude and comprises

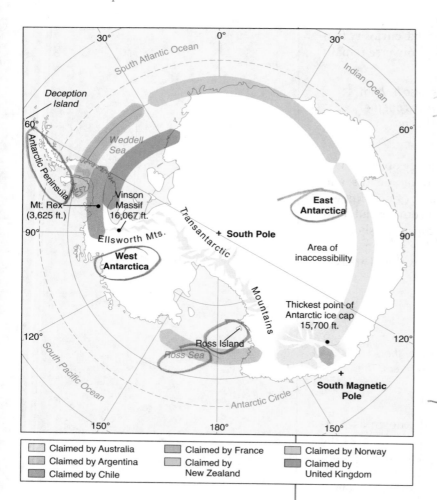

Claimed by Australia	Claimed by France	Claimed by Norway
Claimed by Argentina	Claimed by New Zealand	Claimed by United Kingdom
Claimed by Chile		

an area more than twice the size of the United States. The waters are deep—from 13,123 to 16,404 feet (roughly two to three miles)—with the deepest point being 23,738 feet (more than 4.5 miles) at the South Sandwich Trench. Not everyone agrees that the Southern Ocean deserves to be a separate ocean, but the trend is in that direction. (For example, although the latest atlas of the National Geographic Society does not label the Southern Ocean, the text includes an explanation of it.)

PHYSICAL GEOGRAPHY

Antarctica is shaped like a pear. East (or Greater) Antarctica lies at the fat, rounded end. At the other end lies West (or Lesser) Antarctica. Dividing the two ends are the 1,900-mile-long Transantarctic Mountains.

EAST ANTARCTICA

East Antarctica is a high plateau covered by a thick ice cap that is more than a mile deep. In fact, the weight of the ice has pushed the land down to form a great basin that is 9,840 feet (a little less than two miles) below sea level in one spot.

The Antarctic Plateau is famous for its cold cyclonic storms that whirl almost endlessly from east to west. Gales can reach two hundred miles per hour. The average temperature of the interior during the coldest months is -94° F (compared to -22° F on the coast).

The extreme cold of the interior prohibits life. Nothing lives here—not even a bush or an insect. However, the cold is a blessing. Because cold air cannot hold much moisture, the interior receives less than two inches of snow per year. The desert conditions prevent snow from building up and depleting the world's water level.

WEST ANTARCTICA

In West Antarctica, the **Ross Sea** and **Weddell Sea** cut in on either side to form the neck of Antarctica's pear. Glaciers that flow into the Ross and Weddell seas slide out onto the water to form solid **ice shelves**.

West Antarctica is mountainous rather than flat. The Ellsworth Mountains near the Weddell Sea—the highest mountains on the continent—peep up above the ice cap. Elsewhere, solitary mountains, called **nunataks**, stick up like rocky islands in an ice sea.

At the tip of West Antarctica is the **Antarctic Peninsula**, the most coveted piece of property on the continent. It is the only part of the continent that extends beyond the Antarctic Circle toward South America.

At the edge of this seeming desert, the coastal waters are teeming with life. Plankton forms the basis of the food chain. Small shrimp-like krill and many different species of fish thrive in the ocean. Squid,

Elephant Island is one of the northernmost islands on the Antarctic Peninsula.

BIRDS THAT WEAR TUXEDOS

Penguins are curious birds whose dark backs and white fronts make them seem to be wearing tuxedos. These pudgy gentlemen look awkward on land as they waddle, and they cannot fly. But in water they are skilled acrobats with flipper wings. They can even leap out of the water like flying fish or dolphins. They have to be fast. Catching fish is not easy, and eluding leopard seals and killer whales is even harder.

Antarctica's mainland has two species of penguins. The emperor penguin is the largest of all penguins, growing up to four feet high and weighing up to one hundred pounds. The Adélie penguin is named for the coast first claimed by France. A third species, the gentoo penguin, lives on islands along the Antarctic Peninsula.

Penguins are a common feature of Antarctica.

octopuses, whales, porpoises, seals, and dolphins are abundant. Penguins are the dominant birds.

ROSS SEA AND MCMURDO STATION

Between West Antarctica and East Antarctica is the Ross Sea. It is separated from the South Pole by the **Transantarctic Mountains**. About half of the Ross Sea is covered by the Ross Ice Shelf. On the side closest to East Antarctica is **McMurdo Station**, the largest settlement in Antarctica.

EXPLORATION

The ice-choked seas surrounding Antarctica are the stormiest known to man. Until the nineteenth century, the continent eluded discovery. Captain Cook circumnavigated the Antarctic region in 1773 in search of a fabled southern continent, but his ship could not penetrate the ice pack. In 1820, an American sealing ship, a Russian sealing ship, and an English sealing ship each claimed to be the first to sight Antarctica. Finally, in 1895, a Norwegian businessman named Henryk Johan Bull became the first human to set foot on the continent.

McMurdo Station is the headquarters of the U.S. scientists in Antarctica.

This sign at Scott Base, which is operated by New Zealand, indicates distances "back home" for the international community of scientists there.

Antarctica's harsh environment requires the use of special transportation equipment.

THE ANTARCTIC EXPLORERS: HALL OF FAME

Thaddeus von Bellingshausen (Russia): sailed around Antarctica, discovered Peter I Island (1819–20)

Carsten Borchgrevink (Norway): first explorer to winter in Antarctica (1899)

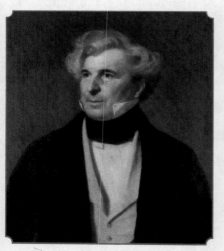

Sir James Ross Clark (Great Britain): made three expeditions to Antarctica (1839–43), during which he discovered Cape Adare, Ross Island, the Ross Ice Shelf, and McMurdo Bay

Scott's Last Journal Entry

Scott set out for the South Pole on November 1, 1911. Five men reached the pole on January 18, but to their dismay they found a note saying that Amundsen had already been there. As they struggled back to the coast, they grew steadily weaker, carrying their own supplies on sleds because they had scorned the use of dogs. Even as their strength declined, they kept hauling thirty-five pounds of rock specimens among their gear. Two men had died by March 18. The last three men got within eleven miles of supplies, but then a snowstorm struck. When searchers found their final camp, they discovered Scott's diary. He had scrawled the following last words:

we shall stick it out to the end but we are getting weaker of course and the end cannot be far, It seems a pity but I do not think I can write more —

R. Scott

Last Entry —

For Gods sake look after our people

Scott's final journal entry before his death

"Thursday, March 29. Since the 21st we have had a continuous gale from the W.S.W. and S.W. We had fuel to make two cups of tea apiece and bare food for two days on the 20th. Every day we have been ready to start for our depot 11 miles away, but outside the door of the tent it remains a scene of whirling drift. I do not think we can hope for any better things now. We shall stick it out to the end, but we are getting weaker, of course, and the end cannot be far. It seems a pity, but I do not think I can write more. R. Scott. For God's sake look after our people."

Sir Robert Scott (Great Britain): made first expedition in 1902; in 1911 set out with goal of being first person to reach the South Pole, but Amundsen beat him; died on return trip when only 150 miles from his final destination

Sir Douglas Mawson (Great Britain): member of Shackleton's 1908–9 expedition; led his own expedition in 1911, discovering Shackleton Ice Shelf; made two more expeditions (1929–31)

Roald Amundsen (Norway): became the first human to reach the South Pole (1911); left a letter for his competitor Robert Scott, who found it a month later

Ernest Shackleton (Great Britain): led first expedition (1908–9), traveling farther south than anyone else to that time; discovered Beardmore Glacier and was only 97 miles from South Pole when he had to turn back; his ship became locked in ice floes (1914), and he spent the rest of his expedition finding help and rescuing the crew.

Jacques Cousteau (France): became the first person to dive beneath the ice of Antarctica (1975); filmed a TV series documenting his explorations

Through Christian Eyes

What inspires humans to achieve feats such as reaching the South Pole?

The "heroic age" of exploration began in the twentieth century. On December 14, 1911, **Roald Amundsen** planted the Norwegian flag at the South Pole. At the same time, a British explorer named **Robert Scott** was struggling to reach the site. He did reach it; however, his entire party perished on the return trip.

Other records followed. Admiral **Richard Byrd** flew a plane over the South Pole on his 1928–29 survey expedition. In 1958, Vivian Fuchs successfully crossed the 1,550-mile width of the continent.

INTERNATIONAL COOPERATION AND DISPUTES

Foreign powers began establishing bases on Antarctica in the 1940s. Once they started, no seafaring nation wanted to be left out. Scientists from the United States and other countries prevailed on their governments to reserve the earth's last great wilderness for pure science, unspoiled by the Cold War tensions. During an eighteen-month period from 1957 to 1958, twelve nations coordinated their efforts in building sixty scientific bases and sharing all their findings. The following year, twelve nations signed the Antarctic Treaty, agreeing to ban military bases and weapons testing on the continent, to freeze all land claims, to exchange all information freely, and to open all camps for inspection at any time. Many other nations later signed the treaty. In 1991, the "Antarctic Treaty Parties" extended the treaty indefinitely and agreed to ban mining for fifty years.

Scientists have studied all sorts of phenomena in Antarctica. Many of those scientists are looking for evidence that world pollution is increasing. The discovery of an ozone "hole" above the Antarctic has raised fears that the atmosphere might be warming. A warming of the earth could have serious consequences. More than 90 percent of the world's ice is locked in the ice cap of Antarctica. Some scientists predict that were the ice cap to melt, the sea level around the world would rise as much as two hundred feet, sinking many islands and every major coastal city.

Core samples and radio soundings provide tantalizing clues about what is under the ice cap. Extensive coal fields and mineral resources may lie under the ice, awaiting the development of economically feasible methods of mining. Some far-off nations have even set up sham research stations to ensure a right to participate in any bargaining over mining and land claims.

SECTION QUIZ

1. What two large seas lie beside Antarctica's coasts?
2. What long, narrow peninsula extends from Antarctica?
3. What are ice shelves?
   - Should the United States claim part of Antarctica?

II. THE OCEAN DEEP

He gathereth the waters of the sea together as an heap: he layeth up the depth in storehouses.
(Ps. 33:7)

God created the deep (Gen. 1:2), broke it up in the great Flood (Gen. 7:11), and put boundaries on the new oceans and deeps (Job 38:8–11). For thousands of years the secrets of the deep have been hidden from human eyes. But new technology is finally allowing man to discover a whole new world of unusual life forms and valuable resources.

THE UNDERSEA LANDSCAPE

The Bible says that God covered the foundations of the earth with the deep (Ps. 104:6). Only in the twentieth century did deep-sea explorers discover what this means. The continents are thick slabs sitting on a foundation of rock. The submerged edges of these slabs are called the **continental shelf**. They slope gently down from the shore to a depth of about 650 feet. At the edge of the continental shelf, the continent drops off sharply. The steep sides of the continents, called the **continental slope**, descend to a depth of more than two miles (about thirteen thousand feet). Deep ocean basins stretch across the vast empty spaces between the continents.

The sea creatures that mankind harvests live in the upper seven hundred feet of the ocean, a region that is called the **photic zone** because it has enough light for photosynthesis. However, no plants grow below the photic zone. Some light filters down to two thousand feet—about the same amount of light that you see at dusk or on a starry night. This twilight region is called the *mesopelagic* (midsea) *zone*. Perpetual darkness reigns below that depth in the *bathypelagic* (deep-sea) *zone*, where man has discovered some unusual fish. The angler fish, for example, has a light hanging in front of its mouth to attract prey.

The ocean floor consists primarily of deep **ocean basins**, which typically range from thirteen thousand to eighteen thousand feet deep. Soundings have uncovered a varied landscape, much more dramatic than the weathered landscape where people live.

Creatures that Live at Each Level of the Sea

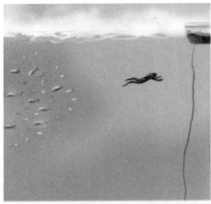

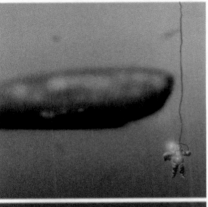

Undersea Surface Features

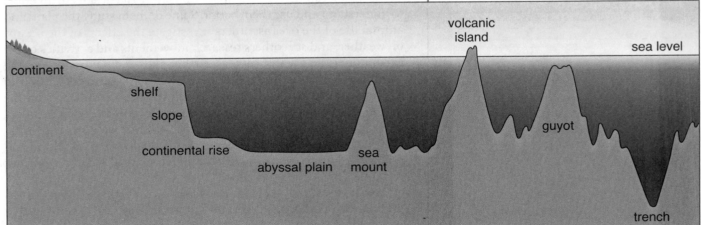

Sediment from continental rivers and debris from landslides have caused a buildup at the base of the continental slopes. This buildup is known as the *continental rise.*

Like continents, the ocean basins have three major physical features: mountains, plateaus, and plains. The plains are known as **abyssal** (uh BIS uhl) **plains**. They begin at the edge of the continental shelf and continue in an extremely level and featureless plain that is covered by silt as deep as a few miles. They are the flattest areas on earth and make up about half of the ocean floor. A few plateaus and hills, usually extinct volcanoes, rise above the abyssal plains.

The sea floor map on page 589 shows that a number of deep canyons, called **trenches**, scar the ocean basins. The Pacific Ocean has more trenches than all the other oceans combined.

Less than 1 percent of the ocean floor descends below the ocean basin. The word *deep* refers to depths beyond 18,000 feet. The Milwaukee Deep, located in the Puerto Rico Trench, is, at 28,231 feet below sea level, the deepest point in the Atlantic. The deepest deep in the world is the **Mariana Trench**, and its deepest point is the **Challenger Deep**, which is more than 35,000 feet below sea level—a mile deeper under the sea surface than Mount Everest is above it.

Mountain ranges form along the **oceanic ridges**. Every ocean has ridges, but scientists have conducted the most studies on the Mid-Atlantic Ridge, a ridge of volcanic mountains that divides the Atlantic Ocean in half. Occasionally, the ridge rises above the surface to form islands. Iceland is such an island.

Isolated underwater volcanoes called **seamounts** dot the basins. Sometimes a new volcano breaks through the ocean surface, forming an island, such as Surtsey off the coast of Iceland.

Scarred areas on the ocean basin are creased by numerous earthquake faults. These regions are called *fracture zones.* Sometimes hot springs, or **deep-sea vents**, spew hot lava and sulfur into the dark, frigid waters. A wide variety of unique life forms are found around the vents.

EXPLORATION

> *They that go down to the sea in ships, that do business in great waters; these see the works of the Lord, and his wonders in the deep.*
> (Ps. 107:23–24)

Oceanographers are scientists who study the oceans in an effort to understand and use them better. Some of them study the plant and animal life of the oceans; others investigate the effects of the oceans on weather; and still others research movements and activities of the earth under the oceans, such as earthquakes and volcanoes and the tsunamis they sometimes produce. Historical researchers try to find and raise (or study on-site) various shipwrecks and artifacts on the sea floor. Engineers help such scientists develop the equipment required to do those tasks safely and efficiently. A well-trained Christian working in any of these fields can do much to help mankind and honor the Lord by learning to be a better steward of this important resource.

As long as man had undiscovered or unexploited lands to explore and conquer, he tended to ignore the oceans, assuming that they held less value for him than the landmasses offered and using them as a mere transportation route. In fact, however, the opposite is true. Man has only begun to learn what the oceans can teach him about any number of subjects and benefits.

PIONEERS AND PROBLEMS OF OCEANOGRAPHY

History suggests that Alexander the Great might have been the first person to go underwater (in a glass barrel) to examine what was there. For centuries, sponge divers all over the world dove—without any special equipment—to harvest their products for sale, but they were severely limited in both how deep they could go and how long they could stay down. (Even the best divers can hold their breath for only about two minutes and can descend only about one hundred feet unassisted by special equipment.)

The three biggest problems to be overcome were providing a reliable oxygen supply; preventing the divers from being crushed by the pressure, which increases with depth; and avoiding "the bends," a painful condition that develops when nitrogen bubbles form in the bloodstream as divers ascend. Over the centuries, people developed various kinds of suits and vessels (generally called diving bells) for going underwater safely.

Two underwater vessels became famous in the eighteenth and nineteenth centuries, but they were intended for warfare, not science. In 1776, early in the American War for Independence, **David Bushnell** built an egg-shaped submersible named the *Turtle* by which he hoped to slip under British warships, drill holes in their hulls, and attach and detonate explosive devices. His plan failed when the drill hit metal on the hull of the first British warship he tried to sink, the frigate HMS *Eagle*. (One theory is that the ship's hull was sheathed in copper, but it is more likely that the drill hit a metal band or a bolt.)

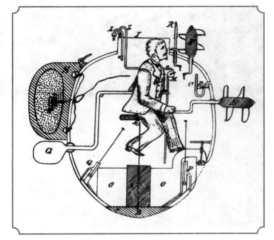

Bushnell's *Turtle* was an early attempt to construct an effective submersible for use in warfare.

"THE PATHFINDER OF THE SEAS"

Sometimes the people who make some of the greatest contributions to a field of study do not get the public honor they deserve. Such is the case with **Matthew Maury** (1806–73).

Maury grew up on a farm in Middle Tennessee. He followed his older brother's footsteps and joined the U.S. Navy. During ten years of sailing the seas, he rose in rank and conducted intensive studies of navigation.

While ashore between voyages, however, he was severely injured in a stagecoach accident that prevented his return to sea duty. Much to his dismay, he was reassigned to the Navy's Depot of Charts and Instruments.

Bored with being a mere caretaker of dusty maps, charts, and ships' logs, Maury began to study them closely. He noticed a pattern with the ships that had wrecked and were disabled and consequently drifted aimlessly on the seas. He suspected that the ocean had continuous currents in certain locations. His naval colleagues laughed at his idea and dismissed it.

But then a ship lost its rudder off Sandy Hook and drifted out to sea. Most people gave up on ever finding it, but Maury obtained the last known coordinates of the ship and, using his theory, calculated where the ship should be. A rescue ship was dispatched. Using Maury's calculations, it found the otherwise doomed ship and rescued its crew. Maury became a recognized expert on currents and even published *The Wind and Current Charts of the North Atlantic* and *The Physical Geography of the Sea*.

Later, Maury served in the Confederate navy and taught meteorology at Virginia Military Institute.

Matthew F. Maury, "Pathfinder of the Seas," charted ocean currents.

The CSS *Hunley* was the first submarine to sink an enemy warship.

In 1864, during the American Civil War, a group of Southern investors financed and built a submarine named the CSS *Hunley*. It became the first successful wartime submarine when it slipped out of Charleston Harbor under cover of darkness, attached an explosive devise to the hull of the Union sloop of war USS *Housatonic*, and sank it. Unfortunately, the *Hunley* did not make it back to the Charleston shore; it sank, and the entire eight-man crew perished. (The *Hunley* was discovered in 1995 and raised in 2000. Scientists and researchers are examining and displaying the sub to the public at the Charleston Naval Yard.)

TWENTIETH-CENTURY UNDERSEA EXPLORATIONS

The first humans to venture below the photic zone (beyond about seven hundred feet) were **William Beebe** and **Otis Barton** in 1930. They used a steel ball-shaped vessel called a **bathysphere**.

In 1943, Frenchman **Jacques Cousteau** invented the Aqua-Lung, or self-contained underwater breathing apparatus (SCUBA), which dramatically increased the time one could spend underwater as well as the range of depth accessible for human study. He purchased and retrofitted a ship named the *Calypso* and used it for numerous underwater studies around the world. He filmed many of his expeditions and used them to develop documentaries that made his name almost synonymous with undersea exploration.

William Beebe contributed to undersea exploration with his bathysphere.

Jacques Cousteau was a famed undersea explorer and the co-inventor of the Aqua-Lung.

FLIP is towed into place and then flipped into a working position.

Another type of ocean exploration tool is the Floating Instrument Platform (FLIP). It is a 355-foot, spoon-shaped ocean laboratory. Developed in 1960, it is towed by boat to the site researchers want to study. Ballast tanks in the handle-shaped end are flooded with seven hundred tons of water, causing that end to sink and flipping the bowl-shaped end into the air. The upper fifty-five feet remain above the surface of the water. Crew members live and work aboard this unique laboratory. *Alvin* is a much smaller, three-person submersible that is highly mobile under water.

Alvin is a three-person submersible exploration craft.

Nautilus 90° North

In the summer of 1958, the USS *Nautilus*, the world's first nuclear-powered submarine, slipped into Seattle with a problem that threatened to doom its secret mission. The sub had a leaky condenser unit. The secrecy surrounding the mission prevented its repair through normal channels, so Commander William Anderson resorted to unconventional methods. He ordered his sailors to don civilian clothing and to fan out throughout the Seattle area to gas stations and auto repair shops in search of a product called Bar's Leak, which was normally used to repair auto radiator leaks. The sailors got every can they could find—one hundred forty of them—and poured half of the product into the condenser unit. The leak stopped. They prayed it would hold throughout their dangerous voyage ahead.

On June 9, under cover of darkness, the *Nautilus* slipped away northward and under the polar ice cap. The sub traveled 1,830 miles to 90° North—the North Pole. You can read Anderson's first-hand account of the experience in the book he wrote in 1959: *Nautilus 90° North*.

Some undersea crafts, however, are unmanned and operate by remote control, photographing the sea floor and environment and sending the images to monitors aboard surface ships. *Jason/Medea* is a team of two vehicles, one

DESCENT INTO THE MARIANA TRENCH

Hundreds of people have summited Mount Everest or traveled into space, even walking on the moon itself. But only two men have descended into the deepest part of the ocean depths.

The Mariana Trench is the deepest trench in the world. The deepest place in the trench, the Challenger Deep, is 35,800 feet below sea level. The first people to descend into this spot were Jacques Piccard, son of the engineer who invented the bathyscaphe, and Don Walsh of the U.S. Navy. The trip took nine hours. During their twenty minutes on the bottom, they spotted a flounder, which proved that certain fish can survive the tremendous pressures of the cold, dark deep.

Auguste and Jacques Piccard built *Trieste*, the bathyscaphe, for deep-sea exploration.

Jacques Piccard and Lt. Don Walsh are seen here in *Trieste*, the bathyscaphe in which they descended to the Mariana Trench in 1960.

NOAA

The National Oceanographic and Atmospheric Administration (NOAA) was an outgrowth of the survey of the U.S. east coast that President Thomas Jefferson authorized in 1807. Although NOAA is most commonly thought of as the organization that tracks and warns the United States of impending hurricanes, it does much more than that, as its name indicates.

In 2000, President George W. Bush formed a panel of "ocean explorers, researchers, and marine educators" to develop a national ocean exploration strategy. In *Discovering Earth's Final Frontier: A U.S. Strategy for Ocean Exploration,* the experts recommended an interagency program to explore in U.S. waters under the authority of NOAA. NOAA then organized the Office of Ocean Exploration. They began cooperative explorations with the Woods Hole Oceanographic Institution and several colleges and universities. In 2002, they helped recover the turret and engine of the Union ironclad USS *Monitor.*

The National Ocean Service offices deal with coastal ocean science, studies of red tide, geodetic surveying, marine sanctuaries, coastal resource management, and response to natural (or man-made) disasters and restoration of the environment afterward.

NOAA scientists regularly collect water samples from the ocean to monitor the quantity of harmful algae.

large vehicle and one small vehicle, that are tethered together and work in tandem to take photos, collect temperature and other data, and gather physical samples from the sea.

Using another such device named *Argo*, **Robert Ballard** discovered the wreck of the HMS *Titanic* in 1985. Ballard has also used such equipment to locate and explore the wrecks of other vessels, including the Nazi battleship *Bismarck* and John Kennedy's famous

Perhaps Dr. Robert Ballard's most famous underwater discovery was the wreckage of the HMS *Titanic*.

Robert Ballard on the Difference Between an Explorer and an Adventurer

A newspaper reporter once asked ocean explorer Robert Ballard what he considered to be the most important quality for an explorer, to which Ballard replied, "Curiosity. I think you also have to be a risk-taker, but not foolish. The difference between an explorer and an adventurer is that we go places as disciplined observers. We keep journals, we make maps—we're not just there for the thrill, although the thrill is there. We want it to have meaning. We want to bring back new knowledge."[1]

[1] Quoted from "The World According to . . . Robert Ballard," *The (London) Independent* (Oct. 26, 2004).

patrol-torpedo boat, PT-109. Ballard's high-tech explorations continue into the twenty-first century.

DISPUTED WATERS

Almost every speck of dry land on earth has been claimed by one nation or another, but claims on water have always stirred controversy. The United States and many other countries support *freedom of the seas*, the view that any nation can fish and trade freely on the open seas. But this position has become complicated. Modern high-tech ships compete for a limited supply of fish to feed the growing world population. The discovery of offshore oil has given waters a value they never had before.

During the seventeenth century, seagoing nations developed the concept of **territorial waters**, the right of a nation to exclude ships of other nations from a three- to six-mile-wide strip of water along its coast. Ships of other nations enjoyed the "right of free passage" only if they came in peace to trade. Beyond the territorial waters were the **high seas**, which were open to vessels of all nations.

In the twentieth century, nations began extending their territorial waters to exorbitant distances from the shores. These claims often overlapped the valid claims of neighboring countries. One country's refusal to recognize the claims of another sometimes led to shooting. In 1958, nearly ninety nations agreed to limit territorial waters to a twelve-mile *contiguous zone*. However, narrow straits, such as the Strait of Gibraltar, were to remain open. Each nation was permitted to develop oil fields on its adjacent continental shelf, but the ocean basins were to remain free of claims. Disputes continued, however, because some countries did not want to comply with the agreement.

The United Nations drafted the Law of the Sea Treaty (LOST) in 1982 to address those problems. The treaty recognizes the previous twelve-mile zone and an additional two-hundred-mile **exclusive economic zone** (EEZ). Each signatory country has exclusive rights to fish and drill for oil in its own EEZ. The treaty went into effect in 1995 after sixty nations signed. Although the United States played a significant role in drafting the treaty, it balked because of provisions in the final treaty concerning deep ocean mining and sovereignty. Nonetheless, the United States complied with all other treaty provisions as though it had signed. Its concerns were eventually resolved, and the United States signed the treaty and the Senate Foreign Relations Committee approved it. As of 2007, George W. Bush was urging full Senate approval.

SECTION QUIZ

1. Name the three ocean layers based on the amount of light received.
2. What are the three major features that the sea floor shares with dry land?
3. What is the deepest trench in the world?
4. Name the major pioneers in undersea exploration and state the contribution of each.

Territorial Claims in the North Sea

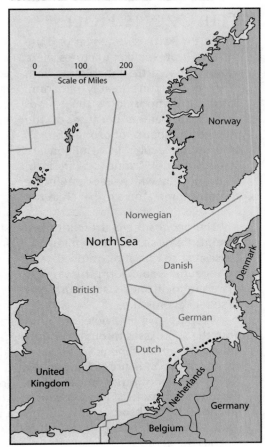

Internationally Accepted Zones Dividing the Waters of the World

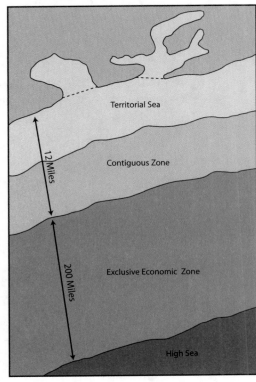

THE OZONE HOLE

As the earth revolves around the sun, a delicate blanket of atmosphere protects the earth's inhabitants from much of the sun's deadly radiation. Particularly important is the ozonosphere, so named because of the relative abundance of ozone (though only six molecules in a million are actually ozone). Ozone is a rare form of oxygen in which each molecule contains three atoms rather than the usual two.

The ozonosphere stretches from an altitude of six to thirty miles. Because air is so thin at that altitude, the total ozone would form a layer less than one inch thick were it brought to sea-level pressure.

As shortwave ultraviolet radiation from the sun passes through the oxygen in the ozonosphere, it produces ozone. Other radiation of a slightly higher wavelength then breaks down the unstable ozone. These chemical reactions help absorb some of the sun's dangerous radiation before it reaches the earth.

Recently, governments have become concerned because laboratory experiments have shown that ozone is destroyed by nitrogen oxide from car exhaust and by now-prohibited halogenated refrigerants and aerosols. In 1985, scientists noticed that dramatic changes were taking place in the ozone layer above Antarctica. They discovered an "ozone hole" that appeared each spring and grew until November, when it started to shrink. The size of the hole steadily increased, raising fears that it was only the beginning of a worldwide catastrophe.

In the Montreal Protocol of 1987, ninety-three nations agreed to regulate or ban ozone-destroying chemicals and to search for less damaging alternatives. Citizens of the United States and other nations began paying hundreds of dollars to change their air conditioning systems. The estimated cost to the world economy could exceed four trillion dollars.

Yet the cause and significance of the hole is still uncertain. For one thing, no similar "ozone hole" occurs in the Arctic, even though continental air currents carry pollutants from temperate regions into the upper atmosphere. Theories about the culprits causing the ozone hole include volcanic eruptions, springtime upwelling of the air, and increased chemicals in the atmosphere (fluorocarbons, chlorine, and other trace gases). If mankind is to be a good steward of the earth and its resources, we must seek ways to correct the problem or at least avoid making it worse.

�🔆 Should the government require families, such as yours, to pay large sums of money to use new substances because of an unproven environmental concern? Should taxpayers fund environmental research in Antarctica? (Support your answers.)

III. THE HEAVENS

For thousands of years, the grandeur of the night sky has thrilled human observers.

The heavens declare the glory of God; and the firmament sheweth his handywork.
(Ps. 19:1)

In the twentieth century, man began to realize his dreams of exploring the heavens, both inner space (the atmosphere) and outer space. But space flight has introduced new problems. Nations now have another "border" to guard from enemy warplanes, missiles, and nuclear weapons.

THE TROPOSPHERE

Psalm 147:8 says that God "covereth the heaven with clouds." This part of the heavens—the atmosphere—extends about six hundred miles above the earth. It has various layers defined by differences in temperature, pressure, and gases.

The lowest nine miles of the atmosphere is called the **troposphere**. It contains the air we breathe and the clouds that water the earth. The temperature drops about 3.5° F for every thousand-foot increase in altitude. (See lapse rate on page 40.) God filled the troposphere with just the right mixture of gases for breathing—78 percent nitrogen, 21 percent oxygen, and 1 percent other gases, including carbon dioxide.

THE STRATOSPHERE, MESOSPHERE, AND THERMOSPHERE

The upper atmosphere consists of three regions. The *stratosphere* extends from nine to thirty-five miles above the earth. Unlike the troposphere, the stratosphere increases in temperature with altitude. It contains most of the *ozone layer*. The mesosphere extends about sixty miles from the earth. This region has decreasing temperatures; the coldest place in the atmosphere occurs at the top of the mesosphere. The *thermosphere*, extending about six hundred miles from the earth, is so named because it retains warmth from direct sunlight. Its inner half, the *ionosphere*, protects the earth from harmful radiation and meteors. The outer half, the *exosphere*, reaches the limits of our atmosphere, where particles can escape into outer space.

SECTION QUIZ

1. How are the four main layers of the atmosphere distinguished?

2. In which region is the ozone layer?

3. In which region is the ionosphere?

⚬ Based on how nations have solved disputes over territorial waters, how should they resolve disputes over space rights?

Can You:

Define These Terms?

iceberg	trench
ice floe	oceanic ridge
lead	seamount
ice shelf	deep-sea vent
nunatak	bathysphere
continental shelf	territorial waters
continental slope	high seas
photic zone	exclusive eco-
ocean basin	nomic zone
abyssal plain	troposhere

Locate These Places?

Antarctica	Antarctic Peninsula
Southern Ocean	Transantarctic
Ross Sea	Mountains
Weddell Sea	

Explain the Significance?

McMurdo Station	David Bushnell
Roald Amundsen	Matthew Maury
Robert Scott	William Beebe
Richard Byrd	Otis Barton
Mariana Trench	Jacques Cousteau
Challenger Deep	Robert Ballard

CHAPTER REVIEW 24

HOW MUCH DO YOU REMEMBER?

1. Describe two major differences between East Antarctica and West Antarctica.

2. How is an iceberg formed? an ice floe?

3. Which nations claim part of Antarctica? Why has the United States made no claims?

4. How thick is the Antarctic ice cap?

5. Why is it a blessing that the polar regions have very dry climates?

6. Based on a 1958 agreement, how far do territorial waters extend?

WHAT DO YOU THINK?

1. Other than raising the sea level drastically, how do you think the melting of the Antarctic ice would affect the world?

2. Some dry countries would like to tow large icebergs to their shores to provide fresh water. What difficulties can they expect?

3. Should Antarctica be open to tourism or remain a wilderness?

GLOSSARY

A

aborigines The earliest known settlers of a region

absolute monarchy Government by a hereditary ruler who has complete control of the government

abyssal plain The broad, level areas on the depths of the ocean floor

acculturation The process of adopting foreign values and practices

Afrikaans The language that developed when the Boers of South Africa blended their native Dutch with words from African languages such as Zulu

air mass A large area of moving air with a similar temperature throughout

alloy A mixture of two or more metals

alluvium Sediment deposited by flowing water

alpine zone The zone above the timberline that is too cold for trees to grow

anarchy Whenever no form of governing authority exists and people are doing whatever they want

animism Religious beliefs that ascribe spiritual powers to animals and plants

anthracite coal A hard coal with a high carbon content that burns with little smoke

apartheid A rigorous racial policy that severely regulated life for blacks, Coloureds, and Asians in South Africa through segregation

aquaculture Cultivation or farming in a controlled, artificial environment

aquifer A layer of underground rock that yields water

arable Able to be cultivated

archipelago A large group of islands

arid Lacking moisture

artesian well A source of water in which water rises from the water table by internal pressure

ASEAN Association of Southeast Asian Nations

atmosphere The layer of gases that surrounds the earth

atoll A ring-shaped island formation formed by coral

autocrat A ruler with unlimited authority

autonomous regions Areas that have limited self-government within a sovereign country; used especially of areas in China where ethnic minorities have been granted some autonomy

autonomous republic A self-governing republic; used especially of the countries that were once part of the former Soviet Union

ayatollah The highest title of honor that a Shiite Muslim can hold

azimuthal projection A type of map that uses a flat-plane map; because it is most accurate in the center but becomes increasingly distorted near the edges, it is useful for compact areas

B

Baha'i A religion developed in ancient Persia that emphasizes the unity of all religions

balance of trade The difference between a nation's total imports and its total exports

Balkanization The tendency of ethnically and religiously diverse territories to break up into small, hostile nations

barrier island An island that lies near the coast and is created by silt deposits

bauxite The principal ore of aluminum

bayou A swampy area along slow-moving, meandering streams and rivers of the Gulf Coastal Plain, especially in the Mississippi Delta

Bedouin A nomadic shepherd of the Arabian desert

bicameral Having two chambers or houses, as in the legislature of a government

bight A large bay formed by a long, curving coast

bilingual Using or knowing two languages

biome A large geographic area that contains a particular group of plants and animals and has a specific physical environment

bituminous coal Soft coal that occurs frequently and is of varying quality

bluffs A steep riverbank or cliff

bog A spongy area that looks dry but is covered with wet organic materials

Bosniaks Muslims who live in the Balkans, especially in Bosnia

Brahmins Priests and teachers, who, along with the Ksatriyas (rulers and warriors), occupy the highest caste of Hinduism

Buddhism An Eastern religion founded by Buddha that offers release from the suffering of the world through meditation and following the Eight-fold Path

buffer state A neutral state between two rivals that is intended to prevent conflict

Burma The former name of Myanmar

C

caciques Local "party bosses" in Mexico who rule as small-town dictators, making their money by selling alcohol at pagan religious festivals

CAFTA Central American Free Trade Agreement

Cajuns Residents of Louisiana whose ancestors were French refugees from an area of Maine and Canada known as Acadia

cantons Self-governing districts in Switzerland

capital Money used to build or operate a business or industry

capitalism A free-market economy in which anyone may go into business in an attempt to make a profit; most businesses are privately owned instead of government owned

cargo cult A religion that Melanesians developed when they were exposed to the riches of European traders; they had no idea how the goods were made or where they came from and concluded that they came from the spirit world

cartography The art of mapmaking

cash crop A crop raised specifically for sale rather than for personal use

cassava A shrubby tropical plant grown for its large, starchy roots

caste A system within Hinduism that assigns people to different classes, each with its own privileges and responsibilities but also limitations, and strictly determines one's social status

cataclysm A violent upheaval or change in the earth's crust, especially a flood

census An official government count of the entire population within a nation's boundaries

civil war A war between factions or regions of a country in which both sides are trying to take over the government

climate The usual temperature, precipitation, and wind conditions of a certain area

climograph Charts that show the average temperature and the average total precipitation of a particular place during each month

commercial farmer Someone who grows crops for sale and profit rather than merely for personal use

communism The most radical form of socialism in which the government owns everything (in the name of "the people") and no private property or free-market business transactions are allowed

condensation The process whereby water vapor becomes liquid

confluence The point at which two rivers join to form one larger river

Confucianism A Chinese philosophy that teaches harmony through proper treatment of others

conic projection A type of map projection made by placing a cone-shaped piece of paper on an imaginary wire globe and tracing the shadow onto the cone; most accurate where the cone touches the line and good for showing wide regions

conifer A tree that produces its seed in a cone (e.g., a pine tree)

constitutional monarchy (or limited monarchy) A government that includes a hereditary ruler whose powers are strictly limited by law (a constitution)

continent One of the seven primary landmasses of the earth's surface

continental divide A chain of mountains that divides the flow of river systems between oceans

continental drift theory The idea that the continents were once one landmass but at some point drifted apart (see also **plate tectonics theory**)

continental island An island, usually large and high, formed near a continent out of the same landmass

continental shelf The border of a continent that lies underwater and slopes at first gradually and then more abruptly toward the ocean floor

continental slope The gradual decline of the continental shelf toward the ocean bottom

contour lines The lines that separate colors on a relief map and that indicate all points on the map that have the same altitude

convection precipitation Precipitation that occurs when an air mass warms and rises rapidly, then cools to the dew point as it gains altitude

copra The dried flesh of a coconut from which coconut oil is extracted

coral Any of various types of skeletal sea creatures that attach themselves to objects by secreting a glue-like substance and then harden to form reefs

cordillera A chain of mountains

core The central portion of the earth that lies below the mantle

coup A sudden overthrow of a government by a military leader or government official (from *coup d'etat*)

Creation Mandate The unique calling of God to humankind to exercise dominion over the earth; based on Genesis 1:26

Creole A language that mixes French and African words and is spoken by Haitians; or a person with Spanish ancestry who was born in South America

crude birthrate The number of people born each year per one thousand people in the total population

crude death rate The number of people who die each year per one thousand people in the total population

crust The solid outer part of the earth

culture A people's way of life, including their political, economic, religious, lingual, social, intellectual, and artistic practices and beliefs

culture region A distinct area in which a specific culture thrives

cylindrical projection A type of map projection made by shaping a chart into a cylinder, placing it around a globe, tracing the shadows cast by the light, and then unrolling the paper to get a flat map; the most important such projection was done by Mercator

Cyrillic A modified Greek alphabet used for Slavic languages such as Russian

czar The title of rulers of Russia from 1547 to 1917; also tsar

D

deciduous Plants that shed their leaves before a period of dormancy

deep Ocean depths below 18,000 feet

deforestation The cutting down and clearing of trees; often viewed as a negative activity

demilitarized zone (DMZ) A neutral zone separating hostile countries; used especially in reference to North and South Korea

democracy A form of government whereby the people rule themselves

demography The study of population characteristics

desalination The process of removing salt from water

desert A dry area with little vegetation

desertification The changing of arable land into desert

developed country A country that has a wide range of industries that take full advantage of its people's skills

developing country A country whose industries do not take full advantage of its natural or human resources

dialect A regional variety of a language

dictatorship Rule by a person or group with the authority of military strength

dikes Strong walls of stone and earth built to restrict or restrain the flow of water

drainage basin The area drained by a river system

durable manufacturing The mass production of goods that are expected to last more than one year

dynasty A family whose members rule over a country for several generations

E

E pluribus unum The motto of the United States, meaning "From many, one"

economic self-sufficiency The ability of one country to produce everything it needs without buying or selling from other countries

economics The study of the process by which people make decisions; includes ways by which people make a living, buy and sell, grow crops, manufacture goods, and provide services

embargo A prohibition on trade

emirate A country ruled by an emir

empire Lands gained outside the national borders of a country

equator The imaginary line that divides the earth into the Northern and Southern hemispheres

erosion The natural breakdown and removal of materials on the earth's surface

estuary The widening mouth of a river as it nears the ocean where it has a tendency to form a delta

European Union An organization of twenty-seven countries that seeks to form a single European community that can compete on the world stage economically and politically

evaporation The process whereby liquid water changes into a vapor

exclusive economic zone A region up to two hundred miles offshore from a country in which that country controls fishing and mineral exploration and exploitation by any other country

export Any product that one country trades to another country

extended family The nuclear family (parents and children) plus grandparents, uncles, aunts, and cousins

F

fall line The area of the eastern United States where the rivers drop from the Piedmont to the Coastal Plain and where many waterfalls occur

fault A crack in the earth's surface where two pieces of land have moved in different directions

favela A slum district on the outskirts of (or sometimes even within) cities of Brazil

federal republic A representative government that also has both individual state governments and a more powerful national government that share power

fjord A long, narrow bay carved by a glacier and filled with sea water

fold A bend in a portion of the earth's crust caused by pressure

fossil fuel Remains of once-living organisms that can be used as a source of energy; includes coal, petroleum, and natural gas

free enterprise capitalism An economic system in which private individuals own most of the factors of production, make most of the economic decisions, and compete with other individuals or companies to earn money

free market An economic system in which the law of supply and demand is restricted very little if at all (see **free enterprise capitalism**)

free trade An economic concept whereby countries trade with the fewest possible restrictions, such as high tariffs or embargoes

front A line along which two different air masses meet, producing changes in weather

G

gap An opening through a mountain (see also **notch** and **pass**)

gaucho A cowboy of the South American pampas

geocentric theory A view that states that the sun, stars, and planets revolve around the earth

geography The detailed study of the earth, especially its surface; a description of humanity's God-given abode—and everything and everyone on it—and how people interact with it and on it in fulfilling their role as stewards of God's creation; from two roots meaning "earth" (*geo-*) and "written description" (*-graphy*)

geometric boundary A boundary usually drawn as a straight line to connect specific points or to follow a line of latitude or longitude

geothermal energy Power derived from heated water and steam beneath the earth's surface

ger A collapsible round tent used in Mongolia; called a *yurt* in Russian

glacier A large mass of ice, formed from compacted snow, that slowly moves over a land area

glen A narrow valley carved by a glacier

gore One of twelve paper strips that are used to cover a typical globe

grassland A region with plenteous grass but few trees

great circle Any imaginary line that can be drawn around the earth to cut it into equal hemispheres

grid A regular pattern of intersecting vertical and horizontal lines superimposed on a map to assist in locating places; first introduced by Hipparchus

Gross Domestic Product (GDP) The monetary value of all the goods and services produced for sale within a country's borders over the course of a year

groundwater Water that has seeped into the earth's crust and is held below the surface of the earth

Group of 8 (G-8) The group of eight countries that produces more than ¾ of the world's manufacturing value

growing season The time from the last killing frost of spring until the first killing frost of fall; when most crops are grown

H

hacienda A vast ranch in Mexico

Hamas An Islamic terrorist group of Palestinians that is dedicated to the destruction of Israel

harbor A sheltered body of deep water next to the shore

heliocentric theory A view that states that the earth and other planets revolve around the sun

hemisphere Either of the two equal parts of the earth, as divided by the equator or a meridian

Hezbollah An Islamic terrorist group in Lebanon, supported by Syria and Iran, that is dedicated to the destruction of Israel

high island A volcanic island that usually rises above the sea, displaying hills and mountains

high pressure An atmospheric condition that generally indicates good or improving weather

high seas Areas of ocean outside of any country's territorial jurisdiction and free for everyone to use

Hinduism The prevalent religion of India that emphasizes reincarnation, a supreme being with many forms, and the caste system

Holy Land The biblical region of Palestine

humidity The amount of water vapor in the air

humus A soil ingredient produced by the slow decomposition of leaves and other organic materials

hydrologic cycle A cycle whereby water evaporates from oceans, lakes, and the soil to form clouds that, in turn, precipitate water to the earth; also known as the water cycle

hydrosphere All the water that exists on or around the earth

I

iceberg A large chunk of floating ice that has broken off the edge of a glacier

ice floe A large, flat sheet of floating ice that has formed from seawater

immigration The movement of foreigners into another country

imperialism The acquiring of an empire

import Any product that one country buys from another country

Indochina The mainland portion of Southeast Asia, including Vietnam, Laos, Cambodia, Thailand, and Myanmar

industrial country A country in which the majority of people work in secondary or tertiary industries rather than primary industries

infant mortality rate The number of infants per one thousand live births that died before their first birthday

infrastructure The basic energy and equipment needs of all industries, such as electricity production, bridges, and roads; divided into three types: utilities, transportation, and communication

insular countries Countries that are isolated or cut off from other countries

international date line An imaginary line near 180° longitude; time on the east side of the line is one day behind time on the west side

Inuit The name by which Eskimos call themselves; means "real men"

Islam A Middle Eastern religion founded by Muhammad that emphasizes good works

Islamic Jihad A doctrine of Islam that teaches that true believers are to conduct "holy war" against all "infidels," or non-Muslims

island A landmass surrounded by water

isthmus A land bridge; a narrow link of land that spans an expanse of water between two bodies of land

J

Jainism A religion of India related to both Hinduism and Buddhism; some people classify it as a heretical version of Hinduism

Juche Worship of the North Korean state as represented by Kim Il Sung, also known as Kimilsungism

Judaism The religion of Israel and the Jews based on the Old Testament law and Jewish tradition

K

karst An area of water-carved limestone formations, such as caverns and rugged peaks

khat An East African shrub with leaves that are chewed as a stimulant or made into a tea

Knesset The legislative branch of the government of Israel

Koran The holy book of Islam

krai A territorial district in Russia

Kremlin The large walled fortress in Moscow that is the center of the government of Russia

L

landform A feature of the land, such as a hill, peninsula, or mesa

landlocked Completely surrounded by land; having no direct access to the sea

language family A group of languages that share many common characteristics

lapse rate The rate of decrease in temperature with increase in altitude

latitude The distance north or south of the equator; measured in degrees

leaching The dissolving of soil minerals by water and their removal downward through the soil

leeward Away from the wind; the direction opposite of that from which the wind comes

life expectancy The number of years a person can reasonably be expected to live following birth

lignite Brown coal with high moisture content

literacy The ability to read and write

literacy rate The percentage of the adult population of a country who are literate

lithosphere The area of solid matter on the surface of the earth

loch A deep, narrow lake carved by a glacier

loess A very fine silt that has been deposited by the wind

longitude The distance east or west of the prime meridian; measured in degrees

lough A freshwater lake in Ireland

low island A coral island that does not stand high above the water

low pressure An atmospheric condition that generally indicates bad or deteriorating weather

M

madrasah An Islamic seminary

malaria A highly infectious disease spread by the Anopheles mosquito and common in wet, tropical countries

mandate Authorization for one country to exercise administrative control over a territory

mantle The portion of the earth's interior lying between the crust and the core

manufacturing The process of making finished goods from raw materials

map projection A method of drawing features of the earth's surface on a flat map

market People or businesses interested in buying a product

marsh A wetland area with standing water, grasses, and small water plants

mass communication Communication intended to reach a large number of people

megalopolis A combination of several metropolitan areas that have grown together; similar terms include *metropolis* and *megacity*

meridian A line of longitude

mestizos Latin Americans of mixed European and Indian blood

metal A substance that can conduct electricity and is usually shiny, malleable (can be shaped), and ductile (can be pulled into a wire or hammered thin)

middle latitudes The temperate regions between the Tropic of Cancer and the polar region in the Northern Hemisphere and between the Tropic of Capricorn and the polar region in the Southern Hemisphere

mineral A solid, naturally occurring, inorganic material with a definite chemical composition and crystalline structure

monarchy A government with a hereditary ruler, such as a king or a queen

monsoon A seasonal wind caused by the heating and cooling of large landmasses

moor A wasteland on a high, treeless plateau that cannot be cultivated but that often has patches of peat bog or sphagnum moss; often called a heath because of the heather that grows on it

Mormonism A religion founded by Joseph Smith that claims to have revelation beyond that given in the Bible

mosque An Islamic place of worship

mountain range A formation of many mountains together

Muslim A follower of Islam

N

NAFTA The North American Free Trade Agreement; between Canada, Mexico, and the United States

nation A group of people with a common heritage, culture, and homeland

nation-state A nation with its own established government and political boundaries

NATO The North Atlantic Treaty Organization; originally formed to counter the threat to Western Europe by the Soviet Union after World War II

natural boundary A boundary drawn along prominent landscape features such as coastlines, rivers, and mountain ranges

natural gas A gaseous form of fossil fuel

natural resource Any useful substance that can be found in the earth

navigable river A river on which deep-draft boats can move great distances

near abroad The term that Russia applies to the Commonwealth of Independent States, countries that were once part of the Soviet Union

Negev An arid region in the extreme southern portion of Israel that, although it is desert, produces abundant crops with the help of irrigation and has rich deposits of potash, bromine, and copper

Nippon What the Japanese call their country

nomadic herding The wandering of stock and herdsmen from place to place in order to find new pastures

nondurable manufacturing The mass production of goods that are expected to last for less than one year

nor'easter A severe storm that blows from the northeast; common in the Northeast of the United States

notch An opening through a mountain (see also **gap** and **pass**)

nuclear family The parents and their immediate children

Nunatak An isolated mountain that sticks up above an ice sea

O

oblast A large region or administrative district in Russia similar to a state or province

oasis A watered, fertile area in the desert

ocean current A basic path of water flow within an ocean

oceanic island An island that rises from the ocean floor rather than from the edge of a continent

oceanic ridge An undersea mountain range found along the edges of some tectonic plates

okrug A large, sparsely populated area of northern Russia

OPEC Organization of Petroleum Exporting Countries

outback The vast, sparsely populated interior of Australia

ozone A form of oxygen that appears in the upper stratosphere and helps to shield the earth from harmful ultraviolet rays

P

Pacific Rim The countries that touch the Pacific Ocean, especially those of East Asia

parallel A line of latitude

parliamentary government A representative government led by a parliament and a prime minister

pass An opening through a mountain (see also **gap** and **notch**)

per capita GDP The Gross Domestic Product (GDP) of a country divided by the number of people in the country

permafrost Ground that remains permanently frozen even though the top few inches may thaw during a short summer

petroleum Liquid fossil fuel

physiological density The population of a country divided by the area of available land in the country

Piedmont The region of the eastern United States that lies between the Atlantic Coastal Plain and the Appalachian Mountains

plain A broad, level expanse with no visible elevation

plantation economy An economy based on large-scale agricultural operations that employ and house many workers and produce one product, such as rubber, sugar, or cotton

plate tectonics theory The view that large sections of the earth's crust move, producing earthquakes and volcanoes (see **tectonic activity**)

plateau A large, relatively flat area that is elevated above the surrounding landscape; a tableland

PLO Palestine Liberation Organization; an organization of Palestinians who worked to destroy Israel and to secure a Palestinian homeland

polar regions The areas north of 66 ½° in the Northern Hemisphere and south of 66 ½° in the Southern Hemisphere

polder A parcel of land reclaimed from the sea

political boundary A boundary that divides the territory of one country from that of another

population density The population of a country divided by its area to reveal the average number of people per square mile or kilometer in the country

prairie Rolling plains with high grasses

precipitation Any form of moisture that falls from the atmosphere, such as rain, hail, sleet, or snow

preemptive strike A military attack launched by one country to prevent an attack on itself by another country

prefecture An administrative district

premier A chief administrative official similar to a prime minister

primary industry Work that makes natural resources available for use, such as agriculture, mining, and fishing

prime meridian The meridian passing through Greenwich, England, which is the base line for determining longitude and the reference point for the various time zones around the world

Protestantism Christian churches that follow the broad teachings of the Reformers

R

rain forests Dense forests found in tropical or temperate areas with heavy precipitation

rainshadow The area opposite the windward side of a mountain that usually receives little precipitation

Ramadan A Muslim holy day

raw material A material used in making manufactured items

reincarnation A belief in a constant cycle of birth and death; each person supposedly lives one life after another

relief The different heights and depths of a surface or region

renewable resource Energy from sources—such as the sun, wind, rivers, and tides—that are unlimited in supply

republic A government characterized by a representative system and operated according to a constitution

reservation A portion of land set aside by the federal or state government for American Indians

retail business A business that sells goods to the general public, usually in a small quantity

Ring of Fire A string of volcanoes that encircles the Pacific Ocean

river basin All the land drained by a river and its tributaries

river system A main river and all its tributaries

rogue nation A country that ignores the most fundamental principles of international relations and willingly uses chemical weapons, terrorism, or any other means it deems necessary—even against its own people—to get its way or increase its power

Roman Catholicism The portion of Christianity that follows the teachings and traditions of the Roman Catholic Church and the pope

rural Of or related to the country, as opposed to things that relate to city (urban) or suburban life

S

savanna The vegetation of tropical areas with a long dry season; has grasses and scattered drought-resistant trees

sea A partially enclosed arm of the ocean

secondary industry A manufacturing industry that produces products from raw materials or from manufactured materials

sediment Particles of sand, silt, and clay produced by the weathering of rock

self-determination The ability of a group of people to determine their own form of government and/or economy

selva A dense tropical rainforest in the Amazon

separation of powers A system that ensures the independence of a country's legislative, executive, and judicial functions

shah The title of the traditional hereditary monarch of Iran; overthrown in 1979 by a radical Muslim regime

sharia A social and governmental system in which all activities are judged according to the Koran and Muslim laws

shatter belt A region that is under continual political pressures and is often fragmented by warring factions and invaded or heavily influenced by surrounding rival countries

Shephelah An area in Israel where, inland from the Plain of Philistia, the land rises into an area of low hills

Shiites A sect of Islam that tends to be more conservative or fundamentalist

Shintoism A Japanese religion that promotes the worship of many gods

Siam The former name of Thailand

Sikhism An Indian religion founded by Nanak that tries to combine the teachings of Hinduism with Islam

Six-Day War A war in which Israel launched a devastating preemptive strike against the surrounding Arab states, capturing Gaza, the Sinai Peninsula, the West Bank, and the Golan Heights

slash-and-burn agriculture The cutting and burning of a vegetation area to provide fields for temporary use; also called shifting agriculture

socialism An economic system in which the government owns the major industries and promises to make production decisions for the welfare of society; a command economy

society A group of people who share common characteristics, relationships, institutions, and culture

Soviet bloc During the period of 1917–1991, the Soviet Union and its Eastern European puppet governments

Special Economic Zone One of six industrial and trading areas established by the Chinese government to attract foreign trade, investment, and technology

specialized farming The raising of only one crop or one type of stock

station An Australian ranch, especially one for raising sheep

steppe A rolling grassland area, particularly of Central Asia and Eastern Europe

subcontinent The general term applied to the area of Asia that is bounded by the Himalayas on the north and by the Indian Ocean on the south; bigger than a peninsula but smaller than a continent

subregion A smaller area within a larger region

subsistence farming Agriculture that supplies only the basic food and material needs of the farmer and his immediate family

suburb A residential community outside city limits but not in the rural area farther away

Sufi An Islamic mystic

sultanate A Persian Gulf country that is ruled by a sultan

Sun Belt The southern third of the United States from the Carolinas to California; the greatest growth in population has been occurring there

Sunnis The largest sect of Islam (about 80 percent of all Muslims) that is more secular

survey A count of a small sample that is considered to be representative of the total population

Swahili A language spoken by Bantu tribes living along the eastern coast of Africa from Somalia to Mozambique

swamp A wetland area of standing water in which large trees grow

T

taiga High-latitude evergreen forests such as those in Canada and Siberia

Taoism A religion of China that promotes the belief in two matched forces called yin and yang

tariff A tax on imports or exports

taro A tropical plant that is widely cultivated in Asia and the Pacific islands for its starchy roots

technology The application of science for practical and industrial purposes

tectonic activity The movement of the earth's crustal plates and the resulting seismic and volcanic activity (see **plate tectonics theory**)

telecommunications Sending messages through electronic impulses

tell A mound in the Middle East that is formed when successive settlements are built one on top of another

temperate zones The middle latitudes with seasonal changes caused by nearly direct sunlight half of each year

territorial integrity A country's ability to defend its borders

territorial waters A zone off the coast of a country that it claims and exploits as its own sovereign possession

terracing The building of level areas that stairstep along hillsides or mountainsides to reduce erosion and provide areas for efficient cultivation

tertiary industry A service industry involving the distribution of goods and services rather than the manufacture of products or the harvesting of crops or other natural resources

till plains Flat to gently rolling areas of deep fertile soil left by glaciers

timberline The altitude of a mountain system above which trees do not grow

topographic map A map that shows the shape and elevation of an area

topography The shape and elevation of the land features of an area

totalitarian government A government that totally controls the affairs of a country and limits the freedoms of its citizens

township The smallest organizational unit of local government in New England states

trade Buying and selling among countries

trade winds The common easterly winds of tropical regions

transitional zone An area that lies between two other regions and has characteristics of both

trench A long, steep-sided valley on the ocean floor

tribalism Strong identity with and loyalty to a tribe

tributary A river that flows into and feeds another river

tropics The latitude zone lying between the Tropic of Cancer and the Tropic of Capricorn with warm temperatures caused by direct sunlight

truck farming The raising and selling of vegetables and fruits for their special uses

tsetse fly An African fly that spreads sleeping sickness

tsunami A seismic (earthquake-caused) sea wave

tundra The vegetation regions of cold climates displaying little vegetation other than mosses, lichens, and similar small plants

typhoon A hurricane that occurs over the waters near eastern Asia

U

unicameral Having one chamber or house, as in the legislature of a government

uniformitarianism The belief that only those forces that are presently acting on the earth have shaped the earth in the past

Untouchables People in the Hindu caste system who belong to despised occupations, such as tanners and garbage collectors, and are considered so low that they are beneath caste

urban area An area where the population and industry are centralized and developed; city areas, as opposed to rural or suburban areas

urbanization The movement of people from rural areas to cities and the growth of those cities

V

vegetation The plants in an area or region

village A small group of dwellings in an isolated area

voodoo A pantheistic religion practiced in some Caribbean countries, especially Haiti, that blends West African animism with elements of Roman Catholicism

W

wadi A usually dry streambed in a desert area

watershed An area of land that drains into a certain river or river system

water table The level below which the ground is saturated with water

wattle A wall, roof, or fence that some Australians make by weaving, or "wattling," acacia trees together

weathering The degenerative process that contributes to the breaking up and alteration of rock materials

westerlies Storms that come from the west

wetland An area of stagnant water, such as a swamp, marsh, or bog

wholesale business A business that sells goods in quantity to be sold to consumers by other businesses called retailers

WTO World Trade Organization

XY

yellow fever An infectious tropical disease transmitted by mosquitoes

Z

Zionist movement A Jewish movement that seeks the growth and development of the nation of Israel

Zoroastrianism A religion founded by Zarathustra during the ancient Persian Empire

INDEX

PHOTOGRAPH CREDITS

The following agencies and individuals have furnished materials to meet the photographic needs of this textbook. We wish to express our gratitude to them for their important contribution.

ACT Heritage Library
Africa Bible College
Alamy
American Geological Institute
anthroarcheart.org
Art Resource
Asiafoto.com
Associated Press
David Astley
Chris Barton
BiblePlaces.com
BIGBAMBOOSTOCK.COM
BigStockPhoto.com
Pat & Chuck Blackley
Ray Boren
Bridgeman Art
The British Museum
Dave Bunnell
Rhett A. Butler
Chesapeake Bay Bridge-Tunnel
Clipart.com
George Collins
Corbis
Denis Cordier
Corel Corporation
Jan Csernoch
Department of Defense (DOD)
Digital Stock
Digital Vision
Dover Publication, Inc.
Gary Eaton
Wally Ellison
Haldun Erdinc
Carlos Estape

FEMA
James Fields
Fotolia.com
Genesee & Wyoming
Getty Images
Gospel Fellowship Association
M.D. Guiry
Attila Gulyas
Brenda Hansen
Harry S. Truman Library
Hasbro, Inc.
The Heritage Canada
  Foundation
Douglas Himes
Steven Hoffmeyer
The Hunley Organization
Indianapolis Motor Speedway
Iron Range Resources
istockphoto.com
JupiterImages Corporation
Elly Kalagayan
KarlGrobl.com
Gard Karlsen
Tim Keesee
Breck Kent
Joyce Landis
George P. Landow
Peter Langer
Library of Congress
Dr. Anne Livingston
QT Luong
Mall of America®
Stephen Mendes
Middleton Place

MODIS Land Rapid Response
  Team
MRP Photography
Gary Mullis
NASA
National Archives
National Park Service
National Portrait Gallery,
  London
National Science Foundation
Navy Historical Center
R. Neal
New Brunswick Tourism & Parks
New Market Battlefield State
  Historical Park
NOAA
The Nobel Foundation
John Nolan
OAR/National Undersea
  Research Program (NURP)
OSCE
Outback Photographics
Outer Banks Visitors Bureau
O Vaering Eftf. AS, Norway
Ozoutback.com
Jerry Peek
Gilbert Pellet
PhotoDisc, Inc.
Photo Researchers, Inc.
Photoway
Jacek Piwowarczyk
Pridenestrovie.net
The Red Cross
Reuters

Joe Rizzo
Royal Canadian Mounted Police
Saudi Aramco World/PADIA
SCDOT
Andre Seale
Sarah C. Strawhorn
Studebaker National Museum
Travel-Images.com
Michael Trezzi
UK Coal
UNHCR
United States Geological Survey
University of Oregon
Unusual Films
Andreas Urban
US Army
US Coast Guard (USCG)
US Department of the Interior
US Marine Corps
US Navy
US Navy Submarine Force
  Museum
John A. Visser
Visuals Unlimited
Jim Wark
Mike Warren
The White House
Wikimedia
Wikipedia
World Bank
worldofstock.com
Worldwide Slides
Rafal Zurkowski

Cover
www.istockphoto.com/
VisualField, www.istockphoto
.com/aaussi (background photos); www.istockphoto.com/
Evgeny Kuklev (tag), www
.istockphoto.com/Stephen
Green (circle stamp); Copyright
© 2003 by Dover Publication,
Inc. (luggage labels)

Title Page
www.istockphoto.com/Evgeny
Kuklev (tag), www.istockphoto
.com/Stephen Green (circle
stamp)

Front Matter
Copyright © 2003 by Dover
Publication, Inc. v-ix (luggage
labels); www.istockphoto.com/
VisualField, www.istockphoto
.com/aaussi v-ix, x, xi (background photos); www.istock-
photo.com/duncan p walker x,
xi (map background); © 2008
JupiterImages Corporation/
Photos.com x (pistol); www
.istockphoto.com/Fitzer x,
xi (photo frame); © 2008
JupiterImages Corporation/
Goodshoot Image x (camels);
QT Luong/terragalleria.com x
(Wailing Wall); www.istock-
photo.com/Stefan Klein xi
(envelope); www.istockphoto
.com/ranplett xi (card); www

.istockphoto.com/blackred xi
(journal); www.istockphoto
.com/Lyle Koehnlein xi (passport); Fotolia.com/© Andrey
Armyagov xi (Spasskaya Tower);
GeoNova Publishing, Inc. xii
(map top right); www.istock-
photo.com/puchan xiii (top);
Wikimedia/US Marine Corps
xiii (bottom)

All Unit Opener Background Images
www.istockphoto.com/
VisualField, www.istockphoto
.com/aaussi (background photos); www.istockphoto.com/
duncan p walker (map background); www.istockphoto
.com/Fitzer (photo frame)

All Chapter Opener Background Images
www.istockphoto.com/
VisualField, www.istockphoto
.com/aaussi (background photos); www.istockphoto.com/
duncan p walker (map background); www.istockphoto.
com/Fitzer (photo frame); www
.istockphoto.com/Stefan Klein
(envelope); www.istockphoto
.com/ranplett (card); www
.istockphoto.com/blackred
(journal); www.istockphoto.
com/Lyle Koehnlein (passport)

Unit One Opener
www.istockphoto.com/Nikolai
Okhitin xiv (compass); Cunard
Line promotional brochure for
the Franconia c. 1926-30 (colour
litho) by American School (20th
century) ©Private Collection/
Ken Welsh/ The Bridgeman Art
Library, Nationality/ copyright
status: American/copyright
unknown xv (ship); NASA/
Goddard Space Flight Center,
Scientific Visualization Studio
xvi (globe)

Chapter 1
© 2008 JupiterImages
Corporation/Photos.com 1; ©
2008 JupiterImages Corporation
4 (both); © Erich Lessing / Art
Resource, NY 5; BATTLESHIP ®
& © 2008 Hasbro, Inc. Used
with permission 7; © 2008
JupiterImages Corporation/
PhotoObjects.net 8; National
Park Service/U.S. Department
of the Interior 12; © 2008
JupiterImages Corporation/
Comstock Images 14

Chapter 2
www.istockphoto.com/Georgios
Alexandris 17; PhotoDisc/Getty
Images/C Sherburne/PhotoLink
18; www.istockphoto.com/Jeff
Logan 19 (top); www.istock-
photo.com/Tom Marvin 19

(bottom); NASA Goddard Space
Flight Center (NASA-GSFC) 20;
Photo by Steven Hoffmeyer at
www.hoffmeyer.com 21;
© 2008 JupiterImages
Corporation/Photos.com 22
(top), 30 (bottom right), 44
(top), 45; © 2008 JupiterImages
Corporation/Thinkstock
Images 22 (bottom), 43; www
.istockphoto.com/Brasil2 24;
PhotoDisc/Getty Images/
Scenics of America/PhotoLink
25; Elly Kalagayan 26 (top);
www.istockphoto.com/Ivars
Zolnerovichs 26 (bottom left);
NASA Johnson Space Center
- Earth Sciences and Image
Analysis (NASA-JSC-ES&IA)
26 (bottom right); © 2008
JupiterImages Corporation/
Comstock Images 27; U.S.
Department of the Interior/U.S.
Geological Survey 28; Image
Courtesy K. Segerstrom, United
States Geological Survey/
earthscienceworld.org 29 (left);
Robert Simmon, SSAI/NASA
GSFC 29 (right); National Park
Service 30 (left); PhotoDisc/
Getty Images/Robert Glusic
30 (top right); PhotoDisc/
Getty Images/Kent Knudson/
PhotoLink 31 (top); www
.istockphoto.com/Laurence

Gough 31 (middle); www .istockphoto.com/Falk Kienas 31 (bottom), 44 (middle); © Marc Epstein /Visuals Unlimited 33; Sarah C. Strawhorn 41 (top); www.istockphoto.com/William Walsh 41 (bottom); Stockbyte/ Getty Images/Bruce Heinemann 42; © 2008 JupiterImages Corporation/AbleStock.com 44 (bottom left); www.istockphoto .com/John Billingslea jr. 44 (bottom right)

Unit 2 Opener
www.istockphoto.com/Mercedes Brea 48 (pen); www.istockphoto .com/Arielle Walrath 48 (journal); AP Photo/ACME/Michael J. Ackerman 49 (Morocco); © 2008 JupiterImages Corporation/AbleStock.com 50 (power plant)

Chapter 3
Digital Vision/Getty Images 51; www.istockphoto.com/Shaun Lowe 53 (top); Yosef Hadar/ World Bank 53 (bottom), 54 (right); Ray Witlin/World Bank 54 (left), 70; PhotoDisc/ Getty Images/M Freeman/ PhotoLink 55; ©M.D. Guiry, www.algaebase.org 56; © 2008 JupiterImages Corporation/ Photos.com 57 (top); www .istockphoto.com/Jim Parkin 57 (bottom); www.istockphoto .com/Steffen Foerster 58 (top); www.istockphoto.com/Michael Fuller 58 (bottom); Courtesy of Genessee & Wyoming, Inc. 59 (top); Image copyright © The Metropolitan Museum of Art / Art Resource, NY 59 (middle); Photodisc/Fotosearch 59 (bottom); MRP Photography/UK Coal 60 (top); PhotoDisc/Getty Images/Kim Steele 60 (bottom); Gary Eaton, Summerville, SC 63 (top); National Archives 63 (middle); US Army 63 (bottom); www.istockphoto.com/Ingvald kaldhussæter 64 (top); www .istockphoto.com/Greg Nicholas 64 (bottom); www.istockphoto .com/zennie 66 (top); www .istockphoto.com/Eric Bechtold 66 (bottom right); PhotoDisc/ Getty Images/Kent Knudson/ PhotoLink 66 (bottom left); AP PHOTO/POOL/Remy de la Mauviniere 67; www.istockphoto.com/Jeffrey Hochstrasser 68; Library of Congress 69

Chapter 4
PhotoDisc/Getty Images/Neil Beer 77 (Tokyo); Edwin G. Huffman/World Bank 82 (top, bottom); www.istockphoto .com/Jeff deVries 82 (middle); Ray Witlin/World Bank 83 (top); Unusual Films, courtesy of Wei Family 83 (bottom); www .istockphoto.com/Loh Siew Seong 85 (top left); www.istock-photo.com/Klaas Lingbeek- van

Kranen 85 (top right); www .istockphoto.com/Eun Jin Ping Audrey 85 (top middle); John Nolan 85 (bottom); Brenda Hansen 89 (top left); www .istockphoto.com/Jason Stitt 89 (top middle); www.istockphoto .com/Kevin Russ 89 (top right); www.istockphoto.com/Nancy Louie 89 (bottom); Jacek Piwowarczyk/www.jacekphoto .com 90 (top); www.istockphoto .com/Volodymyr Kyrylyuk 90 (bottom); World Bank 91 (both); www.istockphoto.com/Joe Gough 92 (top); www .istockphoto.com/Roy Boncato 92 (middle), 92 (bottom); Associated Press Photo/Ed Wray 92 (bottom); DOD photo by Helene C. Stikkel 93 (top); Associated Press Photo/Karim Kadim 93 (bottom); PhotoDisc/ Getty Images/Hisham Ibrahim 94; The White House by Bill Fitzpatrick 96 (top); www.istock-photo.com/Jeremy Edwards 96 (bottom); © 2008 International Committee of the Red Cross 97 (both)

Unit 3 Opener
www.istockphoto.com/ Pavel Lebedinsky 100 (ice ax); www.istockphoto.com/ René Baumgartner 101 (Alps); PhotoDisc/Getty Images/ Emanuele Taroni 102 (village)

Chapter 5
www.istockphoto.com/ur-bandevill 102 (Eiffel Tower); © Andrew Dunn, 29 September 2004/Wikipedia.org 108 (top); www.istockphoto.com/Tomasz Resiak 108 (bottom); www .istockphoto.com/Mark Breck 109; Photo taken by G-Man, Sept 2004/Wikipedia.org 110 (top); commons.wikimedia.org 110 (bottom); Jacques Descloitres, MODIS Rapid Response Team, NASA/GSFC 111 (top); www .istockphoto.com/mike morley 111 (bottom); www.istockphoto .com/Ingvald kaldhussæter 113; www.istockphoto.com/Jonas Engström 114; PhotoDisc/Getty Images 115; NASA 116; www .istockphoto.com/buchwerkstatt .com 117; www.istockphoto.com/ Kenneth C. Zirkel 118; www .istockphoto.com/sublimation 119 (top); © Richard Walker/ Corbis 119 (bottom); www .istockphoto.com/Rafael Laguillo 120; www.istockphoto .com/Thierry Arnould 123; Associated Press Photo/Lionel Cironneau 124; www.istock-photo.com/Monika Simpkins 126 (top); www.istockphoto.com /Bernd Klumpp 126 (bottom); www.istockphoto.com/cjmcken-dry 127; www.istockphoto.com/ Philip Aschauer 129; NASA Jet Propulsion Laboratory (NASA-JPL) 131; www.istockphoto.com/

juanolvido 132; www.istock-photo.com/Fabio Ficola 133; ww.istockphoto.com/Mary Lane 134; DigitalSTOCK/Corbis 135 (top); www.istockphoto.com/ Alexandre Caron 135 (bottom); www.istockphoto.com/Michael Palis 136; Lucretious/stock. xchng/commons.wikimedia.org 137

Chapter 6
Associated Press Photo/ Sergei Chuzavkov 140; © 2008 JupiterImages Corporation/ Photos.com 143; www.istock-photo.com/puchan 144; www .istockphoto.com/Marc C. Johnson 146; www.istockphoto .com/Falk Kienas 147 (both); PhotoDisc/Getty Images/Emma Lee/Life File 149 (top); www .istockphoto.com/Wojciech P?ONKA 149 (bottom); Tim Keesee 151, 154; Dave Bunnell/ Under Earth Images 152 (top); www.istockphoto.com/ Tomasz Resiak 152 (bottom); J.Kaman / Travel-Images.com 153; DIMITAR DILKOFF/ AFP/Getty Images 156; priden-estrovie.net 158; AFP/Getty Images 159; Image courtesy the SeaWiFS Project, NASA GSFC, and ORBIMAGE 160 (top); Associated Press Photo/Viktor Pobedinsky 160 (bottom)

Chapter 7
Fotolia.com/© Andrey Armyagov 163, 171; www.istockphoto.com/ © 2008 Michael Westhoff 166; Time & Life Pictures/Getty Image/Photo by Mansell 167 (top); John A. Visser 167 (bottom); Associated Press Photo/ Boris Koltsov 168; Associated Press Photo/Ivan Sekretarev 169; www.istockphoto.com/cloki 170; Library of Congress 172 (top), 175; Wikimedia/Dims 172 (bottom left); © B. & C. Alexander/ Photo Researchers, Inc. 172 (bottom right); © Kristen Soper/ Alamy 174; www.istockphoto .com/Nikolay Starchenko 176; Jacques Descloitres, MODIS Land Rapid Response Team 178 (top); Wikimedia/ Emmanuel Varoquaux 178 (bottom); Wikimedia/ de:Benutzer:Sansculotte 179; © B. & C. Alexander/Photo Researchers, Inc. 180

Unit 4 Opener
© 2008 JupiterImages Corporation/PhotoObjects.net 182 (wheel); National Archives/ Jackson 183 (farm); PhotoDisc/ Getty Images 183 (bridge)

Chapter 8
Royal Canadian Mounted Police 185; NOAA 188 (top left); 2008 JupiterImages Corporation 188 (top right); Wally Ellison 189; Credit of New Brunswick Tourism & Parks 190 (top);

Breck Kent 190 (middle, bottom); Joyce Landis 191; Wikipedia 193; www .istockphoto.com/Ashok Rodrigues 194; www.istockphoto.com/ Steven Miric 192; www.istockphoto.com/Sang Nguyen 196 (top); www.istockphoto.com/ Julie de Leseleuc 196 (middle); www.istockphoto.com/zennie 198; Corel Corporation 199 (top), 200 (both); www .istockphoto.com/Jason van der Valk 199 (bottom); www .istockphoto.com/Falk Kienas 201 (top); www.istockphoto. com/Natalia Bratslavsky 201 (bottom); Getty Images/James Balog 202; Wikimedia 203; Studebaker National Museum 204 (left); Library of Congress 204 (top right, bottom); © 2008 The Heritage Canada Foundation, www.heritagecan-ada.org, Reproduced with the permission of the Minister of Public Works and Government Services, 2008 205

Chapter 9
www.istockphoto.com/Stacey Putman 208; www.istockphoto .com/Nick Suydam 209 (top left); Getty Images/Richard Laird 209 (top right); www.istockphoto .com/Larry Boston 209 (bottom left); www.istockphoto.com/ Philip Dyer 209 (bottom right); AP Photo/Canadian Press, Jason Kryk 210 (top); Airphoto/ Jim Wark 210 (bottom); 2008 JupiterImages Corporation 211; www.istockphoto.com/Klaas Lingbeek- van Kranen 212 (top); www.istockphoto.com/ KateLeigh 212 (bottom); www .istockphoto.com/Darinburt 213 (top); www.istockphoto.com/Jill Fromer 213 (bottom); www .istockphoto.com/Loic Bernard 214 (top left); PhotoDisc/Getty Images 214 (top right); www .istockphoto.com/Michael Braun 214 (bottom); www.istockphoto .com/dtsuneo 215 (top); NOAA/ Collection of Dr. Herbert Kroehl, NGDC 215 (bottom); U.S. Navy photo by Photographer's Mate Airman Jeremy L. Grisham 216; © Bridgeman-Giraudon / Art Resource 218; www.istockphoto.com/Robert Kyllo 221 (top); PhotoDisc/Getty Images/John Wang 221 (bottom); www.istockphoto.com/ Tom McNemar 221 (middle); COREL Corporation 224 (top); Mark Wolfe/FEMA 224 (bottom); www.istockphoto .com/Jan Tyler 225 (top); AP Photo/Richard Drew 225 (bottom); Wikimedia/US Marine Corps 226; © PAT & CHUCK BLACKLEY 406 AUDUBON ST STAUNTON, VA 227

Chapter 10

Fotolia.com/Gerald Engler 229; www.istockphoto.com/Joachim Angeltun 232; Worldwide Slides 233 (top); Library of Congress 233 (middle); US Navy Submarine Force Museum 233 (bottom); www.istockphoto.com/Graham Prentice 234; Wikimedia 235 (top); www.istockphoto.com/Amy Seagram 235 (bottom); www.istockphoto.com/Klaas Lingbeek- van Kranen 236 (top); Photo courtesy of the Chesapeake Bay Bridge-Tunnel 236 (bottom); Getty Images/Sisse Brimberg 237; Courtesy New Market Battlefield State Historical Park 239; Gary Mullis 240 (top); Outer Banks Visitors Bureau 240 (middle); www.istockphoto.com/JOHN UPCHURCH 240 (bottom); www.istockphoto.com/Ronna Nichter 241 (top); R. Neal 241 (bottom); Rob Thompson/SCDOT 242 (top); Middleton Place, Charleston, South Carolina 242 (bottom); PhotoDisc/Getty Images 243 (top); www.istockphoto.com/Cezary Gesikowski 243 (bottom); www.istockphoto.com/Eric Jackson 244 (top); Copyright © Marli Miller, University of Oregon 244 (bottom); Bob McMillan/FEMA Photo 245 (top); www.istockphoto.com/Juliana Halvorson 245 (bottom); IMS Photo by Bill Watson 247; www.istockphoto.com/Tom Marvin 248 (top); PhotoDisc/Getty Images 248 (middle); Iron Range Resources 248 (bottom); Courtesy of Mall of America® 249 (top); www.istockphoto.com/Jose Gil 249 (bottom); www.istockphoto.com/Tony Colter 250, 251; www.istockphoto.com/Sonja Foos 252; © 2008 JupiterImages Corporation 255 (top), 259 (bottom); www.istockphoto.com/James Phelps 255 (bottom); George Collins 256 (top); Wikimedia/Dundak 256 (bottom); Ray Boren, scenicutah.com 257 (top); www.istockphoto.com/simon dvorak 257 (bottom); www.istockphoto.com/Carol Afshar 258 (top); www.istockphoto.com/Elena Korenbaum 258 (bottom); www.istockphoto.com/Tina Sbrigato 259 (top); www.istockphoto.com/Ashok Rodrigues 260

Unit 5 Opener

www.istockphoto.com/Dave White 262 (binoculars); www.istockphoto.com/Bryan Faust 263 (birds); www.istockphoto.com/Gabor Izso 264 (ruins)

Chapter 11

www.istockphoto.com/Asbjorn Aakjaer 265; Wikimedia 268, 272 (top); Wikimedia/Jens Uhlenbrock 269; www.istockphoto.com/Jim Parkin 270 (top); www.istockphoto.com/aolr 270 (bills); James Fields/Eclectec SA de CV 271; www.istockphoto.com/Marco Regali 272 (bottom); Wikimedia/Gustavo Benítez 273; www.istockphoto.com/Humberto Ortega 274; www.istockphoto.com/Firehorse 275 (top); John E. Poling 275 (bottom); © 2008 JupiterImages Corporation 276 (top); © Greg Dimijian/Photo Researchers, Inc. 276 (bottom); © Joe Rizzo, Cosmic Circuit Studio, cosmic-circuit.com 279; Wikipedia/P199 281; Wikimedia/Luc Viatour 282; www.istockphoto.com/Steve Geer 283; Wikimedia/Manuel Dohmen 286 (top); USCG photo by Fireman Greg Ewald 268 (bottom); www.istockphoto.com/Steven Miric 287 (top); U.S. Marine Corps photo by Cpl. Eric Ely 287 (bottom); Dr. Anne Livingston 288; Courtesy of Stephen Mendes, http://barbadosphotogallery.com 290

Chapter 12

Rhett A. Butler/mongabay.com 292; Getty Images/Alfredo Maiquez 295 (top); Jan Csernoch 295 (bottom); www.istockphoto.com/francisco burga c. 296; www.istockphoto.com/Heidi Kristensen 297 (both); Getty Images/Ed Darack 298; Ertugrul Kilic (http://www.ertugrulkilic.com) 299 (top); Fotolia.com/Daniel Pissondes 299 (bottom); www.istockphoto.com/Mark Van Overmeire 300 (top); www.istockphoto.com/Nancy Nehring 300 (bottom); Jacek Piwowarczyk/www.jacekphoto.com 301 (top); Wikipedia/Brad Mering 301 (middle); www.istockphoto.com/Dan Cooper 301 (bottom); © Jim Zuckerman/Corbis 303; www.istockphoto.com/Kevin Su 304 (top left); © W. K. Fletcher/Photo Researchers, Inc 304 (top right); © Theo Allofs/Visuals Unlimited 304 (bottom left); © Tim Hauf/Visuals Unlimited 304 (bottom right); Wikimedia/Claire POUTEAU 305; Wikimedia/Miguel A. Monjas 308; www.istockphoto.com/Nancy Nehring 309; Georg Gerster/Photo Researchers, Inc 310 (top); Clipart.com 310 (bottom); © 2008 JupiterImages Corporation 314 (left); Fotolia.com /© Sascha Felnagel 314 (right); www.istockphoto.com/Vincent Mosch 315; www.istockphoto.com/Mark Van Overmeire 317 (top); www.istockphoto.com/Luis Carlos Torres 317 (bottom)

Unit 6 Opener

www.istockphoto.com/Kjell Brynildsen 320 (camera); Library of Congress 321; Courtesy of Gospel Fellowship Association 322 (missionaries)

Chapter 13

© 2008 JupiterImages Corporation 323; www.istockphoto.com/Henk Badenhorst 327; Copyright © AJ Mandolesi, American Geological Institute 328; Copyright © The Nobel Foundation 329 (all); Wikimedia/Teo Gómez 331; Michael Trezzi 332; Fotolia.com/Oleg Khripunkov 333; George P. Landow 334; Africa Bible College 335; www.istockphoto.com/Suzan Charnock 336; www.istockphoto.com/Boleslaw Kubica 341; Digital Stock 342; www.istockphoto.com/Stephanie Kuwasaki 343; © Joe McDonald/Visuals Unlimited 344; www.istockphoto.com/Klaas Lingbeek- van Kranen 347; Image courtesy of MODIS Rapid Response Project at NASA/GSFC 348; T. Loynachan/Image Courtesy United States Geological Survey 350

Chapter 14

Curt Carnemark/World Bank 352; Fotolia.com/Thomas Pozzo Di Borgo 353; Martin Dohrn/Photo Researchers, Inc. 356; UNHCR/S. Schulman 359; Mauro Campagnoli 360 (top); Chris Barton, photographersdirect.com 360 (bottom); Douglas Himes 361; B.CLoutier/Travel-Images.com 363 (both); Brynn Bruijn/Saudi Aramco World/PADIA 366; Associated Press Photo/Kurt Strumpf 368; Rafal Zurkowski 369; Jack Fields/Photo Researchers Inc 370; Market of Gorum Gorum - Province of Oudalan - Burkina Faso Photographer: Denis Cordier (denis.cordier@laposte.net) 371; www.worldofstock.com/Anthony Asael 372 (left); Associated Press Photo/van Zuydam 372 (right); Associated Press Photo/Ben Curtis 373; Dolores CM / Travel-Images.com 374; Andreas Urban 376; Wikimedia/Robin Elaine 377; © Copyright the Trustees of The British Museum 378

Chapter 15

© 2008 JupiterImages Corporation 379; Georg Gerster/ Photo Researchers Inc 382; Monique van Gaal 383; Stephenie Hollyman/Saudi Aramco World/PADIA 384; © Rene' Goiffon 385 (top); U.S. Geological Survey 385 (bottom left); NASA/Goddard Space Flight Center Scientific Visualization Studio 385 (bottom right); www.istockphoto.com/Tomasz Resiak 386 (bottom left); www.istockphoto.com/Claus Mikosch 386 (bottom right); www.istockphoto.com/Jean-Claude Gallard 387, 388 (top); Visuals Unlimited 388 (bottom left); www.istockphoto.com/Jacques Croizer 388 (bottom right); www.istockphoto.com/Amy Evenstad 389; www.istockphoto.com/Iwona Adamus 390; Gilbert Pellet 391; Associated Press Photo/Eric Gaillard 392 (top); www.istockphoto.com/Matej Michelizza 392 (bottom); Fotolia.com/Bartlomiej Kwieciszewski 393 (left); www.istockphoto.com/Dainis Derics 393 (right); Fotolia.com/FRANCK CAMHI 394; U.S. Navy photo by Kristopher Wilson 395; Phillip Homer 396

Unit 7 Opener

© 2008 JupiterImages Corporation/Photos.com 398 (antique pistol); © 2008 JupiterImages Corporation/Goodshoot Image 399 (Bedouin and camel); QT Luong/terragalleria.com 400 (Wailing Wall)

Chapter 16

www.istockphoto.com/Eli Mordechai 401; www.istockphoto.com/ron wiersma 404; www.istockphoto.com/Gustavo Fadel 405; www.istockphoto.com/Valentin Mosichev 407 (top); www.istockphoto.com/Bulent Ince 407 (bottom); R.Khalilov/Travel-Images.com 409; George Baramki Azar/Saudi Aramco World/PADIA 412; Todd Bolen/BiblePlaces.com 413 (top), 415 (left), 418; Tor Eigeland/Saudi Aramco World/PADIA 413 (bottom); www.istockphoto.com/Konstantin Kalishko 414; William L. Krewson/BiblePlaces.com 415 (right); REUTERS/Gil Cohen Magen 416; Kim Guess/BiblePlaces.com 419; www.istockphoto.com/Grzegorz Wołczyk 421 (top); www.istockphoto.com/Mikhail Levit 421 (bottom); Harry S. Truman Library 422; Associated Press Photo/KHALIL HAMRA 423; 2008 JupiterImages Corporation 424; www.istockphoto.com/Christian Peeters 425

Chapter 17

Getty Images 427; Wikimedia/Ali Mansuri 431 (top); Fotolia.com/abdelali lahmaidi 431 (bottom); Photoway 432; Tor Eigeland/Saudi Aramco World/PADIA 433 (top); www.istockphoto.com/Hasan Shaheed 433 (bottom); www.istockphoto.com/SimplyRecorded 434; www.istockphoto.com/arne thaysen 435; Fotolia.com/© Philippe Perraud 436; NASA-Johnson Space Center 437 (top); www.istockphoto.com/AravindTeki 437 (bottom);

www.istockphoto.com/John Sigler 438 (left); Associated Press Photo 438 (right); Reuters/Raheb Homavandi 439; U. S. Marine Corps photo by Michael Molinaro 440; Department of Defense 441; Attila Gulyas 444; Wikimedia/Ginolerhino 445; www.istockphoto.com/Natalia Bratslavsky 446; © Damir Sagolj/Reuters 447

Chapter 18
Yuri Mechitov/World Bank 449; www.istockphoto.com/Tauno Novek 452 (top); ilse schrama/Alamy 452 (bottom); Wikimedia/Henri Nissen 453; M.Torres/Travel-Images.com 454; Haldun Erdinc 456; Ria Novosti/Photo Researchers 457; Image courtesy of the Image Science & Analysis Laboratory, NASA Johnson Space Center; NASA 458; Anvar Ilyasov/World Bank 459; OSCE/Lubomir Kotek 460, 461 (bottom); www.istockphoto.com/Rob Broek 461 (top left); OSCE/Soeren W. Nissen 461 (top right); Thorne Anderson/Saudi Aramco World/PADIA 462

Unit 8 Opener
Fotolia.com/Aleksandr Lobanov 466 (antique bike horn); public domain from *Across Asia On a Bicycle* by Thomas Gaskell Allen, Jr. & William Lewis Sachtleben, Publisher: New York: The Century Co. 467; © 2008 JupiterImages Corporation/Photos.com 468 (sushi)

Chapter 19
www.istockphoto.com/Jiew Wan Tan 469; National Portrait Gallery, London 471 (top); www.istockphoto.com 471 (bottom); www.istockphoto.com/Michael Chen 473; Jacek Piwowarczyk/www.jacekphoto.com 474, 482 (left), 487 (bottom); ©www.KarlGrobl.com 475; www.istockphoto.com/Simon Webber 476; Getty Images 477 (top); Library of Congress 477 (bottom); www.istockphoto.com/300dpi 479 (top left); © Philip Baird/www.anthroarcheart.org 479 (top right); Fotolia.com/Alex Lapuerta 479 (bottom); PhotoDisc/Getty 480; ArkReligion.com /Alamy 481; Curt Carnemark/World Bank 482 (right), 483 (top right); www.istockphoto.com/Hendrik De Bruyne 483 (left); Associated Press Photo/Jim Cooper 483 (bottom right); Peter Langer 486 (top); Wikipedia.com/James Mollison 486 (bottom); CJTF-76, 10TH MOUNTAIN DIVISION (Army.mil) 487 (top); © 2008 JupiterImages Corporation 489 (top); www.istockphoto.com/Tan Kian Khoon 491 (top); www.istockphoto.com/

Paul Cowan 491 (bottom); Wikimedia/Shahee Ilyas 492 (top); REUTERS/STR New 492 (bottom)

Chapter 20
Fotolia.com/benjamas thanapade 494; PhotoDisc/Getty Images 498 (top left); Bridgeman Art 498 (top right); www.istockphoto.com/Arjen Briene 498 (bottom); Getty 499 (top); Fotolia.com/Anjo Eijeriks 499 (bottom); www.istockphoto.com/Sining Zhang 500; Associated Press Photo/Greg Baker 501 (top); PhotoDisc/Getty Images 501 (bottom); © 2008 JupiterImages Corporation 503, 507 (bottom), 514 (bottom); Associated Press Photo 504 (top left, right), 518 (left); Harry S. Truman Library 504 (bottom left); Associated Press Photo/Xinhua 504 (bottom right); Associated Press Photo/EUGENE HOSHIKO 505; Fotolia.com/Jason Maehl 506; Fotolia.com/Gerold Setz 507 (top); www.istockphoto.com/Alan Tobey 508 (top); www.istockphoto.com/tcp 508 (bottom); Fotolia.com/Christian Quest 510 (left); www.istockphoto.com/Chris Ronneseth 510 (right); © Eric Martin/Alamy 511; Associated Press Photo/John Leicester 513 (top); Associated Press Photo/Xinhua, Yao Dawei 513 (middle); Wikimedia 513 (bottom); Associated Press Photo/Greg Baker 514 (top); © Jon Arnold Images/Alamy 515; www.istockphoto.com/Andy Hwang 516; Digital Stock 517; Associated Press Photo/Itsuo Inouye 518 (right); www.istockphoto.com/John Leung 519 (top); © John Leung. Image from BigStockPhoto.com 519 (bottom); Fotolia.com/Norma Cornes 520

Chapter 21
www.istockphoto.com/oneclearvision 522; asiafoto.com 525 (top); © Robert Harding Picture Library Ltd/Alamy 525 (bottom); www.istockphoto.com/Lorenzo Pastore 526; © Darby Sawchuk/Alamy 527; Fotolia.com/Jean-Francois Perigois 528 (top); Associated Press Photo/Andy Eames 528 (bottom); Curt Carnemark/World Bank 529; Library of Congress 530; Fotolia.com/ RENE DROUYER 531; PhotoDisc 532 (top); © 2008 JupiterImages Corporation 532 (bottom); Associated Press Photo/Bullit Marquez, File 534; Gard Karlsen 535; Photo by David Greedy/Getty Images 535 (bottom)

Unit 9 Opener
www.istockphoto.com/Steven Kratochwill 538 (flower); © 2008 JupiterImages Corporation/liquidlibrary 539 (fale); Getty Images/Penny Tweedie 540 (aboriginal women)

Chapter 22
CORBIS/DigitalSTOCK 541; © 2008 JupiterImages Corporation/Photos.com 543 (top), 546; www.istockphoto.com/Bryan Davies 543 (bottom left); www.istockphoto.com/Paul Brian 544 (top left); www.istockphoto.com/Wouter van Caspel 544 (top right); Clipart/© 2005 JupiterImages 545; PhotoDisc/Getty Images 547 (top), 548, 550 (bottom), 551 (top right); Fotolia.com/seraphic06 550 (top); www.istockphoto.com/KJAphoto 551 (top left); ACT Heritage Library 553 (left); www.istockphoto.com/_Kit_ 553 (right); Outback Photographics 554 (top); Fotolia.com/Colinda McKie 554 (bottom); S.Lovegrove/Travel-Images.com 555 (top); © 2008 JupiterImages Corporation/Goodshoot Image 555 (bottom); www.istockphoto.com/Matthew Scherf 556; Wikimedia/Guillaume Blanchard 557 (top); ozoutback.com 557 (bottom); Tom McHugh/Photo Researchers, Inc. 558; www.istockphoto.com/mike morley 559; Joyce Landis 560 (top); www.istockphoto.com/Edyta Pawłowska 560 (bottom left); Fotolia.com/Al Teich 560 (bottom right); www.istockphoto.com/Edward Tsang 561

Chapter 23
www.istockphoto.com/christine balderas 563; Library of Congress 565; Fotolia.com/Lucky Dragon 557 (top left); BIGBAMBOOSTOCK.COM 567 (top right), 571 (bottom); Fotolia.com/Nella Star 567 (bottom left); www.istockphoto.com/Jeremy Edwards 567 (bottom right); COREL Corporation 568; Wikimedia/Nicole Wallace 569 (top); Fotolia.com/Nicolas PAULIN 569 (bottom); www.istockphoto.com/colin ochel 570; DOD 571 (top), 577 (top); www.istockphoto.com/Edwin Verin 572; Copyright © Douglas Faulkner/Photo Researchers, Inc. 573; Andre Seale/ArteSub.com 574 (top left); Photomondiale.com/Jerry Peek 574 (top right); Alexis Rosenfeld/Photo Researchers 574 (bottom); Carlos Estape/imagequestmarine.com 575; U.S. Army Space & Missile Defense Command 576 (top); trekearth.com/David Astley 576 (bottom); NASA 577 (bottom); © Douglas Peebles Photography/Alamy 578 (top); QT Luong/terragalleria.com

578 (bottom); www.istockphoto.com/Xavier MARCHANT 579 (top); Mike Warren/www.onlinepitcairn.com 579 (bottom); www.istockphoto.com/Michal Wozniak 580

Chapter 24
Dr. Ken MacDonald/Photo Researchers 582; www.istockphoto.com/Markus Karner 583; Peter Langer 584; www.istockphoto.com/Patrick Roherty 585 (top); Wikimedia/Sgootzei 585 (middle); NOAA Corps/Commander John Bortniak 585 (bottom left); National Science Foundation/Elaine Hood 585 (bottom right); The Mariner's Museum, Newport News, VA 586 (top left), 591 (top); O Vaering Eftf. AS, Norway 586 (top middle); National Portrait Gallery, London 586 (top right); Associated Press Photo 586 (bottom right); Library of Congress 587 (top left), 591 (bottom); Getty Images 586 (bottom left), 592 (middle left); Time Life Pictures/Getty Images 587 (top right); The Hunley Organization 592 (top); AFP/Getty Images 592 (right); U.S. Naval Photographic Center 592 (bottom); OAR/National Undersea Research Program (NURP); Woods Hole Oceanographic Inst. 593 (top); Navy Historical Center 593 (bottom left); Wikimedia 593 (bottom right); NOAA 594 (top); Associated Press Photo/Michelle McLoughlin 594 (bottom)

Map Credits
© 2008 GeoNova Publishing, Inc. 105, 112, 118, 130, 141, 164–165, 186, 231, 238, 246, 250, 253, 267, 279, 294, 327, 339, 358, 366, 381, 402, 428, 450, 472, 496, 512, 523, 542, 564, 584
All other maps were provided by Precision Graphics, Brian Johnson, © 2008 Map Resources, or BJU Press art department.